WARRIOR
IS

WARRIOR IS

First Edition

HARLEY L. ZEPHIER & ROBIN L. ZEPHIER

WARRIOR IS
FIRST EDITION

iUniverse books may be ordered through booksellers or by contacting:

iUniverse
1663 Liberty Drive
Bloomington, IN 47403
www.iuniverse.com
844-349-9409

Interior Image Credit: Harley Zephier, Robin Zephier, Derek Zephier

ISBN: 978-1-5320-2854-0 (sc)
ISBN: 978-1-5320-2856-4 (hc)
ISBN: 978-1-5320-2855-7 (e)

Library of Congress Control Number: 2017912494

Print information available on the last page.

iUniverse rev. date: 05/11/2021

CONTENTS

Introduction ix
Prologue xi

1   Origin 1

2   Human Being 6
         The Great Race Around He Sapa 12
         Star Connection 14

3   Earth People 17
         The "Asking" 27
         Mirrors 30
         The Cannumpa 33

4   Cycle of Life 39
         Lakota Life 40
         Campsites and Hunting Territories 43
         The Plant Beings 45
         Holy People 47
         Medicine and Healing 49
         Time and History 53
         Family and Relationships 54
         Education 58
         Brown Eagle 64
         Saved By Bear 66
         Mato Cikala 72
         The Grattan Incident: An Unfortunate Spark to Light
         the Flame of Conflict 80
         Family Is Paramount 85

The Female Is Sacred... 86

Teaching the Truth... 88

Naca.. 90

Protection From Within 92

Seeking a Balance with All Life on Turtle Island............... 96

First Contact with Foreigners to Turtle Island:

Foreign Concepts 99

5   Transitional Growth...102

    Spirit Horse.. 104

    Jealousy as a Weakness 107

    The Dog Man 110

    Grandfather's Talk..113

    The Shiny Mountains 115

6   Spirit Gathering 123

    The White Stone Pony.. 129

    Warrior: An Age-Old Ritual 135

    The Gift of Heyoka...145

    Yellow Rocks..151

    Entering into the Sacred Heart 170

7   Broken Hoop..177

    Sovereignty 186

    Unrest and Corruption in Minnesota 205

8   Whirlwind Passage...218

    Hanbleceya in He Sapa 222

    Thunder Butte 230

    Sinte and Sunka 230

9   Encroachment 237

    The Media Provides Assistance to the Policy 240

    Washita Tragedy.. 249

    Tatanka Nation: Family to the Lakota 252

    Cheyenne River Agency: The Beginning of the Loss

    of Free Living.. 259

    Wanbli 266

| 10 | Strong Heart | 274 |

    Sacred Stewards, Sacred Protectors...................275

    Sinte Is Called Home................283

    Sunkmanitu Tanka 286

    Horse Nation................289

    Conscience, Philosophy, and Spirituality................297

    Ista´................314

11   Call to Believe 320

    The Pale Moon of the Morning Reveals a Creeping
Shadow over He Sapa 320

    A Conspiracy to Steal the He Sapa................ 328

    Long Hair: A Rising Symbol of Genocide 343

    An Accumulation of Desperate Circumstances................ 345

    Spiritual Instructions and Permission 354

12   Spirit Speak................ 362

13   Preparation................ 377

    The Old Stone Warriors 392

    Owl's Nest................ 403

14   Approach 420

    The Military Plan for Annihilation Moves Forward 423

    Spiritual Messages Are Sent................431

    Leaving Fort Lincoln 434

    Deer Medicine Rock 442

15   Arrival................ 489

16   Our Battle 507

17   Spirit Keeper 537

    The Rhythm of Life Needs Cleansing and Healing 540

18   Victory and Defeat................ 547

    Lieutenant Bradley 549

    Prayer at Mato Paha 557

Epilogue 567

Acknowledgments 573

Appendices
Appendix A Chronology of Critical Events 585
Appendix B A Fulfillment of a Legacy (Harley's Story) 599
Appendix C Reaching Out, I Will Show You (Robin's Story) 607
Appendix D Dog Man Warriors 611
Appendix E Image List of Photos, Maps and Sketches 615

       Appendix photos and images 616
Glossary 627
Sources 633
Index 635

INTRODUCTION

THIS STORY IS THE TRADITIONAL and cultural account of the life of Mnincoju Lakota warrior Mato Niyanpi, Saved By Bear, also later known as Scar Leg. *Warrior Is* is based upon a true story.

What you are about to read has been told to us through our family, passed down as oral history from generation to generation. Every family has its own story. This is ours.

It is up to you to visualize and experience the events described herein in order to determine what you believe or what you choose to accept from what you learn from these pages. You have likely never read a story quite like this one before.

In *Warrior Is*, the reader is able to visualize and experience the events and circumstances of Mato Niyanpi's life. Many times the story is told in the present tense, such as if you were walking with Saved By Bear and his people as the events unfold. That was our original manner of storytelling. Other times the story is narrated in the past tense to account for a past perspective. There are those of us who may not be entirely fluent in particular words or specific language, as much as we may be fluent in spirit and honest communication. The life messages, many times, can be more meaningful than just the written or spoken words.

Warrior Is follows the timeline from the time of Creation, moving through Saved By Bear's birth in 1849, and going up to July 1876, two weeks after the Greasy Grass Battle.

Please exercise your free will and follow your conscience when reading his story. The spiritual side is calling for you to open your spirit so that you may read this tale and learn about these events through your own spirit, that part that may be seeking something that you may have felt for a long time yet did not fully understand. You know who you are.

You know yourself. You know how you feel. You know how you think. Trust your spirit.

One can justifiably condemn the practices, policies, beliefs, or actions of those people who did bad things in the past. But at the same time, we acknowledge that those who live in the present may not share in, or condone or applaud, those past practices, policies, beliefs, or actions.

You do not need to believe as your own ancestors may have once believed, although you may choose to do so. Their past actions are not yours, unless you choose to embrace those past actions and take them as your own in your present beliefs.

All human beings have weaknesses and flaws, including the Lakota. The Lakota were not, and are not, perfect. No one is or ever was. But the Lakota are honest and true as to who we were and are. People of all races and backgrounds can be honest and true. The connection to one's spirit is the key to being honest and true to oneself and to others.

Please view the events told in the story of our great-grandfather through the lens of openness of mind and possibility, with an openness of heart, and mostly with an openness and freedom of your spirit.

We welcome you to join us. We welcome you, whoever you may be or wherever you may come from, to become a part of our story, to become a part of our Circle, for the present.... and for the future.

PROLOGUE

HE SMELLED THE YELLOW OF the sun. His spirit was alive and energetic. He felt the energy in his chest and all along the blood running through his veins. He looked to his left to see his great friend by his side. The strong scent of sage caressed his nostrils and reminded him of home. The movement over the high-running hilly ridge to the south caught his eye. He and Swift Bear sensed and felt the pathway opening up. So much had occurred so quickly. So suddenly. So dramatically. Their call to duty, his call to duty, filled his mind, his heart, his spirit. Today was meant to happen. It was presented to the people from the Creator. The plan was made. The warriors summoned. The preparation was done. It all led to this place. This portal in time.

The sparse clouds to the west resembled mares' tails. And for a brief moment, he remembered his white stone friend in the White Mountains. He remembered his spiritual commitment to protect his people, Grandmother Earth, and the sacred He Sapa. And time stood still for a moment—a small moment in time, through all of the ancient and original history of all the moments of time. And as the group of the horse-mounted soldiers rode briskly over the far ridge, the Creator shined that warm, nurturing light upon these warriors. Such as Creator had been doing since the beginning of time, since the beginning of Grandmother Earth and Grandfather Sky, and at the beginning of all things. All the moments of time forever, had arrived here, now. It had come to this.

Creator's strong will and great invisible hand had placed them here. It was the Creator all along. It always was. And always would be.

For one to know what led the young Lakota warriors to be here at this fateful site near the Greasy Grass River on this warm, sun-drenched day, one must go back. Go back in time. Way back, to the beginning.

When it was only the Creator. And the Creator of all things decided to create a new world.

Her name would be Unci Maka. "Grandmother Earth." And she would be created to hold and sustain life. All kinds of beings, all kinds of peoples, will be given and placed upon and within her to show her love of life. And this is how it all began.

1

ORIGIN

THE HUMAN BEINGS EVOLVED FROM the spirit. Before arriving in Wind Cave, we were star people. Many of us came from a place called the Pleiades, the "Seven Sisters," an ancient star grouping and constellation that contains worlds comprised of the gift of life-giving water. Water is life—*mni wiconi*. The Pleiadian influence is an absolute. But those of us who claim to be relatives of the Pleiadians, share a common bond with other indigenous people, regardless of where we are geographically on Earth. We will always remain Pleiadian star people. Spiritually, we have become human beings of different races and ethnicities, but the origin of our spirit is the water. And for us, as to who we are, as the tribal people in a family way, our name *Mnincoju* is evidence. It means "life's subsistence through the gathering and planting by the water and/ or river." The Mnincoju spend their lives living by the waters. This is something that many of our own people do not know or understand, but this is our history, not only of our physical existence but also the history of our spiritual existence on Unci Maka.

The strongest connection goes back to Creator. The Creator is the one who has taken the time to engineer, develop, *create*, and bring forth life in every unique being. In this way, the Creator is the one who has helped and furthered life by continually providing amenities so that life will be enjoyable but productive. This is the inclusive part of the Creator's grand plan for all things that goes beyond the imagination of the human being. The human being needs to understand that our place is to be exactly where we are—not to dominate, not to devastate, but to live and commune. To coexist appropriately with the already existing beings, places, and things, that Creator wanted us to be a part of.

Creator will not instill fear. Creator will not mandate or dictate. Creator will not oppose anything that is done willfully and positively. The Creator is here to support, and provide guidance and elements to help, all beings that exist upon Unci Maka. The Creator is the keeper of life. Creator will decide how life is to begin and which elements will be included for starting up the feeling and the gift of life.

In the beginning, there was darkness set before all things. This darkness is infinite. It extends in every direction and is empty, void of the Creator's life. It is the first step in the arrival and gifting of this life. The space of darkness contained all the fragments and pieces that would become the Circle of life.

As the darkness waits, in silence and stillness, the Creator gathers the life forces. The life forces resemble orbs of light of various shades and are made up of the colors of the rainbow.

Creator then takes these life orbs in hand and releases them into the new universe, spreading them near and far. It is pure energy. Energy is life. Life is energy. All things are made up of energy. All things created are created out of energy. The first being to be gifted with this life force is the stone. As the orbs are approaching their positions in the galaxies, they become planets, particles of matter, and become a tangible physical presence. The first being, stone, *inyan*, will become the oldest of the beings of life. The planets and pieces of stone, are life, for they are the foundation of every life that will follow throughout time. Constellations are being formed. There are planets and entities, and beings who will be inhabiting these places in the future.

Let us focus on the area of what will come to be known as our home, the one called Unci Maka, Grandmother Earth. She is not there yet, but her foundation for life is waiting for the next step of Creator. These planets, these spheres and centers of energy, are established in our realm of life and in their respective places. There is a constellation which is created made up of the Water Planets. This constellation is the Pleaides. Time is being extended now. No one can say exactly what the time frame was. From the Pleaides, the gift of life and water comes to Unci Maka.

When the arrival of the water comes to be on the stone, life begins. Unci Maka becomes who she is. The Mother, the bearer of every new being who will be sent to her to keep. These beings will come at different times.

We begin with the essence of life from the stone and the water. There are species that come first through the water. The majority of life at the beginning has a water-based foundation. These life forms swim and live in the water. As the water gets older, different species are introduced. We go from the smallest, which may not be seen by the human eye or any eye, to some of the largest and most beautiful creatures of creation. So through the bare beginnings of organisms, life evolves.

As these life forms populate Unci Maka, Creator sends more and more beings full of life to this place. Additional orbs arrive by the hand of Creator. And as they come and begin to exist in their own times throughout the ages, we focus on the ones that come into existence nearer to the time frame of the coming to existence of the human beings. The smaller beings, the organisms, are beginning to exist as beings coming forth next in the chain of life. And as the population increases with the vast number of species, creatures, and beings, the waters become full of life. The plants, the animals, and the element of water itself, all continue to birth creations and life forces. As the beings keep coming, they become more mobile. They become more capable in their own existence throughout this water world. They populate certain geographic areas on Unci Maka. And they ask with a special purpose to maintain the water. Water is the most precious element of Creator's beings. Not only are we composed of it, but also we must have it to thrive and live.

We see the coming of these species, and we now look, and we see that these water people have become very capable of movement, preying, and surviving. They also have become very, very intelligent. These beings turn into what many may recognize in time, as the dolphins, the sharks, the turtles, and the whales. Some of the oldest beings that have existed on Unci Maka. These beings are approaching our time, the time of the human beings. For millions and millions of years, this has occurred. Over time, the species evolve, becoming stronger, smarter, better adapted. But the two-legged, or the human being, has not yet been sent to Unci Maka by Creator.

The time comes when the people of the waters are thriving. But now a land base on Unci Maka has been formed. The land base at the beginning, was one big contiguous land base. Later it would be separated by the movement of the Earth and by the great flood of waters. The land base of Turtle Island—North, Central and South America—came into being. The Earth settled upon the back of the Great Turtle. Creator determined that life will be on foot, on top of this foundation of Grandmother Earth. And again life forms begin fundamentally, through organisms populating plants and the smallest of beings, to begin a recycling process for the future. Each of these species goes through its time and then perishes. However, their bodies, their spirits, their presence, is recycled by the coming generations of life. Recycling of all things is the design by the Creator. The Creator created all things in such a way, in such a beautiful and magnificent way, so as to take into account strengths and vulnerabilities, and the recognition that all life would be important in many natural and significant ways, to all other life.

The world is populated by Creator's life forces in ways that are intact, beautiful, and wonderful. These life forces' coexistence is totally dependent upon need, rather than want. They need to eat. They need to drink. They need to repopulate. This is the purpose that they follow, as they are truly connected to the presence of Creator. Every being born of life upon Unci Maka is sacred, and becomes a child of Grandmother Earth and the Creator.

The land beings will continue to grow, from the smaller animals to the larger ones. There are now more and more kinds of land animals: the ones that will eat the grasses, the ones that will live in the earth, the ones that take and understand that this place is here not only for them to live in, but also for them to perform and live by the purpose of Creator's intention.

At this time now, there is a world populated through the waters and the Earth. The skies begin to see the same effect. First there are insects, and then birds. Various kinds of those beings begin their presence on

Grandmother Earth. And they all work together. They all manage. And somehow there is no bad, is no hurtful means of existence between one another, only a creational *asking* and intention.

There also is an adaptation and natural development of the need to take prey in order to survive. This world is built on the recycling of one another's bodies. It is a hard fact to accept that we must in essence take and consume another's livlihood. But it is not a question to analyze or have pain over. The Creator simply asks that it be this way.

Among all of these peoples, new and older, the most important thing that they have done as a species or a life grouping is to have established tradition and culture to live by. This enables civility and necessity to be two separate affairs, one of emotion and the other of satisfaction. And when you combine the two, you have an adherence to the purpose of this life.

As we move throughout the time frames and the eons, we begin to look at Grandmother Earth as she is, just before the time when the human being is sent to Unci Maka. The beings that are already here wait with an understanding and with very patient minds and spirits, looking forward to our coming—the coming of the human being. All existing beings have been told by Creator of a being that will have reasoning power beyond that of most of the others who have already been living here. These new people will be called human beings.

As we approach this time frame for the human, we see that we are in a position of looking down from above, upon the Earth, as though gazing from an eagle's eye. We are focusing now on a place on Earth that will bring the red man into existence. This place is called He Sapa, the Black Mountains (also known as the "Black Hills"). This is a very special place on Unci Maka because it is considered the heart of all of the lives that have come here. Unci Maka is the Grandmother of everything that surrounds her. We see at this point that sacred sites have been established. These sacred sites were sent by Creator with the inyan, the stone. Now they are full of life and waiting for the presence to commune with, nurture, and provide guidance to all of her children.

2

HUMAN BEING

WHEN CREATOR DECIDED TO GIVE the red man life, Creator also decided that the heart of Turtle Island would be the entry point of the people from Wind Cave, Wasun Wiconiya Wakan. Creator would gather spirits in many shapes and of many forms with particular duties and responsibilities to Grandmother Earth. While these spirits came from beneath the surface of the ground, Creator gathered these spirits, and asked each one of them to become these new people, so that others would be able to rely upon them and coexist with them. A great many things were sent forward, such as the grasses, and the trees that would provide us with berries for gathering and eating, and for use in our ceremonies.

Certain animals would come forward, in particular, the eagles, the bear, and the buffalo. Following a certain order, each people was given approval to appear upon the surface of Unci Maka, exiting from the spirit side of life, and entering the physical. Each kind of people knew their place and their duties as an individual people. As they were all being placed out in the world, there was one who was very full of activity and energy, flying inside of the Wind Cave, nonstop. Creator asked this spirit, "Why are you so anxious to become a part of this new world?" The spirit's reply was that he wanted to be a part of this world so much that he wanted to go out there right now. He wanted to be on the Earth, contributing to it. As such, it didn't matter what shape, what form, or what existence the Creator would give this one. The people of this particular spirit would willfully accept their place and do the providing and caretaking that was asked of them. This anxious spirit was given the name *tatanka*, and Creator sent him on his way onto the surface of Grandmother Earth.

There is a place just outside of the He Sapa where the being called the tatanka, the buffalo, has come forward as a sacred life force. The buffalo take care of the plains in the manner that they live. They migrate to ensure that their people have enough of everything needed to survive. As these beings were approaching He Sapa, there first is seen a cloud. The cloud gets bigger as the first piece of this cloud is coming closer. And through this cloud, emerges the beings called tatanka. They are led by a bull. The bull is running gracefully, leading his people to He Sapa. He follows the path of his ancestors to this place, the Pte Tali Yapa, the Buffalo Run. He takes his families there, knowing that this was the right thing to do for their lives

And as tatanka arrived, the buffalo knew that their role would be to help the human being. They would be very close, like a brother or a sister to the human being. For the Lakota's dependence on the tatanka people would mean living or dying. Tatanka came forth with this commitment to the human being who was still yet to arrive on the Earth. Everybody else was in place, all with the knowledge and wisdom that each of the species would follow forever. The human being was the last to be asked to take its place.

The Creator said to the human being, "I will give you reasoning power, which will give you an extreme amount of responsibility and a great capacity of choice. Now you must learn to coexist with all the other people who have come before you." And the human being agreed. And when the human being came out and stood on the surface of the Earth, it was as a red man and a red woman. The human being came forth out of the Wind Cave in the heart of Unci Maka, in the sacred He Sapa. And this is how we came to be.

We, the red man and red woman, were the first human peoples to emerge upon Turtle Island. So our place is to make sure that Turtle Island always remains intact, and populated with Creator's beings. The red man, and specifically the Lakota, are the *Protectors* of Turtle Island. This was so in the beginning of all things. And it will be so, forever.

If one goes back in time to the recent history of man, approximately four thousand years ago, one discovers that during that time frame, the modification of metal was introduced. Metal, and the mining for metal, created a distinct deterrent to life on this planet and brought worry, death, and suffering to the indigenous peoples and Grandmother Earth. What has happened to the Chinese people is a prime example of this. For thousands of years, the Chinese have had metal, yet it has devastated their own people. Dynasty after dynasty was affected, including the rich and wealthy, and the consuming, abusing, and murdering factions. This situation has been repeated for the last three to four thousand years across most continents on the planet, following and coinciding with the bringing forth of metal and the mining for metal.

Let us consider a perspective from the spiritual side. During all of this time, our Turtle Island, and the North and South American continents, were basically hidden from the awareness or knowledge of the rest of the world, even from the activity or foreign landings of the other humans. Turtle Island was hidden from the people who were traveling to seek riches, wealth, and resources from other peoples. Throughout history, many peoples have spoken of a place called Shambhala, saying that it is like, and imparts a feeling of, utopia. In Shambhala, there was no war, there was very little disease, and there was enough to feed, shelter, and educate your own people. It was a safe place protected by wonderful spiritual beings. So an aura of safety covered the North, Central and South American continents, making us practically invisible to the rest of the world, and particularly, to the potentially evil side of the world. Wonderful people who connected to us spiritually always knew we were here, because we prayed together. But there was that distance, whereby other humans were not so spiritually connected. We are speaking about physically coming to Turtle Island and then leaving. So the place called Shambhala may actually be Turtle Island. This is the place where life began. This is the place where everything that a human being eats or consumes was gifted by Creator, starting from Turtle Island itself, and going out to the rest of the world.

During the early stages of the human being's existence across Grandmother Earth, there were circles forming of very spiritual people. The Creator gifted tradition and culture to help every nation to advance and prosper. As these circles continue to form, the Sacred Hoop is created, which is the total spiritual effect of the human being and our connection to Unci Maka, Wakan Tanka, and Creator. In the end, the Earth is in the center of this Circle and this Circle represents an aura of life, of gifting, and of wonderment. This is the intent of Wakan Tanka and the people who live upon Unci Maka: creating parallels in spirituality.

This story of origin is told through our history and tradition. From the Pleiades, we acknowledge an *asking* of Creator. To become the human being, we live in Pleiades spiritually first, among the water and the water spirit. And when it comes time to send those who are willing to be sent and to go forth from the Pleiades to Earth, these people are initially known as the star children. They have a bloodline that will run throughout all time, since the inception of the gift of life through Grandmother Earth. These people have been born generation after generation in many indigenous cultures. They remain here today, although they are not as numerous as before because of what has happened to many indigenous peoples across the globe. But there is one particular area of these type of human beings who are also spiritually connected to the Pleiades.

Our responsibility today is just as important as the responsibility on the first day of the coming of the human beings and all beings. We must always remember that we are all one life force from Creator. We exist only to perform and be an example of the intent of the wonderful ways and cultures that Creator wants us to live by.

The aforementioned spiritual people in many cultures are looked upon as just that. They have a connection to the stars and beyond, which gives them an opportunity to share with the world and their surroundings, facets that are not known, not documented, and not ever spoken of before. The spiritual people come with knowledge and wisdom with a unique connection to Creator. They can organize. They can criticize. They can do everything a human being can do. But for the most part, you will recognize them by their communal state of unification. They live their lives trying to fit in to this new, unorganized world. When they come into the presence of a being that is in need, they contribute positively, for this is the gift of coming from the stars. And this is the gift of water, the rejuvenation of life.

Also from the Pleiades, along with life, came all of our sacred ceremonies and sacred sites, which were established at the same time as the emergence of the human being. Whether it be a mountain, plains, any other sacred place, or plants. It all depends on water for it to either replenish or to evolve. Therefore, the presence of the human being and the sacred sites is a direct connection to Creator, a very old connection that we have pretty much forgotten, as evidenced by present-day behavior. The tribal people seem to worry about only certain ceremonies now. Originally, there were many various and separate sacred ceremonies for the people. Many of the ceremonies, that would no longer be practiced, were forgotten by many. The people should have been trying to learn and teach the oldest of the sacred ceremonies so that they can find purpose again. Because there is no life without purpose. And the people should be well versed in purpose, in light of the changing world to come.

The influence of the Pleiades on life, is not something specific to Earth. It is believed that life went out to other, similar worlds, worlds with people who also need water to exist. There are many people like this throughout the universe. So these people, being a part of the Pleiadian world, should have a workable and peaceable contact with other worlds as well. Maybe these other worlds are the ones that are going to help our world. In saying "*mitakuye oyasin*," which means "all my relations," we do not limit our relatives to only those we see and know on Earth. Instead, we are relating ourselves to everything that is a part of creation, even those things beyond our imagination, well beyond the distance we can perceive, and beyond even thought itself. For this is how creation is. We are basically given the opportunity to live through creation. But Creator wants us to understand that this life is to be lived equally, communally, and also spiritually. This is the significance of *mni*, water. All beings share the need for water. Say you are out in the hot sun, sweating, hurting from the toil of what you are doing or performing, and needing water. The body needs water to survive. The second you ingest that water, you begin to feel alive again. This is what we need to do: bring that life force back from the Old Ones, the original spirits and beings, who taught us how to live in the first place.

Turtle Island in the beginning was one massive dense continent. Geographically, the red man was placed at different points on Turtle Island: north, south, east, and west. This presented an opportunity for diversity, and to have variations in dialect, ritual, tradition, and culture, but also an opportunity to assimilate with the parallels and the rites of the spirit world. The spirit world was what kept us bound together during this time. For eons, people got along and helped one another.

But then there came the problem with mankind again, the intervention of the evil side. Whether it comes from this planet or not, evil has been here, and is here today. It is more prevalent now because there are many more peoples and populations on the globe. When there was peace and civility, people could travel, enjoy their lives, share with each other, and advance in society. But once the turmoil emerged, and began to raise its ugly head within families, communities, and all the nations, Creator and Unci Maka decided that Turtle Island would be divided. The logic of this was that if the peoples were separated, then maybe they would sense that they may be in the wrong. Keep in mind, however, that not all of the people were causing the chaos. Only a select group was causing the chaos.

Also during this time, a sensibility and peace among all indigenous peoples was realized, as they were able to communicate with one another as if they all spoke one language. Of course, there were variations in dialect and emphasis on certain words with a somewhat different meaning, but the people still understood each other. They did not have to go to a new land or a different nation and relearn everything. If there were things to be learned about another culture, then these indigenous peoples were willing to learn it, just as others were willing to teach them.

The turmoil and chaos came about because of the interruption caused by evil-minded, bad-hearted, bad-spirited human beings. And that group of human beings, for generations then and to come, would seek to obtain control of our planet. Through history, this will become true. More and more, they are removing indigenous people from their places of origin.

The Great Race Around He Sapa

There was a time upon Grandmother Earth long ago when the human beings were in a bad way. There was a lot of evil occurring, and not just on Turtle Island. This was occurring because the human beings were taking evil and trying to make it spiritual. Their practice of destroying and taking life, and everything in between, began to consume everything on a planetary scale. At one point, all of the animal beings, the animal people, decided that the human being had gone too far. The animal peoples decided that there needed to be a discussion about the human beings' presence. Was it worth keeping them here?. Or should they be gotten rid of, along with their problems in dealing with all of the other beings in creation? So the animal peoples asked each of the different peoples—the birds, the four-legged creatures, the two-legged creatures, those who crawl on their bellies, those who grow from the earth—to be a part of this conversation. Their goal was to make a decision about the human being. During the discussion, it was found that only a few of the animal peoples supported the idea of letting the human beings remain. But the majority of the other peoples said, "We want them gone. They harm us. They harm our children. They harm our families. They harm Unci Maka. And we are not even involved in what they believe in."

After the animal peoples had held their council, they would decide to hold a race. It would become known as *the Great Race*, a race to be held around the "Race Track" of the He Sapa, the *Oki Inyanke Ocanku*. The winner of this race, after four days, would decide the fate of the human being. Included in this race were beings who are swift, beings who fly, and beings who crawl.

The reason that the area of land surrounding the heart of Grandmother Earth in He Sapa, the racetrack, is red is because many of the beings involved in the race will sacrifice their lives in this race in order to give their people an opportunity to live equally in coexistence and according to Creator's ways. On the first two days of the race, some of the animals were trampled. Others died because they did not have the stamina to keep up or the endurance to continue. The blood of the beings who would die, creates the color of the red track. On the other hand, there were those who were constantly strong and always in the lead. And there were the birds, who were strong in their own way since they were able to fly, which gave them a big advantage over all the other animals, as they weren't subjected to being trampled to death like some of those who moved on the ground.

After the third day, the weaker animal peoples were weeded out, leaving only the strongest ones in the race. For example, the turtle people didn't make it very far. They were trampled. The mice, and other small people like them, the ones that were not big beings, essentially gave up their existence in running this race.

On the fourth day, as all the remaining contestants were nearing the finish line, the buffalo is in the lead. The buffalo was the swiftest of all creatures known of here on the plains. However, while the buffalo was running and feeling his purpose and what he believed in, the magpie jumped on his back. As the buffalo came closer and closer to the finish line, the magpie remained on his back. When the buffalo reached a certain point just before the finish, the magpie took off, flew in front of the buffalo, and crossed the finish line ahead of him. The magpie had won the race.

So it became the responsibility of the magpie and the winged people to decide the fate of the two-legged and the human beings. The remaining animal people sat and held a council once more, based upon the outcome. They said to the magpie, "What is your decision?" The magpie replied, "I wish to give them another opportunity, because I am one of the closest to them. I am two-legged as well. You all said that you would remove all the two-leggeds. A human being has two legs, and a bird has two legs. The Bear people also have two legs. They stand up and walk like a human being. Therefore, I support the humans. We give them another opportunity, one more chance." With that, the matter for which the Great Race had been held, was settled. And Creator accepted the decision from all of these different peoples. The humans were spared. However, at some period in the future, the two-legged humans may again threaten the survival of all people and all things. Mankind, again, may become the problem.

Star Connection

THE SEVEN SISTERS ORIGINATE FROM the Pleiades and the constellation configuration in the Pleiades. The constellation and planetary configuration represents *seven*. In our Lakota culture, these seven stars and the associated celestial bodies became our sacred sites on Earth in the He Sapa. During our time of preparation as spiritual beings, readying ourselves for coming to Earth, these sacred sites were set before us by Creator. These sacred sites include many of the He Sapa sites that are widely known today: Pe Sla, Mato Paha, Mni kata, Mato Tipila, Owl's Nest (Hinhan Kaga), Wasun Wiconiya Wakan (Wind Cave), and Inyan Kaga. Each of these places is a sacred site to the Lakota and many tribal Plains people. Before human beings were sent to Grandmother Earth, these sacred sites were established. They were all placed and made ready for use by the human being called the Lakota, as well as the other humans. Once the Lakota came to Unci Maka, then our dependence upon these sacred sites resulted in the seven sacred ceremonies that we would perform to keep the people in good health, in good spirits, and of good mind. These were the primary objectives of Creator in asking the Lakota to populate the Earth. Human beings came into existence and learned, adapting to a world wherein they had to provide for their own needs and the needs of their family. This is a part of being human, whether one was here on Turtle Island at the beginning or came after the time of the first red peoples and the division of Turtle Island into two parts. The red man and the red woman, who gave rise to the Lakota, have always, since the beginning of time, been spiritually connected to the stars. The viewing and knowledge of the stars has always been a generational gift passed through family. It is critical to know of and about the stars, and how to plan.

Through each successive generation, it is known and has been told that in the Lakota culture, when any child is born they are given a spirit, a *wanagi*, from a star in the great vastness of Grandfather Sky. The child grows and matures, hopefully into adulthood, and hopefully becoming fortunate and blessed enough to become an elder. Each Lakota lives his or her whole life on Grandmother Earth with that spirit. And when the Lakota dies and passes on to the other side, the spirit world, that spirit leaves the physical body and rises to Grandfather Sky, to the middle of the Big Dipper, *Wicakiyuhapi*.

Once there in the Great Cup, on a special spiritual blanket stretched between each of them, the four stars of the Great Cup Wicakiyuhapi, who are referred to as the carriers, carry the risen spirit of the passing one to the great Spirit Trail—the Milky Way, the Trail of the Spirits—to the home of the Great Beyond, where the people initially came from.

The three bright stars that follow the carriers, and which make up the handle of the Big Dipper, are called the mourners. The three mourners follow the carriers, who perform the age-old sacred duty of carrying the loved one's spirit to the *Wanagi Tacanku* in the north, and beyond. Then traveling to the south, the spirit, accompanied by its devoted sojourners, travels on the Spirit Trail, until this individual spirit of the Lakota returns to its origins, its home, the first destination: Pleiades.

The Lakota belief in, tradition of, knowledge of, and philosophy of the stars memorializes the prehistorical notion of *mitakuye oyasin*, which—again—means "all my relation" or "we are all related." This is demonstrated succinctly and naturally through the cyclical movement of the Lakota spirits from the stars, to the Lakota in the physical world, and then back to the stars. The stars are a nation of relatives, breathing, living entities whose organization, order, and natural and predictable movements can be realized and comprehended by witnessing the pattern of movement of the clusters and constellations in Grandfather Sky. They are always there in the sky, day and night. Wi (the Sun) lights up the daytime skies and casts a bright cloak over Grandmother Earth. This makes it so the human eye cannot always see the stars clearly during the day. But during the absence of Wi, and the introduction of Hanwi (the Moon), or simply when it is dusk or nighttime, the magnificent serenade of the celestial bodies is revealed to any and all beings who choose to look up and turn their gaze beyond the horizons of the physical presence of Grandmother Earth and to the very edges of earthly imaginations and into the universe. It is a free show, one that has been playing for billions and billions of seasons. It is a grand exhibition for all who have been chosen to occupy the physical and spiritual realm of Grandmother Earth and Grandfather Sky.

The vast ancestral homelands of the Lakota people have always been the perfect setting for the personal witness and experience of the relationship between the stars and the Lakota. The Lakota country night sky is a gift from Wakan Tanka and Grandfather Sky. It has forever provided people of all origins—including the four-legged and the winged too—a way to know where and what may be happening on Grandmother Earth at any given time or in any given season. The unbelievable open landscape of the He Sapa and the open rolling plains and hills of Lakota territory provide a great ability to clearly observe the stars. From within these areas, the Lakota recorded their individual and collective accounts of their relationships with the stars and other beings in their universe. These recollections and narratives of the Lakota's knowledge of their own universe, serve as an intricate blessing and treasure. A treasure that was eagerly handed down from ancestor to descendant, from grandparent to grandchild, from a holy man to his people. It was readily told, and received in stone drawings, etchings, hide pictures, the ceremonies, the prayers, and the winter counts, but mostly through the oral histories told by families to each other, season after season, generation after generation.

3

EARTH PEOPLE

On Earth, there are many peoples and many seasons. Ceremonies and prayers are performed throughout the seasons. When the women are doing their things for the home life of their families, when elders are teaching the children about their people—these types of things need to be addressed so that there is a full-circle effect for a family unit, with each member functioning well for one another.

An important aspect of understanding the Lakota is to know how the traditional Lakota society dealt with individuals. The Lakota society was so advanced as to take into consideration all aspects of humanity. The society involved the recognition of right versus wrong, and this involved teaching children, through adulthood, to discern the difference, and to recognize that every individual has a right to self-determination. Still, everyone must exist within the society and conform to the rules of that society so that there is no harm done to individuals or to the people as a whole. The earlier people were thinking beyond the materialistic plane, into the very soul and spirit, which is the Circle of life, and the people themselves.

How these individual groups and the individuals involved in those groups actually dealt with these particular issues and problems, was significant. This just shows how truly advanced the Lakota society was in the sense of being civilized. The Lakota knew and taught that all things were connected. There was a reason for this, and a reason for that. Much thought and ingenuity of spirit went into the formulation of how to deal with individuals and their issues and problems. One can easily see how truly advanced Lakota society was.

For example, the Akicita, the peacekeepers, maintained order and balance in Lakota society. When someone violated the people, the people were at risk. This is why the matter was immediately attended to. The violation of one of our own tribal people was dealt with swiftly and seriously. Because of this, spiritually, there must be a reinforcement of the important teachings that were gifted to a Lakota in order to show what one will be reminded of before severe action needed to be taken.

The special sacred sites, rituals, and ceremonies are there to help us. The horse, the dog, the eagle, and the bear are vital to our having a spiritual presence and staying in a good way as human beings. We must always recognize all the animals in the air, on the ground, and in the waters, because they are the ones who brought us here. Those beings cared for the first human beings when the human beings first arrived. They nurtured us at one time, long ago. The humans learned every aspect of their lives and existence from the animal beings. We must acknowledge their importance to all the human beings. We drank water to get to the battle. We hunted and consumed beings to stay healthy. We asked, in dependence upon the plants, for the plants to provide us their gifts for our lives. This means that what has happened to and with human beings is not the entire story. What was happening to human beings came full circle to affect all life the Creator had made, and the individual connections that all of these beings have to everything else on Earth.

The Lakota took the time to honor individually, the gifts and the existence that has come from each brother of every species and from every type of people, such as the bear, the elk, the turtle, the frog, and the bird. This includes all things that contribute to the Sacred Hoop of life. In recognizing the importance of all the other peoples in the animal world, the connection that exists for certain human beings to see other human beings in a way in true empathy and compassion, is enhanced. For understanding their way of life, and their existence and beliefs, is to show the relationship between the human and the animal. And if the human is motivated or moved by the suffering of the animal, then he or she can use that as the basis for the connection to recognize and understand the suffering and the anxiety, and the existence of a fellow human being. Which also leads to recognizing the connection that can be made that way through that path, from one being to another. That is the gift provided to us, in knowing and accepting these similarities in us all. An ability to appreciate Creator's gift and plan to lovingly place a part of every people, every type of species, within the Circle of life.

Each tribal nation has in its tradition and culture, its own ways of connecting to Creator. Many people today are familiar with some of the more prevalent tribal peoples, like the Hopi, who are known globally for their stories and prophecies of the origin of this world. In the world of the red man and red woman, of whom the Lakota, Dakota, and Nakota are a part, there is a responsibility to take care of the spiritual part of the human being by bringing each other messages, and sharing one's experiences with all peoples communally. A lot of these things that come from ceremony, and to those individuals who are highly connected, are warnings, for the most part. There is a forewarning of something to really have caution about, and as to how humanity is walking and conducting itself. We have, in a Lakota way, some things that were delivered through the sweat lodge. These prophecies are being told by not only Lakota people, but also by others. There is a common thread to all of them.

Family is an extremely important bond across all things. It is extremely important that what was done at the Greasy Grass, and why, involved family members. It was that connectedness of the family that allowed the spirit to be so strong. This connectedness was why the particular members of certain families were chosen to do what was needed to be done.

Our great-grandfather Mato Niyanpi (later known also as Scar Leg) had something among his possessions that he gave to his daughter, Mary Scar Leg Bagola, who has now left it to her daughter, Alverda Bagola Zephier. The item is a very old quiver with a set of blow darts. The darts have extremely sharp tips that are blackened with what appears to be a natural poison. The quiver is made of bamboo, with an insignia or symbol etched on the outside, which appears to represent the Pleiades star system. The quiver is also decorated with a partial piranha jawbone.

This is indicative of the tribes in South America, particularly the tribes in the aboriginal Ecuadorian area, quite possibly the Huaorani people. The partial piranha jawbone indicates a communication and kinship between the indigenous peoples across the globe. And this possession—the quiver and darts—indicates in particular that Mato Niyanpi/Saved By Bear ended up owning it after it belonged to someone from among the indigenous people of South America.

This container with the poison blowgun darts in it is usually associated with the jungle. Jungle dwellers need this type of weapon for subsistence. In the jungle, you have to shoot through the lush tree canopies to get to the animals and the other beings that live in these areas. The blowgun darts are essential for the survival of people who dwell in the jungle. How Saved By Bear came to possess these things is not only because of our indigenous relation as red men and red women. This was an offering, a gift, to the Lakota, in particular, to our families, and other families connected to those peoples from the Amazon. The Lakota may have been there to aid those people or protect them from something that was threatening them, such as battle, conflict, or encroachment. That is likely what happened, and the quiver and darts was part of an exchange of gifts, not only for services, but also for maintaining the contact and friendship between what people now recognize as the continents of North America and South America. We did travel, and we did commune with one another. It is not as if the Lakota merely stayed within the Plains of North America ever since the day they first came into existence. Turtle Island was the responsibility of all indigenous and tribal people, and the Lakota were placed here in a very unique and specialized manner, as human beings. The Lakota were given the gift of *protection* and, if need be, battle. We were physically capable. We were mentally and spiritually prepared for conflict on our lands and in other peoples' lands. There were times when we were called upon to settle disputes and even finalize disputes. This type of gifting among the indigenous peoples occurred throughout time.

As mentioned before, the South American tribe from whom Saved By Bear received the gift was likely the Hauorani of Ecuador. They have forever lived along the Amazon River. Everything they know comes from the Amazon, just like everything we know comes from the plains, our mountains, and our waters. Though we Lakota are geographically separated from the Hauorani, there are parallels in spirituality and practice between our two peoples that are undeniable. The color schemes that represent our sacredness are very similar, with the colors green and gold together representing the spirit of life: green for the earth, and gold/yellow for the sun. Our rituals are very similar. Our ceremonies are done in a similar fashion. The ceremonies for our genders, and for the cycles of age in life, are similar. What we authors believe is that our family was gifted this bamboo quiver with its darts in recognition of a task and for communing with our relatives on another continent.

There also are some very similar connections between the indigenous peoples across the globe and the Lakota. Many of these indicate that at one point, or so it appears, everybody was of the same origin. There are parallels between indigenous peoples from many cultures across the Earth. Some of these parallels include rituals in relation to spiritual presence; ceremonies; the similar use of beings (whether they be plants or animals); and the reference to the sacredness of these beings, such as the eagles and the condors—all these types of people who were allowed to help, and who were asked to help, the human beings as they lived on this planet.

The parallels that exist between the Lakota people and the indigenous peoples of other places such as Australia, New Zealand, Tibet, Appenzell (in Switzerland), the Scottish Highlands, Kenya, Ecuador, and Scandinavia (where the Sami peoples live) are numerous. Similarities exist in the usage of certain colors, whether they represent directions or have other spiritual meanings to each and every people. The astrological connectedness is similar as well. This includes the constellations, the seasons, and times of the year when specific rituals or ceremonies are performed. The reference to the sun is always a big parallel in all these cultures. In Lakota culture, we honor the sun with a ceremony called the sun dance. Other indigenous cultures do the same. The other indigenous peoples may not dance and pierce like the Lakota and Plains people do, but it is the same essence of practice. The other indigenous people also do these things for their people, so their people will have identity, culture, and tradition to rely upon, whether in wonderful times or in times of conflict, or worse…. such as times of enslavement, extermination, or even genocide. So that the indigenous had a strength and spirit to stand together.

The parallels are also prevalent with many of the other aboriginal indigenous peoples, in particular, the contacts and connections that the Lakota had with the people in South America, especially with the tribe of Ecuadorians known as the Hauorani people. The Hauorani's practices paralleled in a sense, the Lakota's, when it came to preparing to hunt and take animals for sustenance. It was the Lakota way, to pray and give ceremony to the Buffalo Nation while preparing for the hunt and after the hunt. In the same manner, the Huaorani people used blow darts and blowguns to do their hunting. But those darts and blowguns were blessed by their medicine people. The Huaorani viewed the taking of an animal as violating the animal's spirit unless this blessing was done in preparation. Then it wasn't as much a killing of the animal as it was a harvesting of the animal for purposes of sustaining the people. This is the parallel between the peoples of South America and the Lakota, but both practicing the same spiritual belief to honor those that are respectfually taken and giving life to the people.

Concerning some other familiar indigenous nations on the globe, the Aborigines of Australia are a very old people, just like the Lakota. They are some of the first peoples. Many of these tribal peoples claim to have come through the *rainbow* to Australia, again, from the Pleiades. So like the Lakota, their origin is from Pleiades, the Seven Sisters. Also, the planetary alignment is very familiar to them. The Aborigines also have their own sacred sites, just as the Lakota do, for prayer, for life, and for everything they need as human beings. Every continent currently has indigenous people who still believe in, still practice, and still rely upon astrology, and the heavens beyond Earth. And a strong belief in the Creator. Pleiades was known by some of the Far Eastern indigenous people as the "Subaru." The indigenous peoples across the Earth still believe in the connection of spirit and origin coming from the Pleiades.

To learn about yourself, your family, and your people, you have to have a strong belief system. You must have something foundational that allows you to continue generation after generation with success, prosperity, and commitment. This is the asking of Creator, for all of the first peoples and indigenous peoples of Unci Maka, Grandmother Earth.

The Aborigines believe in an origin story involving the rainbow. When they came to Earth from the Pleiades, they emerged from the rainbow, which is made up of water and vapor. They arrived in a way similar to the way the Lakota arrived, which was through Wind Cave. The parallels involve water, the constellations, and a belief system. When combined, these three components are very successful. These things have inhabited this planet for millions and millions of years. And these first peoples are now the ones who are left to help and protect Unci Maka. It is time for those who are asked to come here to be keepers of the Earth, to begin that preservation process again, keeping everything intact, teaching, and holding on to the truth in this life.

When one looks at a map of the constellation of stars called the Seven Sisters, or the Pleiades, the Seven Sisters duplicate the appearance of the Lakota sacred sites in He Sapa. In other words, those sacred sites are configured in almost the same way as the seven stars in the Pleiades. These sites in the He Sapa are: Mato Tipila (which is commonly known by white society as Devils Tower, but which actually means "Bear Lodge"); Mato Paha (Bear Butte), which is on the northeast edge of the He Sapa; Pe Sla, in the middle of the He Sapa, which is a high sacred clearing among the mountains and forest; Inyan Kaga (Home of the Stone), to the west and near the buffalo-shaped mountain; Hinhan Kaga (Owl's Nest), the highest peak east of the Rocky Mountains; Wind Cave (Wasun Wicanya Wakan) the sacred place of origin; and south of that, Mnikata (Hot Springs), the therapeutic healing warm waters. Not only do these seven sacred sites replicate the appearance of the constellation of the Seven Sisters, but also each is related to the seven main sacred ceremonies of the Lakota. The significance to the Lakota people has not only been set in stone on Unci Maka, but also has been set into the skies forever, and in the universe, in the stars of Pleiades.

When one looks at the night sky when the stars are visible, one can see that the Lakota have been here forever. Unci Maka granted us the gift of having these seven sacred sites placed the way they are, and with the star knowledge of the people. This is the connection. Each of these sites from the Pleiades is a separate entity with a special purpose and intent determined by Creator. Just as each of us has a life—we live a daily life full of routine, encounters, and experiences—it is the same for these sacred sites. They are here for us to practice our beliefs, learn from, and teach about. They are also here to aid in the earthly presence of everything that has ever lived here.

Recycling is a natural process that has always been present on Unci Maka. Recycling is a way of life on Earth. Things that human beings experienced millions of years ago remain prevalent, running through our veins. Every human being, every being that is a biological piece of Grandmother Earth, comes forth after being recycled from previous beings or elements. The water and the Earth, and its particles and minerals, make up the bodies of all beings. Our bodies eventually return to dust. And that dust returns to Unci Maka, and continues on to be recycled into the Mother, through the gifts of water and time, to become life in some other way or form, again. The gift of life includes the gift of death. Each entity has its place in the cycle of life and death. This is how we function. If we have a need of spirit or body for sustenance, we go to a certain place. If we have a need for a conflict to be settled or resolved, however, we go to a different place. These sites are our relatives, our older relatives. We may not share a shape or form with them, but we do indeed share their spirit. These sacred places are all unique individuals themselves, and are ready to perform their individual duties. This is how connected we are to the Earth, to every bit of the Earth, to every being, to everything. It is the Circle of life, a never-ending circle. The Circle can be interrupted and broken, but it can also be mended. It can be recycled. And the Circle can always be healed. It is never too late to heal the Circle.

Many stories going back millions of years tell of the story of the tree of life. It is a sacred story about a sacred being among all other beings on Unci Maka. Wakan Tanka grants a spiritual pathway to the intersection of life and truth. When Creator creates, it is done with a miraculous sense of purpose, connectivity, truth, and honor, and the deepest of meanings. Miracles of life are beautiful. The nature of life is miraculous. The creation of life is a beautiful miracle. The meaning of life is found within itself. The mystery is the miracle.

It is true that the human body is a gift from Creator. Since Creator had created most all other beings before the human, Creator was loving, caring, and intelligent enough to borrow the best and most useful attributes from one being and apply it to the next being. The womb resembles the tree of life because the womb *is* the tree of life. The placenta even resembles the tree of life. The wonders of Creator are everywhere, in everything. Our physical lives are too short in duration to waste any part of them not enjoying the gift of life.

Many of the oldest and original societies and civilizations on Unci Maka started out in the beginning, as matriarchal societies. Beginning with the most obvious female, Grandmother Earth, the giver of all life on this planet. This includes everything from plants, to animals, to humans, to birds, to all that exists in the water. All of these things involve birth in some fashion as we understand it. For the human being, specifically, the female is the giver of life. She carries forth in tradition just as Unci Maka, Grandmother Earth. The reason for this is that for procreation to occur, there must be a life giver and a partner to help create that life and give it presence. The female is the vessel. Her presence in our world is paramount in most everything that we do.

Traditionally, we are a matriarchal society as Lakota people. This means the women have the majority of the say in matters of livelihood and existence concerning the Lakota. Everything that we know as far as daily living, routines, and practices, and the experiences that come with those things, we know because of the female. In the Lakota way, it was the female who would own the tipi. She would own the possessions. She would be the leader when it came to how to manage and change the daily life of families. Her presence is always revered in the sense of ceremony. When we perform a ceremony, one of the places we use is called the sweat lodge, the *inipi*. Taking part in the inipi is symbolic of being reborn. It is symbolic of the womb, through which every male and female has passed to become a human being. It is vital when we are in ceremonies that we appreciate and respect the female's role in giving us this opportunity to experience. Had she not been there as a mother, as a grandmother, and as an original mother of the Earth, we would not have the separation of genders. We would not have life.

Many Lakota believe that societies have changed over time for many reasons. One of these reasons may likely be the development of organized religion. Religions exist in modern-day society, and for thousands of years prior to the present day, organized religions have existed. Religion was created by mankind. That is what is meant in the literal sense: "*Man*"-kind. Man eventually interpreted these religions in his own image, to reflect his own thought patterns and his own wants and desires. When religion and societies became male dominant, the role of the women became a subservient one. Women, for the most part, became basically possessions of men and participants in procreation. They became objects for the male, and the male-dominated society as a whole, to potentially abuse and subject to indignity. This is something that we all need to always remember today.

Mato Niyanpi (Saved By Bear) and the other Lakota males, took pride in their societal life because of their mothers and grandmothers. Mato Niyanpi defended the right to live that his mother and grandmothers gave to him. To show, preserve, and protect that right was what he was taught as a boy and as a man. He was not taught to disturb or abuse the balance of the female. Instead, he was taught to give the female the rights and respect that she deserved in every facet of society, and to respect her mind, body, and spiritual presence. When we speak about a warrior, we must realize that *a warrior is a gift from a mother.* From that mother, this warrior will have an honor and a responsibility to her and to the other females of his kind. He must do whatever is needed to provide protection for her and to provide comfort in exchange for the things she has given to him in a loving, caring, and wonderful way. This is the balance that existed before the times that we see today. As far as couples were concerned, neither male nor female was the leader or played the dominant role. Each person knew their role, and everybody assumed their designated role, in time learning to love and nurture that role.

The human societies over time changed and developed according to the changing times and circumstances. Those changes were not always for the better. A long time ago, there was no deception or dishonesty when people spoke to one another. People spoke the honest, the simple, and sometimes a shortened version of the truth. If you were concise with what you said to one another, there was no further explanation needed. People understood. They were allowed to make a proper choice because they were given proper information. The use of truth as a foundation was both an educational and evolutionary process of the people.

All my relation. Mitakuye oyasin. Everything and everyone on Grandmother Earth is related to each one of us. It is all a part of everything: people's lives, people's everyday existence, the way people spiritually recognized and performed duties and tasks, and how people behaved among their kind and among all of Grandmother Earth's children and beings. Each independent nation is related, whether it is the two-legged, the four-legged, the winged, the insects, the plants, or the beings of the waters. We should have reverence for the entities of this Earth; for the sun, the moon, the wind, the Wakinyan (Thunder Beings); and for all the beings that are not of human origin but that exist upon the Earth, because all are related.

Given that all beings are relatives of one another, the needs of each kind of people—the two-legged, the four-legged, the winged, the water people, the stone people, et al.—need to be met. All people of every kind have needs if they are to exist and survive, but most times those needs cannot be met by the efforts of the peoples alone. If the needs cannot be met or realized, then survival and existence of the people may require an *"asking"* from the people.

The "Asking"

Asking is a word known to all the people. It is a word that grows in the heart, the soul, and the spirit of every Lakota, from the time of the very first breaths, and from the time of the first learning. It is a sacred word of action, a sacred word of expression of need, of communication, of life.

Asking, in a simple sense, is exactly what it means. To *ask* is to request. To *ask* is to honestly express one's need, a need for something, someone, some way, some hope. The *asking* is the act of communicating to another in a manner to truthfully make it known that help is needed, that guidance of some form is needed, that a way is sought, to attain a goal. When one *asks,* one may be seeking help for oneself, for a loved one, for their family, or for their people, collectively. The subject of the asking can be singular or plural. The scope can be widespread or narrow. To *ask* is to convey that one is open to being helped, ready to be helped. Ready for anyone who will listen to or receive the *asking* to come to help, or to act in furtherance of fulfilling the need of the one, or of the many.

The *asking* itself may be done to the Creator by way of prayer, praying and asking in an honest, good way that Creator provide some help. To ask that Creator provide someone or some way to deliver the help, and that Creator be aware of the urgent or persistent need of the one or of the many. The *asking* of Creator is meant in a good way to speak to the spirits directly in a fashion involving Creator. To *ask* Wakan Tanka to help It is intended to seek the spirits' assistance in the need.

The connection is always there between the spirits and the people, and with all of the spirits that exist and remain through all portals of time and throughout all events. The *asking* merely focuses upon the opening of the door, the portal, the heart and the spirit, to allow the connection to become direct, pure, and thorough. The purpose is to clarify the communication, to make clear the talk. The talk that can happen without words, that can occur without motion or time, and which is within the utility of each and every spirit that has ever lived or existed at any time or in any place.

The connection is always there to be called upon by way of the *asking*, or by way of the unspoken thought or prayer. The connection is never broken. The connection may merely lie dormant and unused by those individuals or groups of individuals who either do not know it exists, or who are not fully aware of their natural ability to ask to rejuvenate, reconnect, or to wake up the connection with the spirits, with Wakan Tanka, and with Creator at any time, anywhere, anyhow. The connection is always available.

The *asking* is an opening of the portal to receive an answer, a vision, a guide, a sign, or a deliverance. The *asking* is a learned method of focusing on a particular means of purposefully waking the spiritual connection, a way to seek a specific type of help at a specific time for a specific reason.

The *asking* can and will be done by anyone—any being or any spirit—at any time and in any place. There is no magic time or place, if your intent is good and you ask in a good way and for a necessary good reason. It is difficult for the *asking* to be used in a bad way, for a bad intent, for a bad purpose, or in an evil way. Creator designed it that way. But Creator always provides for free will and freedom of spirit. So, good is better than bad. Good is better than evil. But good, unfortunately, is not always what is asked for.

The *asking* is the formal recognition of the confirmation of our dependence upon Creator. Creator made every part of us, and every part of what and who we are. Our spirits exist because of Creator. Our spirits occupy our physical bodies because we were created in that image, and by that spiritual design. The miracle of life is the miracle of the Creator. The miracle and purity of the spirit is one and the same with Creator.

We depend upon our Creator for everything. Our dependence is complete. Our dependence is, whole and meaningful. Our dependence is everything and everywhere. We all depend upon Creator. It is our essence, our need, our life, and our existence. We depend upon Creator. I depend upon Creator. We are dependents of Creator. We are beneficiaries of the dependence that we have upon Creator. Our dependence is accepted completely by us all, and by our Creator.

Therefore, because we depend, we must *ask*. When we need help, we are dependent upon receiving that help, so we must *ask*. Our *asking* is the fulfillment of our dependence upon Creator. If we ask, we are acknowledging not only our dependence but also the fact that we need help. The *asking* is the way to show our dependence, to honestly and completely show that we know, and pray, that help will be provided. This makes it so that that which we depend upon can be received. The Circle is twined together by those who ask. The Circle is made up of those who depend. The Circle is us. We all ask to be a part of, to remain, and to forever become the Circle. The Circle is dependent upon those who ask and those who depend. Therefore, we are all the Circle. The Circle is all of us.

Mirrors

The Lakota philosophy of life was always that all things in life are spiritually connected. That philosophy was carried forth into all things. All things in life from the beginning.

If the eyes are the mirrors to the soul, then looking into the eyes of the new life is the mirror into all that a soul will ever be.

Let us begin where the story must: at the beholding of the first glimmer of the promise of the new life; a mother lying next to her newborn, holding, kissing, and caressing the child, and a father realizing this new little soul's total dependence. Those very young eyes are looking into his with unconditional and absolute dependency for everything in life: food, water, shelter, comfort, protection, and love.

This one is a part of you. Not just in the flesh and the blood, but also in the sharing of the eternal connective tissue that mentally and emotionally strings from your very own heart and spirit in a direct line to that new little loving, beating heart and spirit. That connective tissue is never to be severed, never to be impinged, never to be forsaken, and never to be forgotten.

Even though that little beating heart will grow old and weathered over the years inside of a withering physical body, whenever the father and mother look at that being and into those eyes, that same old eternal connective tissue breathes and beats as if a part of that very first day and in that first hour when they first laid eyes upon eyes and shared the joy of life.

The mother buffalo sees this in her newborn calf as he struggles to nurse or to stand on new shaky legs. She nuzzles him for encouragement, and he feels strong and confident at the loving caress of her strong wet nose and the comforting warm breath coming from her nostrils. He will run and prance beside her on the prairie in good times and hard. And they will never forget.

The mother and father horse see the young one stretching those long legs and panting hard to catch his first breaths. He is so lanky and awkward now that it is hard to imagine him running like the wind along the top of a crested ridge with the breeze in his hair and his head bobbing with the nobility of his ancestors that comes with being free and strong. These parents, too, take note of the moment. They have beating hearts and minds. They speak mostly through their conduct and thoughts, but they all understand. Again, the eternal connective tissue runs deep and is secure. And no matter how long or how far the separation as adults may be, they will recognize each other again when and if they are blessed by Creator to have such a moment to share. They will run to each other and they will know, and they will never forget.

The forever faithful mother dog lovingly licks the faces of each of her newborn puppies as they emerge, in an attempt to let them smell her and feel her loving tongue for the first time of many thousands of times to come. Her loving licks are meant to urge them to come forward into the world and to take the first few breaths of air into their little lungs so as to give them a better chance to survive. And they will never forget.

Consider the way that the moving water of the stream reflects the sunshine against the rocky cliff walls in a glimmering, dancing portrayal of the language of old. The moving waves of reflecting light float and ripple in a natural way of communicating on a spiritual plane. It is not just seen, but is also felt. Each view may bring a different shape, a different message, for each set of eyes and each imagination.

The ability to know, to share, to feel, to understand, to remember, and to love, is universal. This is a truth created by Creator and manifested in all things through Wakan Tanka. No one species of being, and no one kind or race of people, owns these things. They are for all to own, all to cherish, all to know, and all to remember.

Life is meant to be shared and enjoyed. This is indiscriminant. There are no rules to confine this fact to only those with two legs, or four, or eight, or to those without. It is not even confined to humankind or animal kind. People of all origins know and feel and emote. People of all shapes, sizes, colors, contexts, and substance, share equally in the gifts granted by the Creator. This is the ever-living and ever-loving gift to all of the children of Grandmother Earth and Grandfather Sky.

It is a message and intellectual understanding of, and a confirmed belief of the Lakota people. The Lakota claim no unique ownership of or control over this belief. They are the ones who speak openly about this magic, the magic derived from all, for all. To each of his or her own. To each, the free will to look, and to experience—to look, and to really see.

The mirrors are everywhere. The mirrors have mirrors inside themselves. The world is made up of mirrors. It is the open heart and the open spirit, and not necessarily the eyes, that is needed to see all the mirrors in the world. And especially those mirrors that we sadly do not take the time to seek out, and to embrace, the ones which we should truly look at, and see into. The reflections within our spirits reveal the original lessons of life. These are the things that form the bedrock of one's existence, individually and collectively, within the family of Creator. The mirrors know no time line. No distance or obstacle can impede their message. It is the binding eternal connective tissue that twines it all together. And if given the honest chance, this message can draw us together so that we want to care about each other as individual beings, which we all once were. We all were once that helpless and dependent fledgling which was so in need of protection, understanding, acceptance, and love.

If we saw, and see, each other in this original way, then violence, harm, and war would not—could not—exist. Such things could not be allowed to enter into the mirror's reflection. They could not, would not, be allowed to sever or impinge, forsake or forget, that eternal connective tissue.

The eternal connective tissue is the miracle of life and living. It inspires us to choose with our own free will to care for and about each other no matter who our father or mother may be. It is the common thread of life and existence. It is the way of Creator. It is the path chosen by Grandmother Earth, for all of us to begin on the path she laid out for us. It is the gift from Wakan Tanka, which is reinforced in all of us. We are the mirror. The mirror is us. We are one and the same. We are a reflection of ourselves—all we were, all we have become, and all that we shall forever be.

⸻ «❂» ⸻

The Lakota paid great attention to the nighttime of Grandfather Sky. The Lakota had a very old, very good knowledge of the stars. The Pleiades featured prominently in such knowledge. The seven sisters of the Pleiades are symbolic of the seven most prominent sacred ceremonies, the seven sacred rites or virtues of the Lakota, and the Seven Council Fires, the Oceti Sakowin.

Even certain constellations among the stars mirror the geography of the He Sapa (Black Hills), as mentioned previously. Cangleska Wakan (Sacred Hoop) corresponds with the Great Racetrack (Oki Inyanke Ocanku) around the He Sapa. The configuration of stars of the Pleiades align with the sacred sites, such as Owl's Nest (Hinhan Kaga), Mato Tipila (Bear Lodge, Devils Tower), Mato Paha (Bear Butte), Mni Kata (Hot Springs), Wakinyan Paha (Thunder Butte), Wasun Wiconiya Wakan (Wind Cave), Inyan Kaga (Home of the Stone), and Pe Sla. Wakinyan Paha, (Thunder Butte), also a sacred site, is not located in the He Sapa, but was near the homeland of the Mnincoju along the Owl River and Bear Creek. As the stars moved across Grandfather Sky, they guided the Lakota people's seasonal movements in and around the He Sapa. For example, when the sun rose in the Pleiades, the people went to Owl's Nest to welcome back Wakinyan (the Thunder Beings).

The He Sapa was at the center of the Lakota world. The topographical features of the sacred land have overwhelming spiritual significance because these features mirror the connection to all things, including the Earth, the sky, and the stars. The He Sapa links the heavens to Grandmother Earth's surface, while He Sapa's underground caves link Grandmother Earth's surface to the very depths within her, where she became the wellspring of the human beings and the buffalo people, tatanka. The seven directions (west, north, east, south, above, below, and center) are manifest and ever present in everything within He Sapa. Therefore, to the Lakota, the He Sapa were *wakan* (sacred) in every way, not just because of their geographical meaning and landscape, but also because of their relation to the Lakota's spiritual meaning and landscape.

The Cannumpa

Unci Maka cradles the red stone of the pipe, the cannumpa. This red stone is the blood of our ancestors. The same blood runs through the veins of the human beings called the Lakota. The place of the red stone is a blessed, sacred place that was given to the people by the Creator for the purpose of making the bowl of the cannumpa. The place of the red stone was known as Pipestone. The Ihanktowan Dakota people were the original "stone keepers."

The pipestone was a gift for these purposes, a gift to be cherished, nurtured, and shared. The red pipestone from the sacred quarries can be carved easily by a person who is knowledgeable and determined. It is softer than most other of the inyan, yet it is hard enough to be heated up by fire without breaking. The stone is known as catlinite. Its durability is what was necessary to smoke, cleanse, and pray, alone or in ceremony. The pipestone became the commonly accepted stone to be used in almost all sacred ceremonial and personal holy cannumpas of the people.

When the sacred White Buffalo Calf Woman had come, she had taken the time to teach the people about the sacred ceremonies and the sacred rites of the Lakota. The Sacred Cannumpa was the gift that the White Buffalo Calf Woman presented to the people for and on behalf of Creator. The Mnincoju Lakota were chosen to be keepers of the Cannumpa because they were the *Protectors*. The sacred pipe would be presented to and kept by these people, who became known as the pipe keepers.

Cannumpas, commonly known as sacred pipes, were usually made by the Dakota, Nakota, and Lakota craftsmen, and given to others as gifts of honor and respect and of special holy designation. It was learned, and has often been said and repeated by the people, that a sacred cannumpa finds its own way to its true owner. This means that many or most times, the cannumpa comes suddenly to the man, woman, boy, or girl who is supposed to have it, and it becomes theirs. This is how it was at the beginning, and the same has been carried forward generation after generation since the beginning, many thousands of years ago. This has been the way, since the onset of civilization, of practicing the civilized sacred ways.

The pipestone quarry was a special holy place where all people were welcome. No one had a right to control it or to keep others from coming and cutting their own piece of the sacred stone, as long as the people came in peace, and in a good way of mind, intent and spirit. The people protected the sacred pipestone site, of course, from pillagers, hooligans, and those who would seek to destroy it. Since the sacred pipe was given to the people, the pipe keepers, they were also chosen to protect the pipestone. The pipe keepers were also the teachers of the way to harvest the pipestone and then on how to make and use the pipe. If another band of people wished to learn about the cannumpa ways and how to use the pipestone, the keepers would show them the ways, and let those other people use their own free will to decide to adopt the holy ways of the cannumpa if they wished to.

This was true as long as the other people had good hearts and good minds. If such were the case, then they would be allowed access to the pipestone. And if they chose to learn these ways, they were taught them. The keepers viewed Grandmother Earth and the natural environment as sacred. They believed that there was a Supreme Being, the Creator, who created all things, created all life, and provided everything for the people, who depended upon Creator. Creator gave all human beings a spirit and free will. Creator provided spirits to all beings, not just the human beings. But it was the human beings who used their free will to increase their knowledge of and to spread the spirit of Wakan Tanka to and for all things.

This area, which was shared among the Dakota, Nakota, and Lakota people, was located in the southwest Minnesota Territory, the land of the Dakota, the eastern relatives of the Lakota. This area was created by Creator to provide the blood-red stone to be used for ceremony and prayer. The stone would be known by the peoples as *pipestone*. It was a natural deep red moldable stone that naturally emerged from a river quarry in this particular special sacred place. The people would travel for days or weeks to get to the pipestone quarry in order to cut and take the portions of the pipestone to make their own cannumpas.

The spirit was what connected everyone to each other and to everything. The sacred pipestone also had a spirit, that of the inyan people, the stone people. And the inyan gave of themselves for the benefit of all other beings. This included allowing others to use the blood red of the inyan in prayer and in ceremony for the benefit of all beings and all things.

White Buffalo Calf Woman has come to present this unique cannumpa and the wisdom of the seven sacred ceremonies to the people. Creator asks for three women of one family bloodline. The three sisters will be taught all knowledge pertaining to this sacred gifting of the Cannumpa. They receive instructions for preparing the people for changes coming in the future. A time when a new people will walk our lands. They will leave footprints on the ground and in the spirit, that can't be washed away. A new era begins for the people and our extended families. Saved By Bear is a lineal descendant to one of these chosen sisters.

The White Buffalo Calf Woman brought the Sacred Cannumpa to the people so that the people could use the Sacred Cannumpa to pray to Creator and the spirits to help the people in times of need.

The Sacred Cannumpa is great medicine in and of itself. That is the greatest reason why Creator sent the White Buffalo Calf Woman to gift it to the people and then show the people how to use it. The Cannumpa is medicine—good, helpful, pure medicine. The Sacred Cannumpa is capable of being used in a good way to accomplish great things for the people, but only if used in the proper way as taught by Creator. Therefore, to be given the duty and responsibility to look after the Sacred Cannumpa was indeed an incredible honor and sacred recognition, something that also had to be handled in a good, respectful way, the way that Creator intended. Since the Cannumpa is medicine, it was delivered to the band of people of the *mato*, the bear, the medicine being at Bear Creek among the medicine people. For that reason, the Sacred Cannumpa was to be kept by the designated families of the pipe keepers.

Because the Sacred Cannumpa was specifically brought to the Lakota people of the Mnincoju, and specifically to the families thereof, it became the sacred honor, duty, and responsibility of the ones receiving this sacred gift from Creator to keep and protect the sacred pipe. The Sacred Cannumpa carried with it the blessing of, the knowledge of, and the energy from Creator and the spirits. It needed to be cared for, protected from harm and abuse, and made available to all of the people as their individual and collective needs arose.

The Sacred Cannumpa was to be kept safe from any person, entity, or spirit that would seek to use it in a bad way, such as to create evil, to bring death or destruction upon others, or to assist someone in a personal gain of wealth or notoriety, or for the purpose of vanity, jealousy, false pride, conceit, superiority, or false prophesizing.

The pipe keeper, in addition to having the duty of ensuring the Cannumpa was safe at all times, was to move Cannumpa throughout the day according to the phases of the sun, and to allow the people with good intentions and good spirits, who came in a good way, to pray to and with the Sacred Cannumpa when they *asked* and needed the help from Creator, which was the purpose of the Sacred Cannumpa. The Sacred Cannumpa was not intended to be kept in such a way as to be used or seen only by a select few. The Cannumpa was supposed to be available for use when needed, really needed, by the people, whoever it may be, not just those who may have known the pipe keeper or who had done a favor for or given compensation to the pipe keeper.

The family who would be the pipe keepers were selected by Creator to watch over and keep safe the Sacred Cannumpa, to make sure that it was not harmed, stolen, misused, corrupted, or destroyed; to be ever mindful that the ways of the Sacred Cannumpa must be honored and practiced at all times; and to respect the Sacred Cannumpa for what it is, namely, a gift from Creator, to do good, to help the people, and to protect Unci Maka. For these reasons, the family of pipe keepers had to be trustworthy, solid, reliable, good, and honorable people.

Long ago when the White Buffalo Calf Woman brought the Sacred Cannumpa, gifted it from Creator to the people, and delivered it into the hands of the original pipe keeper families near Bear Creek on the sacred land, the instruction from Creator and the spirits was that the pipe keeper would be known as *Elk Head*. The elk, *hehaka*, is a noble, sacred, strong, trustworthy being on Unci Maka, a noble people who protect their family and others. So when it was deemed by Creator that the pipe keeper should be called Elk Head, that meant that whomever was the present pipe keeper should be called Elk Head regardless of his or her birth name. So the original pipe keeper was called Elk Head. Once the pipe keeper passed on, after having designated the next person in line from among the original families of the Sacred Cannumpa to assume the role as pipe keeper, then that successor had to assume the name of Elk Head. And so it was intended that this role and this name would be passed in this fashion, from generation to generation, always to keep the Sacred Cannumpa within the same family or group of families of pipe keepers—the family of Elk Head.

This is how the Sacred Cannumpa, the gift from Creator, delivered to the people by the White Buffalo Calf Woman so many years ago, came to be within the Mnincoju tiospaye of Saved By Bear. It was his family and their direct tiospaye (extended family) who were the original intended keepers of the Sacred Cannumpa. They were, and are, the original pipe keepers, the origin of the Elk Head people. As mentioned previously, the Cannumpa was intended to be passed down from generation to generation within the pipe keepers' original line. This was foretold, and told again, by the Great Grizzly Bear medicine holy man also. This was a trust granted by Creator, knowing that the Sacred Cannumpa would remain sacred, pure, and accessible to the people.

4

CYCLE OF LIFE

THE CYCLE OF LIFE REFERS to the peoples' existence by the things that they do in their everyday life, including how they choose to perceive each other, how they treat each other, and how they prepare for the events of life.

The rejuvenation of life itself within a society occurs upon the birth of an individual, with the newborn's spirit and body becoming a part of the Circle. This is also how the rejuvenation of the people occurs. This is a continuation, repeated generation after generation after generation. Although each child, individually, is nurtured in a specific way, all are in a sense nurtured in the same way.

Saved By Bear's birth occurred in late April of 1849 in the He Sapa. Swift Bear was also born in the same season of the same year. Upon his birth, Great-Grandfather was given a name, Wanbli Gi, or Brown Eagle. The first year of Brown Eagle's life was spent entirely in the He Sapa region. He would grow amid the passage of the seasons. His communication with and nurturing by individuals of his nuclear family and extended family would teach him the virtues and morals of the Lakota Nation. Compassion, love, protection, honesty, and courage—all of these things were demonstrated by the family members' behavior. Brown Eagle's upbringing would provide a good picture of the domestic growth experienced by every individual of these family units.

Upon his birth, Brown Eagle was shown the interaction of the caring, compassion, and love that he was given by his relatives and family. When he was two or three years old, and up until he was the age of six, he was taught social mores. He was educated by the women first, until he was about six years old. Most children were educated that way. He and the other children were primarily raised by the women, who taught them about emotions and showed them how to behave with others. The male learns how to feel and how to act properly when he is required to nurture the spirit or heart of someone who is in need. In early childhood, most of the activities were centered around the camp and the lifestyle that the Lakota enjoyed on a daily basis.

After that stage, at about the age of six, the male would be taken by the men and the warriors to begin his education on how to become a man, a warrior, and part of the family. The cycle of occurrences and events involving the people on the Plains showed both changes and consistency.

Lakota Life

The Lakota people enjoy sharing stories. This is the way of knowing the past and foreseeing the future. Our mother and grandmother told us stories that had been passed down through the oral tradition by the storytellers. For life truly is a story that you walk through and experience during all the cycles of your life. Some things are mentioned by the elders, the grandparents, the aunts, and the uncles, who teach the Lakota children about our culture. The storytelling always includes symbolism. Metaphors and positive messages are often used.

An example of this old practice is the type of story that is told to the children when they are very young. This story is about a wolf that lives in a round type of structure. When the wolf enters the structure, he goes through the first entryway. Next there is a walkway. It is you who now becomes the wolf. In front of the walkway, as you start to walk, you encounter a wall. And on the left, there are more entryways, more doors. Each door that you open gives you access to an entirely different world with different lessons to be learned.

This is how our people were educated early in life, by telling and hearing stories of our people's existence and their ways, so that we can make a connection with our part to play as a member of a family, a community, and a society. These stories are imperative to the Lakota's educational system, which encourages curiosity and assertiveness, in the sense of not being afraid to speak to people, to ask questions, to do as your spirit asks you to do. We are taught to live by your spirit, to speak through your spirit, and most of all to hear from the spirits who love you. The most important part of the story being told has always been the love and compassion of the elders. That actually is a never-ending story.

The Lakota people flourished and enjoyed a mobile lifestyle upon the Great Plains of North America, on Turtle Island. The Lakota followed the great herds of buffalo because the tatanka people were a major source of the Lakota food supply. A nomadic lifestyle enabled the Lakota to follow the buffalo herds' migrations across the plains, into the He Sapa, and back out again, year after year, generation after generation.

The buffalo that were tracked, hunted, and then taken during the summer and fall, furnished many of the things that were necessary for the Lakota people to survive. Nothing, no part of the buffalo, was ever wasted. It was an unspoken, unwritten, yet solemn practice that the Lakota would never kill more of the tatanka people than were needed. The buffalo meat that was taken and not cooked immediately was cut into strips and hung out to dry in the sunshine for future use. The sun-cured meat was stored away in hide-skin bags and pouches, and used later while traveling or for the winter's food supply. Bones from the tatanka were used to make lard for cooking and for greasing hair, utensils, and weapons. Some of the bones were used to fashion or use as utensils or weaponry, such as sinew for bowstrings and to tie arrowheads. The leg bones were used specifically for club handles. The buffalo hides were used to make tipis, clothing, coats, and warm heavy robes. There was hardly a material or a hide on Grandmother Earth that was as tough and thick as a buffalo's. The lining of the stomach, or tripe, of the tatanka was a delicacy called *t'aniga*, which was served as a special treat. The bladders were used to carry water and perishable food items. The hollowed-out horns were used as ladles, spoons, or even cups. The skulls, robes, hooves, horns, and tails were all used in one way or another in Lakota ceremonies, including the sacred sun dance.

The Lakota used almost every part of the tatanka that could be used, including the dung. These buffalo droppings, or buffalo chips, were often used for fuel to burn or heat, or for fertilizer for planting. Literally, no parts of the buffalo were wasted or left unused. This is indicated in the rough sketch and diagram of the buffalo and its parts, as follows:

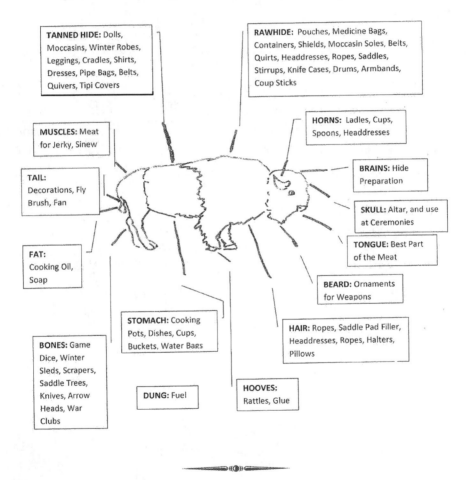

TANNED HIDE: Dolls, Moccasins, Winter Robes, Leggings, Cradles, Shirts, Dresses, Pipe Bags, Belts, Quivers, Tipi Covers

RAWHIDE: Pouches, Medicine Bags, Containers, Shields, Moccasin Soles, Belts, Quirts, Headdresses, Ropes, Saddles, Stirrups, Knife Cases, Drums, Armbands, Coup Sticks

MUSCLES: Meat for Jerky, Sinew

HORNS: Ladles, Cups, Spoons, Headdresses

TAIL: Decorations, Fly Brush, Fan

BRAINS: Hide Preparation

SKULL: Altar, and use at Ceremonies

FAT: Cooking Oil, Soap

TONGUE: Best Part of the Meat

BEARD: Ornaments for Weapons

STOMACH: Cooking Pots, Dishes, Cups, Buckets, Water Bags

HAIR: Ropes, Saddle Pad Filler, Headdresses, Ropes, Halters, Pillows

BONES: Game Dice, Winter Sleds, Scrapers, Saddle Trees, Knives, Arrow Heads, War Clubs

DUNG: Fuel

HOOVES: Rattles, Glue

Lakota men wore buckskin shirts and buckskin pants and leggings. They often wore belts made of strips of hide, to which they tied such things as a pouch, medicine bag, and knife holder. Males always let their thick brown hair grow long. It was then usually braided. Headbands were worn, many times with feathers tied into the hair as well.

Lakota women wore long buckskin dresses over high leggings. For certain functions that were part of female society, they would wear a shawl. Quillwork and ornamentation often created beautiful colors and designs in women's dresses, leggings, hair ties, and moccasins. The women also made and decorated the men's clothing, their regalia, and their accessories (e.g., pouches, quivers, and medicine bags).

Campsites and Hunting Territories

When a camp was moved, the Lakota women always performed the required tasks. The women were intricately skilled at erecting and taking down a tipi; they could do so within a matter of minutes. The women would pack each tipi in a bundle, tie it up together with the poles, and secure it to the back of one of the Lakota ponies in a travois fashion, where the tipi poles, sometimes as long as twenty feet, would be hauled along behind, but not dragged. The travois poles would be what would move along the ground. Other belongings and small children were placed on the travois much like on a stretcher, and were pulled along by the strong Lakota ponies. The people packed and unpacked, and set and reset their camps in this fashion for thousands of years. This was their way of movement. Quick, precise, ready, and in unison. If someone needed help, help was always there. After all, they lived, camped, and moved as a community, as if the community itself were a living, breathing, functioning organism. This is how it was to be Lakota. And the community was only as strong as its individual and collective parts.

Campsites were usually selected because of their proximity to fresh clean lakes and clear running streams. These sites were chosen often where the landscape features and geography, such as trees, tree lines, hills, and bluffs, would serve to keep the encampment from being seen or approached by unwanted visitors or potential attackers. Frequently, each Lakota family would place a family stick outside a lodge to identify which family occupied that lodge. The family stick would have unique markings and designs that specifically served as the individual family's mark. These sticks were mainly used where people were outside of their own camp, so unfamiliar people would know whose family occupied the specific lodge.

At times in the warm seasons, the Lakota would place flags made of thin cloth or material around the perimeter of the camp and lodges. The flags, mainly used during times of ceremony or for larger gatherings, were tied to two-or three-foot-high sticks so that they would move or flap in the breeze. These flags were used to indicate the boundaries of the camp and also to see which way the breeze was blowing. The flapping noise made by the flags blowing in the breeze was a good way to keep snakes (*zuzeca*) from entering into the camp, as the sound resembles the noise made by the wings of a bird of prey like an eagle, a hawk, or a falcon. The snakes, believing that the raptors flying around were hunting for them, would be scared off, and have a tendency to stay away.

If there also were other forms of animal people nearby, like deer, elk, antelope, or rabbits, or if the area was an abundant source of berries and roots (chokecherries, buffalo berries, gooseberries, soapweed, bitterroot, turnips, etc.), then the Lakota might even stay in that location for a month or two at a time, and then return to that area during the same season the next year. When they gathered food, it would be gathered for and shared with all of their people.

Knowing the migration seasons and paths of the buffalo, the people would gather at and hunt specific areas along those paths. The men scouting would alert the people of the tatanka's sighting and passing nearer to the camps. The migration habits of the tatanka were very specific. The buffalo stayed within the grasslands. Ceremonies were held to find and locate the buffalo, and for a successful hunt. When a successful hunt occurred, the people prayed and celebrated the gifts provided to them.

The buffalo roamed freely over the valleys and the rolling hills of the Great Plains during the spring, summer, and fall seasons, where no boundaries existed. There were no fences or laws to restrict their movement from one fine grazing land to the next. It was a very satisfactory, often serene, and naturally compatible existence between the Lakota and their buffalo brothers. Because of the commitment forged by the four-legged buffalo beings millions of years ago, they had volunteered themselves to provide for the Lakota, as long as their people's joint existence was secured and protected. It was a holy and sacred alliance throughout the time of Creator and life on Grandmother Earth. This is how it always was, and how Creator had always intended it to be. There was a natural balance, a natural energy, a natural connection, between the two peoples. A lasting respectful bond existed that only unnatural and destructive forces could undermine and potentially alter or threaten.

When it came to community, the Lakota were people of social exchange, celebration, and council. On special occasions, council fires (*oceti*) were lit and ceremonies and dances were held. When a Lakota woman wished to make something special for her family or friends, she would make a large helping of *wasna*, which was also used on a daily basis. This was a very tasty and sweet compacted cake made by mixing and melding ground buffalo, deer, or elk meat and *talo* (fresh meat with fat), with wild berries, many times chokecherries, buffalo berries, raspberries, or currants. The tasty mixture was then dried and stored in pouches. A Lakota could survive on wasna, if need be, for a long while. You could eat it while on the move.

The Plant Beings

Lakota villages grew corn, beans, and squash, which were also dried for winter supply. The Lakota always grew these three crops together, the three main plant food staples, in the same garden plot at the more long-term camps or settlements. This reduced the size of gardening space needed. The corn would grow up, the squash would grow outward, and the beans would grow up the cornstalks. These three crops all occupied the same root system.

Turnips and other roots were gathered. Eggs of local birds were also a nice treat to have when available. Many Lakota also caught fish by hand, net, or spear, or hooks made from small animal bones. Fish and their remains were used to help fertilize the planting ground.

The Lakota loved the natural abundance and bounty provided for by Grandmother Earth. If Grandmother Earth provided it, it was usually good for food. No matter if it was good to eat or pleasing to the taste, the Lakota learned that every kind of plant, seed, root, cone, leaf, branch, and flower provided medicine to help the people stay healthy or overcome illness, or increase energy and stamina for those who needed it for long, hard travels or hunts. Herbs and roots were commonly used as medicines, such as bear root, bitterroot, cedar, sweetgrass, and sage.

By using the plants provided by Grandmother Earth, the people realized that no one is separate from Earth's environment: *mitakuye oyasin*. The one is an individual, but in order to fully exist, the peoples must embrace their relationships with all of the relatives. This is true across all levels of existence. Therefore, the Lakota used sage, sweetgrass, and cedar to smudge or cleanse themselves, others, and their surroundings, including their homes and camps. The sage in particular is sacred. When smudging themselves with sacred sage, the Lakota would pull the smoke toward their bodies with their hands and spread it over their bodies. Smudging could occur also without burning the sage. Sage was used in ceremonies of all kinds. Sweetgrass and cedar were used for purification and ceremony as well. Sage could be used to make tea. Some would put a leaf of sage in the mouth to help with speaking with clarity and precision. Sage can be used in any way by the people to be used for good purposes. It can be used to smudge around the doorway to ward off evil. The sagebrush itself serves to protect animals from weather, as it provides shade from a hot sun.

Tobacco was seen as a gift that could be used to smoke in the cannumpa, the sacred pipe, in times of ceremony and prayer. Tobacco was used as a sacred plant to make prayer bundles. These prayer bundles were offered in ceremonies, along with a request for health, forgiveness, vision, guidance, protection, or permission, or for the purpose of paying honor, expressing gratitude, or showing respect.

Many personal medicine pouches and prayer bundles contained items of medicine for the purpose of healing, or items of personal significance relating to honor, heritage, sacrifice, or accomplishment. These pouches were worn for purposes of guidance, gratitude, peace, healing, health, knowledge, wisdom, or protection from evil or harm.

Holy People

The holy men and holy women—medicine persons—among the Lakota used Grandmother Earth's gifts to heal people or other beings. Usually a male, the medicine person had spiritual powers that came from his own relationship with Creator and his preparation and sacrifice in the eyes and presence of Wakan Tanka. The holy man was often referred to as *hokowo*. A medicine man's presence can be felt, not just seen or heard. People may find themselves standing up involuntarily when a medicine man enters the room or lodge.

A medicine man is in connection with and guided by the Wakinyan, the Thunder Beings who approach from the west. The blue light or color of healing often is near or around medicine people. Their medicine is powerful. But in order to be of Creator and Wakan Tanka, they can never use their powers for evil or to do bad. If a medicine man seeks to use the spirit and his spiritual gifts for ill intent or evil motive, the risk of self-destruction is great and likely. So strong is the strength of good within Wakan Tanka.

The holy ones can heal by communicating with those who caused the issue in question. This may be done not just in the typical sense of speaking out loud, but also by praying and *asking*, seeking permission, so that the unwanted beings will leave the place they are currently inhabiting. Sometimes the newer diseases are brought on by beings so tiny that the human or animal people cannot see them with the naked eye. When the healer speaks to those tiny beings and asks them to leave, they can be persuaded to leave, to go elsewhere. If they do choose to leave, then the body can heal without their presence.

The sacred touch of the holy man or holy woman carries the connection of the energy of Creator, which assists in direct conversation with Wakan Tanka so that a clearer relationship can occur through which to send and receive messages and prayers. The presence of *wanbli*, the eagle, the messenger, is frequently seen nearby the holy man or holy woman, in the sky or on a branch. The medicine person often uses the eagle feather and the eagle feather fan. These practices and articles are sacred.

The holy people were physically, human. But they were more than that in reality. They are also not merely physical. Many would have the ability to move without walking, to fly without taking flight, to enlighten without light. To guide by sheer will, to foretell the future through visions, to interpret signs and dreams. To seek permission from Creator. To seek protection from threats and danger by asking the Creator. And to translate the spirit's word and intention into real life and real events.

Sitting Bull was such a man. Saved By Bear would become one also. The Lakota people and their spiritual leaders lived and created history together through the guidance and permission of Wakan Tanka. As the story of the history of the people unfolds, the life of the Lakota would never be the same.

Traditional Lakota culture includes rituals that are practiced daily, seasonally, or amid life-changing or life-ending affairs. The Red Nations use these rituals throughout their life. In their daily life they will feed their families. This is a ritual. It is a prayer in itself, to keep the family healthy and secure. They will have a tipi that comes from the buffalo nation, so they will offer a prayer to the buffalo for the providing of sustenance and strength. The spiritual side of life dominates the ritualistic practice of the Earth people and the Lakota.

When Lakota children are being nurtured and reared, they are given hands-on contact, because this is needed by human beings. It is vital for a child to have the physical touch of a loved one and the warmth and energy that is passed by that touch. The Lakota men are able to ritualize their lives around protection and family matters so as to enjoy happiness and celebrate the people in their immediate family and extended family. All these areas are rituals of some type in the traditional manner. The Lakota culture also encourages a daily practice of giving and caring of the heart and spirit.

Ceremonial practice is more specialized, requiring people to follow a protocol. There are certain items, relics, and entities that are commonly called upon to help in specific *askings* in prayer. These things are a part of the spirit and also Unci Maka's gift to us so we can survive. This ritual behavior can be done anywhere on the planet. These rituals can help and be a part of the life of any being of the planet. Prayer is not something that you are told about and told how to do. Prayer is a gift that you give back to creational beings and the Creator. Prayer is the way of the human being, the red man, and the Mnincoju Lakota.

Medicine and Healing

Oftentimes, Lakota people, by and through the advice and assistance of a medicine person, or even by themselves, seek to heal those who are sick, injured, or dying. As in any human endeavor, the Lakota seek the gift of living a healthy, pain-free, enjoyable, long life and existence. When a human being becomes sick or injured or is dying, the situation cannot be appropriately addressed unless or until there is an *asking* done or made by the sick, injured, or dying person or that person's family or friends.

When a Lakota person learns the healing ways of the old traditions of the people as passed down from generation to generation, that person becomes capable of using those old ways to try to do what they can to help another.

The ways of healing are practiced in a way that makes the people and the healers confident and comfortable in the manner and methods used to perform the traditions. There are of course, differences in the details of practice that each healer follows in his or her own way. One way of healing involves a direct conversation between the inflicted individual and the healing one. Through this detailed dialogue that includes a description of the affected area of the body, the healing one comes to understand fully what the real problem is. Or the healer may engage in a laying on of hands to feel the afflicted person's body and come to know and feel where the disease or injury is located. Once this step is accomplished, the healing one considers what may be the best way to heal the afflicted individual.

The healing one must now go through the process of *asking*. This requires a cleansing of the spirit and a cleansing of the person. Sage, cedar, and sweetgrass are used to purify the healer and the sick one alike. If the people are standing together or within the same physical area, this is done by smudging, bathing both healer and the one in need with the smoke of the sage, cedar, and/or sweetgrass. In the process of smudging, the healer is asking for the spirits that are good for and necessary to the healing process, to come and help in this moment of need. If the sick or injured person is not within the same vicinity as the healer, then the healer can do the *asking* by holding an item that belongs to the one in need, or that the one who is in need has recently handled, held, or worn. Whatever the item may be—a stone, a necklace, a doll, a shirt, a cloth, a strand of hair—it can be used as long as it still carries the *tun* (essence) of the one in need. The *tun* can be found in the item since the item belongs to the one in need. That person's tun remains with the item unless or until it is destroyed, or until it is or becomes the personal item of another person.

The healing one uses the gifts of knowledge, tradition, and ceremony, to accomplish the *asking* of help. In the *asking* process, the healing one will receive guidance from the spirits as to how to go about the process of healing. The healing one may receive specific instructions regarding how to use the power of the spirits and the presence of good thoughts and intentions to accomplish the goal of healing the one in need. The instructions, including the steps of the process, may be different each time according to the need, the sick one's specific problem, and the natural elements used to accomplish the goal. If the sick, injured, or dying person is to be healed, he or she must possess a willingness and an acceptance. This is critical. If the person is not willing and accepting, then he or she will not be healed.

In the case of a broken bone, the healer may ask that the blood and tissue in the limb come together, that the two seek each other out and join together—seal their union—to make the bone stronger and hasten its mending. If the problem is a loss of hope, or discouragement occasioned by an episode of heavy grief, the healer may call upon the grieving one's ancestors and their spirits, and other benevolent spirits, to come and touch the one in need. The purpose here, in the case of grieving a death, is to have the spirits come and bring the light of positive energy to the afflicted person's soul, body, and spirit so as to spark a brighter view of the place where the spirit of the loved one has gone and remains, forever with the grieving one, and to ensure that their spirits will be united always. This process brings the energy from the spirit world into the physical world for the one in need, so that the darker, hopeless, and grieving notions do not dominate the spirit and mind of the grieving one. Those feelings are nudged into their proper place, of presence, and prevented from assuming a position of dominance. This allows the good notions, good feelings, and hopeful feelings and thoughts, to flood into the void, to try to cover, soothe, and heal the darker feelings. Also, this process allows the gentle, kind, and benevolent spirits to take the hand of the grieving one's spirit and lead it back into the realm of again being able to feel the notions of peace, unity, tolerance, and love. To convince the grieving one to again see the light at the end of the cave of darkness, so that their spirit can stand up, and take the first steps in the dark, and to start walking toward that benevolent light, the healing light.

For someone who may be suffering from a disease of the blood, of the bone, of the flesh, or of some other part of the body, the healer must and will focus on the specific part of the body of the one in need. The *asking* will seek the specific approach as to what needed to be done to spiritually and physically target the area of the disease or affliction. This healing process demonstrates the human being's true, real, ancestral connection to everything. An ability for the human being to be the living conduit, the living connection, between the physical world and the spiritual world, and between all beings that exist, whether inside or outside the human body.

To use as an example, if the one in need has a disease of the blood that is causing weakness, loss of energy, and deterioration of the body, then the healer will use the physical, emotional, and spiritual gifts given him or her by Creator. The healing one may use bear root or sweetgrass dipped in cedar-soaked water to wet the afflicted area. Whatever the instruction from the spirits, that process will be used. The healing one may burn sage and pray while asking the spirits to help. The healer then may speak directly to the beings that are causing the problem. As mentioned before, these beings may be so small that they cannot be seen by the naked eye, but nonetheless they are present inside the sick person's body, causing harm by their presence in the body alone. So the healer asks these beings, all of them, to go, to leave, to let go of the sick one's body, to come out of there and go away. This can be done by moving the hands over the sick person's body, specifically over the affected body part. Prayers, songs, focus, connection, and spirit are key.

As in all things, singing is a critical part of the healing process, so healing songs are sung to help focus and intensify the spiritual energy that brings healing. The gift of total belief, in heart and spirit, that the sick one can be healed in this way is the gift of fulfillment. It allows the good and benevolent spirits to take hold and to help. The good spirits may come in and join in helping the small beings to vacate the sick person's body, by merely asking them to leave.

If the healing process is effective and the one in need is helped or healed, then the *asking* is fulfilled. In any event, when the *asking* occurs, things are done, and results are realized, a *wopila* is necessary to give thanks to the spirits and to Creator for helping the sick person and for responding to the *asking*. The process of healing will not and cannot be completed without this last natural step of the wopila. If the wopila is skipped, ignored, or forgotten, then the ailment or condition may return. This is how important the fulfillment of all steps of the old ways are necessary to reach the goal of any type of asking. It is as old as the beginning of time and life.

An a*sking*, a healing, or any type of ceremony may be done anywhere. It is important to have a good spirit. However, sometimes a ceremony will carry more personal or original significance if it is performed at a specific site such as a home, a camp, a mountain, a birthplace, a holy place, or a sacred site.

Life is made up of energy, life energy. Energy, in turn, is medicine for life. To live is to have the energy of life. To sustain the life energy, sometimes medicine is needed to preserve health and to preserve life itself.

Medicine (*pejuta*) is not owned by anyone, really. Medicine is intended to be used, to be shared, and to be free to all peoples of all kinds, no matter who or where you are. If you need medicine, then you shall have it. It is wrong in the eyes of Creator to withhold medicine from someone, or to deny them medicine for immoral purposes or selfish reasons. If medicine was available to be used, then it was used for whoever needed it, no matter the situation. No one was more deserving; no one was less deserving. Medicine is life. Life is medicine. Life is naturally bonded with medicine, which is combined with life. This is why Creator provided medicine to the people and gave us the means and ability to find, use, and share it. The value of medicine is only in how it is used by the people for the betterment of the lives of all people, as the need arises.

Time and History

The Lakota counted years by the number of winters that had passed. A winter count is a recording of historical events of a tiospaye. Almost every family had a winter count, made up of symbols or figures. The most significant events or occurrences were represented in painted colors and images on a buffalo or deer hide. These hides were kept by the families as personal historical keepsakes and convenient personal records of events. If some important event was not recorded, then there was usually a good reason for the absence of a record. For the larger group, there was usually a winter count historian.

The Lakota counted months by the phases of the moon. The phases of the moon were important to the traditional Lakota knowledge of the universe. *Hanwi*, the moon, would control the nighttime, and *Wi*, the sun, would control the daytime. In the Lakota universe, the time from one full moon to the next full moon established the period of a month. The month was also the time interval for the natural cycle of the woman. Each month's moon had a certain name. For example, December's moon was "the moon when the deer sheds its horns." There were twenty-eight days in each month, to conform to the natural menstrual cycle of the female. There were thirteen moons, and therefore thirteen months, in the year. The moon was a vital part of the seasonal changes.

A great flood of long ago was spoken of, which washed away many forms of life, including human beings. Creator started again. After the waters receded, the land base became that which was on the Turtle's back. The He Sapa and the Wind Cave were in the center, or the heart, of Turtle Island. The Turtle has twenty-eight small plates along the rim of its shell, (ke nunujela), which wrapped around the main oval section of the turtle's back. Twenty-eight represents the fertility of the female, as the female's monthly cycle consists of twenty-eight days. The turtle has thirteen individual plates on its back. The turtle (Ke ya) was a sacred being and a symbol to the Lakota and their ancestors, going back to the very origin time period of the Lakota. The Lakota have always resided upon Turtle Island. The turtle itself represents time. The ancient spiritual connection is recognized by the making of the sacred site on Medicine Mountain in the great Shiny Mountains (the Bighorn Mountains) where a ceremonial and astronomical stone formation memorializes and honors Turtle. Twenty-eight cairns form the center, representing the twenty-eight days of the female cycle. Then there are six appendages (representing one head, four legs, and one tail). The turtle figure on Medicine Mountain was a means of tracking the stars, which permitted the Lakota to navigate their way as they traveled upon Grandmother Earth. As it was then, and as it has always been. The people often traveled to the turtle to know these things, and for ceremony and hanbleceya.

The Lakota measured a day according to the period of sunrise to sunrise. And when a hunter was leaving on a journey, he may not say that he would be gone for so many *days,* but for so many *sleeps.* This was relative to sleeping during the night, at the end of a day. So if a hunt took ten days, it may be referred to as "ten sleeps."

Family and Relationships

The Lakota did not marry young. The males and females waited to mature to the point where they understood how to be adults who were responsible for themselves and future spouse. If a young Lakota person was not mature enough to know and understand what it meant to be in a loving, committed relationship, then he or she would not marry until gaining this understanding. Being mature meant being ready to be a husband or a wife. It also meant being ready to become a parent, as it takes responsibility to bring forth a new life and adequately care for a child. It should be noted, in light of marriage, that some Lakota men in the mid 1800s had more than one wife at a time, it was usually done so to bring in or to care for the family of another who becomes disabled or widowed as a result of death or absence of a husband.

Like many indigenous peoples, the Lakota have known, and welcomed into their own oyates and tiospayes, persons who were intersexual and/or androgynous people, feminine males and masculine females. These Lakota were referred to as "two-spirit people" and were held in high respect. Instead of focusing upon the two-spirit one's preference of a partner, the Lakota focused upon their unique spiritual gifts. The Lakota viewed a person's basic character as a reflection of his or her spirit.

The common Lakota way of viewing things of this nature was that since all things that exist come from the spirit world, androgynous, homosexual, or transgender persons are seen to be doubly blessed. This is so because they have both the spirit of a man and the spirit of a woman. Therefore, the two-spirit people are oftentimes viewed as spiritually gifted, in their unique way, to bring unity to the genders of the people. For those reasons, the Lakota, rather than stigmatizing such people, often looked to them as an example of comfort in both worlds of both genders.

It was seen by the Lakota, that instead of placing emphasis on a person's physical body, the Lakota emphasized a person's spirit, or character, as the most important attribute. Thus the two-spirit people were respected not just for their spirit, but also for practical matters. Since the two-spirit persons' gender role involved a mix of both masculine and feminine traits, they could do both the work of men and the work of women. They were often seen as hard workers and creatively gifted, and therefore were of great value to the Lakota society, the extended families and the community, the tiospaye. The two-spirit ones frequently assisted the tiospaye's children and grandchildren, took care of elderly relatives, and many times served as adoptive parents for orphaned or homeless children.

When the two-spirit ones paired up or married a spouse, this was seen as an added benefit to the family, and to the oyate, as more roles could be served with less people.

In Lakota culture, it has always been wrong to discriminate against the two-spirit ones. It was appropriate to allow the two-spirit ones to live their lives just as any other member of the oyate. It was only important to see them for who they were and the way they lived their lives—what they do and how they interacted with the people—and not to focus on whom they lived with. It was right to treat the two-spirit ones the same as others, and to let them practice the honesty of being who they are, so they didn't have to hide anything about who they really are. It was inappropriate for the people to treat the two-spirit ones as less human or less tolerable. It was wrong to make the two-spirit people feel diminished in self-worth or value. Every human being deserves respect and to have pride in self.

Many believed that it would be the influx and influence of some of the much more homophobic and rigid European religious beliefs and social structures, that would unfairly diminish the human value of the two-spirit people. Thus creating a situation where some would feel they needed to hide who they truly were, and at the same time tending to damage and harm to their beautiful gifted spirits, because of prejudice and misunderstanding.

These special gifted beings are called upon to strengthen the hand of virtues and morals during this time of losing much of our old ways. The two spirit ones will stand strong for both genders.

A Lakota does not always need to marry only a Lakota. At times, it is desired and available, and could be a wonderful thing. But there are also times when the Lakota people may fear becoming too interbred to function, and take care of themselves. These are the things that some worry about regarding the marrying process. To dispense with this notion, Lakota, Dakota, and Nakota commonly intermarried these cultures and within this dialect difference. Because of this, each family normally had a member from one of the other bands or tribes. The primary reason for this intermarriage was for the health of the gene pool. If you saturate a gene pool with the same genes for generations, then you will not have a healthy people. In Lakota society and tradition, there is a way to avoid mutations and interbreeding: by educating family members through the elders. The elders kept an oral record of who was married to whom, and which family each spouse came from. Using this information, they allowed certain persons to marry another who belonged to their own band. The marriage protocol had safeguards of definitive accepted morals and values as to what the culture of appropriateness was for any given marriage pairing. This protocol permitted Lakota to safely marry healthy, mentally capable, and spiritually practicing people from the other tribal nations, as well.

In Lakota society, a couple planned for the children that they brought into the world. The month in which the child would be born was planned out so that the mother would not have to go into labor and give birth during the harsh seasons. The births of children were usually clustered in the warm months, when it was easier to give birth and to care for newborns. The Lakota followed these natural ways, much like all of the other peoples, such as the horses, the deer, the buffalo, the wolf, and the bear. After all, human beings learned everything about life, existence, and survival from their brothers and sisters, the animal people. The babies and little ones usually made their first appearances in the spring, the time of new birth for most forms of life, including plants. Also, most Lakota families made sure to properly space out the period between the birth of their children so as to not have too many children too soon. It was not fair to the new child or the parents. Time was needed to properly care for, teach, and love each child, before bringing another child into the world.

All Lakota children were named after an animal, a bird, an object, or a human being who had some special importance to the family, or by receiving a special name from the spiritual side. Each child was given a name at birth. This shows the love that the family has for the child. The expectant parents, anticipating the coming of their child, asked the spirits for help in choosing the proper name for each child. If a family was associated with the eagle, then the children from that family would usually have "Eagle" (Wanbli) as part of their name. The same was the case with a family associated with the bear (mato). Each person from the bear people band would have "Bear" as part of their name. This was true of little Brown Eagle's family, being of both the Eagle and the Bear families.

When Lakota boys grew to manhood or became warriors, their names were usually changed as a result of some brave deed or some significant event. As an example, Sitting Bull as a young brave, before becoming a warrior, was known as Slow. Sitting Bull's full name was Sitting Buffalo Bull (or Prone Buffalo Bull). Because of a deed he performed, Sitting Bull was given his now recognized name. The same was true for most men and warriors, including Spotted Elk (also known to the whites as Big Foot). It was common for fathers to pass their own names on to their sons at some point in the son's life. Because of this practice, most families, at one time or another, had multiple members, usually succeeding generations of men, but sometimes women, with the same exact name as their parent. This would prove to be confusing for those whose job it was to write words for the purpose of recording history. Those members of the white society who made written records of the Lakota found it quite confusing to try to record the name of certain Lakota people. The confusion came from the fact that fathers passed their own names onto their sons, and also out of the fact that all Lakota, boys and girls, men and women, were given different names throughout their lives. This would create some confusion for those who wrote history, wondering which person was from which generation, but the Lakota were not confused on this point.

Education

Education was extremely important for the children as they grew. Education was a Lakota necessity and right. It was a part of the spiritual fulfillment also, for the remainder of each child's life. Without an education, a human being may become unwilling to learn about differences in things and people. Without an education, a human may become intolerant of anything not familiar to themselves. Education is a gift from Creator to allow for the individual universe of the one, to be vastly expanded to include the universe of the many. A lack of necessary education, harms the ability of the human to be curious about life and the world. If curiosity is harmed or diminished, then so is the opportunity to learn and to discover the truth, to know right from wrong, and to know and appreciate the difference. A lack of curiosity and education allows for fear, anxiety, and selfishness to consume a person's thoughts and perceptions. Curiosity is the key to unlock a human being's abilities, opportunities, and destiny to become who they choose to be or what they are asked to become.

The typical daily education of the Lakota children would occur in this fashion: the instructor and the children would assemble, and the instructor would ask the children to form a circle and sit in the grass (when the weather allowed, that is. When it did not, the instruction occurred inside, within the family unit). This way, the instructor would have the full patience and attention of the children, as the instructor would become the center and focus of attention, with no distractions. This natural connection between the instructor and the children within the circle, strengthens the education. The children are educated in ethics and morals, with curiosity and questions being encouraged by their instructor, not discouraged.

The instructors would be made up of elders, grandparents, parents, and other respected adults and relatives. These instructors would teach the children about life, tasks, and spirit, according to the instructor's own knowledge and wisdom. The children would therefore have numerous instructors, with one instructor teaching about some particular thing, and another instructor teaching another aspect or a lesson on another matter entirely. At early ages, likely up to the age of six years, children passed through the first, communal stage of education. The next phase of childhood education was gender specific. Boys were taught by the males, and girls were taught by the females.

The ones who teach the young ones are dearly valued in the Lakota culture. It is through their loving talent of transferring the knowledge from one generation to the next, that honorably passes on the greatest of tradition. The greatest of humanity and understanding of the priorities of the world, Grandmother Earth, of life, and of existence, are gifted to those that they teach.

These teachers, whoever they may be, and of whatever age, relationship, or gender, have accumulated the goodwill and trust of the fathers and mothers, the grandmothers and grandfathers. With the knowing and grateful understanding, that the transfer of guidance and trust will be fulfilled.

In many cultures and societies, the leaders are given greater recognition and respect than the teachers are. In the white culture, healers are deeply honored and respected. But in the Lakota culture and society, healers and teachers are equally recognized as absolutely necessary and honored.

The passing on of knowledge, respect, integrity, and justice from one generation to the next, was considered by the Lakota to be a substantial gift, provided to the young and naive at an impressionable time in their lives. And it was something encouraged by parents and grandparents, and even great-grandparents, who especially rejoiced, as they were grateful to Wakan Tanka that they had lived long enough on Grandmother Earth to witness the honorable passing of knowledge and history to their own flesh and blood. All were gratified that education developed the independent minds of their young descendants, so as to continue the cause of seeking a more full and just life for all human beings, and to become an honored individual spirit in the grand picture painted by the loving and giving hand of the Creator.

When a member of the Lakota left the band to act on their own and ends up doing something to harm other people for mean, spiteful, unnatural, uncaring, and inhumane reasons and intents, it was the responsibility of the band to do something about it. To be true to the Lakota commitment to peace, unity, tolerance, and love, we must, instead of sitting idly by and turning our eyes away, confront the provocateur among us, challenging him or her to stop, to change, or to leave.

The Lakota people accepted and professed that it is easier to love than to hate. It is easier to be kind and gentle than to be hateful and hurtful. We are taught when we first can hear and comprehend, that it is better to treat others in the way that we would prefer or hope to be treated ourselves. As very young human members of the family and of the people, we are told to watch the older ones—parents, grandparents, sisters, brothers, aunts, uncles, and elders. We are told to watch how they carry themselves, how they treat each other, and how others treat them. It is through this process of example, right before our eyes, that the learning of the spirit is allowed to occur. And the spirit becomes one and the same with the heart, the eyes, the ears, the mouth, the hand, and the mind. This is how the attributes of honor, respect, dignity, integrity, compassion, kindness, understanding, empathy, and love are recognized and learned. Once recognized and learned, these attributes become a part of life, of our being, of our spirit. Once these attributes are allowed to become a part of our entire self, we can become a conduit and an example, and a role model for the others. This benefits especially the young ones, who watch us, see us, learn from us, notice what we are doing, and recognize, comprehend and accept what we are doing. So that they may become like us and become who they choose to become. This is how the Circle is formed, how the Circle grows, how the Circle nourishes itself, how the Circle re-forms and heals itself. How the Circle rejuvenates itself. And how the Circle becomes whole again.

Lakota boys lived a natural, carefree, physically active life, learning to ride and race ponies, shoot bows, make arrows, track, hunt, and fish. Boys learned to use the bow and arrow by six or eight years old, using blunt points first, and then actual arrowheads. Then, by age ten or eleven, they could shoot well enough to go on hunts with the adult male hunters. The boys were taught to make their own bows and arrows. They were taught by the warriors and other older men how to use a rolling hoop for target practice with the bow and arrows. This way they learned how to shoot an arrow or throw a spear at a moving target, which is beneficial for hunting and for battle. This was a talent passed down from hunter to hunter, father to son, and so on. Boys occupied themselves doing errands for people, tending and watching over the horse herds, gathering firewood, swimming, and running.

A young Lakota male is referred to as a brave simply because of his age. A Lakota male is considered to be a brave during the early years as a boy, on up to his early teens. He is an apprentice to the warriors. He will observe them, listen to them, and do as they say in order to learn. Patience is of primary importance in this phase. Braves become warriors when they do certain things and receive recognition for a performing a brave deed in battle, or for doing something to significantly benefit the community, such as protecting people's lives and hunting territories. The warriors teach the braves these things. It was true that when a group or community of Lakota men, were seen, a great number of the younger men were not yet recognized as warriors. The status of being a warrior needed to be earned. It could not just be given.

Lakota girls were taught by their mothers, other women, and the older girls, how to gather food, prepare hides, sew, and cook. Girls played with dolls and learned sewing designs, how to make clothing, and how to pound grain and berries for food preparation.

Boys wore buckskin clothes according to the season. They also wore moccasins. Lakota girls wore ankle-length buckskin dresses.

Boys and girls who had a background involving the spiritual side, were nurtured in those ways.

Horses were commonly trained by adults who had experience. When boys and girls began to interact with the horses, strong bonds between pony and young Lakota rider were forged. Many times these bonds lasted for twenty or thirty years, the typical life span of the horse.

Many of the ponies used by the Lakota were descendants of the wild mustangs, the paint horses, and the spotted horses—the Appaloosas— that roamed the western lands of Turtle Island. They were all proud and honorable members of the horse nation. The ponies were usually somewhat smaller than the horses brought and used by the white settlers and miners, and members of the US Army. The Lakota ponies were certainly smaller than the Kentucky thoroughbreds often used by the US Cavalry.

Although smaller, the Lakota ponies were lightning quick and had high energy and endurance. These horse brothers were blessed with the gifts of speed and agility. The ponies were treasured by the Lakota. A family usually owned four or five ponies. The warriors many times had several ponies: ponies for the hunt, ponies for traveling, and ponies specifically trained for battle and conflict.

The ponies were trained by their warriors beginning when they were foals. The foals imprinted with their human being friends. This relationship grew from a mutual respect and companionship between foal and child, between horse and warrior. Since the Lakota rode bareback, the ponies were accustomed to the feel of the rider's legs, knees and thighs, and the manner of particular pressure and position on the horse's ribs and flanks. The subtle shifts in body weight and the rider's lean when the horse was running and turning, and especially when turning while running, indicated the rider's intentions to the horse. The rider knew the pony and the pony knew the rider. The relationship was one of trust: during the hunt, in the midst of a herd of buffalo, and especially during times of conflict and battle, amid the heat of the charge, the clash, and hand-to-hand combat on the field. These ponies were proud spiritual descendants and representatives of the great horse nation. They would never forget or lose sight of the spiritual roots they shared with all their brothers and sisters. The strength and bond of their individual and collective spirits served them magnificently and reliably in their times of need, suffering, and change. The horse people were a part of the Lakota family. The horse nation was a necessary part of the great Circle of life, the great circle of being.

The Lakota lived in camps and settlements strategically selected for offering the best security and the most benefits. Campsites and known settlements were often situated beside lakes, streams, rivers, or creeks, reinforcing the tiyospaye name Mnincoju, which relates to life's subsistence through the gathering and planting by the water and/ or river, as it was in these places that the people's sustenance would be available. And because campsites were often by water, water games and swimming were popular for Lakota of all ages.

The Lakota loved the water, the *mni*. And they regarded it as the precious gift of life that it is. Water is sacred, and therefore was always intended to be respected and not forsaken or contaminated. There is an old saying passed down from the wise ones: "The water always remembers." The water does always remember. She will take care of you if you take care of her. Always protect the water. Always honor the water for what she is: life. Without the water, there can be no life.

The secure locations of the camps and settlements allowed Lakota families to gather and commune. In the evenings, the families would enjoy each other's company around the campfire within the lodges. Here, with joyful and thoughtful optimism, they would tell stories about the legendary great deeds of their relatives and sing their favorite songs. What they shared with each other had been passed down from generation to generation by word of mouth, the oral history. Many of these stories, songs, and legends are very old. The elders and older warriors entertained the people by telling the legends of the oyate and the people. The storytellers were always expressive with voice, eyes and hands...and lips. Lakota traditionally spoke with creative hand gestures. Serious tales were mixed with funny ones. Grandfathers told the stories to their grandsons, and when the grandsons themselves grew old, they told the same stories to their grandchildren. Grandmothers, too, got in on the act, and usually added more to the stories, singing melodies or uttering the occasional tremolo. Songs, singing, and music were always extremely important to the people. There were often different variations of each story or song because the different storytellers or singers of other regions or families changed things over time. Therefore, each family had its own stories, or had its own special way of sharing parts of a story. This was how actual history was told, heard, learned, and told again. In any event, the moral, the lesson, or the outcome of the story was always strong and good, no matter if the details were somewhat different each time it was told.

In listening to the stories of their ancestors and relatives, each family member had a hope that they would one day be a contributor to the stories themselves. The belief was that one day there would be a story told about them around the campfire.

This is the story about the Lakota. And within that story about his people and their history and traditions, began the story of the man who the world would know as Mato Niyanpi. And this is how his story begins.

Brown Eagle

The little Lakota son was born to the young Lakota couple Fights the Bear and Iron Hat. He was born in a lodge in April 1849 near the sacred mountain Mato Paha in the sacred He Sapa.

Brown Eagle was the name given to him at birth by his mother. It was Lakota tradition for a respected relative to think of and then provide a name for a new baby. Brown Eagle was named after his mother's favorite maternal aunt, White Horse Woman, who had helped raise Iron Hat. Since Brown Eagle was a boy, and since he was of the bloodline of the bear, medicine, and wanbli people, Iron Hat chose the name Brown Eagle. She knew, of course, that he would likely be renamed at a future naming ceremony by one of his elder relatives when the time came. For the time being, though, he would be known formally as Brown Eagle, although his family just called him *hoksila* (boy) early on.

Iron Hat's aunt White Horse Woman was there when Brown Eagle was born, assisting in his birth, as was customary. When she saw the new baby boy and knew that both mother and child were fine and healthy, she could no longer contain her happiness for her niece and Iron Hat's new son. White Horse Woman let out with one of the loudest and longest tremolos known to Lakota kind. "Le-le-le-le-le-le-le-le-le-le-le-le-le-le-le-ah!" It could be heard throughout the small camp along the Mato Creek near the sacred mountain. Her joy could not be contained, or concealed from the others. The women who were preparing hides looked up and smiled to one another. A couple of them even gave a shorter, more brisk tremolo of their own to acknowledge White Horse Woman's call of pride. Even the paint ponies tied to the pikes near the tipis jumped a little, but they quickly settled down, having heard the noises before.

So there he was, the newborn son of Iron Hat and Fights the Bear, the second child for the couple. Their first child was a girl whom they named Turning Bird. Just prior to Brown Eagle's birth, Fights the Bear had been out scouting for a herd of elk. He could not shake the warm feeling of energy glowing in his chest. The spirits were letting him know that a good moment had come.

Later he would return to his lodge to greet his wife, and to take his new son into his strong, deeply browned arms for the first time. This would be the first of many close embraces that the two spirits would share in their lives. As Fights the Bear looked at his son's face and his small O-shaped mouth, he noticed that the infant's left eye was barely starting to open. As he held his boy in his arms and smelled his newborn freshness mixed with the scent of newly burned and anointed sage, he returned the gaze into his son's newborn eye. A tear rolled down Fights the Bear's cheek closest to his son's head. He noticed that the tear dropped from his high cheekbone and tenderly fell upon his son's forehead just below his thick dark hair. The baby jerked slightly. Then, as if to absorb his father's emotion through the tear, he reached his left hand up and grasped the cheekbone from where the tiny tear had come. The energy of Wakan Tanka was there in plain sight, in particular, in the two beating hearts. One of those hearts, the older one, had seen its fair share of pain and difficulty, but also joy and fulfillment. The newest heart had just begun the journey of life, but it beat mightily with the drumbeat of the deep and old bloodlines of both Brown Eagle and his grateful father. And the family was one. They would be nurtured by the whole tiospaye in a way of tradition, caring, and love. This is what it meant to be a family among the Lakota on Turtle Island.

Saved By Bear

When Brown Eagle was one and a half years old, his *ina*, Iron Hat, was cleaning clothes in the fast-running creek in He Sapa with Brown Eagle at her side. Iron Hat heard the voice of Good Voice Woman, her dear and trusted friend several years older than she. Good Voice Woman started talking about the new romances starting among some of the young people in camp, especially the one between Night Bird and One Eagle, two beautiful young Lakota teenagers who seemed quite dashing together. As Iron Hat washed cloth shirts, a shawl, and dirty buckskin pants on a rock, Brown Eagle was sitting at her side, about fifteen feet from the rocks along the edge of the water. He was playing with a carved-out buffalo bull horn that had shells attached to it to make a rattle—his favorite teething toy. He stuck it in his mouth and chomped. Then, gripping it with his tiny teeth, he swung it about while growling slightly, like he had seen the family dogs doing when they ate bones for snacks and supper. This went on for several seconds.

The two women continued to talk and laugh. They discussed two of the camp elders, Big Hairy Bird and Thunder Woman, both in their sixties, who had lost their spouses over the past three years. The women spoke of how the couple had been seen looking and smiling at each other. Good Voice Woman said, "*Aaay!* But it is *wastè.*" Laughing, they went on with their washing.

Meanwhile, Brown Eagle looked across the creek and saw a very young grizzly bear cub approaching the edge of the water on the opposite bank. The cub looked cute, soft, and cuddly, much like the stitched toy that his grandma had made for him and that was on his bed back in the tipi. He remembered it fondly. He now saw the cub as its animated image come to life right in front of him. The cub was at a point where a rock jutted out to reach, and was almost parallel with, a similar smooth dark gray rock on the bank where the Lakota family were.

The cub, who was looking down at the ground and sniffing, suddenly raised his head, jutted his snout into the air, and sniffed mightily. He had caught the whiff of honeysuckle growing in the bushes just downstream, but the bush appeared to be on the other side of the stream. Having smelled the deliciously sweet fragrance, the cub decided that he needed to follow that scent to see if it led to something delicious to chew on. Something that smelled that good must taste good. And he loved to eat, proven by his nearly chubby baby bear body. He was a light brown rounded version of his parents, probably several hundred pounds or so lighter than they. He was only seven months old and had a lot more meals to consider and pursue.

The cub gently pushed his right paw into the edge of the very cold (*osni*) crystal-clear rushing water. He glimpsed a big trout swimming by but was too surprised to do anything about it. He quickly lifted his cold wet paw out of the water and then gently, as if testing the true nature of its makeup, placed it upon the smooth rock jutting out from his side of the creek.

The rock was so shiny and wet, it almost looked like water itself. Having gained a solid foothold, the cub then reached out his other front paw. He now had both front paws on the large rock. His belly and midsection hovered over the small expanse of rushing water below him, as his back paws were anchored to the grassy cleft along the bank. There he stood for a few seconds surveying the situation.

It was at this point that he spotted the young human child crawling, then standing, then tripping, then partially standing, and then giving up and just crawling toward him from the other side of the stream. The child appeared to be heading in the direction of the gleaming, shining rock that stuck out from the edge of the stream opposite the bear. From the way the two parallel rocks were positioned in the stream, it appeared that they were reaching out to each other. Maybe the rocks had even been connected as one, not so long ago—or maybe a few thousand or a million years ago. That didn't matter right now. The two rocks reached out toward the middle of the rushing stream like old shining wet gray hands, the two index fingers of shiny gray granite extending out and trying to touch each other. The rocks could not touch, though, as about two and a half feet separated their rocky tips.

Once the cub noticed Brown Eagle moving in his direction, his young mind temporarily forgot about the honeysuckle, and began focusing on the little human being in the buckskin pants that was crawling toward him. The child now looked like he was walking like a bear. His "paws" were not as big or hairy as the cub's. The grizzly noticed that the baby's head and snout were both smaller than his own. His mouth looked small too. But that little mouth was open and smiling, smiling in his direction, smiling at him.

The cub recognized in this little being a potential friend, someone who was there like he and his mother were, his mother currently being behind him in the trees. The baby must have been here with those two other, bigger humans across the way.

The whole situation was nonthreatening to the cub. The little bear liked the little one crawling toward him and smiling. The larger ones were smiling and laughing too, although they appeared to be engrossed in whatever they were doing along the edge of the water with those bright-colored things. They appeared not to mind at all that the little one was coming his way, smiling, appearing to want to come and see him, maybe to play with him like the other small cubs back at the den in the mountain rocks.

The cub smiled back with his eyes. At that point, the two little ones locked gazes.

Their eyes met, both dark brown in color and focused. It was as if there was a greeting, but there were no words. It was the old way of communicating with another being.

They stared, and they knew. Both wanted to meet; both needed to meet. They were instant friends, partners on the road of life, although each had only just begun.

Little Brown Eagle crawled to the edge of the grassy cleft of the creek. He slowed temporarily because of the shiny gray rock that jutted out toward the cub, who was on the other side of the wetness. His small hands reached out to touch the wet surface of the shiny rock. Seeing progress toward his new friend the cub, the baby dragged his knees onto the rock as well. The two youngsters continued to stare at each other in awe with the simple joy of meeting a new friend, a new playmate. It mattered not to them the color or appearance of the other baby. Neither, of course, prior to this chance meeting, really knew what he himself, looked like to others. So this was a pure instance of wanting to reach each other, to make contact, to start communication and begin a new friendship. No prejudgment did, nor could, take hold here. Because the two knew nothing different. Neither of them viewed anyone else as anything but a friend whom they wanted to meet. Their eyes did the talking.

The little bear, upon seeing his new friend getting close, became excited and pounded his front paws up and down, twice, keeping his front legs stiff and straight. The baby, seeing this, attempted to mimic his new friend. However, little Brown Eagle did not have wide, firmly padded front paws like the cub. When he beat the ground with his arms stiff, his right hand slipped out from under him, so he stopped. It was at this point that each nudged forward to the very edge of the shiny wet rock each crouched upon. They were close enough now to smell each other's distinct scent.

Gaining the edge, each looked at the other. Almost simultaneously, they each raised their right arm to reach forward across the water to make contact with the other one on the other rock. In doing so, both little ones had moved to the very edge. They strained and stretched forward just above the innocent-looking yet fast-moving water below. It was an innocent but determined gesture by both, an exercise in contact and communication, and of learning about life, that was taking place upon this mountain stream. How many previous encounters had occurred in similar ways? How many times had human reached out to bear, and bear reached out to human? It was happening now, and no preventative warning or scolding could prevent it from occurring. But the laws of nature, and fate itself, intervened.

In an effort to gain just another inch, the little cub let out an excited yelp. "Yap." It worked. As little brown-skinned fingers touched little black claws, the Lakota women stopped talking. They had heard the cub yelp, and quickly glanced in the direction of the sound. Iron Hat's heart leapt into her throat. Seeing the situation, and the young grizzly, she screamed, "Mato! No. Stop. No!"

Trying to stand quickly, she caught her foot in the hem of her dress and fell face first into the muddy grass. Good Voice Woman jumped to her feet and scrambled toward the baby on the rocky edge. As she lunged, and closed the gap between herself and the little boy, the little grizzly got frightened, stood on his hind legs, and yelped again: "Yapp, yapp aoow."

Suddenly, from the trees on the other bank, a huge light brown body sprang, leaping forward in a great gulp of earth and bear paws toward the creek. It was the cub's mama. She had heard the yelp of her son, and her heart, too, had jumped into her throat. Having risen quickly from her task of digging grubs out from under a dead tree stump, she lunged toward the sound of peril in the creek. "Grawwww!" was heard as she ripped through the tree branches and entered the scene.

Iron Hat had regained her footing and scrambled so fast to the creek's edge that her feet hardly even touched the ground. Then, abruptly, she stopped and stared.

There they stood, on opposite sides of the bank of the rushing creek, remaining still, staring into each other's eyes, one mother to the other, scared, alarmed, confused, and frozen in action.

Then it happened. The little Lakota boy's knees slipped off the edge of the slippery rock. He fell face first into the cold rushing water below. His little body disappeared immediately. The cub screamed now, and pounced up and down in his spot, howling.

Iron Hat and Good Voice Woman screamed his name at once: "Brown Eagle! No!" Iron Hat jumped feet first into the rushing water after her little son. She reached out frantically to grab him, if only he were there within reach. Nothing.

It was at this moment that the large grizzly mother saw the fright, pain, and love in the human mother's frantic eyes. And she sprang into action.

Knowing the creek and its rough and fast current from many years of fishing and swimming there, the mother bear sprinted quickly downstream several tree lengths. Glancing quickly and knowingly into the rushing, churning water, she dove paws first, into the crashing waves and current.

Her great body created a tremendous crash and splatter, for a moment submerging entirely, only to surface several feet ahead. Then she quickly dipped again. This time, when her great brown head broke the surface of the rapids, her jaw was clasping the waistband of the little boy's buckskin pants at the back. She lifted him clear of the rushing water and briefly held him aloft. The little boy gurgled water from his mouth before he coughed, and then began to cry, barely finding the breath to let out a wail following his previous intake of air.

With great strength but abundant care and gentleness, the huge mother bear stood on three legs and lifted Brown Eagle out of the rushing current, gently clasping the little human with her right foreleg and paw, carrying him to the opposite shore.

Once there, she gently and slowly lowered the little one to the grass. Then she stood on all fours above him, as he rolled onto his back and continued to cry for his mother. It was at this point that the mother bear lowered her great massive head, briefly studied and sniffed the little human—his face and nose and eyes—and then kissed him. Her rough large pink tongue wetly licked along Brown Eagle's left cheek and came to rest on his forehead. She then gave a gentle growl, stood up, turned toward her cub, and growled again. At that, the little bear rose up and walked over to his mother. She sniffed and licked his face too. Then she lowered her head and, catching him along his furry haunches from behind, nudged him forward and into motion, toward the trees. Getting the signal, he quickly broke into a trot and disappeared into the brush at the edge of the trees. Before following her cub into the trees, the great bear calmly turned and looked directly into the eyes of the human mother, who was frozen in her position, standing in a shallow point of a pool along the edge of the creek. She knew. They both knew.

Then the great grizzly turned and slowly lumbered off toward the edge of the trees, to follow her own son.

Iron Hat cried. She shook. Then she looked up and thanked Wakan Tanka for her son's life and for the bear.

She quickly jumped across the rocks, avoiding the limbs along the way, and came to lie down beside her sobbing son. He was not crying as hard now, as he had begun to calm. She hugged him close and felt their leaping hearts beating against each other. Then, touching his cheek, she remembered the bear and what the bear had done. Iron Hat then kissed her son lovingly on his cheek and his forehead. Creator would be due a feast soon to give thanks.

So the feast was held. The wopila ceremony of gratitude was performed. Prayers were made, carried aloft by wanbli. And little Brown Eagle was given a new name, a noble name to recognize the kindness, the strength, the empathy, and the love of the great mother bear. He would be called Mato Niyanpi—Saved By Bear. This name carried great energy, great medicine, great aspiration.

Mato Cikala

When Saved By Bear was very young and just learning to walk, his grandmother Fire Cloud made him a little brown bear stitched out of deerskin and sinew and stuffed with sage. The little bear, the size of a large squirrel, was sewn together with the determination and detail of a grandmother's love. The little bear had some actual bearskin and bear fur sewn on to cover the deerskin, so as to make him look and feel more real. His eyes were made out of a cluster of small black pebbles forming two shiny round circles around the triangular patch of dark buffalo horn hair that served as his hardened little nose. The ears of the little bear were rounded and raised, kept sturdy by the toughest part of the deer hide that remained firm.

The first time Saved By Bear saw him, he fell in love. He hugged him close to his chest, pressed his cheek against the little bear's face, and kissed the rounded belly. His grandma had really outdone herself this time. This was truly one of the best gifts that the small *hoksila* (boy) had ever received. Little did he know then that it would also become one of the greatest that he had received in his entire life, as time passed and the years would go by.

The little bear was named Mato Cikala: Little Bear. Saved By Bear called him Mato for short. This was a blessed little gift of love, but it also had a deep symbolic meaning for the child's family, the bear clan, the people of the bear medicine. Mato the bear, as the spirit and the two-legged-walking being found everywhere in the land of the Lakota, was powerful, majestic, strong, and graceful, and had magical healing powers. That is why the Lakota and the mato people themselves, looked upon the bear as a being of medicine and healing. Ferocious, as genuine real bears seemed or acted when threatened, they were also kindly, gentle family people, always willing to nurture and care for their young through thick and thin, and to defend their own kind against danger, threat, and destruction, to the death, if necessary.

The gifting of Mato Cikala was also to forever remind Saved By Bear and his family of the huge loving gift that was presented to them by the great mother bear at the banks of the fast-moving creek a few years earlier. Saved By Bear's life had been preserved and given back to him and his family by the kind motherly acts of the good medicine being, the mother bear. This would prove to be an eternal link between Saved By Bear and his family and the bear family, much more so than they had ever envisioned or known.

Mato Cikala became Saved By Bear's constant companion at play, in the lodge, and especially at night when he lay down to sleep. The comforting feeling of the little bear's solid fur and round tummy warmed Saved By Bear's heart. It gave him a feeling of comfort, of safety, in an often uncertain environment.

As the years passed and Saved By Bear grew older and turned to the deeds and desires of becoming a Lakota boy, and even a young brave, he often put his little bear aside, placing it into the larger buffalo hides of his mother, for safekeeping. It was not appropriate in his eyes for a young brave such as himself who was striving to prove himself as a courageous future warrior, to be seen carrying around or cuddling with a little toy bear. So Mato Cikala was mostly consigned to being tucked away with other personal items of the family within the buffalo robes.

Now and then, however, especially at times when he was lonely or feeling like he needed a friend close by, Saved By Bear would quietly and secretly dig through the buffalo hides and find his little trusted friend. His companion over the years had become worn by constant handling, hugging, and rubbing. So much that much of his bear fur had been worn down almost to the deerskin beneath. The little black eyes had grown loose, but still hung in place. As if to signify a slight droop of that eye that a being would experience through the process of aging and loving upon the Earth for so many years. But the love for his little companion never diminished over time. It was just not so readily available for such times to be shown in the private way he was accustomed to, as he was trying to become a courageous young brave, projecting that image outward to the people.

When Saved By Bear was about six years old, the people were in the process of moving camp from the White River basin near the great sandstone cliffs of the Badlands, to the warmer confines of the creeks within He Sapa. While packing and loading their tipis and other belongings onto the horses' travoises for the long journey through the Buffalo Run (*Pte Tali Yapa*) to the entryway to the southeast corner of the He Sapa, the people were alerted to an approaching garrison of cavalry.

The scouts along the eastern perimeter had seen a column of marching bluecoats twenty miles or so south, in the distance. It was certain that the garrison or its soldiers had not seen the scouts, or the camp, because their pace and demeanor never changed during the observance. It was likely that this particular garrison, numbering somewhere between one hundred and two hundred men and horses, and some buckboard wagons being pulled by mule trains, were likely heading toward Fort Robinson, which was well below the Mnincoju Lakota perimeter.

However, to be on the safe side, the scouts informed the *naca* (leadership council) of this discovery. The naca discussed the situation hurriedly with Bull Bear, and then decided it was best to hasten the pace of the departure. But they would shift the route to the north for a while, in order to completely avoid any contact or convergence with the white army group.

As a result of the change in plans, the women and young people, including Saved By Bear, quickened their pace, running and scurrying about to load all that was needed upon the travoises for departure. Unbeknownst to Saved By Bear and his family, one of the buffalo robe bundles, got hurriedly tossed near a travois for loading and inadvertently rolled some distance, coming to rest behind a large clump of chokecherry bushes. There it opened, and the contents came free, to be spilled upon the ground. Since the objects had rolled down a slight incline, no one in the group saw the bundles or its contents or its final resting place. Not knowing otherwise, everything else was packed and loaded with great speed, and then the ponies were mounted and the journey embarked.

Among the strewn objects left behind, at the foot of the chokecherry bushes, was Mato Cikala, his shiny eyes staring upward to the sky and his arms raised over his head. It was almost as if he were gesturing them to stop, to wait, to let him come....

Two weeks later, after some good fishing was done at one of the sparkling creeks in the He Sapa and the trout were brought back to Saved By Bear's mother to cook over the fire, Saved By Bear went into the tipi to look for an additional robe to wear in the coming evening chill. He searched near the back edge of the lodge and found several robed bundles. Selecting his smaller buffalo covering, he threw it over his shoulders. He thought of Mato Cikala, his little bear, since at the moment he was very close to the bundled belongings of the family.

He reached in and began looking for the bear. Soon, it became apparent that his friend was nowhere to be found within the bundled belongings. Saved By Bear stopped and tried to think of the last time he had taken him out to kiss his worn-down face or to hold him tight as he drifted off to sleep in his curled-up state on the floor of the tipi—but he could not remember. Then it occurred to him that he had taken his little friend out and held him close to his chest while sleeping one night in the Badlands after a particularly long day of riding. That was the last time he could recall seeing him. The memory made him smile, temporarily. Then it hit him: Mato Cikala was not here. Where was he? Did some other child take him? Did his mother, father, or grandfather finally get rid of the little bear, so as to end the boy's childlike ritual of sleeping with the bear from time to time? He was not fully aware at the time that his elders did in fact see him with the little bear in his arms during particularly deep sleeps.

Saved By Bear felt embarrassed and worried at the same time. The little bear was not even human, not even living flesh, so why should he feel so panicked over his disappearance? Why was there this sense of emptiness in his gut when he thought about the loss of the little bear and his soft fur? It was silly. It was not a thing that a future warrior should even be thinking about. And yet he was thinking about it, panicking over the loss of his little friend made of deerskin, sinew, and sage stuffing. It was silly. It was childish. It was unnatural, he presumed. And yet, as he scrambled and fumbled through the strewn bundles in the lodge, not finding his friend, a tear formed in his eye. He was thinking about the little shiny eyes that seemed to look into his soul, understand him, and give him comfort. And the transference of warmth between their bodies as they slept. And then it made sense. The little bear was gifted to him out of pure love, and therefore, became pure love. This was why he had not outgrown, and could not he see himself outgrowing, that love, that symbol of love.

It did not seem logical to Saved By Bear at that moment of panicky loss of a trusted friend that he would grow to allow these human emotions and feelings to flow from within him to other things, to other beings, to other humans in the future. His emotion, his love, would flow as strongly and as purely as it once did for his little bear. He would one day understand what it meant to feel love for, caring of, and commitment to others, and what it felt like to experience their loss, when that too came. His little bear, his little friend, Mato Cikala, had somehow enriched in him an ability to open himself up, to truly feel— to feel life with his heart, with his soul, with his spirit, to feel beyond himself, and to know that it was wonderful and meaningful to care for another, to care for and about others.

But at this moment, the pain of loss of his little friend was great. He felt lost. He felt empty. He felt lonely, and so he cried. This was not a simple quiet letting go of a single tear down the cheek. No. This was an outburst of emotion that he had not known could well up inside him. It came thundering out of his chest, and burst like a burgeoning, rushing waterfall. It gushed from the inside of his heart with a guttural wail. It showered and sprayed from the corners and the whole of his eyes and wetted his hands and his buckskin shirt. His nose became a faucet of mucus and snot, which dripped and flowed uncontrollably down and over his lips, some getting into his mouth, where he tasted the salt and the tartness of the mixture. He believed that others could hear him, but he didn't care. It came upon him quickly and mightily, and without warning. But it was real. It was raw. It was human.

Rushing into the lodge, his mother grabbed him by his shoulders and hugged him close, believing he may be hurt. She quickly and breathlessly asked him, "What's wrong? What's wrong, Saved By Bear? Why are you crying? Tell me. Tell your mother."

After a minute, he could not gush any more. His shaking body calmed. In his ina's arms he felt safe and loved, but he also felt the loss of his friend, as the embrace only reminded him of that which he had done from time to time over the years with the little bear. And he sobbed some more.

"What is it? What is wrong? Are you hurt? What happened? Where does it hurt? Are you sick? Why do you cry? Why do you cry so hard? What has happened?"

It all came out of him so quick. He couldn't think quick enough. But again, the feeling of guilt and embarrassment came, the silliness of the notion. How could he admit this to his mother? As he was nearly seven years old, she would think he was just being a baby. She would be embarrassed to have a son acting like a little baby. He was no baby.

But she held him in her arms, and hugged him tighter as if to emphasize her question. "What is it? You can tell me. Please tell me, Son. Can you tell me what is wrong? Why not? I am your mother. Please tell me, Son."

Then it hit him between the eyes, and between his heart and his spirit. She was his mother. She had raised him all this time. She knew him inside and out. She would not forsake him. It showed in her teary eyes as she stared at him with sadness, as it pained her to see her son this way. He could not deny her the truth—not here, not now, not ever. She would understand, wouldn't she?

At the moment, having heard the commotion, the crying, and the urgent questions, Saved By Bear's grandmother Fire Cloud came running through the tent flap and flung herself beside her daughter and her grandson, falling to her knees. Although she was no longer a young woman, she still moved surprisingly quick and well, as if the years had taken nothing from her energy. It was the urgency in her heart and in her mind that set all else apart, from the notion of just getting to her grandson to help ease his pain, whatever that pain may be.

She hugged them both in her strong embrace. So there they were, all on their knees in the corner of the lodge among the strewn-about robes and other personal items, hugging, kissing each other's cheeks, and crying, the two women wondering what this was all about.

So Saved By Bear calmed. Regaining his breath, he looked into the tearful eyes of his mother and his grandmother. Then he looked down at his knees, and at the open bundles.

And he told them. He feared the shame. He feared ridicule, but he got none. They calmly listened. They stroked his arms, his face, his cheek, and his hair. And they both understood.

There had been no act of taking the little bear from the bundles to give it to another child. There had been no purposeful effort to remove the bear from Saved By Bear's possessions, although it was known that he kept his friend securely in the bundles, and periodically took him out to hold him and sleep with him. There was a calm, smiling manner of understanding and acceptance shown in the eyes of the Lakota mother and grandmother. They understood. They understood because they themselves, as little girls, and then as young girls, and then as women, kept such things close to them too. They kept items and things that meant much to them, things that caused good memories and feelings to come flooding back. So they understood. Although they understood, and all was known and accepted between them, no reasons could be found for Mato Cikala's mysterious disappearance.

Nothing was known about where the little loved bear was or what had become of him. Not until one night, several nights after the events with the bundles in the tipi, when Saved By Bear's grandmother had a dream.

She always had dreams. Sometimes they seemed strange and unexplained. Many times they seemed quite real. She was a dreamer, and a good one at that, because she remembered her dreams. She had taught herself at an early age to savor her dreams. She had learned that if she'd had a good dream, or one that she wished to savor or know more about—or continue—she should immediately upon waking, talk to herself about it, to tell herself what she had dreamed, what she felt, and what she believed it was all about. It was like having a conversation with herself. Be that as it may, she became aware of the fact that by doing this, she was able to retain the dream, and to readily or more easily remember it. This practice was one she carried forth all her life.

When Fire Cloud had this particular dream, she knew right away once she awoke that she needed to talk about it as quickly as she could. She spoke with herself about it. And later that morning, she gathered her daughter and her grandson Saved By Bear around her in the lodge and relived the dream to them. This is what she said:

"I heard someone crying. Someone little, someone lost, was crying in the night. The stars were overhead. It was quite full of stars, the sky was. The crying was lonely, as if whoever it was, was feeling lost, lonely, left behind. It was a confused type of crying, as if questioning why, at the same time."

In the dream, Fire Cloud had found herself walking in a field at night, with jagged peaks in the distance against the night sky. She was wearing her moccasins, and the fringes at the end of her buckskin dress were dragging and swishing against the prairie grass and scraping against an occasional cactus. The scent of sandstone was heavy in the night air, along with the fragrance of a tart fruit, weak and dim. And yet the smell of the fruit got stronger and more tart as she continued to walk. She heard a distant wolf howl at the night moon. Then she heard it again, a soft sobbing, a little voice sobbing. As she moved forward, the sobbing grew louder, but it was still a quiet sobbing in the night, in the distance. As she moved, with her hands stretched out before her in the darkness so as to feel for trees or other things she may encounter, the sobbing continued. The tart smell grew stronger. She felt an unevenness to the dusty ground she walked upon, like she was walking over slight ridges and grooves in the dirt, not very wide, and a few inches deep each. These reminded her of the tracks and ruts left by the people when their camp travoises were dragged over the dirt behind the ponies, weighted down with the heaviness of the tipi poles, the tipis, and the personal belongings of the families.

Then it dawned on her to stop, so she did. She stooped and felt the earth, the deep gouge of the dusty rut. She smelled the fresh fine dust rising from the stretch of her fingers and her knuckle. She felt the crinkly prairie grass at the edge. She smelled again the sandstone, and the tart of the berry. That is what is was: chokecherry. Then, while still kneeling, she looked at the deep dark blue of the night horizon, and followed the craggy edge of the jagged peaks that seemed to jut up, and then slope down to the trough, and then jut up again, all across the distance.

And she heard the sobbing again, the little voice, the painful crying like that of someone who had recently lost a friend.

In an instant, within the dream, she found herself lying in the dirt upon a mat of some crinkly prairie grass, her eyes open and wet with tears. Staring straight up at the night sky, with the brightness of the Milky Way overhead. She felt both her arms extended up over her head. And in between sobs coming from her chest and throat, she smelled the tartness, so close that it was overwhelming. Turning her head slightly to the left, she saw it: a large bush of clumped, ripened chokecherries outlined by the moonlit star-studded night. And she felt overcome with sadness, the sadness of being alone, the sadness of being out in the middle of the night world, all alone. Sadness. A sadness of being left behind, of not knowing where everyone went, or why. Then she found her mouth and her lips forming the words. A name. "Saved By Bear"… And her eyes filled with tears, washing away the vision of the chokecherry bush and the stars through the sobs.

And she woke up.

The next day, Fire Cloud and her grandson rode on the trail once taken. Into the Badlands and to the site of their previous camp before moving. And looking behind the largest chokecherry bush. They found a friend. And took him home.

The Grattan Incident: An Unfortunate Spark to Light the Flame of Conflict

In the late summer of 1854 near Fort Laramie, west of the Spotted Tail camps of the Oglala and Sicangu (Brule), a young military officer named Lt. John Grattan was commissioned to oversee matters for the Sixth US Infantry Regiment at the military fort. Grattan was an arrogant, belligerent man who had no patience or tolerance for the Lakota people and their ways. It was a mistake for the army to send him there under those circumstances. It would only be a matter of time before things erupted between this provocative, short-tempered, arrogant young officer and the Lakota.

At the time, a Sicangu named Conquering Bear, headman of the

Lakota at the camp, served as the go-between and as spokesman for the needs of the Lakota who chose to stay and live near the fort.

As a result of the annuities and goods that were to be provided to the Lakota and Cheyenne as a result of the 1851 peace treaty (Fort Laramie Treaty I), the Lakota who stayed near the fort, under the guidance of Conquering Bear, attempted to take the "go along to get along" approach with the white people and military personnel at the fort. Conquering Bear proved to be a good diplomat for these relations. He held a much more passive position toward the whites than that of many of the young warriors and braves among the Lakota who lived at the camp, or those young Lakota who frequently visited their relatives at the camp. Among the Lakota at the camp of Conquering Bear at this time was a thirteen-year-old Mnincoju brave known as Curly.

The inevitable trigger to the escalation of conflict between the military at the fort and the camp occurred on August 17, 1854.

A group of white Mormon settlers had come through the fort on their way west on the Oregon Trail, traveling to the coast in search of gold and better opportunities. Along with their wagons, they were also escorting a small herd of cattle. On this particular day, a Lakota brave named Straight Foretop had been at the camp visiting his own relatives. One of the cows had strayed away from the Mormon herd. Straight Foretop and some young friends came upon the lone lame cow. It was said that Straight Foretop shot and killed the cow with his arrows and a spear, because he and the others believed the cow to have been abandoned and seeing it therefore as fair game, for becoming … game.

The Mormon cow owner, learning of this taking of his cow from some of the other Lakota and the white people at the fort, complained to the officers at the Fort. Later the white cow owner went with Lt. Hugh Fleming to speak to Conquering Bear to seek compensation. Dissatisfied with the response, the Mormon complained to the post commander, Grattan. The Mormon embellished the event and declared that he wanted the cow killer to be arrested and held by the soldiers at the fort. Grattan's envoy spoke to Conquering Bear, who invited the Mormon to come to the camp and select a pony to take as compensation and as a substitute for the dead cow. But the Mormon continued to demand more for the cow, as did the officer envoy, and insisted that Conquering Bear turn Straight Foretop over to the soldiers to be arrested. Conquering Bear spoke to Straight Foretop. He refused to be taken into custody. He did not feel he had done anything to warrant his arrest.

Word got back to Grattan. He was not pleased. Grattan's interpreter, a man named Auguste, had been drinking liquor that day. Grattan, who had a tendency to be arrogant in his own right, developed an angry mind-set and sought to get the Lakota to succumb to the demands of Grattan and the US military authority and turn over Straight Foretop.

Conquering Bear and many of the other warriors at the camp sensed that emotions were running high over this matter. The Lakota came to the conclusion that a physical conflict was fast becoming unavoidable. Conquering Bear and the Lakota believed that they had made a fair conciliatory gesture to make amends for what Straight Foretop had supposedly done wrong, and for the loss of the cow. After all, that is all that was required to do under the terms of 1851 treaty.

Grattan, using the interpreter Auguste, summoned a contingent of soldiers from the fort. They mounted up, toting firearms and a Hotchkiss gun, and rode into the Lakota camp to try to forcibly take Straight Foretop into custody. This is how something that seemed somewhat trivial and easily resolvable by reasonable thinking men turned ugly and sour. It had now become a show of might by each side, all because there was no agreement as to what needed to be done about the cow and Straight Foretop. So in effect, the whites and Grattan had chosen in the broader sense to place the value of a slaughtered cow over the value of the life of a Lakota, or over the value of peacefulness and coexistence with the Lakota. Grattan was not about to be the one to back down, especially given his animosity toward the Lakota. This situation incited his temper and arrogance. He was further egged on by the scout's behavior in mocking the Lakota as the soldiers advanced into the Lakota camp.

Grattan approached the lodge of Conquering Bear, who had taken Straight Foretop inside before the soldiers' arrival. He yelled for Conquering Bear to show himself and to bring "the Lakota cow-killing thief" out to him for arrest. Conquering Bear, in face paint, walked out and addressed Grattan, advising him, "I have already provided a good exchange for the white man's loss. We do not believe a Lakota man's life to be equal to the loss of a white man's cow. We will not force Straight Foretop to come out to be taken by you and to be jailed. We do not trust that he will ever return."

Grattan was getting angrier by the moment. The drunk interpreter again mocked the warriors standing by, by whooping at them and laughing. He mocked Conquering Bear, saying he was a coward protecting a thief. Tensions were high. On all sides, fingers pressed upon trigger, bow, and knife. Grattan demanded that Straight Foretop be turned over. Conquering Bear, continuing to try to reason, raised his arms and advanced. The soldiers behind Grattan jumped the gun. Rifle and pistol shots rained down upon Conquering Bear, the bullets entering his chest and his torso, his buckskin shirt turning into a bullet-riddled bloody mess as he fell to the ground.

The warriors had flanked the contingent of the twenty-nine-strong soldier group. Now that the first, and deadly, shots had been fired at their spokesman, and now that Conquering Bear lay there dying, the warriors quickly reacted.

Shots rang out, arrows slicing through bone and flesh. Warriors leaped upon and slashed and clubbed the nearest soldier from the side, or in groups from the front and back. The Hotchkiss was not able to be fired. In a matter of minutes, all twenty-nine of the solders, including Grattan and the annoying interpreter, were dead. A few Lakota lost their lives

The whites immediately pounced upon this event as the Grattan "Massacre," without ever revealing the entire true story or how it all started. The whole situation got completely out of control because of the military officers' unwillingness to listen or compromise.

The declaration of the event as a massacre only described the end result of what appeared to be an almost wholly one-sided military conflict. This is an example of how the whites and the US military distorted history and the reality of the events that took place between the whites and the Lakota.

Emboldened by the relative ease and the dominating manner in which Grattan and his troops had been taken out, many of the younger warriors wanted to take the opportunity to overtake and destroy the fort and all the whites there. However, with Conquering Bear mortally wounded, elder warriors assumed control of the heated situation, and talked the young warriors out of creating more of a violent mess than the situation already had created.

Instead of overtaking the fort, the Lakota, mainly the participating warriors and their families, decided to leave for other camps to the north and to the east. They did so to get away from what would surely be an immediate uptick in the military's desire to strike back at the Lakota. The young brave named Curly left with them. He would later become the warrior named Spirit Horse. It was suspected that regardless of how or why Grattan and his men had come to be at the camp, to provoke conflict, and then to be wiped out, would not matter. Circumstances did not mean much to the military in matters such as these. To the US military, the results spoke for themselves.

This episode ignited the terror and the anger of the United States government and its military, who now stepped up their campaigns against the Lakota and the Cheyenne. Gen. William Harney and his army were brought in to Blue Water Creek, which is in western Nebraska, in 1855. On September 3 of that year, they massacred an entire Lakota village of mostly women and children. At least eighty-six died. This military massacre is now referred to as the Blue Water Creek Massacre or the Ash Hollow Massacre. As a consequence of this massacre, Harney traipsed his way through sacred territory and near the He Sapa on his way back to Fort Pierre in the Dakota Territory. He did this basically as a complement of his act of terror, to send a message to the Lakota for the Grattan affair that took place in August 1854. Military personnel took it upon themselves to later name the highest peak in the Black Hills after this man (Harney Peak), which is an utter travesty, not just of all things factual and circumstantial but also of all things spiritual. The Lakota refer to this sacred peak by its original, aboriginal name, Hinhan Kaga, meaning "Owl's Nest" (which is presently called Black Elk Peak). Harney would become known to the Lakota as "the Butcher" as a result of this massacre. Ironically, he would later participate in several "peace treaty" meetings with the Lakota.

Family Is Paramount

For thousands of years, and specifically in the middle 1800s on Turtle Island, the Lakota lived in a civilized society. Saved By Bear's Mnincoju (Hohwoju) Lakota band of families and extended oyate existed within a simple yet highly sophisticated civilized community. To an outsider with no understanding of the people and their community, or to someone who purposefully chose not to try to understand these ways, the Mnincoju Lakota oyate community may have seemed primitive or unorganized. However, that could not be further from the truth.

Initially, to understand Saved By Bear as an individual Lakota, and the Mnincoju as a community of Lakota, the basic concepts of kinship, community, and family must be understood on their most basic levels.

To the Lakota, kinship is at the heart of identity. The fact of knowing where you belong, and that every Lakota has their place in the camp's circle, was absolutely crucial to the welfare of everyone in the community.

Families extended beyond the boundaries of the nuclear family, and included cousins, aunts, uncles, grandparents, and good friends who were not necessarily blood relatives. Family, as extended to encompass the greater group, created the tiospaye. Family status was freely given and granted among the Lakota, with the only restriction being that of what each Lakota felt was right in their own relationship with the people whom they loved and cared deeply for. Individuals, of course, made up the family and then the extended family, the tiospaye, which in turn became the foundation for the community of Lakota.

The community was made up of the groups of families and individuals who chose to be together and share their lives with one another. Bonds were deep, whether of blood, friendship, marriage, moral responsibility, or choice. The community of Lakota many times were referred to as "bands"—for example, Mnincoju Lakota, Two Kettle Lakota, Hunkpapa Lakota, and Sicangu Lakota. The bands routinely shared their lives with one another and participated in events together. Most bands of people had relatives and friends in other bands. It was perfectly normal for Lakota bands to live and travel together as if one.

Again, it was a matter of free choice, kinship, and personal relationships, which were the keys to these unions.

"*Toksa ake*," the Lakota would say to each other—"until next time" which is akin to "until we meet again." That is what it is: much like, "I will see you later," not "good-bye." "I will see you again at the next time we meet."

It was always important to the people that when it came time to depart a camp or leave a loved one or a friend, or any person at all, something be said to the special people left behind. So you said "Toksa ake." It was not good-bye, however, as there is no word in Lakota for "good-bye."

The special reason of the separation is meaningful. The special moment of departure is also meaningful. "Toksa ake" was something said to let the other person know that you were mindful of and hopeful for your next meeting with them.

The Female Is Sacred

From the very beginning of Lakota civilization and throughout the generations, theirs has been a maternal society. This was the way it began from Creator. This was the way of the teachings from Wakan Tanka. Unci Maka, Grandmother Earth, is female. She is the mother of all life, past, present, and future. The Grandmother is the center, the origin, of all life.

The significance of the woman was paramount within Lakota society. The female was always the one to run the society. The female would define the norms of the individual, the family, the oyate, the society, and the community. The female would create and prescribe the laws of the people. This natural, instinctive status derived from the breath, and from the calm guidance of the hands of Wakan Tanka. The female was the one who was in charge of the human from birth, throughout life, and until death. The female was the common natural link to all that was life. She alone could give birth to life, give birth to the human. All humans had a mother, a grandmother, and a great-grandmother. Without the woman, there was no life. She was life herself. Her responsibilities were great because she was the life giver and the life nurturer. While the male was chosen by Creator to be the preserver and the protector of life, the male could never give life. He could only take life. Or more compassionately and humanely, he could enrich, preserve, and protect the life that had been given already by and through the female. Because of her blessed gift of being the giver of life, the female was *wakan*. She was pure; she was innocent; she was life. Because of this, she should be the one to speak for those who had been given life. Through her guidance and counsel, life could be sustained, nurtured, and allowed to grow and mature. She provided the home. She owned the home and the property. She raised the entire family. She took care of everyone.

Males were born with natural instincts of survival and protection. And if need be, they could utilize their mental and physical aspects in confrontation, conflict, and even war. War, being the least preferred consequence or option. Because of the wakan nature of the female as a leader of the people, the female had a more instinctual ability to know and recognize a means of resolution or conciliation with regard to conflict or differences, without violence or war. This is because she has greater affinity with what it means to create and bring forth life, as life is created from and within her. She is far less prone or quick to condemn or to escalate matters into a set of circumstances that lead to or culminate in the taking of life.

A society not based upon a maternal foundation or grounded in female leadership, often finds itself upside down. Such a society may find itself with an opposite set of priorities for life and a lack of respect for those things that enrich and preserve life. Indeed, such a society may find itself more focused instead on death and destruction.

The societies and cultures wherein the woman is deemed subservient or second class to the male, mostly suffer from a loss of perspective on humanity and an absence of respect for Grandmother Earth and her children and peoples. In those societies and cultures where the female is dominated or controlled, or relegated to a lesser role in leadership, the concepts of family, community, and sharing with and caring for others, many times become lost attributes, or are viewed as weakness to the male-dominated influence of those societies and cultures.

If a culture practices control or domination of women, the

prominence of the value of each and every life that exists, is diminished. The value of life diminishes in the present, and surely over time. The value of each life loses its sacredness and is no longer revered as equal to every other life in existence. This is because the woman, as the giver and keeper of life, is diminished. Her influence is controlled or subdued.

In such societies, it becomes easier to make war, to engage in violence, to kill and take lives, at bay. The natural moral force of the wakan nature of the woman is not present to remind the people, always, that each life is truly sacred and equal to every other life. When a society is structured as a matriarchy, the people do not so freely or eagerly kill or wage war on other people. This is because the people do not believe that they should kill a mother's child. In a purely female-dominated society, war and destruction would be less, or altogether nonexistent, in a perfect or nearly perfect, world.

However, the world of Turtle Island during Saved By Bear's lifetime was highly civilized and functional, but not perfect. The Lakota society tried to survive and exist within that world and keep to itself, despite the unpredictable circumstances influenced by outsiders. This is why the structure of a civilized community and society was so important for the people.

From the beginning, the community of Lakota was a living, functioning thing. It was a multifaceted living, breathing organism in and of itself. The community members existed within a civilized collective involving group responsibility, organization, duty, education, and order. The community, therefore, was only as strong and as committed to its goals of sustaining a happy, enduring, civilized existence as each of the individuals making up the community. This was the foundation of Lakota society. This is why it worked.

Teaching the Truth

The Lakota means of civilization created a society based upon sharing and concern for each other. This was done so as to ensure equality in success and opportunity for a full, happy existence, to each and every Lakota in the society. At the foundation of this society, was the communal education.

The education of the Lakota began at birth. Once a Lakota baby was born into the society, the baby was raised within that very society so that everyone knew about the baby and its needs. Nothing happened within the Lakota society that the community did not know. The entire structure of civilized society was designed to create a circle of communication and information from the very moment of birth. And so the education of the baby would begin, because everyone knew that it must, proceeding in the same way as it had for every other baby in every other Lakota family.

In educating the young, the expectations for the child would always be focused upon the positive aspects of life, family, love, and friendship. There were no notions held back for the child to guess about. There was no testing as to right versus wrong. Education was all about truth and about the truthful way everything was handled and done. The child was presented with the truth from the beginning, from the very first time he or she was taught about some thing, some way, or some process. Children were told the truth about the matter and nothing else. Those that taught, taught the child the truth of things from the very beginning. This way, there was no question in the child's mind about what the truth was. The truth was the only way that the Lakota child would live within. The Lakota child would know things to be no other way. They would not have to guess about the truth. They would not be presented with a false positive or with a distracting test seeking to discover whether or not they could pick out the truthful thing from among multiple untruths. There were no deceptions and no competition. No one had a greater claim than anyone else to the truth.

The Lakota taught the children the truth of their society. The Lakota society had morals and ethics, both for individuals and for the whole community, from the beginning. Therefore, the children knew these things from the beginning. They would only know the truth of things. For example, if the Lakota child was being taught about a certain flower in the pasture, the teacher would show the flower and show the child what it looks like, and what the flower cures, and how it is used to cure. The child is therefore being told the truth about the flower and what it does. The child was not expected or required to ever guess about it.

This is how every Lakota was raised and taught without exception.

There were no deviations in the manner or method. Stick to the truth, and it is simple. More pure. Through the years, this was the greatest foundation for the education of the human. It set the stage for those moments in life when one's body, mind, and spirit is challenged to respond to something new, something strange, when one is asked or forced to adapt to a set of unforeseen circumstances or events that have little or nothing at all to do with the truth. In those moments and at those times, the Lakota, because of their education, felt prepared to face the prospect of adaption. However, adaptation is not assimilation. Adaptation is positive. Assimilation is not.

The civilization of the Lakota was derived of its ability to contribute to, and to preserve and protect, the peaceful, calm existence and survival of the community as a whole. This was accomplished by way of the Lakota's education in the truth of things from the very beginning. It was also brought about by the use of honest and meaningful communication within society as to the needs of the one or the many.

Naca

Among the people, there were individuals referred to as *naca*. (pronounced Nah-cha). These were the ones whom the people informed of the needs or requests of an individual, of a family, or of the oyate as a whole. The naca themselves were all members of an individual oyate, each serving as the head or the spokesperson of his or her oyate. The naca would bring forth and communicate the state, nature, and condition of the oyate so as to keep the community up to date so the community would know. The naca would communicate if the oyate needed things or assistance, and where, why, and when these things were needed. The naca were the ones who brought forth the concerns of the individual, or an individual oyate, to the community as a whole.

The system of the naca worked well, bringing matters of concern and interest from one oyate to another, and to the heads of the council of the communities. It worked like this: The common family would be experiencing a problem, such as hunger; or the tiospaye would be suffering from a drought; or the families were in a position of having lost a large number of their warriors in a conflict or similar event that left them short of help and without the strength to carry out the functions of the family. The matter at hand would first likely be brought to a head council, a group of delegated women who listened to these concerns. The women then spoke to the head council of the tiospaye or nation of the community (the headmen) about these concerns, seeking a solution to the problem or a way to satisfy the need. For example, in the case of having lost a number of warriors in battle, the head council may ask a neighboring nation (such as the Hunkpapa) to send men to the community to help the families in need, to perform duties that had been previously performed by the men when before they were lost in battle. The neighboring naca council may then in turn offer to send a number of men to help those families fulfill that specific need.

The concerns or issues of the people were brought forth truthfully without shame or the fear of ridicule, and with the knowledge that the community would wish to help. The concerns and issues were always dealt with quickly, addressed within a matter of days or a week, and in the most positive way. It was seen as harmful to delay the process of implementing a solution to the problem at hand. Therefore, it was a virtue to act thoughtfully but quickly in a time of need. It was not virtuous or just, to procrastinate, or do nothing.

This is how matters of concern to the Lakota were dealt with within the community. Needs of the individual, the family, the oyate, and/or the nation were calmly and rationally made known to the naca plainly, simply, truthfully, and without reservation, absent of shame, humiliation, and ridicule. To ask for or seek help when in need was considered truthful and honest. It was a representation of a truthful condition. The truth was the truth. If a truthful need was necessary to be addressed, then it was addressed. If one could not tell the truth when seeking the help of the community, then the truth and the process would not work for everyone when the inevitable time came, when others had a time of need and it became necessary for them to approach the naca.

If the naca relayed the need or concern to the head council and the need was met within the community, then nothing else was required. If the need or concern could not realistically be met within the community, then the head council of the nation would feel no shame or reservation in seeking help from their friends among the neighboring Lakota bands or nations. Again, truthful pleas for help or expressions of need from the individual Lakota, or from one Lakota nation to another Lakota nation, were nothing to be ashamed of and were not viewed as weakness. In the circle of community, and within the circle of civilized society, what was done to assist or comfort a neighbor in need could easily be returned and showered upon one's own people in the future when they experienced a time of need. Again, nothing was easier or more simple than to just truthfully and openly ask for help.

It is this truthful means of communication that provided real and honest solutions to the problems and needs of all Lakota. Food and water was shared. Workers were sent to help as needed. Buffalo hides were presented. Horses and ponies were lent or gifted to those who needed them. Medicine was given. Shelters were bolstered or constructed to house the unsheltered. This process worked for those in need, because it worked for all who could meet the need. It was community. It was a sharing of aid. It was a sharing of the burden. It was a sharing of resources. It was a sharing of humanity. It was a truthful presentation of caring—truly caring for each and every individual member of society. It was expected. It was practiced. It was self-satisfying. It was a self-fulfilling prophecy of all that had been taught by Creator. This is the way that it was, the way that it is.

It was believed that if an issue or concern affected one person within the nation, that issue or concern affected the nation as a whole.

Protection From Within

Every society must have a peacekeeping force to maintiain stability and the confidence of its citizens. In the Lakota tradition, this group of men and women is known as Akicita. The men dominate the physical control of a threatening volatile situation. Priority of intervention is for detainment and removal of a violator. After this first action of the men is secure and safe, the headwomen can enter the tipi to care for the individual and family that has been harmed. The women know and practice their healing methods for this family. The culture of Akicita is based on a proven philosophy of sharing duty and responsibility.

These practices are required to protect the people from harm or fatal experiences. The Akicita behavior is evidence of each individual's commitment, and is reinforced by the morals and ethics taught to them and the people, since birth. They are good hands when called upon.

The women and men combine their wisdom and experience to be the first responders to every violation that may occur. The akicita are present and prepared to engage wrongful behavior at a moments notice, day or night. This method of approach will always be used as the initial physical contact when an emergency has occurred. When one of the people is wrongfully harmed, all of the people may be in danger. This is the first, in a sucession of four levels of akicita responsibilities. The remaining three levels will be under the authority and decisons of the men. The women will take care of the families and their needs, each and every time a crisis arises.

The akicita levels of responsibility utilize the personal attributes of the elder and younger warriors. The first level exemplifies authority to protect life. The elder of this group will use diplomacy as he speaks to the violator.

The violator is now informed of traditional protocol and is taken to a predetermined secluded area. The reason is to completely isolate the perpetrator away from any contact with the people of the camp. Families may resume normal daily activities when the removal is accomplished. The reeducation process of this individual's spirit and mind begins. The severity of the violation dictates the duration of the confinement time. This time frame is needed for the violator to understand and take full responsibility for the harm committed. The more egregious the wrongful act, the higher the level of akicita that will be needed. Each degree of violation will dictate which level of akicita is called in.

The second level is comprised of a more intense immersion of traditional practices. There is still hope that this individual may be rehabilitated and enter society as a trusted member again. Emphasis is placed on the service to community, rather than placing self, first. Rituals of practice focus upon contributions to the welfare of the people. The violator will learn to give of self, labor, and personal possessions. Future subsistence responsibilities will be mandated and performed by the violator, for the family that was harmed. These first two levels focus on healing the lost spirit through reason and ceremony. If the good of this human being is fighting to stay alive, it will be willing to learn and accept these offerings of the akicita. They observe all behavior and emotion of this person who is confined.

The time frame for this personal spiritual growth is solely determined by the discussion and eventual decision of the warriors. The akicita have had to leave their families to protect and preserve peace and order in accordance with our laws. At these two levels, seclusion with no camp contact may be for weeks or may extend into a number of months. The wrongdoer has the best opportunity to eventually return home with the people at this point.

The third level of akicita includes mainly warrior society members. They are trained and prepared for battlefield situations. Under this watch, communication of any kind, is initiated by the command of a warrior. The individual wrongdoer who has reached this level, is guilty of causing extreme physical fear, abuse, maiming, and potential life threatening violence. This bad energy has forever harmed an innocent human being. The conditions of this confinement will involve rigid instructions that must be followed exactly and immediately upon command. Resistence will be met with harsh physical treatment if necessary. The violator of this kind of crime, must be taught to understand the loss of privilege and societal rights. This person may never be able to enjoy the true celebrations of the camp again. The good people have earned this secured peaceful time for the heart and spirit to feast and share with one another. They deserve to be protected from such wrongdoers.

At this third level, the violator will be given instructions of support to accept the new reality of daily existence. The warriors and spiritual advisor discuss the consequences of their decision for action. The violator may try to return to the camp, but will be recognized as one who looks in on the people from the outside. There will be a lack of respect and trust for this person throughout the camp fires. There is another choice to consider for the violator. To willfully leave the camp and relatives and start an entirely new life without the families. When the violator makes the choice of which path to walk, the akicita will announce this decision to the people. They also have a say if re-entry is to be allowed. The decision of the camp is final, no negotiation. Life will be hard for the violator. The consequences of one bad decision that changed everything in a once promising life.

The fourth and final level of the akicita is the most forceful group of celebrated warriors. They respresent the last approach in dealing with the violator. The violator has committed one of the most heinous acts upon another person. The injured member has experienced life threatenting trauma, or the member has passed on to the spirit world. The akicita at this level understand that time is of the essence. They must decide the fate of this menance to society. The warriors are prepared to relay their decision to the violator. All warriors stay present and on guard to contain this evil being. From the horrible event happening, then removal, and then secured by all the warriors, away from camp. The akicita make their decision as quickly as possible to permanently correct the violation. The violator is given their decision that goes into effect immediately.

As the warriors surround the violator, the headman speaks of a choice to be made right now. Then, the akicita will force one of two ways to send the violator away from our campfire forever. Walk as you are now, never return in this life, you are banished from our nation. Any resistence to this demand will necessitate action for the taking of the violator's life. The akicita remove this dangerous being from walking on our sacred earth.

Through these traditional practices the Akicita have remained a constant and reliable protector of all people of Grandmother Earth. A civilized society provides the necessary teaching to continually maintain law and order through the generations. Where there is peace, there is the Akicita.

At the highest level of the structure in place to protect the people, preserve their lives, and preserve their way of life was the fourth group. Saved By Bear and Swift Bear would become a part of this group that, along with some of the other elders, had a tremendous responsibility and duty to the people. This was why certain members of this fourth group, the fourth level of warriors, including *heyokas*, would be asked to participate in the preparation for the time of the breaking of the world at the Greasy Grass, the Little Bighorn.

Seeking a Balance with All Life on Turtle Island

A civilized society such as that of the Mnincoju Lakota remains civilized as long as all of its people remain committed to a spiritually connected way of life and existence. The continuation of civilization required that the Lakota provide the necessary amount of care, empathy, respect, and honor to all of the other peoples and beings that share their existence with the Lakota upon Grandmother Earth. A civilization, if it is to exist and endure, must be balanced within the truth of its environment and surroundings. The life forces and the spiritual energy must be in balance with everything around them.

The balance must include all of the peoples: the air, the water, the stone, the dirt, the plants, the humans, and the animals. Each type of people is as worthy of respect, dignity, and presence as the other. To have balance in life means to share each other's life force, to share each other's life energy.

This balance begins with knowledge and understanding of each other, which in turn begins with the curiosity and the desire to learn what there is to be learned about the other peoples, including their similarities and differences and what they must do to survive. When you learn these things, then you know how to help other types of people survive.

We all learn from each other. One people watch and learn from what another does. Then they adapt their own behavior, using those things or ways that are most beneficial not only to their own survival, but also to the survival of the balance in life. It is helpful and meaningful, for example, to watch how the raccoon handles his food with his five-fingered hands, or how the robin meticulously builds her sheltering nest with anything she can find to add to the strength of the structure.

It was through the constant pursuit of maintaining a balanced life and spirit that the Lakota grew to accept and love their brothers and sisters among the other species of people.

This virtue was exemplified by the relationship between the Lakota and the mato. The bear, the mato, is the giver of life medicine. This is true throughout the Circle of life. Since mato is medicine, and since medicine is life, mato is life. An understanding of mato and all that mato represents furthered the balance in life. Both species of beings—humans and bears—benefited from this relationship of balance and respect.

These lessons of balance were found everywhere. In the mid-1850s, Fights the Bear had found himself on a long-distance scout for tatanka with four other others warriors along the southern fringes of the territories bordering the wagon trails of the whites beyond the Niobrara River. It was here that he witnessed the struggle for survival of another kind of family.

A mother cougar and a mother wolf worked in unison to take down a huge longhorn bull. Their cubs and pups looked on from the nearby tree line. They all were starved after the long, harsh winter. The bull's meat would be greatly needed nourishment, something that would sustain them for weeks. The warrior watched, knowing what it felt like to be desperately hunting for life-giving food for his family to save them from starvation. He felt in his heart the same pangs of need, commitment, and love that the two four-legged mothers were feeling at the time of killing the large beast.

It was through this soul-driven role reversal gift that Fights the Bear could empathize with the cougar's and the wolf's desperation, intent, and drive, and their devotion to family, their love for their own. This was made clear by their willingness to do such a thing in obvious view of the white settlers, who would see their predatory action as a reason to hunt them down and try to exterminate them for taking one of their prized beef bulls.

The mothers did this with desperate love and with that sullen knowledge in mind—because they had to. It was their obligation. It was their duty. This is how it has always been and how it always will be with Creator's four-legged beings. The warrior, knows that the two mothers' families would survive only if the mothers themselves survived the inevitable vengeful hunt and the coming consequences. He felt that he needed to do something to prevent the young ones from becoming motherless.

Being true to his connection to Grandmother Earth's balance of life, Fights the Bear quickly convinced the four warriors he was with, to ride hard toward the temporary encampment of the white wagon train. As they rode by the cougar and the wolf, who were with their kill, the warriors slowed. They made it seem as if they were the ones who had taken the bull. The whites, seeing that fearsome gesture, quickly loaded up their wagons and scrambled to be on their way, hoping to get far away from the area. The mothers could now feed their young in peace.

The Lakota recognized that in order to live true to the spirit of balance in life, it was important to know and respect their grandmother Unci Maka and not to use up or waste her beautiful, bountiful gifts. They could appreciate and enjoy her, but they were not to disturb her in such a way that she could not heal herself by natural means.

One concept was "walk on the rocks when you can." Walk on the rocks so you do not leave a physical footprint. It will make you less trackable when your opponent tries to find you, and it will leave less behind for Grandmother Earth to deal with after you have gone.

If your footprints are meant to remain, they will remain. They will be left behind for those who knew who you were, where you were going, and where it was you walked. They will know in their hearts and spirits that they are following in your footprints even though they do not see them with their eyes. They will feel you and your honorable direction, with the guidance of the spirit within their souls. And they will thank you for showing them the way.

First Contact with Foreigners to Turtle Island: Foreign Concepts

Prior to the arrival of the white European peoples to Turtle Island from across the waters, the North American indigenous people did not believe that they would need to put markings on a piece of paper to indicate one person's word to another or one people's word to another people. Like the introduction of the "foreigners" to Turtle Island, the notion of having to document or write promises and commitments between peoples and their nations on a piece of paper, was *foreign* to the indigenous tribal people, particularly to the Lakota.

The word *treaty* was not a part of the Lakota language. It was not a part of any conversation or discussion. The word *treaty* was not even within the realm of imagination or thought of the Lakota people, who were closely connected to Grandmother Earth and all that was provided by her to the people. There was no need to enter into such flimsy and phantom-like arrangements with another people, especially those people who were foreign to Turtle Island and who had no connection with Unci Maka in the lands of the Lakota—and certainly not those who were trespassers and invaders.

The Lakota never deemed themselves as *wards* of any kind of the European immigrants. The Lakota and their brother bands and tribes of the indigenous people on Turtle Island viewed themselves as the caretakers of all of the lands of, and all the waters within and around, Turtle Island. The Lakota and the other tribal people simply viewed themselves as the true stewards and *Protectors* of all of Turtle Island and all the peoples who resided there. One does not become a ward upon one's own land and territory.

As the number and frequency of the contacts with the white European immigrants to Turtle Island, beginning in the late 1600s, increased over time, the indigenous people, of course, were forced into dealing with these new people. It was difficult at first, because the new people did not speak the same language as the indigenous tribal people. And it was soon learned that most of the early white immigrants did not share the same beliefs, have the same respect for the natural world and the natural progression of life, or believe in the freedom of existence for all beings.

The white immigrants often brought with them to the eastern shores of Turtle Island dark-skinned humans of indigenous origin. The whites usually controlled these dark-skinned people, treating them as servants and forcing them to do work. There seemed to be an arrogance and contempt emanating from the white Europeans toward their dark-skinned captives, like the whites had some innate *privilege* and as if they were supreme over the races of people whose skin was not as white as their own. As the indigenous people of Turtle Island—or "Indians," as the newcomers called them—became more and more familiar with the motives and intentions of the ever-increasing, ever-encroaching white immigrants, they became more and more uneasy in their dealings with the white Europeans who were newcomers to their land.

The intents and motives of the new people bore through clearly when they just started to advance and take…, advance and take…, advance and take…, with no permission or consent from the indigenous peoples and with no concern for indigenous rights and interests. They advanced upon all that could be advanced upon and took all that could be taken. They took what was once the free land and territory of the indigenous tribal people. Then the whites decided to begin to use force to advance and take—to remove, strike, or kill those who got in the way of or resisted their advancing and their taking.

The white Europeans would advance and take, and then afterward try to obtain the consent and agreement of the indigenous people whom they had just advanced against and took from. The white European immigrants would try to convince the indigenous people that it was in the latter's best interests to just allow the whites to go ahead and advance and take all that they wished to take. But the white people and their new government made up of white people only, decided that they would or should at least provide some form of proof of their advancement and their taking of the lands and other property interests. So it was that the new white government in the eastern part of Turtle Island began in 1778 to draw up "papers" to acknowledge and document what was taken, and what was *agreed upon* between the parties. Of course, the term *agreed upon*, would be defined according to the whites. This is how the word *treaty* came about for the first time for the indigenous people of Turtle Island.

When each of the treaties was created, the government fashioned it in the form of a proposed peace treaty. However, these *agreements* were never really intended to be peace treaties. Instead, they were intended to be a step-by-step approach to genocide and the removal of the indigenous peoples from areas from which the new government wanted to extract more and more resources.

5

TRANSITIONAL GROWTH

THE LAKOTA PEOPLE WERE TRYING to lay a foundation for themselves and their children, such as Saved By Bear, within the society as it existed then in the 1850s. However, the society was under tremendous outside pressure to change. Saved By Bear and all the Lakota at this time were more or less learning to survive as humans and trying to retain their humanity in a changing world.

Saved By Bear was being taught traditionally, but the times were changing. The wilderness was changing, as were the pathways to and from the settlements. Things were becoming faster and quicker. People had less time to focus on all the aspects of their lives. The word coming in from all other indigenous groups was that the advancement of the whites was making it so that peoples had less and less time to live in their customary fashion.

The people were experiencing growth and transition. In a sense, they were trying to learn and grow according to the old ways, while simultaneously recognizing that the old ways were now being threatened by the new influences and the changing world.

The approximate time frame was the late 1850s, the time when Saved By Bear was being taught and when the Lakota were securing their sources of subsistence. This was a time of transition for the entire tribal nation. They were being hurried, pushed, and rushed, sometimes facing deprivation in the absence of staples that used to be part of their normal life.

The original Fort Laramie Treaty, entered into in 1851, was the first major encroachment upon the lives of the Lakota. It heralded a series of clashes between the Lakota and the new government over the government's entry into Lakota lands and the subsequent interference with the Lakota way of life. When Saved By Bear was a very young boy, Lakota society was entering a transitional phase. And this transition, of course, would end up increasing as each year went by. The changes were occurring more quickly and more immediately for our Nakota and Dakota relatives in the east, because they were closer geographically to the approaching white population, which was moving westward.

Between the ages of seven and ten, Saved By Bear was nurtured and taught by the men. The male of each family unit had the responsibility to teach the young boys all that was required of them. The boys would learn how to listen, how to be students. They would learn how to be patient with their instruction. They would be curious, but the questions they asked would be directly related to becoming a brave, and eventually a warrior. Much of this time period would be spent in the settlement area in the Bear Creek region, and sometimes in another settlement called Cherry Creek. Also, significantly, the people were moving to and from the He Sapa. This last place was where the warriors were the primary focus, as they spent their time not only teaching the young but also maintaining their own experience and knowledge and keeping the people safe while they were thus engaged.

It was during this phase of life, that there would be an encounter with Spirit Horse, a very respectable warrior who would meet Saved By Bear and Swift Bear, and be presented to the boys and the young men as an example of what a warrior is. He would speak and inform the young ones of his deeds and practice.

Saved By Bear's grandfather Iron White Man would also give his talk to his people, as he was a proven warrior and a society member. His experience and knowledge helped the people and the warriors to gain the confidence and courage needed to take the best next step.

During this period of time in the lives of the Lakota, particularly the lives of Saved By Bear and his family, there was a special recognition of the heyoka way in Saved By Bear and Swift Bear. Their spiritual connection was highly recognizable by the people, including the elders and the medicine leaders. Upon this recognition, the two boys would enter into a process of nurturing and education aimed at helping them to become special people, warriors, and defenders. As part of this experience, they would communicate directly with other beings as though they were of the same species. This is a connection that a heyoka has. They would also be observed as they connected to the entities, the bodies, and the beings on the spirit side of life who are reached through ritual and ceremony. The spirit side was very, very strong in Saved By Bear and Swift Bear.

Spirit Horse

Saved By Bear and Swift Bear first met the young man Spirit Horse in the hunting season after they each turned nine in 1858. They had been told by their fathers and other adults, mostly the warriors, of this brave young man who had been raised in the tradition of the warriors of old. They were told that this one was especially gifted in his ability to ride, track, hunt, fish, and fight. It was understood by all that this young warrior, Tesunka Witko, was gifted by Creator with the attributes of someone whom men and warriors would follow into the hunt and into any battle, on any day and under any circumstances. Spirit Horse was young, bright, and serious. His father was Spirit Horse I (known to the whites as Crazy Horse I). The mother of Spirit Horse II [known to the whites as Crazy Horse II] was a Mnincoju named Rattling Blanket Woman who died when Spirit Horse was only four years old. Likely born in 1840, he was first given the name Curly Hair, or Curly, for his long, slightly curly brown hair, light complexion and lightly colored eyes. He went by that name for many years, but he would also at some point, be known as His Horse in Sight for a short while. It was the young boy's desire to be great in battle that drove him to rely upon his courage and his quiet ability to act on matters, whereas others sat by and watched. When Curly was about thirteen years old, he was one of the young braves present when Conquering Bear was shot and the warriors at his camp then wiped out the soldiers in the Grattan Incident. By the time he was fifteen years old or so, Spirit Horse had already experienced adventures and episodes of conflict and war. Through his early life he was engrossed in the life of a warrior. Counting coup and going on raids for horses were things he relished. By the time he was eighteen, he was already known through Lakota lands as a warrior whom the people talked about. He was someone whom the people looked to as an honorable and respected leader and protector, even at a very young age.

It was a long-followed tradition for the Lakota that a father would celebrate and recognize his son's accomplishments with a wopila, a thanksgiving with a feast for the people and a gifting of items to honor the son. For example, if the son had gone out on his first hunt and succeeded in taking his first tatanka, the boy's father, being proud, would make it known to the people that he would honor the boy for his feat, which was a step to becoming a man. The people in the camp would be fed to honor the son's deeds. Also, the father might choose to give away a horse, or maybe several horses to people in need of them. Again, this would be done in the son's name, to give him recognition.

The ultimate way for a father to honor his son was to give the boy the father's name. This was a very old tradition of the Lakota people. A good example is Spirit Horse II (referred to by the whites and others as Crazy Horse II).

The Mnincoju warrior known by the outside world as Crazy Horse, was known to many Lakota as Tesunka Witko. *Tesunka*, is one of the Lakota words used for "horse". However, another Lakota word for "horse" is sunkawakan, a sacred horse, or likewise, a "spirit horse".

The Lakota word for *Crazy* is Witkotko Ka or gnaskinyan. The word for *courage* is Woohitika. The word for *brave* is Ohitika. The word *witko* could mean "folly," "foolhardy," or "foolish," but those meanings appear to have little or no connection or significance to a great warrior or his life. A warrior and his horse have spiritual power and significance together. Neither the warrior nor his horse is crazy, foolish, or foolhardy. They are spirit. They are sacred. This warrior's name is Spirit Horse, according to how Saved By Bear's family knew him.

Prior to being named Spirit Horse I, the father of Spirit Horse II was known as Waglula, translated in English as "worm." When his son earned such great accolades of bravery and leadership after a conflict with the Crow, enemies to the Lakota, the father determined that it was appropriate to honor his son His Horse in Sight by giving the boy his own name. Spirit Horse I gave his own name to his son, who became Spirit Horse II. It was an incredibly great and meaningful honor. The father then reclaimed his prior name, Waglula. It is believed that he kept that name until he passed into the spirit world.

The name Crazy Horse appears to have been passed down by the whites who interpreted the behavior of a horse that Spirit Horse rode at one time on a particular raid, when the horse acted erratically, like a *whirlwind*. So the whites may have interpreted that to mean akin to *crazy*. The whites frequently interpreted Lakota words to mean something in a demeaning or derogatory way (e.g., "Crazy Woman" or "Big Nose"). However, the name Spirit Horse seems to be a much more accurate and honorable translation of the name of the father first (I), and then the son (II). Again, the Mnincoju families of Saved By Bear and Swift Bear knew this warrior as Spirit Horse, or High-Spirited Horse. Some, obviously, still refer to him as Crazy Horse.

A maternal aunt of the young Spirit Horse II, had raised the boy and taught him, along with the men and warriors in the camp. Spirit Horse was taught by his relatives how to ride, hunt, shoot a bow and a gun, and conceal himself to remain unseen by prey or an enemy. Even at a young age, he was known as a fierce warrior.

The boys, Saved By Bear and Swift Bear, were anxious to meet this young warrior, with the hope that Spirit Horse would choose to spend some time with them. This would make the boys feel that they were closer to becoming men, despite the fact that both of the boys' mothers still had a strong influence in their lives at that time. Spirit Horse was, as previously mentioned, the son of the elder Spirit Horse, a Mnincoju warrior whom the boys now knew as a trusted relative in the camp.

Spirit Horse decided to teach the boys some things while they were together. It was one of the ways he could pass along the gift that he was given by Creator. This opportunity to help and mentor the two boys in this way, the Lakota spiritual way, as a warrior, would be Spirit Horse's way of lending his hand, not just physically but also spiritually, to the generation following him. Spirit Horse was usually aloof with most people, including children, but he made an agreement with the

Mnincoju warriors that he would help the young ones in the camp and show them how to become warriors.

Spirit Horse had no children at this point in his life (later he would be blessed with a baby girl that, tragically would pass away at a very early age, and he would leave no direct surviving, natural lineal heirs). He did not speak much, but he taught them by showing what he could and what they must know to become warriors. And they did learn from him, as they learned from all of the others. They never stopped learning. The two young Mnincoju braves would be eternally grateful to Spirit Horse for helping them on their journey to become warriors.

Jealousy as a Weakness

Saved By Bear and Swift Bear were born in the same month of 1849 in the He Sapa of the sacred land. They became like brothers from different mothers. They grew together; they learned together. It was acknowledged throughout moments in their shared lives that sometimes one would excel and the other would not. It was confusing at times for one boy to see his own father take the other boy into the sweat lodge ceremony, and not himself. Yet it was not jealousy, that was felt. What was felt was a longing to be with the other and to be included.

As young Lakota boys, Saved By Bear and Swift Bear had been advised by the adults and the teachers of all things, not to feel jealousy, not to let that disease of jealousy to gain even a foothold. The boys were taught that the people survived because everyone has a role. It was expected that each individual perform his or her role. When an individual succeeds in his or her role, it is a gift not only to the individual but also a gift to all the people. Therefore, when one person realizes a success, everyone benefits. The successes of one individual Lakota should not be seen as something to use against that person. Instead, one should be true to Creator and Wakan Tanka and celebrate the other's success, instead of feeling jealousy or animosity toward the person. The Lakota people, especially the impressionable young ones, were always taught not to allow jealousy to get a foothold in one's life. It was wrong to feel jealousy, as jealousy would only lead to self-destruction of the individual, and damage to the whole of the people's goals and purposes.

Jealously, if allowed to take root in one's consciousness and spirit, spreads like a virus and infects all the thoughts and actions of the affected person. It is not honorable at all to lose control of one's free will and allow such a thing to happen. Permitting jealousy to flourish was not in line with the spiritual trail of a Lakota's life. Jealousy was not to be seen as an alternative or accepted way of living. If the teachers saw signs of the presence or growth of jealousy within a Lakota, especially within a young one, it was the teacher's duty and responsibility to sit down as soon as possible with that person and explain that jealousy, was not wakan. Jealousy is bad. Jealousy must not occur. Instead, it is taught that the feelings that lead to jealousy can be changed from a quiet animosity toward another or another's success, to an outward, positive commitment to try harder and work harder in one's own role so as to become successful themselves, whatever that role may be.

Saved By Bear and Swift Bear were taught, like all Lakota children, to follow the spiritual trail of honor, respect, and integrity. Both for themselves and all others. This included honoring, respecting, and treating with integrity Unci Maka and all her children of every type of species. They were taught and they learned, that their thoughts and beliefs were important to their development as good human beings. They embraced these concepts and principles, and not just because the adults, their teachers, lived that way. It was easy for the boys to now envision and accept their individual roles in the great Circle of life. And they embraced it as a challenge to themselves, and to each other. This would carry forward for the rest of their lives. This way of honor, respect and integrity became a part of their spirits. The teachings of the past would come to serve them well as they matured and became men. These virtues would turn out to be extremely valuable when the time came for duty. The time came to open up their hearts, their minds, and their spirits...when they sought and received the permission from Creator.

To the Lakota, age did not matter. If it was time for something, then it was time, no matter what age the person was.

Age has always, throughout time and history, been a barrier to those who are needed in a particular situation to rise to the call. Sometimes the needed ones, because of their age, were not able to see and hear or recognize the call. And for the imposters, because of age, it serves as an excuse to forestall or disguise or to discourage the call of those who are truly needed.

Age is not relevant to anything except age. If age is a requirement or a detriment or a prohibition, then it is an obstacle to having the best person with the best intellect at the best time, for the best social and spiritual end. If a young man is able to perform a task as well as, or even better than, an older man, then his age should not prohibit him from doing it.

The fact that a person is young should be no barrier to his or her ability to be a leader of all people. Age does not equal wisdom; wisdom does not equal age. Respect goes with age, but is not purely granted, without being earned. To lead, one must be chosen. A leader is rarely born with the privilege. But sometimes, one is born, and even at a very early age, is chosen by the spirits to assume a role in life, to perform a duty, to fulfill a destiny. If the spirits choose to touch a young one at an early age, and if the young one is able to recognize and receive the message, the symbol, then this is the way that things must be, spiritually. He was already old enough to do the task, to fulfill the destiny. This could hold true for a female as well. The young one will know, and will grow into, his or her calling. The spirit within will guide him or her to the path foreseen by the spirits, as if a torch lights the way for the young one to follow. This type of spiritual destiny cannot be denied or set aside. For it will forever be a part of the one. Forever be a spark in his thoughts, his instincts, abilities, devotions, and his courage. The ability to see, accept, and then embrace this spiritual gift and destiny, is the key to making his life, his call and his spirit, whole.

The Dog Man

Being a warrior was a noble pursuit and a cherished accomplishment for any Lakota. Becoming a warrior was, most times, the achievement of a lifetime, the fulfillment of a dream. One did not just become a warrior by the passage of time, by age, or by birthright. In every respect, one had to earn the status of warrior in the traditional way. But mostly, the honor was earned and achieved by becoming so spiritually connected with Wakan Tanka and Creator that one's blood was infused with the energy of being a warrior.

A warrior exemplified a true status of respect and honor among the people. This honor and respect was not given to just anyone. The spirits must have the overriding consideration and recognition as who became a warrior and who did not.

Becoming a warrior took a vast amount of education, preparation, and training. It was a physical journey as much as it was a mental one. As with most things in Lakota society, the spiritual side of becoming a warrior was the most significant attribute and accomplishment. Becoming a warrior was not easy. It was not intended to be easy. It was hard and took much work, desire, and commitment. A warrior did not achieve warrior status on his own. It was a joint endeavor, a journey and an accomplishment for him, his immediate family, his other relatives, and his Creator.

There were many warrior societies to become a part of once a Lakota brave became a warrior. There was the Brave Hearts Warrior Society, the Kit Fox Warrior Society, the Owl Feather Headdress Warrior Society, the Akicita, and of course, ultimately, the Dog Man Warrior Society. All of these warrior societies were unique in their own way, and each had different tasks, duties, and responsibilities to perform for the oyate and the families. A warrior had to be inducted as a member of whichever warrior society he was accepted into. Membership was not something that was just given. It had to be earned.

One of the most cherished and respected of all the Lakota warrior societies was the Dog Man Warrior Society. Since it was quite elite, a warrior had to undergo a difficult and challenging process to obtain membership.

The Dog Man Warriors were among the most honored and trusted of the warrior societies of the Lakota. Members of this society were feared. A warrior became a member of the Dog Man Warrior Society as a result of deeds, not words, inheritance, or bloodline. The Dog Man had to earn his status as a warrior of a very high-level. It was a recognition of honor, of gratitude, and of extreme responsibility and duty. The duty and obligation of the Dog Man was to the people, and to Grandmother Earth, Wakan Tanka, and Creator. They have always been and shall always remain the *Protectors* of all things. Dog Man warriors have a sacred duty to lay down their lives if necessary to protect the people, to protect the Grandmother, to protect the Lakota way of life, and to protect the sacred He Sapa, the Black Mountains.

The Dog Man's symbol, is the sacred dragonfly. This is the symbol that every warrior of the Dog Man Society wears on his clothes in times of battle or conflict. The symbol is connected to all that is the Dog Man warrior, and what he is and what he stands for. The connection is spiritual.

The dragonfly is a special being put on Grandmother Earth at the beginning, many millions of years ago, when the Grandmother was much younger. Therefore, dragonfly has seen many things, has lived through many times, and has seen many types of peoples, including the human being peoples at their various stages of existence. The dragonfly learned to become who he is by learning to survive, learning to exist, and adapt, and by learning how to persevere in any environment under any set of circumstances. Dragonfly is a hunter and a tracker. He is also a carrier of things from one world to the next, from one threshold to another, from one life to that which comes hereafter. He listens and learns.

The dragonfly is resilient, tough, and enduring. He is born of the water as a water nymph, coming forth into life from an egg in the ground or upon a reed under the surface of the water. That's where he grows and nurtures himself, until the energy and curiosity of life, and the desire to discover what is beyond his watery boundaries, becomes too much of an earthly drive and a sacred motivation. It is then that the nymph moves up the reed of the underwater plant until he breaches the surface of the water. Once the plane between water and air is broken, he cannot return to those he left behind at his beginning. He will grow and sprout, and show his masterful ways and his ever-roving, ever-seeking eyes. He will become that which he is chosen to become. He will become the flying dragon. The dragonfly.

The young dragonfly must survive his early days of being without his whole arsenal of bodily tools, before he is mature enough to own and master the use of his wings, his skills, and his mind. If the young dragonfly does survive these first moments after leaving the water, then he will alight upon his new and exciting world of discovery, hunting, tracking, and living life to his fullest potential.

The dragonfly can fly up to forty miles per hour in straight flight, and can abruptly come to a complete stop in an instant. The dragonfly has been given many gifts, one of which is to use his physical and mental skills, as well as his instincts, to hover in one place thanks to the tremendous speed of his multifaceted set of four wings. He can dart at any angle: to the right, to the left, up, down, sideways, looping, straight up, swooping down—whatever it may take, whatever may be needed. He can turn at a ninety-degree angle and hover. Then, using his quickness and agility, he can dart up and down, forward and backward, with lightning speed. He also has the gift and the ability to move quietly with great energy and speed, making no sound that would alert his prey, or his enemy. There is no sign left on his trail to be found by those that seek him or wish to catch him. He does not expose himself without his willingness and desire to allow himself to be exposed. His ability to blend in with his natural surroundings provides him with a means of hiding, sometimes hiding in plain sight, as he has the ability to actually become his surroundings, to camouflage himself so that he is not recognized by those who are not knowledgeable about the world around them.

The dragonfly's strength is immeasurable in comparison to his earthly stature. His gifts of movement, strength, and agility combine to make him a warrior among warriors. When dragonfly needs to strike to catch his prey, or to render a blow to kill his opponent, he does so with a speed that cannot be avoided, and with a determination that cannot be denied. He becomes one with the wind, one with the grass, one with the sunshine, and one with the dimming of the dusk. He becomes what he chooses to become, because he has been blessed to know and understand his connection with Creator, and to do all that he is intended to do, all that he believes he can do, and all that he knows that he must do. And dragonfly will spread his wings and become the one Creator created.

When dragonfly strikes, he strikes before his opponent can react. Some may not even realize they have been struck by the him until after he has done his will. By the time, that occurs, it is too late for the prey, too late for the opponent. Only later will the prey know that it had been struck by the dragonfly, once the prey beholds the vision of his spread wings, the grace of his manner, and the determination of his actions, and the completion of his goal.

So the Dog Man prepares. They pray. They cleanse. They emerge from the water. They emerge from their humble and innocent beginnings. They acquire their mental and intellectual skills from their education, and from those who love them enough to teach them all that they must know. And they grow and nurture their connection with Creator. They energize and grow more, gathering more energy, more knowledge, and more strength from that connection. And their physical and athletic strength and skills flourish and develop, as they spread their own wings and find their own way, their own path in life. With the Dog Man, they know, and they feel, with their hearts and within their spirits, that Creator is always there to guide them, to provide them with the necessary energy and the will, to succeed. It is all of these attributes that the Dog Man as warriors, as the embodiment of the dragonfly warriors, must rely upon to carry out their duties and obligations as *Protectors*. As warriors, their spirits will spread their wings as well, when the time comes to act.

Grandfather's Talk

Saved By Bear's grandfather Iron White Man gathered the Mnincoju families together around the campfire one late summer evening to talk. The children sat at his feet, close enough to see the details on his well-worn moccasins. All of the other people of the oyate sat in a big circle around the fire with a look of anticipation reflected on their faces, along with the gleam of the crackling flames. They knew it was time for his talk, for his hopeful speech of encouragement, which was specially intended for the young ones in his presence. With his low and deep voice, he began:

"Remember always that you come from a very old people. We have been around for millions of years. Embrace that. Embrace your lineage, embrace your ancestors, embrace your bloodlines, and feel proud to be Lakota.

We have been selected by Creator to be the Protectors of Grandmother Earth. We are the ones that must stand in her defense, and in the defense of all of her children of all of her people, no matter their color, shape, or size, and no matter the strength or magnitude of the obstacle. Come forward and be recognized. Be counted. Be proud to be Lakota.

We are not better than the other people of Grandmother Earth as a whole. We need not view ourselves that way either. But we do have the special responsibility to act when other people cannot, or will not.

That is why Creator made us all with the ability to connect to the spirits at will, if only we open our hearts and put the distractions and barriers of the mind aside, to gratefully accept Creator's gift of the everlasting current of life of all things, including ourselves.

We can do great things for Grandmother Earth and all her people if only we allow ourselves to be ourselves. To believe and to freely give of our openness to receive Creator's gift of commitment to continue to learn and embrace that which is dear to every living being no matter who they are or where they come from.

It is an honor and a sincere privilege to be chosen as the Protectors. It is why we come from the water, why we come from the heavens and the stars.

When we near the end of our physical days of walking upon our Grandmother, and when we each look back at the path we each have walked, both alone, and together, we will see the footprints that we have left for the little ones and the other people behind us and those yet to follow. We can go to one another, and to our relatives and ancestors on the other side camp in the great Milky Way, and recognize that we each did that which each one of us could, while we could, when we could. We can look at each other and say that we did all we could to allow Grandmother Earth, and the life of all her children, of all her people, to survive and to keep growing, or for them to learn to walk on that good road, the honest road of one's life. And we can be happy and share all of those good stories around that happy and loving campfire. It is then that we will each know that we have honored our duty and our commitment to Creator, and that Wakan Tanka will too smile with us. And the stories told by the people to the young, will now include ourselves, when the young ones and those yet unborn, too, look up to the night skies and know that we watch over them as continuing loving guardians.

I thank Creator for this life. I give thanks to Wakan Tanka for the privilege to do my part. I thank my people for listening to me, and I thank our ancestors for leaving those footprints for us to follow. Let our feet barely touch the ground as we walk the walk of life with peace, unity, tolerance, and love for each other. Oh, ha!"

Saved By Bear looked keenly at his hunka brother, Swift Bear, and saw the bright brown eyes that were like his own. And they both smiled. Saved By Bear felt a tingle move up his spine. His heart beamed with joy and pride upon hearing the words of his grandfather about the people, his people.

He felt the same current shooting through his chest that he had experienced being upon the sacred mountain at ceremony at the top. And it was at this moment, being among his people, his relatives, and standing beside his brother, that he knew one day he would surely be called upon by Wakan Tanka to do his part. To do his part to help his people, all people, and the Grandmother. He didn't quite know or understand what that would be or when the call would come. But he knew deep down, caressing the current of life with his own heartbeat… that he would be ready.

The Shiny Mountains

Hanbleceya is a male ceremony for self. The man stands on the hill and cries. He cries for the understanding and strength of his belief and role in society by performing this ceremony. The man asks for a vision to occur so that he has a better path to Creator. He can cry out

in anger, in happiness and in tears of sadness or sorrow. This is what
we call growth. Patience is a necessary virtue as one meets the beings
of Creator's world.

In the Lakota way, the old ways, the hanbleceya usually occurred
when a man was asked to make a sacred act of sacrifice for his people. It
was a special moment in a Lakota man's life when this *asking* occurred.
He might be asked by a holy man; he might be asked by an ordinary
man, a *wicasa*; he might be asked by a leader; he might be asked by a
respected family member; or, in many cases, he might be asked by the
spirits themselves to do something for his people.

It was a tremendous sacrifice of body, soul, and spirit to go through
the hanbleceya. It required preparation. It required the man to sit or
stand on a hill or high place by himself within a sacred altar constructed
of prayer ties and sacred sage. There could be no water, no food, no
nourishment at all, for four days and four nights while the man prayed,
sang, and talked with Creator, the spirits, and anyone or anything else
he chose to talk with while there. A fire was kept for the man's sacrifice.
If visions came, then they came. If the man realized his own spirit was
changed or speaking to him, then that was what was meant to happen.
At the end, a special wopila, a thanksgiving ceremony, was held by
those who had asked the man to do this and by the hanbleceya man. A
feast was held, gifts were shared, a fire was kept, and songs were sung.
The hanbleceya was a highly sacred event, a life-changing event.

Saved By Bear knew of many of the warriors and the elders who
had done the hanbleceya. Most used the bluffs and hills either in the
sacred He Sapa (like on Owl's Nest, Mato Paha, or Pe Sla) or along the
Owl River near the Mnincoju camps along Bear Creek, overlooking the
Chien (Shay-enne/Cheyenne) River, or by Cherry Creek. For efforts that
involved a longer journey, the one doing the hanbleceya chose the high
mountains near Greasy Grass or else the Shiny Mountains, also known
as the Bighorn Mountains.

In fact, when Saved By Bear's father, Fights the Bear, had done his
hanbleceya when Saved By Bear was only nine years old, he had gone
to the summit of the great Medicine Mountain where the sacred Turtle
Shell Circle was located. On their long journey to the mountain, the
traveling group of Lakota weaved their way through the mountain

valleys and passes beyond the eastern rim of the highest peaks, which appeared to touch the clouds. The families rode and walked along well-worn trails from the past, and camped at well-worn recognized campsites with preestablished tipi and campfire circles. Many of those camps were along the Ten Sleep River, which was named after an ancient hunting story of the ancestors. To get to the western edge of the Shiny Mountains was a trying, long, but magnificently beautiful journey. The people saw many families of bear, deer, elk, bighorn sheep, and buffalo. They also saw many families of the statuesque moose people, who thrived among the thicketed bushy areas along the various creeks and slough areas along the way. It was always a treat to see the moose, as the moose did not frequent He Sapa very much.

The Medicine Mountain was over ten thousand feet above sea level, and it felt like being on top of the world. One could see for a great distance all around, and especially to the west, as the high mountain drops off dramatically on the western slope and opens up into a prehistoric-looking western area of desertlike stone formations and wind-carved landscapes.

On the summit of the mountain, is a very old formation of rocks set out in a large circular shape. This is a place that has been frequented by the indigenious people of Turtle Island for thousands of years. This stone design in the form of a very large circle was placed there long ago, either by humans or by non-humans. It is now commonly referred to in the present as the Medicine Wheel formation. This Medicine Wheel formation consists of six different short appendages with twenty-eight lines, or cairns, emanating from the center of the circle. Some believe that this formation depicts a medicine wheel, which is part of the reason why the mountain it sits upon is called Medicine Mountain.

However, when seen from way up in the sky, as the wanbli may view it, this design resembles the shell of a turtle. There are twenty-eight separate plates along the ringed perimeter of the turtle's shell. The Lakota have always referred to the turtle as a sacred being because this is Turtle Island where we reside. And we live upon the Turtle's back. Creator placed a large amount of earth upon Turtle's back in order to create Turtle Island. Turtle (keya) is the caretaker. Turtle is sacred, symbolizing healing, wisdom, spirituality, patience, long life, and fertility.

The Turtle also has thirteen individual plates on her back shell that stand for the thirteen full moons of the seasons of the Lakota year. (e.g., the moon when the ducks come back, and the moon of the deer shedding its antlers). The number of the twenty-eight individual side plates is significant in that the length of the female's monthly cycle is twenty-eight days. With these things in mind, we may conclude that this stone formation that was set in place many, many generations ago is not actually a depiction of a medicine wheel. A medicine wheel would have significance in and of itself. This stone formation on Medicine Mountain is more appropriately a symbol to mark that the place is a part of Turtle Island, therefore serving as Unci Maka's recognition of the beginning of life on this land. This is one of those special sacred places that offers an opportunity for those with open minds and spirits to communicate directly with the Creator or with any spirit that one chooses to communicate with.

However, in a traditional, aboriginal sense, these individual lines that are part of this stone formation on top of Medicine Mountain are significant since there are twenty-eight of them. These twenty-eight individual cairns on the Turtle's back may be the guide to the astrological alignment of the planets with the sun, the moon, and the stars. It is said that the people used this particular formation to measure time, given its relationship to the seasons and the movement and positioning of the stars and constellations. It was an astrological guide to the seasons and for time and travel.

It was during the time of his father's hanbleceya on Medicine Mountain that Saved By Bear's grandfather Iron White Man led the group of warriors, elders, and other adults from the tiospaye. They had set up the fire camp in the open circular area near the large ancient turtle. Wanbli, marmots, mountain goats, and bighorn sheep were seen frequently up here.

It was during the time of waiting during the four days of his father's hanbleceya that Saved By Bear first saw the people use the Great Turtle to communicate with the spirits in the stars. Since the mountain summit was so high, it almost seemed as if one could reach up and touch the stars, especially the billowy-looking Milky Way as it stretched across the night sky like a wonderful gleaming trail across the entirety of the expanse of the horizons, from the southwest to the northeast. And it was inside the Turtle's round shell that the holy men studied and engaged the areas on Grandmother Earth, going from point to point within the Turtle's twenty-eight sections, and unlocking solutions of time and travel, in coordination with the positions of the constellations. It was a magnificent realization for them all, and gave then an unforeseen energy to stand inside the sacred circle and pray.

Saved By Bear's uncle Running Elk helped guide the young Mnincoju boy into the Great Turtle's back circle. Running Elk took his hand and they both went to the west side of the Turtle, near the its tail, facing the west, the direction of Wakinyan and the west wind, the zephyrs. And Running Elk told Saved By Bear that he must always enter the sacred circle, all things sacred, and especially those things that were ceremonial from the west, and then circle to the right around the edge of the circle from the west, moving to the north, then to the east, and then the south, returning to the west once done. In the great circle of the Turtle's back, however, they entered from the west after making the walk around the entire shell. Then Saved By Bear and his uncle walked into the center. Even as a young boy, Saved By Bear could feel the spiritual energy there and the connection of this special place to the Earth. He could feel the energy tingle in his young chest, mixing with his quickly beating heart. He could feel the energy seep up from the ground through his deer-hide moccasins and penetrate the soles of his feet. And he felt good. He stood in the center and looked around. It was as if he was the tallest and highest boy that Wakan Tanka had ever allowed, without flying. He tilted his head back, looked up into the sky and at the heavens, and prayed like his father had taught him. And it was good. He would develop a great fondness for this place over the span his life, and would return one day to gaze at and measure the connection to the star spirits at night.

During the remaining time of his father's hanbleceya on the Medicine Mountain near the Great Turtle, Saved By Bear would learn many valuable things from the elders and the warriors. He was taught in the old way by seeing, doing, watching, and listening. He received honest answers to his curious questions about why certain things were done and in the sequence they were done in. And he learned. It was as if this huge, beautiful place on top of the world was his personal classroom to increase his knowledge and develop his intellect. He absorbed it all and asked for more. His energy remained at an extremely high level the whole time he was there, so much so that he found it hard to sleep. His nighttime blanket turned out to be a truly wonderful blanket of Creator's stars and stellar combinations slowly moving across the biggest sky that he could imagine, even bigger than at the Pe Sla in He Sapa. He was anxious to wake up and start living and learning in the next cherished day to come.

Throughout the four days and four nights of Saved By Bear's father's hanbleceya on the western rim of the mountain summit, the warriors made sure to keep the fire burning. The drum beat solidly and methodically throughout most of the days and nights. Like the heartbeat of the Grandmother Earth, it was a soothing sound that energized Saved By Bear's heart and spirit. The men and the women sang many songs to encourage and honor the man standing on the hill and crying. It made him proud that his father would make such a sacrifice to help his family and all of his people.

When the last night of the hanbleceya had been completed, and Fights the Bear emerged from his altar site looking thin, parched, and tired, he hugged the medicine man, Strong Buffalo, who had sponsored him to the hill. Then Fights the Bear looked for his son. When the father and son met eyes, they ran to each other. There on top of the sacred Medicine Mountain in the early morning dawn of the new day, father and son embraced, holding each other close and strong. Despite his physically weakened state after four days and four nights without food or water, Fights the Bear lifted his son high up into the air. It was then that Saved By Bear received the sacred gift of looking directly into the soft brown eyes of his father. All that he saw in those eyes was love, honor, and life. His father's eyes were strong, blazing with energy and enthusiasm despite his bodily weakness. It was the strength and the energy of his spirit that had come to shine brightly in his eyes, that energy flowing into the eyes of his only son, whom he loved dearly. It was the same look from those same eyes that had looked upon the same newborn son years before by the Mato Paha in the He Sapa. On the day Saved By Bear was born. His father was rejuvenated and enlightened by his experience on the mountain. The son could see it all in his father's eyes.

Soon, the rest of the people gathered around Fights the Bear and gave him warm honoring embraces. The meal and fire tenders set about laying out the goods for the thanksgiving and celebratory wopila. And it was all good.

When the time came the next morning to leave the sacred mountain and the Great Turtle, Saved By Bear once again entered the massive circumference of the Turtle's back. He stopped one more time in the center, among the twenty-eight lines, and prayed to the sacred directions, both starting with and ending with the west. Before he left the center of the circle, he reached into his pouch and pulled out a tasty hunk of wasna and some sage. He then placed the wasna and the sage in the center of the Turtle's back, as an offering, to give thanks to the Great Turtle, and to give thanks to Unci Maka and Creator for having granted him, his father, and his family such a wonderful life, such a wonderful existence. Saved By Bear then gently picked up a small piece of one of the ancient white stones that had broken off one of the larger ones nearest the center of the circle. And he placed it into his pouch as a reminder—a piece of the sacred energy he could take home with him.

The line of Mnincoju left the Medicine Mountain and wound their way out of the Shiny Mountains. They again camped along the clear, clean, fast waterways. On the last day of their journey, leaving the high regions of the large mountain range nearest the eastern edge just above the Tongue River valley below, the people came to one of their favorite lookout stopping points. They knew it as the Sunrise Shelf. A nearly flat area among the raised-up and slanted gargantuan gray slabs of stone that lay slanted toward the west, this shelf was near the northeastern ridge above the Tongue River and faced due east. When the sun would come up, the viewer would be treated to a grand spectacle, the beautiful genesis of the new day as the sun crawled over the dark-shaded Wolf Mountains to the east.

This was a great stopping place for any group of traveling Lakota, as it was located upon the threshold between the high grandeur of the great Shiny Mountains to the west, south, and northwest, and the lush fertile valley of the Tongue River lay nestled down below. One could see for great distances from this spot. It was easy to make out the aboriginal travel routes and trails to one of the most beautiful and bountiful places on Unci Maka, the magnificent and sacred Greasy Grass valley to the northeast, about two days' travel.

When Saved By Bear looked east from the Sunrise Shelf and took in the beauty of Grandmother Earth from above, he moved his clear, anxious eyes toward the Wolf Mountains and beyond, farther north, toward the valley of the Greasy Grass. And felt a familiar tingle, as if inside him, his spirit was showing his eyes and his mind, something important that was to come to him and his family. He would never forget that day, or that energy.

6

SPIRIT GATHERING

BETWEEN 1855 AND 1862, THERE was greater frequency and intensity of change as it rippled across the plains into the territories of the Nakota, Dakota, and Lakota. The people oftentimes refer to this field of energy force, the tapping of the energy, as being basically akin to the spirit within every individual or everything. When there was change or disruption, the indigenous peoples referred to it as something much like a disturbance in the energy. And in a sense, the world that the people were living in, the relatives, and Saved By Bear, being a young brave, felt this, not just in the mere physical presence of people who were bringing news from other parts of the land, but also in the feeling of disturbance in the spirit. This was something that was beginning to gather, like a gathering storm, and it needed attention. Saved By Bear became alert to and aware of this as a very young man. The elders were searching for answers themselves. There was a new urgency to find these answers, and to return to old familiar places, old familiar feelings, and the old familiar energy found in the He Sapa and other places of spiritual rejuvenation. This could help not just in the mental and physical sense but also in the spiritual sense. It would help people get in tune with how best to deal with these concepts, these new negative forces, these new influences, that were on the verge of changing our lives forever.

During this time, there was a sense that there was a new awakening to come, an awareness of change occurring that was beyond our control.

Something was needed to awaken our spirit to deal with these new problems, these new issues, on a different level than anything that had been dealt with before. This was something that not only the elders and the adults recognized but that also filtered down through the children. As part of a cohesive society and community, it was the responsibility, the duty, and the obligation of the adults and the elders to prepare the children to best deal with this gathering storm.

As a young boy, Saved By Bear, was taken on a hunt with the warrior band, and encounters a very sacred (wakan) place and a figure in stone and is asked to give a gift to this stone being. There is significance to this event and this time, as it will affect this Lakota boy's future. Saved By Bear's father, his uncles, and other elders are with him, as they always were on these trips out west. They are fully aware that Saved By Bear has a place within himself that loves to be nurtured and allowed to grow as an individual warrior, in time. It is imperative what he, and the others like him, are taught to do, is done diligently and wholeheartedly, because the time is now short for growing up to defend the people.

These warriors who are with him make their presence known, whether they are medicine people, warriors, or just companions there to make sure the band of warriors come and go properly.

In learning how to blend the spirit with the mind, and how to teach the mind to step aside in favor of the spirit when needed, the warriors taught Saved By Bear to cast aside that which he feared or that of which he was uncertain. To open the realm of possibility and potential. He was also taught about Creation and the relationship between the people and the stars, and how those connections remained strong and meaningful. Included in his education were things such as star travel, a concept involving people, spirits, and worlds moving through portals in time, or becoming one small speck up to the time of the creation of life on a planetary scale. When you feed that into the human brain and it deals with the concept of reality versus fantasy, or possibility versus impossibility, the only parameters that exist are those put up by the individual's mentality. The spirit has a means of punching holes in the fences and the barriers that the mind creates. The heart and the spirit are the truth seekers. And if they are left unchained and unbounded, everything is a possibility. Sometimes we deal with individuals who exist in this world or any world, who close their minds to the mere concept of the possible versus the impossible. Those who do not believe that anything is possible except for that which is a reality, something visible within six inches in front of their faces. These people need to be touched in such a way that their spirit is motivated to remove the barrier that their mind has created, to open up the portal of the possible.

This concept is very easy to understand if you think in terms of being a young soul, a young being, whether you have two, four, or six legs, whether you have wings, whether you are human or not human. Every experience in our lives is a series of firsts. There is a first time for everything. We only learn when we experience something for the first time. Whether we will accept it as a good experience or bad experience, we won't know until we experience it. For instance, you don't know what it's like to be submerged in water until you yourself are submerged in water. Perhaps you do it willingly, cautiously, or recklessly. For example, stepping into a pool of water and lowering yourself until your nose and your eyes submerge, you feel engulfed by the water. Now you know what it is to be submerged. Until that time, you don't know. Also, only those who are willing to take that risk, to chance doing something for the first time, will know themselves what it is like. They will walk into it willingly, taking that risk of the possible versus the impossible. Some will step willingly and know for themselves, while others will not take that step by themselves. These people may need to be thrown into the water.

Once that happens and the experience becomes reality for the first time, some may not like it. Some may say, "This is not for me, I want to go back." But others may see it as a confrontation of their own fear. These people may embrace it and say, "This is not so bad. Why didn't I step forward sooner? Why did I close my mind to this possibility? Why did I let my mind close itself off to this possibility? From here on out, I am going to listen more to my spirit and my heart, and put my mind aside, so as to feel the truth for myself."

The teaching and the learning began and was constant in Saved By

Bear's life. The men, his father, his uncles, the older males, and the older boys among the Lakota, began to teach him and take him on hunting trips at a very young age, including him in the things that a man does in order to teach him how to be a man and how to begin to become a warrior. And so, having gone through the teachings and the nurturing of the women in his first six years of life, in this phase of Saved By Bear's life, it was now the men's duty to take on his education, to help him fulfill his destiny and become the man he was intended to be.

Saved By Bear was taught all the things that a Lakota man and a warrior was supposed to learn, such as how to make a bow; how to prepare a knife; how to use a knife; how to train and take care of a horse; how to dress; what to look for when out gathering necessary materials for purposes of preparing for a hunt or making a fire; and other things that the men did in order to prepare for ceremony, for the hunt, or for battle.

It was during this training that Saved By Bear was allowed to go with the men on hunting trips. On these hunting trips, the men, of course, traveled on horseback and took whatever supplies were necessary. They went to various places depending upon the time of the year, depending upon the season, looking for where deer, antelope, buffalo, or elk grazed or gathered. These are the types things that were and are learned from generation to generation. Being familiar with their world, the Lakota knew the migration habits, the activities, and the planned movements of the herds. So when the men planned hunts and decided to take the boys, including Saved By Bear, these were the specific types of things that the Lakota boys would be expected to be familiar with. They were also expected to be able to hold their own if they were going to go on a hunt with the men. These particular hunts usually would take a day, but sometimes they would take days or even weeks. It all depended upon the movement of the peoples that were being hunted. Normally when going on a hunt, the Lakota would get on horseback and then travel to a particular area looking for game. One of these areas was known by the people as the White Stone Mountains, or the White Mountains, which were off to the west, along the Owl River and to the west and the north, into the areas near the Montana Territory and the Powder River hunting territories.

Each hunting season, the Mnincoju men and boys went for a hunt into the White Mountains north of the He Sapa. This year, Fights the Bear, Saved By Bear's father, wanted Saved By Bear and Swift Bear to be a part of the hunting group. Both Lakota boys were now ten years old. Both Saved By Bear and Swift Bear had been hunting for two years by this time and were excellent horsemen and hunters, especially with the bow.

Saved By Bear was riding his favorite horse, which he had trained since it was a foal. He called his pony Wildfire. Wildfire was two years old now. The young pony was full of life, energy, and personality. But Wildfire, Saved By Bear knew, trusted him with all of his heart and soul. Wildfire was quick, strong, and courageous. He could care less about wolves, coyotes, or snakes. He loved to race the other ponies with or without riders. This always overjoyed Saved By Bear.

Wildfire was spotted with a mix of brown and white. He was a descendant of the great spotted horses, the Appaloosas. He had huge brown expressive eyes. He had a way of looking at you out of the corner of his eye, especially if you had food.

The scent of Wildfire's hide was unmistakable. It smelled of sweat and grass and was strongly reminiscent of the most recent ride. That smell conjured up the image of walking along a narrow dusty trail, or of galloping up a craggy-rock-strewn hillside trying to gain the ridge. The smell is that of speed, of strength, of adventure, and of home. Wildfire's scent could be recognized without even seeing or hearing him. You would know he was there or that he would come walking around the corner of the lodge when you smelled his smell, that pure, comforting horse smell. The smell of his pony never failed to cause Saved By Bear's heart to lift, because in smelling it he knew that his friend and traveling companion was near by his side. Wildfire also recognized and embraced the smell of his trusty rider, his caretaker, his friend. So it was that the two often smelled each other's presence. And they drew a feeling of safety and companionship once they caught that whiff of friend in the nostrils.

The Lakota ponies such as Wildfire were born with an innate sense of loyalty and courage. Their lives were tough and rough from the very beginning. They had no time to be pampered or treated like a beast of luxury. Once foaled, the Lakota pony had to stand for the first time on skinny, shaky, very long, gangly legs and assume the instinctual duty and responsibility of bearing a heavy burden for his people, the two-legged whose family he had become a part of. There was no option for the foal other than to view the future with a head-on approach, and with a young and vibrant enthusiasm equal to that of few others. There was no time to sleep or lay around all day, or at least not as much time as the foal would have liked. There was little time to just remain a baby, little time to remain a colt. The pony would grow by leaps and bounds, its muscles and bones seeming to expand and extend each day before the eyes of his mother. The young pony would be too anxious to run with the mares and stallions, too impatient to wait to be a part of the most recent chase or run.

With feet seemingly too large for his legs and body, the pony's early awkwardness momentarily belies the truth of what he will become. The newness of youth and his clumsiness will, as a result of brief learning sessions, be overcome and surpassed. He will become strong, tall, coordinated, and fast. He will even amaze himself at times. And he will become adoringly handsome to the eye, sporting a champion's physique.

The young pony spends most of his youngest days working on becoming who he was meant to be, becoming what was expected of him by his mother and his family, becoming the trusted and true friend and companion of his Lakota brothers. One of those two-leggeds shall become special to him, as if the two decide to become companions by way of dreaming about their plan of connection.

Ages and ages, generations and generations, have passed for the horse people, who have emerged in life to live, exist, and flourish this way. They have been proud of who they are, the horse people. They quickly recognize their own strength, endurance, and utility. They come to know their great individual and collective value to the herd, and also to the group of families of Lakota, who share their lives with them.

The White Stone Pony

Wildfire had helped Saved By Bear hunt antelope in the spring earlier this year. At first, he was somewhat apprehensive of the fast jumpers, but he found out quickly that he should try to stay clear of them and not run too close, because of the quick jerky turns they could make. Wildfire performed magnificently in his first hunt. So when it was suggested that Saved By Bear be one of the hunting group going to hunt in the White Mountains, Wildfire was excited to be going on the long trip. The purpose of this hunt was to look for deer, antelope, and maybe some elk, all of which were commonly seen in the areas of the White Mountains the Lakota frequented.

The White Mountains themselves were sandstone and granite, carved out of a prehistoric ocean or swamp. As a result of their history and creation, the mountains contained devastatingly beautiful white cliffs, ravines, canyons, jagged peaks, and unique formations reaching hundreds of feet in height. There was layer upon layer of whitish-hued rock in each set of spires and plateaus. One could get lost in the vast number of ravines and canyons if one was not careful or accustomed to the trail. The area was also thickly populated by the great raptors, the great birds of prey. It was not unusual to see great owls of all kinds and all colors, and all kinds of hawks, turkey vultures, falcons, and of course the great messengers, wanbli, the eagles. There were always bald eagles and golden eagles, young and old, flying among the grand white sandstone cliffs and peaks of the White Mountains. This fact created a useful and yearned for opportunity for the Lakota to pray to Wakan Tanka, knowing that the wanbli were close by to carry their prayers directly to the Creator.

It was well-known and believed by the generations of the Lakota that the eagles had a special gift bestowed upon them by Creator. When the Creator created all things, every spirit individually chose to be who it is. The horse chose to be the horse, the companion and carrier of humans. The bee chose to be the bee, the tireless worker and the sacred pollinator of plants, so that the plants could grow and thrive, and all other beings could survive by eating the plants. The human being chose to be human and to serve as the steward of Grandmother Earth and complete the Circle of life with peace, unity, tolerance, and love. But the eagle, the wanbli, chose to be the eagle. It also chose to be the messenger, the carrier of prayers from all the beings to the Creator.

If you have ever watched the eagles in their natural environment in the skies, you know that they are unique. They have the ability to swoop down and skim the water at great speed. They also have the superpower to fly straight up through the sky and then disappear. This is how they deliver the prayers from below.

It was always a special moment when one saw these messengers wherever they may be. It was a wondrous, beautiful sight to see the wanbli and watch them fly in and above the majesty of the White Mountains, where they nested and hunted.

It was on this hunting trip in 1859, when Saved By Bear was ten years old, that the Lakota hunting party came upon a certain area in the White Mountains. As all of the men and boys and their horses entered the mountains, it was getting to be late afternoon, so they looked for a place to set up camp. They found a place down by a small stream amid the white rock spires and caverns within the White Mountains. There they staked out a flat place along the waterway, and then they set up camp.

After they finished setting up the camp, Saved By Bear got up on his young pony Wildfire and joined a small group of scouts who were looking for signs of the herds and also making sure there was no danger from others. Swift Bear stayed behind with his uncles. As the group neared a coulee dropping toward a small stream, the young brave told the rest that he was trailing off that way. Saved By Bear and Wildfire rode even farther west, away from the campsite. As he and Wildfire rode through a nearby canyon, following the stream, he came upon a vision of a white horse in the distance. It appeared to him that this white horse was all by itself. The horse's head was bowed down as if the horse was drinking water. As Saved By Bear looked at the horse from afar, he decided to ride up to where the horse was standing. Once he got closer, he noticed that the horse did not move. And as he got even closer, and closer still, he realized that the horse had still not moved. The head was still bowed and remained perfectly still. It looked as if this horse was in a position of prayer. Saved By Bear took particular notice of that, in light of the fact he was alone himself. This was something that he had never seen before. As he took in the vision of this figure, this animal suspended in time and position, a feeling came over and rushed through him, moving throughout his body and his spirit. It was a strong feeling that he had just encountered something of great significance. As he got even closer, the horse remained silent and perfectly still. He noticed that actually the horse's head was dipped toward the running stream, not in the stream, but near the edge.

To Saved By Bear, the horse appeared frozen. It did not move— could not move. Wildfire realized the same thing as the young brave dismounted. Saved By Bear approached the white horse and placed his hand on its shoulder. He then realized that the horse was made of a smooth white stone. He felt along the mane and moved his hand down toward the horse's face, gently grazing his fingertips against the white stone locks of hair covering one eye. This was a beautiful white horse. And the horse was tall, standing slightly above Saved By Bear's head.

This is a moment that Saved By Bear would have etched upon his spirit and soul for the remainder of his life. There was an energy racing through his body, moving from the top of his head to the soles of his moccasins. This energy indicated to him that what he was encountering here was a vision, a symbol, a sign from the Creator, something that he was intended to see, something that was meant for his eyes and his spirit. He realized that this stone being from another place had been placed there by the Creator for the specific reason that the young Saved By Bear would encounter him. He felt the need to take care of this beautiful white stone pony. It was as if he had met a long-lost friend, somebody who shared a common bond with him, though not just an acquaintance from an earlier time but from a friendship that existed amid the oldest and most sacred portals in time.

Saved By Bear and Wildfire remained with this horse, with this stone being, and Saved By Bear prayed. He prayed to all the directions for help in understanding the meaning of his encountering this particular being. Seeing three messengers flying overhead, he sent his prayers drifting up to their winged embrace for a comforting and dependable delivery to Creator.

As night fell throughout the canyons of the White Mountains, and as the air grew crisp and cold, Saved By Bear stayed with his new friend. He felt at that time that the purpose of this meeting had a deeper meaning to him both for now and for what may come in the future.

With this feeling in mind, he gently unrolled the bright red scarlet blanket tied to Wildfire's back, took it down, and cast it across the broad shoulders of the white stone pony. He grasped the edges of the red blanket and pulled it tight around the horse's neck. And for a moment in time, he draped his arm against the horse's neck and felt a pulsating bond, something that he would later describe as a feeling of love. Giving the stone pony's face a last gentle stroke of his warm hand, Saved By Bear lay down next to the pony and felt his presence as he stared up into the bright, beautiful night sky and the wondrous spectacle of the gigantic expanse of the great Milky Way, the Trail of Spirits. Wildfire stood by quietly and calmly, as if to sanctify the moment for his human friend. Saved By Bear brought out some wasna for the stone pony, and laid it down by his mouth. He prayed for safety and protection for his family, himself, Wildfire, the hunting party, and his new friend standing in solid silence just next to him. Then Saved By Bear quietly drifted off to sleep.

When he awoke, the sun was beginning to crawl over the edge of the cliffs and he heard the meadowlarks in the distance, chirping. He realized that he had slept soundly through the night. The memories from the night before came flashing back in his mind instantly. He turned and looked for his friend. However, he saw that the horse was gone. He felt something in his heart, as if he'd lost a companion, lost a friend. At that moment, he looked within his spirit, and he asked again for an answer. Following what he had been taught by his father, his mother, and his grandfather, he searched for a meaning. Raising his hand to the west, he said a prayer. Suddenly the meaning flashed in front of him, and he understood. The stone pony had been a gift that was given to him, and him alone. It was a symbol of strength, a symbol of courage, a symbol of hope, a symbol of commitment, a symbol that he could carry with him as a man, as a Lakota, as a human being, and as a brother.

Somehow, as he felt deep within his heart and spirit, a sense of longing for his friend, he knew that one day he would see his friend again. He also knew that this moment in time would serve as a reminder to him—and as a motivation, a meaning, and a purpose—that his life would turn in a way that he could never have imagined. And yet he felt confident that Creator was watching over him. As he climbed upon Wildfire's trusted back once more to begin the ride back to the camp and to the others, he felt his mind meld with his spirit. He had the feeling that his spirit had taught him an ability to let it shine brighter and more truthfully, than his mind. As he and Wildfire climbed out of the canyon with the gentle flowing stream, he took a last look down at the area where the white stone pony had once stood, and he felt a comforting serenity about the experience and what was to come. He would not know the true magnitude at the time, however, or that this would be a story that would be passed down from generation to generation among his family from that time forward. This story would live forever in the oral history told by our grandmother and our mother, to us.

—————————⟫«⟨⬤⟩»⟪—————————

There is significance to this story, and in particular to the fact that the horse was white. In the Lakota tradition, the white horse is a unique, special horse to the people. Since horses have always been our brothers and sisters, and since we have depended upon the horse nation for our livelihood, we look upon them as very sacred. There is ceremonial significance for their presence in our lives. A white horse is normally a gift to one Lakota from the rest of the people, the medicine people, the grassroots people. It is gifted as an honor to a warrior who has earned it and is recognized for his practice in helping the people, protecting the people, and serving the people. So when one would see a white horse, one would immediately know that the warrior atop it, the man who rode it, was a man of good spirit, highly developed in strength in his heart, a man who had compassion for his people and who had a presence that earned him the right to be recognized on hoof. In doing his part to earn the pleasure of the white horse and the respect shown by its being given to him, the man can feel comfortable in what he has become as a wicasa, a red man. And it can be discerned that the people are confident that he has the qualities, leadership skills, patience, and knowledge to help them when a time of need arrives, or when the time comes to celebrate.

To Saved By Bear, the white stone pony would serve as a symbol to him throughout the stages of his life. It had appeared at a place where he reached out and called for help from the Creator, asking for courage, knowledge, wisdom, and hope. Throughout the trying times in his life, he would remember that Creator had granted him the gift of this experience with the white stone pony. Saved By Bear knew that his friend would come to him in his time of need.

Often, throughout his life, Saved By Bear would think back to the stone pony. He did this at pivotal times. The memory of the stone pony came upon him in moments when he needed someone, or needed something. At a time of *asking*. At a time of trial. At the times of conflict. At the times of duty. At the time of seeking to fulfill a promise. At a time of delvery upon a permission granted. At a time of fulfilling a destiny.

The experience that Saved By Bear had with the white stone pony also served as a precursor to what he would later do in his life on the Greasy Grass battlefield, on the *hill*. It was a sign of things to come, a sign that he was chosen to do things of great consequence to his people and Grandmother Earth. Another significant aspect of this experience with the white horse, is that it was the spiritual confirmation of Saved By Bear as a heyoka. The hunting party went to the west. The west would be an important factor in Saved By Bear's life for the remainder of his days and beyond. And he would remember.

Warrior: An Age-Old Ritual

Following his experience in the White Mountains with the white stone pony, Saved By Bear, along with Swift Bear and a number of other younger boys and men, will pursue and be taught the warrior lifestyle and begin to experience the warrior way on every level. They will be taught about the proper warrior regalia and weaponry. They will be given the opportunity to do everything that a warrior does, and to know what being a warrior is about. They will be taught the labor-intensive measures required every step along the way, such as the tactics, geography, and military strategies, and the horse training. Man's dependence upon the horse was stressed. Hand-to-hand combat will be taught in a way that will make Saved By Bear ultimately become a lethal weapon, a skill that he would use when necessary. The warriors in training went through the ceremonies and were encouraged to develop the spiritual side of the warrior. All of these experiences gave each young man an opportunity to achieve his goal of being a warrior.

As part of their warrior education and teaching, the young apprentices were also told and taught by the warriors and elders what it meant to become a warrior, versus merely growing up and maturing to become a common man. The young Lakota braves were taught how a warrior acted and carried himself in both group settings and private relationships. How a warrior spoke and communicated. How the warriors were chosen for and inducted into the individual warrior societies such as the Old Men Warrior Society, the Owl Feather Headdress Warrior Society, the Brave Hearts Warrior Society, the Kit Fox Warrior Society, the Crow Owners Warrior Society, the Badger Warrior Society, the Akicita Warrior Society, and the Dog Man Warrior Society.

The young apprentices were taught about what it meant to carry on the tradition, adhere to the culture, and accept the honor of being a warrior and a member of a warrior society. They learned how the warriors wore their hair, made their weapons, painted their faces and horses, and how they dressed.

———— ‹‹◊›› ————

The warriors of the Lakota took pride in how they dressed. The warriors of the Mnincoju had their own customs and ways as to their manner of dress and regalia. It was important to follow tradition in order to stay on the right path of the honorable tradition of these ways, so as to respect those ways and preserve them for the young ones who would follow. These things were significant. This is the way that our tiospaye did things. Our brothers from the other bands and oyates may have differed somewhat in particular ways, but for the most part, the old ways were followed in a consistent manner.

A warrior's attire often reflected his accomplishments in performing deeds of bravery for the people and in battle. Long pants and long-sleeve shirts made of buckskin were standard attire for any Lakota warrior. The Lakota women were the ones to prepare and make the clothing and the animal hide accessories for the men and boys. The Lakota females therefore became a part of every individual warrior through their practical and spiritual support. Each individual warrior may chose how to create his own unique look, by adding some aspect indicating something personal to the warrior himself. Eagle and hawk feathers were commonly tied in the hair. A headdress was worn by accomplished and respected leaders. This method of respect required that these traditions be recognized and used. The headdress is a combination of many feathers gifted to us by the sacred wanbli. It was rare to wear a full headdress of feathers, unless for very special ceremonial and leadership occasions.

The shirt sleeves may be decorated with painted or quilled designs, usually the symbol of the family or the band (like the symbol of a bear, an eagle, or an elk), or with the symbol of a particular warrior society. The best example is the symbol of the Dog Man Warrior Society, the dragonfly. The dragonfly was painted, etched, or burned into the sleeves of the warrior's shirt, and often into the legs of the warrior's pants. The dragonfly symbolized agility, speed, quickness, great precision, and training, regarding the uncommon approach to matters of life, protection, and battle. But the Dog Man symbol was usually only put upon warrior regalia, not on the warrior's everyday clothing.

Symbols were used for his role as a warrior. But each warrior was also a common man and did not always have to wear his symbols. If he did not respect what a warrior is, he couldn't be a warrior. If you don't believe in yourself as a warrior, you certainly are not one.

Often the warrior ponies were painted with the symbols and designs of the warrior. Handprint symbols, commonly appearing on the flank and shoulder, were placed on the horse to protect both horse and warrior in preparation for battle. The horse and the warrior knew strength as *two*. Lightning bolts were sometimes painted on the horse. Sometimes the horse's eye was circled to symbolize the completeness of the two, the warrior and his horse.

The number of feathers and the angle at which they were worn in the warrior's hair also had significance. If a warrior had actually taken a life in battle, he was entitled to wear the eagle feather tied to the back of the hair and pointing straight up. A single red mark may be made on the feather to indicate this as well. The Dog Man warriors commonly wore two feathers straight up on the back of their heads. If a warrior had counted coup on an enemy or opponent, then the warrior would clip out a portion of the eagle feather to indicate he had had that honor. All warriors, of course, would wear feathers in their hair in battle. Warriors often braided parts of their long hair. The Lakota usually had full heads of long hair that was quite thick. Their hair was dark brown, not usually black.

Warriors often painted their faces in various combinations of colors in preparation for battle. The significance was in the design and the coloring. Warriors usually painted their faces to depict visions or the individual warrior's feelings about battle. In painting his face, the warrior is trying to do everything he can to gather protection. The faces were painted in a way distinctive to an individual given warrior society, as well. The paint was sometimes used to project the courage, determination, and mystery of the individual warrior, and to depersonalize his identity in any potentially deadly meeting. Many times, warriors could not be recognized in battle unless they chose to reveal who they really were. They painted their faces so that the enemy only saw the warrior face, not the face of a family man or an ordinary man. This both confused the enemy as to the warrior's identity and showed the ferocity and courage of the warrior.

A coupstick was one of the Lakota warrior's most honored possessions. It represented the Lakota warrior way of demanding attention without killing. In Lakota culture, it was more honorable and brave to draw close enough to your opponent or enemy in order to touch him with your hand or with a coupstick. To do so was called "counting coup" upon your enemy. To be able to count coup on a person rather than kill them was a great achievement. It allowed the person you counted coup upon to remain alive. This way, the receiver's next thought would still be in this life, not after death. Counting coup was the Lakota way to briefly bring honor and diplomacy to a situation involving a clash of cultures, to allow human beings to take a step back from war and aggression. However, counting coup sometimes was not enough to save the lives of your own.

War clubs were made of a piece of hard wood (ash) as the handle or shaft. The handle was topped with a heavy round or oval-shaped stone tightly bound to the end with tough rawhide and buffalo sinew, which would shrink up when dried. It had to be strong and resistant so that it would not break when used. This weapon, as was every weapon used by the Lakota, was made to be in proportion to the size, length, and width of the user's arms and hands.

The warrior shield was a protective battle instrument designed to ward off enemy arrows or hand weapons. It was not designed to stop bullets. Shields were made according to an intricate design, the shield being carefully curved in a way to deflect arrows away from the warrior's body. A shield was also designed to be form-fitted to the warrior's arm and hand, to allow the warrior to move the shield into the best position to deflect the arrow away from his body. Also, the shield fit so tightly to the arm that it could be thrusted with the forearm to deflect the blows of an enemy's club. Much like the making of a bow or a war club, the shield was made of the tough hide of the buffalo, moistened, cut, stretched, and tied tight to garner the most strength and durability. In the oldest way, the Lakota used the hide of the buffalo hump, as this was the thickest part of the hide and it, therefore, afforded more protection. The handle straps on the inside of the shield had to conform to the warrior's forearm. The width and length of the warrior's forearm dictated the fit and size of the shield. The shield was formed in such a way that it could move easily and smoothly with the arm while the warrior was riding, running, or fighting in battle. The straps allowed the warrior to drop or clutch the shield at will. The fingers could still be used. As with the warrior's regalia and horse, the shield bore the design and decoration particular to the warrior. The colors and shapes were uniquely significant to him.

To understand the importance of the bow and arrow to the Lakota people, one must understand the history of this weapon. The Lakota story of how the bow and the arrow came to the people goes like this: A very long time ago, too long to even situate it within a contemporary time frame, the bow came to the people. The story involves a man who was a warrior himself, a family man and society man who was respected and trusted. His ways were in tune with Creator. He had passed his warrior time agewise and was now a teacher, an instructor of the younger men whose time had come to fill the positions needed in Lakota society. One day as this man was taking a stroll along a stream, he was made aware within his spirit of an address to him from Creator. Gazing into the sky, he listened to what the Creator was saying to him. He recognized that he himself had been chosen for a very special task. This task, once completed, would enable the people to defend themselves with much greater ease, in a quicker, faster, and more lethal way. This was something that they had never had before.

As the man was walking next to the stream, he looked into the sky again. Lightning came down from the sky and struck an ash tree close to him. It was so intense that he was shocked. The lightning had set this tree on fire. The tree was burning in front of him, turning black with soot. As the man stood there, his spirit received messages from the Creator. "This is the tree that will be used as a weapon and for domestic purposes. This new amenity will enrich the people's lives in many ways." Creator said to him, "I give you the authority and knowledge to pass this on to your people." As the warrior stood there, all the messages and other information was placed inside of him. His spirit welcomed his new role to fulfill for the people.

He then went back to his camp and explained to the elders and others what had occurred. They listened in amazement, knowing that Creator does nothing that does not have a positive impact on the ways of the family. This man, now full of the knowledge of what he is to do, begins. He goes back to the ash tree and takes the first wood for the first bow. He takes the wood back to his camp, with the knowledge in his brain, and begins to make the first bow. He shapes the wood first by shaving and carving it down. This takes him a number of days as he learns his new trade on his own. The people watch, intently paying attention to what he is doing, because he is now the teacher of a new aspect of their civilization. He continues on with the shaping of the bow. Holding the bow of ash wood over his campfire to make it pliable, he bends it and shaves it at the same time, shaping it so that it will be able to cast the projectile, the arrow, which is to come as well, at its target. Using the bow and arrow is one of the swiftest and most precise means of taking a life without causing suffering or needless pain.

The man continues this process, assembling each piece of his bow. As he finishes each part, he advises those who are willing to learn how to do the task too. After he has shaped and formed his bow, he takes buffalo sinew that has been dried in rawhide form. He uses hide glue from his animals of prey. The buffalo sinew glued to the shaft of the ash bow reinforces the bow's strength, enabling it to bend and then instantly spring back into shape. This allows for force of impact as well as speed when in pursuit of prey or an enemy.

The next piece is the bowstring, which is also made of the sinew of buffalo (or perhaps elk), which is braided with the strands tightly meshed together, just like the tribe and the people. Intertwined, they become strong, flexible, and directed. These are the teaching tools, along with this weapon and its use.

The man has been working for weeks now. Many who watch him are very interested, asking to be taught this new trade. He knows this is exactly what Creator wanted.

The man then turns to making the arrow, for which has been given instructions. The arrow comes from a different wood, a lighter wood, but very strong. It is often called dogwood. It grows very straight like the brush in creek, stream, and river areas, and it is very abundant. From one patch of dogwood, one can fill a quiver with ease. Once the dogwood is procured, it is shaped to be as straight as possible, so that it will glide through the air like a bird. The man will use stone and bone utensils to shape this arrow, shaving it down to a proper thickness so that it is not too cumbersome and also not too thin or flimsy. The shaft of the arrow will be run through a hole, or a notch in a stone. It will be glided and moved through in this manner until the shaft is smooth, straight, and sleek. To the end, the man will attach three feathers that come from various birds, perhaps a turkey or a prairie chicken, but in any event a bird that predominantly is frequently seen by the Lakota in their daily lives. These feathered pieces will be cut into a uniform shape so that they will help the arrow fly through the air. Elk glue and sinew are used to attach the feathers to the shaft. This way, they stay strong and remain bound very tightly.

The arrowhead begins as stone. The man is taught how to knap the different types of stones that he was instructed to use. Knapping involves flaking bits and pieces of the stone so that the arrowhead will be sharp and have the ability to enter its target with ease. This arrowhead will take time and effort to make, just as the bow and the arrow took time. When it is complete, the arrow shaft will be notched and the arrowhead will be inserted at the point. It will then be tied with sinew so that it will stay in place.

After a period of intense labor, the man finishes the original bow and a quiver of arrows. The bow is then brought to the people, and the man demonstrates this new weapon, which is widely accepted. The men and the women thank him for his commitment and his receivings from Creator. And he is now the bow maker, the one who makes every bow for his people. He started with one, and then the number increased as he got better and better at this art of bow making. He then begins the teaching process to show others how to make the bow and arrow. This trade will be passed from the original bow maker down through the generations. And that is the story of how the bow and the arrow came to the people so long ago.

For the most part, a bow maker is the expert relied upon by the warrior, who will use the weapon to obtain food and defense from an enemy. The bow maker's place in Lakota history is revered. Each tiospaye is taught about the bow and arrow. And since the first bow maker continues to teach the people, his way of making the bow and arrow becomes the traditional way. To Creator we give thanks. We offer our lives and the presence of those whom we may take with this newfound tool. Our lives are enriched; our lives are protected. We are now more of a people thanks to Creator and the gifts for our life.

The bow and the arrows were designed according to the old way, a skill that was passed down from generation to generation. The bow and arrow was the primary weapon for the warrior while on the move, while chasing prey during the hunt, or in the midst of battle. The arrow was important and necessary in that it provided the warrior the gift of being able to strike the prey or an enemy from a short or a great distance. The length of the individual arrow was important for each warrior. The arrow needed to be the same length of the warrior's forearm, from elbow to fingertip. This was so the arrow's length equaled the length of the warrior's reach when he pulled the arrow into firing position at the peak of bowstring tension, just before releasing the shot.

The bow maker had a specific, and very important, role to play in the old ways of the Lakota. According to the old ways, the role of bow maker was something passed down from generation to generation, even following bloodlines. The bow maker's role was to make the bows for all the people in camp or for the oyate. The bow maker specialized in making a good, strong, reliable bow. Time and talent were necessary if one was to be a bow maker.

The shape of the bow needed to conform to the length and contours of the user's bicep, forearm, and hand, taking into account his physical ability. The Lakota bows were short, never longer than the distance from the ground to the warrior's hip. The short bow was chosen because the bow was used while riding a horse, while running, and for shooting through a tree line. A buffalo hunt required that the hunter be quick and mobile, with the ability to move the bow in any direction necessary. The shooting angle could be changed according to whatever the warrior may encounter or need. There was an incredible strength in the pull of these short bows (100 to 200 psi). A single arrow could cut through the body of a buffalo or an elk. This capability was necessary because the Lakota needed to be able to rely upon his bow in situations where precision and quickness were imperative. On the hunt, a missed shot could mean that the hunter wouldn't be able to provide life-sustaining food for his family and his people. In conflict and battle, of course, any slight deviation or flaw could be the difference between life and death.

Every piece of the Lakota warrior's weaponry was made according to his bodily proportions and physical attributes. This is why most of the warriors made their own weapons.

The Lakota were tall people. It was not uncommon at all for a Lakota man to reach a height of six foot four or six foot five. The Lakota were naturally muscled and toned from all of the physical demands of life. Warriors were mostly gifted to be athletic, and became more so with training and preparation. Compared to other peoples, the Lakota had longer legs and longer arms, their bodies built for the geography, terrain, and topography of the lands they lived upon. The Lakota, because of their size as compared to the whites in the middle and late 1800s, instilled fear in the whites, who were intimidated by their physical power and stature.

These physical attributes made the Lakota physically superior to many of the white soldiers on the battlefield. The Lakota's physical strength and ability combined greatly with their spiritual strength.

It was this combination of the physical world and the spiritual world that gave the Lakota the ability to confront and deal with the problems of the new world, allowing them an opportunity to act upon their beliefs and their sense of duty in protecting their people, Grandmother Earth, the He Sapa, and their way of life. The warrior embodied the Lakota way of life. The warrior is that life. The warrior is… the spirit of the Lakota.

⟫ ⟪⟨⟩⟫ ⟪

The Gift of Heyoka

It came to pass that the spiritual balance in life provided a welcoming open door to Saved By Bear to follow the spiritual path that his dreams and visions had been suggesting.

One day, at the break of dawn, the young Lakota boy awoke to the sound of a large bird calling out repeatedly from a nearby pine tree, several footsteps from the flap door of the family's lodge. Saved By Bear knew the bird's position because, as he turned on his side to look in the direction of the sound, he saw the slight movement of the wings in the branches. He was still lying on the robe upon which he had slept. He noted that the rising sun had crept up over the crest of the forested hill in the distance. Looking in that direction, he could clearly see the outline of the large bird perched on the branch, facing the rising sun. As he lay there on his side before getting to his feet, he could tell it was a large bird with long tail feathers and a somewhat hooked beak.

Saved By Bear's grandfather Iron White Man had taught him much about the bird people, speaking to all the children together at the teaching sessions in the circle, or to Saved By Bear alone in their private walks through the trees, when it was just the two of them. During these talks, Saved By Bear always intently listened. He knew that when the older ones spoke, it was his place to listen, not to talk. Then, when the time was right and his questions were encouraged, he could talk and seek to quench his curiosity by asking all sorts of questions. The elders and the adults knew many things, and they were always anxious to share their knowledge with the young ones upon a moment's notice. This was the way, the old way. It was how things were taught, how things were learned, how things were accepted, how things once new and different became known and familiar. How the tales of the Circle of life found their way into the mind, memory, consciousness, and spirit of the young eager ones. And the gift of the old way was one that the Lakota were eager to pass on, and carry forth in word and deed, to show the young ones the aspects of life that were all around them every day, everywhere, every moment.

This is how Saved By Bear came to absorb knowledge of all the animal peoples: the four-legged, the two-legged, the water peoples, the insect people, the plant people, the stone people, the winged people, the bird people.

Saved By Bear found the bird people to be extraordinary. When he first saw them, he was amazed. They had legs and feet, and interesting faces with big eyes and long noses. The fact that they were adorned with beautiful blazes of colors and designs in their feathers made them a wonderful sight to his eyes and his mind. The thing that made his heart jump, his spirit light up, and his imagination spring into action, was the fact that these beautiful interesting people could stretch out their arms... and fly.

It was amazing to the young Lakota that such a being could be calmly sitting perched on a rock or a tree branch one second and then, in the blink of an eye, spread those magnificent feathered wings and take off, flying through the air with the greatest of speed and agility. It was as if it was pure magic. As if these beings had been chosen by Creator and gifted with the magic of flight. Saved By Bear learned to love to watch them fly—so fast, so far, so high. He often imagined being able to ride along with them on their backs, or being lifted into their grasp.

Saved By Bear even began to imagine. Then those images from his imagination snuck into his nightly dreams, where he found himself with wings and felt that it was he who could suddenly spread his arms, flap his wings, and take flight. He would fly over villages, over forests, and over rivers, circling the mountaintops. It was as if his heart and spirit could actually feel the sensation of weightlessness and easy energy as he flew among the clouds and looked down upon all the peoples who lived below and were confined to merely moving along the Earth's surface. These images, these thoughts, these dreams, always brought a joy to his heart and a smile to his face. His mother sometimes would ask him when he awoke what it was he had been dreaming about when such things presented themselves to his subconscious sleeping mind. He did not hold back in describing it all to his mother, who smiled when he spoke of such things. Iron Hat remembered having such dreams as a child, and even now as an adult. But it always felt the same. It was understood by all ages that the honoring gift of flight was indeed a sacred gift granted to certain beings by Creator. Still, it never hurt anyone or anything when the hearts and spirits of human beings of all ages imagined or dreamed of experiencing the great gift of flight that the bird peoples had been given. Having such dreams is what began Saved By Bear's special affinity with the winged people. He grew to celebrate them, their lives, and their existence in his life, honoring them every time he encountered one in his presence.

For several years now, Saved By Bear had been feeling in his mind and his heart, but mostly in his spirit, that somehow he knew what the animal people were thinking and what sort of things were important to them. He envisioned what it would be like to be one of them. To be a four-legged one, a mato, a winged one, a swimming one in the water, a bee in the hive, an ant on the ant mound, or a bluebird on a branch. These thoughts and feelings seemed to percolate out of his spirit where it felt as if there was a warm buzzing energy coming through his chest and spreading into his arms, into his fingers, to the top of his head, and into his mind. Almost as if the energy was seeking a route of its own to venture beyond his own body to the outside world, to seek out and find a connection with the other energy out there in the great big wonderful world. It was this feeling of an inner energy and the innate consciousness of its existence in his mind and within his very spirit, that caused him to act upon what it was that he felt.

So Saved By Bear began to emote his thoughts and feelings to those other beings and peoples he would encounter in his physical presence. It started by willing and pushing this energy within himself to go forth from his mind toward the other one that he wished to receive his message of energy. He used no words, no physical signs. Just thoughts, emotions, and a conversation from his mind and his very spirit. And in the process of experimenting in this manner, he felt the wings of his soul, his spirit, open up wide and spread. And his spirit carried forth his message as if the message had its own invisible wings and flew to the one he wished to communicate with.

And once the other being showed signs of receiving his message, to him, it now all made sense. He had been given a gift. A precious, sacred gift, from his Creator. A gift that was once unknown, untested, and unopened. But now, a gift that he had become aware of, and one which he now accepted and did not fear. It was a gift now to know, to understand, to accept, that he could do something with his mind and the unseen energy of his spirit, to emote a part of himself to share with other beings. To share with other beings whoever they may be. And he did not even need to speak or mouth the words of his messages. He could do it by merely willing himself to do it. And it worked. It worked like magic. And he thanked Creator, which was something his parents and grandparents had taught and encouraged him to do when he received a gift. And it was wonderful.

So Saved By Bear began to communicate with the animals... and the birds.

When Saved By Bear heard the big bird outside the lodge this morning, he had not yet communicated his energy with such a large bird. So he got to his feet and started walking in the new dawn light, toward the tree where the magnificent five-year-old red-tailed hawk was perched. As he slowly approached, he gathered the inner energy in his chest, and sent it to the hawk in the direction of the rising sun. "Hello. How are you this fine morning, my friend?"

The hawk turned her head and stared at the young Lakota boy walking slowly toward her tree. And her large brown eyes softened, and she opened her beak and made her earthly hawk sound. "*Wasté!*. It is good to see you, to hear you, to hear your heart, to hear your spirit."

Saved By Bear, now getting close, returned the glance and said, "I hope you are not scared of me or my family. I think that not everyone speaks to you this way, with the mind message."

The red-tailed hawk turned and ruffled her rust-tinted tail feathers as if to highlight her joy in conversing with the human boy: "No. I am not frightened. It is always good to see the people. I know that I am safe in your presence. My family is near too, and we are feeling safe and good to be near the Lakota. It makes me feel good and happy to be able to speak with you, little one. It is okay, if you wish, to talk to me with the words from your mouth also. I will understand because we can hear and understand both ways. It has been a gift to all of us, the old people on Unci Maka. And it is rare to be able to speak to and share thoughts and feelings with our brothers, the humans. But it is good to know you can."

"*Pilamaya ye,*" Saved By Bear said, verbally now.

Then he and the hawk spoke about their families and their favorite places to visit. After awhile, the large hawk said that she needed to check on her children at home in the nest, so she bid farewell to the Lakota boy. "*Toksa ake.*" She meant to say—"until next time." And she flew over the tops of the trees and toward the steep cliffs along the river. As he watched her fly home, Saved By Bear felt alive. He felt good. He was grateful to have made a new friend.

For many days while Saved By Bear's family was at this campsite, the hawk came to talk to him and to sing. She flew along with him on walks and rides into the trees. She looked over him, literally. And the word was spread among the bird people, the hawk family, and other peoples. That a special young Lakota brave had the old ways about him. The red-tailed hawks would follow him and look over him for the remainder of his life. And it was waste´.

After his experience with the red-tailed hawk, Saved By Bear spoke to his grandfather about what it all meant. Iron White Man sat and studied his grandson. Then he calmly said, "Takoja, you are heyoka. It is good. It is a gift. You are one with the Thunder Beings. You must use your energy, however, to do only good. If you remain true to your heart and your spirit, then you will see wonderful things. I am proud of you. Be honorable. Be humble."

--------⊗--------

To the Lakota, a heyoka is an extremely connected spiritual person. He can be a medicine person, a healer, a holy person, and/or a warrior. This person is gifted the way of the heyoka while still in the womb, and will carry this life long. The abilities are recognized in early childhood, and nurtured through the childhood and teen years. This special connection is with the Wakinyan, the Thunder Beings. The Thunder Beings are the most powerful entities of creation and Grandmother Earth. Their commitment to life is to spread the water to rejuvenate and to bring about a rebirth of family. The Thunder Beings are associated with the color blue due to its healing qualities. Thunder Beings are also associated with the west direction.

A heyoka is gifted with spiritual assimilation based upon experience or need. By feeling the needs of another's presence or emotion. The heyoka has the ability to connect instantaneously with all beings. The gift is the direct connection to all spirits. This ability allows him to open the door to the spirit in all beings out of necessity and compassion.

The heyoka is sacred. These society members are a mirror to the people to help them see themselves. His teachers are the Wakinyan, the Thunder Beings.

The Lakota recognize the heyoka society. These heyoka have their own rituals and ceremonies which only they perform. They are inducted into this male society.

The heyoka way originally begins in dreams, normally in the earlier phases of life or at an early age. The Thunder Beings present visions and messages to these individuals. They nurture the man as a father would his son, teaching him and giving him the understanding needed as he matures to take his place in society.

The heyoka spirit will go through certain passages and education in preparation for entering this sacred circle. The child will live in a family way. The child will become a brave and will be taught the ways of a common man. He will be introduced to ceremony and patience through the sweat lodge. Here he will learn to pray in many languages and hearts. The passage continues with a ceremony of hanbleceya, a man cries on the hill. This experience is for self-enrichment and understanding. The final passage is to become a sun dancer. The sun dance ceremony is for the people, all the people of Grandmother Earth. That they will live in a good way, in peace and harmony, for another year.

The heyoka will walk in society with his ways and spiritual presence to provide assistance and strength of spirit. Each experience with another being is unique in its presentation. The heyoka is capable of bringing forth the faces needed to help his people.

A heyoka is not a clown or a trickster, or someone to ridicule or make fun or light of. They do not do everything backward or in an opposite fashion. No walking backwards or bathing with dirt instead of water. The one who is being assisted by the Heyoka presence, is being taken backward in spirit and time. Providing both people a familiar feeling of comfort and safety during this experience. Clowns are just that: clowns. Heyokas are serious, sacred people who are chosen to fulfill destinies, the destinies of others and their own destinies. The false statements made about the heyoka in contemporary times are merely a stereotype arising from the forced removal of Lakota tradition and culture.

Yellow Rocks

Swift Bear looked at the sheer cliff wall as they passed on horseback, riding north along the beaver creek in the northwest canyon within the He Sapa. Interspersed in the rock wall were yellow lines that curved and flowed from the top to the bottom of the thirty-foot outcropping. It glittered in the sun and caught your eye as you moved by. One could not avoid the bright beacon of its call.

This was the area that the boys had come to know as the high cliff falls area with the ancient canyon in the northwest region of He Sapa. There were numerous waterfalls of all kinds and sizes in this ancient stone cliff canyon that the boys had been coming to all of their lives. The high waterfalls came from the natural mountain springs that popped up out of the rocks here and there. These cliff falls are in the area of the three-faced warrior rock overlooking the canyon. There was also an area close by that had been used as a winter survival shelter and hiding place for the people, a high inlet cave concealed by a series of thirty-foot waterfalls covering the big opening. The cave opened up to a large cavern, where the people could gather, and tailed off into a seemingly never-ending series of smaller caves and tunnels in the stone walls within the cavern. Also, nearby and to the south, there was the falls that resembled a large eagle fan, like the one the Lakota holy men used in ceremony. It sprayed a veil type of waterfall from the cliff's top edge that cascaded down to the creek below.

This particular outcropping of rock that Swift Bear had just gone past and noticed, was near the eagle-fan-shaped falls and not far south from the high cave falls. It also held a stone figure of a great wanbli flying with wings extended, with sharp beak, and with keen eyes focused toward the falls. It was a recognized symbol in the stone that Swift Bear always enjoyed seeing. He got off his horse and walked up to the side of the sheer rock wall.

When he was younger and had visited this place, Swift Bear enjoyed how the golden sparkles glinted off the rock surface and onto his skin. He could not avoid wanting to touch it. Upon gazing closely, with his cheek and chin pressed to the rock, he grazed his right finger along the golden seam. It was smooth, as smooth as a heavily polished grinding rock or the head of his father's war club. He touched his finger to his tongue to gather some spit, and then he touched the seam again. This time he brought his finger to his lips. His tongue lapped at his fingertip, he found that it tasted of metal, like some of the old pans that had been found at one of the old white people's camps after being abandoned following a winter storm.

Saved By Bear had also seen the shining rock in the He Sapa as a young boy, when he was with his mother Iron Hat wading in a creek near Owl's Nest Peak. It was in pebble form sitting at the edge of a small waterfall. The crystal-clear water bounced cleanly off the gilded stones. The bright beacon of the sunlight beams glancing from the rocks, commanded the attention of the eye. Saved By Bear's mother saw his interest. She told him to grab some of the pebbles and put them in his pouch. He did so, grabbing four. They were heavy rocks, and quite pretty when cleaned up.

The people knew of these rocks from before, using the pretty little heavy stones to decorate their necklaces or traditional staffs. The people thought no more about the stones' usefulness, as they did not appear in large enough sections to use them for making any useful tools or weapons. They just seemed to look nice. However, the undeniable fact was that these yellow rocks were a part of the He Sapa, which was and remained the sacred aboriginal home of the Lakota, always.

Little did the people know at the time, that these yellow rocks growing in the stones, looking like the earthlike veins in the human arm, were one of the rarest of the rare elements on the planet. Nor did the Lakota and Mnincoju people fully appreciate the monetary value that the whites and white society would ascribed to these yellow stones. Nor did the original people of the He Sapa immediately come to appreciate that the non-Lakota people could be driven nearly insane in a never-ending search for the yellow rock, as such a thing was inconceivable to the Lakota. One day in the not so distant furture, however, would bring forth a much more threatenting understanding of these yellow rocks within the Lakota way of life.

It was known as "gold," one of Grandmother Earth's most beautiful and rarest of natural elements on Turtle Island. The intrinsic value of gold to the European world was extreme. At a time when money was scarce for individual people and enterprises alike in the new American country, even the government, which would come close to bankruptcy and economic collapse as a result of the very costly Civil War, would develop a twisted imperative and immediate need for caches of gold. That is why anywhere that gold was to be found—or particularly, discovered—and ultimately mined, the US government and the white population felt the urgent wealth-driven need and purpose to move in and take over. Wherever there was gold, there was money and wealth. Any place where gold could be mined, extracted, and converted into money, was a greedy man's paradise. The presence of gold drove all sorts of men, filled with greed and covetousness, to the ends of sanity in their search to become rich, influential, and powerful. In a sense, the need to have and to possess gold would drive men to commit any act of greed, atrocity, destruction, or annihilation necessary to achieve their goal of having wealth, status, and power.

Gold is an ancient material found upon Grandmother Earth, one of her natural stone resources. It is not plentiful or easy to find or obtain. But this mineral called gold was different. It was a metal, but resembled stone. Yet, it was abundantly shiny, and malleable when heated. It had the natural capacity to be melted into a pliable liquid by extreme heat, and then bent, shaped, formed, and cut into whatever size or shape one could ever imagine.

Outwardly, gold had an awesome beauty, very pleasing to the eye. It was a splendor to behold just looking at it. Its sparkling and glinting properties seemed to capture individual rays of sunlight, holding them and then releasing them when the gold was turned on an angle. This natural effect made an obvious impact on the beings who came into contact with the element throughout all the ages of the Earth and the stars. For Grandmother Earth was quite possibly the only place where such a truly beautiful and mesmerizing metal could be found. Therefore, once it was learned that gold was at home within Grandmother Earth, beings from all over the universe were attracted to the exquisite and rare element throughout the ages.

Gold is a living organism. It is like the blood of Grandmother Earth. The veins of gold seem to be just that. They are her veins. This is how the yellow rocks exist, as yellow, golden veins.

But it was not just the outward beauty of the gold, or even its unique malleability that set it apart from other elements. What appeared to be the most fascinating and attractive attribute and quality of this rare metal was that it could serve as a natural conduit, a natural connector, a sinew of sorts provided by nature. Because of its unique nature as a metal and its malleability, the element was part and parcel of a great network of conduit, connecting things and allowing for the transference of natural energy. The type of conduit that was capable of transporting a blast of natural energy along its veins and sinew and delivering it to another place. Gold is a carrier of electrical energy, and flashes and surges of connective force, within Grandmother Earth herself. This quality makes it special beyond its beauty and beyond its use as a source metal for trinkets and coins. Because of its natural tendency to transport energy from one source to another source, from one place to another place, from one being to another being, and from one soul to another soul, gold would be coveted by many beings from all sorts of civilizations in the universe, whether native to Grandmother Earth or not.

The characteristics and value of gold undoubtedly attracted visitors from other stars and other worlds who were also in search of such a rare element. This coveted value is why gold is capable of taking the minds of ordinary humans and other beings and turning those minds themselves, into their own malleable shapes and forms, and selfish desire. Gold is natural to Grandmother Earth, but it could become unnatural. It could be corrupting to beings or forces who would only wish to worship it and to use it to serve the means and ends, to steal, to cheat, to deceive, to murder, to corrupt, to defraud, and even to exterminate all of those who possessed or controlled the gold. The drive to obtain gold will have such evil and disastrously inhumane effects on those beings who, in seeking it at all costs, allow its mere possession, to control their souls.

The Lakota would know about the metals of Grandmother Earth for a very long time; the iron, the copper, and of course, the gold metal. Gold is found naturally, in the streams and on the banks in certain areas of the Black Hills. This metal, and the pursuit of it, will become one of the triggers for the biggest dispute between the Lakota nations and the white people.

There are two ways of looking at this resource. The Lakota would view gold as a natural part of the earth. The gold emits an energy or frequency. It resembles the veins in a body. The intersection of mind, body, and spirit can occur when one is viewing the gold, when one is touching the gold, and certainly while one is taking the gold. The white man and his government would view the gold through eyes of greed. Acquisition of this resource would be imperative for future warring across this continent. The accumulation of wealth that will occur once the gold is mined, extracted, and altered, will come to be the motivation to claim our sacred land.

That is the keyword: *altered*. When the gold is altered, it becomes more than just a piece of a stone or a replica of something in nature. It is now capable of paying bills, paying politicians, paying for influence over the government to keep the indigenous people from truly possessing and managing their own lands. For many hundreds of years, the white man has used altered gold and other precious metals to devastate people. Gold brings wealth to the elite as a result of an inequality and the presence of the evil money. The countries that these new people and cultures come from have been known to be under this type of ruling hierarchy and this type of elitist wealth for generations. Generationally, they have been accustomed to war and the destruction of resources and families. Their spirit has been deadened. They think only from a selfish point of view. They come to our lands and our territories with the expectation of accumulating wealth to satisfy their economic needs. They are the reason for the formation of the government, which would allow them to do what they would do to the indigenous tribal nations. It appears that most of them would not know any better. It is already within many of their bloodlines. Therefore it would be difficult for them to see things differently.

In the beginning, there was Grandmother Earth. The gold is a part of her total existence. It is a part of the natural way she allows us to live and coexist with every other being. The gold itself is a conductor of energy, spiritual energy. The Lakota left it alone for the most part because we did not want to alter the things that were gifted to us by Grandmother Earth. So for the Europeans to come and think they would just take it for their own profit, would pose a direct conflict, without belief in the natural presence on this land. This land has always been preserved and protected with the idea of looking after the sanctity of Grandmother Earth first, so that all of her beings and children would have enough to share and to survive with.

The obsession to find gold, to obtain it, and to own it is really an obsession borne of the disease of greed and domination. Ultimately, the disease would lead to the attempted removal and genocide of the Lakota and the theft of their He Sapa, in the coming years (1874, 1875, and 1876).

And yet, as previously mentioned, gold is a natural part of Grandmother Earth. It comes from within her, her earth, her ground. It comes from within her soil, her dirt. One might wonder why this is so, but the answer is simply that because gold is as natural to Grandmother

Earth as is her own dirt, the gold, like the dirt, is a necessary part of the Circle of life. Unci Maka has reasons, purposes, and uses for all things. All of her natural elements are good when used in the proper way. The key is in how human beings use those elements, whether with a good intention or a bad intention. We were all born of Grandmother Earth after our origins as a people. We come from her earth, we come from her inner self, from her elements, from her dirt.

Like gold, dirt has many kinds of special things within itself. Dogs dig in the ground and roll in the dirt, smear it all over. Children dig in the dirt to play. They rub it on their hands and faces, and they bury their fingers and fingernails into it, smearing it all over. This is how they first learn to truly feel the Earth, to know it, to touch it, to smell it, to wallow in it. And not, to fear it.

The Grandmother provides nutrients, and particles of all the beings that have existed throughout time, within her dirt. It serves as strong medicine to bring immunity against disease and skin disorders. In the earth is where the seed is planted and where Grandmother nurtures and caresses the seed, giving it the nourishment to grow. The nourishment allows the seed to become a sprout, then a stalk, and then a plant. That plant, in turn, becomes food or medicine.

In effect, Grandmother's dirt is a form of natural protection afforded to anyone for free. There is no cost or price. One need only to dig in and feel it. Dirt was never intended to be "dirty." Dirt is a pure part of the Earth. It is only made dirty by the corruption of other things, or of other beings, like Man.

It seems then that the grand meaning of having both dirt and gold together, mixing with one another in Grandmother Earth, is that there is a good reason and purpose for both to exist. It is only when the actions of the human beings seek to corrupt or disturb the natural elements in an unnatural way, that the good reasons and purposes for all things set forth by Creator on Grandmother Earth, are violated.

Saved By Bear's father, whenever he would be departing on a hunting trip or, more infrequently, going out to clash with an enemy on the trail, would say to his wife and children, "Keep the fire burning."

Fights the Bear was a sincere, quiet man, not very talkative to many at all, unless he was in the mood to tell and hear good stories around the campfire. Once settled in and started, he could sit and listen, and tell and animate all kinds of stories around the campfire. It seemed as if the setting itself, beside the warm, flickering, crackling flames, with the smell of the wood and sprinkled cedar filling the tipi, and with the breeze blowing on a clear night, ignited his own inner fire, which he could not help but share with others.

The fire seemed to warm, spark, and then engulf Saved By Bear's father's inner self. As if the campfire's flames reached out like a willowy hand and touched a lighted finger to the strong heart in his chest. As if the fire was fluidly transferring its burning flame and energy to him and igniting his own fire. It seemed that the flames sought to ignite the thoughts and imagination of Fights the Bear, springing into the part of him that was the best storyteller, which all of the tiospaye had seen from time to time. Everyone who knew Fights the Bear knew of these moments, and could sense, predict, and then witness his metamorphosis from solemn father and warrior to freewheeling and easy-talking storyteller. Available for anybody within earshot who is ready to be entertained. As long as the fire in the circle continued to burn, and as long as his own inner fire flickered with that otherwise dormant energy that could not be contained. They could all see it happening to him, the change. His posture would become more relaxed, his face would become more easy, his voice would become more soothing and yet excitable, and his eyes would become brighter and more animated, even his eyebrows. The change in him was the result of allowing himself to become like a hidden flower exposed to the early morning sun.

It was a sight to behold. And those who knew him, and saw the moment approaching and then appearing, could only smile, as they mentally mounted up for a long, joyful, and many times educational journey on a steed of unbridled quest and energy. This was Saved By Bear's father at his relaxed best. These moments of his life were both enduring and special to those who knew and loved him.

It was as if that old fire was his long beheld old friend that would show up to sit beside him, wherever he was, to ease the trials and issues of the day. Easing him into the moments of life that could and should be shared with others for the benefit and fulfillment of all.

As long as the fire was fed and burning, the stories continued, until weariness sought to slowly close the eyes of the audience and even of the storyteller. Time passed quickly this way. The wood and rocks burned with darker shades of yellow, orange, and red as the old fire seemed to want to hang on as long as possible so as not to miss any of what was going on around its flames and embers.

It was only natural that Fights the Bear came to acknowledge these moments, these feelings, as a means to communicate with his family and friends, so that when they were apart, they would think of the time when they would all meet again and be together, and share each other's stories, their love, and their lives.

"Keep the fire burning." No other words could describe the bond felt by the family at those times. It was part of being human. Saved By Bear would always think back on those moments, remembering his father saying, "Keep the fire burning." It was a good thing, reminding him of family, of life, and of love. Upon remembering, he would smile. It was a ritual that he would carry forth into the next generation, saying those words to his own children just as his father before him had said the words to him. It was a good thing, and seemed to leave open a door of promise, presaging a future meeting with those whom he loved.

A wise human being once told Saved By Bear that a burning campfire loses none of its strength or brightness when its flame is used to light another campfire. That means, he said, that that wise human being recognized that we can all give of ourselves, that which we know and possess, without having to fear that the passing of that knowledge will leave us empty or diminished in any way. We are not lessened in any way by giving a part of ourselves to help another human being or to make someone else's light brighter.

This is a part of the Circle.... a very wise human being has said that. One's whose own campfire was once lit by the bright campfire of another. Take that to heart, and remember. Never look down on those who give to others, and never look down on yourself for doing so either.

The Circle of life suggests, and Wakan Tanka knows, that we live in a good way and we travel the true trail, when we do not lose sight of these things. We must always see where we are going, but we must never forget, the trail we have walked, or those who walked with us along the way.

No human being ever truly stands alone at any time. It may seem from time to time that our body is alone, but it is at these times that the spirits, the thoughts, and the love of the others, alive or passed, are the hand on our shoulder, the strong grip on our arm, the gentle yet firm push at our back. To keep us going, to help us overcome the obstacles in our path. To light the way with hope and understanding. To show us that, no matter what, we are loved and we ourselves, love.

This is a gift from Creator. To keep the fire burning.

Another instance when the young Lakota Saved By Bear became more fully alerted to his inner strength and spirit in relation to communicating with the spiritual realm, occurred when he and Swift Bear were fishing in the He Sapa along Deer Creek near the great meadow the people called Pe Sla.

The families had come through in the springtime on their way to the Shiny Mountains in the west, the Bighorns. The leaders decided it would be a good idea to set up camp at the old site along the base of the gleaming cliff rim to the north of the highest crest in the sacred high meadowland. It was a holy magnificent place within the sacred He Sapa to come and give offerings to Wakan Tanka, to pray, and to plan the trips. But it is truly a blessing to come here on a clear starry night when a Lakota could stand or lie on the ground and look up and see the brilliantly magnificent portrait of the night sky with the trillions and trillions of stars in the heavens.

Pe Sla was a magical place in that it was a very high open meadowland with soft high grasses, very few trees (if any), and an opening among the mountains and cliffs of the He Sapa. The great opening of the high meadow allowed one to see, with little or no obstruction, the entire beauty of the open sky, and at night, the majesty of the celestial brilliance of all other worlds out there with the numerous constellations and symbols, including the one of the origin of the people, the Seven Sisters of the Pleaides system, the water worlds. One could also clearly see the Big Dipper, where the Trail of Spirits begins, the Trail of Spirits being the great Milky Way; the hand cluster of stars off of the Hunter; the Dog Star, signifying the humans' closest friend and companion; and the abundance of falling stars, the gleaming showers of light moving across the sky.

The camp area was very old. It had been used by the Lakota for many generations. The camp was always set up at the base of the huge cliff drop-off where the crisply running cool, clear water of Deer Creek ran just at the base, in front of the rocky walls. The camp circles were strategically set according to plan, hidden away from distant onlookers, should someone trespass and come upon the area. All that strangers may only see was a clear, open, gradually sloping dome of high prairie, and nothing else, except for two or three lone birch trees spaced out accordingly. A stranger, not knowing of the camp, may entirely miss seeing the camp nestled snugly into the base of the hidden cliff, which more or less cradled the low-lying campsite circle areas nearest to it. The high rocky walls also protected the camp from the direct wind or the periodic driving rain, hail, or snow that world blast from the west or north. It truly was a piece of paradise tucked away in the high country of He Sapa.

Many night ceremonies were held at this site because it offered an unobstructed view of the constellations. There the people could pray to and communicate with the spirits from the Milky Way and beyond. And sometimes when Hanwi, the Moon, presented herself, and added a lighted show of deep blue and purple hues that outlined the landscape, one could walk about as if it were nearly daylight. And of course, the full or almost full moon provided the impetus for the other peoples of He Sapa—the frogs, the nighthawks, the owls, the coyotes, and the crickets, but mostly the old wolves and their packs—to gather close and break into song. The sight of the moon struck a chord in their spirits and drove them to lift their own voices into the nighttime air, to be carried afar to distant relatives and acquaintances, either across the plains and hilltops, or across the universe or the wonderful threshold of the spirit world. It was a gift to hear and witness these things, and to know that everyone is all connected to each other. Everyone has a beginning and an end. Everyone has a mother and a father, at least at the beginning. Everyone has someone to care for or to care for them. Everyone feels a need not to be alone. Everyone has a reason to exist, to be heard, and to be recognized. It was Creator's plan. It was Creator's will.

Saved By Bear, Swift Bear, and their families had traveled to this wonderful place and had set up camp. In the morning after the first night, which had been full of nocturnal activity, sights, and sound, the two Lakota braves sought out a place to catch fish. Having gotten up early, they grabbed their hooks and lines and a short spear, and headed for the gathering ponds Fights the Bear had mentioned to them on earlier trips. It was an area on the Deer Creek, just to the east of the camp circles where the quick-running waters slowed at a series of bends. It was these bends in the creek that created areas of slight pooling, and it was in these pooling areas that, the people knew, the trout, bass, and perch collected in groups to swim. It was these areas where the boys were most likely to catch a fish or two or three.

So the boys walked to the pools, their moccasins hardly getting wet as most of the hike did not require any wading or crossing of the creek. Once they arrived, Swift Bear, being most eager, cast his hooked line into the nearest pool. Saved By Bear chose to just wait. He sat by his friend and looked over Swift Bear's shoulder at his progress in hooking a fish.

Saved By Bear put his right hand on his best friend's shoulder and, unbeknown to Swift Bear, smiled a little smile to himself.

Swift Bear was having trouble getting any fish to latch onto his bone hook, so he pulled it up onto the ground with the buffalo sinew fishing line he had wrapped around his right wrist. *This is how it is supposed to work,* he thought, remembering the hundreds of times he had caught fish by the Owl River, the Cheyenne River, the White River, and the old familiar Cherry Creek. He knew that these mountain fish were quicker, probably from having to dart and jump to avoid rocks in the fast-streaming waters, so he thought it would just take patience. Saved By Bear still stood by, watching his friend, exhibiting his own patience, and letting himself smile off and on.

It was not an amused, but an anxious smile that the young boy showed. He was waiting for the right moment to show his friend something that he had discovered after the time he first had his conversations with the birds and the animals, which had been not too long ago.

Saved By Bear waited patiently until his friend's patience ran out. Swift Bear was now growing tense and frustrated because no fish had grabbed his line. He did not feel like wasting his time just dangling his fishing line in the water, pulling it in, and recasting it, with nothing to show for it. Shaking his head, with his braids swinging around to bang against his shoulders, he pulled his line free of the water just as a big trout broke the surface not more than four feet from where he had had his line and hook. All Swift Bear could do was to turn and look at his friend with a bewildered look. Then he hung his head and dropped his line.

Feeling sorry for his friend at that moment and thinking that now was as good a time as any to try to brighten Swift Bear's mood, Saved By Bear calmly reached for the fishing line laying in the thick green grass on the bank. As he picked it up, he noticed it was still wet and a little slippery from a fine coating of green creek moss that had gathered along its length when Swift Bear was trying his darnedest to catch a fish. Saved By Bear stretched the line out between his arms and held it wide, keeping it taut like that for a second or two. Then he looked at his friend, smiled, and threw the line to the side. It landed on top of a low-lying flat rock along the creek's edge.

Swift Bear looked at him quizzically and then frowned, sensing he was being made fun of. It was then that Saved By Bear put his right index finger up to his own lips as if to signify quiet. He reached over and put his left index finger on his friend's lips in the same manner. Swift Bear quickly swatted it aside and merely stared at him. It was at this point that Saved By Bear pointed to the pool where the fishing activities had just occurred. His hands now at his sides, he stepped as close to the edge of the grassy bank as he could, his light-colored worn moccasins hanging over the edge of the water slightly. For a moment, Swift Bear thought he was going to dive in.

But what Saved By Bear did instead was to lean over the pool area, which was four to five feet deep, take his right hand with the palm down, hold it parallel to the surface of the water, and slowly move it clockwise, left to right, in a series of four circles.

Wondering what was going on, Swift Bear could not help but look at the water below his friend's hand. There, he noticed a slight movement, then a bubble, then a series of bubbles, and then more and more bubbles. After several seconds, the shiny dorsal fins of the trout and the perch broke the surface, and the fish started swimming in the same clockwise circles as the movement of Saved By Bear's hand.

Swift Bear caught his breath and held it. Not knowing what was happening or how, he remained anchored to his spot on the grassy bank as if there were stones in the soles of his moccasins. What he saw next would forever remain in his memory, coming to mind when he thought about the times with his friend.

Seeing the fish come to the surface, Saved By Bear turned his wrist so his right palm faced upward. Now he curled his fingers up and in, as if taking hold of something invisible. He did this four times. The fish kept swimming in circles. Gradually, they lined up in single file, one after the other. Then Saved By Bear brought his fingers inward, and moved his right arm toward his body, making the motion one makes when waving someone closer. And the fish followed his lead. One by one, the trout and the perch swam forward.

Each fish, approaching Saved By Bear's hand in turn, brought its head and face out of the water and stayed still as Saved By Bear reached down with a single finger and touched it on the nose. After each contact occurred between the fish and boy, the fish sunk under the surface and swam away in the opposite direction. One by one all of the fish took their turn. When the last one, a trout, reached out to be touched, Saved By Bear instead spoke to him: "It is okay. Climb into my hand. I want to show my friend how beautiful you are and how you move your tail to swim and to jump so fast and far. Come up here with us. It is okay."

Saved By Bear cupped his hand. The trout gave a slight jump, and was cradled in the young Lakota's hand, who then gently lifted the trout up and away from the water. Saved By Bear turned and held the fish in both hands, stretching them forward to show his friend what the fish wished for them to see. Swift Bear stared with open mouth and wide eyes, as the fish turned and wiggled its wet tail fin for both to see.

It was then that Saved By Bear said, "We know you need to go back to your family now. Thank you for showing us and for being so kind. We are thankful to your people for helping us survive. We mean your people no harm and will only ever take from you and your people when we need to, and never more than necessary. You are a friend to us and a gift in our eyes, from Creator. So we will let you go, and wait for another to come up to latch onto our lines when we must. We say thank you to you and your people for providing yourselves to us from time to time. We know that we all need the clean, fresh water to live, so we will always and forever protect the water and, with it, your ability to survive. You can and must always depend upon us to do that for you. Thank you, my friend. It is time for you to go."

And with that said, the young Lakota heyoka turned and stooped down, lowering the kind fish back into the water, its home. He watched as the trout gently turned, wiggled its tail, and then swam away toward the small quick falls downstream.

It was at this moment that the other boy knew. He knew what he had previously suspected but had not actually witnessed. His greatest friend was, in fact, a true heyoka. He felt proud of his friend, and that his friend loved him enough to show him in a manner consistent with the oldest of the old ways. As the two boys looked at each other and said nothing verbally, they knew that their lives were changing in ways unimagined, in ways within their control, and in ways beyond their control.

Swift Bear bent down, picked up his line, and looked as his friend. He smiled. "Maybe we should just eat some of Grandma's wasna tonight instead." Both smiled and laughed at the same time.

"Wanna race back?" asked Saved By Bear. No sooner had he gotten the words out than Swift Bear started running his swiftest down the trail back to camp, trying to outrun his friend.

It would be several months later, after Saved by Bear had described his ability to emote his life-force energy to other beings, that Swift Bear would realize that he himself had that same heyoka energy and spirit.

He would discover this on one of the family trips made by the tiospaye into the He Sapa in the middle of the fall season, when many animals are preparing for winter. All throughout the journey, Swift Bear had noticed his aunt Jumping Bear appearing to walk and ride slowly and painfully, as if she were suffering from some kind of injury or ailment. Jumping Bear was having a hard time even drinking water, and she refused to eat anything at all when the families gathered by the campfire for a meal. Swift Bear, becoming concerned, asked his mother what was wrong with her sister. His mother, Ghost Horse, told him that she did not know what the problem was, but she did notice that something was affecting Jumping Bear a day or so before the journey began, which was two weeks prior. Jumping Bear had not taken the time to consult with one of the medicine people back at the lodges near the Owl River before their departure, so she was continuing to suffer from whatever it was that had made her sick. Now, after many days, hardly able to walk, she was staying in the lodge and sleeping most of the time.

Swift Bear went to speak to her one morning, as he had some questions. He found out that Jumping Bear had come across a bag of flour and a blanket that an Indian agent had given to the family back at Fort Bennett by the Big Muddy River to the east of the Owl River encampments. She had recently used the blanket back at home before leaving on this trip, and had prepared a meal from some of the flour before she left. She had been the only one to eat the bread prepared from the flour, because the rest of the family had been gone to visit relatives in a neighboring camp. It tasted bad, she remembered, so she threw the rest of the bread into the fire and ate no more of it.

Also, she noticed that ever since she had been using the agency blanket, a red rash had appeared on her arms and legs, and it was itching her most times. She did not particularly like the looks and feel of the blanket, so she thought of tossing it onto the fire as well. Just before she did so, she looked closely at the seams of the blanket and saw some tiny insects moving in and out of the stitching. She had not seen them before. The view of the bugs made her itch more, so she shook the bugs out over the ground, then threw the blanket on the fire.

It was during the next day and into the night that she started feeling weak and queasy. She did not give it much thought, knowing that the trip to the He Sapa was coming the next day. She figured it would pass. It had not. Now it had been with her for ten days.

Swift Bear thanked his aunt for speaking with him and then left her so she could sleep. The medicine woman who was to travel with the tiospaye had been delayed at the home camp and had not yet arrived. Swift Bear thought about what to do. He remembered that his grandfather had told him that when he needed to think clearly about a problem, he should go to a high point and pray. So he got on his horse Spotted Smoke and rode. After a while he spotted a craggy rock ledge hanging over the creek's canyon, about 150 feet beyond the canyon walls.

He and Spotted Smoke rode and eventually came to the rocky high summit. It did in fact have an overhead view of the camp. Swift Bear could see the people below in the distance.

It was here that Swift Bear tied the rope for Spotted Smoke to the nearest pine. Then, walking to the very western edge of the overlook, he put his hands up and out, toward the camp and Jumping Bear's lodge, and prayed. As he was praying, he heard a noise to his left in the trees, a shuffling sound of pine needles and loose earth, being made by hooves. It was not Spotted Smoke. Spotted Smoke remained behind him and to the right.

When he looked closer, Swift Bear saw him: a strong buck, a member of the black-tailed deer people. Proud and beautiful, the buck had a large set of antlers on his head and an air of confidence and pride in the way he stood at the edge of the lower cliff to the left of the rock edge Swift Bear stood upon. A memory floated into Swift Bear's mind. It was of his hunka brother Saved By Bear saying something to him. It was coming through as if Saved By Bear were standing right beside him and speaking to him—except Saved By Bear was back at home by the Owl River helping his own family right now.

"You know you can do it. You know that you have the gift. You know that it is there inside you too. Just reach real deep within yourself, and speak to your spirit. Ask your spirit to come out and to help you show yourself to the deer being across the way. You know you can do it. Just try."

With the memory and the encouragement of the two braves' spirits, Swift Bear looked directly into the deep brown eyes of the black-tailed buck. Without opening his mouth, his spirit spoke to the deer.

"*Hau,* brother. Thank you for coming to see us. I wish you and your family well." Then it happened. The proud buck looked back at him, and Swift Bear heard him speak.

"Thank you, my Lakota brother. I see your family down below, and I heard your spirit speaking and praying. You have a sick aunt. I felt it. We know sometimes what ails the humans. We know it often comes from poisonous goods delivered by the white humans at the forts."

"Yes, you are right. What can we do? Can you help us?"

"Yes, we can help. I only ask that you and your family give my family safe passage this time in the hunt. That is all I ask."

"It is agreed. I will speak for us all. Thank you. What can I do?"

"Follow me down by the creek. I know of some sacred roots that would be the best thing to help her to release the poison from her body and spirit. The bad spirits sometimes crawl into the shells of those tiny people. They do not even know it themselves, but that is what happens."

"I will follow you. Lead the way."

With that, the young Lakota brave untied Spotted Smoke, hopped on his back, and watched as the big buck calmly walked and then trotted, down toward the sloping coulee leading to the creek. The buck led them to a lush clearing hidden behind thick bushes of buffalo berries and dogwood. It was here that the big buck stopped. He sniffed the air and sniffed the ground, and then began digging with his front hoof at the base of a cactus-like growth. The deer dug deep with his sharp hooves. When he was done, he looked up and said, "There. It is a very old medicine that we have used from the beginning of all time. Please take it to your aunt. Have her put it in her mouth and suck on it for at least two days. Ask her to pray to Creator, and to pray for the protection of us all. I only ask that you protect these medicine plants when you see them, and respect them as much as you would us."

"Thank you, brother. I will honor your wishes. I give my word, and honor to respect what you have done for me, my aunt, and our people."

Then the big buck nodded. Just as he was turning to walk away, he emoted to his friend: "Toksa ake."

"Toksa ake, my brother," said Swift Bear, as he and Spotted Smoke watched the magnificent buck jump nearly seven feet off the ground and over the buffalo berry bushes. Their last vision of him was his long black tail waving in the air as he gained ground on the other side.

Three days later, Jumping Bear came out of her lodge and walked up to her nephew while he sat by the fire. She was walking straight and strong. Her color was back. She reached out and placed her hand on Swift Bear's shoulder. Then she touched his forehead. "Thank you. My dreams told me what you did for me. I want you to know that if Creator sees fit to bless me with a child, I already know the name I shall give to her or him."

"What is that, Auntie?"

"Black-Tailed Deer." Both smiling, they turned to gaze into the beautiful dark pines in the thick forest of the He Sapa.

Entering into the Sacred Heart

The group of Mnincoju and their warriors rode all day in the early autumn season, when the time for the falling leaves had not yet come. They were out scouting for the herds and trying to determine a way along the northeastern edge of He Sapa, looking for areas for winter camps along the fast-running creek in the canyons that the Lakota referred to as Fast-Running Creek or Rapid Creek—the Mninluzanhan. The night before, they had camped along the Cheyenne River at the point where the river valley contained hundreds and hundreds of ash and willow trees along the banks of its numerous bends. It was here that many times, very good pieces of wood were found for the people to use for their bows, arrows, handles, inipi lodge poles, and numerous other tools and utensils. Before harvesting the tree parts and branches, the ones doing so, of course, gave an offering of sage and wasna to the spirits, giving thanks to the tree people for providing such gifts to the people. A great many of these gifts were gathered up, bundled, tied, and taken on one of the larger travoises.

This campsite by the Cheyenne River was quite convenient in that it was in a low protected area along the banks of good river land, with abundant water for the purposes of washing things and filling the water bladders. Since the firewood was extraordinarily abundant, there was always a huge, welcome campfire built here, big enough for the whole tiospaye to gather around and tell and listen to the wonderful stories about the past and the ancestors. It was also a well-known and well-used campsite for the Mnincoju because it was the last stop-off on their journey from the home camps, before the land started lifting toward the great sacred He Sapa range in the west.

As one climbs out of the Cheyenne River valley and ascends to the high rolling hills that are lined with the lush growth of tall grasses, and sees the sagebrush-covered tips and ravines of the high ridges and bluffs on the western ridge of the river valley, the traveler gets their first glimpse of the Black Mountains along the western horizon.

Saved By Bear always experienced a sense of pride, honor, and joy, and a realization of beholding beauty, when he first gets a glimpse of the sacred mountains to the west. On a clear day, a being could see a very long distance to the west. And when you see the horizon and follow the line of the mountainous terrain, it is truly a wonderful scene, a scene that becomes permanently etched in one's mind, heart, and spirit, as it is one of sheer beauty and magnificence. It is especially meaningful and positive, if the one viewing the scene of the sacred mountains on the horizon has already set their feet upon the sacred sites one sees in the distance. It brings a sense of belonging, of positive magical energy, knowing that one is coming home to the land of the beginning, the land of the ancestors, and the heart of the Grandmother. It never ceases to make a person smile, like Saved By Bear was now smiling, because this was the sacred heart. This was his birthplace.

He panned the horizon, eagerly picking out and placing in his mind's eye each peak, each dip, each range. The tallest one to the south side of the highest range was the magnificent Owl's Nest, the place of wisdom and knowledge. To the left of the Owl's Nest was a high, ruggedly jagged series of sharp stone columns that looked like a set of huge bear teeth from the distance. These were the great gray stone columns of the Old Stone Warriors. The Old Stone Warriors stood tall, straight, and proud in clusters of grand spires and columns, one next to the other, shoulder to shoulder, back to back, supporting and giving strength to each other. These were the extremely tall, slender, looming gray granite stone spires that stood guard over the rest of the sacred mountains. It was the duty of the Old Stone Warriors, their sacred honor given to them by the Creator, to stand guard over and protect the sacred He Sapa for all time. They were ancient warriors whose spirits were committed to serve forever as protectors of the sacred mountains. They were always there, always dependable, always trusted.

There had been many occasions where the young Saved By Bear had climbed up to be in their presence. He visited them by walking to their great stone bases very high up in the peaks just to the south of the Owl's Nest. Each time he went there and visited the Old Stone Warriors, he felt sacred, safe, and protected. And he always prayed to the four directions, and to the stone warriors, to whom he gave offerings of fruit and bread. Always, then, he would stand with his chest pressed to the great gray stone wall at the base of one of the tallest and highest, spread out both of his arms, turn his face, and press his whole body against the stone.

In those moments it was like he was covering himself with a stone cloak of protection and love, an honorable blanket of pride and serenity made available by the Old Stone Warriors themselves.

So it was these types of good, familiar thoughts and memories that flooded into Saved By Bear's mind and heart, as well as his spirit, as he viewed the sacred mountains from a distance. Soon the people would arrive there at the northeastern range of the He Sapa and venture into and inside of Grandmother's abundance.

When the tiospaye did arrive at the gap entrance along the Mninluzanhan, the area was awash with rejuvenation. It was an energetic bath of spiritual awakening, an interjection of growth and understanding of life.

The people had decided this time to come into the He Sapa along the Rapid Creek rather than to come in through the passageway to the north by Mato Paha and the northeast canyon or to enter through the southeastern passageway of the great Buffalo Run in the rim of mountains just inside the red circle making up the Great Racetrack of the He Sapa.

This time they approached through the passageway along the fast and beautiful rapid running creek that flowed from the large crystal-clear lakes in the high regions to the west, about one day's travel in that direction. This entryway was a popular one for all the bands of Lakota, including the Hunkpapa, the Sicangu, the Oglala, the Yanktonai and others. It seemed to be the way that offered the most ease, as the traveling group did not have to encounter much in the way of tough terrain in order to get to some of the more well-used trails at the center of He Sapa. The foothills at the beginning of the gateway to He Sapa along Rapid Creek were a popular area to camp. It was a low-lying, accessible, wide-open area good for camping and communing—a good place to trade, and to prepare the traveling groups for the rest of the journey into the heart of the He Sapa. The clean, clear, fast waters were abundant with brown trout, pike, and perch, along with many beavers, turtles, raccoons, otters, and mink, and waterbirds of every kind, including ducks. The ducks, which appeared to love the creek and its wonderful nesting coves, would follow the boys when they saw them coming to the water's edge. There were also many wanbli. There were natural springs along the creek plain which sprung out fresh, pure water from the rocks. The stories of the Mnincoju tiospaye was that the young warrior Spirit Horse had been born along the banks of this Rapid Creek about nine years before Saved By Bear's own birth.

The stop-off at the base of the most northeasterly range of the foothills provided the passageway along the Rapid Creek. If one followed the creek into the heart of He Sapa, one would encounter a beautiful underlying naturally carved passageway all along the creek. This had been carved out by the millions of years of crashing water, which rushed through the beautiful stony tree-lined canyons over that entire period of time. The fast-running waters had carved out a picturesque canyon passageway with extremely high cliffs, ravines, bluffs, and waterfalls with rushing patches of rocky water rapids that made the water look white. The fast-running creek originated in the high mountain lake to the west.

The people said that if one dropped a light buffalo horn shell into the creek up there at the high lake, and watched and waited for it to float along the fast creek through the deep and twisting canyons toward the open passageway to the northeast entry of the popular encampment area at the base of the foothills on the east end, it would emerge near the entryway downstream. The water's strength and resilience would thereby be revealed. Since the buffalo horn shell is merely made up of hardened matted buffalo hair, it is very light. The buffalo horn shell would travel a complete moon cycle—twenty-eight days—before coming out at the passageway in the gap between the entryway foothills. This story always amazed Saved By Bear. He often wondered how the theory could be tested, but he also trusted that many of the people, especially many of the elders who had seen many things in their lives, knew a great deal about Grandmother Earth. What they said was reliable and dependable. They were trustworthy in what they said because they had the knowledge, the experience, and the life to know such things. They knew how things worked, and cared how things worked. Especially how Grandmother Earth's world worked. So Saved By Bear accepted these things as helpful knowledge and meaningful details.

After the tiospaye members had arrived at the lowland encampment area at the entryway between the opening of the foothills along the

Rapid Creek valley, they looked for a secure campsite area where they could spend the evening. Finding one, they began to set up camp. This gave Saved By Bear and Swift Bear, the constant companions on these types of ventures, an opportunity to go off on their own to explore and view the surroundings.

The two young Lakota mounted their horses, Saved By Bear on his Wildfire, and Swift Bear on his Spotted Smoke, and rode off toward the nearest foothill bluff to the south. The people had often used these fringe-side foothills to climb and scout the area in order to view where they were and where they wanted to go, and to discover if there were any approaching riders, travelers, bands, or trespassers. It was also a good place to get a wonderful view of the activity of the people and their goings-on in the lowland camping areas below, along the banks of the fast bending creek.

Saved By Bear and Swift Bear rode to the top of the nearest hill and then had their horses trot south along the highest backbone ridge, always keeping their eyes to the west. They rode along this high ridge until they reached one of the highest points offering a wonderful view to the west of the Rapid Creek valley as the creek twisted and turned to the west among the great rocky, craggy cliffs and bluffs that lined the canyon. They had come to a high area known to them as Ten Ant Hill, which was a common stop-off for them for just this reason, because it had such a magnificent far-reaching view up the canyon.

As they looked up the canyon, they remarked to each other of its strength and beauty, saying that the Creator had been very artistic when Creator had carved this one out. They both had been told that intermittently over a span of millions of years, the canyons along and from the Rapid Creek experienced times when the rains from the Thunder Beings came down so hard and so fast for so long that the volume of water up in the high lakes got to be too much. So that now and then over that long period of time, there would be a great rushing flood of a wall of water cascading and crashing through the Rapid Creek valley and coming to spill out into the lowland at the entryway to the east between the very foothills that these Lakota and their horses stood upon. It was said by the Lakota elders that these types of floods were extremely powerful and would cause extremely heavy, very large pieces of stone to crack off the walls of the canyons. These boulders would then roll and spin in the creek passageway, moving in the direction the floodwaters took them. The evidence of this type of natural power could be seen when one rode or walked through the valley and the canyon and beheld the huge boulders placed here and there along the creek by the great hand of the Creator. The elders had said that these types of great rushing flash floods occurred usually once or twice every five hundred years. Many, many generations would pass between those events. To Saved By Bear and Swift Bear, this was another example of why the people needed to understand and respect the strength and power of the water. Water was a gift and gave life. But water also needed to be respected in every way, and be allowed to live its own life naturally, the way Creator intended it to do. "The water always remembers," Saved By Bear's grandfather Iron White Man often reminded him.

While looking up the canyon to the west from the top of Ten Ant Hill, the two young Lakota pointed out the great distant cliff that could be seen jutting out, high and provocative, in the midst of the open horizon beyond it to the west. The distant cliff was about six or seven miles from the hill they stood upon. They recognized it as the area frequented by the flying buzzards, an area where the buzzard people commonly gathered and nested. Since it was so high, and since it overlooked the Rapid Creek valley on the north side of the canyon's edge, it was easy to see why the buzzards found it convenient to roost there.

The buzzard people have always been an important part of Grandmother Earth's Circle of life. They have bald heads with sharp jagged beaks and sharp talons. When they fly, they somewhat resemble wanbli, but the people knew how to differentiate between the two in flight. The buzzard's head is kept closer to its body when in flight, whereas the wanbli's head sticks out more. Also, the wanbli's wings are held straight out while gliding. In any event, it is the buzzard people who serve as the great disposer of dead tissue in the Circle of life.

The buzzards feast upon the decomposing remains of beings that die in whatever way, by natural means, by accident, by being killed or wounded when hunting, or by way of war or other violence. If not for the buzzard people, then many of these remains would lay on the

Earth undisturbed, possibly causing disease or contamination. When the buzzard people seek to locate a carcass to feast upon, they do so in groups. One flies and locates the remains, sending a signal to the others, which come and fly in a circle above the target. Seeing a group of buzzards circling an area, people know that there may be such a target down below. This is the way the buzzard people work, their way of survival. Their contribution to the Circle of life does involve death, eating the remains after a being passes. The buzzards have a bodily system that easily and naturally digests the contaminants in the decaying flesh. In essence, they clean these things so that the rest of the beings are not exposed to disease-causing bacteria. The buzzards have been unfairly characterized by those who misunderstood who they are. They have their role in the Circle of life, too.

Saved By Bear and Swift Bear viewed the majesty and beauty of their surroundings, their home, their sacred He Sapa. They looked at each other and nodded. As they had grown accustomed to doing, they got off the backs of their horse friends and walked to the westernmost edge of the cliff they stood upon. With the buzzard people circling in the air above the edge of the distant cliff in the valley of the Rapid Creek canyon as a backdrop, they raised their hands. Starting with the west, they prayed to each direction. They prayed to Creator, Wakan Tanka, and Wakinyan. They thanked Creator for allowing them to live in such a beautiful place and to coexist with such wonderful, generous beings. They also asked Creator to preserve this sacred place, these sacred mountains, He Sapa, for all time, forever.

When they finished, they got upon their horses and, nudging them with their knees, turned and started a slow gallop to the north along the high ridge, toward the sight, sound, and smell of the campfires down below, where they would rejoin their loving families. As they rode, they both believed in their hearts and spirits that Creator had heard them. They also believed that it was a part of their role in life to do everything they could do to protect and preserve this sacred place.

7

BROKEN HOOP

ON TURTLE ISLAND, THE EXISTENCE of all kinds of peoples, the two-legged, the four-legged, the winged, those who lived in water, were all dependent upon the existence of the other. This was part of the natural balance of the environment and in the world, something that had been understood for millions of years by all the existing peoples. However, the new people who had arrived on the shores of Turtle Island did not understand this. Many of the new people saw all of the various species and types of peoples as just something to kill, remove, or take advantage of. The new humans, the Europeans, thought this way, removing from their equation the territories, the lands, and the very existence of these types of people, the two-legged, the four-legged, et al. Any time such an attitude is adopted on Grandmother Earth, an imbalance is created.

When we speak of the spirit existing in all things, saying that it encompasses all things—the air, the water, the stone, and all the species of people—we are saying that this spirit is something that will continue to exist and is connected throughout all of Grandmother Earth and her children. Humans who don't understand this, separate themselves, remove themselves from the natural equation of things. They create a disconnect. They create a loss of that energy path. And when this occurs, the removal of some of the much-needed parts of the natural balance, there are consequences according to Grandmother Earth. Destruction of one species will affect the survival of an ecosystem, and a disturbed or destroyed ecosystem creates a chain reaction of other events and consequences.

When the Lakota people saw themselves as the *Protectors* of Grandmother Earth, they also saw that they were the *Protectors* of all things. They were to protect the natural balance. All indigenous peoples across the world share this common belief system and understanding, because it comes from deep within. It comes from the spirit. When people who don't understand this spirit or don't feel this spirit, try to extract, destroy, kill, and remove parts of the natural world, they are harming us all, including themselves. Therefore, in respect to the disturbance caused by the removal of any necessary elements of the natural world, we Lakota need to be, as we always have been, the ones to stand up as the *Protectors*.

The American Civil War, fought between 1861 and 1865, basically came about because of political coercion, political oppression, and political motivation. There were two factions trying to control the US government. During this struggle, and because of the friction between the North and the South as each attempted to seize control, the United States nearly went bankrupt. The new people didn't know how to manage a government. They didn't know how to manage the resources, including the land bases. Many people throughout history have claimed that the Civil War was fought over slavery. And this is true, as slavery is a horrible stain on humanity through any time period. However, it was also fought over territorial control and over resource management (cotton, sugar, etc.). Slavery also provided a good economic model for the slave owners, and the black people were merely viewed as products in the economy. The overbearing reason that the North and the South were battling was to gain control over the entire government so that then, the winners could dictate how the government would be run.

At this time in history, when the United States would become almost completely bankrupt, much of the money they had, was allotted to fighting the war. A way to diminish debt is to diminish the size of the population. Fewer people to care for, means less money a society needs to spend on its own citizens. War is, and always has been, fought to appease one side's desire to obtain control over the other side, or their land and resources. War is often motivated by greed and the desire for wealth, with humanity becoming second nature to money. And sometimes war is made and fought, so that those with the most financial interest, can extract further wealth in the game of war profiteering. The game is as old as war itself.

It has been believed by some throughout history that each battle leading up to and in the midst of the Civil War, may have been part of a design to effectuate war. The battle sites were strategically selected so that the armies would have easy access to the weaponry, food, clothing, and other things necessary for war. These things would be supplied by rail or wagon to whichever side, the North or the South, needed them. This way, each side would be supplied for each battle. The country's money and resources were all going toward a conflict that killed off many of the people. This was a destructive approach toward the United States' own people. When you kill off hundreds of thousands of young men, you can also greatly affect their families too, as you take away the strength of those families. This way, the family can be broken, lost or decimated. One of the consequences of this Civil War was that the population was depleted.

In war, a victor must emerge. In this case, the victor would be the one to advance west, exploring the remainder of the North American continent. The victor would have the authority to pursue *manifest destiny*. As it turned out, the North won. The South ceded its place in opposition to the newly formed government. But there would not be a unanimous true support for the unification of the two factions. Personal, financial, and societal interests and preferences still clouded the minds of the former combatants. The original sin of slavery, after all, was grounded in racism and white privilege, and alleged supremacy. No civil war could truly eradicate those deeply embedded belief structures. Only a change and cleansing of the spirit will suffice.

The type of behavior that was brought to the North American continent by the new people was a very familiar and steadfast practice in Europe. Most of the people who were involved in the American Civil War had been sent to North America by their European countries as poor people. The only option these immigrants had was to support what was going on and to come to accept what was happening to the indigenous peoples of this continent, Turtle Island. The Lakota's presence and place in this world became pronounced at this time. The Lakota needed to stop what they were doing, stand up, and not allow the spread of war and destruction to happen.

As a result of the Civil War, which obviously entailed much bloodshed, conquest, horror, atrocity, loss of life, depletion of natural resources, and depletion of populations, the country lost an incredible amount of its wealth and resources. As the Civil War continued over a period of four years, the United States became depleted of its financial resources. The government began looking for new opportunities and new areas to seek wealth, as the country was nearly bankrupt. The lands and the territories of the Lakota now became a target. The government sought to try to open up and exploit those lands under the guise of acting peacefully with the Lakota. But the real motivation was to conficate these lands and extract their resources for the personal gain of the country and its wealthy benefactors. The Black Hills area in particular became of great interest to the US government because of the mysterious nature of the purported unfathomable wealth it contained. The government wanted to become better acquainted with what was available to be taken, with the intent of exploiting the natural resources found in the Black Hills.

Between the years 1863 and 1869, the US government had a bad effect on not just the territories and lands of the Lakota people but also on the people themselves, as the whites encroached on the Lakota's spirit and their very existence. There was a gathering storm approaching, something that the Lakota, Nakota, and Dakota had never quite experienced before. It was an inevitable clash of cultures and peoples on the horizon.

In 1862, our Dakota relatives had gone through the terrible experience of genocide. The whites had not only tried to steal and confiscate their lands, but also had placed a bounty on the Dakota in Minnesota, where they were now taking scalps and other body parts. This is where the use of the word *redskin* came to bear in the white man's world, their way of describing who we are. They would take a life for money, for a bounty. The blood is what they speak of with the word *redskin*. It was a terrible way to get a penny or a dollar bill, and an awful way to run a government, without feeling or caring for human life at all. The Dakota were subject to all types of these indignities. These brave ones and their families were trying their best to survive. The people were trying to believe that they still had a place in the New World. The hanging of thirty-eight Dakota men in Mankato would occur in December 1862.

This was a devastating time for the people, with terrible events, awful happenings, and the elimination of an entire natural existence of the people. Imagine what it would be like to have somebody march to your home, break your door down, grab your family, and do evil, horrible things to them as you watch, seeing your relatives being harmed or killed. You would feel an anger, pain, and grief that you probably haven't ever imagined. Being subject to this type of experience would make a person ponder all aspects of life and existence. These things entered the minds of the indigenous people during this period of history. Their choices were now limited. The things that would, in ceremony, aid and guide them, were now even being shunned by many of their own people. The people and their old ways were being persecuted by the US government and its military. We were in chaos trying to find a way to survive.

Revisiting the events previous, between the years of 1855 and 1862, we find that the military was incrementally encroaching on Lakota land, motivated by the California gold rush, which had people moving from the East Coast to California, traveling along the Bozeman Trail. The Bozeman Trail cut through the ancestral homelands of the Lakota and the Cheyenne, which meant that prospectors and homesteaders traveling west inevitably clashed with the Lakota and Cheyenne—a clash of races and societies. This was motivated by the US government's need to ever to be on the cutting edge of money, and by the profit motive generated by the wealth-seeking individuals who were financing this move westward. Along with the miners came the mining interests, the railroads, and the telegraph lines. The need of the United States government to capitulate and accommodate these financial interests by proposing military campaigns to establish forts along the Bozeman Trail increased. The United States tried to come up with neutral-seeming motives for the exploration of *Indian* lands and the control of the Indian people across these western

tribal regions. The government engaged in these explorations despite
the existence of previous treaties that forbid this type of conduct. The
trespassing, once begun, continued in a steady stream.

The military atrocities were occurring mainly as a result of the 1862
conflict in Minnesota, which spilled over into the Dakota Territory to
the west. In spite of the Fort Laramie Treaty of 1851, which separated
the lands of the Lakota from all other territories, the government started
encroaching upon those Lakota lands to build forts so as to protect the
private business entrepreneurs along the Bozeman Trail. Red Cloud of
the Oglala Lakota became more involved in leading fighting groups here
and there against settlers and small groups of soldiers along the Bozeman
Trail. This was the beginning of the period when individual skirmishes
were causing the government to devote more time and effort to manning,
building, and securing military forts on the outskirts of the Great *Sioux*
Reservation, as recognized by the aforementioned Treaty of 1851. The
money interests were trying to expand out to California on account of
the gold rush. One of the natural pathways went through the territories
of Nebraska, into Wyoming, and up into Montana. The Bozeman Trail
illegally trespassed through the unceded hunting territories/unceded
Indian territory that were specifically reserved to the Lakota in 1851.

There was an effort afoot to try to obtain more concessions from the Lakota so that the commercial and corporate enterprises along the Bozeman Trail would encounter no further problems. As a result of this new activity during the 1860s, the government's negotiators and certain tribal people met at Fort Laramie. The 1868 Fort Laramie Treaty, which was referred to as a peace treaty, came into being. All the peoples of the Lakota, including the Mnincoju, were parties to that treaty, which was supposed to protect the entire Great Sioux Reservation[1] from any incursion by the military or any private people or entities. This treaty was to preserve the people's aboriginal rights to all that was there, *forever*: the air above the surface; the waters that ran under and upon the surface, and the total of the subsurface, including all earth, minerals, (including gold and silver); aquifers, and cave and tunnel networks running throughout the total land base. The treaty was entered into also to protect Lakota hunting and fishing rights and to prevent white occupation of the hunting territories and the unceded Indian territory extending into Montana and Wyoming, as well as the areas up to and including the Bighorn Mountains (Shiny Mountains). This included the area of the Greasy Grass valley along the Little Bighorn River, the Greasy Grass River. The 1851 and 1868 treaties included the formal agreement by the US government not to trespass into the Black Hills. It was the "law" to actually protect the Lakota from any trespassers into their lands, and specifically into the He Sapa.

<hr />

This was a burdensome time for the people, so they returned to the ways of sacredness. The Cannumpa, the sacred pipe, had been given to the people a very, very long time ago, presented by a very special spirit known as the White Buffalo Calf Woman, who had been asked to deliver it to the people. Once Creator blessed the Lakota with the gift of the Sacred Cannumpa, they could use it to make their existence

---

[1] Note that the United States government referred to the Lakota as Sioux, and to our lands as a Sioux reservation. We do not accept that name for the Lakota people. When the lands of the Lakota are referred to as the "Great Sioux Reservation" in Warrior Is, it is used for the purpose of ease of comprehension.

and their spirit stronger and more sustainable. But times were becoming tough. New people from across the world were beginning to advance on and take the lands, lives, tradition, and culture away from the people by force.

The cannumpa has always been a prevalent part of Lakota existence. However, during the time of genocide preceding the Greasy Grass Battle and such, many of the Lakota people and their relatives began to use the cannumpa in ways that were not proper. They used the cannumpa to fit themselves into the military world and the political world, and eventually into the leadership of a totally distressed, utterly distraught, and sometimes defeated people. Some of these people used their cannumpas for purposes of self-gain, undermining, and deception. This was not the use as originally intended. There were still those who believed in using the cannumpa in the proper way to address anything in Creator's life, but for others, the cannumpa became almost like a rifle, a weapon used by certain Lakota against their own kind. The fallen heart and spirit of our own indigenous tribal peoples led to the misuse and abuse of the wonderful spiritual practice associated with the cannumpa. Some of these people began to use the cannumpa in a wrongful and unholy fashion.

Take for example a greedy man who is concerned about his own personal fortune. He has a personal choice to assimilate with one of two worlds, or both. In this case, he chooses both. He chooses to follow the new way of the white man, and also tries to hang on to a piece of the cannumpa. He does this so that his people will trust him enough to deal with the white man and with his personal affairs. He is no longer honest with his people, and his improper use of the cannumpa is evident. Sometimes he even introduces himself as a pipe carrier, as a spiritual person.

This situation is best described by the following example, an incident concerning a man who claimed to be very spiritual. He was given a cannumpa by two warriors. The warriors hoped and prayed that he would be able to recognize its worth and presence. But what the man ended up doing is, when using the cannumpa to pray, he rushes and uses the cannumpa in a way that was not proper or acceptable. In front of a group of people, the man prayed and then presented the cannumpa, holding it up in the air toward the sky. This he did wrong, in a backward fashion. Instead of pointing the stem of the cannumpa to Grandfather Sky and Wakan Tanka, he pointed the bowl in that direction. This showed complete disrespect of the cannumpa, and was utter torment to the peoples who had always lived by it. This example shows how quickly and destructively many of our own kind gave in to the ways of the new world and the new ways, which included the oppression of their own people and the old sacred ways.

The two warriors remained standing there with the group, after they had handed the man the cannumpa. The man was acting like he knew what to do with it. When he improperly pointed the bowl toward Tunkasila, the sky, instantly the Wakinyan, the Thunder Beings, came over the top of the mountain and sprayed the ground near the men with hail. All who were present and watched, quickly ran for cover from the hailstones. What the Thunder Beings were doing was showing that this man was not a part of the people anymore. He mocked the cannumpa, reducing its significance to nothing. He did not respect the cannumpa ways enough to know, or to ask to know, how to use the cannumpa. He believed he was more valuable and sacred than the cannumpa itself. The warriors who watched this knew better. They knew that the man had done wrong. But since they were a part of what had happened, they were also witness to the Thunder Beings, who were fully aware of the people's presence, the people's activity, and the people's prayers. The sacred power of the cannumpa cannot, and should not, be taken lightly. It should not be abused or misused. The sacred power needs to be respected and trusted.

<hr />

Because of the gathering storm and the impending threat to the Lakota people and their way of life, many of the Lakota began to fall away from their culture, their beliefs, their spiritual connection. As a result of the erosion of the people's sacred beliefs and practices, which occurred in the wake of the whites' encroachment on their lives, the very sovereignty of the Lakota was threatened and attacked.

Sovereignty

Sovereignty to the Lakota means more than just recognition of a government or a nation. Sovereignty means to us, an innate right to live our lives as we choose to and as we always have in the past. When the United States breached any of the treaties it had made with us, it attacked and violated our sovereignty as the Lakota nation. But the United States also violated our aboriginal and indigenous way of life, our very existence. So in that respect, the U.S. also violated our personal and our communal sovereignty.

Sovereignty promotes our prosperity and evolution as a society. It entails the right to breathe, not only for the human being but also for the human beings' necessary cultural advancement. Sovereignty also entials the right to birth, not only for the individual human being, but also for that human being's culture. These are the innate rights that genocide takes from you.

Sovereignty gives an entire nation choice and control over its own decision making. This is how you maintain a constantly peaceable, protected, and civilized society: by exercising the contribution of the individual while following the guidelines of Creator's gift to you in placing you here. In essence, sovereignty is the right to be, and the right to do your bit or piece to keep your nation and all your natural surroundings intact throughout the cycles of life. Without sovereignty, you have no balance, no direction, no life to truly live. The new people and their government wanted the Lakota to live without any inalienable rights whatsoever. Not one of these inalienable rights to life, culture and a way of life, would be considered under the English word *sovereignty*.

Two conflicting notions to sovereignty existed between the European settlers and the indigenous peoples. Sovereignty to the government of the United States meant a right to do as they pleased, to take what they wanted, and to remove what they wished so that their path for approach was totally clear. They had no qualms, and asked themselves no questions, about imposing their will, and their own definition and philosophy of sovereignty, upon the Lakota.

The Lakota nation's view, however, as we have just discussed, was the opposite. The Lakota believed that sovereignty allowed for the advancement of civilized human beings. It was not used as a reason to destroy, take from, or disrespect the lands or other peoples, especially not with utter arrogance and the display of evil as exhibited by the whites and their new government. The difference in the Lakota idea and the United States' idea of sovereignty is best made apparent by one point that everybody must consider. The land beneath the feet of any occupant of the United States was once taken care of by our indigenous peoples. The comfort that you feel at night when you sleep, the stars that you look at, the mountains that you cross, the waters that you drink from—sovereignty of the indigenous nations made it possible for you and me to be taught better about such matters of life.

Sovereignty is more than a word or a legal concept. Sovereignty is a way of life. When the white society and its government, through the process of making treaties, committing genocide, and forcing assimilation, took the Lakota way of life away from the Lakota, the Lakota lost their sovereignty. It wasn't lost through any treaty, any formal governmental agreement, or any court decision. It was lost when the people lost their spirit. What that means is, that if that is how it was lost, it can be regained. Through strength of spirit and the courage to reclaim that sovereignty, it will come. But first the indigenous peoples must understand the concept of sovereignty and not believe that sovereignty is something that is contained in a book—because it's not. It's not something imposed by a court case decision. It's not something contained within a treaty. Sovereignty is not capable of being found in the words of a treaty. You must rely upon yourself and where you come from, and the way of your ancestors. That is sovereignty. Human sovereignty.

Sovereignty is of the Earth. It is your space to move. Sovereignty has nothing to do with legality. Sovereignty is a natural law. You cannot protect you sovereignty if you have nothing left to protect it with. You cannot assert sovereignty if you never had it to begin with. Sovereignty really is just a teaching tool. If you do not protect it, if you have not protected it, then there really is nothing for you to pass on to the next generation.

Sovereignty is not determined by the ink of a pen signed by an evil hand.

When one wants to impact the real lives of a man and a woman, you hit them in the heart with the spirit—not a word, not a phrase, and not an empty promise. It is the sovereignty of the spirit that endures. It is the most important sovereignty any being can have.

The concept of sovereignty is the biggest piece of the human being's life. Sovereignty is the right to choose how to live. It empowers one to feel confidence and optimism when they wake up to the sun in the morning. It gives them thanks, appreciation and gratitude when the night comes. In the time frame before the encroachment, advancement, and incursion of the white society and military, the Lakota, Nakota, and Dakota were safe, secure, and protected. The children could laugh, be innocent, enjoy life, and be taught the lessons of life. These amenities were theirs to have and to hold for the remainder of their lives. The people could take their time to enjoy their sons and daughters, converse with other headmen and other warriors, and also travel where they chose to, taking the time to enrich themselves through ceremony and membership in societies. All of these things are available to human beings when protocol, heart, and spirit are followed.

Sovereignty is an issue for the indigenous peoples of Turtle Island. It always will be, because this is our own land. Anyone else who has ever come here, came as an immigrant. We tried to work with them. We tried to care for them. And then they tried to take everything, and left us with no sovereignty at all. The choices we have are to stand up and believe, and to go and practice these old traditional ways to enrich our lives for the purposes of enjoyment, celebration, defense, safety, and ultimately the passage back home to Creator through the Milky Way. It can be a wonderful life if managed in your own way, as guided by your heart and spirit and through your people, if all are committed to life.

The Indigenous people have been inhabitants of Turtle Island from the beginning of time on Grandmother Earth. It is our home on Unci Maka. When the first Europeans came to Turtle Island, they encountered the indigenous peoples, the tribal nations of peoples. The Europeans usually came as explorers or curious travelers, but the historical record seems to show that, always, they came seeking new resources that could be used to further the wealth and/or dominance of their peoples or their nations. To those early "explorers," the indigenous peoples were mostly viewed as just another species of animal, something to be exploited, hunted, killed, raped, used, captured, and enslaved. There was little or no recognition of the indigenous peoples' humanity or their individual and communal right to live and exist undisturbed and unharmed. No recognition of the survival of the indigenous people or the survival of their race of peoples; no empathy or compassion for the indigenous values or ways; no respect for their cultures, their societies, or their spirits; and no recognition or acknowledgement of their sovereignty.

When the individual Europeans came to Turtle Island, they were not just immediately killed or repelled by the indigenous people. That could have been one outcome, but it was not. This is because the indigenous people, and particularly the indigenous of Turtle Island, viewed the new people as people, as humans with valuable lives, individual families, and their own existence. The indigenous values have always included peace, unity, tolerance, and love. So when they first viewed these new people, their initial thought and intent was to get to know them, to find out about them, to assist them. The indigenous tribal people were curious about the new people, wishing to become knowledgeable about their ways, their intents, and their goals.

It was only when the European foreigners, the new arrivals, sought to harm the indigenous peoples and take away their ways and lives, that the conflict, confrontation, violence, and killing began. And the killing and violence began at the hands of the new people, because eventually they became convinced that the indigenous people could be removed, could be tricked, could be enslaved, could be taken advantage of, and could be killed and exterminated. However, the true intent and resolve of the Europeans remained hidden from the indigenous people until it was too late. Until the new people had gained a foothold on the indigenous peoples' lands and territories by way of theft, population displacement, enslavement, and genocide.

Christopher Columbus and his expeditions into the "New World" in the west, including the Caribbean Islands and North America, provide us with a historical example of how the Europeans used exploitation, greed, and genocide, to take over land, claim it, possess it, and occupy it, and kill the people who were already there. Columbus and his people were not noble explorers. They were not innocent travelers. They were state agents seeking wealth for themselves and the destruction of other societies, hoping to claim riches, gain land, and have political influence over indigenous interests. No just or empathetic human being should ever celebrate Columbus or his party's deeds and accomplishments. Columbus was not a hero. Columbus is not a human being to be honored, or to be recognized for anything but death, theft, and destruction.

North America had been hidden from the rest of the world until these Europeans, including Columbus and his people, and other earlier explorers, showed up on the shores of the lands in the Western Hemisphere, including Turtle Island. The introduction of the new people on Turtle Island did not, according to actual real history, get off to a very good start for the indigenous people. It was the first step toward *manifest destiny* and outright genocide of the indigenous peoples, including the Lakota.

History suggests that the Mayans from the southern peninsula of Turtle Island exchanged gifts and stories with the Lakota headmen in the 1860s. This is how the peoples of the south knew of the Lakota, and how the Lakota knew of them.

The Mayans spoke of the whites who came on ships, of the gold and land they sought, and of the slaves they took on the ships back across the sea. The Mayans told of the horrible atrocities the whites with the iron helmets wreaked upon the indigenous peoples of the peninsula and the southern islands.

The white soldiers and aristocrats slaughtered the people. They cut off their legs, hands, and arms without killing them, or else cut their heads off. They also cut out their insides, especially the women with children or unborn children. They took the tops of the head with hair—the scalp—and regarded these things as trophies of conquest and death. They raped most women and girls, and particularly liked to mate with the very young girls, even molesting the young boys. They were horrible and evil, and sought only gold, riches, and slaves. These were the experiences that the indigenous peoples of Central and South America had with the first white European people who came to their lands.

Through the South American and Central American region, the indigenous peoples had similar stories of atrocities committed by the white European peoples who encroached on their lands and their lives, bringing their weapons with them.

Across the oceans, in the lands of the Australian Aborigines, the New Zealand Maori, the Hawaiians, the Samoans, and the Africans, the stories were mostly the same: the whites brought a disruption to the life force and energy, and damage and destruction to the people, their ways of life, their cultures, their existence. The new people brought this destruction to the indigenous peoples across all of Grandmother Earth, all in the name of exploration or "discovery."

The white man, the white government, and white society sought a means whereby they could control the "Indian,"[2] as the North American indigenous peoples of Turtle Island were called by the whites, which effort became known among the European settlers as the *Indian problem*. Because many people within the European white society did not understand the Indians, and in particular the Lakota, the whites were often without empathy, sympathy, or conscience when developing their plans and policies that would directly affect the Indians.

It can be said that the white society and its new government of white men, many of them landholders, came to view the Indians, including the Lakota, as less human than themselves. This view was common, as can be discerned by the stories, accounts, and tales passed on by many of the white people who encountered people of indigenous descent and racial makeup, either individually or in groups, throughout the eighteenth century on Turtle Island.

These accounts, usually told firsthand to others or written in individual journals, oftentimes described the Indians in quite derogatory

---

[2] Elsewhere in Warrior Is, when the word Indian appears without quotation marks, it is to be assumed by the reader that the authors do not accept the term as applied to the indigenous peoples of the North American continent. The term is to be regarded as one used by the white people of European descent who colonized North America, stealing the lands of the indigenous peoples.

terms, with little to no regard for these people's humanity or culture. The accounts, of course, were the subject of great embellishment and contriving, in order to sensationalize or dramatize the individual encounters of the reporting whites. This embellishment was done so as to create a good story that could survive many repetitions, and carry weight so as to popularize the storyteller or the storyteller's deeds of bravery and courage in dealing with these dark-skinned aboriginal people.

The tales often stereotyped the Indians by overcharacterizing their physical traits and image, which included descriptions of overgrown body parts—big feet; a big *pasu* (nose); dark gleaming "red" skin, like the devil was commonly believed to possess according to certain selective interpretations of scripture; or strong-smelling odors resulting from gross behavior and unhygienic habits. Many of these unsophisticated characterizations of the Indians, and especially of the Lakota, were of course great exaggerations or purposeful distortions and misrepresentations. It seemed that white storytellers often compared the Indians to the devil and attributed to them devilish ways and characteristics, in an obvious attempt to literally "demonize" the aboriginal peoples, whom the whites believed to be undeserving of compassion, honest depiction, or empathy. These *red skins* were less than human—less than white. And they were interfering with the god-given natural rights and *privileges* of the white people and the entire white race. The whites saw it as their *manifest destiny* to obtain, own, and utilize all of the lands and resources that these *savages* occupied and held. It was therefore convenient, and a misguided leap of faith to view these *red heathens* as mere pagans.

In an aboriginal sense, the oldest stories of the Creation handed down from generation to generation spoke of the ancestors of the Lakota as the "red man" and "red woman." This phraseology acknowledged their aboriginal appearance provided by Creator, but the terms were never intended to be used in a derogatory fashion. The new peoples, in their perception of the indigenous people of Turtle Island, created racial and ethnic slurs to use when describing many nonwhite peoples. Such misinformed and ignorant perceptions caused some to coin phrases to connote that the indigenous people were something less than human.

The term *redskin* referred to the bloody body parts that a white person had to produce in order to collect one of the bounties paid for dead Indians that were springing up across the continent as part of the genocidal policies. *Redskin* is not an acceptable or honorable term for anyone to use.

It became easy for many whites to view the Indian as possessing no serious godly importance and subsequently to view them as having no long-lasting consequence to the whites' best interests or general welfare. This was an easy conclusion for most whites, and certainly for the white-male-dominated government, to come to. It was a conclusion that allowed a pervasive mind-set and belief structure to take hold and then be hammered into place by the iron will and resolve of the white society. The white belief structure then embraced the notion that these dark-skinned *primitive* beings needed either to be killed and forever removed or rounded up and controlled, so that their continued physical presence would no longer be a threat to the *manifest destiny* of the ruling race of white men.

It is believed to have been foretold by the white people's leaders, in their vision of conquest and of the deliverance of white European society, that all reaches of the expansive "new" continent would be simply laid out in front of the white people for the taking. *Manifest destiny*: the inevitable right of those that have, to rule over those who have not. Manifest destiny was derived from the *doctrine of discovery*, which was adopted from the old European dogma utilized to claim the superior right of ownership and possession of the lands of indigenous peoples just by declaring it to be so, in the name of the Crown or of the white people's god. The doctrine, of course, was nothing more than a convenient way to ascribe a false status to something that was being stolen from the indigenous people.

The *doctrine of discovery* created a belief system in the minds of many of the first white Europeans that set foot on the Eastern Seaboard of Turtle Island. The mind-set prevalent among the white immigrants was that they could freely take anything from the indigenous people and destroy them in the process. Therefore, the whites began to commit ugly and horrible atrocities, such as the massacre of the Lenape tribe (near present-day Bowling Green, New York) on Manhattan Island in 1643, the Pavonia Massacre (along the Hudson River in New York) in 1643, and the massacre at Corlears Hook on Manhattan Island in the same year, 1643. The massacre of the Lenape tribe in 1643 was particularly heinous: "Infants were torn from their mother's breast and hacked to death in the presence of their parents, and pieces thrown into the fire and in the water," wrote Dutch witness to the massacre David Pietersz de Vries, on February 25, 1643. "Other sucklings, being bound to small boards, were cut, stuck and pierced, and miserably massacred in a manner to move a heart of stone. Some were thrown into the river, and when the fathers and mothers endeavored to save them the soldiers would not let them come on land but made both parents and children drown."

On Turtle Island in the 1800s, the foreboding belief structure of white people, who saw themselves as being privileged and therefore free to take what they wanted from the Indians, including the Lakota, set the stage for an Indian "policy" that was lacking human and cultural empathy and was borne of greed, conquest, and genocide. The greed aspect could be overtly held and spoken of in public (i.e., "We must obtain their holdings and seek their cession of their territories, so that we can take and possess those resources for the concerns of the wealth of the individual white settlers, miners and entrepreneurs, as well as the economy as a whole"). The conquest aspect could not be so boldly advertised or spoken of in public forums. The intent of conquest needed to be disguised in policy-making ideas and subsequent implementation and actions. The notion of conquest was cleverly cloaked in overtures made regarding obtaining and maintaining the peace between the whites and the Indians.

However, the aspect of genocide was a whole different matter. Genocide would be at the very heart and soul of all that was to be done for, done with, or done to, the Indians. The outright extermination of the entire race of these "subhuman beings" was the only real goal of the new US government, which had been founded upon principles of life, liberty, and pursuit of happiness for all men. However, instead of to "all men," the US Declaration of Independence only afforded that right, recognition, and privilege to white men who owned land. (This would become a well-known fact of history, as learned later by historians, not by the intent of the written word, but by the actual deeds done by these men and their immediate descendants).

The notion of genocide was simple. Once the plan was agreed upon by the leaders of the new country, things could be set in motion to accomplish that very raw and basic goal. But it could never, ever be spoken, written, or confirmed that genocide was the original intent of the white government toward the Indian people. If the word *genocide* were ever mentioned or used in an inquiring or reactionary sense toward the government's actions, all officials, to a man, would adamantly and vehemently deny that genocide was ever even contemplated as a potential outcome for, let alone being part of a *policy* toward, the Indians. No one was allowed to discuss it except in the most secretive and private of affairs. Nothing was to be written, so as the plan would not be uncovered or seen by nosy information seekers. No official or citizen confidant was allowed to know the whole truth in carrying out their duties under governmental policy.

Even some of the clergy, often used by the government as agents and go-betweens to communicate matters between the government and the Indians, oftentimes were oblivious of the true nature of their involvement in the recruitment and development of new Christian flocks from among the masses of Indian people. (Some, however, absolutely knew the truth of the matter).

In any event, the truth about the government's genocidal policy toward the Indians remained a great secret that was never to be revealed, because if the secret were ever to be discovered, then the new government could and would be viewed as a complete hypocritical farce, and not worthy of its professed honorable goals to promote humanity and ensure justice for "all men," who were supposedly, created equal.

Critics viewing a government that had the motive of committing genocide and wiping out the indigenous population, would conclude that such a government would not go down in history as being consistent with a democratic republic. The grand experiment embarked upon after the breaking of the bonds of tyranny and repression from the European lords and oligarchies would be viewed globally as a hoax and a failure. So the great secret needed to be kept, and cleverly disguised within deeds that would be understood by gullible and ignorant third parties as a noble, honorable attempt to deal peaceably with the aboriginal race of people, consistent with the principles of faith, justice, and righteousness.

In the decades beginning in the 1800s and proceeding through the 1850s and beyond, to the end of the nineteenth century in and upon Turtle Island, Saved By Bear, his relatives, and their ancestors were faced with the onset of a secretive, invisible, hidden genocidal movement. The Lakota were initially lulled into passivity. This happened because they believed that since they dealt with fellow human beings according to their own cultural belief structure of peace, unity, tolerance, and love, they themselves would be dealt with in the same fashion.

The Lakota viewed these new, lighter-skinned people as visitors coming in peace, and treated them with the dignity and respect that would be due to visitors who were just seeking to pass through. Peace could be had and shared. Coexistence and cooperation could prevail. Tolerance of each other would foster peace, understanding, and cooperation. The whites would be allowed into the Lakota communities as peaceful visitors, everyone unified by their own humanity, respecting the fact that humans can help and understand each other.

However, over time, more of them came and passed through. And then they stayed. The situation, having become more complicated, now required more consideration among the Lakota. Because the people had voiced their concerns to the naca, the headmen, and the oyate councils, an honest and open discussion of the motive of the white people needed to be had so that an understanding could be reached. So that no one would misinterpret or misunderstand each other.

Through these councils, the Lakota decided that it was permissible to share resources with these visitors, whom the Lakota should expect to assist and accept, as long as they were just visitors. It seems only fair that the Lakota inquired as to the long-term intent of their visitors in the territory, as they were concerned about hunting and gathering, especially in the seasons when food and shelter were scarce.

White visitors were appearing with more frequency in Lakota territory and were staying longer. Some were even making land-set lodges, structures secured to the Earth. No longer a matter of visitation, it was now a matter of permanent occupation. So the time came to speak of such things in an honest and open way.

These talks or councils with the whites started a dialogue of expectation. For the Lakota, the expectation was focused on their land and resources; for the whites, on their use and occupation of the territories they sought.

This began the talks of maintaining peaceful relations with the whites, as long as they did not try to challenge the Lakota or Lakota rights to their own land and territories. Disagreements arose. Disputes occurred. Sometimes force became necessary to assert the right to expel visiting whites from areas that had not been discussed and therefore in which the whites were not allowed to be. Sometimes, arguments led to unfortunate skirmishes, which sometimes resulted in confrontation and injury and, rarely, death.

The need arose for recognized agreements so as to avoid breaches of the peace between the Lakota and the whites. This was when the government and its armies came into play, acting on behalf of the white visitors, the white trespassers.

Very few Lakota spoke the whites' language. Very few of the Lakota on the plains in the 1800s had any comprehension of the written word. Almost none of the Lakota during the nineteenth century on Turtle Island had ever seen written language or words. Hardly any Lakota understood English, the white word language, except for a scant few who had encountered European fur traders along the rivers farther east in the land of the Dakota. Literally, the Lakota communicated through speaking Lakota, through sign language, or through pictographs drawn on rocks or hides. Very few, if any, actually wrote *words*. Very few, if any, understood what it meant to record what one spoke. No one ever really thought that the words they said to one another could be etched down on hide or paper or a piece of wood, in such a way that another, just by looking at an etched inanimate object, could know what had been said by mouth.

The written word, therefore, was the great advantage the whites had over the Lakota when it came to these meetings where people *spoke* about things that could be agreed upon by the Lakota and the whites, things related to the camping territories, the hunting areas, the right to hunt or fish, or to take animals or food, and how often and in what amounts. The purpose of these meetings was to reach an agreement so that no one would end up arguing with or committing acts of violence against the other. The Lakota hope was for diploimacy and peace.

The Lakota disadvantage when it came to communication in English, and understanding written and spoken English words, was actually a great and distinct advantage to the white participants who understood the meaning of the words or who understood the confusion and deception that those same words could create and conceal.

Sometimes, albeit rarely, a Lakota had a cursory understanding and comprehension of the language. But for the most part, the Lakota were subject to having an interpreter provided by the whites or their government. The interpreter was supposed to "assist" the Lakota in understanding the words, and the nature and extent of what the Lakota people were supposedly agreeing to. This became a big problem when the interpreter chosen and used by the government had his own personal agenda, such as a desire for wealth or notoriety. Often, in the end, the agreement reached in such cases was detrimental the Lakota. This was more likely to occur when the interpreter had no familial connection to the Lakota or was not of Lakota, Dakota, or Nakota descent. The white governmental officials purposefully chose such people as interpreters, as it was their motive to easily manipulate the Lakota and cheat them after reaching an agreement. Using interpreters who did not have the interests of the Lakota at heart allowed the government to gain the upper hand, resulting in, say, a lower price paid for land or a greater amount of land and rights received in exchange for less consideration.

There was very rarely a chance to have an honest and true meeting of the minds when the whites and the Lakota and/or Dakota were negotiating the terms of an agreement. Almost always, the Indian parties were cheated by the dishonest white negotiators and deal makers. Many a bad agreement came out of these unequal and unfair negotiating sessions—bad for the Indian participants, that is. (Later, many dishonorable and unethical reviewing courts and judges would add to the harm to the Indians and their legal interests by unfairly and deceitfully deciding that the Indians had forfeited their land and rights in favor of the whites and governmental interests. These decisions were mostly based upon the false fantasy of the existing *doctrine of discovery*. Little was ever done by the government to prevent or correct these dishonorable and harmful judicial decisions, over time. This process would even exist subsequently into the twentieth and twenty-first centuries as well).

Once written *agreements* were made, the need arose to fulfill and enforce the terms of these agreements, regardless of how unfair or inequitable they were to the Indians. To perform this function, the government appointed and employed white men, usually from the east, and usually from the business world or the military, to serve as Indian agents. This would become an unfortunate and tragic element in the lead-up to the breaking of the world.

The Declaration of Independence states, "We hold these truths to be self-evident, that all men are created equal, that they are endowed by their Creator with certain unalienable Rights, that among these are Life, Liberty and the pursuit of Happiness." However, King George of England, attempting to control his subjects in the New World, issued the Proclamation of 1763, which set a boundary at the Appalachian Mountains and declared essentially that the American colonies no longer had the "right of discovery" of the residual Indian lands west of the Appalachians. Through this proclamation, the so-called right of discovery of these Indian lands was now reserved solely for the Crown of England. The position taken by the king obviously did not sit well with the colonists, who wished their westward expansion into all of North America to be unrestricted.

Thirteen years after the Proclamation of 1763, the leaders of the American colonies wrote a letter of protest to the king, accusing the English monarchy of "raising the conditions of new appropriations of land." The colonial leaders went on to indicate that the king "has excited domestic insurrections amongst us, and has endeavored to bring on the inhabitants of our frontiers, the merciless Indian savages." This letter of protest later became known as the Declaration of Independence, dated July 4, 1776.

Although the phrase "all men are created equal" is part of the beginning language of the Declaration of Independence, just below that widely known statement is a less-known—indeed, mostly unknown—recitation of the real intent of the *founding fathers*. The Declaration of Independence refers to the indigenous people on Turtle Island as "merciless Indian savages." By including this specific statement in the historical Declaration of Independence, the *founders* of this *new* country made it clear that the only reason that the inclusive language of "all men" was used was that they had a very narrow, exclusive definition of who was and who was not a human being—a narrow, exclusive view pertaining to which human beings were "men." Therefore, according to the new country's founding document declaring its own independence from England on July 4, 1776, it is clear that the indigenous people are dehumanized "savages," and that these less than human savages obviously stood in the way of the unrestricted westward expansion of the new country and its white "men." It is clear, then, that manifest destiny was in the works as intended from the very beginning by the new government of the new country. The new country, its founders, and its new government would chose to use the *doctrine of discovery* to proclaim white supremacy and privilege as being over and beyond any indigenous peoples' personal or communal rights, or right to land ownership. This was the usurped "right" of white dominion over the indigenous peoples of Turtle Island.

In furtherance of the planned westward expansion of the new country to follow its manifest destiny, the United States passed a law known as the 1787 Northwest Ordinance. The hidden agenda involved expansion, land acquisition, and genocide, although the words of the ordinance paid lip service to Indian rights.

The 1787 Northwest Ordinance describes the preferred relationship with the Indians as follows (emphasis added):

> Article III. Religion, morality, and knowledge, being necessary to good government and the happiness of mankind, schools and the means of education shall forever be encouraged. *The utmost good faith shall always be observed towards the Indians; their lands and property shall never be taken from them without their consent; and, in their property, rights, and liberty, they shall never be invaded or disturbed,*

unless in just and lawful wars authorized by Congress; but laws
founded in justice and humanity, shall from time to time
be made for preventing wrongs being done to them, and
for preserving peace and friendship with them.

The Louisiana Purchase was a massive land transaction carried out
in 1803 between two foreign nations, France and the United States,
neither of which had any legal right to possess, occupy, use, buy, or
sell such land, as neither country owned North America, especially not
North America beyond the Appalachian Mountains. You cannot buy
or sell property that you do not rightfully own. It is well established
in the opening of the new country's *doctrine of discovery* that its *right* to
buy, sell, own, or control the lands of the Lakota, Nakota, or Dakota is
rotten to the core, all the way down to the roots. The transactions and
confiscation of lands and property resulting from this rotten core would
merely be fruit from a poisoned tree.

Combined with the true intent addressed in the Declaration of
Independence in 1776, most, if not all laws or treaties entered into or
enacted affecting the North American indigenous people, especially
the Lakota people in the entirety of the Great Plains region, were based
upon lies, subterfuge, trickery, false claims of ownership, fraud, deceit,
and unfair dealing. When the very foundation of the bedrock principles
of an entire body of law concerning an entire race of people and their
property is a flimsy sham, then there is no surprise that almost every
treaty, every promise, every obligation, entered into by the United States
government with the Indian people (or tribes) would end up being
breached, reneged upon, and broken.

Most or all of the "laws" that were to follow the foundations of the
treaties and agreements, and the statutes and enactments concerning
the North American Indians, were mostly a sham also. An entire body
of developed law which would follow, would ironically be referred
to as a separate, specific category of laws called "federal Indian law"
or "tribal law," or just plain "Indian law." These laws and principles
would be designed to supplement and carry forth the true intent of the
treaties, agreements, and statutory enactments affecting and involving
the Indians. If the true intent of the government was to complete

the long-term goal of genocide and the total removal of all Indians and Indian interests, then the government needed an arsenal of legal weapons to use in order to meet its objective. This is why *Indian law,* as a body of law, would become riddled with exceptions, loopholes, clever defenses and principles, complex hidden tricks, and judge-made tactical escape hatches. Whereby the government and private wealth interests would be afforded a *legal* avenue to circumvent any and all obligations that appeared to be negotiated or agreed to by the Indians. These enacted and crafted loopholes, exceptions, and many times, dubious *Indian law principles,* would be used by the government and its wealthy benefactors or resource-hungry constituents, and usually with the knowing and willing compliance of many of the courts and many judges. The laws and many resulting court decisions would be used with the intent of divesting, destroying, manipulating, terminating, and denying the rights, privileges, immunities, protections, holdings, assets, and alleged benefits of, the indigenous people. Some benevolent and scholarly citizens of integrity, would try over time to do what they could to help the indigenous peoples in their legal struggles against their occupying government, but successes were few and far between in a system designed to have the Indian lose almost every time. Since the beginning of all US government transactions with the indigenous people on Turtle Island, dating back to the 1700s, this is how things occurred.

Unbeknown to the people at the time, the new government would choose to deal with the indigenous people on Turtle Island by forcing them to relinquish their territories. And if they would not do so or if they would resist or object, the government would seek to simply eliminate them by whatever means necessary. The policy was old. It was called genocide. It had, as an evil act and idea, been practiced in Europe for ages. Now the policy came full force upon the indigenous people of Turtle Island by the hand of their oppressors and the new government, which was hungry for land and resources.

This theft and confiscation policy was exemplified by the passage of the Indian Removal Act of 1830 by the U.S. congress and its president, the notorious Andrew Jackson. It was a so called *legal* means to steal the lands of the indigenous people by forcibly removing them from their aboriginal and ancestral lands. This racist law was used to steal millions of acres of land from the people. This process resulted in almost completely eradicating the Seminole nation, and forced the Cherokee people to leave their homes in the southeastern states and to walk their way to Oklahoma territory. In 1838, this horrible event killed over 4,000 of the Cherokee on the way. It became known as the *Trail of Tears*. As time moved forward, this process would be repeated time and time again by the US against the indigenous people. Hundreds of Trails of Tears would occur in the next 150 years as millions of the indigenous people of Turtle Island would die and have their lands and homes stolen from them by the government and its benefactors.

Some Lakota people would eventually choose not to become a part of the treaties or agreements with the new government. They would know and perceive that any and all of these agreements were going to be of little, if any, benefit to the Lakota people or the Lakota way of life, either in the short term or in the long term. So they would eventually refuse to participate or to sign. These individuals, of course, would eventually be tagged as nontreaty *hostiles* by the United States, in events to come in the future.

⋯⋯≫⟪◉⟫≪⋯⋯

When the new government chose to take from the people, and when the people resisted, the guns and iron weapons were used to murder the people and pillage their properties. Efforts were made to destroy, burn, or contaminate their food supplies. The government knew that the people had no natural immunity to many of the European diseases the new people had brought over to Turtle Island. So the indigenous people were vulnerable to these diseases previously unknown to them, such as measles, rubella, influenza, dysentery, and smallpox, which wiped out and killed the people by the millions.

The government even took the extremely devious and secret approach of infecting the food and goods provided to the tribes, and bands and camps, by placing disease-laden items among them. In particular, during the time when the government was seeking to divest the Dakota, Nakota, and Lakota of all aboriginal lands, the government's agents, many times private business partners and profiteers, provided blankets to the Dakota, Nakota, and Lakota as fulfillment of some of the numerous treaty provisions. These blankets were intentionally infected with smallpox. This evil was carried out with the apparent blessing of the new government.

It was as if the government and its officials were dropping poison and disease from the sky and the clouds, as if the poison and the disease rained upon the people with no shelter from the drops. It was germ warfare used by a government against the people. It was a form of terrorism. The people could not fathom that something so devious, so vile, so destructive, could be consciously thought out by a human being, to wreak havoc and death upon another human being or upon a whole group of human beings.

Creator had blessed the Dakota, Nakota, and Lakota people with, in addition to a strong will, a strong body that could deal with every sort of illness-causing bacterium, germ, or organism. However, Creator had not provided enough time for the people to become immune or protected from these new alien diseases brought with the white people from Europe. Creator usually has enough time to provide the people's bodies with the natural ability to become immune, but these new diseases took hold too fast and with such frequency that the people's bodies were unprepared. Creator could not protect them in the natural way because of the fast invasion of these new people and their new and different diseases.

The death songs, death ceremonies, and death fires were occurring with far greater frequency, as were the cries—the moaning and the wailing—of the people when their children, grandchildren, sisters, brothers, cousins, mothers, fathers, and elders began to get sick with no meaningful way of healing or saving them. The people's medicine, which usually provided help and ensured health over thousands and thousands of years, was not useful or efficient against these new white diseases.

So the vast numbers of the people began to diminish. They suffered. They died. The death multiplied and continued. And the policy of genocide flourished. The grand scheme was working, the goal becoming attainable. The genocide was really happening. It was time for the people to seek out Wakan Tanka and Creator. It was time for another great *asking*.

⸻⸻ ⊙ ⸻⸻

Unrest and Corruption in Minnesota

In Minnesota Territory, and later in the state of Minnesota (*Mni sota*), following the "signing" of the various treaties with the *Sioux* (actually, the Dakota bands of the Mdewankanton, Wahpeton, Sisseton, and Wahpekute) of 1825, 1837, 1851, and lastly 1858, white settlers, white profiteers, and white entrepreneurs became obsessed with confiscating more and more of the Dakota's aboriginal lands and their natural resources. Corrupt businessmen such as Henry M. Rice, Gen. Henry H. Sibley, Maj. Gen. John Pope, Maj. Samuel Woods, Franklin Steele, Alexis Bailly, Samuel Stambaugh, Gen. James Shields, William Chapman, George Brackett, Alexander Ramsey Nininger, Henry Welles, George A. Nourse, Charles Flandrau, and Minnesota governor Alexander Ramsey saw riches that could be stolen and exploited, if only those *damn Indians* would disappear or be removed. Many of the greedy businessmen became politicians. For example, Rice and Ramsey, acquired their ill-gotten gains by mining copper near Mankato ("Blue Earth"), through the railroad interests, or by way of theft, speculation, and sale of confiscated Dakota lands (including the land rights) for purposes of homesteading and development.

By the time Minnesota became a territory, the indigenous populations in the area had been reorganized by the movement of colonization. The Dakota were no longer crucial to the survival or profit of the Europeans who flooded into the Minnesota Territory. This process of colonization and diminishment of the indigenous influence began with the signing of the treaties that ceded title to huge areas of land to the United States, which in turn opened that land up to settlement, homesteading, industrialization, and commerce. The treaties created an economic system that was wholly dependent upon Indian business, which was based upon the receipts of the annuity monies owed the Dakota from these treaties. The Dakota rarely received the benefits themselves. This credit system was diabolical and corrupt, with white European businessmen and profiteers creating illusionary debts. These credit debts were supposedly owed by the Dakota people for goods and services, and these white interests convinced the politicians to write prepayment of these debts into the treaties. The private businessmen in the area became wealthy off the Dakota's money payments, while the treaty annuity money almost never got to the Dakota.

The theft and scheming for ill-gotten gains using the property of the exploited Dakota reached a zenith with the despicable, fraudulent, deceptive, and conniving confiscation of the 1854–55 Half-Breed Land Scrip, which was partially obtained from many of the desolate prisoners at the Fort Snelling internment camp in 1862 through 1863.

Initially, within the 1830 Treaty of Prairie du Chien with the Dakota, the U.S. agreed that a fifteen by thirty-two mile area of over 320,000 acres of land were to be assigned in 640 acre tracts to the "halfbreeds". It was to be called the Half Breed Tract and was on the western shores of Lake Pepin near and within the present day city of Wabasha, Minnesota. In 1854, Henry M. Rice was instrumental in passing legislation to issue land scrip certificates granting the "half breeds or mixed bloods of the Dakota or Sioux nation of Indians" up to 640 acres on unoccupied, unsurveyed lands not reserved by the federal government in exchange for relinquishing all rights in the Half Breed Tract. A set list of *halfbreeds* or *halfbloods* was recognized. The law allowed the land scrip to be sold in fee or to be negotiated and or swapped for unoccupied public land anywhere in the U.S.. So these certificates of land scrip turned out to be quite valuable. Therefore, the scrip was attractive to thieves of the day.[3]

So, again, a hidden agenda of genocide was incorporated into the very intent and purpose of the successive treaties with the Dakota bands. The Dakota lost more and more of their lands through cessions in exchange for monies they were promised but never received, and, by losing their Half-Breed Land Scrip, annuities and other support. Even when the Dakota specifically negotiated clear intent in their end of the treaty agreement, the US Congress would just modify it to the

---

[3] Millikan, The Great Treasure of the Fort Snelling Prison Camp, p.8

Congress's own wishes, and ratify only parts of the treaties that were most desired by the corrupt politicians. For example, in the 1837 Treaty of Traverse des Sioux, the Dakota specifically negotiated to have granted the Dakota interpreter Scott Campbell, $450 per year for twenty years, plus a five-hundred-acre tract of land west of Fort Snelling (where the Minneapolis–St. Paul International Airport is today), but Congress just decided to strike that provision from the ratified treaty, despite the Dakota's insistence that it was part of said treaty. Promises were broken, treaties were breached and violated, and subsequent "laws" were passed to try to cover up the breaches and violations as much as the politicians could. The treaty-making period of history was a very dishonorable time for the United States and its government.

It was always the same with many in the white business circles back then, when it came to Indian dealings. The time was filled with moneymaking schemes to defraud and steal from the Indians. The corrupt people in business and government planned and conspired how to carry out these schemes and criminal activities, usually under the guise and protection of some law, some statute, some regulation, or even some treaty. But it always almost certainly involved greedy, uncaring operators who were willing to take and steal from the indigenous people in whatever manner or in whatever amount they could get away with. The Indian be damned. This was part of the onset of a legalized kleptocracy which was enabled by the governmental policies to allow the wealthy and well-connected to steal from innocent victims such as the Dakota, Nakota and Lakota. Whole business coalitions and families of white grifters emerged to prey on the opportunities presented from the money derived of cheating the Indians out of their land and property rights.

In 1862 many Dakota Indians who continued to live by the hunt began feuding with traders over the issue of these past payments for "debt." Funds from the 1858 treaty, it was believed by the Dakota, had paid all past debts owed by the individual Indians. Traders, on the other hand, argued that the Indians had received credit after the treaty. By the spring of 1862, white traders and their Indian customers were on the verge of a violent break. Many of the mixed-bloods were caught squarely between the two groups, Dakota and the whites. A white trader in New Ulm, when confronted with the starving Dakota asking for more credit so they could buy food from his grocery store, arrogantly said, "Let them eat grass."

Regardless of how the contemporary media or government reported why and how the 1862 Dakota Conflict arose in Minnesota, it was directly as a result of the United States' failure to provide the annuities, food, and obligations to the Dakota that were promised to them in the treaties of 1837, 1851, and 1858. The Dakota were losing their lands, their resources, and their way of life, and they were starving. It was surprising that there was not an uprising assertion of their rights and interests before 1862. In any event, those Dakota who did take part in the uprising, realistically and rationally, appeared to be justified to do so. The treaties were breached and their people were dying. It was unfortunate that violence rose to the level that it did. Many Dakota were thrown into an impossible tragic position because of those events.

According to many accounts, the events of the 1862 conflict began when four young Dakota men from Shakopee's village found themselves in Acton, Minnesota. The tension had escalated in early August 1862. Several small hunting and war parties had left the reservations. These groups were made up of young men, some of whom were angry about the way whites had treated their people and the failure of traders to assist the Indians. One of these groups from Shakopee's village on Rice Creek met and quarreled with Robinson Jones, a settler, after they had taken eggs from a chicken nest, near the small community of Acton. The impassioned warriors turned on Jones, killing him and several members of his family, which created a spark that ignited the conflict.

Another account of the conflict was recorded by Cecelia Campbell Stay on the first day of the conflict at the Redwood Agency, where she lived with her Dakota mixed-blood family. She wrote the following:

> Another incident I want to bring before my readers is that same day [August 18, 1862], [I] shall name our family first for we lived at that house, where some taken prisoners were congregated. There was Grandmother Mrs. Margaret Scott Cambell [Campbell], Uncle Hypolite [and his] wife Yuratwin (a cousin of Standing Buffalo) and two children

John & Theresa, Uncle Baptiste, Uncle Scott, father A.
J. Campbell, mother, sister Emily 15 years old, myself
(Celia), 13 and Mary 9, Joseph 7, Martha 5, Willie 2, Stella
about 7 weeks old. All those who were fleeing fugitives
[and were] brought back to us were Mrs. Antoine Findly
and step-son Billy Findly, Louis Martin [and his] wife and
three children. Mrs. Matilda Vanosse [with] one child on
her back ... she would fall in a fit ... Uncle Scott went,
met them and between them they got her to the house ...
Mrs. Findly never left us during the seven weeks of our
captivity until [she was] safe back to Traverse des Sioux
[and] out of danger. Cecelia Campbell Stay's Account.[4]

The Campbell family was one of those Dakota families who had
mixed heritage, Dakota, Scottish, and French. They were a prime
example of how the mixed-blood Dakota families had a horrible choice
at hand: to fight against the whites because of the treaty violations
and depredations, or to try to assist the noncombatant white settlers
and help keep them from being captured and killed by the factions of
the Dakota who were against governmental policy. Many had to make
urgent harsh decisions.

In the midst of the fight during the conflict, the New Ulm,
Minnesota, white trader who had proclaimed earlier, when speaking
about the plight of the starving Dakota, "Let them eat grass," had an
ironic fatal encounter. Andrew Myrick was found by his store dead, with
his mouth stuffed with grass.

The Lakota's relatives to the east, the Dakota bands of the
Mdewakanton, Sisseton, Wahpeton, and Wahpekute, were of the
full-blood and mixed-blood background. When the August 17, 1862,
events broke out, many of the Dakota relatives found themselves torn
between the two worlds: one group of the Dakota who chose to actively
participate in the war with the Minnesota white settlers and the US
military soldiers, and the other group, the Dakota, who chose not to
raise up any arms, but instead chose to protect or save the white settlers
who lived among them along the Minnesota River in southwestern

---

[4] Anderson, Woolworth, Through Dakota Eyes at p. 51-52.

Minnesota in 1862. The friendly *Sioux* (actually, friendly Dakota) found themselves scorned by those on both sides of the conflict. These Dakota friendlies were ostracized by many Dakota who fought against the whites and were also hated and demonized by the whites, the white government, and the white US military. The so-called friendly Dakota families endured the worst of both worlds. They had all of their land, property, treaty rights, and privileges forever stripped from them by the government, effectively stripping away their way of life. Some were hanged or killed in another way by the military when captured. Many were imprisoned at interment camps, like at the base of Fort Snelling in Minneapolis along the confluence of the Minnesota and Mississippi Rivers, for over a year from 1862 through 1863.

Some of the sixteen hundred prisoners who were forcibly marched to Fort Snelling from Camp Release near Redwood Falls were half-breeds/mixed-bloods. The United States determined that they would take the full-and mixed-bloods from Camp Release and hold them in captivity at Fort Snelling along the river. The Campbell and Renville families were among this group. As the Dakota were marched on foot through the town of Henderson, Minnesota, which was on the way, the white townspeople threw stones and sticks at them, even killing a young infant being carried in the arms of his young Dakota mother. These Dakota people were then imprisoned at the internment camp at the base of Fort Snelling, where they lived with extreme disease, starvation, and hopelessness. The Dakota prisoners began dying at an alarming rate while imprisoned there. Some of the half-breed men were eventually allowed to become Indian scouts ("Half-Breed Scouts," "Sibley's Scouts," "Renville Rangers," etc.) in exchange for their freedom from the prison camp. (Later, some were granted warranty deeds of 160 acres of land from the US president, but in most cases they lost that land too, thanks to white land thieves and corrupt governmental officials.) Through it all, the corrupt thieves like Rice and Steele, continued to fleece the Dakota halfbreeds of their valuable land scrip. Gabriel Renville would lose more than 500 acres of valuable land scrip to these corrupt grifters, when he sought to negotiate the freedom of he and his family from Ft. Snelling in 1863.

Many of the captured Dakota were later forcibly removed by steamboat, the *Davenport*, which was akin to a packed, deathtrap-style slave boat. The Dakota forced onto this boat were hauled twelve hundred miles down the Mississippi River to Davenport, Iowa, where the boat turned north and traveled eight hundred miles up the Missouri River, and were dumped at a desolate reserve along the Big Bend of the Missouri River in Dakota Territory at a place called Crow Creek. Over one-third of the people died from disease and starvation either on the trip or at Crow Creek that next year. The graves would populate the hillside overlooking the Missouri River and serve as a permanent haunting reminder of the horrible events and forced removal.

Many of the Santee Dakota, or "Isanti," were forcibly relocated to a new reservation outside the state of Minnesota near Niobrara, Nebraska, along the Missouri River. The Santees had to start a new life there in an unfamiliar land away from their relatives. Over time, many of them would seek out the Dakota relatives left behind in Minnesota.

Those of the friendly Dakota who had chosen to remain in Minnesota after 1862 found themselves hunted down like prey. Men, women, children, and the elderly were indiscriminately slaughtered or wounded and imprisoned. The violence touched every family of Dakota. Some were captured and committed to insane asylums, like at St. Peters, Minnesota, where they were tortured, subjected to inhumane medical experimentation, or perversely mutilated. Many died while committed, and all their property was stolen. The dead were often buried in unmarked pauper graves. Many Dakota were forced to become fugitives and vagabonds. Most were hated by a majority of the whites because of the way the government and local media had portrayed the events of the conflict. The corrupt politicians such as Gov. Alexander Ramsey wanted blood and revenge, as well as the extermination (as punishment) of the Dakota, no matter what their involvement was in the 1862 conflict. This edict would also include many of the mixed-blood Dakota and the *friendlies*. "The Sioux Indians must be exterminated or driven forever beyond the borders of the State," Ramsey was quoted as saying. Ramsey instituted a bounty of $25 to anyone who would kill the "redskins," the "red devils," and provide the scalp as proof. A local newspaper reported as follows:

The State of Minnesota, feeling aggrieved by the Government's slow and humanitarian mode of conducting war against the hostile Indians within her borders, has lately adopted some very decisive but questionable measures of her own for getting rid of the "red devils." A proclamation appeared offering a State bounty for every "scalp" of a Sioux that should be brought in by volunteer and amateur hunters. The document rested upon the official authority of Gov. (now United States Senator) RAMSEY, and greatly shocked some of that gentleman's Eastern friends who made haste (too much haste it seems) to repudiate the proclamation as a forgery and a slander.

But later accounts confirm the authenticity of the original document, which, however, has since undergone some modification. The hunters of the redskins were no long required to produce the scalps torn from the head of the slain victims, but they did have to furnish "satisfactory affidavits" of their exploits in bringing down their human (or inhuman) game. A St. Paul correspondent of a contemporary gives the Minnesotan view of the subject as follows:

Whatever exceptions humanitarians might take to the scalp bounty, they would soon be convinced of the wisdom and necessity of the present order if they would come among us, and expose their own scalps, instead of keeping at a safe distance, and prating about humanity. A "Moral Minnesotan" is informed that he doesn't need to defend Senator Ramsey from the imputations of issuing the order, as it is an act he is free to acknowledge, and read to sustain.[5]

It is undoubtedly true that a protracted residence on the Western frontier is fatal to the existence of sympathies once cherished for the "poor Indian." The feud between

---

[5] Waste of Warriors in the West, The New York Times, August 18, 1863

man and the serpent, begun in the Garden of Eden, is not more implacable than that between a frontiersman and a Sioux. Hence Minnesota will continue, without shame or remorse, to pay bounties for Sioux scalps, as other States pay for wolf scalps. It is a "State right" that will not be given up.[6]

On November 5, 1862, in Minnesota, 303 of the Dakota were tried in front of a military tribunal. Each case was heard for five minutes or less, with no attorneys for, or witnesses to speak on behalf of, the accused. All 303 were found guilty of either murder or rape, or both, of white settlers, and were sentenced to death by hanging. After some consideration, President Abraham Lincoln signed a death warrant for 38 of them who were to be hanged all at once in Mankato, Minnesota, on December 26, 1862. When Lincoln signed that death proclamation, he became a part of the history and spirit of those men and their families, and the ways that make up the traditional Dakota culture. He must have taken us in, in spirit. This deed forever remains an inhumane stain on Lincoln's reputation as an *emancipator,* and may be a reason why his spirit is yet unsettled (it is said by some that his spirit still roams the White House and the Capitol Building in Washington, DC). The Mankato hanging, the largest mass execution in US history, was attended by the local white population and had a somewhat carnivalesque, hate-filled atmosphere to it. Many of the corpses of the 38 decedents were stolen or purchased by local physicians to be used for study or exhibition. It was alleged that Dr. W. W. Mayo was one of the local physicians who confiscated the dead bodies of the Dakota men who had been hanged.

The Dakota men whose sentences were commuted were imprisoned in Davenport, Iowa, from 1862 to 1865, where more than half died. The treaties of 1837, 1851, and 1858 were abrogated by the government, and the annuities due the Dakota, even the innocent *friendly* Dakota, were instead paid to the white settlers for reparations. The government could not bring itself to pay reparations to any indigenous or black citizens, but it gladly did so for the white people in Minnesota. An Act of February 3, 1863, was passed to supposedly assist the innocent *friendly*

---

[6] Waste of Warriors in the West, New York Times, August 18, 1863

Dakota by providing them eighty acres of their own land, for themselves and their heirs, *forever*. But Congress and the courts later stole that right to that land from them as well.

Those of the Dakota who did escape Minnesota in 1862 fled toward their relatives to the west, the Nakota and Lakota, in Dakota Territory. The US military, however, regrouped and formed hunting parties to track them and hunt them down. This revenge-motivated military campaign, led by Gen. Henry H. Sibley, Gen. Alfred Sully, and others, led to many more conflicts with the Dakota people who were on the run for safe haven, as well as their relatives among the Nakota and Lakota. This military campaign to hunt down the Dakota led to massacres of large groups of innocent men, women, children, and elderly people at various sites throughout Dakota Territory.

As the remaining Dakota, finding themselves fugitives in their own aboriginal homeland in Minnesota, moved west, many sought refuge with the Yanktoni in Dakota Territory, with the Hidatsa and Mandans near Devils Lake, and also with the Lakota of the Hunkpapa, Mnincoju, Sans Arc, and Two Kettle bands. However, while the Dakota were in the process of seeking refuge, the US military did catch up with many of them.

On September 3, 1863, six hundred and fifty soldiers under Gen. Alfred Sully attacked a Yanktonai hunting camp at White Stone Hill, Dakota Territory, south of present-day Jamestown, North Dakota. At least three hundred Dakota and Lakota were killed. Sully mistook the Yanktonai as being involved in the Minnesota Conflict. There had been a handful of women and children that had fled Minnesota to seek safe haven with relatives. Sully ordered that the wounded be killed. On September 4 and 5, 1863, Sully ordered total destruction of the Yanktonai camp at White Stone Hill. The remaining Yanktonai that there not dead, were taken to Crow Creek Agency as prisoners of war. Later, in July 1864, Sully again pursued whom he believed to be bands of Dakota from Minnesota, but instead confronted a hunting camp of about sixteen hundred Yanktonai, Hunkpapa, Blackfeet, and others near the Little Missouri River at Killdeer Mountain in Dakota Territory, killing about one hundred. The soldiers destroyed everything in the camp. Sully chased the remaining bands into the North Dakota

Badlands and attacked them along the Yellowstone River. Many more were captured and died.

Volunteer militias rose up across the new country during the midst of the Civil War. Some of these mercenaries were out to kill Indians. At dawn on November 29, 1864, led by a former Methodist minister named Col. John M. Chivington, the Third Colorado Cavalry Militia volunteers surrounded and then attacked a sleeping Cheyenne village headed by Black Kettle at Sand Creek, Colorado. Black Kettle had just swore peace with the government. The fanatical Chivington had ordered the women and children destroyed. He was quoted as saying, "Nits make lice." The seven hundred volunteers obeyed orders and chased down the Cheyenne, killed them, and then mutilated their bodies. Men and women were dismembered and decapitated; children, bayoneted and piked; pregnant women, cut up, their fetuses removed. Genitalia were sliced off and kept. The militia members even wore the Cheyenne body parts, including women's genitalia, in a parade held in Denver to celebrate once they returned after their "victory."

So it was that Saved By Bear, and his people of the Mnincoju, became increasingly aware of the atrocities, the horror, the death, and the unspeakable genocidal acts occurring among their relatives to the east and south.

One day, in particular, in the hot, dry late spring season of the year of 1863, two young riders approached the Mnincoju camp along the Owl River. It was shortly before dusk. The Akicita perimeter scouts noticed these riders in the distance and cautiously rode out toward them to find out what their story was, before the riders could get close to the camp. Goes Along and Blue Bear stopped them. Upon learning that the two young men were Mdewakanton Dakota from the Yellow Medicine River Valley near Lac qui Parle and the holy area of the sacred red pipestone, the Mnincoju Akicita warriors escorted them into camp, all on horseback, the two Dakotas looking extremely exhausted and starved, as did their skinny horses.

They were taken to the center lodge of Iron White Man and his wife, Fire Cloud. It was here that the *naca* were called for, and came to the lodge to meet with the two young Dakota warriors. The Mdewakantons were extremely hungry, soiled, and weary, and appeared to have a look of disdain and hopelessness about them. The naca, and the elders who arrived, both men and women, gathered around the two young men, while the men were given large portions of meat and corn to eat, and water to drink. They ate as if they had not done so for weeks, like they were afraid that the food would be ripped from their hands before they could place it upon their lips. They guzzled the horn cups of water offered to them, spilling half of it in their haste to quench an obvious long-lived thirst. After many minutes of the Mnincoju respectfully allowing the two men to attend to their overwhelming human instinctual needs of the body, the older-looking one of the two spoke first.

"Pilamaya yelo, Kolas. I am One Plume from the land of the Spirit Lake. This is Black Bird, my cousin from the quarry area. We are forever grateful to you for taking us in and providing your hospitality and your food and drink. It has been many nights since we have eaten anything but bugs and dandelions, or since we have closed our eyes for more than a moment."

"Wastè, kolas, relatives," said Short Neck, the elder female member of the camp's naca. "We are happy to help, and to see you alive. Tell us what it is that you have been through."

One Plume slowly turned to Black Bird. The two locked weary eyes. Black Bird then nodded at his cousin. One Plume sighed deeply, bowed his head, and sat in a meaningful yet uncomfortable silence for a moment. Black Bird reached over and placed his dirt-soiled hand upon his cousin's shoulder, as if to signal an acknowledgement of the difficulty of the task at hand: to tell the story. One Plume raised his head and looked at Short Neck, and then at the faces of the others pressed around the fire in the lodge. All could see the tears welling up in his eyes. His dried, chapped lips opened, but he stayed temporarily mute.

From across the blazing tips of the fire, Fights the Bear looked at the young One Plume, nodded his head, and said, "It is okay, brother. It is good for you to tell us, to let it come forth from your heart and your spirit, so that we can all know what it is that casts such a sad shadow upon your heart. It is okay. We must hear what you have to say, good or bad. You are a friend here, our relative. You are safe. We will honor our commitment to all our relatives."

One Plume nodded. But before he started telling the Mnincoju people the horrific stories he had to reveal and describe, he acknowledged the age-old recognition of the bonds between the peoples of all the lands. "We knew we could come to you, the Mnincoju. We knew from our ancestors' words and stories that you would welcome us and take us in, give us safe haven, and protect us. We know who you are. We know your role in all things. We knew it was right to come to you, and that you are the ones to know, who must know." And then One Plume tearfully told his story of all that had occurred in the east. The Mnincoju listened and learned. They took it in. At the end, they thanked One Plume. And they all remembered.

Later, Fire Cloud, overcome with grief, worry, and anxiety for all of the Lakota's relatives to the east who were going through such horrible times and atrocities as painstakingly described by One Plume, walked up to the high ground overlooking the river. There she made offerings to comfort the spirits of the dead and to pray for the safety and guidance of the living. She then prayed to Creator and Wakan Tanka, and asked all of her ancestors and the spirits of those who had passed before, to help. She wept longer and harder than she had in quite a while.

It would be a foreshadowing of the gradual, yet increasing, encroachment of the white settlers and armies into Lakota territory. The people would need to take notice and become aware, become conscious of the coming changes, become aware of the need to plan.

8

WHIRLWIND PASSAGE

Now comes a time in the people's lives when Saved By Bear is taught to be a good human being and also be taught about what is happening to the people, how they are having to undergo dramatic changes, how things once familiar, are now becoming nonexistent. Travel, settlement, and nomadic behavior are definitely on the decline.

What we are seeing now is our own people turning from and shunning their tradition and culture. As they are given so-called amenities and promises from the new government, some turn against us and help to destroy the culture of the people. These tribal members are now somehow wanting to be a part of the white government and its military. They now are treating our families as a mere obstacle to their getting what they want in the new world. They have absorbed the greed, the anger, the hatred, and even the racism against their own. Because of this, they are helping to search out and find those of our families who are called hostiles, who will not adopt the trading post life or any other submissive way of life. Now, particular Lakota families are beginning to lose their nomadic livelihood. Rather than traveling to their own hunting grounds and settlements, they are now having to take each tiospaye almost regularly into hiding, traveling to and from the homes of trusted relatives only. If you were to let word out to one of these informants who wants you out of the way, they would alert the military, who would come and murder you. So the people now fear murder, torture, and other atrocities—the inhumane acts committed by these people. These atrocities are more prevalent than ever before.

Saved By Bear sees this. He is coming to understand now that his place in society has changed. He may be but in his early teen years, but now he must become a warrior, and quickly. This is also realized by all the families, by males and females alike. Life and culture is dramatically changing. We will have our own ways, but they will now have to be practiced in secret. This secrecy will allow us to have an opportunity to survive. Our prayers go directly to Wakan Tanka for *wiconi*—life. How can we maintain life, how can we survive what is happening, and what will we be without our tradition and culture? These are the questions that almost all of the indigenous tribal people are asking as they come westward now. The whites come for possession, money, and politics, There is no human quality that we want to associate with. As they come through, it is like a cancer. It starts in one place and then spreads to all directions. And if you happen to be in their vicinity, you will be infected or destroyed.

Saved By Bear is now approximately age thirteen. Now he and the other braves of his age group, throughout the tiospaye and extended families, are called to become warriors. This they must do confidently and quickly. It is essential for the livelihood of the people. The elders and their support, including their memory and past accomplishments, add the spiritual component of the medicine, and the lodge, and the other things that are included in the rite of passage to manhood. All of these young boys will be mentored now, and they will bear a greater responsibility than have other Lakota their age throughout the history of our culture. But they have been informed, so they understand why there is such haste to ready them for what is coming. The Lakota numbers are reduced, and all we have are those whom we trust and live with. These young braves are going to be another small group of our warriors in the near future.

The braves will be taught the physical requirements, and there will be an emphasis on their physical conditioning. Certain physical abilities will be needed in the case of attack, or if we are trailed in the process of seeking safety and refuge. The mental capabilities will be another thing that the young ones will need to develop. They will require very good direction from their elders and the warriors, because to kill another man or to be killed at that age is different from what the brave would normally be doing, such as watching the horses, watching someone making weapons, or helping Grandmother. The brave now has the responsibility of a *wicasa*, and he must act the part and behave in a way that reflects the proper mental state. The elders and warriors will prepare him for life and death. But they will accept his abilities and nurture them accordingly, much the same as the process for the true warrior who has already been decorated.

This life now is dependent upon the youth. They will carry the hopes and dreams of the elders. They will carry the future of the adults and families, tending to their needs. This is because they are the remaining labor force. It is up to them to help us, to keep us secure, and to fulfill our needs. We depend upon these young men, these young braves. We respect them.

When Saved By Bear is going through this quick training with the others, the most important thing that he is going to learn is who he is and what his capabilities are. He will learn what a true warrior is.

The role of the women is also changing. Things that once were normal and routine to them, such as providing sustenance, tending to relatives, and making visits, are now scarce and sparse. Their life is changing so much that they now will be called upon to be warriors in their own sense. The things that they do will have to be done in haste. The stores of food and necessary items will have to be filled quickly and hidden away, so only a select few will know where these things are. It is hard for anyone to try to adapt to a new way of life in a day, a week, or even a year, but these are strong human beings and their commitment to one another will come full circle in the end. The women will perform their duties to help the warriors accomplish the goal of saving our traditions and culture. They will be strong and they will pray.

The medicine women will access what is needed from their perspective, the female side. Grandmother Earth will be their guide, as she is the life giver and they have given us life. Now the women will take many new avenues or paths, even at times being victims of or witnesses to the genocidal behavior that is approaching. Since the lives of the young people are changing very fast, there is not enough time for the youth to truly grow up. And since the lives of the women are changing just as fast, they do not have enough time to truly take care of their family. Now the Lakota have to live in such a way that mere seconds and minutes may mean the difference between life or death. The youths, the parents, and the elders are all learning to relate to one another and communicate in a different manner now.

There is now a need to do a lot for preparation in a short amount of time, because time is valuable and there is a sense of urgency. Still, the braves must have the patience and diligence to do things right. Sometimes when a person looks up to the sky, he sees only sky, but if he opens up his spirit and looks beyond that which is ordinary and easily recognized, he may miss the clouds, or miss the whirlwind forming within the clouds. This is the kind of detail in even common things, that the people were searching for to help them in their moment of need in light of preparing these young Lakota braves to assume their roles as warriors at a hastened pace.

In the Lakota world, those who still believe and practice the traditional cultural ways are the last ones to hold this sacred behavior and connection. They are going to keep this throughout time. During this brief period when the Lakota are adapting to the changing world and becoming different human beings than they were before, they experience great turmoil within themselves. And the mind plays a major role in how they come to adapt to the changing world while retaining their traditions. The reason that the Lakota culture remains intact is because of the elders, the medicine, and the people. The headmen and headwomen now play prevalent roles, performing the ceremonies and including parts of the tradition and culture so as to keep these things alive. They will give everything of their existence to ensure that we do not lose everything we were given from Creator.

These wisdom keepers will do their absolute best to teach us to hold on to our prayer.

In facing an uncertain future, one also faces the danger of losing what one already has, what one cannot afford to lose. So the preparation needs to be extra careful so as not to leave behind that which we are, to attain something that you choose to become. Don't lose your spirit along the way. Because if that is allowed to happen, then the goal can never be attained.

Hanbleceya in He Sapa

In the early summer season, Iron White Man told Saved By Bear that he had received a vision from Wakinyan during the recent inipi. In the vision, his grandson Saved By Bear was asked to stand on a hill for his people. He is asked by Creator and the spirits to participate in his own hanbleceya. It was then decided between Saved By Bear and his grandfather that the hanbleceya would take place upon a high hill in the He Sapa. Once the preparations were made, the people traveled to He Sapa, to the sacred mountain, Mato Paha. A camp was set up, and the spiritual fire was lit. On the morning of the start of his four-day hanbleceya, Saved By Bear had set himself upon the hill within his natural altar. And he started to pray. The people by the fire started the drumbeat, and then the songs began.

At one point during his fouth day of hanbleceya on Mato Paha, Saved By Bear's vision began to become locked on certain aspects of those things that his human eye could see.

His mind was jumping from prayer to prayer, from gratitude to gratitude, from question to question. His thoughts bounded within his mind like so many pony herds galloping in a common direction all at once. The ponies became diverted, in unison. They quickly and abruptly switched direction to avoid an approaching obstacle, only to individually separate into a hundred different tracers upon the same sloping prairie before the great expanse of the universe laid out in front of them: one leaping over a mountain; another splashing through a shallow ocean tide; another leaping up from within a molten volcano; another sprinting along a high narrow mountainside trail; another galloping through groves and groves of pine trees, brushing the treetops with his front and back legs, above the hooves; and another one jolting up and into the horizontal lighting of Wakinyan as it lights and advances across a dusky, stormy summer sky.

So much to see. So much to hear. So much to feel. So much to experience. So much to know. So much to learn. And so much time, yet not enough. As Saved By Bear sees his face age within a few seconds, as his empty hands are grasping for a levitating cannumpa billowing a fine puff of white smoke. He feels the ground giving around his bare feet as the sun races across the sky to set, to be immediately replaced by the night sky and the billions of stars. His face refreshes before his mind's eye, resuming the form of the young Lakota brave, on his white horse at the edge of the cliff looking out over a great canyon and upward, beyond a full moon, and then into the bright and infinitely trailing and revolving Trail of Spirits, the Milky Way. Looking up closely, he sees the reflection of the great starry trail in his dark brown eye. Looking closer yet, his eye zooms in to see the people carrying the buffalo-robe-wrapped earthly bodies of the ancestors, solemnly walking their way toward the sparkling Big Dipper in the far west horizon at the end of the milky Spirit Trail. The *Wanagi Tacanku*.

One of the stars suddenly flashes, and explodes, sending millions of flaming and trailing embers up and out. Saved By Bear's eyes follow a group of them. One of the blue-colored embers glowingly flies and falls at the same time, alighting upon a high rocky peak in the sacred He Sapa. A great eagle soars down to grasp the ember in his huge claw, and lands on the rocky ledge. The wanbli gently turns, offering the glowing light to his neighbor the great owl. The owl was sitting there near the high ledge tending to her four owlets, who were waiting to be fed. They were snugly positioned one by one beside each other at their mother's feet in the great round nest. The wanbli presents the blue glowing ball to the owl, who reaches out. Then the wanbli squeezes the glowing ball, and smaller blazing spheres gently drop into the mother owl's right calwed foot. She hops on the other foot to her children and gently places one small sphere near each of their beaks. With their huge bright eyes, they look at the glowing spheres at the ends of their noses. One sphere drops from the mother owl's claw, bounces on the rocky surface, and breaks into a hundred smaller, yet just as energetic, balls of light.

One of the smaller spheres falls off the edge of Owl's Nest Peak, bouncing and rolling down the gray rock cliff, off the trees and stone outcroppings, and coming to rest at the foot of a big pine tree, which is gently swaying in the brightly lit night sky.

The sphere comes to a rest. Then, still smoldering, it begins to burn its way through the pine needles and twigs, and into the powdery glinting dirt. Soon, within a few seconds, it is gone. A few seconds after that, the young Lakota's eye witnesses the earth beginning to move at the foot of the big pine. The earth slowly but constantly pushes up and outward. A small yet definitive mound forms. A hole begins to form at the top and center of the mound. The dirt begins to churn upward, and then within itself. Slowly, a small head, a dark brown shiny head, appears at the hole. Then a set of skinny triple-jointed legs come out. The whole scene plays out before Saved By Bear through the lens of his human eye.

The ant emerges. He slides himself free of the hole and looks about, antennae wriggling. He appears to study his surroundings. He busily ducks back down into the earth, into the hole. The dirt covers his body. Abruptly, a round brown metallic-looking pebble emerges from the hole as if levitating on its own, yet below the bottom curve of the shiny pebble is the head and the front legs of the ant. He pushes up. The pebble dwarfs his head, his legs, his body. And yet with the gift of unbridled strength and determination, he pushes the pebble up and out of the hole at the top of the mound. He moves the pebble to the side and carries it on his back, grasping as he goes, until he reaches the base of the mound. There the ant leaves the pebble, turns, and following the same pathway, goes back up and disappears into the hole.

As the young Lakota watches, the next pebble emerges in the same way, toted by the same ant. Again the same movement, the same result, and the same return. Again he disappears, and reemerges with yet another shiny pebble, again and again, never tiring, never stopping to rest. The same thing, over and over again. Soon a small pile of pebbles has formed at the base of the mound. As he is turning to reenter the hole, the ant is obstructed momentarily by another ant coming out, pushing his own shiny pebble. The first ant kindly gives way, as if to politely grant passage to the other. Then, once the hole is clear, he goes back in himself. Soon after, another ant emerges, then another, then another, and then another. It now seems as if fifty ants are scurrying and hurrying in and out of the hole at the top of the mound. Each time, each ant brings forth a new shiny pebble, only to leave it at the base of the mound and return for another. The pebbles are stacking up. Soon they completely cover the exterior of the anthill. Each shiny pebble seems the same, much bigger than the ant. There are very many ants, all of them moving in a smooth orderly fashion, so diligent, so determined. They have built their home by bringing parts of Grandmother Earth up and out from within, the sacred building blocks moved by each one, for the benefit of all. It reminds him of the sacred life work of the brother bee who pollinates the plants so all life can exist.

As the young Lakota watches, the individual pebbles at the base of the anthill itself, begin to glow and flicker as if carrying their own force within. It is at this point that the young Lakota eye with the brown pupil, suddenly becomes a shinier, more solid orb. Saved By Bear sees it is his mind. And that orb is now looking up, up toward the starry night sky as if up and out of a hole in the ground. Then the focus turns around, and in. Now, it is as if the young Lakota is seeing through a new, different set of eyes, not his own human eyes, but those of another. It appears now that the new eye and the new vision sees the triple-jointed legs ahead of him. Those skinny legs are taking him down the dark hole, until a bright opening appears at the end. The opening grows larger and brighter with each small forward step of the skinny legs. Soon, the hole opens up into a vast cave of shiny rock and dirt. A shiny round glowing sphere is nestled in a campfire ring in the center of the cave. It is from here, from the base, that the shiny metallic spheres come.

The small skinny legs reach out, grasp the nearest shiny brown round sphere, haul it in front of the set of ant eyes, and lift upward. Swiftly and momentarily, the round pebble emits a small blue energy, which then calms. Then the young warrior feels himself seeing and feeling those skinny arms and legs moving up and back into the hole. Going up, up, up, and then out of the opening, where the shiny pebble is taken to the bottom of the hill to be piled with the rest. And then the small skinny legs turn and move back toward the hole again, just as the ant head clears the hole and starts down again. Now, Saved By Bear's view moves quickly up again to the great Milky Way above the Owl's Nest Peak, and along that great starry trail, until the light begins to brighten, and then suddenly turns into a blazing star, Wi, the sun.

The eye closes, but the reddish-orange shape of the sun remains even through the covering of the eyelid. Slowly the eye opens, and the slanted view from behind dark eyelashes reveals that Saved By Bear's head is on its side, and the bright sun is beating down on him, warming his face.

He is still on the hill, and he is still within his fasting period. He blinks his brown human eye to ward off some of the brightness, and slowly focuses on the scene in front of his face.

There, not more than a foot in front of his eye, a small metallic pebble is being pushed out of the small hole at the top of the mound laden with small shiny brown pebbles. And the shiny head with full shiny eyes and two skinny triple-jointed legs emerges, pushing and lifting the pebble. The pebble is many times larger than the small head and skinny legs. It is pushed up and out of the opening of the mound. With uncanny strength and determination, the small ant person carries the shiny pebble up, then out, and then down the outside slope of the mound, down to near the base, where it is placed on top of and next to other similar shiny pebbles. There the ant lets go and leaves it. Then he turns his body and starts back up the side of the mound toward the hole. And as Saved By Bear watches with his human eye, he notices the quick, slight, almost imperceptible flash of a blue light of energy crackling from the ant's recently deposited shiny pebble. The blue light briefly takes the shape of a horse… head down, appearing to be drinking from a stream… or praying. And now he understands. It is a part of his journey, and the sacredness of the miracle that he has been gifted by Creator to see. It is all connected—always has been, always will be. Saved By Bear sits up on the ground, and he prays. It is another gift, another lesson to be learned, thanks to the ant people and their sacred pebbles.

All the lessons to learn, all the things to sense, and all the spirits to feel, hear, and speak with. These things are all a part of the young Lakota's learning experience, all a part of the nurturing of his spirit, all a part of his journey to become a man, to become a warrior.

As Saved By Bear regains a view of his present earthly surroundings, he realizes it is dark. The billions of stars shine brightly overhead amid the warm night breeze. The hair near his ear wisps to and fro, and now allows a soothing rhythmic sound to gather, then dwell within his ear, his hearing. It is the steady, calming, comforting beat of the drum by the distant campfire. The campfire that his family and his mentors have kept for him…for his hanbleceya. And the singing begins all over again.

———— «◎» ————

Whoosht… Whoosht.

In quick succession, with lightning speed, the arrows shoot through the sky. The first flies through the air and strikes a tree. The second, however, enters the body with a thud. There is silence, then the rustling of the pine needles, and then a gasp and the sound of the body crashing to the earth.

The young Lakota peers over his outstretched arm still gripping his bow, waiting. Then he slowly lowers his bow and listens as hard as he can. The piercing screech of an eagle's call can be heard in the distance. Previously crouching, the brave now stands. The pine needles that have collected at the knees of his buckskin pants fall to the ground. His moccasins, well-worn from the many miles behind him, move slowly toward the sound of the thud following the last shot.

He crouches again but slowly moves forward. A light warm breeze moves through his long brown hair, which is tied into pigtails on the sides of his head. He sniffs the deep pine smell of the trees and the cones. In a few steps, from around the border of the low-lying gray granite rock, he sees the tip of the antlers. He knows for sure now that his last arrow connected.

Twenty feet in front, he can hear the somewhat labored breathing, and see the slight twitch of the antlers. Having done this many times before, he knows what the sound means. He knows that the buck, as his prey, is in the last moments of his physical life on Grandmother Earth. He knows that it is a gift to him and his family that the buck was here at this time, on this day, for him to sight, pursue, and then take. It is what he and his people had been taught and had done for thousands of years. His grandfather, and then his father, prepared him for these moments, teaching him not only the fine art of tracking, hunting, sighting his prey, and shooting his target where it would be most efficient. But also what to do after his target was hit, and now at this time, in nearing the end of the buck's life.

Out of respect for Wakan Tanka and for his four-legged brothers, the young Saved By Bear recognizes and accepts his sacred duty to the four-legged brother that is now giving his own life so that Saved By Bear and his family may survive. Saved By Bear's father, having also been raised in the He Sapa and surrounding prairies of the great lands west of the Big Muddy, had taught Saved By Bear that now was the time to honor the being that allowed himself to be taken for his meat, his hide, his horns, and his energy.

Saved By Bear walks among the crushing pine needles and cones, his footsteps no longer concealed. He draws his bone knife from its beaded leather sheath slowly, with his right hand. He had anticipated that he would need to use it to assist the buck brother on his way to the other side.

Saved By Bear comes upon the ten-point buck that is still slightly wheezing and barely moving, his big brown eyes staring. It is as if the big buck knows that his life was not taken, or given, in vain. He had seen this young Lakota before on the hunt in the hills and trees, and up until this time, he had been fast, strong, and quick enough to keep a safe distance from the hunting parties.

But now the buck sees the bow shooter's face and smells his body and his buckskin. His nostrils flare with the knowing sense that it was okay for him to have been taken by this one. The buck senses that he now is becoming a brighter part of the grand Circle of life. He had lived many years in these sacred hills and was grateful for the experience and for his life. Now, he sees Saved By Bear standing, and then kneeling, over his wounded body, the body whose breath is about to leave. The arrow had struck near his heart. He knew that it had been a near perfect shot, in order to more quickly and efficiently end his physical life. He suddenly looks into Saved By Bear's eyes, acknowledging to him that it is all okay. He will not fight. He is ready. In fact, he is anxious now to see what the spirits on the other side are like and how he might be greeted by his ancestors and relatives.

Saved By Bear sees this look and acknowledges it with a nod of his head. Reaching out, Saved By Bear caresses the buck's forehead to soothe his pain and suffering. Saved By Bear, too, knows the end is near. He looks at his knife, which could be used to cut the throat of his brother deer to quicken the onset of death, but he realizes that he does not have to use it with this one. Saved By Bear looks into the buck's eye, seeing the eye flash and then begin to slowly close. He reaches for the end of the deeply embedded arrow. It had been a very true shot. The precision of the shot made it easier for the buck to begin his next journey.

Saved By Bear places his left knee near the deer's softly beating heart, feeling it lurch and then slowly pulse. He again strokes the buck's forehead and begins his prayer that he had been taught by his father and the others: "Be still, my brother. It is okay for you to go now. Wakan Tanka awaits you. I want to thank you for what you have given to me and my family, brother. It is okay, brother. No pain awaits you. May Wakan Tanka be with you. Thank you for giving us life, brother."

Then the big round brown eye closes for the last time, and Saved By Bear feels no beating or movement against his knee. The great buck has provided the ultimate sacrifice to the people. The brother buck's part of the Circle of life is now complete. Wakan Tanka will be good to him.

Saved By Bear, and all Lakota, were taught how to respect those that contribute to the chain and the Circle of life, those that accept the giving of themselves or their physical life, knowing that their life is not given in vain, that their bodies and their energy will be used for a greater good, that thanks are given to them, each of them, no matter how big or small, when their lives are taken and their bodies and energy are ultimately received. The wise elders always say, "Do not kill for the sake of killing. Remember, all things—all beings and their existence—are connected with us. With all of creation and with all of what Grandmother Earth offers to us so that we can enjoy this gift we are given called life, only kill when necessary. It is more honorable not to kill if you can avoid it. When taking the life of our brothers, the tatanka, the deer, the elk, the bear, the fish, always know that they are giving their lives so that you and your family can survive. Remember that, and thank them."

Thunder Butte

Back along the Owl River, almost all the time, clouds would form over Thunder Butte, Wakinyan Paha, but it would not really rain. Wakinyan Paha was one of the ancient sacred sites gifted to the people by Creator. The Thunder Beings were among the most powerful of all spirits. The gift of the Wakinyan, in the form of lightning and rainwater, was a gift of cleansing and nourishment, and of rejuvenation of the natural world on Grandmother Earth. At Wakinyan Paha, it seemed as if the lightning (*wakan gli*) and the thunder emanated from somewhere within the butte itself. As the times in the world grew tougher and harder, Thunder Butte appeared to be more active.

There were times when Saved By Bear and his family would go up to the top, where there was a natural stone table positioned near the center. They would hold the cannumpa and pray to the sacred directions. There was a particular focus on starting into the west, and then moving to the right, to the north, to the east, to the south, to the earth, to the sky, and back to the west. West, the direction of the Wakinyan, the great Thunder Beings. Some within the Mnincoju were fearful of praying to the west, fearful of the strongest of medicines, apprehensive of the Thunder Beings and their reaction. To the spirits of Saved By Bear and his family, Wakinyan, the west, was always the direction that was home. He and his family felt the most comfortable and the most natural when praying to the west, facing the Wakinyan to speak to the Thunder Beings. Never neglectful of any of the directions of life or of Creator and Unci Maka, Saved By Bear always regarded the west as the starting and ending point of all things.

Sinte and Sunka

She came to Saved By Bear as a small one that fit into his hand. In the spring season of 1860, one of the loyal female dogs in the camp had recently given birth in the tipi next to his. The gray mother dog's name was Isota. The young puppies' mother had been with the family of Runs Many for over six years and had been a wonderful, loyal, and lovable dog. When she gave birth to a batch of four newborns, it was quite easy for the family to find each of the new pups a home. All dogs were given a home with the people under any circumstances.

The first time Saved By Bear laid eyes upon her was when he was almost fourteen years of age. Having been invited to go over to Runs Many's family lodge to see them, he went. He looked into a corner at a circular pile of elk hide with pieces of warm buffalo hair. In the middle lay Isota and her four little babies.

The pups were now about three weeks old. They could barely walk or see. The little ones were motivated by their mother's milk, her comforting licks, and her body heat, more than anything else in the world. When Saved By Bear came to the puppy nest in the lodge, a little white female pup with floppy ears and a straight short tail ceased her snuggling. She stood, slightly stumbling on her tiny paws, crouching and moving toward his hand where he knelt. She came to him by way of his warmth and smell, and the small kissing sound he made with his lips. Her tiny brown eyes for the first time looked into his. At this moment, all of Saved By Bear's previous encounters with the beings of the wild, the four-leggeds, the winged, and the other people, were second nature to him. However, the energy he felt from this little life and small beating heart positively jolted his own heart. He smiled. She came to him as if she had been waiting for his arrival.

As he caressed her small black nose and felt her little puppy teeth nibble on his fingertip, he fell in love with her. She licked and sucked on the edge of his finger, never losing eye contact with him. She wagged her straight short little tail enthusiastically. He carefully picked her up and held her close to his face to feel her warm body heat against his chin. The fine soft white hair on her chest caressed his skin.

She never ceased her loving and incessant licking. It was as if she were trying to get to know him by tasting him. He kissed the top of her small head, and breathed in her fresh newborn puppy scent. He remembered similar encounters throughout his life in the various camps, moments of his young life when he witnessed those newborn and the new joys of life and love that were presented. He'd even had encounters with other litters of puppies and other babies of the wild, as they had their initial contact with the human beings.

But Saved By Bear had nothing in his memory to compare to the smell of a puppy, the smell of the beginning of life of the human being's best friend, the *sunka* kind. The smell was unlike anything else. From the smell of the paws, the soft hair, and the soft belly to the unmistakable smell of puppy breath, it was like a dash of love manifesting itself within the spirit through the nostrils. This was the introduction of the young brave Saved By Bear to a being that would prove to be a genuine, loyal, and forever loving and soulful friend and companion. He laughed and smiled. He hugged the puppy close to his chest, to his heart. She stopped licking long enough to appear to be listening to his heartbeat. He felt her tiny heartbeat through his shirt and against his own.

He looked over at Runs Many and his wife, High Hawk, and smiled. They smiled back at him, acknowledging the connection between human being and young dog. And they all knew. Saved By Bear had just found a companion for his journey in life, someone to help him through good and bad times, comforting and tough moments, trying and enjoyable moments, alike. He knew this little one would grow with him. They would grow together, and love each other, for life. It would be like the connection he had with his Wildfire, the same on many levels, but different in the sense that sunka assumed the role of being the extension of the human heart and spirit. The horse did the same; however, it not only carried the connection of the heart and spirit but also served as the physical means of literally carrying Saved by Bear's body at times. With sunka, they loved and shared their spirits and care for their humans, but their burden was to carry the human heart and conscience, as well.

So it was that the little girl puppy was gifted to Saved By Bear, not so much from Runs Many, as from Creator. He would name her Sinte, honoring not only her short straight tail but also the fact that she would try to be with him always unless he told her to stay with the family. It was like she was his tail… his Sinte.

As she matured and grew that first year, her fur naturally thickened and became more coarse. She grew strong and agile. The fur of her front legs grew in such a way that her small legs appeared to be wearing leggings, the type that the warriors often wore for celebration dances or other special events. Those leggings of hers would serve to be Sinte's way of reminding Saved By Bear that her life was part of the celebration of his own life. She was his little four-legged warrior, his protector, his warmth while sleeping, his kind and loving companion through all the moments in life that he would be expected to face and endure. And through her love and commitment, she would always be there to show him kindness, give him warmth, give him laughter, and entertain him with her antics.

She loved to chase and run. And when she ran or pranced about, her straight tail would stand on end as if she were a loyal warrior carrying her spear into camp in a show of friendship, strength, and protection. She could nearly climb trees with her strength and agility. She could jump over three times her height. She sprinted with the best horses, even Wildfire. She could walk ten miles a day if necessary, and still run and jump in the evening to entertain Saved By Bear and his family, making them laugh. When he needed strength at times, he would reach for her paw. It would always be there. But always at the end of day, when the sun caressed the western horizon, she found her best friend, searched out his warmth, and cuddled up next to him as if to relive and reshare those moments of their first meeting so many years ago. And that is how the two slept most nights, the Lakota with his loving and loyal dog by his side, just as Creator intended.

The story of Saved By Bear and Sinte is a story of a life shared with true loving friends. True friends whose souls join your own while you live. Souls that penetrate your very being and existence because of their ever-present, reliable, trustworthy, and unconditional love for you no matter what.

To look into the eyes of a soul that loves you unconditionally is to reconnect with what life is all about. Life was intended by our Creator to be a spiritual miracle of experiencing events, happenings, and moments that enhance our existence while we occupy the physical realm with our earthly presence. Those who love unconditionally are those who will always be there during your life, no questions asked, no reason put forth, and indeed no reason needed, except that love exists and is there—and nothing else matters.

A wise Lakota once said long ago that the dog represents the west direction, which is also the direction of the Wakinyan, the Thunder

Beings. It is also the direction of the hail, the rain, the horse, the wolf, and the coyote. The dog is a very close relative of the Lakota, just like the buffalo is. The dog is by far the most domesticated relative that the Lakota people have ever had. The dog protects us. The dog warns us of danger. The dog is strong enough to drag a travois. The dog protects the children. The dog is the being from whom the children learn about all of the other four-legged peoples. The dog has become a source of enjoyment, entertainment, and comfort for human beings. Dogs are funny when they choose to be, like when they get wet and run around with their wet birdlike legs, and when they roll and spring about while wet. They are our brothers, our companion souls. They depend upon us as we depend upon them.

Dogs were sent here to the Lakota by the Creator to help us. And they have helped us. Dogs have a long history with the people as companions, friends, and helpers. The people should always remember to treat their dog, and their horse, like a member of the family. In return, they will help the family. Remember to feed your dog every day, much like one feeds one's own family and one's own spirit. Good things will come from that.

Because the dog had been so close with the people throughout the ages, dogs became a significant part of the Lakota family and way of life. Also, the character and loyalty of the sunka became a model for how a Lakota should live and view life. There are many things the people can learn from a dog. These things include the following: Allow the experience of fresh air and the wind in your face to be pure ecstasy. When loved ones come home, always run to greet them. Run, romp, and play daily. Sleep when you need to. Eat with gusto and enthusiasm. Chase your own tail, because you are strong enough to know that even you are not perfect. Sniff out the stranger to check to see if he or she meets the smell test. Be loyal. Never pretend to be something you're not. If what you want lies buried, dig until you find it. When someone is having a difficult time, be silent, sit close by, and nuzzle them gently. Don't be afraid to kiss the ones you love. Don't be too proud to be patted on the head. Shower your loved ones with love. Allow others to scratch your belly for you if they so choose. Don't demand it, but hinting about it is okay. Avoid biting when a simple growl will do. On hot days, drink lots of water and lie under a shady tree. Dive into the water headfirst to save time. Let others feel your love for the water and the joy it gives you by shaking it off and sharing it with them all.

Sunka is the one that never deserts man. A man's dog stands by him in prosperity and in poverty, in health and in sickness. He will growl at and scare off those who would seek to harm his human family or his dog family. He will follow his family anywhere they may go. He is dependable. He is reliable. He will sleep on the cold ground, where the wintry winds blow and the snow drives fiercely, if only he may be near his human's side. He will kiss the hand that has no food to offer. He will lick the wounds and sores that result from the toughness and harshness of life. Dogs know when a person is sick or in need of loving care. A dog will never, ever abandon those that are most vulnerable or weak, or whimpering for help. Dogs can detect illness or sudden calamity. They sense danger before danger clearly presents itself. They sense bad people and bad spirits, and will speak loudly against them. They will make us smile. They will make us laugh. They will make us think. They will make us cry, when we think of them when they are gone.

Dogs have character. They have empathy. They care for each other and for us. They absorb our love like a loving vessel that is naturally incapable of ever filling totally, or ever running over. They are exceptional parents and loving caretakers of their own. They will die to protect their own. If a puppy dies, then the parent will even bury that puppy, to keep its body from harm. When a dog knows she is about to die, she will go away somewhere, so as not to burden her family with the grief or the burden of what to do with her remains.

Through it all, sunka remains loyal, remains a friend, remains a committed and loved family member. He is as foundational, as trusted, and as sturdy as a stone. His unconditional love for his family exists from the first day as a puppy, to the last days with the failing eyes, ears, and legs. His spirit loves us throughout all of his, and our, physical life, and even dwells in our hearts and our spirits when the time comes for us to visit all our relatives in the spirit world and on the Trail of Spirits. Sunka's star shines the brightest in the sky because he tries to remain the closest to us on Grandmother Earth. Dogs are love. Dogs are life.

Dogs are a gift from Creator, the gift of love, and love of life. Human and dog: the bond that is never broken.

Sinte was always a great climber, a great runner, and a great companion on their trips. She never shied away from walking long distances or climbing high craggy peaks or trails. She never whined or complained about jumping over logs or walking over tough rocks, up steep slopes, over narrow passageways, or through fast-moving streams or creeks. No, she never did. In fact, she enjoyed it all, every minute of it. No matter how long the trail, how high the peak, how difficult the path, she used her skill, stamina, and determination to stay with Saved By Bear and the pony. Her heart, he imagined, was the size of a bear's, when it came to courage, fortitude, and attitude.

She went everywhere that Saved By Bear did, despite the turmoil, despite the weather, despite the danger. She lived up to her name always: Sinte.

9

ENCROACHMENT

THE ADVANCEMENT OF THE WHITE race, the military, and their followers showed the whites' clear desire to take over the lands of the Lakota. This period of encroachment included the government's establishment of the fort system and how it chained itself throughout our lands, and influenced the culture of our people. This was a time of skirmishes for wood, food, and possibly even clothing and such—a very difficult time for the Lakota. During this time, the people become aware of the real threat to their existence posed by this encroachment of the whites and their interests.

Red Cloud from the Oglala band engaged the United States government and the private and military trespassers who were coming into Lakota lands during the mid-1860s, particularly the years between 1864 and 1867, the period of Red Cloud's War, as it became known to the white population. Red Cloud frequently led bands that encountered, and had military confrontations and conflicts with, not just the United States armies but also individual groups of settlers, miners, and entrepreneurs who were invading the territory of the Lakota. There was a series of conflicts and skirmishes that occurred along the Bozeman Trail.

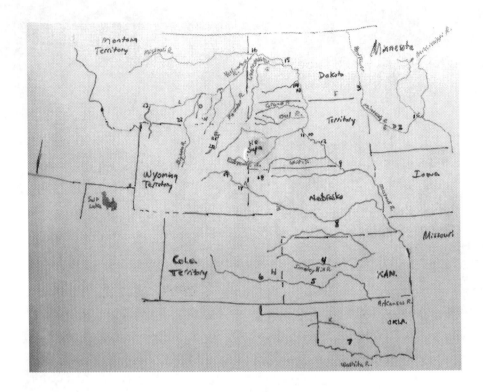

LIST OF FORTS AND CRITICAL EVENTS

Forts		Events	
1.	Ft. Snelling	A.	Grattan Incident
2.	Ft. Ridgely	B.	Blue Water Creek Massacre
3.	Ft. Abercrombie	C.	Ft. Snelling Prison Camp
4.	Ft. Hayes	D.	Battle of Birch Coulee
5.	Ft. Dodge	E.	Battle of Wood Lake
6.	Ft. Lyon	F.	Whitestone Hill Massacre
7.	Ft. Sill	G.	Killdeer Mountain Massacre
8.	Ft. Kearny	H.	Sand Creek Massacre
9.	Ft. Randall	I.	Fetterman Fight
10.	Ft. Sully	J.	Wagon Box Fight
11.	Ft. Bennett	K.	Washita Massacre
12.	Ft. Pierre	L.	Baker Fight
13.	Ft. Rice	M.	Yellowstone Expedition Fight
14.	Ft. Lincoln	N.	Battle of Rosebud
15.	Ft. Stevenson	O.	Greasy Grass Battle
16.	Ft. Buford		
17.	Ft. Laramie		
18.	Ft. Robinson		
19.	Ft. Fetterman		
20.	Ft. Reno		
21.	Ft. Phil Kearny		
22.	Ft. C.F. Smith		
23.	Ft. Ellis		

Almost all of these battles or skirmishes between the whites and bands of Oglala and others led by Red Cloud, occurred along the wagon trails, railroad routes, and telegraph lines of the government and the private white business interests. It was believed by many that these conflicts and skirmishes led by Red Cloud may have not been purely random. This notion of predictable incidents arose mostly out of the consideration of the political needs of the major parties to these incidents. The government and its moneyed business interests and wealthy investors needed a good purpose and foundation for forcing the Indians to discuss a peace agreement potentially involving even further cessation of land and resources. Red Cloud, the Oglala leader, known to many Lakota as the leader of the *Bad Face* people within his agency, the Red Cloud Agency, needed the government to recognize him as a Lakota leader and spokesman. Red Cloud needed to be viewed as someone capable of pushing for and entering into agreements between the government and the Indians about land and resources, particularly the Black Hills. So this notion that Red Cloud's War was a foreseeable prelude to future treaty discussions, fueled these beliefs. The fact that the government did recognize Red Cloud as a Lakota leader, and sought his leadership and influence for the making of the future 1868 Fort Laramie Treaty, somewhat confirmed these suspicions in the minds of many *nontreaty* Lakota. Many Lakota remained suspicious of Red Cloud's motives and conciliatory actions toward the government, seeing them as consistent with the intent and goals of the *bad face* people whom Red Cloud led, among the Oglala bands.

In essence, Red Cloud's War occasioned the first major experiences that the US government and its military had with fighting forces of the Lakota in the west. The bands of warriors who were involved in these conflicts were well armed, were well prepared, and had actual battle strategies. The government was not able to just swoop in and massacre villages of old people or children and women. They were now dealing with actual strong men and warriors. During this phase of history, Red Cloud, on the Lakota side, engaged the government and its armies, and also groups and bands of settlers, miners, and entrepreneurs who were trespassing on the lands along the Bozeman Trail area in violation of the 1851 treaty. It was during this phase that Red Cloud appeared to serve a noble purpose in standing up for the rights of the Lakota to protect their hunting lands as well as their resources, trying to ensure that there would be no violation of the treaty by establishing military forts without the full knowledge and consent of the Lakota people. This period lasted between the years 1864 and 1867. Red Cloud became recognized as a war leader during this time by the white society and the military. As a result of these various skirmishes, which involved the Fetterman Fight, the Hayfield Fight and the Wagon Box Fight, all near Sheridan, Wyoming, Spirit Horse also gained his reputation as a skilled warrior and tactician in battle. He also obtained the reputation of being antisocial and easily roused to conflict and confrontation. Some of the Lakota viewed him as aloof and impersonal. However, his legend would grow over the next decade.

The Media Provides Assistance to the Policy

A government intent upon carrying out an agenda with specific goals that it wishes to keep concealed, and for which it needs to influence public opinion in its favor, needs a compliant and willing press to present such an agenda to the public. In 1867 in the United States, the public mostly obtained news about all things—politics, government, entertainment, and business—from newspapers. Since the US government knew that it could likely control, influence, and manipulate the American news media in 1867, it took the necessary time and effort to draft, create, and promote its social and political propaganda for how to deal with the so-called Indian problem in the west. And for the most part, the press delivered.

For issues dealing with the American west, and specifically dealing with the Great Plains and Dakota Territory, and the Lakota people and their lands, the government fed information to the dominant Midwestern periodicals that were printed daily, weekly, monthly, or quarterly. Newspapers from the areas of Dakota, Nebraska, Colorado, and Montana were the dominant sources of news coming out of the Lakota territories during this time. These periodicals were, of course, owned by white people, which meant that they had white editors, white writers, white reporters, and lastly, mostly white readers. These newspapers included the *Rocky Mountain News Weekly* out of Denver, the *Bismarck Tribune* out of Bismarck, Dakota Territory, the *Bozeman Times* from the Montana Territory, and the *Omaha Daily Herald*, the *Omaha Bee*, the *Omaha Weekly Herald*, and the *Omaha Republican* out of Omaha, Nebraska.

The United States government sent a group of treaty commissioners into western Nebraska to try to negotiate an end to what was referred to by the government as Red Cloud's War. This group of so-called peace commissioners included individuals such as Nathaniel Taylor, John Sanborn, Samuel Tappan, Gen. Alfred Terry, Gen. William S. Harney (the "Butcher"), and the nororious Indian-hater, Gen. William Tecumseh Sherman. Most of these men were career military officers, private businessmen, or both. All had some degree of relationship on a personal level, in helping the United States acquire more Indian land and resources. Some just wished to annihilate all of the Lakota. The commissioners invited the Lakota bands to meet with them at Fort Laramie on September 13, 1867, for the supposed purpose of discussing peace, but more likely for the purpose of getting the Lakota to cede more land. Fort Laramie was closest in proximity to the Red Cloud Agency, which was located near Fort Robinson in northwest Nebraska Territory.

But Red Cloud of the Oglala Lakota and the Iteshicha, the Bad Face band of the Oglala, refused to meet with the commissioners. Red Cloud, instead, sent word to them that the purpose of his war against the whites was to save the valley of the Powder River, one of the only hunting grounds left to the Lakota nation, and to keep the United States and the whites from trespassing on that land. Red Cloud demanded that the military posts at Fort Phil Kearny, Fort Reno, and Fort C. F. Smith be closed, saying that only then could the conflicts between the Lakota and the United States come to an end.

The *Omaha Weekly Herald* wrote on February 5, 1868, of the potential success of the Fort Laramie Treaty. It blamed much of the current animosity toward the treaty on the recent violent actions of Col. John M. Chivington, a former Methodist minister, and his Third Colorado Cavalry Militia volunteers, during the atrocious and inhumane Sand Creek Massacre of November 29, 1864, in Colorado Territory. The *Herald*'s story indicated the following:

> *The Rocky Mountain News* and other organs and echoes
> of Chivington and his piety will be pained to learn that
> the authorities of Fort Laramie are in receipt of messages
> of peace from the most powerful Indian warrior of the
> West …

> We hope that the bloody-minded Chivington
> exterminators will be patient under the prospect which
> offers a fair promise of no more massacres of White
> people. We remember the time when, for more than 10
> long years, the lives and property of White people were
> safe on these plains against Indian attack … We remember
> when the lives of defenseless White women were safe in
> Indian hunting grounds as they are in Omaha today. What
> caused the change need not be recounted here but we may
> say that every White life lost or captive child or woman
> taken by the Indians in the last four years has been due
> alone to such diabolisms as the Chivington massacre and
> the continued wrongs practiced on the Indians. We hope
> the messages of Red Cloud presage the return of old-
> fashioned peace with the Indians.[7]

The *Omaha Weekly Herald* listed some other people who sought
to obstruct the treaty process, including unscrupulous and thieving
Indian agents and greedy beef contractors. An *Omaha Weekly Herald*
story published on March 15, 1868, stated the following:

> Throwing chaff into the eyes of the Eastern press is not only
> done by the Indian agents but also by beef contractors and
> others who hope to sell goods to the Indian department
> for "those poor peaceable Indians." Discharge lying agents
> and put Indians under the control of the War department.
> Every citizen of the country will be satisfied and help
> whip the Indians to a good peace if necessary.[8]

---

[7] Reilly, Bound to Have Blood, at p.32.
[8] Reilly at 33.

On May 6, 1868, the *Rocky Mountain News Weekly* wrote: "It is the opinion of the oldest settlers that the treaty will be a farce ... While the commission is waiting, their 'children' are making some very friendly demonstrations in the way of stealing stock and scalping the whites when they have a good opportunity."[9] This was an obvious racist view of the circumstances. In a story dated May 6, 1868, the *Omaha Weekly Herald* even focused upon the derogatory stereotype of the "murdering red devils" to describe the situation on the plains:

> We believe in the wisdom of making peace and removing Indians to far reservations. But why sit idly by and talk of peace whilst your neighbor and friends are being murdered by these red devils? Why not declare war and wage it? We are for war, if we cannot have peace, because that is the only alternative. We are for anything and everything that can stop or lessen these accumulated outrages upon our people.[10]

Red Cloud's band had insisted that the United States abandon its three military forts on the Bozeman Trail:as a treaty violation. Ultimately, President Andrew Johnson, on March 2, 1868, ordered that the forts be abandoned. This move angered many, as reported on in the white press.

The *Rocky Mountain News Weekly*, on May 13,1868, commented upon Johnson's decision and reported the following:

> A gentleman told us the other day that he had helped to make 12 Indian treaties, not one of which had ever been fulfilled in a single item. We do not want the forts dismantled and the road abandoned through the Powder River country, but we cannot blame Red Cloud for putting no faith in the government or its agents.[11]

In reporting on the treaty progression in May 1868, the *Omaha Weekly Herald*, in a story dated May 20, 1868, wrote as follows:

---

[9] Reilly at 33.

[10] Reilly, at 33.

[11] Id at 34.

Generals Harney, Sherman, Tappan et. al. have concluded a treaty with the northern Indians who have agreed to go on reserves. Red Cloud will come in as soon as the Powder River country is abandoned. If true, and we do not doubt it, this is glorious news. We believe, and have long maintained against the idle clamor and natural Spirit of revenge aroused amongst our people by Indian massacres, in an ultimate and enduring peace with the Red Man. It has been the White Man, and not the Red Man, who has violated agreements under which the former has nearly crushed the latter out of existence. We are, as we have been, for peace with these savages. Captive Whites in Indian lodges exposed to horrible lusts and cruelties were unknown in this country for ten long years. Until the red-handed Chivington and their Colorado backers and apologists made worse then [sic] savage war on bands that were friendly, we had no real war, and now these men lament a peace. Peace is not yet. It will come. The Indians will go on reserves and live out the remainders of their days in a state of semi-civilization like the Cherokees. Settlements will advance without fear of the tomahawk and scalping knife as they did in years gone by; commerce will go unvexed to the mountains; lives will be safe from the Indian incursions; millions will be saved by the government. These and other blessings will fall on the heels of an enduring peace with the Indians just as certainly as effect follows cause.[12]

It was, of course, ironic, that General Harney (the Butcher), who was the military leader of the Blue Creek Massacre in 1855, ultimately ended up on the treaty commission for the government to negotiate the so-called peace treaties involving the Lakota, in particular, the 1868 Fort Laramie Treaty. It is said that during one of the treaty meetings, Harney would say to the Lakota, "We know that you have been treated badly for years, we will take care that you shall not be treated so anymore."

The *Omaha Republican*, on May 26, 1868, declared: "The Indians

---

[12] Id at 34.

known as the 'Bad Faces' have not yet come to terms, and if they don't behave they are to be 'cleaned out' by Spotted Tail and Man-Afraid-of-His-Horses, who have engaged to undertake the job provided the government will furnish them with arms and ammunition."[13]

The statement by the *Republican* that Spotted Tail and his people would be given arms and ammunition to take out Red Cloud and his band of *bad faces* if they did not behave was very presumptuous, describing an unlikely occurrence. A significant number of Red Cloud's people at the Red Cloud Agency (later, Pine Ridge Agency) were known as the Iteshicha, the bad faces, because of their history. The bad faces were known by many Lakota to have many difficult and self-centered people within their band. However, it should be noted that not all of the Oglala people were bad faces nor were all the bad faces as bad as some said. Certainly there were many Oglala who followed the good red road with honor and integrity. The bands of the original headman named Oglala (true Oglala), the bands of the Kiyuska and Old Bull Bear and others, were not always in sync with Red Cloud and many of the bad faces. Many of the Lakota people affected by the treaty signing and negotiation, felt uneasy about the dominance of Red Cloud and his bad face people in the treaty negotiations because many of the leaders and headmen of the nontreaty Lakota were absent when said treaty was negotiated and signed. The nontreaty Lakota viewed it as another potential deceptive subterfuge by the government to try to steal more of the Lakota lands, believing that they could not trust the government to enter into any treaty honorably.

As a result of the conflicts that occurred during this period, a contingent of members of the Lakota, including the Mnincoju, Brule, Oglala, Yantonai, Hunkpapa, Cuthead, Two Kettle, Sans Arcs, Blackfeet, and the Arapaho and the Santee Dakota, were able to reach a consensus among themselves to stand in unity against the government. This resulted in the Treaty at Fort Laramie in 1868 that was supposed to guarantee the peaceful ownership, recognition, occupation and enjoyment of the entire Great Sioux Nation, which encompassed the entire western half of of the future state of South Dakota. This territory

---

[13] Reilly, Id at 35

also included all of the *unceded hunting territories* and *unceded Indian territory* which extended into the eastern edge of the Bighorn Mountains (the Shiny Mountains) and included the area of the Greasy Grass valley (See the 1868 Fort Laramie Treaty map). These unceded territories were to be preserved for the Lakota people forever, or "so long as the buffalo may range thereon in such numbers as to justify the chase."

It was this particular *peace* treaty of 1868 that was supposed to preserve the entirety of the sacred Black Hills for the undisturbed total ownership, use and occupancy of the Lakota. If there was to be a treaty, then all the people would hope that it would be a basis from which to be able to live in peace and secure their future with what they had left of their way of life. The terms of this treaty were decent as long as those terms would be lived up to by the government. The 1868 Fort Laramie Treaty did not *give* the Black Hills and all of the Lakota territory to the Lakota people; the treaty recognized and *reserved* the Lakota's existing aboriginal title to, occupation of, and ownership of the Black Hills, and all other rights not specifically ceded or relinquished, *forever.* This original ownership of the entirety of the Lakota lands, including the He Sapa, encompassed all natural and aboriginal rights, even to the air above, the water running over and below, all natural resources within and upon (including all gold, silver, ore, timber, etc.), and the limitless ground underneath, including the cave networks within Grandmother Earth, for all time forward. (This aboriginal right to these lands preceeded the encroachment by the European white people, and such enactments such as the Magna Carta, the doctrine of discovery, the Declaration of Independence, the Northwest Ordinance, the Louisiana Purchase, etc.). It was a result of this treaty, this *agreement*, that the Lakota people used the whites' treaty method to become more aware of their own self-determination in a changing world. They were becoming more attuned to their ability to adapt to it and to preserve their own way of life. And this was a means that the peace agreement could be used to try to stop the massive continual encroachment upon Lakota lands and territories. Essentially, the treaty could provide a way to strengthen the Lakota's holdings and to protect what was theirs, without having to fight and shed blood over it. The treaty could be used to protect and preserve their lives and to try to civilly protect their way of life. If the treaty could be honored and trusted, that is.

The *Rocky Mountain News* had previously blatantly encouraged genocide of the Lakota, but in May 1868, it seemed to be willing to give the Fort Laramie Treaty some possibility of success. It even admitted some culpability on the part of the white settlers for the present problems of the Lakota. In an article dated May 20, 1868, the paper stated the following:

> They admit … they have occupied the hunting grounds of the Indians, and in various ways made game scarce and that an Indian must eat to live … They will admit further, though they deprecate the policy, because of its failure to secure peace, that the making of treaties with the Indian is a recognition on our part of their right to the country.[14]

Once the military forts on the Bozeman Trail had been closed by the government, Red Cloud did in fact report back to the commission, and did sign the treaty on November 6, 1968, as a representative of his people. Other Lakota headmen obviously signed as well. The treaty was ratified by the US Senate on February 16, 1869, and became formally recognized on February 24, 1869. Despite its flaws, the treaty became the *law* in modern terms.

The racial assertions and media attempts to stereotype and incite hatred for the Indians continued. The *Omaha Weekly Herald* used the stereotype of the "murdering red skin" many times in its media reports of the Fort Laramie Treaty discussions. The *Herald* blamed bloody-minded Colonel Chivington for instigating much of the conflict and stated that whites bore more responsibility for violating agreements than the "redskins" did. The use of these derogatory terms to describe the Lakota was intended to drive a negative public perception of the Lakota, to invoke fear of them, and to show them as less than human. These "savages" were not to be considered equal to whites. It was a clever propaganda tool used by the government and the media to dehumanize the Lakota, and to generate fear of them in the public arena

---

[14] Reilly, at 35-36.

so as to leverage that fear in order to promote its policies of genocide and land theft.

The 1868 treaty did not satisfy the various Omaha newspapers' minimal expectations. Within a few years, the treaty was being ignored. The government's false treaty-based promise to protect the Lakota lands and the He Sapa from white intrusion and exploitation would be blatantly broken by Lt. Col. George Armstrong Custer, who would flagrantly violate the Fort Laramie Treaty during his 1874 *expedition* of the Black Hills. Miners and settlers would end up flocking into the He Sapa, the sacred mountains, driven by Custer's claim of finding gold "from the roots down."[15] In the end, the treaty that was supposed to last forever would be breached by the government in less than five and a half years. To the nontreaty Lakota, this would be confirmation that the U.S. government could not be trusted to live up to any promises.

———————⊙———————

At this time, the Cheyenne River Agency of which Saved By Bear and our families reside, was formed under this treaty of 1868. The actual agency came into existence in 1869. To many, the formation of the agency was the genesis of a prolonged confinement to a metaphorical *prison camp* of our people and relatives. A confinement created out of economic, racial, social and legal consequences. The 1868 Treaty to many Lakota in those times, was controversial in the sense that many Lakota believed that the treaty negotiators and signors may have held some ill manner or dishonest presence. To many Lakota, the overriding intent of these people in attendance at the treaty meetings would appear to be selfish and greed motivated. Appearing to be a securing of position and place in the new white society. Many Lakota people considered some of the treaty participants as those who may have been tribal members, but who may have also become traitors, and are now allowing the regular committed, traditional families to be slaughtered and massacred. To many of the Lakota, the opening and the gifting of vast parts of the 1851 treaty lands to the new white people is the biggest mistake that will ever be made by some of our own people.

---

[15] Reilly at 37.

The trust that we tried to believe in with the government, was never there. The promises in the treaties for possessions and the amenities to the people, were never to come. The treaties were changed as they left the tent after they were signed. By the time they arrived in Washington, DC, the government was rewriting everything to their own advantage so that they could militarily, and politically and economically, devastate everything that we are in this world.

Washita Tragedy

In 1867 and 1868, the US government initiated a military campaign against the Cheyenne in the Southwest Territory. The Cheyenne and Lakota were friends and shared many relatives over time. The government was intent on wiping out or capturing as many of the *hostile* Cheyenne as they could. Black Kettle's band of Cheyenne had a peaceful encampment along the Washita River in Oklahoma Territory. The Seventh Cavalry of the US Army, led by the young commander Lt. Col. George Armstrong Custer, located the encampment on November 26, 1868. Custer developed a plan, deciding to attack at dawn. He would split his regiments into three separate groups and would utilize the element of surprise by attacking simultaneously from three different parts of the camp, from the south, from the east, and from the north. One of the regiments was commanded by Capt. Frederick Benteen. At the time that this attack was planned, the camp was made up of mostly women, children, and elderly men and women. Hardly any warriors were there at the camp. When Custer and the Seventh Cavalry attacked the Cheyenne camp along the Washita the morning of November 27, they slaughtered and massacred almost two hundred people. Since most were women, children, or elderly people, there wasn't much of a fight. Many of the people were shot as they ran and hid. The cries of fear, anxiety, pain and death echoed throughout the river valley. Mothers were calling out for their children, children screaming, yet nothing could deter the committed assailants from completing their task. At the end of the destruction and the carnage, a young officer got separated from the cavalry group. Maj. Joel Elliot had taken seventeen other soldiers with him to pursue a group of escaping Cheyenne. However, the eighteen soldiers did not return to the Seventh Cavalry's location at the camp. Custer decided it was the better course for he and his men to leave those individuals there and let them fend for themselves. Major Elliot was a close friend of Captain Benteen. Elliot and his men would be found dead and frozen two weeks later. It was said that Benteen held that against Custer.

As a parting decision before he left the encampment of the bloody Washita Massacre on November 27, 1868, in order to make sure that the Cheyenne did not have any ponies that were to be utilized by the people or their relatives to use, Custer and his men gathered all of the nine hundred or so horses from the camp. Rather than take those horses with them as part of the army, Custer made the decision that all of the horses should be killed. So they were rounded up. The cavalrymen stood along the perimeter of the group of horses and shot every one of them, slaughtering all of these horse people, many of them mares and colts. Cries, moans, and torturous whimpers rose from the group of innocent horses. They were calling out to their relatives, but nobody was there to help. So the horse nation suffered a tremendous loss along with the Cheyenne nation, all these lives extinguished in one slaughtering campaign. This particular campaign would prove a harbinger of what would come in another eight years, as some of the very same three pronged attack tactics that were used on that particular day, resulting in the massacre of many human lives and horses' lives, were again used by the same military leader, and the same regiment, the Seventh Cavalry of United States Army, along the Greasy Grass River in Montana eight years later.

⸻ ⸻

On November 27, 1868, in the early morning hours in Oklahoma Territory, the deliberate killing and brutal execution of over nine hundred horses, mostly mustangs and their foals, by the Seventh Calvary, including Custer, at Black Kettle's camp along the Washita River was remembered by the descendants of the horse nation. Blue Streak's mother, Cahansa, had been present. Standing among six other four-legged brothers and sisters in a high, hidden tree line overlooking the scene, Cahansa painfully stared at the horrible scene, her beautiful relatives being suddenly and evilly extinguished right before her big brown eyes. A misty resolution formed in the crisp, sharp, biting-cold air, her long lashes desperately trying to filter out a clear, albeit unwanted, vision of the horrible carnage. She saw the dark blue of the army coats, their flag, their guns, and their utterly determined purpose…To kill, to take, to extinguish, and to deny life and existence.

She even witnessed it in the eyes of the army's own horses. As the shooting commenced and continued, those horses had a harsh disturbing stare of their own, one of disbelief and sadness. It was as if they knew a hidden truth of these men's brutality, their plan, their commitment to destruction. Cahansa felt this through the message of their minds and emotions. It came to her in her own spirit that the cavalry mounts knew, because they had seen it before—and would most certainly see it again unless or until something changed. Cahansa felt in her heart that the cavalry horses wanted to be free from this life of war, assault, destruction, and death. Except through the soulful communication of their inner thoughts and feelings, the cavalry horses emitted an air of being trapped, like lost, hopeless prisoners, prisoners to the will of their masters.

One brown roan caught her eyes from afar, slightly in the sunshine and early morning mist of the valley. Cahansa saw the wide, expressive eyes searching for the assault to end, and crying. The tears glistened on the horse's face. For a moment Cahansa felt his pain. She also felt his inner wish to switch places with the watching mustang, to run free with the free people, to live with a human family that respected his life and his existence, one that would treat him as a loving being, rather than as a mere tool of destruction and killing.

<hr />

The Cheyenne people heard what had happened to their relatives along the Washita. Those who had been lucky enough to survive got away. The Cheyenne ended up heading north toward the land of the Lakota, their friends and allies. The Lakota were known to protect people, offering safe haven when needed. Many of the relatives who were affected either directly (that is, the survivors) or indirectly (that is, the relatives of those who had been killed) would carry that burden, that pain, that anguish, and that loss with them to their new homeland up north. And those families would remember, Those families would carry that burden and would eventually use that burden as a motivating force to participate in the events to come.

Furthermore, the horse nation also suffered a tremendous loss. The spirit that was involved in the horse people carried forth from that atrocity. And those that knew, those that felt, those that carried that spirit and that energy across all the miles, all the terrain, and through all the channels of energy, felt it as well. Like Cahansa. And the horse people too, one day in the future, having to carry that burden on behalf of their relatives, would use their burden as their own motivation.

Tatanka Nation: Family to the Lakota

In the beginning, the buffalo nation gave of itself at the will of the Creator, becoming the provider for the Lakota. Tatanka gave of its own flesh and life to feed the Lakota, and the Lakota became the people who followed the tatanka from place to place, from season to season, living and surviving because of the eternal gift given by the tatanka to the Lakota.

Tatanka provided for the Lakota people's every need and provision, sheltering them from the weather and the cold with their hide, and offering their skins for use in making clothing, robes, tipis, and moccasins for covering their feet. Tatanka also gave of its bones, sinew, and horns, providing the people with utensils, tools, weapons, needle and thread, awls, bowls, pouches, bladders, and satchels. The tatanka proved itself to be a true relative to the Lakota, giving life the chance and possibility, preserving and protecting life for the people.

The tatanka skull and symbol are a part of almost every Lakota sacred ceremony and event because the tatanka provided a critical foundation for life itself. The symbol serves as a constant reminder to the Lakota of their tatanka brothers, which thoroughly gave of themselves on behalf of all Lakota generations since the beginning of time. The triad formed between the sacred sites in He Sapa of Owl's Nest, Mato

Paha, and Mato Tipila symbolized the head and skull of the sacred tatanka. Tatanka is truly a magnificent symbol to the Lakota of self-sacrifice of the one for the good, the protection of, and the preservation of the many. The tatanka gave of itself, its body, its parts, its energy, its very life and existence, until it had nothing left to give.

The symbol of the Lakota brother-provider the tatanka holds such prominence in the lives and sacred well-being of the Lakota because it mirrors the intent, motivation, and goals of the Lakota people themselves. In the grandest sense of love and respect for their provider-brother the tatanka, the Lakota's lives are devoted to these goals: to be generous and give what one has, and what one can, to others in need; to honor life and Creator, and others in need; to live one's life in accordance with the principles of respect and dignity for all; and to seek to obtain a world where peace, unity, tolerance, and love have a higher level of existence in one's life than war, violence, greed, hate, and destruction.

The tatanka were strong, resilient, and brave. When a storm gathered on the horizon and tough times were at hand, the tatanka would not shy away from the storm. Instead, tatanka would stand strong, tall, and proud. Tatanka will turn to face the oncoming storm, to meet it head-on with no fear. This is unlike the cattle herds brought forward by the white settlers that cannot survive harsh conditions and will easily die.

The tatanka, through its genuine, reliable, devoted sacrifice for and on behalf of the people, was a model being. The tatanka was to be emulated. The tatanka stood for the principle that one's acts in life determine the value of that life to others, and also for what it means to preserve and protect the people.

It is said that if a buffalo herd lives together for years, they form an extended family—an oyate. It is the same for the Lakota. If a buffalo calf is abandoned by its mother, or if the parent is killed, another female will step in to nurse and raise the calf as her own. It is said that when a buffalo dies, the whole herd comes by the body, one at a time, with bowed head and a nudge with the nose, to pay homage to and show respect for their fallen loved one.

These spiritual beings serve as providers for the Lakota. Long ago, the Creator gifted the Lakota with the great herds for such a purpose, to protect the human from the ails of life and from hunger. The tatanka served that role in a sacred manner that likely no other being could.

The Lakota respected the tatanka, and forever gave thanks for the gift from Creator. The pact was made that the people would take and use what they could and what they must, never wasting any part of the offering and sacrifice made by the tatanka for the people. The Creator intended that the people only take as many buffalo as needed and no more. The circle of respect for these ways caused restraint and practicality in such things.

The Lakota learned from the buffalo, as they did from the other four-legged, and the winged and water people. Every being has learned how to live and survive in the world in its own way. There was a sacred trust and a sacred circle that was formed between all beings. This was the plan of Creator.

The order of creation has only been disturbed or broken by the acts of some of the two-legged, the humans. This is especially true of the two-legged who decided to commit evil deeds and follow evil motives, creating destruction for and bringing despair to the rest of the beings and Grandmother Earth. That is what the running of the First Great Race around the Great Racetrack in He Sapa was all about.

When the disruption of the Circle of life occurs, it is like a ripple in the center of a pond, spreading out to splash and affect all other beings' lives. Strong is the effect of evil ways and evil deeds. Yet stronger must be the counterbalance of the good in beings, like the humans who follow Creator's plan as set out at the dawn of time. Do unto our brothers and sisters as you would wish for them to do unto you. It matters not whether your brother has four legs or two wings or two gills. The Circle is intended to remain forever, and to run eternal as long as our spirits are given the opportunity to seek out the life intended by the Creator, hoping to live up to those things in our lives, in our hearts, and in our spirits. The wise Lakota holy men and women, seeing the Creator's way laid out like a path in life, say, "We do not control how much time we have physically upon Grandmother Earth, but we can control what we do with that time while we are here."

The buffalo were the *safety net* of the Lakota people. When the devious intentional decision was made to kill all the buffalo, then the decision was made to exterminate the Lakota. The evil intent was to remove the Lakota's safety net, thereby removing a significant, critical part of the Circle of life. This was an intentional breaking of the Sacred Hoop.

———————◦◉◦———————

On almost every hunting trip made into the Powder River country, when riding back to the He Sapa, when the hunters rode south of Mato Tipila (Bear's Lodge, a.k.a. Devils Tower) and then rode back east toward the old buffalo jump and the Spearfish Creek along He Sapa's western edges. On the way, they passed the Buffalo shaped Mountain, "he tatanka" (now in the city of Sundance, Wyoming). The mountain was referred to in this way because of its magical resemblance to a lying buffalo bull facing the north. The travelers would say, "Look! Tatanka!"

The mountain is abruptly high at the northwest side, giving the image of the majestic head of the great bull, and is deep brown in color. The great bull's massive head leads to the right (the south) into a lush stand of pine trees growing on the steep mountainside. This group of trees bears a sincere resemblance to the thick hide over the hulking shoulders and grand hump of the great buffalo. The flanks of the great tatanka in mountain form is mostly barren of trees and consists of brown rock, to the right (the south) of the rocky mountain summit, forming the image of the smooth backside of the bull's large, muscled body.

When the warriors see this vision, heading east, they know they are not far from their sacred home, the He Sapa, the Grandmother's heart of all things.

The buffalo-shaped mountain, He Tatanka, is located about two days' ride from Mato Tipila to the north. This had significance to the people in that the sacred symbolic tatanka triad included Mato Tipila. He Tatanka, the mountain, actually directly faced the towering gray striated-stone columns of the dramatic nine-hundred-foot butte of Mato Tipila, the Bear's Lodge. So it had significant spiritual meaning. Mato Tipila was one of the Lakota's most sacred sites.

The route to and from Mato Tipila had been taken and traveled for thousands of years by the people. When traveling back from the Shiny Mountains, in the west in the Montana Powder River country, moving east toward the He Sapa, the Lakota traveler would come upon the buffalo-shaped mountain. The traveler then could direct his route to the north toward Mato Tipila.

Before 1859, Mato Tipila had not ever been seen by any white man, but had only been seen and visited by the indigenous people and tribes in the regions, such as the Lakota, Dakota, Nakota, Cheyenne, Arapaho, Kiowa and Crow, and maybe some others. For that reason, Mato Tipila did not appear on any map.

One of the humans who knew the territory of the He Sapa and Mato Tipila well was a Dakota scout and interpreter by the name of Zephyr Rencountre, who was born in 1800 and was of Yanktonai descent. As a young man, Zephyr learned to speak many languages (Lakota, Dakota, Nakota, French, Italian, German, Latin, and English). He was skilled in his knowledge of the aboriginal lands and routes.

In midsummer of 1859, the US government decided to put together an exploration party to make an expedition into the lands of the Lakota and Cheyenne. Capt. William F. Raynolds headed up what was called the Yellowstone Expedition of 1859, the purpose of which was to obtain additional information about the Indians, record climatological data, catalog mineral resources, and search out several wagon routes for future travel in the country. Frontiersman Jim Bridger was also with the team.

This Yellowstone Expedition of 1859 would actually be considered a breach by the government of the 1851 Fort Laramie Treaty, which was intended to keep all white trespassers and explorers out of the lands of the Lakota. The expedition needed an indigenous scout and interpreter to guide the party into the territory, so Raynolds convinced Zephyr Rencountre to be their guide. Rencountre decided to go partly to steer the party clear of the He Sapa and partly to report back to the people about the government's plans and motives. It was on July 20, 1859, that Rencountre guided some of the party to Mato Tipila, the Bear's Lodge. The first white men now observed the sacred mountain butte. After having guided them there, Zephyr Rencountre decided that he needed to return to his home on the Yankton Agency in southeast

Dakota Territory along the Missouri. He was respected by his people and had done much to help them. At one time, he had owned all of the land in Bon Homme, Dakota Territory. The French name Bon Homme means "good man." The area was named after Rencountre.

———⊛《◉》⊛———

When negotiating the Fort Laramie Treaty of 1868, the leaders of the Lakota who participated in the treaty discussions were trying their best to preserve their lands and their way of life as much as they could while attempting to understand the white man's language. At first, when the white representatives of the government included language in the 1851 treaty stating that the Lakota lands would forever be the property of the Lakota people, "so as long as the buffalo may range thereon in such numbers as to justify the chase," it was somewhat of a problem for the government. According to the natural balance of Grandmother Earth, the buffalo would always roam, the water would always flow, and the grass would always be green, unless a drastic change occurred. So the government came up with yet another subterfuge. If the United States could not get rid of the Lakota people by killing them directly, what better way to get rid of them than to remove their very sustenance by destroying the buffalo and, thus, their natural world? The plan was literally to take the buffalo out of the picture, to make them extinct, which would therefore make the people extinct. Once the buffalo were gone, the United States could claim that the treaty was no longer in effect, being able to proclaim that the buffalo no longer ranged. The government would then declare that the *unceded Indian territory* was now ceded to the United States since the Lakota could no longer hunt the buffalo there. It was a brilliant strategy by the new government— brilliant, but horribly unjust, vile, deceitful, fraudulent, and rank.

———⊛《◉》⊛———

The scene is of a group of thirty hunters with elephant guns, Gatling guns, and various assorted long rifles. They have gathered near the train station by the river. An overweight balding man in a suit, accompanied by a young man wearing a tailored suit and carrying a briefcase, walks to the front of the group of gathered men, who are wearing a varied range of outfits, from furred coats and furred hats, to high leather boots with denim pants and suspenders, to tattered overalls and long-sleeve undershirts. Most of them are bearded or have stubble. All have the same steely look in their eyes, as if they cannot wait to start shooting, to start killing, to start slaughtering. As the balding man speaks to this impatient crowd, the view pans to the young man's briefcase, which bears his name and place of employment, "Thomas Smith, Department of War," and then to the poster near the boarding dock: "25 cents for every buffalo killed: proof of kill must be shown. "Jordan & Co., Inc., Investments".

The men are embarking from the train station at Yankton in Dakota Territory, traveling westward into *Indian Country*. These men are just a mere handful of the army of hired killers who have been enticed and lured by the companies seeking the buffalo kills. They are not here to *hunt*. This is not *hunting*, which can be done honorably if done out of necessity. These are the slaughter teams, the slaughterers, who are here to carry out the United States government's plan to bring about the quick extinction of the buffalo. The government has agreed to pay the private companies to bring in these killers of beings, these annihilators of tatanka. The public word had been sent out that there is an urgent need for buffalo hides and buffalo oil to be used by consumers back east.

However, the real intent is the planned extinction of tatanka, to wipe out the main food source of the Lakota, to in effect quicken the genocide and removal of the Lakota themselves by killing off all the buffalo people.

The armies of slaughterers will have their travel expenses paid and be given free and room and board, as long as they are willing to spend weeks on end riding around to find the herds so they can be killed. Once found, the great herds will be slaughtered by the thousands from the windows and platforms of the freight cars, or from wagons. Most of the tatanka will be killed and left to rot where they fall. Providing proof of the kill was not altogether important to the government. What was important was to have the killing done.

The buffalo slaughter was an opening up of one of the ancient, yet ever-present, doors to the evil side of existence, the doors that should remain shut. But the doors which are too tempting for men who have no conscience or caring. These doors become the beacon for these men, whose only goals are to seek their own personal wealth, and the survival and ethnic advancement of their own kind at all costs. To do this, they must rid themselves of the *redskins* and their beasts. This policy of slaughter of the buffalo, intent upon the genocide of the Lakota, did swing open the door to the bad side, where the evil spirits dwell and flourish. Death and destruction can serve as an aphrodisiac for those who lust for killing and domination. The bad side feeds the evil part of man in such a way that his appetite will no longer be able to be satisfied. When a man discovers that it is much easier to gain power, influence, and wealth by just killing his opponent, then it follows that compromise, peace, civility, and humanity, no longer are important or necessary. The drive to control all things, and to be in control, is too great sometimes to be denied by the nuisance of life and empathy. Empathy and conscience are the first casualties when the door to the bad side is flung wide open.

So the slaughter began. The willing participants in Yankton will be joined by thousands more, willing to flood the plains and mountains with killers and killing. They were now nothing but exterminators, nothing but a bloodthirsty gang of slaughterers. Grandmother Earth and the people will always remember how this came to be.

Cheyenne River Agency: The Beginning of the Loss of Free Living

Although the Second Fort Laramie Treaty was entered into in 1868 by the Lakota leaders who did sign the agreement, the Cheyenne River Agency was established in 1869 in Dakota Territory in what is now north central South Dakota west of the Missouri (Big Muddy) River and north of the Cheyenne (Chien or Shay-enne) River. It was made up of 5,000 square miles within the Great Sioux Nation. At the time, the Cheyenne River Agency was bordered on the north by the Grand River, which made up the shared southern border with the Standing

Rock Agency to the north. This was the time before the states of South Dakota and North Dakota had even been established, which ultimately would occurr in 1889.

The land was part of the age-old aboriginal lands of the Teton (Tetonwan) Lakota people. The Lakota were people of the trusted campfires, which were the lifeblood of the people. The Lakota, Dakota, and Nakota chose their representatives and leaders from among those who had the people's trust and according to whom they were committed. The chosen person would represent many extended families and attend the Seven Council Fires (Oceti Sakowin) gatherings that were called for. Those who were chosen would decide upon matters affecting the welfare of the people and concern themselves with the lands and territorial boundaries. It was an honor to serve the people in this way. The Mnincoju, an extended group of families of the original Hohwoju people, were an original band of the Lakota. Saved By Bear, his family, and their tiospaye resided along the banks of the Owl River just a few miles east of the Thunder Butte, and just west of the confluence of the Owl River and Bear ("Mato") Creek. Bear Creek is the area where the sacred White Buffalo Calf Woman brought the Sacred Cannumpa to the Lakota people many years ago. The Mnincoju/Hohwoju people were the original pipe keepers, and Saved By Bear's family, are descendants of one of the original three holy women who were the original pipe keepers long ago.

When the White Buffalo Calf Woman brought the Sacred Cannumpa as a gift from Creator to the Lakota people, she also brought with her, the wisdom of seven sacred ceremonies to the people.

Through all time, it has been said by the old, wise ones that the Lakota were originally gifted with many sacred ceremonies. It is, however, the seven most prominent of these sacred ceremonies that are referenced here: (1) the *sun dance*; 2) *the inipi*, or sweat lodge; 3) the *hanbleceya* (the vision quest, or "the man stands on the hill and cries"); (4) the *hunka* ceremony; (5) the *tatanka lowanpii* (female rite of passage); (6) the *tapa wanka yap* ("throw the ball"); and (7) *nagi gluha* (keeping and releasing the spirit).

These seven sacred ceremonies would be performed by the Lakota as rituals to celebrate and honor life, Unci Maka, the spirits, Wakinyan,

Wakan Tanka, and Creator. The purpose of each ceremony was to address a specific need—whether the need of the one or the need of the many. These new ways would be practiced and used for generations, until they became tradition. And tradition became the way. And then these practices and ceremonies would become known as the "old ways."

The Lakota people also practiced the seven sacred rites for proper, balanced living according to Creator: (1) *wocekiya* (prayer); (2) *waohola* (respect); (3) *waunsila* (compassion); (4) *wowicake* (honesty); (5) *wawokiye* (generosity); (6) *wahwala* (humility); and (7) *woksape* (wisdom).

These seven sacred rites or virtues served as a perpetual guide to being a human being first and a Lakota second, teaching people how to become a good and respected member of society, a good parent, son, daughter, husband, wife, grandfather, grandmother, friend, and/ or relative, a good person, a good Lakota, a good human being, a good citizen of Grandmother Earth.

The seven stars of the Pleiades and of the Big Dipper also symbolize the indigenous people's main seven council fires. The seven council fires, the Oceti Sakowin, were made up of the following peoples: Mdewakanton (Dakota); Wahpeton (Dakota); Wahpekute (Dakota); Sisseton (Dakota), Ihanktun Wan/Yankton/Lower Yankoni (Nakota); Ihantunwana/Upper Yankonai (Nakota); and the Tetonwan (Lakota). The seven bands of the Lakota or Tetonwan are:

1) Mnincoju (Hohwoju)
2) Itazipco (Sans Arc)
3) Siha Sapa (Blackfeet)
4) Oohenumpa (Two Kettle)
5) Brule (Burnt Thigh, Sicangu)
6) Oglala (Bad Face, True Oglala, Spleen, Kiyuska, Oyukpe, Loafers)
7) Hunkpapa (Standing Rock, End of the Horn)

There were four bands of the Oceti Sakowin of the Lakota located on the Cheyenne River Agency: the Mnincoju (the Hohwoju), the Siha

Sapa (Blackfeet), the Itazipco (Sans Arcs), and the Oohe Nunpa (Two Kettle). Three other Lakota bands of the council fires, the Sicangu, the Oglala (Bad Face et al.), and Hunkpapa (Standing Rock), all had their own agencies.

The Cheyenne River Agency would contain the aboriginal lands between the Grand River in the north and the Cheyenne River in the south, both of those being bodies of water that drain into the Big Muddy, the Missouri River, to the east. Most of the camps of the various bands congregated along the various winding waterways running through the agency territory. A high land ridge runs down the middle of the agency, west to east. The creeks and streams that flow from the high middle ridge run off into the lower waterways of the Owl River to the north, and the Cherry Creek and Cheyenne (Chien) River to the south. The French, some of the first whites in the area, traveled up and down the rivers by canoe. The French had a language that was somewhat similar to the Lakota. The Lakota indicated that the river by the Cherry Creek settlement was known as the Sunka or Dog River, after the Dog Man warriors of the Lakota. The French word for "dog" is *chien*. So it is believed that when the French were told that it was the Sunka or Dog River, they gave it the name "Chien," the French word for "dog" (or "sunka"). Through the years the Europeans mispronounced and misspelled the word *chien* as "Shay-enne," which led to the word *Cheyenne*. The Lakota did not spell any of their words, so many Lakota names were distorted by and misrepresented in many things, such as the naming of the Cheyenne River. It is apparent still that many historians attribute the name of the river to the Cheyenne relative of the Lakota. We know it is a wounderful and respected waterway, another gift from Creator

In the Cheyenne River Agency, the land base is made up of the large amounts of rolling grasslands with medium-range hills and buttes throughout. The grassland terrain and the moderate to harsh climate creates a vast prairie land of open, beautiful sloping lands with abundant game and plant life. The winding and bending rivers, creeks, and streams allow for abundant water sources for the people and all beings. The waterways flow through beautiful bending routes of magnificent carved out bluffs and cliffs.

There were small villages and encampments on the agency that served as centers for gathering and trading for the people. These would eventually include places like Eagle Butte, Thunder Butte, Iron Lightning, Cherry Creek, Green Grass, Bear Creek, White Horse, Swiftbird, and Red Scaffold, in addition to Wakpala, Bullhead, and Little Eagle (which originally were within the 1869 borders). Stations were set up at some of these sites to deliver treaty-promised goods and annuities to the Lakota, when the government chose to do so. A large indigenous trading and gathering site was frequented northeast of Thunder Butte. The people navigated their travels by using the buttes and natural landmarks as guides.

The western boundaries of the Cheyenne River Agency were within five to seven days of travel by horse or wagon of the He Sapa to the west, where the people visited quite often for food, hunting, prayer, ceremonies, gathering, and wintering.

Because the Cheyenne River Agency was bordered on the east end by the Missouri River, north of Fort Sully, Fort Bennett, and Fort Pierre in Dakota Territory, and because it contained travel routes through the agency and into the fertile He Sapa, the agency became a target of the US government for purposes of starting an infrastructure for financial, military, industrial, and commercial enterprises. This was the case despite the fact that it was a breach and violation for any whites or the military to trespass upon the Lakota lands all across the Great *Sioux* Reservation, including the Cheyenne River Agency. Although the 1865 treaty with the Mnincoju band of the *Sioux*, (ratified March 5, 1866) indicated that the Mnincoju would not attack or create war upon other bands or whites, unless first assailed upon the "routes overland" that were already established or were to be established through their country, the Mnincoju still held the right to protect themselves and their territory against trespassers and invaders. The 1865 treaty was a so-called peace agreement, but it served as a means for the whites and the government to believe that they could plan or build an infrastructure that would provide a route to the valuable He Sapa and its great natural resource wealth of timber, game, water, land, and potentially gold and silver. What the United States could not obtain through open negotiations in the Fort Laramie Treaty with the Lakota in 1868 (i.e., a relinquishment of, or unfettered access to and sale of, the Black Hills), the government and its money-motivated private interests pursued anyway, with their hidden agenda. And the Cheyenne River Agency would eventually play a part in this.

In order to establish a sound, useful infrastructure for the military and the business interests to have a route to the He Sapa, the planners of the matters in Washington and in the financial institutions back east needed to have the basics: food for the soldiers, easy business transportation access, and a compliant and willing leadership group within the agency so that all things could be put in place with the least interruption, resistance, or cost of doing business.

This process attracted eager and vivacious entrepreneurs, opportunists, and vultures, who swooped in and took advantage of cheap access, cheap prices for land and other resources, and cheap associations with corrupt politicians and leaders. The railroad industry, of course, jumped at the chance to supply the means of quick and easy transportation on a large scale. The banks back east were eager to finance the railroad men, and the rights of way were obtained from the government and the agency, as easy as stealing.

Then, the agency officials had to be compromised or bought off to allow these things to happen, which turned out to be an easy feat. That was no problem at all, as the United States had become quite good and downright professional at hiring and appointing some of the most corrupt, compromised and greedy individuals to serve in the capacity of government superintendents or *Indian agents*. All that was needed was to skim some part of the ill-gotten gains off the top for these corrupt officials. And the word *no* was not ever uttered, except when a Lakota asked for assistance. In any event, compliant tribal leaders were quickly identified and utilized.

Then, last, the commercial business profiteers and opportunists needed to play their part in supplying the goods for subsistence of the business employees, soldiers, and government officials who were needed to fulfill the operations for the infrastructure, namely, gaining and using the access routes to the Black Hills. These goods came by way of the cattle industry. Established in 1870, the largest cattle company in the western United States, the Diamond A Cattle Company, ultimately would come into the agency years later.

It would be at or soon after this point in time that the Cheyenne River Agency would start to become engrained and historically embedded in the cattle industry. It would become the greatest and most devoted commitment that the agency made initially, or would ever make (even into the 1900s and the 2000s, up to the present day). The cattle industry on the agency would quickly become predominant, the cattle becoming like gold to the businessmen, the ranchers, the government, and the agency officials. Cattle would become more valuable than the people themselves. All efforts would be made by governmental officials to cater to the cattle industry—the cattle companies such as the Diamond A, and other, smaller cattle companies—and to the cattle owners, ranchers, and dealers who would come to use, and ultimately misuse, the agency resources to gain incredible personal wealth, personal influence, and great and everlasting political dominance and entrenchment.

The cattle industry, and companies like the Diamond A Cattle Company in particular, would eventually obtain over a million acres of almost free grazing land and privileges, infringing upon the best interests of the Mnincoju people. And the government, local and federal, allowed this to happen. It would set the stage for future generations and would create a corrupt permanent hierarchy within the agency government for ages. Cattle would be given more privileges than the people. Ranchers and their cattle would be given the best and free access to the best water, waterways, and grazing lands, and would enjoy the greatest of economic and legal protections against anyone or anything that would threaten to interfere with the darling industry of the agency.

This practice would ultimately create a distorted sense of privilege and governmental entitlement in those who would obtain, hold, and perpetuate their cattle holdings and personal influence. It would become widely known that there were many families on the agency that would become a fundamental part of the agency's cattle empire from the beginning. The investors and cattle industry moguls who were white, often would secure their status on their holdings into the future, many times by taking Lakota Mnincoju wives and husbands and starting families whose children would be directly linked to the Lakota bands. This would allow the whites to secure and protect their interests against any resistance which might be based upon a lack of band or tribal membership status for generations into the future.

In the years immediately following the 1868 Fort Laramie Treaty, the stage was set early to mold and permanently earmark the plan to create the infrastructure for an easy-access route to the Black Hills. The plan was in place so that when the time came, the government and its profit-hungry white profiteers could at long last seize or steal the He Sapa from the Lakota. It took good planning. It took persistence and determination. And most of all, it took guts, and a lack of empathy, conscience, and humane consideration, to do what was needed to pull it off. As history played out, the government and the white profiteers would ultimately meet their goal.

Wanbli

In 1871, Saved By Bear believed that he needed to go and visit the Butte of the Wanbli to try to obtain more of the sacred eagle feathers for the people's ceremonial use. On an early autumn morning, he got on Wildfire's sturdy back and rode.

Since the wanbli's feathers were treasured and important to all ceremonies and honorings, it was an honorable task to be chosen to be the one or ones to go and collect the feathers. Many times, the wanbli themselves, because of their close spiritual connection to the people, would leave a feather or two at the lodge or camp of the Lakota, as a gift, or as a result of just being near the people. Many sacred feathers are gathered and collected this way without having to try to obtain them directly from the wanbli. Special care needed to be taken in handling the feathers, and placing them in a protective cover of some sort, until such time as they could be used or worn. The feathers are considered a sacred gift from wanbli and Creator, and must be respected and used in a sacred manner. Many times the feathers could be seen and located around the nest, and obtained that way, if one is lucky to have that happen. When that is not the case, then the respectful tradition of seeking the feathers, only a few at a time, would be used in a respectful manner.

It is unnecessary and wrong to take the life of wanbli. This is because the wanbli are, after all, the messengers of all prayers to Creator. It is wrong to knowingly kill or hunt the sacred being. The spirits would be saddened and disturbed to know a human intentionally killed a wanbli for selfish or prideful reasons. But it was honorable to remove the feathers after they had naturally passed onto the spirit world. Thanks and prayers would still be offered. Therefore, whenever a Lakota went in search of wanbli feathers, every effort was made not to harm the wanbli. Instead, the Lakota would try to distract and catch the wanbli, taking feathers directly from its tail. The tail feathers of the wanbli were the most treasured of all since they held the magnificent beauty, strength, and breadth of a lively chiseled fan or knife. The tail feather had to withstand flights of thousands of feet through the air and at tremendous speeds. It is a finely durable feather with a stout and reliable shaft, which is long and circular and perfect for use as the natural handle of the feather. The shafts made it easy to attach the feathers to bits of clothing, staffs, coupsticks, buckskin shirts, fans, and weapons, and to braid directly into one's hair.

The wanbli tail feather has a whitish translucent shaft that joins with the quill. The individual barbs of the feather are a deep brown. Sometimes there is also a natural fluffier type of downy feather (like that of a duck's breast) near the quill of the tail feather. The barbs are closely formed together, growing upward and outward and away from the body to create the natural cascading fan look one sees when examining the feather up close.

The deep brown colors blend into a softer brown and become grayish, joining the brown with the white tail feather tips on the baldeagle. The magnificent whiteness of the tips of the feather tapers off to a near point at the end—not exactly pointed, but more blunt and narrow. And yet these tips are wonderfully beautiful. The defining difference between the deep brown of the overfeather suddenly blazing into the bright white ends gives a truly dramatic sense of brazen strength and invincibility. Wakan Tanka took great care in outfitting wanbli to be the beautiful being that wanbli is.

Standing nearly three feet tall in adulthood, a full-grown bald eagle is smaller than its close relative, the golden eagle. The female in each wanbli family grows larger than the males. If lucky enough to survive the first year of life, most wanbli can live to a ripe old age of thirty to forty years. Some, after painful sacrifice, actually live to be sixty.

Wanbli chooses a mate for life and raise their generations of young together. The wanbli family is centered around caring for the young, hunting, carrying messages for Wakan Tanka, and playfully maneuvering through the brilliant skies. Their nests are usually made in high cliffs or on rocky ledges, or in high tough-wooded trees, mostly near a waterway such as a lake, stream, or river. Hunting, to the wanbli, a survival instinct, represents their existence as a being.

Wanbli's eyes were made specifically by Creator to be able to see great distances. One could perch on a mountaintop two miles from a town of prairie dogs and see each one clearly, with the ability to pick them out individually. A wanbli can also gaze through the gleaming clear layers of still or fast-moving river waters from hundreds of feet above and, moving quite fast, swoop, dive, and grab the swimming fish from within a foot or so below the surface of the water. It is a genuinely magnificent thing to see.

Wanbli's eyes are clear and precise, constructed to provide the gift of accurate vision for all of wanbli's life. Such great vision is needed for all the activities and tasks that wanbli needs to carry out while they serve the physical realm of Grandmother Earth. With strong wings and great vision, wanbli have the ability to appear when summoned. Wanbli is asked to carry prayers and messages upon its great wings to Creator from the people or from any being who chooses to seek its help. Wanbli is indiscriminate in the carrying of prayers and messages. Wanbli's life has been a gift from the beginning, as wanbli was chosen to play this role. They were chosen to move between the physical world and the spiritual realm. The wings beat, and the breath rustles at the portals of that threshold every time wanbli is asked to perform these duties on behalf of Creator.

It is at those moments when wanbli is chosen to carry a precious, urgent, pleading, or thankful message and prayer to Creator that wanbli is at its finest. Those moments call upon all of wanbli's abilities to become a keenly working element, a chosen being who would hear, then know, then receive, and then carry those precious messages and prayers.

The wanbli is unique in that it is a sacred being made by Creator that can fly, moving at extreme speeds and reaching great heights, through the sky carrying that prayer, that message. Wanbli was blessed by Creator to be one of the few that could fly high enough to look down upon all below, as if in space and beyond. One may see wanbli come, moving its way over the hillside and valley with that piercing call, and then zooming, hovering, and circling to alert onlookers to the fact of its arrival and its willingness to listen and to carry. Wanbli oftentimes will circle above those whom they know or feel they must watch over, without necessarily being called upon to carry messages or prayers. It is this type of relationship between wanbli and that particular being that is most treasured, because from this display it is made known that a gift is coming or is to be given. It is a blessing and a thrill to the heart to know of and to feel such a thing. The Lakota always viewed the presence of wanbli as sacred, and as a good sign in that one is leading a good life.

When wanbli seeks to serve and deliver the message or prayer to Creator, wanbli comes, hears, receives, and circles. And then it happens. It is one of the most unbelievable, magnificent, and unforgettable visons one can have when the wanbli has come, has just received the message, and starts out on its great journey to deliver the message or prayer to Creator. Wanbli often will circle, beginning with short concentric circles. As wanbli gains more speed and determination, those circles gain size and height. Then comes the moment. As wanbli attains a level of permissible delivery entrance, it seemingly stops abruptly in midair, and then immediately, with incredible speed and agility, zooms straight up to Wakan Tanka in Grandfather Sky. Wanbli in effect disappears. Those who witness this great act can stand, breathe, feel the goodness of Creator at that moment, and appreciate the oneness of all creation, because it is at these moments in time and life that one may give thanks for having been granted the gift of life, the gift of grace, the gift of peace, the gift of unity, and the gift of love—true, unbridled love for all things in creation, with no concern for war, territory, disagreements, or turmoil. These times of unity must be savored, captured, and then stored in the vessel of one's heart, and deep within one's spirit. This is the great giving of the grandest gift.

We have connected with Creator, with our heart and our spirit much more than with our mind or analytical thought. It is a moment of rejuvenation of the spirit accompanied by the sense of being a human being and a child of Grandmother Earth, coexisting with all her beings, sharing the same gift for all time, and cherishing this gift with others for all time. This is why the gathering of wanbli's feathers is so important, so genuine, so critical to survival, and so critical to moving on in our collective lives.

So that task begins. The wanbli nesting or hunting areas must be discovered and explored. It is wrong to do this at a time when the wanbli couple are raising their young in the nest. This is not right. It must be a time chosen when the big adults, male or female, can be lured to an area that is safe for the human being and the wanbli. A site is chosen usually in a high bluff, on an open cliff, or amid a plateau. A shallow hole is dug, long and wide enough to hide one's body in. Then a covering of brush or light branches can be used once the human crawls into the hole. The bait can be laid on top of the cover brush to lure the wanbli. Then comes the task of silent, concealed positioning, hiding, camouflaging with the brush, and waiting.

———— ««◉»» ————

On this particular day, Saved By Bear was on a mission. He had been watching a particular group of wanbli over the Eagle Butte bluffs, the great messenger's namesake territory. They had already raised their young wanbli that year. There were plenty of adults of all ages to be seen near the top of the butte, mostly bald eagles with their white heads and bright white tail feathers.

Saved By Bear knew the butte well from his previous trips up there to scout for approaching herds, or to go meditate, think, or pray. It was a good site to look for feathers. The wanbli frequently came here to hunt or socialize. There was also plenty of room to dig a good hole, and the more level ground near the top was not as hard as some of the rock-laden ledges. He selected a midmorning when the wanbli would likely move up the nearby Owl River to hunt, search, or visit others for most of the day, as he had observed many times before.

He grabbed a stone hatchet, his digging rock, a big knife, his elk-hide bag, and his foot-long parfleche feather holder, which would secure and protect the integrity of the feathers if he was lucky enough to get some. Sometimes, as mentioned earlier, the wanbli came in a manner like a giving friend, willing to provide the gift of its feathers as a spiritual fulfillment to the particular Lakota. Other times it had to be lured and caught, its feathers taken. In any event, Saved By Bear was prepared to handle the situation. It was a little cool for an early fall morning, but the colors and sounds of the late summer were still there. Since he had been to this area before, he was not unknown to the people who lived there: the swallows, the coyotes, the larks, and the occasional porcupine. He was not an unwelcome stranger, so to speak. What was different today was that Saved By Bear carried all of these other things with him and may have looked out of place to the other peoples.

He had been taught by his father, his grandfather, and many of the Lakota elders always to respect the homes of the other beings, even beings who were not human. Every creature was a person in its own right. There were the winged people, the water people, the ant people, the four-legged people, the wolf people, the bear people, the plant people, and the stone people, each being people of Grandmother Earth just as much as Saved By Bear was. And his human Mnincoju people were of the same Grandmother Earth. We all have our natural unci, but we all also have our great and nuturing Unci, Grandmother Earth. We can all exist in the same world and share with each other for the betterment and continued existence of all. This was the great teaching. This was a cornerstone lesson taught to all of the young of all the peoples. *Let the time never be seen,* Saved By Bear hoped and prayed, *where we lose sight of or lose touch with each other, where we lose that connection. Grandmother Earth will be saddened by the loss of any of her children.*

With that understood, Saved By Bear started to dig his hole before wanbli came back and he lost the chance to hide himself. This he did with large scoops of dirt and small stones. A few small roots of some brush plants were taken and put on his pile of cover. The hole was deep enough for him to kneel in if he tucked his knees in tight and kept his face near his thighs. He hoped that once he hid, he would not have to be there for a long time. The hole was cramped and not very comfortable.

He chose as bait one of the rabbits that had been taken on a hunt recently. Wanbli would often snatch the prey off the grassy prairie at such speed that it was hardly believable. The rabbit would be a good treat. With the bait in place, the only thing left to do was to wait.

When wanbli finally showed up, Saved By Bear stayed perfectly still, barely breathing. Then he felt the heavy weight of wanbli on top of him in the hole, clawing at and eating the meat. Carefully, he adjusted himself to spring forward. However, since he sensed that wanbli was at ease and was not sensing any danger, Saved By Bear decided to ask wanbli if he could take some of wanbli's tail feathers today, rather than using the traditional means of grabbing and holding onto the wanbli's feet. So he turned his mind and his spirit toward the message to wanbli. "Is it alright with you if I take four feathers from your tail for me and my people? We need to have a few more for our ceremonies and for the young warriors. You can decide which ones. Will you help?"

Wanbli heard him with the spirit. Wanbli stopped working on the prey, and lifted off the brush covering the hole. Wanbli said: "Yes. You can take four of my tail feathers. I see you were hiding. You need not do that anymore. We can help when you need it. You can just ask us." And with that said, wanbli spread its wings, flapped them quickly a few times, and then rose to a hovering position above where Saved By Bear crouched. With deliberate and steady movement, the warrior pushed aside the covering, and reached up toward wanbli with both hands outstretched. "Pilamaye, Brother", he said. He was presented the opportunity to take ahold of both of wanbli's feet at once. Wanbli, a strong bald eagle, pulled him partially out of the hole, but he hung on. Then wanbli just stayed hovering with its feet held. Wanbli had kindly and generously agreed to provide some of its tail feathers to this warrior on this day. Acknowledging this, Saved By Bear quickly but gently removed four of the wanbli's larger tail feathers. Then he let go. Wanbli flapped its great wings and remained hovering for a moment. Then wanbli said, "Look after your people. We all need to do the same. Toksa ake". And then wanbli lifted up in the sky, and turned its wings to the west, and flew fast and far, toward the distant tree line. So it was that

Saved By Bear received the gift of four eagle feathers from the kind being that day. And he thanked wanbli with a four-directional prayer. He left some more rabbit for later. Then he climbed down the butte. With his valuable feathers, he got up on Wildfire and had a happy ride home.

10
STRONG HEART

To maintain the strong heart of our people, would involve the Lakota adaptation to a rapidly changing world, and the necessity to pass wisdom about all aspects of life to the next generation. This wisdom included the spiritual instructions given to men and women about their own life experiences. Gender-specific topics were brought forth to ease this transition to a much more difficult time. Tradition and culture were beginning to fade from practice and memory. Rituals were performed less frequently since the people had to provide for their more immediate subsistence needs. The movement of the tiospaye to areas of known abundance and safety would become a priority. The seasons could not provide enough sustenance to meet the people's need as the difficulty increased. It was more difficult to gather and hunt in our previously safe and secure areas. Conversations of concern and questions occurred much more frequently, and with increasing urgency. The questions came from children, women, men, elders, warriors, and spiritual leaders. They all spoke as individuals. Disease was becoming a deadly problem. The health of the people was suffering. That's why movement had to be very carefully organized and planned. Basic human necessities were very scarce and insufficient at this time. The people suffered, their energy levels and their practices decreasing. They could not always keep up with things that were rapidly disappearing. The number of people who needed to be fed, clothed, and sheltered was large. It was harder to find the resources that were needed to accomplish these simple tasks of daily life.

Sacred Stewards, Sacred Protectors

One of the most critical elements which called for the Lakota to take a stand and seek permission to act, was their sacred duty and obligation to protect the sacred He Sapa, the magnificent heart of Unci Maka—to protect her sanctity from the encroaching hordes of greedy destructors and pillaging human vultures. They must protect and preserve the natural positive spiritual energy of the sacred ground and her entire family of beings: the stone, the tree, the elk, the buffalo, the grass, the air, the waters, the deer. In order to tap back into that sacred positive energy, the warriors needed to feel Unci Maki's ground and her essence all around them. They needed to feel this true connection and recommence the ceremony of life.

Actually, anyplace in the sacred He Sapa was always an appropriate place for ceremony. The land itself there is rich and full of the connective natural energy of the spirit of life and Creation. A person, if truly connected by the spirit, could actually feel the energy and the connection by merely standing on the ground and thinking with the heart instead of the mind.

This connective energy is there at many of the Lakota's sacred sites where the natural spiritual Earth energy of life is abundant and free to use and to be absorbed by all of those who come with free will and good hearts and spirits. If the open heart and spirit are allowed to freely absorb the energy at these sacred sites, then the connective energy of the spirits can flow freely to receive and carry forward messages of prayer and the answers to questions.

The energy is often perceived by the people as an electric current that passes gently through the heart (chest) and through the feet and hands, and even through the top of the head. This is a signal to the physical body that the spiritual connection is present. To many who know, it is like turning a switch on in the body, activating tissue, nerves, and blood, setting them into motion in order to prepare the physical body for the energetic spiritual experience. One can freely invite and accept this warming glow of connectivity and the forthcoming messages and communication. Alternatively, one can choose to block these things. It is truly an exercise of free will.

No innate ability is required to receive the connectivity to the spirit world. All that is needed is a sense of belief, an open heart, an open and free mind, a willing soul, and a lack of fear to truly feel the connectivity to the spirit and to Grandmother Earth. If free will is lacking, or if fear of the unknown is present, or if evil thoughts and intentions are at the forefront of the human mind and purpose, then the natural current may be interrupted, broken, or worse yet, perceived as something evil, unwanted, or harmful in and of itself. This is why it is unproductive for a nonbeliever in the spirit world to close his mind and spirit, allowing analytical and documentary thought processes to overtake and overwhelm his ability to receive the spiritual connectivity of the moment and the place, and the gifts being offered.

When a human or any being would enter a sacred site with an intent not to give and receive in the connective exchange of prayer, messages, and answers in a good way, but instead enters with an evil intent to pervert, steal, destroy, manipulate, impugn, corrupt, or usurp that goodness, the spirit world knows. It is not wise for such beings with such designs to enter that arena while in that mind-set, as it could end up being a rather bad experience for that individual or group of individuals. Corrupted individuals, or anyone else who would seek to pervert the good connectivity and energy and use it for evil intents or purposes, may find that they convert a haven of peace, love, and giving, into a spiritual battlefield that turns upon them when the truth of their bad intent and purpose is revealed. It would be much like when Wakinyan sprayed hail upon the man who used the sacred cannumpa in a bad way.

It happens that once a nonbeliever of the spirit and connectivity to the spirit world has a bad experience at the sacred site, that the reactionary comments, rumors, statements, and criticisms surface. The natural energy of the sacred places and the gift of good that is intended to be received, may then be seen or perceived as something bad or evil by the nonbelievers or would-be corruptors. They may tell others of their bad experience or bad feelings about the place. Maybe they felt the energy moving through their body as a physical attack upon their health, an attempt to harm them. Maybe the fear of these unknown feelings and perceptions brought on at the sacred site struck fear so strongly in their heart and mind that they were compelled to tell others to avoid going there, or to claim that the place is possessed by demons or evil spirits.

When those who seek to obstruct, corrupt, mask, hide, or destroy a sacred site's energy or its magical connectivity to the good in life, obtain a means of knowing what they are truly encountering, then they may take measures to purposefully conceal the reality of the sacredness of the place. This often leads trespassers, thieves, conquerors, destroyers, and occupiers to erect physical barriers to try to contain, conceal, or obstruct the sacred good energy itself.

Those who would seek to vanquish, corrupt, or destroy a people's sacred sites and portals of the connectivity to the good energy of life, would often build stone or metal structures or monuments over the top of these sites, in an attempt to physically bury the natural ability of the energy to flow freely to and from the open spirited ones. If the corruptors gain the ability to occupy or control the land, then they will undoubtedly choose to encase the site in cement, stone, or brick. Sometimes even putting up structures upon the holy sites to block the energy and to conceal even its natural appearance. They may even seek to bring their own nonbelieving ways to the place so as to further corrupt or interrupt the energy, placing foreign materials upon or underneath that which is aboriginally sacred.

They will bring the names of their own leaders, their conquerors, their generals, their headmen, and others, to transform and further disguise the true natural identity and meaning of the sacred places. Good will be called evil. That which is godly will instead be referred to in the devil's name. Sacredness will be masked and perverted. The connection will be intentionally blocked.

<hr />

The sacred ceremonies of the people are oftentimes performed within the inipi, the sweat lodge. When the inipi lodge is constructed, the design used is one that is as old as the people themselves. Sixteen branches of willow are used as the column poles. The willow branches should be long enough to penetrate the ground a foot or so. Once buried, the moist, newly cut branches are bent over, toward the center, and joined with the willow branch column poles from the opposite side of the lodge, where they are held together and then tied off. This way they form an arc across the center of the lodge. The height at the center of the lodge should be between four and six feet.

The fire pit is dug in the center of the lodge circle. The earth that is dug up to make the fire pit is taken from the earthen womb, so it is used to build a mound for the ceremonial altar and the placement of the cannumpa and other ceremonial items. Some of the remaining earth is dropped onto the grass between the inipi's entryway and the mound, to create a pathway between the two. This earthen pathway is a pathway to the Creator. The pathway should only be traversed when entering or leaving the inipi.

What one takes into the lodge, one also brings out. That which we bring out is the good path. One enters the inipi from the left and exits the inipi on the right, the directions being dictated by the four directions: west, north, south, and east. According to the individual holy person, medicine person, or ceremony leader, the opening of the lodge may face the east. However, the heyoka, and the families of Saved By Bear, always used the west because of its significance to the Wakinyan. The Wakinyan, or Thunder Beings, prefer to have the people engaged in prayer and ceremony use the west entrance of the inipi.

When the lodge frame is fully constructed, secured, and tied off, the interior of the lodge, where the willow branches meet and intersect, forms the eight-pointed star. The origin of all life is revealed by this connection.

As the lodge is intended to represent the womb, the inipi ceremony serves as a representation of a rebirth into the world, a rebirth of body and spirit. The connection to the heavens and the stars is natural and spiritual. The inipi fire is usually started with time enough to heat the inipi stones, usually sandstone or lava rock, so that the rocks are ready to be used when the inipi begins at dusk. When the four doors, four phases are done and the inipi ceremony is completed, the people leave through the opening, exit on the pathway to the right, and are embraced by the starry night sky if the night is clear. The purity of feeling like a human being on Unci Maka is once again gifted.

———— «(❀)» ————

In Lakota philosophy, a deep current runs within the flow of humanity upon Grandmother Earth. As long as humans fulfilled their duty as stewards and protectors of Grandmother Earth, the two-legged humans would be free to live in civilized societies upon Turtle Island. The destiny and responsibility of being stewards of Grandmother Earth, is great. Being such a steward is honorable. It is also forever.

If there were to come a time when all things set out by Wakan Tanka and Grandmother Earth in the great plan for life and coexistence, were to be threatened or thrown out of balance, then the great hand of destiny may seek to rise up and to pluck offending organisms from within and upon the Earth. This is the philosophy of the Lakota based upon the millions of years of their existence, a history known and believed. A Great Race was once held….. at a time of imbalance of all things that was present on Grandmother Earth. That should events and history be repeated, would and may come again. A vision of what was once the truth, and what may lie ahead as a future truth, must be understood if it is to be learned and known.

Whereas the Lakota society was based upon community, with an outlook of sharing with and respecting one another and of caring for nature and all of Grandmother Earth and her children. The emerging society of man in the industrialized world will come to complicate and threaten the natural balance of things. If the encroachment of machines and air-depleting menaces would be allowed one day to accumulate to the point of dominating the Earth's surface and all societies, then the trusted and reliable hands of time may cease to move in the expected way from sunup to sundown, from season to season, from storm to storm. If the wondrous balance of the natural Mother is challenged and weakened, then she will be asked by Wakan Tanka to adapt herself.

A good spiritual prayer of protection is commonly made, as follows: "Creator, we pray for Grandmother Earth and for her protection, for her to protect herself from all destructors, and for us to protect her and all of her people to the best of our ability in good faith, in good will, and with good intentions. We pray for her healing, and we ask that through her healing, we be healed, so that we may live our lives in the manner of Wakan Tanka, with peace, unity, tolerance, and love."

If Grandmother Earth is asked to adapt to the ensuing imbalance of her former self, she will do so in ways that will create an unexpected change for the peoples. What was once ritual and reliable will no longer be so. The expected ways of things will become unexpected, unpredictable, unknown, unfathomed, or unnatural.

Creator created Grandmother Earth long before Creator created humans. If Creator were pressed by the circumstances caused by humanity to make the future decision between the survival of Grandmother Earth or the survival of her inhabitants, then the millions of years of history and natural cycles of existence may be rewritten, and played out again, as they had before.

The greatest moments in the history of Lakota society, when the people were the most free to live, to learn, to exist, to love, and to grow, were also when the people were most at peace with themselves in the great Circle of life among all beings, all peoples, of Grandmother Earth. These were moments when all that could be shared was shared; all that could be learned and known was sought and cherished; and all that had any value was within an arm's length, such as holding onto a loved one or nourishing the young, or celebrating the great sacrifices provided by the buffalo people to fulfill all the needs of the Lakota.

It was the time of riding free upon the horses until there was no more light on the horizon, and then riding some more at the insistent hoot of the owl people or the yapping of the midnight chorus of wolves and coyote brothers.

The land was wide open, the breeze strong and sweet-smelling. The water gushed quickly and purely over the rocks and between the clumps of pine and ash, and nourished parched, thirsty lips at the dunking of one's face into the stream. The trails were long, trusted, and reliable— much like an old friend whom one goes to visit frequently. The four-legged people, the winged people, and the water people went about their busy lives, in harmonious existence with the Lakota, because it was known that each leaned upon the other at times in their lives within the great Circle.

Life was good. Life was joyful. Life was natural. Life was adventuresome. Life was spiritual. Life was trusted. And, life was reliable and dependable.

Oftentimes during prayers, the people looked upward and raised their offering to the sacred directions, saying, "Wakan Tanka, I depend upon you. We depend upon you. I depend upon you for all things. I give thanks for your help in providing for us, and for being there for all that we need."

It is this loving respect and dependence, which the Lakota would feel most lost, if that which is depended upon, no longer were to be provided. The dependancy is for the opportunity to live, to survive, to grow, and to love—for all time, until the end of time.

Should the great balance of life be shaken and harmed by the deeds and intents of man, especially the industrialized future human being, then the people who depend upon Creator will realize a need for that which was once dependable and reliable, but which has now become unreliable and undependable.

This would be the time of the crumbling of the Circle. This would be the time when the human being's place in the Circle will be viewed as indeterminate. This would be the time when life itself will be unbalanced. Life, as all have known it before, will have been changed. It could result in a breaking of the world.

Should the great unbalancing occur as a result of humanity's greed and errors, then man's very existence will be threatened. Many will not survive. Those who will survive will need to be strong in heart, strong in body, and strongest in spirit. Those people closest to Creator in spirit will be those who have the greatest ability to withstand the imbalance and the retethering of the world. The four-legged and winged will have an advantage over the two-legged.

But should the time of readjustment of the spirits and the building blocks on Grandmother Earth, calm and settle upon stable ground, then those who shall survive to live again, shall live again in a time of new beginnings. But it will also be a time of bringing back many of the older, reliable and dependable means of existing, resulting in a new dependence upon things and a new manner of trusting what is to be worthy of trusting.

It is in these times that well-worn customs and ways will reemerge through kindness of heart and courage of will. The new ways will be much like the old. Old friends will find each other in the new age and the new existence. The two-legged will join the four-legged in compromise and selfless coexistence. The winged will observe while aloft.

The time to reconnect and to regenerate will be at hand. The time to dream again will be here. The time to know what to forget, and what not to forget, will grow out of necessity.

The breeze will blow gently again, with less violence and less harshness. The waters will flow kindly, clearly and cleanly once again. The ground will spring forth the roots and shoots for abundant foods and medicines for all. The sun will joyfully rise and set, in exchange with a brighter, happier moon. The creatures, the people of all sizes, shapes, and colors, will come forth once again in the community of life.

And the human being, the Lakota, will get up on his friend's back once more, and the two will ride toward a new, brighter horizon on newly blazed and trusted trails that seem subconsciously familiar. Riding upon lands that have the ability to breathe and pulse with the energy through one's soles of his feet, and through one's hooves.

And the time will again be simple. And the days will again be known. And the nighttime will again be reliable. And the seasons will come, and they will change. They too will become expected again. And the Grandmother will show signs of growing trust and love for her children once more. And she will allow her memory to fade into history, as to the past mistrust, misdeeds and betrayal.

The Circle will be reformed. The Circle will be mended and healed. Creator will mold it in Creator's great hands, and touch the surface of the gift with a love that a parent shows for the newborn child.

The Lakota belief in the virtues of peace, unity, tolerance, and love, holds true for all things, all peoples—not just the Lakota, and not just the human beings. The Lakota plan and pray that life will survive. We pray that the Circle, if broken, will be healed. That the Circle will be eternal.

In the times of encroaching danger and change forced upon the

Lakota by the new people and their government and military, the fear and the sense of uncertainty is real. The people long for the times of the old. But now, like their brothers the buffalo, they look to the future with an acceptance of reality. And like the buffalo people, the Lakota will stand up, they will rise, and they will face the coming storm, and walk forward into it with the strength of the spirit.

⸻⸺◈⸺⸻

Every Lakota, when the time came, felt the need to have made their own medicine pouch. Most times, it was the women who designed and made the pouches, much as they did with all the clothing for the people. The pouch was usually made of hardened hide so as to protect the treasures inside. Frequently the medicine pouches were carried on one's waist or were tied to one's sash with a rawhide tie or with a tether made of deerskin or buffalo skin. The medicine pouch was meant to be with the Lakota at all times—at every step, during every hunt, on every venture, for every meeting.

The pouch commonly contained things that were dear to the individual Lakota. For example, sage for smudging as needed; bear root for a clean mouth and spirit; cedar for protection of person and place; sweetgrass and sage for prayer and cleansing; stones for Grandmother Earth and special spiritual sites and events; wasna for quick nourishment; the hair of a loved one; the hair of a dear horse or dog; things that memorialized some of the most important things in the individual's life; and usually anything else that the Lakota held dear within his or her heart. This included their hopes, their dreams, their memories, and their prayers.

Saved By Bear and Swift Bear wore their own medicine pouches in their daily lives, everywhere they went.

Sinte Is Called Home

Saved By Bear felt the cold of early winter closing in. One night, as he settled down to sleep, he looked closely at his Sinte as she struggled to get close to him.

He knew Sinte was getting sicker and sicker, and weaker and weaker, and that her physical body was giving out on her. He wished that he could give her part of his flesh, his blood, his bone, to heal her and to make her stronger. Through it all, she never failed to look at him with those soulful deep brown eyes full of love, trust, and loyalty.

He wondered more persistently these days, seeing her age and condition, and knowing that she was coming closer to the end of her physical life. He grew somewhat sad and confused, not knowing why a spirit so good, so loving, so wakan, was not allowed to live upon the Earth for as many years as he or his human two-legged kind. Why was it that she and her sunka relatives could not live long enough to grow old together with their Lakota family, to live and love and share for all the years, staying together, running, walking, playing, and loving. It did not seem right. It did not seem fair or just.

One night while stroking Sinte's soft white fur at the base of her belly and along her cheek, Saved By Bear studied her. And for some reason, he looked up, out through the tipi flap atop his lodge, and saw the stars of the Trail of Spirits, the great Milky Way. This is the spiritual trail where all the spirits of the loved ones travel upon and sit around the campfire of Creator and the ancestors—not just the human being ancestors but all ancestors, including the sunka ancestors. It was then that it struck Saved By Bear in the middle of his thought, catching his spirit by surprise.

These ones such as Sinte who love totally and unconditionally, are so full of love and bring so much joy and comfort to those who share their lives with them, that Wakan Tanka decided long ago why it was to be. As Saved By Bear lovingly stroked his dog's warm cheek and listened to her deep, slightly labored breathing, he realized it to be true.

She, and her kind, gave so much love, joy, and happiness that they were given shorter physical lives than humans. Because they were so loved and could love so much, the spirits could not wait as long to see them again. Sinte would be able to rejoin all the relatives, sunka and human, who had passed, sooner. This was designed as a means of sharing their love and joy. This is why they were called back sooner by the spirits. Once Saved By Bear realized this, he knew that regardless of how much time he and Sinte would have together on Earth, they would find each other in the Milky Way when it was his time to look for the ancestors and for her. And she would find him. They would run to meet each other, sit with all of the ancestors, hers and his, and share their love unconditionally, once again.

It was as if a sign had come to Saved By Bear, a sign that he now understood, a sign indicating that their physical time together was coming to an end. He knew it one night when Sinte painfully and slowly lay down by his side in the lodge. Her breathing was labored and irregular. She periodically let out a small whimper. She closed her eyes and snuggled up by his chest. He closed his warm arm around her body and held her close—not tight, but close enough to feel her heartbeat and her warmth. He caressed her ears and her cheek, softly singing to her the song he had sang when she was a puppy. Then they fell asleep together—for the last time.

When Saved By Bear awoke at dawn, Sinte still lay by his side, wrapped in his arms, but she no longer had labored breathing or whimpers. There was no painful movement of sore old joints. There was no movement at all. He knew that while he and his dog had slept, Wakan Tanka and Sinte's relatives had come to visit her, to visit them. And they all welcomed her to come, to go with them across the green prairie, over the hilly way, across the stone bridge, and into the safe and loving embrace of Wakan Tanka and Creator. Sinte would now be able to run and jump like a puppy, and to kiss and love all her ancestors, her mother, her father, her brothers, and her sisters—her kind. But she would also greet and be with Saved By Bear's kind, all his ancestors and relatives.

Saved By Bear took some of Sinte's hair to place in his medicine pouch, which he wore close to his heart. She would now become one of his closest spirits, always there in his heart, his thoughts, his dreams, and his spirit. He knew that he would need to call upon her, and that she would be there no matter what, no matter the circumstances. But mostly, he remembered. As the tears flowed down his cheeks, he remembered the good, the love, the devotion, and the friendship. And he remembered the promise that he had made to her, that when the day came for his ancestors to call him home too, he would look for her.

She would hear him coming, her ears perked up, her tail straight, her gaze directed toward that stone bridge. And they would find each other.

———— «⦿» ————

Through the years, among the people, the sunkas were a constant presence, a kind, loyal, noble presence. The people respected sunka, and sunka respected the people. The bonds of love and commitment were strong between the Lakota and their dogs. The sunka were an amazing race of peoples in light of their physical and mental abilities. They were intelligent and loving. They showed empathy and communally cared for their sunka and human families. The sunka were much like their close relatives and ancestors, the wolf people.

Sunkmanitu Tanka

Wolves are a species of people that the humans misunderstand. Throughout recent history, the European humans have been taught to fear the wolf, the claim being that the wolf is wild, vicious, scary, and carnivorous. The myths and tales tell of wolves attacking people, stealing children, and killing lost or wandering human strangers.

However, to the wolf, nothing is as important as life itself, and its family. Wolves live in packs. *Sunkmanitu tanka*, the wolf, is an empathetic, caring being. The wolf packs usually have one alpha male and one alpha female. The wolf mates for life. The pair of united mates bear children almost every year and raise their children until such time as the pups are mature enough to go out on their own to start their own families. The families usually live in dens that are inside natural caves or enclaves for protection from the weather and wind. These dens are also a good place to hide from the sight of humans or from those human beings who would track and kill the wolves.

Human beings sometimes believe that they are the most special people on Grandmother Earth and therefore are better than all others. However, they are not. The humans are the youngest of all the peoples on Grandmother Earth. The other peoples, like the wolf, came into existence upon the surface of Grandmother Earth long before the humans. So too did the other peoples who came before, the buffalo people, the bird people, the stone people, the water people, the grass people, and on and on.

As previously mentioned, the wolves have always been devoted to family. The wolf family will take in an individual that is lost, hungry, injured, or scorned, even if that individual is a human being. Obviously, the wolves are great hunters, using this instinctive talent and way of life to survive. They must hunt and kill other species from time to time to feed themselves and their families. They do not kill just to kill. If they kill, they will almost always come back to the scene of the taking to retrieve the meat. The wolves, misunderstood for the manner in which they hunt and take other species as game, are feared for their howling and their sounds of attack when they hunt.

Wolves are compassionate, taking care of and revering their elders, and those individuals who are sickly, injured, or most vulnerable among them. The alpha male will hunt in packs made of other males and some females. They will communicate with each other by their howls and barks, coordinating their positions and announcing the presence of prey or humans. Because they travel in packs, they are feared for their sheer numbers, especially when on the hunt. They do in fact have strength in numbers. However, this is the wolf family merely working together with the common goal of securing food for the survival of the entire family, for the feeding of their own, even the ones that cannot hunt or run on their own, such as the very young and the very old, the sick, and the injured among the family.

When the wolves need to move, travel, or track, they first move from their safe haven den to find another. Often, the wolf family goes from one previously established den to the next in one season. They may move back and forth from one home site to another as long as the den still exists.

When the need arises to move the pack, the wolves will form a line. The lead hunters and scouts, three or four deep, spearhead the moving pack line, and the rest follow. Next comes the rest of the family, including the most vulnerable, those that are young, sick, injured, or elderly. These ones in the middle move along at their own pace. The lead group of wolves will not move so fast or so far ahead that the more vulnerable ones are forced to catch up. In the rear are more of the strongest and fastest. These members of the wolf family bring up the rear to secure the safe and easy passage of everyone else no matter the circumstances. They make sure that no one falls behind, is attacked, or falls away. They will not leave a sick or injured wolf behind if it becomes too tired, too sick, or too feeble, or is too old, to continue. When this happens, the strong ones in the rear alert the rest of the pack, who then will stop and wait. The wolves will not leave the vulnerable one behind. They are full of care and empathy for all the members of their group, their family. In this manner, the wolf family and the Lakota act alike.

The Wolf, in many respects, is like the warrior. A strong belief in protection and family exists for both. With its devotion and caring, the wolf portrays the character of its people, as the warrior does: Do not mistake my kindness or my calm silence as a sign of weakness. If you try to do harm to my family, you will see and know my strength.

A common story told around the campfire at night by the people when trying to teach an important aspect of life to the young and curious ones uses the wolf as a symbol of the dichotomy in one's life. The story is as follows:

> An indigenous grandfather is teaching his grandson about life. "A fight is going on inside me," he says to the boy.
>
> "It is a terrible fight, and it is between two wolves. One is evil—he is anger, envy, sorrow, regret, greed, arrogance, self-pity, guilt, resentment, inferiority, lies, false pride, superiority, and ego." He continues, saying, "The other is good—he is joy, peace, love, hope serenity, humility, kindness, benevolence, empathy, generosity, truth, compassion, and faith. The same fight is going on inside you—and inside every other person, too."
>
> The grandson thinks about it for a minute and then asks his grandfather, "Which wolf will win?"
>
> The grandfather simply replies, "The one you feed."

And so the wolf is viewed sometimes by humans as an outward symbol of this dichotomy. However, that notion has always been unfair to these noble beings. The wolf is a spiritual being. And again, much like the Lakota, the wolf regards song and singing as an important spiritual part of its life. Wolves sing. They howl. In good times and in bad, they sing.

They know. They care. They love. And they remember. So when the wolf howls at night, it is calling out to its family or other loved ones who are on the hunt with them or at home in the den. Or the wolf is calling to those who are waiting for her in the spirit world. In the world of the wolf, one will lay down her life for the good of the many. It is no wonder that the wolf is the ancient ancestor of the human being's closest friend, the sunka.

Horse Nation

To the Lakota, the horse nation has always been a gift and a blessing from Creator. The horses are a part of the Circle of life. Sunkawakan. The circle would not, could not, be complete without horse nation. These four-legged people are viewed as sacred beings, spiritual in their connection to all things and also in the way they use their natural strength, speed, and love of family to enrich the lives of all they come into contact with.

Horse nation relies upon the plant people for their nourishment. They are not meat eaters. Their bodies were created and designed by Creator to be a perfect combination of things important to timely and efficient movement upon the surface of Unci Maka. Their physical presence is enhanced by their incredible beauty and grace. It is a sight to behold merely watching them.

Horse nation was with the people for thousands of years. They came to the human beings as much as the human beings came to them. It was as if Creator looked at the two species of people, human and horse, and saw immediately that both should be together. Of course, the plan of Creator is always benevolent and peaceful, with the aim of supporting life and community. It is the way of life. The Circle is formed, continued, and cherished if all peoples play a role, with all peoples important to the meaningful continuation of the Circle: peace, unity, tolerance, and love. Each plays their part. No one people is selected to dominate or vanquish the others, not according to the original plan of Creator, not according to the perpetuation of the natural ecosystem. If all peoples work together in a harmonious communal fashion, then all life can flourish naturally.

So the interconnection of the peoples on Unci Maka became an important facet of survival of the one, the survival of the many, the completion of the Circle.

The horse nation arose proudly from the parts of Unci Maka that provided the natural things needed for them to flourish, the waterways, open grasslands, and enclaves of natural protection. Many of the original inhabitants of the horse nation on Turtle Island arose in the mountains, prairies, and river basins.

The Appaloosa are a band of the horse nation that wear a naturally spotted coat. The mustangs, or painted ones, had coats of mixed portrait-style design, with patterns of shapes and colors, not so much spots. These are two of the aboriginal bands of horse nation that found their way to meet, befriend, and join forces with the Lakota human beings many, many thousands of years ago. The two peoples have been together as a functioning community for much longer than modern Europeans can fathom or that their books and theories will allow them to accept.

The Lakota and the horse nation were intended by Creator to live together, to take care of each other, and to utilize the best each had to offer in order to live and survive, to continue their generations of life on Unci Maka together for all time. Horse nation was an important part of the Lakota way of life, of the Lakota Circle of life. The Lakota were an important part of the horse nation's way of life, their circle. Together, these two individual circles moved together to join the greater circle, the one intended to be the Circle of all life.

Horse nation survives within their own families. The young are precious and must be protected, cared for, taught, and mentored by the adults. The horses know and feel what happens to each other. They have the same emotions the human beings have. They have spirits. They have empathy, loyalty, and love.

When one among the horse nation suffers, they all can feel it. They all can know it and remember it. In this way, they are no different from any other living being, but particularly their friends the humans.

Members of each species may, from time to time, attempt to dominate, kill, feed upon, or abuse another, or use another people in a manner of enslavement, torture, massacre, elimination, or genocide. As long as the dominators among any type of people are so motivated and act upon their bad intentions or influences, all others remain at risk.

Horse nation, throughout time, has faced dominators, particularly in the form of certain bands of humans. The horses, although they have been used as pawns in times of war, hostility, destruction, violence, and conquest, never wished to participate in this way. It is not part of their natural way of life or in their makeup. It is not a part of their natural circle of life.

In particular, across the world, but especially in Europe and Asia, horse nation has been used for activities related to war and genocide. They have not been volunteers. They have been forced. Horse nation would much rather be of service and live with peaceful, life-preserving ways. The horses are spiritually connected to kindness, diplomacy, generosity, sharing, freedom, and enjoyment of life for all; not just for some. This connectedness would come to bear as members of horse nation witnessed events that troubled them.

The horses knew, so they communicated. They let the people know by sniffing and licking their faces. They knew the secret circumstances of the Lakota death warrant delivered into the hands of the bluecoats in 1868 and of many other campaigns against the people. Their own ancestors had known, and had told them the same stories about these particular humans. Yes, the stories have flowed, and do flow, through all of life.

The horse people have always been some of the most valuable messengers, as they are communicators of the messages of life... and death... and other events, throughout time. It was only natural that they were blessed by Creator with the gift of long life (many times with a life span of up to twenty-five years per foal).

⸺⸻•⟨◉⟩•⸻⸺

The Lakota used their spiritual connection with horse nation to act in pursuit of their goal to enhance the way of life of both peoples. Horse and Lakota worked together for their mutual peaceful survival. Individual horses became a part of the Lakota family, starting from the time they were born and going all the way until the time they passed from the physical world. The two peoples became the same family.

The bond is incredibly strong between the Lakota and the horse. It is this bond that existed between the young Lakota named Saved By Bear and his bright, energetic pony named Wildfire.

In looking at Wildfire, Saved By Bear never ceased to be amazed by what he saw. He looked closely at the horse's head dipped at the edge of the water. The coarse dark brown hair on his head draped along his forehead and fell over the very long eyelashes of his left eye. The pony's lips pressed to the surface of the cool clear water, submerged just slightly, and then curled back to create a sucking motion. But for the color, the vision, and the motion, Wildfire reminded Saved By Bear of his friend in the White Mountains.

Saved By Bear watched as the graceful pony gulped the water in, like he hadn't tasted it for days. And again the young warrior studied his horse, standing there with his long neck sloping down, with rippling smooth short hair, the sunlight lightly dancing off the white patches and spots to shimmer and flash in the young Lakota's eyes. Those strong muscles just below the short hair on Wildfire's neck and shoulders were not altogether visible to the innocent or unknowing viewer. However, those who knew him and his kind, knew how magnificently powerful and how beautifully graceful those coordinated muscles just below the horse hide truly were.

Saved By Bear's gaze drifted along Wildfire's long snout, briefly pausing at the elastic-like expanse of his large nostrils slightly flaring and keeping time with the gulping. He moved his eyes up the horse's face, where the dark brown forelock flopped forward between the upraised pointed ears—one mostly white, the other mostly brown.

This creature, this being, this life, was beautiful: beautiful in spectacle, beautiful in design, beautiful in utility. But the most beauty was to be found in the fact that this young horse was Saved By Bear's friend, his loyal devoted companion. Saved By Bear silently thanked Creator for his Wildfire

Saved By Bear had often wondered how it was that the Lakota had come to know and gain the trust of their horse brothers. As a young boy, he had been told of the horse people by the warriors and the elders, and especially by his father, Fights the Bear. Saved By Bear remembered how his father described, and then showed him, how to build the trust to gain a friend, how to build a relationship with a companion. Fights the Bear described in detail to his son how it was that the Lakota, for countless generations, learned how to become connected to an individual horse. He started by speaking of the human's manner upon first approach, describing the process of easing into the relationship. He used as an example something he'd experienced with a young horse that needed to be taught many years ago.

As Fights the Bear approached, he remembered the spiritual way to know the horse, to let the horse know him and to let the horse see him—really see him—and smell him, watch him move. This way the two could feel connected, as one, and have a companionship, a familiarity, a knowing sense of comfort and friendship.

Fights the Bear quickly looked down at the ground to determine the pathway he would take to the horse. He moved forward, making an open and honest approach toward the four-legged one. Then, once his eyes briefly studied the steps to be taken, they slowly moved up and looked into the eyes of his new acquaintance. He knew that the horse would notice his body, his look, his manner. The horse would study him, and his approach, with caution, awareness, and nervousness.

Having never been ridden by a human before, the young horse looked down briefly at his own feet and noted the difference between his hardened hooves and the man's dark-shaded moccasins. What a clash of difference in their feet. The four-legged pony caught the scent of the man on the breeze and recognized it as the same scent given off by the other two-leggeds he had come close to in his young life. It was not an offensive smell, just something different from the smell of his own hide.

He sensed the human move. The horse's eyes quickly darted up to behold the human, only to be caught up in the stout yet soft gaze of the man's brown eyes. As their gazes lingered, the man's forward motion resumed. Horse stood his ground. He peered into those human eyes with his own deep brown eyes, the large rounded pupils forming a glistening concave half sphere protruding between his long dark lashes.

The human continued to come forward, moving toward the horse, steadily advancing. He was not overbearing, just seeming to be determined to move forward, toward the horse. Their eyes remained locked. Horse wondered how the man was able to walk with such purpose and confidence without breaking eye contact.

The Lakota, trusting his mind and his memory, knew how to perform this age-old dance of trust with a four-legged one. It had been learned generations and generations ago. And once learned, it was a handed-down gift from elder to youngster, from the knowledgeable to the novice. It was an extension of the Circle of life, an extension of Creator's will to allow free will and devotion to form bonds between beings. And the method worked because it was simple. It was something felt deep down in the consciousness and the spirit.

The method consisted of using one's perception of oneself as a being, a once fearful and apprehensive life experiencing things and other beings for the first time. The ability came from looking within one's very own being to discover one's own thoughts, beliefs, and perceptions. This gift of seeing oneself in this manner allowed a being to learn what it was to be another, to think as if in the other's moccasins, as if standing upon the other's hooves. Using this method, one could understand the thoughts and feelings of the other, as if there had been a soothing and magnificent reversal of roles, a transporting of perceptions, a transference of reality, by seeing through one's own eyes what another being saw from his, by becoming those eyes and the consciousness behind them. This was the key to understanding oneself, the key to understanding others, any or all of Creator's beings.

So this is how it was done. This is why it is done. And on this day, between this two-legged one and this four-legged one, it was being done. The knowledge gained from the reversal of roles was valuable, good, and spiritual. It was useful in gaining trust, in gaining a friend.

The human recognized that the horse sensed the differences in their bodies. Aside from the obvious, the fact that the man walked on two legs while the horse walked and ran on four, the horse also observed that both he and the man had noses. When seen from afar with unconnected minds or motives, their noses looked quite different in shape, color, texture, size, and length. A nose is the first point of the face, the outward point cutting through the air when the body is moving forward. It is the tool of smell. It is a force of first impression, a force of first encounter, a force of first familiarity.

It is understood by all beings that to a great extent, one family of beings resembles others of their own kind. Humans resemble their parents, their grandparents, their relatives, their kin. Young buffalos look like miniaturized, less heavily furred versions of the adult buffalo. The owl's beak and powerful claws look the same as those of the young owlet. It goes on and on, through time. So familiarity is borne of family. Family is much easier to accept and to trust by the one. To be familiar is to be more readily welcomed, more readily accepted, more readily trusted.

The human nose is much smaller and much shorter than the horse nose. This fact is easily recognized from a distance as long as the two peoples remain apart. But the act of making a kind and easy approach, and the old knowledge summoned forth by the reversal of the roles, forges a new connection between the two people. It is the narrowing of the space, the distance, between the two that ignites the unseen magic of the new sense of trust, the new friendship. If only the two can see each other as equal, equals in life and equal in purpose, then they can realize their mutuality, their familiarity, and their trust in each other.

The old way contemplated the closing of the gap between human being and horse while the two were looking into each other's eyes. This gave each the opportunity to truly see each other. Fights the Bear came to know that the elders were right. The familiarity would come. The familiarity would show itself and be revealed in the trust.

As Fights the Bear drew closer, the young horse noticed his eyes and also his face, especially the nose. Once the steadily approaching man got close enough to sniff the horse and for horse to sniff him, the young horse noticed that as the man's face got closer and closer to his own large brown eyes, the man's nose grew even larger, wider, and longer. The miracle of the role reversal created an image caused by the slow, even, friendly approach, allowing the natural dimensions of the horse's eyes to see the man and his now long, large nose as familiar. As it was similar to his own long, large nose. Similar to the nose of every member of his horse family. He recognized now that the gently approaching being was not threatening. He began seeing a connection. And now that the man was close, he was familiar to the horse. The first barriers of apprehension, suspicion, and uncertainty were gone. The connection between the minds and the spirits of the two now had an open and honest chance to grow.

This is how it begins. This is part of the process, how it always begins. This is how it is taught, through time and events. Most of the time the connection between horse and Lakota begins soon after the foal's birth. But when it occurs later in the horse's life, this is how the understanding and love for other beings can be helped along, by the things learned, such as the empathy inspired by the reversal of roles and the transference of consciences between Creator's beings. It is old. It is original. It is open and honest. It is life.

In thinking of how his father had taught and showed him, Saved By Bear remembered that when he was eight years old, he tried his hand at training a pony. The father, seeing his son trying to train his pony, came out of the lodge to help.

The son, an independent spirit, looked frustrated as the horse bucks away from him. "If you wish to have my help, you just need to ask," said Fights the Bear. "Sometimes, you need to lean on the older ones to help things along. You must not believe that you know it all yourself right away. And that is particularly true when dealing with our horse brothers." It was always a good memory, and also a good lesson. Saved By Bear took his father's advice to heart and claimed it as his own. Both he and Wildfire would be beneficiaries of their initial bond and their connectivity from the beginning, the eternal bond that grew between foal and boy at the start of their friendship and at the outset of their love for each other.

Conscience, Philosophy, and Spirituality

In examining how the changing times and the broken hoop of events led to a direct challenge to the Lakota way of life, one should also look deeper into the Lakota's basic philosophy and foundational belief structures. Because the Lakota and their relatives the Nakota and Dakota believed in the concept of *mitakuye oyasin*, "all my relation", or "we are all related," the people saw themselves as connected to the spirit of all things. Their communal lives elevated the best interests of the many over those of the few or the one. The Lakota way of life cannot be separated from the Lakota spiritual practice. To understand the Lakota and how they lived, and why they did things the way they did, one has to know that their most precious virtues truly were peace, unity, tolerance, and love.

Human beings function best and in the most healthy way when they act in ways that are consistent with the principles of peace, unity, tolerance, and love. The mental and physical health of the human being is tied to how people live their lives, both individually and as part of a healthy society. Personal health is also a matter of exercising the free will that Creator bestowed upon human beings. The individual choices and decisions made by the human being in exercising that free will have a bearing on how that human being will live his or her life. That life, in turn, may, can, and will, have an effect upon other lives that are part of the collective society and environment that one resides in.

When human beings focus on living with a good spirit, and living a life of good intentions and good deeds, they are naturally healthier in mind, body, and spirit. Living in a good way opens the door to a happier life and existence. There is less worry about harming others or damaging or destroying other humans' lives. It is easier to get along with others, to make and have good friends, to be a good friend, to be a good trusted family member, a good father or mother, a good uncle or aunt, a good son or daughter. People choose to be near a person who is living in a good way, because it makes them feel good too. Good healthy spirits attract other good healthy spirits.

Living in a good way makes it easier to laugh and to joke around with friends and family. It is easier to share life, stories, and feelings with others when a person knows that he or she is doing his or her best to live in a good way. It is easier for others to share the same with you when you are living in a good way. It is easier to smile, and to enjoy all aspects of life, when one sees life, existence, and others in a good way. It is easier, even physically, for the human being to smile than it is to frown or glare. Creator made it easier for humans to live their lives in a good way, in a happy way, in a sharing, caring way, in a way that allows for communal survival within a good society. The Circle of life moves strongly, simply, and naturally when people and all other beings live in a good way. When the life of all beings follows the path of peace, unity, tolerance, and love, the Circle is complete, respected, and dependable.

However, when a human being directs his or her free will toward the negative sides of things, the energy flow is shifted. When a human being lacks conscience, he may not see things in any other way except the way that seeks only his own benefit. When a person lacks empathy for other beings or other things, he may not know how others may be or are affected by what he does. A lack of compassion for other lives can cause a person to lose sight of the bigger world in which he lives, as he remains focused only on his own selfish needs and goals. When a human being lacks conscience, empathy, and compassion, his heart, soul, and spirit make room for bad intentions, bad influences, bad thoughts, bad motives, and bad spirits to move in and occupy that empty space. No longer will this person find it easy to love anyone else but himself. No longer will it be easy for that person to share meaningful moments and things with others. No longer will it be easy for the person to know and feel the consequences that his deeds have in the lives and spirits of others. No longer will it be easy to laugh and to smile. People who lack empathy are in danger of becoming consumed by greed, spite, envy, hatred, prejudice, destruction, war, and death; the idea of having supremacy; and/or the pursuit of wealth, notoriety, power, political influence, dominion, and conquest. It will be harder, if not impossible, for a person who has no conscience to remain connected to the attributes of peace, unity, tolerance, and love.

———— ((◎)) ————

A dishonest person can try to change and become honest and good, but he must work hard and be diligent if he wishes to succeed. He must allow time to earn others' trust, which will be built like a sturdy lodge over time, progressing from the ground up.

There is no absolute when it comes to the rehabilitation and rejuvenation of the soul and the spirit of the human being. The tide can be turned while the physical life continues and the physical heart still beats. The conscience, which resides in the mind and the spirit, must reach deep within itself if the person is to be saved, gaining the ability to stand, then walk, and then build the structure of the good and honest spirit.

It is the human being who throws aside concern for life, decency, humility, justice, peace, and Grandmother Earth, who risks true uncertainty and turmoil of spirit once his physical life force passes over the threshold between the physical world and the spiritual world.

The scoundrel and the greedy man is the hardest one to turn. However, the tide too can be turned for him as well. He may have a harder road to travel before he can return to the realm of respect, humility, and compassion. But it is possible, as a life is not something that is set in stone. Those who have committed atrocities and do not learn, or do not listen for the opportunity to turn the tide, will be too far gone most times to salvage a physical life in unity with those spirits that are peaceful, tolerant, and conscientious. If warnings to avoid or change the course of a life of evil ways and deeds go unheeded, then the chances for honest change may never materialize.

The goal of all the children of Creator is to live in a world of peace, unity, tolerance, and love for one another and Grandmother Earth. Spirits and souls that deviate from these principles may still find the light, the way, salvation, and redemption in the physical life. If they cannot attain that level of understanding and that spiritual sense in the physical life, then hopefully they can seek that same blessing and deliverance in the spirit world thereafter.

It is the challenge of all beings, regardless of origin or appearance, to learn about, come to recognize, and then live a life of fulfillment and purpose while still on the Earth. If that cannot be accomplished, then the spirit world may provide solace in some respects as far as those missed or lost opportunities are concerned.

If believing in Creator and living a life of being honest with oneself and taking responsibility for one's deeds is realized, then the spirit world may truly provide the needed peace and sanctuary that we all seek.

———————⟨⟨◉⟩⟩———————

The force of goodness in the heart and spirit is a beautiful gift given to every living thing. It requires only a natural activation in the system, the soul, and the spirit to become a breathing, growing part of any given being.

The spirit of goodness allows for the growth of kindness, empathy, generosity, and compassion, and for enlightenment. The good spirit is bathed in the bright nurturing light of love—love for oneself, and love for those who are ready to be, and capable of being, loved. For when the bright light of love is turned on inside a person, it is nearly impossible to turn it off. The energy and heat of the lifeblood of love goes deep, beyond tissue and bone, and springs into and molds with the very energy that serves to connect body, mind, and spirit. It is permanently intertwined with the genetics of life itself. The light is intensified in feeling, nature, and extent by each successive injection of love into another being. If and when that light of love is returned and shines back upon you, projected by another who loves you, then the brightness is kindled like the warmest, most joyful, most comforting campfire imaginable. This is why the light of love makes beings feel good and joyful in the mind, in the heart, and in the spirit.

Love is the medicine to cure all ills of the heart, soul, and spirit. Love is the clean, clear, crisp, running stream of water that, when pressed upon love-parched lips and love-starved spirits, provides a much needed and much desired quenching of the *spiritual thirst* that each living being possesses throughout their lives, starting from the moment of birth into the world.

The forces of good cannot ever be used for purposes of harm, pain, or destruction. The goodness of love and life cannot be suddenly or incrementally turned upon another to inflict harm or evil. This aspect has been known by all of humanity throughout the ages. By design, the goodness of life increases the strength of mind, body, soul, spirit, and faith. To hold onto and maintain the goodness of love, life, and all things that naturally pass within aspects of love is more challenging to the human being than to just give up and give in to the charms and enticements of the dark side of humanity, the evil in the world. The age-old conflict between good and bad is always present. Those people and spirits motivated by corrupting influences, destructive intent, and material possessions constantly try to satisfy an insatiable greed, a need for more, more, and more.

It is known by the scoundrels and persecutors with bad motives and ill will, that the powers of good can never be corrupted in the hearts and spirits of the good. They know that they cannot utilize the forces of good as tools of harm, destruction, and hate. Therefore, it remains a constant battle of conscience and resolve to challenge and repel the forces of evil things, as corrupted individuals and entities will never cease trying to gain a sense of superiority over all beings and all things,... even Grandmother Earth.

The challenge to remain strong and committed in the face of the constant barrage from corrupted human beings and spirits is always present, as it has always been there through time. Creator has provided those who believe in and practice the goodness of peace, unity, tolerance, and love with their own tools to challenge and keep the forces of evil at bay. But these tools must be used if they are to be effective. These tools are found precisely where they were originally placed at the time of creation of all things: in the hearts, the spirits, and the free will of all of Creator's beings. To use these tools, one must first accept that they are there. To know that these tools are there within every spirit, able to be used by everyone, one must be able to see with more than the eye. One must be able to see with the spirit, and must welcome that part of the spirit into the physical deeds of each individual faced with this freedom of choice.

"Actions speak louder than words." Many who lead or have led with spiritual courage and by example have lived by this mantra. It is greater to act in a way that aligns with one's beliefs than it is to simply talk about doing so. Lives are not saved by mere good intentions. Souls are not protected by kind, hopeful words. Action is necessary at crucial times in life. When lives and souls hang in the balance. When a way of life of a people nears extinction or vanquishment. When the battle is struck between life and death, good versus evil, moral versus immoral, and humane versus unconscionable, then the true moment of decisive action is at hand. Survival depends upon the outcome. Dreams of a people depend upon the outcome. Generations of those to follow need to have their opportunities for life protected.

This is why, at a critical time in the history of the survival of the Lakota, his people, Saved By Bear accepted the duty to act—at a time when the confluence of the generations of the past collided with a brutal reality of the present. At this critical time in the future, when needed, the forces of good would prevail.

———— ((◈)) ————

The Lakota way did not include wanting to kill on first contact. Our spirit said for us to take time to help the white people, help them survive, in hopes that they had decency and would learn. Their way, however, was mostly to initiate first contact in anticipation of engaging in eventual slaughter. Thus was demonstrated the differences between the capabilities of consciences.

The white European settlers would have suffered and died without the indigenous peoples' help. The white immigrants would not have lasted the first winter. We wonder why the white immigrant people were not more tolerant, more peaceful, or more thankful to us in the end.

———— ((◈)) ————

In examining the changing times and the encroachment of the new people and their advancement and taking, the indigenous people tried their best to rationalize what was happening and to convince the whites to have a change of heart and spirit, which would hopefully result in a change in their ways. It would come down to an ability of conscience and free will. Those people would eventually try to conquer us, destroy us, kill us, annihilate us, and erase us from history. May they, if we survive this, someday, somehow, someway, realize how lucky they are and were, ever to be here upon this sacred land. May they also be forced to see, to know, to smell, to feel, and to swallow all that their own relatives and ancestors did. All that they tried to do, all that they took, all that they made us forsake, all that they killed, all that they destroyed, all that they distorted, all whom they terrorized, all whom they sickened, all that they corrupted, all that they negatively influenced, all that they stole, all that they degraded and made evil. May they see the truth of what has happened, not just with their eyes and analytical minds but with their hearts and in their spirits. Only then will they truly know the truth. Only then will they truly learn. Only then may they be able to use their free will to build a future with an enriched, compassionate, and understanding spirit bathed in the message of peace, unity, tolerance, and love.

When even a small number of people choose to stand up to a force that threatens their way of life and their very existence, all things are possible if they are united in spirit with a goal pertaining to the good of the survival of the just and the reasonable. This is especially true if those forces that create the threat, bring it forth in an unconscionable way with an evil intent to destroy all things.

For true healing to occur, numerous healings must take place: healing of the person, healing of the mind, healing of the community, healing of the planet, and healing of the spirit. Then there must be a great telling of the truth of history, not a sanitized version, but a real, hard, raw actual account of what has actually occurred. It is necessary to lay the raw and brutal truth wide open for all to see.

The ability to separate what is right from what is wrong has always been the torment of humankind. There are no clear marks or warnings for when you are near the barrier between the two, only the regret and guilt that follows when you make the wrong decision—choosing the wrong path over the right one—while at the fork in the road of life.

Each of us cannot know totally which of the two roads to take at the fork, not unless we allow ourselves to know ourselves and have the ability to feel how our decision will affect not just us as an individual but also others, especially those whom we love, care about, and have meaningful contact with. We cannot truly appreciate that impact upon others unless we have spent some time coming to know that our own actions do in fact impact others. If one does not know or accept that reality, that notion, then one is truly selfish and unappreciative of the concept that one has an impact on the society in which one lives and on the greater world. In order to discern between right and wrong, one must open up one's mind and spirit enough to allow the real truth to enter and then find a home in the conscience. To be able to do what is right, versus what is wrong, one must truly first know the difference.

The Creator has created all peoples. The human people, the two-legged, were given specialized gifts, the ability to do many things. The humans are capable of making things that allow them to better survive. The human peoples are capable of utilizing their physical talents to build and invent. They are capable of using their hands and their minds to bring life to ideas that, once implemented, accomplish good things for all. But the humans are also capable of using their hands and their minds to create things that are used for pain and destruction.

Creator's gift of free will to all beings, and especially to the human beings, allows each individual to pursue his or her own beliefs and own direction. The Creator gave the gift for the human peoples to use. How the humans choose to use this gift had a great significance on history and on all the other lives affected by the individual's exercise of free will and the exertion of the accompanying beliefs and life direction. The human peoples have been blessed with the ability to dream the most beautiful of dreams, but they may also make or pursue the darkest of nightmares.

The human peoples were created in all shapes, sizes, and colors, with many backgrounds and varying appearances. The look of the human, or his or her skin color, is never a final determinant of whether he or she should be seen as a good person or a bad person. Each individual, regardless of origin or circumstances, possesses the same capability and capacity for peace, unity, tolerance, and love, according to the Lakota. Regardless of the appearance, origin, or color of the human, the Lakota view all as equally capable, as a part of a good, civilized, functioning world. No prejudgment is made of those with dark skin or black skin or white skin. It is the word and the deed, but especially the deed, that is the great determinant to the Lakota people of whether someone is trusted, or considered to be reliable and good. Only through experience with the individual, can the people know, looking beyond the outward appearance of the human, what is truly in his or her heart and spirit.

The Lakota have never had a definitive, universal, or prejudged distrust or dislike of the *wasicus*, just because of the color of their skin, their hair, or their eyes. The way the Lakota judged people always came down to the way an individual conducted himself, as one's conduct indicates one's character. If a white person was good in heart and deed, then he was worthy of trust, friendship, and respect. The Lakota embraced many, many white people who conducted themselves well and had good character.

As a matter of common belief, the Lakota did not distrust or dislike all white people. The Lakota believe that most human people, regardless of color or appearance, are good at heart, and capable of acting upon the basic tenets of peace, unity, tolerance, and love. But the task of trusting or liking white people seemed to become more difficult over time for the Lakota given the conflicts between their two cultures, and the general disinterest the whites had toward learning about the Lakota's life, culture, and belief. It was this basic concept, learning about that which is new, different, or unknown about another, that proved to be the greatest challenge when it came to the coexistence of the Lakota and the whites.

Creator bestowed upon each human equally, the ability to learn, to accept differences, and to acclimate. However, the *desire* to learn about and come to accept the other's way of life and beliefs, was absent in many.

Regarding the destined meeting that occurred between the Lakota people and the white European people, it must be understood as an undeniable point of history, that it was the white European people who came upon the lands of the Lakota at the outset of their relationship. The whites came from foreign lands to Turtle Island, where they encountered the indigenous people of Turtle Island. The Europeans were the visitors to the aboriginal lands of the Lakota. The Lakota were already here.

Given this significant point about the initial contact between the peoples, the basic Lakota and human tenets of peace, unity, and tolerance became extremely important, as they concerned the preservation and civility of both peoples during their early acquaintance and their subsequent contacts. If one people were viewed as less deserving than the other of common respect, human dignity, and the right to survive, then the two peoples would never have a chance to coexist in a peaceful manner.

Creator, while bestowing upon all peoples free will, formed the basic framework of human relationships and civilization. Since the Lakota had encountered in their homeland human peoples of other backgrounds, beliefs, appearances, and colors before the late 1700s, they knew, as previous generations had learned, that each of the different peoples, including those of other tribes, needed to be dealt with on their own merit. Each needed to be dealt with according to their ability to exhibit good in word and deed, and according to whether or not they understood the Lakota people and their way of life. This is what it always came down to. Each race of people had the opportunity to establish its own track record according to their words and, especially, their deeds. Throughout the story of the meeting between the Lakota peoples and the white European peoples, it is important to understand this backdrop, as it helps one understand how and why the Lakota people came to distrust and clash with the white people. Many of the white people chose according to their own free will, individually and collectively, to exhibit disrespect toward, dislike of, and condemnation of the Lakota people and their way of life.

The historical record shows that although there were many good, honest, and humane people among the white Europeans, there were also many who were not good people. It was the bad men among the whites who seemed to overlook the humanity of the Lakota people, the integrity of their lands, and the dignity of Grandmother Earth. It seemed that during the time of Saved By Bear and his relatives, those bad people sought to draw the other white people in, mesmerizing them and convincing them that the better course of action to take when dealing with the Lakota was one that entailed violence, theft, deceit, destruction, death, and genocide.

It was these bad whites, mostly those in influential positions of power in the government or private enterprise, who instigated many of the events and actions taken against the Lakota and their lands. It was these bad men among the whites in North America who, of their own free will, started down the path of confronting the Lakota, engaging in conflict with the Lakota, and destroying all that was Lakota. It was those bad ones among the whites who therefore sullied the reputation of the white European people and diminished their honor. They did this by way of their *actual* words and deeds against the Lakota and their way of life.

When one views the parents (of any type of being) taking care of their young, one sees and comes to realize the importance of the bonds of love and caring. Each little life has a beginning, is held dear, and is deeply loved by those who bring it into the physical world. Each life is cherished by those who take the time and make the loving effort to raise the child so that child grows to become strong to fend for itself, eventually to become its own being.

Those who nurture and give a great deal of love to the new ones, never forget and never relinquish that connective tissue that forever binds their hearts and souls with the heart and soul of the child. This is a lesson of life, a lesson of time, and a lesson for anyone who has no conscience when it comes to taking the life of any being.

If you look closely at your own newborn, and if you think about this gift from Creator that can cause you to have so much love for, and be so devoted and committed to, the new soul, then you will come to realize that you will do anything to protect that newborn, now and for each day to come. Even when the child becomes an adult, even when the child becomes an elder, because he or she will forever be your child.

One learns a great lesson when opening one's heart to welcome the new soul. If the parent, looking into the eyes and mind of the newborn, can do a role reversal, even for a moment, then the parent, can temporarily become the new one. It is then that you can see what the new one sees, feel what the new one feels, fear what the new one fears, discover what the new one needs to be protected from, and realize the unconditional love for and dependence upon the parent that the new one has.

It is with this new way of seeing, that the parent can realize that all beings, all spirits, and all people of every shape, color, origin, background, ethnicity, and species were once a dependent, innocent, wakan, loving being that needed a great deal of help just to survive. And with this new way of seeing, the parent also comes to realize that every new soul has a mother and a father, a family who cares for and loves him or her at all times in life. Nothing can change that.

A person who is able to see things this way and who chooses to harm, cause pain to, or take the life of another being can, by recalling that moment of reversing roles with his or her newborn, come to the absolute realization that everyone, every being, is someone else's special loved one. Realize that this is someone else's child, someone else's brother or sister, someone else's mother or father, someone else's loving little soul, who will be missed by his or her family and whose absence or harm will cause an extended ripple of pain throughout his or her family and beyond.

Maybe when a person has this point of view, he or she, when contemplating whether or not to cause harm to another, will first stop to think, reflecting on the possible consequences of such an action, and at least briefly examining that which is found within his or her open heart and open spirit. Perhaps this person will remember that consequences of actions committed without concern or care, endure well beyond the present moment. Sometimes those consequences endure forever.

The choice to harm another being or not, is part of the free will granted by Creator. This free will can be exercised with self-restraint, self-reflection, forethought, concern, and care for self and others. With moments of understanding and realization that no soul really deserves to be harmed or killed without due consideration of the consequences.

It is for this very reason that the Lakota, including the families near Bear Creek, the warriors, the Dog Man, Saved By Bear, and Swift Bear, prayed in ceremony for the answer to the question of how they should deal with the people who were trying to take their spirits and the spirits of their families. They sought instruction regarding how to deal with people who acted as if they had no conscience, and no concern or care for the rippling effect that their acts of harm and destruction, and their plan of genocide, would have on the Lakota, all indigenous peoples, themselves, and the whole world.

This is why they pray. This is why the Lakota will ask for, then seek, and then receive the instructions of what to do, why to do it, and how to do it, when the permission is requested.

———————⫷(◉)⫸———————

A good example of tainted perception is the way the white people who migrated from Europe to North America looked at and felt about certain indigenous tribes. Because the Indians appeared to the whites to be a less advanced culture (which they were not), the whites saw them as savages. The European white people compared the indigenous peoples' spiritual belief structures, comparing them to paganism or devil worship. Many of the white people also viewed the Indians as bloodthirsty subhumans who preyed upon white men, women, and children, butchering and mutilating them or simply taking their scalps.

The Europeans' tainted perceptions and prejudgments of the indigenous people on Turtle Island, had their roots in fables and rumors, and were not fairly based on any actual experiences with the indigenous people. These prejudicial and wrongful perceptions were often based on the whites' prejudicial culture and religion, mostly arising from the concepts of white supremacy, religious and cultural superiority, and white privilege. These concepts were clearly entrenched and were in evidence at the times white society would come into contact with people of other indigenous cultures. For example, the whites also showed their tendency toward white supremacy, their sense of superiority, and their self-entitlement when dealing with black Africans, and African cultures.

Many white people who came upon these indigenous peoples and their tribes, including the Lakota, prejudged them, through the whites' own cultural perception. Being unfamiliar with these new diverse cultures, the whites concluded that the Lakota people, their culture, and their beliefs were not as good nor acceptable as their own. Of course, the white people, new to Turtle Island, did not wish to, or actually take the time to learn the true value and depth of the indigenous and Lakota cultures.

It was this critical flaw in perception, arising from the culture and the belief structure of the white people, that prevented the whites and most of white society, including its government and military, from viewing the Lakota culture as the Lakota themselves viewed it. Not many of the whites, the *wasicus*, had the willingness, or perhaps even the ability, to overcome their prejudice, bias, fear, hatred, and animosity toward the Lakota and all the other tribes.

If mainstream white society in colonial times, the society that encroached upon Turtle Island, had allowed themselves to feel empathy, then more of them may have been able to see and understand that in many respects, the Lakota culture, including their spirituality and their way of life, was more advanced, in terms of humane behavior, communal living, and a social structure that permitted freedom, than even that of many of the encroaching Europeans. Had the whites regarded the Lakota with empathy, and had they been curious to learn the truth about the Lakota people, then they may have come to understand that the Lakota lived their lives in an empathetic way. They may have seen how the Lakota raised and cared for their children, their elders, and all their people, and how they honored and cared for all of Grandmother Earth and her beings. "Do not judge a man until you have walked a mile in his moccasins." This proverb imparted a real truth, a practical truth. It was a directive that was always there to be learned from and followed. In the United States, though, this would be a lesson not easily learned or accepted by the white people, not even after a great deal of time had passed.

———— ((()) ————

An age-old scenario confronted in wars and other military conflicts throughout the history of Grandmother Earth became an immediate consideration for the US Army in its conflicts with the indigenous people of Turtle Island and in the Civil War. The prospect of suicide emerged in the thoughts of individual or groups of soldiers when they encountered a situation with seemingly hopeless odds. The thought of suicide came upon a soldier's mind like an escape hatch appearing out of thin air. Suicide served as a way for the soldier to easily pass through a trapdoor, and in so doing, to avoid the ultimate pain and fear of what he perceived would befall him.

According to the Lakota, suicide is a violation of the natural law. The Lakota believe that it is wrong for a person to take his or her own life. Suicide is viewed as a selfish act, something that does harm to the loved ones left behind. After suicide, the spirit can become confused. It was important for the Lakota to teach their children about suicide at an early age so that none of them saw it as an option to consider when encountering difficult circumstances.

A false belief became widespread among the army brass and their ranks of enlisted men during the time of the Indian conflicts in the west: the notion that if US soldiers or other white citizens were ever captured alive and imprisoned by the Indians, they would be subjected to horrific, grotesque, and inhumane torture and mutilation of their bodies and minds. The army taught its soldiers to fear this thing from the Lakota and Cheyenne, in order to provoke a sense of loyalty among the troops, partly in an attempt to cut down on desertion. Of course, the notion of the Lakota capturing white soldiers and torturing them was false and fabricated. Nevertheless, it did create a real fear among the ranks, causing them to view the Lakota as evil, inhuman, disposable, and killable. And suicide was viewed as something the soldiers could do if they feared being captured. An old saying among the troops was a direct result of this false fear: "Save the last bullet for yourself." It was, of course, just a made-up tale that the military leaders could leverage so as to more effectively control the minds of the enlisted men. A fearful soldier is more easily manipulated into doing as he is told. Soldiers can be convinced to kill at will if they view their enemy as evil and less than human.

In reality, it was the European societies, in medieval times and the 1800s, that utilized human torture and mutilation as a means of battle, a method of warfare, in order to gain the psychological advantage and ensure conquest of weak or more vulnerable peoples or societies. This included the age-old practices of beheading (decapitation), dismemberment, disemboweling, stretching, burning, raping, torturing, mutilating, and scalping, which the military did to victims, prisoners, enemies, captives, and corpses. Scalping was a practice utilized by the Europeans when moving from region to region in either Europe or Asia seeking conquest over populations of foreign people. It was the Europeans who had arrived on the shores of Turtle Island who introduced the practice of scalping to the indigenous people on the Eastern Seaboard of Turtle Island.

The white soldiers' fear was fueled by the stories told to them of the things that could happen to them if they were ever captured by these *savages*, these *redskins*, these evil *heathens*.

The white soldiers knew how the whites and white society had come to treat the Lakota once the Lakota were captured or confronted by the whites. And they feared that if the roles were reversed, they would be treated just as badly by the Indians as the whites had treated the nonwhites throughout time.

The whites' fear of scalping, mutilation, and torture by the Lakota was unfounded for the most part. As already mentioned, that fear was instigated by the propaganda of the white military leaders to instill a serviceable mind control over their own troops so that the soldiers would try to avoid capture or desertion at all costs. The US military used this propaganda tool as a means of psychological projection to invoke the fear in the troops, as to what the Indians would do to them if given the chance. The propaganda was easy to incorporate by the military and its european influence of warfare, because they themselves have used it. The corruption or deception of any nation's military, to merely serve the desires and goals of a misguided or destructive leadership, would always be a threat to the Circle of Life. A military and the human beings that make up that military, deserve better. They deserve to be told the truth as to what they stand for and why they fight or kill. Many times, if the truth were to be known, a soldier may look deep within his heart and spirit, and decide to put down his weapon.

The real concern was not that the Lakota would torture or scalp the whites. It was that if the nonwhites ever gained the advantage over the whites, the nonwhites would treat the whites as bad as the whites had treated the nonwhites. The whites knew how they had treated the nonwhites over whom they had gained control, so they feared their methods would be used against them. The whites seemingly always treated the nonwhites badly, and many times horribly, so the fear that their own tactics would be turned against them was a legitimate one in their minds. It gave them an incentive never to allow themselves to lose control over the nonwhites, including the Lakota, because if they did, they feared that they would be treated just as poorly. Again, the whites feared that the roles would be reversed. However, white society's fear was based upon the false notion that other, nonwhite societies would behave as badly as they did toward others.

War and warfare are not natural to the human being or the human spirit. War and warfare bring about death of human beings, destruction of societies, and removal of hope. War and warfare violate the value of human life, and are opposed to the concepts of love and empathy for others.

Every human being who has ever lived and or is now alive has a mother and a father. Many are lucky enough to know and have been raised by both their mother and their father. The even luckier ones are allowed to experience life with their brothers, sisters, cousins, and great friends. Some, less lucky, don't know their birth parents, or have a life absent one or the other of their parents, because of events beyond their control.

But the common thread of human existence is that each and every human being on this planet is born as a child of parents and into a family. This human instinct is why a mother hugs her child close when she cries, why a father will run and cover his son's body to protect the boy against a flying object or threat, why a brother will stand up to a person who is bullying his brother, why an uncle will escort his niece down a dark canyon when she appears apprehensive, and why a child reaches for the hand of the protector when he is scared or confused.

One look into the eyes of those whom one loves and has a natural duty to defend reveals the nature of these things. Every human being is able to realize that this is the pinnacle of life: to love and to be loved. It is that simple. There need be nothing more than that. We are completed as humans once we achieve that one simple, truthful, and magnificent goal.

⟫⟪⟫⟪

Ista´

During the years following the 1868 treaty and the increasing encroachment of the whites, including the military, into Lakota lands, the Lakota people tried their best to hold onto their humanity and to honor their commitment to be stewards and nurturers of Grandmother Earth and all her children. However, it was becoming increasingly difficult for them to do so. In the midst of the development of the encroaching storm, which entailed the losing of their way of life, the Mnincoju embraced what they could. The story of Istà is a good example of this.

Swift Bear had a medium-sized dog whom he named Istà. Istà came from a litter of pups who had been left near the camp, their mother having been killed by a white hunter passing through. When Swift Bear was out on the hunt, he found the litter of six puppies. They were all blackish brown. He stopped to see them huddled together in a brush den between rocks, whimpering, scared, and hungry, their fur matted with burs. Still, as had always been the case with sunka, they were happy to see him, happy to see another living spirit who could help them. They all approached him with wagging tails, squealing and jumping on his buckskin-covered legs.

They all seemed to be skinny and almost starving, but otherwise they appeared to be healthy. As they were jumping up at Swift Bear, he noticed that one of the little males was having a hard time jumping. Looking more closely, Swift Bear saw that the little pup, which was mostly black, had one short leg, on the left side in front. Swift Bear knelt down. The little guy jumped toward him as best as he could. Swift Bear grabbed him by the exposed ribs under the arms and picked him up, bringing him close so that the warrior and the pup were nose to snout. The little pup eagerly stuck his tongue out and kissed Swift Bear's face, while happily whimpering as if he had found an old friend. Swift Bear's heart melted; he fell in love with the little guy. He used his fingers to feel the little pup's left front paw. It appeared not to be injured or severed. A birth defect had caused the front left leg to be shorter than the rest. Plus, the puppy's front left paw was not fully formed and it was small, almost not there.

As Swift Bear examined the paw, the little guy in his hands squirmed and licked his face even more joyfully, as if to thank him for noticing that he was different from his siblings and that it was okay.

When Swift Bear took all the puppies into the camp and showed them to the people, they were all welcomed with open arms and open tipi flaps. Wica (Little Man), the biggest male of the litter, went to Red Deer. Wasu, named after a hailstone, went to Big Bull. Hoksila, the energetic herder of the group, went to Kicking Boy. Pa Pa, named after the buffalo meat jerky he enjoyed to munch on, went to Saved By Bear's sister. Takoja was welcomed into Jumping Elk's tipi. And Swift Bear hung on to the little pup who had stolen his heart, his Istà.

Swift Bear was handy with his hide work and was adept at using sinew. He was also an excellent engineer, able to use forms and angles. He was proficient in the practical analysis of common difficulties, and was a good problem solver. Using these skills, he fashioned a pliable laced moccasin for Istà's misformed paw. This allowed Istà to walk, jump, and run at an almost normal pace, enabling him to keep up with the other pups and dogs. The little boot was soft on the sides, secured by laces of sinew and with a durable sole for walking on rocks, sharp pine needles, or sticky brush. Istà's gratitude for his friend's handiwork, his love for him, and his tending to all his needs, shone through clearly in Istà's expressive deep brown eyes. It also showed in the joyful, playful snaps of his jaws, as if he were mouthing words to his human and sunka family members. Istà was a warm, happy, and helpful spirit to have upon Swift Bear's journey of life.

Istà had a gift of knowing the pain and suffering one was undergoing. He would frequently come to Swift Bear and the family, and lick and kiss the areas that hurt—a knee, if sore; an arm, if cut; a shoulder, if strained; or a heart, if sad. His tender yet strong way was a comfort to his human being friends. He did the same for the other sunkas, and even the horses that would let him.

Swift Bear, his family, Saved by Bear, and all of the Mnincoju people who knew Istà had a special connection to the soulful and happy dog. He, with his huge heart and spirit, would leave his footprint, lovingly misshapen and unique, upon all their hearts and spirits forever. Ista' would forever be a symbol of how the beauty of the spirit exists in all beings despite the flaws and imperfections of our physical bodies. Istà, his siblings, and all the sunkas brought enjoyment and fulfillment to the lives of the human beings. The dogs all fulfilled their needed roles and served as important members of the family.

Istà's story confirms that the Lakota spiritually acknowledge, embrace, and have empathy for all of Grandmother Earth's children, an empathy that is taught to, and learned by, all Lakota at an early age. It is a gift received from Creator to be able to feel what another is experiencing. This proved to be another difference between the Lakota and many of the new people on Turtle Island.

———— ◈ ————

An empty soul (or spirit) need not remain that way for eternity. An empty soul is capable of being made to feel the need to begin filling itself. The person with the empty soul needs only to be shown the light in his or her own eyes at a critical moment in his or her life, when the need to feel, opens the rigid door that has been blocking the sunshine of life's shared existence. People with empty souls live life with little personal experience of what it feels like to cause, or to receive, a true soul wound. The human soul is every bit as capable of being wounded as is the flesh. Soul wounds are quite often shared or witnessed by others.

To witness a soul wound, one must first realize that soul wounds can, and do, exist. It is not enough to be told. It is not enough to imagine. A person can only learn about soul wounds through firsthand experience or by the secondhand account of a loved one or someone else who means a lot to the person who was wounded in the soul, with the witness being an interested bystander at the time of the wounding event.

Suffering and pain, oftentimes, are capable of being transferred through the air, much like a bolt of lightning striking a tree or a rock. If visualized, this transference of emotional energy resembles a shooting current running from the wounded person to the bystander, striking the bystander square in the soul with a solid thud and a sizzle. The eyes widen, moistening slightly. The fingers tingle and then burn. The chest heaves; it is hard even to breathe. There is a veritable punch in the gut. The heart temporarily stings and then aches. The mouth opens, the lips quivering slightly. The blood rushes to the forehead and the back of the neck. The toes curl, the spine stiffens, and the fist closes. The mind reaches for reason. Not finding any, it defers quickly to the aching gut, then to the aching heart. It is the heart, the *cantè*, that is the deliverer of the sensory news to the soul.

This is the moment, the moment of newness, the moment of trying. The moment of rebirth is at hand for the human and his empty soul.

It is like the struggle that occurs when a newborn being is fed for the first time. The new one is hungry and has been so hungry for so long that the first mouthful of nourishment, this new feeling to the soul, is a struggle to swallow without choking. The newborn tries to breathe, swallow, and absorb all at once. This is the beginning. This is the feeling of the new beginning, the first filling of the empty soul. The empty soul may not have known or even imagined how hungry it was, having never tasted or smelled true feeling of any sort. So when the soul wound, however subtly, brazenly, or viciously administered, is witnessed or experienced by the one with the empty soul, the age-old process of filling the soul can begin. For once a sudden influx of the effects and remnants of the soul wound are witnessed, the breach has occurred. Most inevitably, to never be turned in the other direction again.

Empathy is usually the blood of the current of energy that rides that lightning-bolt-like stream that ignites the spark, which lights the fire, which burns its hole through the protective cover of the empty soul. Empathy is the nourishment of the human conscience and of the instinctual sense of right versus wrong, of justice versus injustice, of fairness versus unfairness, of concern for others versus concern for only self. Empathy is like the clear, crisp, clean mountain spring in the middle of the hot scorching summer day with no shade, and with no water for many days. Empathy is the liquid drop that touches the tongue, which in turn convinces the mouth to do its work of producing saliva to help quench the overwhelming thirst—the thirst of the throat, the body, the mind, the soul, and the spirit.

The Creator grants every living being the gift of free will to seek out that which enriches the lives, the souls, the spirit, and the existence of ourselves, and of all those whom we care about and care for.

As empathy pervades the entire body, mind, and soul, it breaks down all barriers, including those that are natural, unnatural, taught, learned, or accepted. Empathy becomes the antidote, the medicine, for the sick and unhealthy soul, or the empty soul. It allows the soul to join hands with the mind so as to achieve a healthier state of being and to gain a better awareness and understanding of the true meaning of life. Empathy, and its continued growth in the being, exponentially expands how the one views the circle of those that encompass the ones he or she cares about and cares for.

Once that contagion takes hold and empathy spreads throughout the mind, the heart, and the soul, it can no longer be contained within the one. The person is mandated to reach out and pass that current of caring and empathy to others, including others he may not even know or have any idea why he would one day care for or care about. He only knows that he wants to grow outward, and that the need to expand this feeling of caring and concern must reach others if it is to succeed and travel its natural pathway. It is much like a newly awakened fresh stream of water, seeking to run out and into the rest of the world. A stream of feeling and caring that can no longer be dammed up, but which must break free to rush downstream in a rush to nourish others who may be thirsty.

It is the fulfillment of the people born of the water. The *spiritual water* of life. The very existence of the people in a home where the water runs clear and clean and fast and deep. A home where the water is plentiful, nourishing, free to all, and forever life-sustaining. In a home where all of the children of all of the people of every kind—two-legged, four-legged, winged, water, insect, plant, stone—beautifully share the life-giving water with the knowledge that through the natural currents of empathy and the water of life, all life, all peoples, can coexist in a world of peace, unity, tolerance, and love.

This seems very simple if one imagines and believes that it is all caused by something as natural as the sun rising and setting. Something so natural that we, all the people, had it all along from our very beginning in life. It is and always has been the water of life. And the *spiritual thirst* that each and everyone of us has.

Empathy is what causes people, no matter their station in life, to act out of concern for, or for the preservation and protection of, those about whom they care. Empathy cannot as easily be taught, as it can be learned. Empathy is easily deflected when someone is indifferent to the plights of others. The less that one sees or learns of someone, the easier it is to avoid having empathy for that person. Oftentimes people prefer to avoid having empathy for their enemy, or their rival, setting aside any notion of caring for and being concerned about the well-being of those *others*.

In the matter of war or genocide, the architects of such policies aggressively promote tactics and mandates to specifically avoid any potential empathy. So as to convince those whom they must convince, to do things, to believe, that when they do things to these *others*, there is no need whatsoever to care for them or their well-being or to be concerned about their present... or their futures.

Empathy is the enemy of war and genocide.

11

CALL TO BELIEVE

The Pale Moon of the Morning Reveals a Creeping Shadow over He Sapa

It is at the break of dawn when the coyotes quit yapping and the meadowlarks start their chorus to welcome the new spread of early-morning sun. The night dew glistens in the newfound sun streaks as the golden hue spreads across the rolling hills of brownish grass and brush. The nearly full moon leans toward the western horizon, still aglow but fading to a lighter shade of blue. If one looks closely, one can still make out the outlines of the moon's crevices, ravines, and deep canyons. Not altogether that different from those on Unci Maka.

The morning brings a freshness of mind and purpose for the Lakota warrior. A noble herd of elk graze in the distance, not fearing the full blast of the daytime showcase. A herd of sixty move around slowly and confidently, feeling as if they are within one of their safe havens where they can roam and graze and not feel intense and anxious. The males let flow their proud bugling in the early-morning air, letting their relatives know of their presence.

The fading moon almost symbolizes an era gone by, one when the Lakota were the only human beings amid the handful of Cheyenne or Arapahoe relatives occasionally seen hunting and moving within the sacred He Sapa. The era and the moment were passing now, however, like the bright moon fading, almost disappearing, as the new day dawns. It is now the time of dealing with the new people, the white people, the wasicus. They have come steadily, increasing in number at intervals within the past fifteen years. And they have even become bold and curious enough to enter into the sacred He Sapa.

Saved By Bear and his group of warriors led by Turtle Back, the thirty-five-year-old veteran of many conflicts and reconnaissance missions, arrived in the He Sapa at dawn of the new day. There were twelve of them in total, including Turtle Back. This was the fifth day, after four nights' sleep. The warriors had been on the trail of the blue-coated US military expedition that had moved into the He Sapa from the southwest and had ventured into the southern reaches of the great forested regions at the heart of Unci Maka. The mostly Mnincoju warriors, with three Hunkpapas, had followed this group from a distance, tracking them ever since Sitting Bull and his Hunkpapa camp had conveyed to them that a large cavalry contingent with wagons, mules, horses, cattle, soldiers, civilians, and even cannons had started on a long journey from the army fort near the home of the Mandans. During the hot days of early July 1874, the cumbersome expedition team had steadily moved south and west. Sitting Bull's Hunkpapa warrior scouts had seen them, after first having heard and smelled them, once the group had crossed Cannonball Creek on the western edge of the Standing Rock Agency and along the western perimeter of the Mnincoju's Cheyenne River Agency. The noise, the dust, the general disturbance of the whole moving affair, did not serve to conceal their presence or their slow, deliberate movement.

A wayward army scout from Standing Rock, half Hunkpapa and half white, had conversed with some of the soldiers at Fort Lincoln before the team departed. Fools Bull had learned that remnants of the US Army's Seventh Cavalry were to be used in this mission. The military expedition team was intent on penetrating into the Black Hills despite the existence of the 1868 Fort Laramie Treaty prohibiting trespass across and into the Black Hills—unless—it were a military expedition to establish a military post, according to Article II of the 1868 Fort Laramie Treaty. The warriors knew that there was supposed to be no trespassing in the He Sapa. So the twelve had been sent to observe.

The public was advised of the alleged purpose of this expedition, namely, that Lt. Col. George A. Custer and his expedition team had been commanded and authorized by the US War Department to explore the Black Hills in order to find a possible location for a military outpost. This was the War Department's story. It was, of course, a lie and a diversion from the real truth.

Fools Bull had learned that contrary to the story told to the public, the real purpose of the 1874 Black Hills expedition was to search for gold in the Black Hills. Reports had been coming out since about 1848 from trespassing claim jumpers, criminals really, and sporadic trespassing settlers and trappers, that gold was all over the Black Hills. A priest named De Smet was shown a bag of "glimmering powder" by a Lakota on his visit to the Lakota in He Sapa in 1849, twenty-five years prior. De Smet recognized the gold then and advised the Lakota not to show it to anybody else. However, De Smet's story did get out.

The United States had recently come out of the bloody, exhausting, and treasury-depleting Civil War, which ended officially in 1865. The country was also in the midst of a severe economic panic over a failing economy. The country was broke, almost bankrupt. The US government was becoming increasingly desperate to open up the lands of indigenous people of Turtle Island, and particularly the Lakota lands, as they thought the He Sapa might be a treasure trove of resources and wealth. The government was desperately seeking any way to obtain the potentially mineral-rich territories.

President Ulysses S. Grant was instrumental in pushing the passage of the General Mining Law of 1872. It was common knowledge that Grant had gotten quite cozy with big business, especially the mining industry, since his election in November 1868. The 1872 Mining Law was written with a view toward the situation the miners and the private mining industry encountered in the gold rush in Montana and California in 1849. The Mining Law grossly favored the mining interests and allowed for miners to pay an outrageously low price to purchase unlimited rights to all minerals found in a claim. The law allowed the miners and mining companies, even foreigners and foreign companies, to mine for gold, copper, silver, and so on, to take all the profits, and to assume no liability for any of the losses to the public. The US public, the government, and the taxpayers, were paid virtually nothing.

The 1872 law was designed to provide the wealthy metal-extraction corporations and their wealthy benefactors, an opportunity to rape the land and to steal the profits, paying almost nothing for those rights or the destruction caused by the extraction. The miners, and the mining and financial corporations, were allowed unfettered access to public lands to steal their fortunes. It is a given that when a corporation is granted a license to steal something... it will. It brings to mind the wisdom-filled observation of Clarence Darrow: "A petty criminal is someone with predatory instincts but insufficient capital to form a corporation." Again, during this period, the government operated more like a kleptocracy than like a democracy. Much like how the powerful white thieves in Minnesota did what they did to the Dakota in the 1850s and 1860s.

In 1873, a financial panic, the worst in the nation's history, swept the country. Taxes were high, and the public debt was enormous. Several eastern banks failed, and the stock market exchange closed for ten days. Again, the government of the United States, and the white society desperate for cash, were thrown into a near Depression-style frame of mind. Since the 1868 treaty prohibited trespassing into the He Sapa, and since the Lakota refused to open up the He Sapa to white interests, the government, by and through President Grant, devised a plan. The plan would be based upon a big lie. It devised this subterfuge as a means to once and for all determine if the stories and rumors about gold in the Black Hills were true. If gold were to be found and confiscated by the United States, then the Black Hills would serve as a newfound treasure trove for the financially and morally bankrupted government that was in desperate need of an immediate influx of cash. The government needed to be sneaky, and camouflage its real purpose. Its young, eager, arrogant, and zealous military officer George A. Custer, was just the man to lead this deceptive, devious charade of an expedition.

Custer fit the mission. He had even urged Gen. Philip Sheridan and Gen. Alfred Terry to authorize the Black Hills expedition. Custer had wished to *explore* the Black Hills on many previous occasions himself. Custer believed that the allegedly gold-rich region would open a rich vein of wealth calculated to bring commercial prosperity to the United States. The mission was to locate and then pilfer ill-gotten gains from any deposits of precious metals, *despite* the United States' absolute sovereign commitment *not* to trespass, or allow for trespassers to enter, into the Black Hills. Generals Sheridan and Terry knew fully well that a gold exploration expedition would violate the 1868 Fort Laramie Treaty. But they went ahead and did it anyway. Intentionally. With the obvious and emphatic knowledge and approval of the President of the United States.

A team of over one thousand men with all of their livestock, equipment, and weapons began moving from Fort Lincoln near Bismarck toward the Black Hills in early July of 1874. They also, as was their habit, brought along five embedded, easily manipulated members of the white press corp. President Grant's brother Frederick Grant went along as well. Also present was a team made up of a geologist, a paleontologist, and other scientists specializing in various other areas who were to allegedly test the soil to determine the proper placement of log columns for the military fort they were *not* looking for. Lastly, a young photographer named William Illingworth, from St. Paul, Minnesota, was brought along to record the movement and spectacle with the newfangled picture-taking machine called a camera.

So it was under these circumstances that the group of twelve Mnincoju and Hunkpapa warriors assembled. The warriors prepared and departed under the cloak of night, and started to track this moving symbol of greed and deception. The goal was not to confront or fight the soldiers, but to watch them. They were there to learn what the expedition group did, where they camped, what they studied, how far they traveled, etc. The warriors were also going to monitor, observe, and familiarize themselves with certain members of the troop, and to report on the movements of the expedition and its military leaders. The warriors would camouflage themselves and their horses so as to remain concealed from the soldiers. The warriors would become the trees, the sagebrush, the stone boulders. They would assume the shape and appearance of their brothers who had lived in the He Sapa for millions of years.

The assignment also was to allow the warriors to see where the soldiers camped, what they preferred in a campsite and in terrain, how they set up camp, where they made their fires, and where they picketed and fed their horses. In light of other things, the warriors were to discover how often the expedition needed to stop, how long and how hard they could go, how often they got sick, how often they fought with each other, what distracted them and what did not, what they hunted and why, what did their uniforms look like from a distance, how high the dust clouds rose when they traveled, from how far away could one see them coming, whether or not they avoided ravines and why, and how they navigated streams and rivers. This would be very valuable information to the warriors and the Lakota people if a battle or other conflict would occur between the two forces. And that likelihood of such an event was greatly increasing, according to the spiritual messages being received by the families near Bear Creek and along the Owl River.

On the way into the sacred He Sapa, the expedition looped down through northern Wyoming Territory. Custer and several of his men climbed Inyan Kara, (home of the stone), a high mountain on the far northwest fringe of the He Sapa. One of the officers carved "Custer 74" into a stone near the top of the mountain. Normally, one could see Mato Tipila from Inyan Kara, but the day was overcast, so Custer and his men did not see it. Although the expedition went very near the He Tatanka (the buffalo-shaped mountain), they did not notice that either. It was from Inyan Kara that the expedition moved into the He Sapa by way of the southwest entry, coming across the Great Racetrack. This was an ironic crossing of paths— the white Europeans' path colliding with a sacred prehistoric remnant of a time long ago when humans had nearly been banished from Earth.

During this tracking mission, Saved By Bear was like a sponge. He and his friend, and fellow Dog Man, Swift Bear, were overly intrigued by and curious about these white soldiers, in particular the man they came to know as "Long Hair"—the young Indian-fighting lieutenant colonel who had a reputation as one of the elite officers the US Army had to offer. The Lakota knew of Custer's reputation among the army and the other military personnel, by encountering such people from time to time when the government sought to meet with the Lakota to try to get them to cede more and more territory to the whites.

However, the Lakota and Hunkpapa warriors also knew of Custer's other side, his alternate reputation. This was his reputation among the indigenous people all across Turtle Island. The dark reputation, the bad, evil side. The arrogant, bloodthirsty murderer of children, women, and old people, and the slaughterer of families and loved ones, and also the destroyer of members of the horse nation. It was this reputation that struck into the hearts and the spirits of the people which was becoming more and more ominous, more and more threatening, more and more imminent. The spiritual visions were confirming all of this, and serving to enlighten the people of the threat Custer posed to their very existence. Custer had a persistent habit of and obsession with challenging Sitting Bull and the Lakota to go to war with him and his army. The Lakota and Sitting Bull were becoming increasingly disturbed and anguished about the potential clash with the United States and its military leaders such as Custer, seeing it as an inevitability rather than as only a possibility.

Still, Sitting Bull and the people had continued to ask for, pray for, and call for peace, requesting a civil dialogue with the government to avoid war. However, the messages to engage peace, instead of war, were being ignored. This latest arrogant maneuver by the US military and Custer to invade the sacred He Sapa was proof of the imminent nature of the direct threat to the people, and also to Unci Maka and He Sapa.

Custer's men were unsavory, wasteful, and mostly unskilled in traveling in the He Sapa. It was as if they were on a hunting and fishing vacation in a new and wondrous land. The area had to feel and look like paradise to most of the members of the expedition given where most of them had come from. Custer would write to describe the Black Hills in a most flattering way. His description of the landscape, the beautiful pine-clad hills, the clear fresh water, the abundant timber, all kinds of game, and all the beautiful flowers and grasses would later instigate the public to demand for the opening up of the Black Hills for white settlement. A *Bismarck Tribune* reporter described the Black Hills as "one of the most beautiful spots on God's green earth," adding, "no wonder the Indians regard this as the home of the Great Spirit and guard it with jealous care."

The wagons tore up large swatches of land as the expedition team moved. The men became drunk frequently. They shot recklessly at anything that moved. They seemed totally unprepared for an attack by any group of Lakota, should one occur. They did not seem to be very proficient or efficient as a military team. Many weaknesses and vulnerabilities were observed. The warriors knew and believed that they could have engaged them or crippled their efforts had they chosen to do so, but the warriors' mission on this occasion was to track and monitor them, and to learn.

At one point, a lone Lakota man was captured by Custer's group. He was somewhat of an elder, maybe in his late fifties or early sixties. It was learned later that his name was One Stab. As a captive, he was used as a scout or guide, but mostly he served the role as prisoner and unwelcomed vagabond. The warriors could see that the white men, including Custer, showed no respect for or humility toward this man.

When one of the group claimed to have found some gold while panning in a small creek south of Owl's Nest Peak in early August 1874, the whole expedition team scrambled, hooted, and hollered, and carried on like lunatics, including Custer. They had scored a victory in locating the gold that they believed to exist. The scout known as Charley Reynolds, Custer's scout, was sent out to the south to spread the news to the newspapers and wires that gold had been found in the Black Hills. Newspapers such as the *Yankton Daily Press & Dakotan* and the *Bismarck Tribune* wrote of the finding of gold in the Black Hills. These stories were picked up, of course, by other newspapers across the country. That was the intent of the mission.

Custer was beside himself with arrogance and self-congratulations. He would end up declaring personal ownership of this part of the Black Hills, and he would press President Grant to reward him and to give him ownership of a million acres of this land, to be called Custerland. The expedition went to his head and fanned the flames of his vanity. He was anointed a hero for having led the way to find the gold and for having ignited the massive gold rush to the Black Hills. To the Lakota, Custer's 1874 expedition into the He Sapa would forever be notoriously known as "the Trail of Thieves." That name was well deserved.

This set of events and circumstances, none of which were caused by or contributed to by the Lakota, served as the fuse that lit the powder keg of conflict. Through 1874 and into 1875, the US government went into action to exploit the news and event, to pursue its own devious plans for the Lakota, and to steal their lands and resources.

A Conspiracy to Steal the He Sapa

The following is a re-creation of what may or would have been said in an Oval Office discussion held in mid-August 1874, based upon information revealed, as allegedly witnessed by a White House aide named Winston Eakdoamy:

PRESIDENT ULYSSES S. GRANT. Well, now it is confirmed.

GEN. PHILIP SHERIDAN. Yes, Custer really came through for us. I knew he would. That is why I knew he was the right man to lead the group. He has always had a genuine feeling that the Black Hills were a paradise of riches that we have got to have, at all costs.

GRANT. I am afraid you are right. We are almost bankrupt from the Civil War and this damn economic downturn that we are going through.

GEN. ALFRED TERRY. Mr. President, we need to take advantage of this opportunity. Our friends in business and industry are chomping at the bit to get their hands on the richness in resources in those Black Hills. Here is our chance. We must not waste it.

SHERIDAN. I totally agree, Mr. President. We must take advantage of this. It is something we can no longer wait to do. We should not concern ourselves anymore with trying to work out some kind of an illusory agreement with those damn Indians. They will not give up that land. It is too beloved, too sacred, to them. They don't even know what they have. They are too dumb and too unsophisticated to know that they have the wealth of fifty nations within their control. They cannot comprehend that, because they are too connected to the land, the image, the feeling of that place. And we should never clearly tell them what they have, so we can continue to lead them to believe that it is just the territory we want for settlement, and not the gold.

GRANT. God no. We must never allow gold to be revealed as our real purpose. Never. Do you hear me? Never! That would be a giveaway to the public and to the Indians, as to what we really need, what we must have, what we must take.

TERRY. That is it, Mr. President. You are on the right track. You have finally come around to know the truth about what we must do—under the cloak of secrecy and benign purpose, of course. Mr. President, we only need you to come along with the entire notion.

SHERIDAN. Yes, Mr. President. It is time. The stage is now set. Our Manypenny Commission has failed. The Indians believe that they have weathered the storm of our encroachment. They have come to develop a sense that they really own and control that territory and those precious Black Hills. I think they actually believe that we would honor their right to live in and occupy the Black Hills undisturbed. They are that foolish and naive. They obviously signed believing that they could trust us to protect their rights to that land. They were foolish to believe that the agreement would last forever, especially with the gold.

GRANT. I know what you are saying, Phil. I know. I know. I have been hearing this from you gentlemen now for the past five years, even before I took office. I know that we were waiting for and looking for the opportunity to seize the moment. And I do now believe that you are right. We never intended to have that treaty with the Lakota stand forever. How could it? It was not meant to be. We are the United States. We own all of this territory. How could we allow these primitive people to control what we desire, or to stop our manifest destiny? We cannot. We must not.

TERRY. Well then, Mr. President. You are the one who can set all the wheels in motion. You authorized the mission to seek gold. We knew then that it was a total subterfuge, and that we had to sell the idea to the public and to the Indians that we were looking for a fort location. Ha! That worked like clockwork. But when you authorized that, you knew fully well that we had crossed the threshold and had acted in a way that could or may be seen as a violation of the terms of that treaty. It could be viewed and argued by the Indians, if they had any intelligence at all, that that act alone was enough to breach the whole affair. But you took the chance. We took the chance, in the face of that prospect, under the color of law. And it worked. Oh, how it worked. We confirmed what we suspected all along: our gold is there, waiting for us to come and get it.

SHERIDAN. And Custer. He has served us very well. I know you don't care for him much, Mr. President. We know that one day he may very likely succeed you in this office. But, boy, did he come through. I told you he would. He has always wanted to travel and hunt in those hills, to explore and to dwell in that paradise. But now, after he has done this grand deed for us, for this country, he is expecting his just reward. He really now expects that we should give him as much as a million acres or so that he can call his own, to use as he pleases. I hear he wants to call it Custerland, his own personal kingdom of sorts. Ha-ha! But he might well deserve something for what he has done for us.

GRANT. Yes, I know. He is too arrogant, too brash, too outspoken at times. He is very cocky. He does not respect me, I think, many times. But you are right, he was the right man to use. He has no scruples. He had no misgivings about the illegality of the endeavor. Yes, he was the perfect man to use. So, let me think about what you say. Once we have secured possession of the Black Hills, then we can talk.

SHERIDAN. Are we a go, then?

TERRY. Yes, sir, we should get our plans in order as soon as possible so as not to waste anymore time. We must act now, before the Indians become too comfortable in their means, and become any stronger than they already are. We must start to put pressure on them from all ends, leading up to the point where we are inevitably forced to declare war upon all of them. Then that opens the door for us to waltz into the Black Hills and to take what is rightfully ours.

SHERIDAN. I know that our friends in the mining, banking, and cattle industries will be very happy. There will be tons of profit available for everyone, even us. We cannot lose this moment.

GRANT. And we will not. We will not lose this opportunity. It is my duty as president to act. It is in the best interests of this country, and of our financial survival, to act. So we must. So we will.

President Grant and his military henchmen, Terry, Sherman, Sheridan, and others, would plan to breach and break the 1868 treaty obligations to the Lakota. It was an intentional plot, a conspiracy among the nation's highest political and military officials, to allow the blatant flooding of the trespassers into the sacred He Sapa. This was done to fulfill the personal desire for wealth and enrichment, to feed the kleptocracy and to enrich the ruling classes.

The 1872 Mining Law covered mining claims on *public* lands. It did not pertain to lands belonging to individual Indians or Indian tribes. It most certainly, in 1872 through 1876, did not encompass lands within the Great Sioux Nation or the Black Hills, which were supposed to be protected against any trespass or invasion by any party, by virtue of the 1868 Fort Laramie Treaty. And yet, after Custer's 1874 *Trail of Thieves* into the Black Hills, when the United States found the gold, the government intentionally allowed miners to flood into the He Sapa at will. This planned intentional breach of Article I and II of the 1868 Fort Laramie Treaty by the government set the stage for white miners to trespass and roam freely within the Black Hills, leading to the inevitable theft and depletion of the Lakota gold and natural resources, which were supposed to be legally protected by said treaty, forever.

In 1875, a miner named John B. Pearson found gold in a narrow canyon in the northern Black Hills. This canyon became known as *Deadwood Gulch* because of the many dead trees that lined the canyon walls at the time. On April 9, 1876 (two months before the Greasy Grass Battle, and ten months before the February 28, 1877, *agreement* stealing the He Sapa was ratified), a group of four white miners from outside the Plains *purchased* a cheap mining claim in the northern Black Hills. Moses Manuel, Fred Manuel, John Henry "Hank" Harney, and Alex Engh bought and developed a "leed" gold placer outcropping. They found a lot of gold, $5,000 worth. They named their mine "Homestake". Later, in June 1877 (four months after the illegal taking of the Black Hills by the United States), wealthy businessman and mining executive George W. Hearst partnered with two San Francisco lawyers, James Ben Ali Haggin and Lloyd Tevis (of Wells Fargo fame), and bought the (originally illegal and stolen mining claim called) Homestake Mine from the four miners for $70,000. The Homestake Mine would operate for 125 years and become the source of over 10 percent of all the gold ever mined in the world by that time. There were approximately 40 million troy ounces of gold extracted over the subsequent 125-year period. The value of the gold taken, *allegedly stolen from the Lakota*, is valued at over $51.42 billion as of the last year of operation in 2001 (i.e., 40 million troy ounces @ $1,285.50 per ounce in 2016 prices = $51.42 billion. This figure does not take into consideration any form of accrued interest on the gold removed since 1875 through 2001, or as to all the gold taken out by new extractors to the present time, and certainly not compounded interest at 10% per annum. Gold would continue to be extracted from the He Sapa by private entities to the present day).

During May and June 1875, while Red Cloud, Spotted Tail, and other headmen of the treaty-signing factions of the Lakota met in Washington, DC, with government officials to talk about the potential sale or lease of the mineral rights in the He Sapa, the Newton–Jenney Expedition was also illegally in the He Sapa with miners and surveyors looking for gold. It is believed that this is when James Pearson found gold in the Deadwood Gulch.

The Newton–Jenney Expedition produced letters and reports that were circulated widely in the *Cheyenne Daily* (Wyoming) in June and July 1875. The expedition's last report indicated the presence of gold in paying quantities. One *Yankton Daily Press & Dakotan* headline stated, "Dakota Mines to Eclipse the World." Even the *Bismarck Tribune* (Dakota Territory) wrote, "Gold Enough to Pay the National Debt."

Thus began the greatest theft of the land, resources, property, and identity of an entire race of human beings, the Lakota, in the history of the Western world. The United States, knowing the consequences of its actions, planned this criminal act anyway. The government officially declared war on the Lakota then and there, all in the name of stealing the He Sapa, the very heart of Unci Maka, from the Lakota people.

The infamous hand-in-the-cookie-jar communiqué between Sheridan and Terry, the "Sheridan letter" would be written and served on November 9, 1875.

What follows is another re-creation of what may have been said in an Oval Office discussion held on November 3, 1875, again based upon information revealed, and as allegedly witnessed by, White House aide Winston Eakdoamy:

SHERIDAN. Mr. President, our plans are coming together.

GRANT. Well, I am getting weary of pretending that the United States is doing everything we can to keep the gold miners out of the Black Hills. General Crook, your previous public announcement served its purpose, but it seems to me, to us, that we could not do anything to stop that tide of trespassing even if we were committed to doing so.

GEN. GEORGE R. CROOK. I understand, Mr. President. I too feel that the warnings we issued to the trespassing miners since gold was found were useless in reality. I do realize that you had to do something publicly to keep up the appearance that we were protecting the Indian borders, but the military really never did much formally, despite the words.

GEN. WILLIAM TECUMSEH SHERMAN. Mr. President, the public statements do not reflect our real policy or our real need at all. Never did, really. We all know that. But in my position as commander of the western forces, I would like to be able to assure our military that they are not expected to act to protect the Indians' interests in the treaty. Almost all of the military personnel are opposed to helping the Indians in any way. Most want to just be rid of them as quickly as can be done. I think it best if we determine what we expect of our military, even if we cannot speak of our position publicly.

SHERIDAN. I believe that is a good idea, General Sherman. I would wholeheartedly support having a clear understanding among the military and the administration, so that the motives are not misunderstood. We have to do this as quietly and covertly as we possibly can. It cannot be known by those who need not know.

CROOK. I agree. But are we going to be prepared to act once the inevitable happens, and the Indians realize that we are turning a blind eye?

SHERIDAN. Some of the nontreaty Indians will eventually catch on, someday.

SHERMAN. Well, would it not be efficient and in line with our overall policy and need if we just turned the whole thing on its head, and used our abandonment of the protection of the Black Hills against the Indians when they do try to strike out against the miners? It could be a good trigger event to just hunt them down and finally take care of our overall problem.

GRANT. Yes. You are all correct. We appreciate the reports as to how good the mining prospects are proceeding. Those interests need to be given a good chance to gain a foothold. The investors are already hard at it. It would be a terrible shame to confuse them over a false proclamation of some sort coming from the president or Congress.

SHERMAN. What are you willing to do then, Mr. President?

GRANT. Phil [Sheridan], I want you to issue a directive to the forces in Dakota and to General Terry advising him that there will be no further resistance against the miners going into the Black Hills. If any miners choose to come into the Black Hills, neither the administration nor the Department of Interior will do anything. We will just wink at it. Do you understand?

SHERMAN. We will need more than that, Mr. President. Our war plans are about complete, but we need the necessary reason and provocation to carry them out in a manner that will have the clean outward appearance of our justification.

GRANT. Do you mean that we need an excuse to formally declare the Indians hostile to the United States government?

SHERMAN. Yes, we do. We should, in order to hurry the process along, set some deadline which we all know they cannot meet. Make some enunciation of our enforcement privileges to separate the compliant Indians from the ones we need to annihilate right away.

SHERIDAN. Yes, Mr. President. Our campaign against them should be seen as one to try to maintain peace rather than to just hunt them down and kill them, although that is the ends to justify the means.

GRANT. All right. I have heard you. Include in our orders to the military that we will send a notice out to the various agencies and bands stating that all Indians must report to their agencies no later than, let's say, January 31, 1876. Those who do not report shall be declared "hostile" against the United States. And the US Army will then consider that an act of war against the United States.

SHERIDAN. Yes, sir. I do understand. I will put that together as soon as possible.

GRANT. We must, of course, maintain secrecy of our intent.

———— ((◉)) ————

Sheridan's November 9, 1875, letter was then issued. It reads as follows:

Confidential

Nov. 9th 1875.

My Dear Gen. Terry,

At a meeting which occurred in Washington on the 3rd of November, at which were present, the President of the United States, the Secretary of the Interior, the Secretary of War and myself, the President decided that while the orders heretofore issued forbidding the occupation of the Black Hills country, by miners, should not be rescinded, still no further resistance by the military should be made to the miners going in, it being his belief that such resistance only increased their desire and complicated the troubles.

Will you there for quietly cause the troops in your Department to assume such attitude as will meet the views of the President in this respect.

Yours truly,

Philip Sheridan
Lieutenant[16]

⎯⎯⎯⎯⎯⎯◎⎯⎯⎯⎯⎯⎯

Many of the traditional Lakota and their families who chose not to participate in the treaty *negotiation* and signing of such things, would have preferred to just go on living their free and truthful lives in the manner intended by Creator, without any need for any type of formal paper agreement with the U.S.. However, since reality indicated that a treaty was entered into in 1868 which at least promised permanent preservation of their lands and way of life in their own territories, even the non-treaty Lakota realized the legal right to expect that the government would honor that treaty. Even if it was highly skeptical whether the government ever would.

A *treaty* is a legally binding agreement between one *nation* and another *nation*. A treaty therefore is a legally enforceable agreement by either party to the *agreement*, the treaty. When the governmental party to an agreement breaches its end of the agreement, it destroys the agreement itself. Since the government has the legal responsibility and duty to protect the legitimacy and sanctity of the agreement, those duties and responsibilities are supposed to be legally enforced by and through the powers of the government. This requires pursuing the treaty's enforcement and any prosecution of the violators of the agreement.

---

[16] Philip Henry Sheridan, General correspondence (1874; Dec. 10-1875, Dec. 31; reel 22), Library of Congress.

If the government intentionally chooses not to legally, responsibly, or reasonably enforce the agreement against those who would violate the terms of the agreement, then the agreement itself becomes illegitimate.

In this situation, where the government is *required* to enforce the terms of the 1868 Fort Laramie Treaty and to prosecute violators of said treaty, according to the *law* of the treaty, when the government fails to do so, then the failure to uphold that legal responsibility and duty destroys the *trust* and reliability of the treaty itself. If a treaty with the government is not legally enforced by the government according to its terms, then the government has clearly breached the entire treaty.

This is especially true when it is the government that has specifically assumed the legal duty of prosecuting violations of the terms of the treaty that could or may occur at the hands of the government or by outside third parties. If that is the case, and if the government chooses not to enforce violations or prosecute violators of the treaty, then no one is left to legally enforce the terms of the treaty except the other party to the treaty, in this case, the Lakota.

If the government is merely negligent, careless, or reckless in failing to exercise its legal duty of enforcing the terms of the treaty and protecting it against violators or violations, then this is still a breach of that legal duty on behalf of the government. Negligence or recklessness does not legally excuse the government from performing its duty of enforcing the treaty and protecting the Lakota treaty rights against breaches or violations of the treaty.

When the government intentionally, with full knowledge and forethought, chooses not to enforce the terms of the treaty, it becomes blatantly obvious that the government has intentionally chosen to breach the treaty. When the government clearly knows that it is legally required to enforce the terms of the treaty against any violations and violators, *and* when the government specifically and purposefully chooses *not* to enforce those violations or prosecute violators of the treaty, this is an absolute and clear destruction of trust and full foundation of the treaty itself, in total. The government has the clear legal duty and responsibility to enforce the terms of the treaty by investigating, determining, pursuing, arresting, charging, and *prosecuting* any violations or violators of the treaty. When the government specifically decides *not* to enforce the treaty, and *not* to pursue prosecution of or to actually prosecute the violators of the treaty, again, no one is left to *enforce* the terms of the treaty or to prosecute the violators of the treaty *except* the remaining party, in this case the Lakota. When the government fails in this way, it indicates a purposeful, deceitful, fraudulent, and oppressive violation of the treaty itself by the government.

The secretive and purposeful concealment of the real intent and motive of the government in *not* enforcing the treaty, and in *not* investigating or prosecuting the known and obvious violations or violators of the treaty, creates an outright and complete destruction of the trust responsibility of the government to honor, respect, and fulfill the legal, ethical, and moral responsibilities the government had undertaken by negotiating and signing the treaty in the first place. This is the most devious, the most fraudulent, the most deceptive, the most rank, the most dishonorable, the most disrespectful, and the most destructive form of dealing that can occur between civilizations, between nations of peoples. This is how the U.S. government viewed the concept of *law*, as it concerned the treaty with the Lakota.

The American concept of *law,* in a general sense, was originally supposed to be just, enforceable and dependable. The United States was supposed to be a nation that followed the rule of *law*, and not the rule of men. Law, according to the Lakota, was intended to be as just and pure as a truthful word said to your neighbor and friend concerning the important affairs of life and society. But the whites' view of law, obviously, was different. To the U.S. and its society, the laws would almost always be written for and by the persons and entities that wished to use it to their own benefit. The original Constitution of the U.S. authorized and recognized slavery and subhuman classifications of certain dark skinned human beings. Many, if not most of the founders of the law, were slave owners and wealthy property owners themselves. The founders were all white men with desires and individual stakes in the economic welfare of their union, and themselves. For the most part, the *law* was written to favor those who were white. Therefore, most American laws were written to not be consistent with empathy. In fact, most of the laws attempt to remove empathy from the equation, either overtly or covertly. The law, generally, was not designed to promote the truth or dignity of *all* humans or their causes. Usually, the *law* was intended to provide a script for the most saavy and analytical to grasp and navigate. It is believed by many that much of the American laws were designed in many situations, to avoid, or to in fact, mask, the truth. It would become a clever game as to who was better at keeping the truth from becoming the desired outcome. To a large extent, many would argue that this remains the case, even in the present day.

In the case of the 1868 treaty, if the prosecutors of the "law", *intentionally* violate the law in choosing not to enforce the law, it destroys all aspects of trust, responsibility and fulfillment of promises. It breaches all codes of ethics, morals, and human interaction. If those charged with the legal duty to prosecute violations of the law, intentionally choose *not* to act and not to enforce the law, then the obvious only alternative, is that the people whose rights are violated or who suffer as a result of the violations of the law, *must* take the law into their own hands. The situation is as if there were no law to begin with. No formal legal agreement (treaty) to begin with. And that all things should revert to the time and status before the existence of the agreement (treaty). Reasonably, fairly, and legally, this particular situation should then revert to the time of the Lakota's aboriginal title and their original rights and privileges to protect their own territory, and to enforce and prosecute violations and violators in their own way, in the way of the Lakota, under the Lakota laws and customs. Much as the Lakota people did before the white man arrived. And before the US government was formed. And before there were white people in their territory violating the sacred He Sapa or any of the other of the Lakota's aboriginal territories. Much like the time of the Naca, and the enforcement of the levels of law and order according to Lakota civilization by and through the Akicita and the warriors. That system had worked for thousands and thousands of years before. It could still work now. At least it was a fair, just, and reliable means of enforcement of duties, responsibilities, and conduct. It was a just means of enforcing the ethical, moral, and social rules and requirements upon the people.

When President Grant and his military officers, including General Sherman, General Sheridan, and General Terry, conspired to breach the 1868 Fort Laramie Treaty, they were acting with purposeful intent, malicious forethought, and an ill-willed motive to oppress. Grant pushed for and obtained passage of the corrupt 1872 Mining law. Then, these governmental leaders planned to invade and trespass into the sacred He Sapa for the sole purpose of searching for and finding gold in 1874. On November 3, 1875, after the flood of miners, settlers, and other white people and private interests invaded and trespassed into the He Sapa, Grant declared that the United States would no longer protect the Lakota's He Sapa from invasion. And on November 9, 1875, Sheridan documented the conversation confirming the secret ill-willed motive of the government executives and military leaders to force armed conflict with the Lakota so that the United States could *steal* the He Sapa from them.

This intentional conduct was illegal and immoral. Article Six of the U.S. Constitution recognizes that treaties of the U.S. are the supreme law of the land. Article One of the 1868 Fort Laramie Treaty referenced a remedy for the Lakota that when "bad men among the whites" shall commit any wrong upon the person or property of the Indians.... then the Indians have the right to "proceed at once to cause the offender to be arrested and punished according to the laws of the United States, and also reimburse the injured persons for the loss sustained." In 1874, President Grant allowed the Army to ignore the gold miners and wealthy entrepreneurs who were trespassing in the Black Hills, and Grant commissioned and directed the 1874 trespass of Custer and his expedition to find gold. Further, on November 3, 1875, there was no federal law in place that superseded the 1868 Treaty, so the Treaty was the supreme law of the land, and the President and his officers were all sworn to uphold the Constitution in the performance of their official duties. The intentional acts and conspiracy to violate the 1868 Treaty by Grant and his federal and state officials, were unconscionable. They all could have been legally arrested and punished according to the laws of the U.S. for their actions as "bad men amongst the whites" in Article One of the Treaty. [17]

When corrupt politicians in a corrupt government realize that what they desire to do, is in fact, illegal, their lack of shame and conscience

---

[17] Lee, Tribal Laws, Treaties, and Government, 2013 at p.31-34

allows them to just rewrite the law through legislation or court decision, to make conduct that was once illegal, now legal. When a human being lacks a humane conscience to the extent that they will do anything to anyone in pursuit of the goal of getting more money or wealth, then nothing matters to that person anymore except the goal of obtaining more money and wealth. That goal, now, actually becomes, their conscience. When the conscience to do what is right, just, humane or compassionate, disappears, so does the ability to feel shame. If a person loses the ability to feel shame or shamefulness, for committing shameful acts, then the conscience also dies the same death within that person. There may be no meaningful or moral road back from that dark pit.

What Ulysses Grant and his officers did in 1872, 1874 and 1875, was a pure criminal and civil conspiracy to violate the 1868 Treaty, and the responsibility to uphold the trust as defined by the Treaty. It was specifically intended. Furthermore, these intentional acts were done to set up and to create a war. Death, destruction, and theft of property was the known goal and design. It was carried out in the most deceptive and dishonorable way, in secret. And the whites would blame the Indians. It would work well, at least up until June 25, 1876.

When the Lakota started to become suspicious of the behavior and intent of the US government in negotiating, then agreeing to the 1868 Fort Laramie Treaty with the Lakota headmen who actually signed the treaty, many of those who did not sign, began to plan for the future. Many Lakota, especially the Mnincoju, the *Protectors*, saw a real threat to the He Sapa by virtue of the 1868 treaty. They did not trust the United States to live up to its promise to forever stay out of the Black Hills, the He Sapa. This idea was prevalent among the nontreaty Lakota, who often viewed those who signed the treaty as having given into the government, and selling out the future of all the Lakota's best interests. So as the signs began to appear and the events began to occur following 1868 indicating what the government may have been up to, many of the Mnincoju started to meet and to plan for that contingency, and when it would be revealed that the US was once more, deceiving them. This became a plan of protection, a plan to secure their way of life, a plan to protect the He Sapa. The discussions were had outside of the words and ink portrayed on the paper the treaty was printed upon. If the treaty promises were a sham, then plans needed to be made for the time when, not if, the United States would break its promises sworn to in the treaty. It was a meeting of minds to see to this protection for the future of the people and the He Sapa, in an "old" way. It was done in an aboriginal way and custom, according to the "old" traditions, taking into consideration the new circumstances, the new threats.

——— ❈ ———

Soon after the events of November 1875, the Powder River Campaign against Sitting Bull and the *hostiles* was planned to start in the spring of 1876. As it would turn out, things would prove to be eerily ironic and sadly prophetic in that many of the sites that were part of the sacred spiritual lands which would end up being stolen by these thieves, the government and its conspiring private profiteers, would become named after the thieves themselves: "Harney Peak" (Owl's Nest), Sheridan Lake, Terry Peak, Custer Peak, and so forth. It was a travesty to honor. It was a travesty to justice. It was a travesty to fairness. It was a travesty to the natural world and Unci Maka. And as the linchpin to it all, again, stood the man called Custer.

Long Hair: A Rising Symbol of Genocide

Since the 1874 discovery of gold in the Black Hills by his expedition, Lieutenant Colonel Custer had been increasingly anxious to do even more to further his military career and reputation. He had accused President Grant's administration, and even Grant's own brother, of corruption while in office. Custer had placed himself in a position with the Grant administration that was causing higher-level politicians in Washington, DC, and military men, including military leaders and officers, to view him as a polarizing influence.

There had already been important military people who disliked Custer with a passion. Many of these people thought that he was too arrogant and that he had been given too easy of path to stardom and hero worship status as a young officer. These people, who knew that some of the top military brass regarded him as the best of the best, or the bravest of the brave, when it came to military campaigns and accomplishments, believed that he was undeserving of praise and accolades. They thought that he needed to be taken down a peg or two for his own good. They saw him as someone who, although he may have been brave or talented as a military leader, was keenly and profoundly reckless and impulsive, with a desire to do things his way.

To others in the military, Custer was seen as a true leader of men and soldiers who had no comparison. These military folks, officers and enlisted men alike, viewed the young lieutenant colonel as a winner and a military genius who could run rings around any other commander or strategist. Someone who could wipe out hordes of Indian savages with the wave of his gloved hand or the slash of his gilded saber. Custer's admirers were many. They included celebrities in politics and in society. They included many members of the newspaper business and the journal-publishing press. Custer himself was well-read, and frequently wrote of his own adventures, goals, endeavors, conquests, and opinions, of which he had many.

Custer had graduated last in his officers' class at West Point in 1860, but he did not allow that to be a blemish upon his life or to tarnish his drive and grand aspirations. He was what some people would refer to as a character of folklore. To those who admired him, none of his achievements was small or underserved. His successes and victories were commonly viewed as stupendously fantastic accomplishments worthy of putting him on the cover of every newspaper and magazine in the country. His image would be die cast in gold and bronze in the eyes of his followers and many admirers and hero-worshipers.

Coming from Michigan, Custer decided early, upon a career in the United States military, and that is what landed him at West Point. Although it was known that he did not fare well in school or achieve high scholastic marks, he garnered enough prestige with his aggressive manner and direction that he was quickly elevated to the rank of brevet general of the Michigan militia at the time of the American Civil War in 1863. He, of course, fought for the Union, although it was well-known that he did not look upon the issue of slavery as any great sin for the country. His ambivalence on that very subject, the domination of another race by the white race, proved to serve him well later in his numerous and repeated campaigns against America's first peoples, including the Lakota and Cheyenne.

An Accumulation of Desperate Circumstances

The white man's year of 1874 begins during the hardship of winter. The hardship of this wintertime would never leave the Lakota. The seasons ahead would see no end to the encroachment upon and illegal taking of our lands and resources. Our families try to keep in contact with others of our relation to see how the people are doing. It is through those efforts that we are made aware of the new people's movements, especially the military. As word passes from extended family to extended family, we become more aware of the troops' movement. Throughout the time of early spring, after the winter has gone, we are informed by those who are out in the plains. The warriors who are doing the patrols between our sacred sites and our settlements, hoping to protect our nomadic means of survival, are aware of an occurrence about which they must advise the people. They tell the families once they arrive home that there have been numerous white men going to and coming from the He Sapa. The US government and its citizens have been using this very same approach since the signing of the treaty in 1868. This total disregard for life and legality, troubles our families. Our leaders are fully aware that they are going to have to make some very serious decisions now. The resources that are contained within the He Sapa are enormously valuable according to the white man's point of view. His idea is to rid the land of us and take anything below or above the ground. To the Lakota, this is a violation of the natural laws of Creation. Our families will plan to meet and discuss these issues that we face concerning the survival of our Lakota nation.

The whites and their government are pressing forward to get their hands on the He Sapa because they see our sacred land as a means to resolve their greed for wealth and riches. Among that obsession to divest us of our land and resources, is of course, the gold that has been recently found.

The gold had no present monetary value to the Lakota. The search for gold became almost a lustful goal for the government and the white society, as they sought to get into the He Sapa to exploit the gold, to take it for their own use and profit. The Lakota knew that Grandmother Earth needed the gold, so they took a stand against this invasion and theft. This is one reason that things developed in the way they did. Once the military discovered gold in the He Sapa, the government's policy of protecting the Black Hills from being invaded and trespassed upon was turned on its head. This was really the beginning of the perpetuation of the genocide of the Lakota. The Lakota were in the way of the financial goals of the United States. And because we were not willing to relinquish the sacred He Sapa, let alone the gold in the Black Hills, the government decided to try to exterminate us. If we were gone, then the wealth from the gold could run freely to the United States and to its wealthy private business profiteers and coconspirators.

The intended confiscation and theft of the He Sapa involved other natural resources as well. The mining efforts also resulted in causing near extinction for many of the nonhuman beings, the most obvious being the buffalo, the beaver, the elk, and the deer, among many of the other four-legged. These beings were now being taken by fur traders. The buffalo were being slaughtered. The government needed political control over regional territories, so it decided to deplete the populations of these beings, knowing that since we needed them for sustenance in our world, our livelihood would be severely impacted.

If the buffalo were exterminated and thereby removed from our lives, then we would starve, we would go without clothing, we would go without the tools that made our daily lives easier, we could make no more tipis, we would have no more hide, and we would not be able to hunt the buffalo. For this reason, the government put out bounties and hired killers to come and kill the buffalo and other game. Whether they were on foot or on horse, whether they traveled by railroad or some other means, they came and killed every buffalo they saw. The more buffalo they killed, the harder life got for the Lakota people.

The beaver was taken for its pelt, which was sold for profit. The waterways were the first to be cleared. The whites familiarized themselves with scouting not only to learn about our people but also to discover those among us who would turn against their own families to show the whites where profit-generating resources could be found. As the white

Europeans advanced toward Lakota country with the sole purpose of taking resources and profiteering, our people became concerned that everything would be lost, taken, and absorbed. Eventually, all we had left was ourselves, with very little support from even many of our own people. Even the gifts of Grandmother Earth upon which we once relied, were not dependable at this time. We were trying to understand that this taking of everything that was ours, would eventually come to claim our lives.

The cannumpa came from the White Buffalo Calf Woman, who gave it to the female and male of our nation. It was used not only so that we could learn about prayer, life, and existence, but also in preparation for the time of the coming of a new type of man, one who was heavily bearded, hairy on the face like an animal, but without color. This new type of man would come dressed in clothing that made him look almost like an animal, so the people sometimes recognized this being as much different from what they knew a human being to be. And the cannumpa was given to us to prepare, from that moment forward, for what was to happen in the future. It was given to us so we could confront, combat, and hopefully overcome the presence of evil and the devastation spreading across our land.

This new man also came with an insatiable appetite. He did not come to bring any good. He just came to harm and disrespect everything that our world was built upon. This new human being was known to bring two critical assets to his people's way of life: One would be science, and, in the future, technology. This is how the white people's presence would disrupt the natural ways of life and cause massive confusion on a global scale. They were encroaching upon every indigenous nation during the colonization periods of the 1500s to 1800s. Their behavior here on Turtle Island was a repeat of what they had done in other countries. What they intended to do here, they had already done elsewhere in the world. The support that they had, came from a system built on *sica*, that which is evil, that which is bad. Our world could not accept this coming of the new ways, which promised to harm everything that we cherish. One facet of the Lakota belief structure concerning our world and our loved ones is *tehicila*, which means "I cherish you." We are a family of true human beings. Whether you come from one part of the planet or you are a direct relative, the cannumpa is here for all of us to live and abide by.

The cannumpa has been in our possession throughout time. It is one of the most important and most necessary teachers in the tradition and culture of our individual peoples. Across the planet there are many diverse variations of cultures. However, each of these cultures has the same premise. There is a focus on spiritual guidance, which the human can access in times of need. The cannumpa is the safeguard of an existence of positive energy and prosperity. It brings the truth out in situations where there is dishonesty. It brings presence and stability where there is confusion and disarray. It brings light to a situation that is dark. And it gifts a presence to those who practice with it, giving them an opportunity to be heard, followed, and even asked by others—to serve in an advisory role. It brings confidence. It sometimes brings any aggression that needs to be brought out in the people when they need to be motivated. It also heralds a time of celebration and thankfulness for all the gifts and blessings of life provided by Creator. So the cannumpa, though it does not live and breathe as a human being, and although it is without arms or legs, is one of the most precious gifts from Creator. We have learned to live through it, with it, and by it, throughout all the ages.

All the efforts to try to deal with the situation with the whites that had developed over the years, resulted in an approaching and gathering storm for the people. It was understood that a peaceful means of resolution was no longer legitimately viable. It became known by the people that war, and taking a stand against the military, including Custer, was inevitable. These are the changes that the people are facing as we move into this period of wondering: *How are we going to survive? Almost everything they do violates everything that we believe. There is no apparent natural similarity between what they do and what we do. Opposition is the only common bond that we have. Outside of that, we are alone. We are on our own.* Once that realization that we were on our own became clear to the people, our whole direction changed. And much like our sacred buffalo brother intentionally turns to face the oncoming and approaching storm, the whole Lakota nation turned toward the spirit. The spiritual preparation for meeting these urgent threatening forces, in a spiritual sense and upon their own level, became necessary.

Leading up to the Greasy Grass Battle, the Lakota, including Saved By Bear and many holy ones, would know through the spirits how the battle was going to come to pass. They knew it for many, many months. Being true to our culture and spirits, we Lakota try to avoid killing and war, engaging in it only as a last resort to protect our families and our own lives. When the Lakota saw that the government was basically determined to exterminate them and take everything they had, including the He Sapa, Sitting Bull and the holy ones repeatedly sent out a spiritual message to Custer and the government's leaders. This message was repeatedly ignored. Custer would have with him a large number of indigenous scouts, including Crow and Arikira, who could not deny their own spirits. These scouts and others who received these spiritual messages would feel the warnings in their own spirits. Those who would be traveling with Custer and the Seventh Cavalry would see that if they continued on the path and joined with Custer and the Seventh Cavalry, they too would perish. This is why we would hear accounts of these scouts singing death songs or praying. Their fear would be based upon their knowledge of what was going to happen to them if Custer continued on his path.

These warnings to Custer were manifested in the hope that something would change, that there would be some means for him not to go to the Greasy Grass area for the purpose of killing all the Lakota. However, Custer could not help himself, even though he felt the warnings, somehow inwardly, knowing that he was marching toward his own death. His own personal goals, aspirations, and arrogance would cause him to ignore those warnings. This was to be the ultimate feather in his cap. If he were to go in and slaughter a bunch of women, children, and old people, then he would be recognized and applauded as a hero and a great military leader. And he was willing to take a risk in that regard for the glory. This is something that the Lakota warriors would come to know, and this was why so much time would be spent preparing for the things to come.

A number of years prior, Custer had contacted Sitting Bull. The messages to Sitting Bull were that Custer wanted a war. He wanted a final war to eliminate the Lakota in one fell swoop. Custer communicated this message just as if he had sent a letter in the mail. He was quite casual in his bad spiritual manner when requesting a war. Custer had much arrogance. All he wanted was death to the Lakota, political advancement, and self-elevation. So his part of knowing already was that the war was under way, and that he had instigated this war. Sitting Bull tried his best to get Custer to understand that the two sides did not need a war to settle their dispute. They could do it with diplomacy, cooperation, and equality. There may be a peaceful solution. But Custer would never consider that idea. So in time, the people and their spiritual leaders decided that if the Lakota people were to survive, there would indeed have to be a war. Otherwise, the agencies, all those considered hostile, and all those not yet contained, would indeed be exterminated. Custer's drive was to have his own war, to have his own world revered and written about, going down in history, American history.

Custer's ambition was not only to possess a region of Lakota land but also, as many believed, to become president of the United States. This was part of his agenda. So Custer initiated these messages of war to Sitting Bull. Our families, hearing of these messages declaring war, began making preparations for what was to come. The Mnincoju, Saved By Bear, and the trusted warriors were called to gather near Bear Creek in the homeland of their ancestors. Creator listened as the families gathered. These would be the people who would be granted permission to act and would be given the instructions to act. They were shown in the spirit, together. They would begin discussing and praying about this conflict, wondering why it would have to happen. As referenced earlier, we asked for the spiritual presence that we invoke on behalf of our lands, our people, and all the other beings. We would send the spiritual presence to Custer and his wife, asking this presence to give Custer those messages and show him that he did not have to go to war. But his desire was to have his war, and we could not satisfy him, so the battle would need to occur.

The situation was like this: you either do this or else you die. Saved By Bear and Swift Bear could not defend the small extended family who remained, by themselves. By themselves, they would be overrun by the sheer numbers of the US military. Every other extended family unit would face the same thing. As the Lakota and their families would be hunted down, the warriors who would stand up to try to defend them would also be taken out. And as the warriors would fall, the elders, the women, and the children, would fall. The Lakota, as a race of human beings, would become extinct—the vanishing ones. So in order to preserve this life gifted by the Creator, the Lakota had to make a stand. Now was the time to act. Now was the time to stand. It had to be done. And every one of the families had to commit to doing so, so that the opportunity to live, to eat, to laugh, to enjoy, to celebrate, and to survive would continue to be existing reality, and not become just a memory. Rather than face the memories of what we had been through already, we looked forward to enriching our lives with these deeds and this desperation to preserve life and to survive: to survive as a people, to survive as a nation, to survive for the future of the children, for Unci Maka, and for the He Sapa.

The cause was firmly recognized and assumed: to protect the very existence and survival of the Lakota people. It was agreed that if the Lakota did not take a stand at this particular moment in time, the US military and its leaders would come and kill them all anyway. It was just a matter of time. If the people did not take a significant stand at this moment in time under these circumstances, then all the indigenous people, not just the Lakota, would be killed and slaughtered. The military would move from village to village, from camp to camp, seeking out and destroying all traces of the Lakota people. The peaceful efforts, the warnings, the invitations to resolve our differences with the white society and the United States and its military, had all failed. Those efforts were ignored or dismissed by the government and its military. Once all those efforts of the Lakota failed, our energies, our spirit, and our thought processes followed the direction to meet them with a force that their government and military had never faced before in history: the force of the spirit.

━━━◆◎◆━━━

The sun brings the shadows of August 1874. Our relations saw that we were casting fewer and fewer shadows. The absence of the loved ones' presence was very keenly felt. The children needed our commitment and contributions for their future survival as true human beings. We prayed that peace would be their gift to the women and men of Unci Maka. Our families and warriors needed to do their best with our belief in the wakan way of life.

And this is when the *asking* began, asking how to go about confronting the approaching storm of encroachment and genocide. It was also the beginning of seeking the spiritual answers, the spiritual guidance, the spiritual assistance, the very spiritual presence, to be able to know and understand, to see how to go about doing this and how to accomplish these things in detail. The purpose of the *asking* was to understand what to be aware of and how to carry out everything that needed to be carried out.

This is why Saved By Bear, Swift Bear and his people, the Mnincoju/ Hohwoju, were called to be the ones to carry this out. The Mnincoju, throughout time, were looked upon as the warriors, the *Protectors*. They were seen as the strong ones who would stand up when called, when needed, to protect the people, Grandmother Earth, the He Sapa, and all that was sacred.

All the deeds that are performed by the Lakota are for the survival of the people. This is how you keep a circle intact. With each spirit using its strengths and positives, everyone can walk a step further together. This is why Creator called upon the tribal people, the Lakota, the Dakota, and the Nakota. These specific people were asked to make their individual contributions to help further the survival of the people and their ways of maintaining all life, and to affirm their sacred role as the keepers of this Earth. If we are not allowed to be in this position, then we truly have no place. We will be without the gifts of the one who brought us here: Creator. And Unci Maka.

With all the preparation of the human being, the Lakota did not forget those peoples not of the two-legged kind. We resolved to defend those who fly, those who swim, those who run on four legs, each given its place as a child of Grandmother Earth. We called upon them to make their sacred contributions to our ceremonies. The feathers from birds and raptors, the horse underfoot, the grass and the grain provided as food as we rest or recuperate, the clean water that we drink. That spirit of the water will thrive within us. The sun will nurture everything inside our bodies and within our environment. Our lives are good.

They have just been horribly interrupted by the evil-intentioned human peoples. We appreciate the comfort and support of Grandmother's children. They have always been here, even before we arrived as a species on Unci Maka. At one time long ago, they raised and nurtured us like their own children. They remain with us. And we pray that we will see them again in the future, not just in memory, but in real communion again, and in a state of wonderment and brotherhood, in a world of renewed hope, trust, friendship, and respect.

The elders and medicine people of our tiospaye of the Mnincoju called for a gathering. This spiritual meeting of families and other tiospaye will be performed entirely in secret. We know that not every person of the Lakota and the other tribal nations can be trusted. Even among our own families, many will not know of what is to come. We must try to keep them optimistic and working together, uniting to perform life deeds and satisfy life needs, helping one another through these very, very difficult times. Our leaders know that genocide will come with the United States military to all who are unprepared.

This secret spiritual gathering will take its first step in an area very special to our families, the region called Bear Creek, a very wonderful place. The natural beauty is in the rivers, the streams, the creeks, and the thermal and cold springs that exist there. These amenities are given to us by our Creator. There has always been a settlement here at Bear Creek. Our tiospaye and other families have spent time here throughout the generations. We have lived here since the first memory of our people. Among this Mnincoju tiospaye are some very old families.

A special family that is known to our bloodline comes from three Lakota sisters. Long ago, these sisters were presented with a cannumpa, the Sacred Cannumpa of the Lakota and the Seven Council Fires. The White Buffalo Calf Woman taught them knowledge and wisdom contained within the cannumpa. These sisters took this commitment to serve as the pipe keepers and embraced their bloodlines as the means to carry on that commitment into the future and for all time. The goal is to help us human beings to keep our connection strong with Creator. Creator asked our people, the red people who walk in the cannumpa way, to play the spiritual role of keepers of the Earth. Over the generations, the keepers of the Sacred Cannumpa have been the men and women of this tiospaye bloodline.

This is the Bear Creek tiospaye of the Mnincoju, our families. We have called for a gathering to discuss our concerns about the recent conditions and the increasing threats facing us. We have decided to depend upon Creator and ask about every step that we should take. The people and families will be given individual instructions and duties. The people will act diligently, courageously, and committedly as they carry out these instructions.

Spiritual Instructions and Permission

The spiritual medicine people and warrior advisors welcome the people. The families settle in, and become part of this special camp. They are greeted by caring, happy relatives. There are sighs of relief, cries of happiness. Eyes meet, glittering upon seeing one another. It is as though everyone is acknowledging a better time in the past, before the coming of these trying times, recalling how life was enjoyable and celebrated with the senses alone. Most know this emotional safety zone is not real. For the next few days the families will commune and prepare for the meetings to come, where the people will instruct and plan.

The scouts have been placed in the areas surrounding our camp. They pass word to the warriors, and then to the headman, that it is now safe to begin the meeting. All age groups had to attend, because all needed to hear the words being spoken in defense of our people. The children are kept separate by their relatives, and of course, all are protected by the warriors within each family. Once silence descends upon all who have assembled, the address begins from our medicine man. He nods his head in the direction of another medicine person, who then begins to smudge all the people in attendance. In one hand, he holds a braid of sweet grass that has already been lit, and is smoldering and smoking, releasing its energy. In his other hand is an eagle fan that he proudly uses. He is our spiritual leader, and we will follow him.

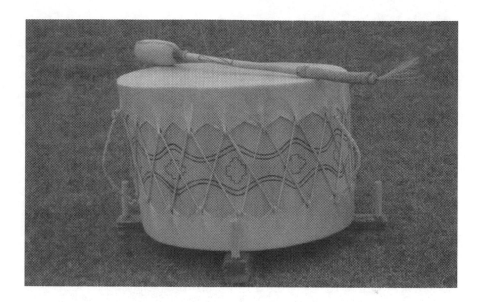

The silence is greeted by the heartbeat of the drum. The medicine man begins to sing a prayer song. The lyrics honor and praise the gift of our spiritual life. We depend upon Creator for the understanding and guidance we need to remain human beings. We ask for the ability to defend and battle for our right to exist. We will stand against the ever-encroaching opponent, the evil. The song finishes and the drumbeat stops. The people gaze about, looking in different places in their surroundings. Some are looking to the sky; others are looking at the ground and the grass; and still others are looking at the human beings and listening to the surroundings. Each has offered prayer and his or her personal strength. One by one, they have been allowed to speak directly to Creator.

In our world, spiritual immaturity can be deadly. One can follow false hope, believing it is a message. This is called self-centeredness and selfishness, greed. By falling prey to greed is how mankind has fallen away from the spirit. Mortal and materialistic distraction, and the emptiness or disregard of the spirit and the spirit's paramount importance in all occurrences and all matters of change, led toward this time of preparation.

This gathering has been called by the families, our families. All the people who were in attendance had come together to pray. No outward announcements would be made. The meeting was intended to be secret and to be kept secret. Even the names and identities of the warriors to be chosen, would be kept secret from the outside world and outside influences. The chosen warriors who are present would have their own separate sweat lodge ceremony where the instructions for the chosen warriors are given to them by Creator.

During this meeting, the sixteen are named. The individual warriors who would follow the plan and undergo the preparation were identified. Sixteen individual warriors were *chosen*. They would become the sixteen *chosen warriors*. They are called for. Most are Lakota, but some are Nakota or Dakota, that we must notify. The individual warriors that are chosen are being notified spiritually, and through their own family and extended bands. During this ceremony, our spiritual leaders pray to the other spiritual leaders among our relations in the east, asking them to identify and notify each of the warriors who have been chosen to be a part of the warrior group to go to the Greasy Grass. When this message is sent through spiritual means during the ceremony, it is confirmed by the scouting and patrolling Lakota (scouting and patrolling is ongoing throughout our territories.). In this way, the three warriors of the Dakota and Nakota are made aware of their selection as a chosen warrior who is being asked to attend and to play his role. They were included so that our families were truly represented by the entire tiospaye of the Nakota, Dakota, and Lakota. We needed to have a relation here and present, so that all of us can benefit from the spiritual instructions.

The sixteen *warriors* were chosen during the process of the spiritual instructions. They were identified and called upon to perform this spiritual duty. The warriors were: Saved By Bear (Lakota); Swift Bear (Lakota); Eagle Fan (Dakota); Buffalo Horn (Nakota); Blue Stone (Lakota); Runs with Wind (Lakota); Elk Whistle (Lakota); Comes from Star (Lakota); Flies Above (Lakota); Spotted Horse (Dakota); Brave Dog (Lakota); Black Wolf (Lakota); Touches Heart (Lakota); Many Thunder (Lakota); Strong Hand (Lakota); and Red Whirlwind (Lakota).

Out of the sixteen *chosen* warriors, Saved By Bear and Swift Bear, will soon be accompanied by five others. This group of seven warriors of the entire group of sixteen was called upon to participate in the ceremony. A spiritual message is given to the Lakota, Nakota, and Dakota through the ceremony. Those present hope and pray that the Nakota and Dakota medicine people will receive the spiritual message. There is not enough time to jump on a horse and head down to the Dakota people's homelands, or head toward the Mississippi. This is why we, the Mnincoju Lakota families, need to rely entirely upon the spiritual communication method of our ever-present spiritual people.

Saved By Bear, Swift Bear, and the other Lakota wait for these two to arrive. Eagle Fan from the Dakota, and Buffalo Horn from the Nakota people And once they do arrive, they greet each other and understand that they have been called to participate in a very sacred endeavor.

Saved By Bear's group of seven, including himself, is the primary first group of the sixteen to assemble. These seven make up the main group that our narrative will follow as they travel the spiritual path that has been set before them. The other nine warriors are just as important and just as needed, but they are mostly needed to perform their individual and collective duties in the battle to come. Their qualities and natural abilities have brought them to the forefront of warrior status. But today, being a warrior means to prove why it is that you are a warrior. And that is why each warrior is chosen by Creator to be a part of it all. When the time comes to leave for the preparation period, Saved By Bear's group of seven warriors will leave together, the other group, which includes nine warriors, is in the process of assembling separately. That group of nine warriors will then take their own path, and will meet Saved By Bear's group in the spiritually designated area. This is how the two groups of warriors will become one force.

After the sweat lodge ceremony, once each of these *chosen* warriors has been identified and notified, it is very clear who has been asked to go fight in the upcoming battle. Most of the families among the Nakota, Dakota, and Lakota are not going to know of this endeavor and are not going to be informed of who these men are. They cannot be. Those who have gathered must keep this part entirely secret, as mentioned before. We have to make sure that these sixteen warriors can gather, commune, learn, and pray together. This is the only way we are going to be able to accomplish what is needed at the Battle of the Greasy Grass. The sixteen represent an elite group of warriors now. This *asking* of Creator is a direct one. It is not assumed. It is not expected. It is simply accepted, as the word. And this word will be followed by deed.

The instructions that Creator gave to the families includes such things as that the individual people of the grassroots nation are told to assume additional responsibilities, at times going above and beyond their normal calling. The scarcity of domestic livelihood is severely affecting the people. The things which we relied and depended upon to look after our common daily needs. The women are the ones who bring the domestic life to the forefront for everyone in the tribe. Their concerns are for food, shelter, and clothing. The animal beings that we normally approach and ask permission to take, whether for clothing or food, have become fewer in number. We are exhausting the means used for survival, that cannot be replenished by the seasons alone.

The needed articles we normally gather and take have also become scarce. It is harder to travel to places where berries and fruits may be plentiful. It's harder to track the buffalo, whose numbers have been greatly reduced. The number of elk, deer, and antelope has also decreased. Keep in mind that genocide is the extinction of any species. It doesn't matter the species' shape or form or language. Committing genocide is these new people's way of dealing with any species believed to be in their way of advancement. Wipe out the means by which the people exist, and the people themselves will cease to exist.

There are sixteen warriors who have been asked to go on foot and on horse to perform one of the most honorable and respectable deeds that we indigenous peoples have ever been called to do in our time on Earth. These men will defend our rights, and will defend the family with their own lives. They know not where they may fall or where they may live in the future, but they leave that to Creator. Their belief is strong, just as their muscles in their bodies are strong. Belief must remain strong if we are to confront the white man and his ways.

We must understand that the land itself will give us advantages. The lands that have been foreseen as the battle sites, and mentioned along with the instructions, already have beings upon them. The familiarity with the territories where we gather, hunt, and travel becomes integral to what we are planning. We were put here in our land to live this way. Those who have come in a wrong and bad way know not what they do. For every wrongful taking of a being, through murder and extermination, there is a chain reaction for those who remain. Each and every time the whites come across and violate any nation of people, whether two-legged, four-legged, winged, of the water, insects, or plants, they are violating the natural life put forth by Creator. Each of these beings has its place on Grandmother Earth. Each has its role to serve, as well. With a combination of trust and unity, we—all of us, all the peoples of Unci Maka taken together—have survived through times similar to this. We hope we will survive through this time, but we fear that our numbers will be decreased.

We are up against a type of weaponry that is mostly unfamiliar to us. *Maza*, iron, has now become an enemy of the people. As it lays in the ground naturally, in He Sapa and throughout our land, it is only a part of the wonderful ways of Creator. But when the new people take it and wrongfully change it, it loses its spirit. The bad human beings' hands and minds take control of it. Iron then becomes a consumer of life, rather than a provider of life.

We must provide what is needed at this time. Creator, in the spiritual instructions, has specifically given us things to pursue and to prepare for. Not only are the warriors given their ways and the right to be who they are, but also the families are given instructions, such as how to take care of the food supplies, how to manage the clothing and traveling, and how to adapt to a more nocturnal existence. Many of our ways that were commonly practiced fully in the daylight, under the sun with the other beings, are now being driven into the darkness. In the darkness is now where we will pray and where we will contend with all the negatives that we face. Because of this, the Creator gifts the families with instructions for how to take care of one another, where to go, how to get there, and where to gather—all of the finer points for existence. All we have to do is listen to Creator and believe.

For the warriors, their ways are separate. They will be asked to carry out many tasks during their time. But again, we come back to Creator. Every topic that we have opened up, and everything that we have asked for or questioned, has been addressed. This is indicative of the trust that we have always had in the one called Creator. We will not fail Creator if we follow this belief system. We will certainly lose more of our loved ones, but the ones who do survive will have that opportunity of creational intent and purpose set before them. It will be their responsibility and their right to carry on with life for the people who remain among our nations.

In these instructions, and particularly for the warriors, specifics are given, such as where the upcoming battle will take place, how to get to this place, how to prepare, what people need to bring, and what the families will contribute from the stock of necessities and belongings still in their possession. The families will give everything, including their lives, to help the warriors defend our way of life. Our lives depend on one another. Our children, our women, and our elders are the supportive strength that the warriors will need in order for us to fight the white man and the destructive ways of many in their society, government, and military.

The elder medicine people who are involved will assist the Dakota holy man Eagle Fan as best they can. Eagle Fan has been identified as the spiritual leader of the warriors. In their most understanding way of supporting Eagle Fan in what he must do, the medicine people's prayers, add to what we have prepared for, and will make the warriors stronger and more determined. This spiritual preparation of so many of these tribal peoples and their culture, including the Lakota, is absolutely necessary to prevent our extinction.

This portion of the preparation is not only for the warriors and their encounters to come. It is also for the families who have committed to forever hold their knowledge of and involvement with the pathway, the permission, and the battle, in secrecy, so as to aid in what is to happen. The families are the strength of the warrior. The people's lives and their way of life, is what is at stake here. With patience and honor, they support and believe in the chosen ones. Still, the life that these men, women, and children will face once the warriors leave to prepare for battle, will get harder and harder. Their spiritual presence will give this cannumpa strength. The families will surround us with this spiritual presence, prayer, and most certainly with their belief that we can accomplish what we have been asked to do as a people, as Lakota, as coexisting human inhabitants of Grandmother Earth, and as members of the family of mankind.

The preparation of the selected warriors will start in the spring, and will continue through the winter of 1874. And in the late springtime of 1875, the warriors will begin their trip to the Black Hills, He Sapa. This is where they will stay for the next year. And then, after their preparation time is over in the following spring, they will take off for the Greasy Grass. May of 1876 is when Creator's instructions reveal that they shall make this departure.

12

SPIRIT SPEAK

THE LAKOTA PEOPLE, BY AND through the families of Saved By Bear and Swift Bear, received a spiritual message from the Creator directly. This spiritual message was gifted to them and the medicine people at the sacred place along the Bear Creek near the confluence of the Owl River, the oldest lands and the area where the Sacred Cannumpa was delivered to the people by White Buffalo Calf Woman. Creator had responded to the people, including Saved By Bear, Swift Bear, and their Mnincoju families, who performed the *asking*. And it was the Creator, by and through the sacred spirits from the west and beyond, who delivered the messages to these families. The Creator gave them an answer when they asked for guidance, providing them with direction and instructions, and granting them sacred and spiritual permission to do everything that was necessary to protect the people, the He Sapa, Grandmother Earth, and the Circle of life.

At this point, the responsibility for survival is bestowed upon Saved By Bear, Swift Bear, our families, and our medicine people. We will rely upon ourselves, and the teachings of our tradition and culture passed down through the generations, to pull us through this difficult time. Leaders will rise to the top. People will assume responsibility for tasks they'd never before performed. Each will contribute to these warriors' welfare in the hopes that the warriors will keep everything alive.

Outside of our family units, there will be no mention of this affair.

There will be no talk. There will be no indication of what we are going to do. Secrecy is maintained because most of the human beings, even some of our own kind, are untrustworthy and unreliable. Times are just too hard. Trust is hard to find among humans.

Our people are the ones who spiritually support this secret affair. Many of them will now take an oath that they will never speak of this spiritual commitment, sacred duty, and this spiritual act, until such time in the future that the message is clear that the world is ready to hear the story and to receive the message.

Saved By Bear will pass on his story to his descendants to carry forth as time goes on. He would provide the spiritual message about what is to be done. It is to become a part of the extended process of this battle, which is not to be fought and settled in just one day. This battle will be a long continuous spiritual one, which will come to last for many decades. The opportunity to be a part of this spiritual process is one that all the designated families would cherish, as each knows that the action of these sixteen men is absolutely necessary. There is no other alternative. Everything else has been tried, and everything else has failed. Now we will come as a force against the whites to prove our point. We will take life, and we will allow life to continue. This will all be recognized one day in the future by the world. This will also be understood one day by the world. Those who are capable of letting positive energy reside within themselves will feel the steps walked, the breaths taken, and the time spent by these sixteen warriors, including Saved By Bear and Swift Bear, who will do as they were asked. They accept their duty. They courageously carry this responsibility in body and in spirit for the purpose of preserving our world. One day the world would come to know. Until then, there would be much work and preparation to be done.

During the giving of the spiritual instructions to the warriors in the inipi at Bear Creek, the story is told from the warriors' perspective as if the events were in the process of happening. When notification came, the warriors' families began the process of preparing for the ceremony and ritual to help the warriors prepare themselves. Our world was going to change. The warriors involved, in particular, Saved By Bear and his spirit brother, Swift Bear, had been given specific instructions for the battle that will come. When the warriors are preparing for what they need to do in the battle to come, they will begin taking those steps to prepare as if they are seeing all of these scenes play out in front of them. They see the mountains, the valley, the water, the birds, the movement of the grass, and the way the sun plays off the rocks and the landscape at any particular time of the day. They are becoming the plan. They become so in tune with the spirit of what is to occur, that they begin to live out their roles even before their roles have realistically begun.

Creator informed them of certain facts and circumstances to aid them, also telling them of the separate involvement of the other warriors who would be at the separate battles. There also was to be a designated call to duty for Saved By Bear and Swift Bear, and a separate duty and need for the expertise of the warrior Spirit Horse.

Sitting Bull and Spirit Horse were called upon by the Creator to play their roles in the upcoming Greasy Grass Battle, Sitting Bull being a respected spiritual holy man and Spirit Horse being a respected warrior and military strategist. Sitting Bull was told of what was to come, where and when it was to occur, and what would be the result. But Sitting Bull was to serve a role. His role. He was to safely guide the people to the sacred place at the proper time and in the proper manner so as to ensure that when the military and Custer sought them out, they would be found. Sitting Bull's role would be to serve as the spiritual presence for the people during the battle by being across the river praying. He was to give the people a showing of hope and confidence so that they would not be afraid. But Sitting Bull would not be required to fight or to otherwise physically participate in the battle. And he would play his role well. We will honor him and respect him for his role, as he would indeed support the warriors and pray for their success.

However, the most critical aspects of the battle to come, the spiritual battle, is in the hands of the grassroots people, the people of the grass, the people of the roots: all of the families. These are the unknowns, these sixteen warriors, unknowns in the eyes of most of the people. But they have been selected by Creator, and are trusted by their own people.

Spirit Horse will receive a separate set of spriritual instructions to direct and command the Lakota and Cheyenne warriors against the cavalry units attacking from the south. His duty will be to monitor and encourage the larger group of warriors from the encampment, ensuring that they move forward in honoring their commitments. According to the spiritual permission granted, Spirit Horse's conflicts, battles, and supervision are not to be directly involved in the individual spiritual pathway battle. Spirit Horse's *asking* was specific. He is to take care of the general group of warriors who will be acting that day, independent of what the sixteen *chosen* warriors would be doing. Those warriors in the larger group will act bravely and fight fiercely, but they will be operating as their own unit under the direction of Spirit Horse. None among this general group of warriors will even know about the spiritual pathway battle plan or the participating warriors. Not even Spirit Horse himself. The larger group of warriors' lives are Spirit Horse's responsibility. He will prepare them accordingly.

All of the warriors that will assemble at the main encampment and that will fight in the Greasy Grass Battle, would have a reason to be there. However, there would also be many warriors who would choose not to be at the Greasy Grass at the time of battle on that day. Why many of them choose not to go, or to remain absent from the scene, will not be widely known, but one can honestly speculate. Perhaps at that time, these men were not worthy of the warrior status they held among the people. Or they may have chosen to work for the other side, perhaps now serving as informants, ambassadors, scouts, or something else in order to aid the white men and the US military. So there are historical figures who become recognized after this battle. Many of these men, or warriors as they called themselves, would not personally engage in this particular battle, but instead would engage with the US military to negotiate a position for themselves. The amenities of this new culture is what they would be promised. But in the end, they were neither recognized nor honored for their role in the Greasy Grass Battle, as they failed to carry out their responsibility to the families and the indigenous tribal nations by refusing to fight. They would rather leave their people in pain and suffering, so that they themselves, behaving with arrogance and selfishness, may benefit from the material possessions, amenities, or even the personal security they were likely promised, intending that only they and their confidants should benefit. This is one of the many things that the group of sixteen chosen warriors would be up against, and why secrecy had to be maintained at all costs. These absent ones would not be a part of the spiritual plan or the permission.

As for the battle that is to occur, the world knows it as the battle that occurred at the chosen *hill*, Last Stand Hill—the Battle of the Little Bighorn, the Greasy Grass Battle. In actuality, there are really three separate battles that will occur during this day. The two major battles will be directed by Spirit Horse and the main group of warriors. The third battle will involve the sixteen warriors seeking to fulfill that for which they were granted permission after making their spiritual *asking*. The different groups of Lakota warriors and various tribal nations in the encampment would be completely unaware of the identity or presence of the sixteen warriors. However, the sixteen warriors will know that the larger group of warriors led by Spirit Horse, will be occupying the soldiers on other parts of the battlefield. The warriors are of one mind and one spirit.

The first battle that will be initiated will be supervised by Spirit Horse, as he will use his knowledge to determine the military strategy, which is his spiritual duty to develop. The first armed conflict will involve Maj. Marcus Reno, where Reno and his cavalrymen will be confronted by the main group of the warriors to the south of the encampment. The advancement of foot soldiers and mounted soldiers will be met with an onslaught of the defending warriors under Spirit Horse's direction. This first battle will take place approximately four miles southwest of the *chosen hill*. If Reno, and his men, should decide not to retreat, then each officer and his soldiers and separate regiments will perish as well. If they do retreat, they will be likely to survive.

The second battle would occur south of where Custer's men would eventually come to be. Again, the warriors from the encampment under the direction of Spirit Horse will push from the riverbanks toward the top of the higher ridge as the fighting continued at this stage of the overall conflict at the Greasy Grass. These warrriors will confront and fight the soldiers at the river, then upon a separate hill, cutting off many of Custer's troops, which would then end up forcing Custer and his remnants north toward the *chosen hill*. The warriors involved will have been instructed and be prepared for battle, much like the sixteen warriors including Saved By Bear and Swift Bear, were prepared. These men would perform with the same courage, attack with ferocity, and perform the ultimate duty of confronting the US soldiers and taking their lives where they must.

The third battle is the spiritual battle to be fought by Saved By Bear, Swift Bear, and the fourteen other warriors. Because of the spiritual *asking*, Creator responded and instructed that Custer and certain soldiers among his cavalry would be confronted and taken at the *chosen hill*. This battle would occur on the northern perimeter of the *chosen hill*, at the most critical stage of the overall military conflict between the warriors and the US military. The responsibility of the sixteen spiritual warriors' group would be to advance and defend this northern perimeter, but to stay within their own perimeter as they advance toward Custer himself. The movement by the remaining group of soldiers from the south to the north, as forced toward that direction by the actions of Spirit Horse and his warriors, would cause these soldiers, the officers, and Custer himself to begin moving toward the northern perimeter. Near the *chosen hill*. These soldiers would move at first out of desperation, but the real reason would be the warriors' *asking* of Creator and the presence of the spirit mostly. What we will do is to take the lives of these men, and we will be proud of what we will do that day against the U.S. military. Every soldier of the US military in the battle to come on the *chosen hill*, will die. If everything follows true, as foretold by Creator, all of them will die.

After the sweat lodge ceremony at Bear Creek near the Owl River in August 1874, Saved By Bear and Swift Bear, as they make their exit, they are greeted by their families and the medicine people. They sit down and discuss in secrecy with only those who need to or must know, the happenings of this unique and very special spiritual encounter in this particular inipi ceremony in the lodge. Saved By Bear will speak as to his instructions for the upcoming battle. Swift Bear is fully aware of these instructions. A significant factor in this battle is that there will be one warrior facing one soldier at a time, to show honor in the battle. The purpose of doing battle in this way is not only to prove manhood or status in the warrior society, but also to prove to the families that one can defend his own family.

Within the spiritual instructions of this ceremony, a priority is placed on two specific items of warfare that are not to be carried onto the battlefield. A commitment that the sixteen warriors agree with. The first is that they leave their shields with the scouts at the gathering site. The second is that they leave their rifles and revolvers with the scouts as well. The spirits speak of altered metal, a weapon of vital importance. This weapon of the United States military will be used against Custer. The symbol of the United States military's power, the carbine with its ammunition cartridges, will be carried to the battle by one of their own, one of the soldiers of the Seventh Cavalry. This particular soldier will not know this, but he will be rewarded in the spirit world and be thanked by the people. This soldier would be the one to carry the carbine, according to the ceremony and instructions gifted by Creator. We will take no guns or bullets onto the battlefield ourselves. That is what Creator instructed. That is the way it must be. Therefore, that is all that the warriors needed to know about this particular weapon. Saved By Bear will be given specific instructions by Creator about how to find and use the military's own weapon against one of its own: Custer.

There would not be thousands of warriors attacking these cavalry soldiers. The number of actual warriors present at the Greasy Grass Battle when this is to occur, will be limited. The number of existing Lakota warriors has already been substantially reduced because of war, conflicts and encounters with the whites, and lack of sufficient food and means to survive. During this battle, to come, the warriors from the encampment will be instructed by Spirit Horse. These instructions would hopefully be followed exactly as they would be relayed. There would be no torture, or desecration after the killing of these soldiers. There would be no taking of possessions. There would be no taking of anything that falls to the ground. If a warrior were to kill a soldier, then he will leave the soldier and go on to protect the warriors who remained.

No torture, no mutilation, and no body dismemberment was to occur. That is the usual way of Lakota battle, but these things will be especially prohibited in this battle, for which spiritual permission has been granted. The warriors will not take pieces of flesh from their opponents, as the whites have done to our people. There would be, however, one exception. Mato Niyanpi, Saved By Bear, has been asked by Creator to take a partial trigger finger, so that the spirit of Custer will be kept and nurtured by Saved By Bear. This will be the special encounter and meeting between Saved By Bear and Custer. This will be the only instance where any of the warriors will take a representative piece of any soldier's body, but in particular, that of Custer himself.

The trigger finger is selected because it is the focal point of a soldier's weapon. When that finger pulls that trigger and releases that bullet, it has been the heaviest influence on the people's lives. It has brought genocide, and suffering in the form of massacres and indignities. Custer has his finger on the trigger of the new country's military. He has his finger on the trigger of the genocide of the Lakota, the Protectors. His finger is on the trigger of the destruction of Unci Maka. We are tyring, by example, to show the United States and the world that we are trying to mend what has happened, and is happening. Custer's trigger finger will give us the opportunity to try to redirect the minds and spirits of mankind.

Custer is one of the leaders who instigates and carries out the genocidal policies and practices for the government. The reason behind the spiritual instruction to take his trigger finger is not only to show that the Lakota can stop him from killing our people, but also it represents every human being whose life that has been taken in such a fashion by that finger: the pulling of the finger against the trigger, the loss of life.

At the beginning of the preparation process at the lodge near Bear Creek, there are specific messages that come to be directed to Custer himself. He has wanted this war for quite a while. The Lakota are going to give it to him. What the Mnincoju families of the Lakota are going to give to Custer first, is spirit. To connect to Custer's spirit through their prayer and their words. Custer will understand that what he wants, has been granted. He is a man who is totally self-indulgent. His spirit is larger than life, because he believes that is what he represents. His mind-set becomes one in which he is ready and willing to come and perform his dastardly deeds again. His feelings give him the strength and the courage he needs to say to himself, *We will go and take care of these hostiles.* In preparation, he knows that his spirit is alive now. The

Lakota and the spiritual messages have revivified this in him. That bit of spirit that he has left. The drive to get to this battle will encompass and overtake everything else, including his daily routine. His arrogant drive to lead this new country is as big as the Lakota's prayers with the cannumpa.

Custer's preparation is not unlike that of Saved By Bear, Swift Bear, and the other chosen warriors. Custer will know what he is going into. He will know what he is going to be faced with. But he has never encountered before, what he will encounter in this particular battle. He will be drawn into everything, every fiber of his body to go to the Greasy Grass, for he believes it will fulfill his destiny. And his weakness of mind will be his downfall, as he will be relentless in pursuit of his destiny and his place in history. He will drive his men almost to the breaking point, both physically and mentally. He will torment his men to perform for him, demanding that they abide by his will. He will be on a mission almost by himself, because he has been called to come. To come forward, and to face…. the warrior.

The spiritual connection that was made with Custer through the warriors' preparation leading up to the battle, and the connection with Custer's spirit itself, will lead him to precisely where he needs to go and where he needs to be, in fulfillment of the spiritual plan that was set in place. He will be led by his own arrogance, and his drive to impose his will and have this war, and to follow through on the policy of genocide. However, it will really be his spirit that will be drawn upon to lead him to where he will go to fulfill his destiny.

Custer's spirit will be awakened by this contact that our spiritual message had initiated. His thoughts will be that he has been granted, as before, an opportunity to go and participate in the game of war. He may feel that the Lakota are giving up, and will be just sitting there waiting for him to come and massacre them, as was the case at the Washita River in 1868. This is how the spirit that has not been connected for a lifetime, or on only slight occasion, reacts. Given that Custer is uneducated as to these spiritual matters, he will not understand the moment or the means to come to a proper decision. This is why we, the Lakota people, and specifically Saved By Bear, Swift Bear, and the other fourteen warriors, rely upon the spiritual part of this battle. The spiritual connection and belief allows the warriors to encounter Custer's spiritual weakness of mind. This will draw him in and exactly as we have been told. He will follow patterns without thinking, but he will believe them to be his decisions. They will not be. Custer will be properly cautious, and painstakingly brought along, step by step, to this inevitable battle of wits, mind, body, and lastly, spirit. The question will be, whose spiritual presence will prevail?

Along with all of the preparation that the warriors will undergo, including the *asking* and the other behavior, it will come to the crucial point of one of the most significant pieces of this whole affair: a prayer bundle. A separate bundle must be made for this battle. The bundle will be made as instructed as well, to prepare its contents. This is a very special bundle, which will be made by the loving, nurturing, courageous and strong hands of the women. A special bundle for a special reason, that will be taken to the battle, the battle yet to come. The contents will be representative of the Circle of life, according to tradition and culture. The bundle will be assembled as preparation ensues, step by step. When the appropriate time comes, and the ritual is performed, the articles and prayers will be inserted into the bundle. A cannumpa is prepared. One that has a recent and specific reason of importance. The prayers that will come and go through this sacred cannumpa are one of the last human and spiritual efforts that these tribal peoples, the Lakota, have to rely upon. This cannumpa is how we will speak, how we will converse, and how we will make decisions about every step of the approach. The north is the home of tatanka, the buffalo nation, and of the cannumpa. The significance will be that these are the times, now, for which the cannumpa had been brought forth.

The spirits and the very old ones said that the times to come would bring an uncertain change in the lives of the people, forced upon them by a new group of people coming from across the oceans to our land. These new people would not come in a peaceful communal fashion, the people were told. They would have come from a long perilous era of behaving violently toward other people. Instead of getting along with each other in those countries from which they came, these new people warred against each other and depleted their natural resources and human factors. Those who arrived on Turtle Island brought with them many bits and pieces of this evil generational behavior that existed among them. Their individual and collective spirit must be reached if we are all to survive.

According to the spiritual instructions from Creator, the bundle, it was determined, would be made from buffalo hide. This is how we would honor tatanka's gift to our lives. A special pouch would be carried, created for the purpose of the meeting on that *hill* near the Greasy Grass River. The pouch is intended to hold something of great significance. It would carry this spirit for a very, very long time, long enough for the spirit to learn, to understand, to be taught, to be nurtured, and then to come back to a life of assimilating as human beings and spiritual beings. As we walk today, we are both humans and spirits. A directed, nurtured, and compassionately cared for being can only benefit from the process of being taken in by those who want a better life for all people.

This plan was predominantly from our people and for our people, our leaders and families who decided that it was time that we stand up or else forever be lost. It was important to all of us, including our children, women, and elders, that we would sacrifice everything we knew in life to accomplish the goal at the Greasy Grass, so that one day our world would be at peace so that we would understand the word *unity*, and we would also live in a spiritual fashion, to preserve our lives, our lands, culture, and to protect Grandmother Earth and all beings, and to prosper in the future.

These sixteen warriors were called upon by Creator during the ceremonies. Specific instructions to prepare the families of these warriors were also given. These instructions concerned the needed articles, the needed rituals, and the specific behavior for the upcoming battle at Greasy Grass, including what the warriors should and should not do. These warriors passed these plans not only through the spiritual side but also through their connection with trusted relatives. Saved By Bear and Swift Bear were called upon for a very specific and important task: to meet Custer. They would have a face-to-face meeting with him, and then the matter would be settled.

The site of the great preparation had been chosen: He Sapa. All of our other sacred sites, all of our generational prayers and activities in this life, have hinged on and focused on this special sacred area. It is very special to the presence needed on the journey of the sixteen warriors, including Saved By Bear.

They will gather and go to the He Sapa, the Black Mountains. The reason they will do this, spending the four seasons in the He Sapa, is to prepare for the forthcoming event revealed to them during the *asking* of Creator. They will be able to take what they need from their families and from the society that they are now going to leave, in hopes of preserving Lakota traditions and culture, in hopes of preserving the people's presence on Grandmother Earth. Saved By Bear and the other chosen warriors will say "toksa ake" to their families sometime around May of 1875. Before leaving their families, they will entrust the warriors who stay behind with their relatives with the task of protecting them. Basically, this is to be an extended family affair. It is predominantly the Hunkpapa, the Hohwoju, Mnincoju, and closely related people who had been chosen and who decided to do this. Many of the other peoples from the other Lakota nations were either not strong enough or connected enough at this point, or were trying to assimilate into the new world of the trading post Indian. The Mnincoju will fight this fight to the very end. After the warriors say their farewells, their families will be escorted to safety by fellow warriors who were trusted by leaders such as Sitting Bull. The families of the warriors will be taken care of, fed, and sheltered during this time when the warriors are gone. It is imperative that these families survive and that they are being taken care of, as they need to participate in the spiritual part of the warriors' preparation activities. Family is the lifeblood of the people.

In the preparation, certain places will be designated and given to the people for those purposes. The warriors will have already been given the spiritual instructions as to what needed to be done on each visit to each of the sacred sites. The He Sapa, with its eternal boundaries and beauty, contains and provides numerous special places to learn, to pray, and to exercise one's body so that it remains healthy and in very good physical condition.

According to the spiritual instructions, Saved By Bear and his individual group of seven warriors will leave for the He Sapa, the Black Mountians. They will stay there for just about the entire year before the battle. This is about how long in advance we knew that the battle would take place. The warriors will go to prepare for this *asking* of Creator, Wakan Tanka. They will stay throughout the winter and prepare themselves to go to the Greasy Grass at the appropriate time late in the following spring.

The warriors will travel from their homes, riding west toward He Sapa. It will be a four-day ride. Their intent is to track around He Sapa. First, the group will head for an old campsite along the river running north of the Mato Paha, the Belle Fourche River.

After making a brief stop near Mato Paha, the warriors will travel south toward the Buffalo Run in the He Sapa. The Buffalo Run will lead them close to the heart of Grandmother Earth, the Wind Cave area. A day's ride to the west, is where they will set up a base camp for all that is needed to be done over the next year. To the south, not far from their base camp, are the hot springs, the *mni kata*, which are also very sacred to us, as they are healing waters.

After they finish this part of their journey, the instructions indicate that they will again return to their camp, which is not far above, and just to the north of, the Wind Cave area. This base camp is a very special place to Saved By Bear, as he has been there many times throughout his life. This special place is located near the Sage Creek and the Sun Mountain.

Saved By Bear will know all these special places in the He Sapa because he had been there before, all throughout his life. Having been born in the He Sapa and having spent a great amount of time in the sacred mountains, he definitely knows these lands quite well. In the He Sapa, one could hide, one can exist without anybody knowing where you are. There was a reason why these warriors will use this area as their base camp, because there is a sun dance ground directly above the campsite, which is where they will stay for the winter. In the sun dance ground there is an inipi, which they will enter to pray and to ask for direction for the upcoming battle, a very important one for the people. Throughout this period, they will sweat and hope to receive what they ask for.

According to the instructions, in the fall, they will go to a place deep in the higher reaches of He Sapa to the place of the Old Stone Warriors.

These Old Stone Warriors have stood proudly, honorably, courageously, and spiritually throughout all time. They have defended and protected the people. They have been the guardians of He Sapa. Swift Bear, as the protector and a military strategist, will head up this meeting as he and the warriors gather amid the Old Stone Warriors. Swift Bear will pray. Then he will converse with and receive his instructions from these truly reliable spirits, who have been through this before during other times on Earth. Swift Bear will enter the spiritual realm and will then devise a military strategy according to the spiritual instructions given directly to him. He, Saved By Bear, and the other warriors of their select group will take their time to ensure that they do all they need to do to prepare themselves for the roles they will play in the upcoming battle. These warriors, including Saved By Bear and Swift Bear, are all Dog Man society members. This spiritual vision, this spiritual guidance, will direct them as they decide how they will behave, how they will assist each other, and what they will accomplish once they get to the *hill* and encounter Custer.

In the springtime, within weeks of the time when the warriors would depart for the Greasy Grass, the warriors will go to the sacred Owl's Nest peak to receive their last spiritual round of preparation and instruction for what lies ahead for them individually, and as a group of united warriors pursuing their common cause of fulfilling the permission granted by Creator.

The warriors' actual journey to the Greasy Grass must be and will be an isolated one, and they must remain under constant cover. No one must see them, no one must speak to them, and no one will be joining them. The duty and the responsibility belongs to the sixteen alone. After everything in their lives that they have accomplished or gone through, and in light of every opportunity they have missed, this will be their chance to redeem themselves. If they did not hold a belief in and care for life, then they would not have been asked to be a part of this most spiritual happening. All of the warriors will look forward to the day when they will leave for the upcoming battle.

The instructions have indicated that on our way to the Greasy Grass, we will find the place where we will stay, farther north of the *chosen hill*. This site too is designated according to the spiritual instructions. We will go to that site along the Greasy Grass River many days ahead of time because we will not want to be seen by anyone, not only by the cavalry and their auxiliaries, like the Crow scouts, but also by the tribal peoples and other warriors who will have already gathered, or will gather, there. Our places of sanctuary and seclusion were revealed to us during the ceremonies, our choices and decisions having already been made for us by the spirit. We will just follow our spirits and use our knowledge, and do our best to get to these designated areas as instructed. We will know these places once we arrive. These selected places and the specific areas will become familiar to us all when the time to act would arrive.

Included in the asking of these sixteen warriors was that these spiritual instructions received at Bear Creek, this permission, this plan, this act, would be kept secret. The warriors will not speak of anything at all involving this event, until the appropriate time for Saved By Bear, and the spirit of Custer, which he is asked to keep, to come forward. When this happens, it will be a much needed revelation, something with great significance for the future, as it will provide the human beings with the opportunity to unite by praying together, eating together, and enjoying life in a communal way. The Creator instructed that this effort will be in the furtherance of a world of rejuvenation for all beings that exist on Unci Maka so that they may live in peace, unity, tolerance, and love. Until that future time, according to Creator's instructions, it shall remain secret, a hidden truth.

Therefore, all of the instructions having been given, and received, and the plans set in place, it was time now, to put all of the plans and instruction into physical action. It is no longer just a plan for preparation. And so the actual preparation begins in the Spring of 1875……

13
PREPARATION

THE WARRIORS PACK THEIR HORSES, including Wildfire and Spotted Smoke. They bring all the supplies and amenities needed for daily life and for ritual and ceremonial practice. Specific items will be needed. They carry their buffalo robes. They bring their weaponry. But most of all, they will bring their heart to the Black Mountains, to He Sapa, and ask Unci Maka, the place of all birth, for strength, for knowledge, and for access to the path that will allow them to bring their people *back*.

During this time of travel to the He Sapa, Saved By Bear will ride with his group, seven warriors in all. There will be nine others who will arrive, later, traveling as a separate group. The two groups will meet in a specified place, known only to these warriors at this time. Not even their own families will know exactly where they are.

As the warriors approach He Sapa, the Black Mountains are ready to welcome them. It is a good day for them to arrive. The animals are abundant; the sounds of life are everywhere. All of the beings are aware that these warriors have come on behalf of their welfare too. The stone and plant people express their gratitude to their warrior brothers. Unci Maka honors the warriors by allowing them safe haven. They will follow this path and toward the sacred place where they will be staying for the coming year.

On the fourth full day of travel toward the He Sapa, Saved By Bear scanned the horizon for a familiar sight. He looked south. The band of Mnincoju had been traveling through the night from the Bear Creek region. Exhausted from the long trip and its events, the warriors and the horses settled down on the south side of the Belle Fourche River to make camp for the night.

Saved By Bear placed his blanket on the ground near the hole last used a year or so ago. It was about twenty feet from the bank and slightly under a large drooping elm tree with a wide ruddy base. The tree was old and had seen many winters and summers. Its age called for, but did not demand, respect and honor. It was known and accepted among the Lakota that the Old Ones knew things that had come to pass, and have seen much from season to season.

The Old Ones grew a ring to mark each successive season of survival, each ring adding to its individual knowledge and protection. Wakan Tanka and Creator had gifted the tree people with wonderful spiritual powers. One of those gifts was the tree's ability to self-heal when cut or nicked. Creator had given tree sap as blood to the tree people long ago, at the beginning. They could let this sap flow over the wound to heal it, as it sealed the wound, protecting it from exposure. This in turn allowed the tree to grow and continue to nourish itself, healing on its own.

The tree people are an important part of the Circle of life for all things. When the Wakinyan, the Thunder Beings, release their life force and energy in lightning, the lightning in turn causes the occasional fire in the forest. The fire causes a rejuvenation of the plants and soil. The pine tree's cones get heated up and release their seeds into the earth. The old is replaced by the new. A tree that burns down serves to nourish the other beings, bringing forth new life, rejuvenation of the Circle. It is all connected. Even the roots that reach deep into Grandmother, drink of the water and eat of the food buried within her. All of the trees and plants nourish each other as needed. The aspens have collective roots, the root system being a family of its own. All the tree people possess a great and lasting memory, something valuable to their own existence. Such is the relationship between the Old Ones and Unci Maka.

The elm, the Old One about which we are speaking, saw that it was time to again welcome some familiar friends. This Old One recognized the warrior known as Saved By Bear and his group from past winters, past summers, and past hunts. They often hung the meat from their hunts in the Old One's branches, leaving it to dry. This made the Old One feel needed and depended upon by the people. The Old One would provide what he could for the people, because he knew that these people would not turn the axe or knife to him unless it was absolutely necessary for them to do this for purposes of survival. The Old One was the guardian of the Belle Fourche basin, which the people often traveled through on their journeys across the land to and from certain sites, before they would go to pray and give thanks at the sacred mountain.

The Old One's high vertical branches could see to the south, beyond the rolling plains of prairie grass and brush, and view the sacred mountain, Mato Paha. This is why the people used this dependable resting site over and over again. The Old One knew he had been selected to stand guard, and to strengthen his roots and arms, to provide for the weary beings as they moved from place to place, returning to the sacred mountain.

The Old One understood what the mountain meant to all on

Grandmother Earth. Even the winged that came to perch on his branches whispered to him of the enchanting beauty of the sacred mountain and its peaceful and soulful presence. The winged ones spoke of the true beauty they beheld when swooping and hovering over the places at the top of the sacred mountain that were used by the people to pray. The winged ones told the Old One how, when passing over these sites with wings spread and vision locked, they felt the energy pull at their chests, inviting them to come closer to the source of the message. The energy clearly flowed through and up from the mountain, at the request and in answer to the prayers of the beings.

The young eagles especially crooned in the Old One's ears, saying that they had danced the previous summer from energy point to energy point, trying to absorb as much as they could before performing the ancient task of delivering that energy in the way they were taught by their own elders.

The owls loved to sit quietly in the Old One's embrace, waiting until nightfall to give the Old One their full account of the magical things that happened on the sacred mountain. An owl's huge eyes light up and shine with their own lunar blaze because of its excitement and its obvious pride in viewing and knowing such things.

The Old One only smiles, fluttering his great leaves.

As he had done many times in the past, Saved By Bear came up to the Old One's large sturdy trunk. With palms open, he laid his warm strong hands upon the tree's bark. This was their way of communicating with each other on a deeper level. This method made it easier for the Old One to share his knowledge and his past experiences, including what he had seen and endured throughout the years. It was as if the Old One were a magical old wooden picture book, free to be used by those who took the time to turn the pages. One could hear about ninety years of history if one were so inclined. And indeed the old guardian shared his knowledge and experiences with the kind warrior, focusing on the things the Old One had witnessed recently, mentioning the groups of soldiers who had passed close to his rooted home. Once the conversation was over, Saved By Bear slowly and solemnly kissed the bark of the tree and lifted his hands. The Old One felt the flow of positive energy zip through his branches and leaves.

The Old One knows the people. The people know and accept him. The Old One has heard all the campfire stories of the people, the laughter at the jokes, the solemn advice of elders to the youth, the loving words spoken by the parent or grandparent to the maturing child, the tales of bravery and adventure, the songs sung by the happy friends, and the tearful, sorrowful crying of the heartbroken. And now and then, the Old One heard stories of spiritual wonderment and gratitude, and stories of the magnificent things accomplish. ...including, something that was spoken about a spiritual plan and preparation, with a mention that the heyoka and the Dog Man warriors had been chosen by Wakan Tanka to make themselves ready. The Old One, however, never needed to be sworn to secrecy, because after all he was a trusted friend, an old, yet loving guardian.

———— ◆ ————

Once the warriors left the camp by the old guardian, passed close by the sacred Mato Paha, and traveled toward the south, they witnessed the late spring activity of all the four-legged ones along the way. The warriors cross the fast-running Rapid Creek, the Mniluzanhan, and turn to travel south along the perimeter of the Red Racetrack of He Sapa toward the Great Buffalo Run passageway at the southeast of He Sapa. The deer, antelope, and elk were thick in the grass and in the tree lines along the Racetrack. The Racetrack was still as red and noticeable as it had been after the legendary race of the beings so long ago. On the second day of travel beyond Mato Paha, the warriors come to the wide entrance of the Buffalo Run into He Sapa. They find an old camp circle area by a nearby creek and set up camp for the night. Tomorrow they will go into the heart of Unci Maka to begin the year of their preparation. The other group of the nine chosen warriors will meet up with them at the preordained place, the old base campsite.

Saved By Bear and his group of seven warriors rise with the morning sun and ride west along the wide, brimming Buffalo Run. Riding north of the hilly crests overlooking the canyons protecting the sacred Wind Cave, the warriors hear the majestic early morning bugling of the sacred elk. Off in the distant west, near a flat tabletop peak clustered with dark pine trees, the warriors see a vast herd of elk slowly moving and grazing on the lush prairie grasses along the edge. It is a great sight to see. The warriors continue moving along the high hogback ridges, traveling northwest deep into the sacred forests of He Sapa. As they crest a particular high bluff that had recently burned in a natural fire brought on by Wakinyan's lighting strikes, the horses impatiently prance, as the warriors look longingly to the west.

When the warriors see the great split Drumstick Rock, they know that they are close to the base camp along the Sage Creek, in the shadow of the great Sun Mountain. It warmed their hearts and their spirits to know that they are close to the safe haven, the cradle, that Grandmother has provided for them for this time of their most important preparation.

Saved By Bear particularly has a great affinity, respect, and adoration for this old sacred site. For as long as he could remember in his life as a human being, he and his family frequented these sacred grounds, where the Mnincoju people had gathered and camped for generations.

The old campsite sat along the Sage Creek, which flows clean, crisp, and fast from the highland canyons to the west. It runs freely and strongly over the dark gray stones. It flows under the streaking, looming granite cliffs among the bends and waterfalls of the onrushing current. Where the clear freshwater creek widens, it becomes more shallow. Where it narrows through the rock crevices, and as a result of the sporadic dams of the beavers, the running stream quickens and deepens. This is the lifeblood of the Grandmother, water, *mni*—the gift of nourishment and existence from Creator. It is the life-giving supply for the people who have been visiting, camping, and drinking from the flowing spring. The water was a main reason why this place was chosen, why this place was so special, why this place breathed with a life of its own.

The beautiful bending stream runs along the north valley of the Sun Mountain. The stream supplies nourishment for the roots of the strong pines, willows, birch trees, and ash trees that cover the circumference of the sacred rise. The warriors saw no need to haul their tipi poles here. The Grandmother's He Sapa had millions of strong young straight pines that were absolutely perfect for meeting this need.

Saved By Bear remembered how the family had followed the herds of tatanka through the Buffalo Run, through a gap to the southeast just beyond the sacred origin place at the mouth of Wind Cave. The tatanka would roam, graze, and run out on the rolling prairies to the east, but they would always return to the cradle of the He Sapa for the late fall and winter seasons. He remembered the significance of the Buffalo Run which is a beautiful natural pathway into the heart of the He Sapa from the southwest. When the great herds of tatanka and all of their individual families and oyate made the big journey through the Buffalo Run every end season then the Lakota would soon follow them. This was the cycle of life that was repeated every year, generation after generation, from the point when time began. Until recently, when the herds were being slaughtered and diminished. The He Sapa was the great food basket for all the peoples. The tatanka would know the proper time to begin their journey from the plains to the Buffalo

Run between the rising hills along the big hilly ring of the Racetrack around He Sapa. The Tatanka Run had been used by the tatanka since the beginning of time, since the origin of the heart of Unci Maka, the He Sapa.

This Run was near the place of origin of life on Grandmother, as it had been when the red man and red woman first walked upon the ground coming from the Wind Cave at the heart of Grandmother Earth. The first human being, having been granted the gift of existence, emerged from the Wind Cave, following the buffalo people, who emerged first. The Lakota and the tatanka have been, and will forever be, joined together as peoples, as beings, as brothers, and as compatible spirits on Grandmother Earth. Tatanka, asked by Creator to go forth upon the surface, became a brother to the first humans, who came after the tatanka. Tatanka, eager to come forth, became a living people on land beneath Grandfather Sky for all time. The two-legged humans, the first red man and first red woman, emerged from the sacred Wind Cave thereafter and joined the world of people on Unci Maka.

It is said by the sacred peoples that the massive network of caves and tunnels beneath He Sapa still contains an abundance of life, peoples, and spirits, and will forevermore. It is all a part of the spiritual energy of the aboriginal land space of He Sapa, within the boundaries of the Great Red Racetrack around its perimeter.

Saved By Bear remembered how the family would visit the warm healing waters of the springs that flowed from the rock openings to the south. These warm waters served as a reliable therapeutic place for meditation, rehabilitation, healing, relaxation, rejuvenation, and spiritual awareness. If the people needed to cleanse and refresh their bodies, souls, and spirits, then they plunged themselves into the warm therapeutic water of the springs, which was always there.

And it was in this secluded, sacred place at the foot of Sun Mountain that the ancient Lakota base camp was one of the old campsites which were set up and used by the people for hundreds of years. This was also one of the sites of the instinctual, ritualistic migration of all the beings, which moved through this area, this portal amid the natural paradise of the great food basket, within the cradle of Grandmother Earth's He Sapa.

The Sun Mountain would be chosen because it had a special natural feature. On the steep wooded mountain's summit was a naturally formed circular meadow of lush grass, with surrounding rock walls to protect it from the wind and weather. And it was high and open. This is a place where the Lakota held their sacred sun dance early each summer to celebrate life, to give thanks to Creator, and to seek guidance for all the families.

The base camp was the perfect place for all of the warriors to gather and collect themselves before embarking on the preparation journey of their lifetime. All was available and provided here. The humans and the horses would be well protected and nourished. There was ample opportunity for planning, prayer, preparation, and spiritual enlightenment. The old camp was close in distance to all the sacred sites that the warriors had to go to, in stages, as part of their sacred duties as decreed by Creator.

When the warriors arrive at their base camp, they are, of course, surrounded by the mountains. But they were also next to a spring, which would provide them and their horses with ample water during their time here. Saved By Bear, Swift Bear and the other five would set up camp for the night. The other group of nine would arrive the next day at the base camp, and then the two groups would become one, according to the spiritual instructions given at Bear Creek.

Upon the second group's arrival at the base camp, the first order of business was to erect shelters. Now that the sixteen had greeted one another, then went out and began to gather willow and chokecherry for the purpose of building two structures similar to a sweat lodge, but with more of a dome shape, large enough to house all of warriors. This is where they planned to sleep, to make and repair their weapons, to confide in one another about the changes to their lifestyle and the raising of a family. Here they would speak of the strength they needed to gather to confront the United States military. They were few, but they were also many, because behind them stood their families and the ancestors' past of prosperity, happiness, and commitment to this life. Standing by them and with them also were all the other peoples of Grandmother Earth, and Unci Maka herself.

Saved By Bear had decided to ride and bring his trusted friend

Wildfire to the preparation, despite knowing that his friend is almost too old to ride into battle. But Wildfire, is a true and trusted friend, so he will accompany the warriors to the He Sapa for the preparation and beyond, when the time came. Wildfire is anxious to be there with his friend at a time when they both need each other's presence. Wildfire will be there in the end to carry his friend away from it all once the instructions would be fulfilled. Swift Bear has done a similar thing. He demanded to bring his own trusted friend Spotted Smoke on this journey. The warriors and horses felt a truer bond because of their inclusion in these important affairs, together.

On the journey to Greasy Grass, the warriors would not need all of the horses they had brought to the He Sapa for the preparation to come, especially the ones that worked very hard to haul the bulk of the heaviest packed burdens to the base camp area in the He Sapa. Four of these horses would not be asked to make the sacred journey west with the warriors. The warriors recalled what they had been told during the sacred ceremonies at Bear Creek. These kind and loyal four-legged ones should be released to roam He Sapa freely, maybe to find and be taken in by one of the wild herds that roamed the southern rim of He Sapa. So that is what must be done.

The packed and loaded contingent of sixteen warriors and their horses led the four ponies down the trail. It was a thankful and somewhat sad journey, the warriors knowing that some of these great representatives of horse nation will not be there with the rest of them at the time of fulfillment of the sacred plan. And yet there was happiness and gratitude just the same, the warriors knowing that these four would find new friends and maybe become part of a new family.

After a half day ride, they came to a low-rise ridge topped with a stand of pine and aspen trees overlooking the vast open plain just north of the warm springs area. It was here that the warriors would let the four horses go. The warriors dismounted, went to the ones they had befriended and become attached to, and gave them each a fond kiss or a pat on the forehead and ears. Eagle Fan took the sage and smudged each of the horses. Each pony bowed their head in recognition of what was being offered for them and their well being.

As the warriors released the ties from around their necks, Eagle

Fan began to sing the honor song for horse nation and these brave, kind souls. It was then, to the west, that Saved By Bear and Wildfire both looked…, and saw him. In the clouds that billowed slightly in the northwest just beyond the highest tree-lined ridge, the image of the White Stone One appeared. The sunlight from behind the warriors glanced off the image in the clouds and gave a glimmering and glow to the horse's head. As Eagle Fan sang, a distant rumble of the Thunder Beings could be heard. In the far distance, Saved By Bear heard. Wildfire also heard, his ears turning forward. Swift Bear and Spotted Smoke heard. They all heard. It was the distant call of horse nation, who were waiting to welcome the four brave ones to the freedom of the herd.

The warriors watched them gallop in the direction of the rim of the far canyon. It felt good. It felt right. It felt sacred. The ponies grew smaller and smaller as they rode toward their new lives.

Silently, with more determination than ever, the warriors climbed up on their horses and started off on their journey north, back to the base camp.

———— ((◊)) ————

The next order of business after erecting the shelters was to start the procedure of cleansing the spirit, the body, and the mind. The first cleansing act was to ride south to the hot springs area, the Mni Kata, where the warriors would spend several days. This sacred region provides enough to eat, as well as spots suitable for prayer and recreation. It is also the place of the healing waters used by our people and many other beings, even the wooly mammoths that once ranged through this area in the not so distant past.

These warm waters of the Mni Kata are medicine. They are also recreational, located within a place our people frequented when coming and going through the He Sapa. Saved By Bear and the warriors will come here to the hot springs as one of their first steps in preparing for the battle, to cleanse their bodies, to strengthen and nourish their bodies, and to ask for spiritual assistance, positive messages, guidance, and for strength. There is a spiritual rejuvenation of the body and spirit to be had by immersing one's body into the warm healing waters. The natural minerals of the *mni* absorb into the warriors' skin, their tissue, their bones, their energy.

Through the water they would gain strength, coming to flow, react, and think as the water does, that element that ever consumes, yet ever gives to, the world that surrounds it.

Mni Kata could always be depended upon as a place to cleanse oneself and wash the bad spirits and bad clutter from one's life. Further south, along the southern edges of the Great Racetrack, were the natural pools of the cool, cascading falls that abutted the vast ranges that were home to the wild mustangs and Appaloosa of horse nation. The horse nation peoples were always a welcome sight to behold for any Lakota at any time in life. A few of them had come to the hot springs while the warriors are there. The reunification of the natons of indigenous man and horse is very meaningful

After the warriors returned home to the base camp from the Mni Kata, they rested a night and then set out for the top of the mountain beside the base camp where they would spend the next several weeks. This was one of their sacred spots, the sun dance ground, a place where a man committed the entirety of his life to his people, and all people.

The warriors found that they needed a certain cottonwood tree, so they asked for the tree's help. When they were given permission, they carefully cut the tree without allowing it to touch the ground. They stripped most of the branches except for some near the top. And then they carried it to the center of the sun dance ground, the harbor circle, while singing the old songs. They then placed the tree into the hole in the center of the harbor while tying their offerings to it. A sacred buffalo skull is used at this point. A fire is made.

The preparation for the sun dance required days of fasting, prayer, and meditation in the sweat lodge. The sun dance itself would last four days. The warriors attached the ties from the tree to the pierced holes in their upper chests. Each had an eagle bone whistle and had purified himself with sage, sweetgrass, and prayer. The drum started. The fire continued to burn. And they danced. Those designated to dance would dance for a long time, and with determination. They would dance in waves, four at a time. While the four danced, the others attended to all other matters as necessary to help and support the dancers. All of these sixteen chosen warriors had already participated in the sun dance previously, so the tradition and the *asking* was familiar to each of them. They danced in the sun and into the night. The drumbeats echoed through the canyons and thumped across the treetops and the stone walls of the sacred He Sapa. The spiritual rhythm beat consistently and soothingly in time with the warriors' steps and prayers. The low thumping of the drumbeat was felt by all beings, who all listened and prayed in unison, knowing that this was being done for them too. The drumbeats and sacred songs would be recorded and forever remembered by the stones and the trees, to be played back at times in the future when prayer and ceremony summoned the old rhythm and spirit.

The flesh that was offered by each warrior was offered so that the people, all peoples, could live and survive. It was also offered for He Sapa, for Unci Maka, and for the life force, the spiritual connection from the physical world to the spirit world. A calling was made, and an *asking* done for help, for courage, for guidance, for strength, for wisdom, for protection, and for the peace, unity, tolerance, and love needed for all peoples to continue into the future.

The warriors would use this sun dance ground as their place for their sweat lodge, to pray, to ask for direction and strength. The time spent here would be a spiritual encounter and a strengthening for every warrior involved. Each had his own unique qualities, his own personality, and each was recognized as a crucial part of the band of warriors who would accomplish our goal. Since each of these chosen warriors, prior to their involvement in this spiritual calling, had already been a sun dancer, this period of sun dancing served as their spiritual confirmation as warriors, as men, as human beings, as citizens of Unci Maka.

When the warriors finished the sun dance ceremony portion of their preparation, they began to make their way to the east. Packing enough to last for a week or so of travel, they got on their horses and headed to the point of origin, the sacred Wind Cave area, where the Lakota first emerged from Grandmother Earth. Here, they prayed to the spirits. They asked the spirits to guide them, and to walk alongside them as they learned and came to understand what would face them in the future. They felt the sacred wind coming from deep within Grandmother, breathing the spirit of life and protection upon their faces and into their spirits.

Here Grandmother Earth spoke directly to each warrior, as war is not entirely a communal affair. It is comprised of individual battles. Each warrior must be proficient and efficient in everything that he does. From the first step to the last step, preparation is vital to survival. The time spent here would strengthen the warriors in these ways. After this period of preparation, the warriors would return to the base camp by Sun Mountain. This was their home now. Soon they would return to the summit of Sun Mountain to spend a few weeks in contemplation, discussion, and preparation.

When the fall season arrives, the time came for Swift Bear to share his spiritual instruction and teaching with the entire group. Swift Bear had been chosen by the Creator when the message and the permission was delivered to the Mnincoju people near the ancient holy site along the Bear Creek. After the first and subsequent powerful spiritual inipi ceremonies held in the lodge, Swift Bear had been named as the warrior responsible for the practical development and implementation of all the various individual and collective maneuvers that the sixteen warriors would learn, practice, and know, and ultimately carry out on the day of deliverance to come.

Swift Bear had been touched by Creator and given specific insight into, knowledge of, and spiritual awareness of the complete battle plan. He had been chosen because of his unique talents and his special ability to see a problem and then use his intellect, his knowledge, and his authentic imagination to quickly and decisively develop solutions so as to result in an optimal outcome. His spiritual presence and the fact that he was a heyoka also played a significant part in his being granted the honor and tasked with the duty of serving in such an important capacity to save his people, to save his home, and to save the Lakota spirit.

The sacred message was ultimately delivered to Swift Bear and Saved By Bear simultaneously in the sweat lodge along Bear Creek soon after the summer season of 1874, when the military group invaded the sacred He Sapa and found gold there. Swift Bear received the message and instructions as if it were etched in symbols upon his very spirit. He remembered feeling the incredible energy within his chest and running through his body. He recognized it. He knew this feeling. It was one similar to that which had come upon him in hanbleceya and during the sun dance. It was the pure energy of Wakan Tanka. It was the hand of the Creator, drawing an immaculately vivid picture for him, in his mind and within his spirit, as if his eyes did not even need to view it. He felt and absorbed the message and sacred instructions, more than he heard it.

But the experience was somewhat different. This spiritual message strongly settled in Swift Bear's left arm. He felt the energy gather as if pulsing, and then it glowed within his flesh and blood, moving along the veins in his left arm. The energy began at his bicep and moved down to his elbow, where it turned and rose within his forearm, and then slowly, precisely, and steadily moved toward his wrist, then his hand, then his palm, and into his fingers, nearly blazing at the tip of his index finger. The warm pulsing energy beat steadily in time with the beat of his heart and made the blood within the palm of his hand tingle, as if he were holding a presence in his open palm. He remembered looking down at his arm and seeing the yellowish-gold pulsing energy surrounding his left arm as if encasing it.

It was at this moment that the image of the group of warriors, including he and Saved By Bear, began to form within his mind. And he saw a sequence of events begin to happen, so clear and so intricate that it was if he had seen it many times before and many lives ago. It was as if he were being shown a moving set of images of the warriors moving from one point to another, and of taking a stance and waiting for another to move, all in a precise collection of individuality and synchronicity. Then he saw the place, and the terrain, and the sky and the grass and the river, and the other participants outside of a golden aura. He recognized where it was, he recognized why it was, and he recognized what it was.

Swift Bear, the courageous heyoka, the proud Mnincoju son of his ancestors, knew his time had come. His calling had been made. His duty was set out ahead of him. Within the sacred pathway lay his destiny—and that of his people and Unci Maka. He bent his head back and absorbed the vision. As he did so, amid the darkness of the lodge, he stared at the ceiling, the eight-pointed star, and saw the magnificent Milky Way, the Trail of the Spirits, the trail of his ancestors. He knew he was not alone. He knew he would not be alone on the battlefield. He would never be alone.

The Old Stone Warriors

When Swift Bear gathered the warriors at the base camp, he was eager to begin playing his part in preparing them all. He told them that they would travel high up to the meeting place at the foot of the oldest of the Old Stone Warriors across the deep valley just south of Owl's Nest. It would be there, at that site of old solitude-based camps, where the sixteen would hold their next gathering to hear and receive their specific individual instructions. The actual placement, direction, movement, timing, sequence, order, and their collective accompaniment which will comprise the detailed plans of what was to happen when they faced the man known as Custer and his army. Swift Bear would teach the fifteen warriors as the Creator and the spirits had taught him…and had showed him. All were eager to visit the Old Ones.

From the base camp, the warriors would ride their horses, bringing all the horses that would go to the Greasy Grass, so that all could be there to listen, to see, and feel the instruction as well. Sixteen warriors and their horses would ride for two days and two nights, riding past the large Bear Paw rock and higher up, to reach the high open meadow along the stone-pillared protection of the Old Stone Warriors. (some of the whites, later, would refer to them as the "Needles"). It is a steep and rocky climb among the deeply carved passageways between the stony protection of the gray colored rim of the tall, majestic and comforting stone columns. The pine, ash, and birch trees along the way seem to serve as the nurturing undergrowth for the brave Old Ones that lived upon Unci Maka once, long ago. These Old Ones were granted the honor and the duty by Creator to forever stand guard over the sacred center, the *canté*, the heart of Grandmother's He Sapa, forever looking after the He Sapa and protecting the mountains and all the beings that existed here, and respected Unci Maka. The Old Ones' duty is to protect the He Sapa from harm and to alert the beings that were able to help, that help was needed. The Old Ones have been sending messages to the people for some time now with all of the unsettling activities and negative energy seeking to infiltrate the He Sapa lately.

The warriors and their ponies arrive in the late afternoon of the second day and begin to set up the camp that they would keep for the next moon cycle. There would be plenty of food, and they would get their water from a nearby natural spring coming from a high table. There was abundant room to run and ride, to maneuver, and to scout if necessary. The formation of the stone columns nearly made a half circle, like the crescent moon before it started to fill and become full. If one looked closely at the Old Stone Warriors as they stood tall and proud, shoulder to shoulder, most facing west and north at this point, one could make out the noble stoic faces, the deep-set eyes and jawbones, the unique Lakota nose, and the strong, graceful backs and chests. In and among the stone warriors, also standing guard and watching, are large gray granite wanbli. One of these wanbli, a large dark gray, sits perched at the southern edge of the rim of the column of warriors, and faces back, overlooking the campsite vicinity.

One of the most intriguing and valuable features of some of the spired warriors, the ones nearest the northeasternmost rim of their area of protection, was their large vertical open walls of solid gray stone. This stone served as the perfect instruction board for teaching what was needed to be taught. It was also the area to which both Saved By Bear and Swift Bear had come many times before, when they wished to connect to the stone guardians and with Creator. One could walk right up to the stone wall base of the biggest stone warrior there next to the old campfire circle and touch him. Saved By Bear and Swift Bear often came up directly to the wall at the warrior's base and put their chests and faces, with heads turned, directly against the solid gray granite of the wall, standing flat against the stone warrior as if hugging an old friend. And they would feel his energy, his strength, his integrity, his commitment. With both arms outstretched and fully connected to the Old One, they would speak through the natural energy that flows through all things. And they would pray with the stone warrior, with them all, thanking the stone ones for their protection. The two friends always left that place feeling better, taking some of that solid fortified positive energy home with them.

Swift Bear will be the director of everything that is done here. He will be the connection to the Old Stone Warriors. He will be the one conversing with the Old Ones in a spiritual fashion. This is the place where he has been asked to be the leader. His concern is for the other fifteen warriors, not for himself. He is committed to listen, to understand, and to help them come to learn the strategy of approach.

The Old Stone Warriors have been through these types of things before. Each of them had already proven in his own time, long, long ago in his own generation on Earth, that he was valuable and needed, and also respected. That is why each of these Old Stone Warriors sits in the cluster of the Older Ones, why each one of the Old Ones was chosen in his own right to be one of the sacred guardians and protectors of the sacred He Sapa, why each of the Old Stone Warriors was granted the honor and sacred duty of being forever present.

At this time, all sixteen of the warriors will be addressed. Each will be asked to come forward, to bare himself, to show himself to these Old Stone Warriors so that they can view him and understand him, give him what is needed, strengthen him where he needs to be strengthened, and most of all, support him in what he is about to do. That is the warrior way. The warrior does not condemn you or disassociate from you because you do not listen to him or agree with his opinion. Everything is on an equal plane in the spirit realm. These Old Stone Warriors have volunteered to sit here forever for the people. This particular time period will be spent with the sixteen warriors sitting upon this portion of the mountain, talking to one another in little groups, sharing with each other, eating together, doing everything that they can to strengthen one another, and talking about life and the changes, the wants, and the desires of the individual. The Old Stone Warriors will listen carefully, as they had the same concerns in their day as the human beings have now. This will be a time when the individual warrior will come forward. This is the portion that is imperative for the sixteen warriors to understand so they can execute what they must do according to the spiritual instructions.

When Swift Bear had the warriors form a semicircle on the morning of the fourth day since leaving the base camp below, he also had the fifteen face the one hundred-foot vertical stone wall of the biggest Old Stone Warrior. It was then that Swift Bear started speaking of the details of the coming battle. Closeby, but to the west of the gathering site of the teacher and his pupils, was another that had come to watch. He stood silently on the peaked ledge overlooking the warriors, and listening intently. His dark fur, keen ears and eyes, and his lean build, showed off his ability to be a warrior in his own right. He was known by the Old Stone ones as Sungila Sapa, Black Fox, and he was here to learn as well. Swift Bear spoke and gestured about the spiritual instructions to this courageous, honorable group, of old, and young warriors…. stone, and flesh, alike. This is how the instructions would be delivered to the warriors over the next several weeks.

Swift Bear used the stone wall as his buffalo hide canvas, as if he were creating a portrait for the other fifteen warriors. He used blackened wood from the fire and some of the colors from the nearby stones and trees, to diagram what he needed to explain. He had joint sessions with all fifteen present. He sometimes counseled and instructed a warrior one-on-one. He instructed the lead-in battle group separately, informing them of their specific movements and advising them on the matter of decision making. He gathered the riders with their horses, because in the moments to come, warrior and horse would need to move together and act with precision, as only warrior and horse know how to. He diagrammed the expected and known placement of the men, the horses, the weapons, the ridges, the ravines, and the sagebrush, noting the slope of the hill, the smell and sound of battle, and most importantly, the existence and presence of the spiritual pathway.

When Swift Bear spoke of the spiritual pathway, he was quite vivid in his description of what it would look like and feel like. He mentioned why all the warriors needed to trust in the spiritual pathway, trust themselves, and trust each other. Many times, Swift Bear could be seen standing to face the Old Stone Warrior and leaning fully into him, face first. On many other occasions, Swift Bear showed the other fifteen warriors what he had felt, seen, and experienced when the spiritual energy moved through him in the inipi at the time he had received his instructions. He explained the energy moving through his left arm, and he spoke to the warriors about the plan, the goal, and the pathway. He would turn and show them with his left arm bent, leaning flat up against his old stone friend, with palm open and fingers extended. And the blood in his veins pulsed, as if knowing it for the first time.

One night after the sun had set and night fell, the coldness of the high mountain air brought a chill to the warriors. They were still camping amid the Old Stone Warriors. As always, they gathered around the main campfire. This was a time to tell stories and to share personal life experiences with each other. The Lakota could hear more about the Dakota's change in life since the Minnesota events. The Nakota could report about things along the Big River. The Lakota could share the solemn experiences with the further encroachment of the whites. But it was not always serious or solemn. There were also times of sharing joyful and emotional things about friends, families, pets, situations, and loves—and also jokes and funny predicaments.

Many Thunder and Touches Heart were chosen by Creator at the time of the *asking*, and the spiritual permission was granted for them to serve as the warriors' scouts on horseback. They were both designated to protect the *bundle*, the *bundle keeper*, and all the horses. They were chosen because of their special talents and gifts in the natural ways of scouting, tracking, watching, and knowing. They had the ability to lead the warriors where they needed to go without being seen. It was a serious, solemn business, and an important role to be given. However, the solemnity of this role did not stop Touches Heart, the younger of the two, from ribbing his friend Many Thunder in a way that only someone who knew him well could do.

On this evening, as the sixteen warriors sat around the fire before sleeping, Touches Heart decided to share some lightheartedness with the rest when he saw Many Thunder get up from the fire to walk into the trees. Knowing that Many Thunder would be walking among the trees in the vicinity, Touches Heart nudged Blue Stone's arm and pointed toward Many Thunder as he began to disappear at the tree line. "Watch this," he said. Touches Heart got up from the opposite side of the fire, silently walked back to a large pine tree, and hid himself behind the tree so no one could see him. The warriors sitting around the tree looked on with anticipation and uncertainty. Touches Heart then raised his voice and called out, "Many Thunder! Can you see me now?"

From the opposite direction, well beyond the tree line, came a voice: "Of course. I can see you hiding behind that tree!"

"You always behave like you have eyes in the back of your head!" Touches Heart replied from behind the big pine.

Many Thunder said, "I do!"

All the warriors looked at each other and burst out laughing. Touches Heart reappeared from behind the big pine, doubling over and chuckling. "See, I told you!"

Many Thunder did indeed have some uncanny and valuable gifts. He had the ability to know where someone was even if he did not see them. He could sense and feel, without his eyes. His vision extended beyond that which was brought forth by his eyesight. Although they could joke about it, the warriors knew that the gifts of the one were intended to help the many on this sacred journey, to fulfill this sacred duty. And all of the gifts were appreciated. They were all important. They were all needed. So it was that the Creator had provided each of them with many gifts, and had brought them together to share these gifts in the way that would be of the most benefit to the others. Most significantly, Creator had brought them together to honor their spiritual commitment at the time when it counted most.

———◉———

Many of us have all been told that many of the holy men and Dog Man warriors are able to assume the shape of anything they choose. This is true. The ability to shape-shift is something that is taught and learned. It is a gift from Creator, a gift of protection, perseverance, and survival. This gift was never intended by Creator to be used in evil ways or abused by those who possessed it.

The gift arises from the energy and spiritual connection between a human being and the earth; between a human and an animal; between a human and a tree, a stone, the sagebrush.

Witnesses say that the shape-shifter has the ability to become invisible to the human eye. However, this is not true in terms of physics. The shifter only becomes able not to be seen, having gained the ability to pass unnoticed by those who do not take the time or put forth the effort to see.

The shifter assumes the essence of those around him. Shifting one's shape is a method of communicating with the deer, the pine tree, the boulder, and the sage. The one gives permission to the other, and to the next. Each participant, in turn, gives of itself or himself or herself. It is like becoming the ground, becoming the sage. This gift of being able to camouflage oneself in this way would prove to be very useful on the way to the Greasy Grass, and within the world that awaited the warriors there.

After the moon had completed its cycle and was full again, Swift Bear finished up his instruction with the chosen warriors and with the horses that would go to the Greasy Grass. Now that he had gone over the detailed precise movements and expectations of each and every chosen participant in this spiritual event, he felt confident that everyone knew their role inside and out. So they broke camp at the base of the Old Stone Warriors.

Eagle Fan gave the Old Stone Warriors and their friends a final blessing. When this was finished, Swift Bear said "toksa ake" to the Old Ones. He and Saved By Bear gave the oldest one the spiritual hug they always gave him, with arms extended. Then all sixteen mounted up and started their trek back to the base camp.

As the line of warriors and horses trailed away from the granite spires near the south end of the rim, the warriors heard the low humming voices of a group of men, very old men, singing. The slow methodical plodding of the horses' hooves upon the rocky trail echoed and played along to the sound of ancient times and ancient alliances. As Swift Bear and Saved By Bear rode past the huge gray granite wanbli perched on the shoulder of one of the Old Ones near the edge, they looked up. The old stone bird appeared to nod in a graceful and meaningful way. They both knew that there were so many beings in addition to them that were hoping and believing that this preparation would work. It was clear to the two friends that what they and the other fourteen warriors were doing meant a great deal to more than just the human beings, or the Lakota in particular. What they were doing truly was meant for the survival of us all.

⚫

The sixteen warriors returned home to the base camp, where they would stay for the remainder of the fall season in preparation for wintertime. They would spend the late fall season hunting, gathering, and doing many of the chores that would have been taken care of by others had they been accompanied by their families. But now, each had to assume responsibilities that were perhaps new and unfamiliar, but that were vital nonetheless. And in doing these unfamiliar tasks, they learned the lesson that one cannot be a warrior all the time, that sometimes one needed to be a common man and take care of common daily needs.

Combining all of these things, the warriors learned to exist as a unique separate group of human beings, a very close, concise, unified, cohesive, cooperative, determined, functioning spiritual entity unto themselves.

During the winter months, subsistence would be a prime focus. Grandmother Earth had blessed the sacred He Sapa to be a natural sanctuary for all life. She created shelter and warm zephyrs of breeze that took away much of the harshness of the usual winter season. This is part of why this area was always a safe haven for people of all kinds, including the Lakota. Another important point to remember is that the spiritual side of life would be a constant here. Eagle Fan had been appointed as the bundle keeper and the leader of ceremonies. He would run the inipi for the warriors and would pray directly to Creator for anything they needed. That was his task. The warrior that he was, was also very powerful on the spiritual side. This is the reason he had been chosen to serve in this capacity for the people.

The wintertime activities would involve many facets of life. The warriors would eat and sleep in a communal fashion, never forgetting the reason they are there. They might get distracted at times with the affairs of the past, but there will be an ever present reminder that they need to accept those things and put them aside in order to accomplish a new deed, which will not be accomplished if they do not use prayer and ceremony daily. This is the part of life proving that as Lakota we originated from the spirit. We must fight for that spirit. We must believe in that spirit. And by the warriors' actions and their potential success, we have our rightful place to continue the commitment to Creator.

Of concern to the warriors was the fact that they had to be very diligent about maintaining their horses, having to make sure that anywhere they stayed had a meadow with ample grass, as you cannot take a starving horse into the battle and expect him to perform well. These horses would be taken care of as well as the warriors took care of each other. Being brothers in this endeavor, the warriors and their horses had to rely upon each other and each other's life forces to accomplish the goal for being here. So, many things were beginning to occur. The entities, the forces of nature, became parents and teachers. The warriors recognize that they are the youngest of all the people they are surrounded by in the Circle of life and in nature. They listened and they learned, doing what they were guided to do. The rocks, the stone people, gave them their wisdom. The grass and the plants gave them their subsistence, providing for their bodily needs. The air and the water allowed them to survive, to continue each day. One must always look at the things one is fortunate to have, things that remain constant. This is the Creator's way.

The spiritual part of this upcoming battle, and the spiritual place in the Lakota's lives from the beginning of the time of the human being, will be focused upon the spiritual existence, which is first and foremost. We are spirit before we are conceived and born. We are spirit before the time frame involved here. Our spirit was created when the first breath was sent out our way, when we knew no other way to exist than to spiritually connect. And we live through the messages of that spiritual connection and practice.

For many of the new people, it is just the opposite, or backward. They know very little of the spirit. They only believe that a person's spirit is to be nourished at any cost. Many of the new people do not believe or know that all things are actually connected to the spirit. The new people have religion and religious belief, which can become spiritual, but which many times is not spiritual. Good-hearted people can live good lives when they are part of an organized religion, but many use the organization of religion itself as a means or justification to pursue selfish goals involving greed, supremacy, or domination. The indigenous peoples and the white settlers had two very conflicting philosophies as to how people should exist. This battle between them was to be guided by the spiritual presence, which would help the warriors understand how the battle would be operated, how it would be instituted, where Custer would end up, and what path he would follow. These things were all preordained for Saved By Bear, Swift Bear, and the other warriors. Without spirit, we could not have communicated. We would not have been strong enough to uphold the belief system that they had a right to live by.

In the early winter season, the warriors are sitting around the base camp conversing and laughing, taking some time out from the responsibilities they were tasked with to enjoy themselves. To one side of the group of warriors, two blurs shoot through the pines along the tree line. When the warriors look all at once, they see it was a young buffalo bull. And it is also Buffalo Horn. The two are running side by side amid the pine trees as if playing a game, thoroughly enjoying themselves. Buffalo Horn is so swift and agile that he moves just like this young buffalo bull. And together they are like music, synchronized. The pounding sound of the young bull's hooves mingle with the sounds of Buffalo Horn's moccasins stirring up the loose leaves and pine needles. They appear to smile at each other. They are a magnificent, joyful sight to see. This is Buffalo Horn's gift, as he has a very strong connection to the animal, the other beings, other than the human being. It is his place to bring peace and harmony with him wherever he goes. It is his gift. He has known this young buffalo bull for weeks now. The young bull has been visiting and watching the camp, very curious and wondering why this group of warriors has gathered for so long in his home territory. His people are used to seeing the women and children, but there is a difference here that he is observing. But the young buffalo bull is also associating spiritually with Buffalo Horn, so he now knows the reason the warriors are here. He helps Buffalo Horn celebrate in the wonderful gifts he has been given. Like his brother, the human being, the young buffalo will enjoy their time spent together.

Owl's Nest

In the early spring of 1876, the warriors, continuing to work on their individual and collective preparation, traveled from site to site. The last site of preparation, which the sixteen warriors would visit once the snow melted, would be the Owl's Nest. The steps the warriors will take at the sacred Owl's Nest will enhance the skills they gained at all of the previous sites where they gathered together and gave to one another. This place is where their wisdom and knowledge will be applied.

The purpose of this time spent at the Owl's Nest is basically to give the warriors the strength of *self*, to give them the knowledge that they are very capable and they know how to react, how to put their best foot forward. Each step that they will take in the coming battle will be a matter of life or death. They must understand the wisdom of the warrior. This is the gift to them.

⸺⸻●⸻⸺

Owl's Nest is the highest natural peak east of the Continental Divide of the Rocky Mountains on Turtle Island. It is significant to the Lakota, one of the sacred sites among six others that correlate with the seven stars of the Pleiades system. The sacred significance of Owl's Nest is that it was used particularly by the people for the purpose of praying or having a ceremony for the purpose of receiving visions and messages. It was a place of sacred energy.

The owl is a very special being and a very revered people according to the Lakota and others. The warrior society known as the Owl Feather Headdress Warriors honored the significance of the owl brother. The owl represents wisdom and knowledge, and is a messenger. The owl's presence can bring solace, wisdom, and confidence. The owl also has the gift of silent flight. He can fly undetected to all around him. He is a night flier, a night hunter. But as a messenger, the owl, if he appears for several nights in a row, hooting by your lodge or camp, he may be giving you a warning that someone is going to pass on to the spirit world. The owl is good and should not be feared.

Owl's Nest is the highest peak of Grandmother Earth's He Sapa. It is a place of worship, prayer, and sanctuary for those in need, or those assisting others in need. It has always been available to us upon request, and sometimes it has requested our presence. The Owl's Nest is widely known by many of the indigenous people. There is also a great stone owl that stands and watches over the sacred Deer Medicine Rock in Montana Territory. That great owl bears the markings of Spirit Horse and is the premonition of his death. Spirit Horse would see his death come to pass in the near future.

When you stand at the summit of Owl's Nest, you are able to look 360 degrees around yourself. You look out at the beautiful wonders of Grandmother Earth and Grandfather Sky. You may be looking through your eyes, but you are seeing with more than your eyes. You are seeing with your spirit and your heart. And when you are on the summit of this sacred mountain, looking across the natural terrain at the stone formations, the beautiful forest, and the many peaks in the distance, you can't help but almost be transformed from a human being into a spirit. It seems there is somebody who is looking at something in front of you, as if you were a three-year-old child. You feel the presence of the spirit dominating your whole being to the point that you are almost at a loss for words. The Owl's Nest often causes you to set aside your natural tendency to analytically approach what you are viewing. In this sense, it magnifies your senses, naturally and spiritually. It is a place where that which clutters the mind has little chance to invade, to pervert, twist, or distort the truth. When you have your feet planted on the sacred soil of the sacred mountain, the energy rises through your being and permeates through your spirit. When there is a message to be received while you are in the presence of such natural beauty and abundance, that message goes directly into your heart, into your spirit, without the clutter of the analysis of the mind.

Many times, many generations of the Lakota found themselves, either by will, destiny, purpose, or intent, climbing up to the summit of a sacred mountain such as Owl's Nest. This is the sacred peak that the young brave named Black Elk described in his sacred vision of 1862, when he was only nine years old.

In the young Black Elk's vision, he was visited by the Wakinyan and taken to the Grandfathers, the spiritual beings of the sacred directions. After they spoke to him, he was taken to the center of Grandmother Earth, to the central mountain of Unci Maka. This was Hinhan Kaga, the place where owls are made: Owl's Nest. Here Black Elk said the following:

> And while I stood there I saw more than I can tell and understood more than I saw; for I was seeing in a sacred manner the shapes of all things in the spirit, and the shape of all shapes as they must live together like one being. And I saw that the sacred hoop of my people was one of many hoops that made one Circle, wide as daylight and as starlight, and in the center grew one mighty flowering tree

to shelter all the children of one mother and one father.

And I saw that it was holy.

Through his vision, he came to understand that it was his destiny to help his people, the Lakota. Black Elk became a holy man who did help his people. His face now naturally appears as the first face on a mountain east of Owl's Nest, as a permanent tribute to his deeds. His eternal connection to He Sapa and to Owl's Nest will be represented here for all time.

Also, many times a person finds himself in the presence of other human beings on top of the sacred mountain. At these moments, the conversations and the messages shared among the humans can also be magnified, underscoring what it means to be Lakota, what it means to be a human being, what it means to life itself. In the context of communicating a truthful message to someone who may be viewing this vista for the first time in their physical life, is that a message may be received more openly, more honestly, more truthfully, and more easily, while standing or praying on top of this sacred mountan. The Lakota would believe that maybe all of the He Sapa and their lands would one day all be seen and declared as sacred, so as to let the truth and the honesty of a good life in a good way, flow uninterrupted.

To understand the sacred importance of Owl's Nest in He Sapa, we have to go back to a time before there was the human being, any human being. This place was originally given a life force by Unci Maka, Grandmother Earth. She was filled with stone. She had her gifts ready to propagate life according to Creator. But this first presence of Grandmother Earth and Turtle Island could not be complete without the Pleiades, the constellation of the water planets, the Seven Sisters. Because water is life. Creator spoke to the Pleiadians, our relations. Many of us were star people before coming to Earth and becoming a human being. Creator asked these spirits of the water worlds to come and to live as human beings, and to call themselves the red man and red woman.

As the Pleiadian spiritual energy of creation left the Pleiades, that energy came to Earth and instantly began to bring forth life on Unci Maka. First to appear were the rudimentary fundamental life forms, which evolved over billions of years into the various different species and forms of life we see today. Eventually, the human being emerged from Wind Cave. Owl's Nest and the Pleiades were even foretold and brought with us. Each constellation had a sacred name that we today carry forth in reverence and respect. The people would practice ceremony to stay in touch. We practice daily living so as to try to be examples of the goodness and wonderment in life that the Pleiadians gifted to us in a spiritual sense. Having come here to Earth, we are water people.

You can always tell when a tribe or indigenous nation is of Pleiadian origin by considering how they name themselves, what their cultural is like, how they live, and what they believe. The Pleiadians will always have the word *water*, or *mni*, as part of their identifying name. We are the *Mnincoju*. Tribes of Pleiadian origin will normally surround themselves with settlements, and their places of nomadic activity will be near water. These are the first of the human beings to truly be connected at the beginning. Pleiadians include beings other than human beings. Pleiadians obviously came with the water and were of different species, assuming different shapes and forms at different times. The Lakota came near the end of the creational gift of Creator. The human being is the youngest of the species. The human being will always be the child of Creation.

Owl's Nest towers over the other naturally beautiful wonders of the He Sapa. We as a people, as the descendents of the Pleiades, the descendents of the Lakota, Dakota, Nakota, and other related tribal peoples, have a responsibility to continue this union of earth and water, because there is nothing on this planet that can continue to exist without this union and this presence. Throughout the millions of years accounted for in oral histories told, and heard, flowing down through to the time of the emergence of human beings, it always has been essential that we recognize what is underfoot and what is supplied to keep us on foot: the two basics of earth and water. When we combine these, life can be sustained, and there can then be planned activity, prosperity, and generational succession. This is what Creator wants for us, not only to be, but also to live, and to show those future generations to come, that this is a good way to live. The Pleiadians are very important across Unci Maka. And they are even more important right now because of the turmoil and distress that Grandmother Earth is in. To put things into context, a human being has a right to live but also has a responsibility to make sure that all life can live. This is an undying spiritual presence of our connections with the stars, from a beginning long before many could even remember or fathom in their imagination.

From the peak of Owl's Nest, when the sixteen warriors each arrive at the summit, they will be able to see in all directions. One of the closest sites they will see, will be Bear Butte, Mato Paha, to the north. The warriors had passed by that sacred site on their way into the He Sapa the previous spring. If successful in carrying out the plan for which they have been given permission at the Greasy Grass, the warriors will visit Mato Paha in the end. At Mato Paha, everything that they have prepared for will be laid upon the Bear itself, for the medicine, for the strength, for the love, and for the commitment. Then, the warriors will leave Bear Butte, knowing that they will have given everything humanly possible to change the course of destiny according to the spiritual plan and their instructions, as long as the spirits continue to guide them.

At the Owl's Nest, Eagle Fan will run the entire affair for all the warriors. When they arrive at the base of the Owl's Nest mountain, they will set up a temporary camp at a stream area several miles below the summit. There they will have enough water for themselves and their horses, a bit of grass, and also seclusion. Once everything needed for their stay is set up, they will take a break. Before sundown, two of the warriors will take Eagle Fan to the top of the Owl's Nest mountain, where he will prepare himself and the area, much like one would prepare for hanbleceya. Eagle Fan will prepare for, and then perform, certain things for the other warriors so that they may grow in personal strength and offer any questions they may have for the asking process. The warriors who take Eagle Fan to the top will not stay there with him. Eagle Fan will stay on the summit through the night, beginning his preparation for the coming morning. The warriors will return to their temporary camp below.

As morning approaches, it will still be dark. The warriors will rise. The four who had been chosen on the first day to be the first group to go up to the summit will ready themselves. Saved by Bear and Swift Bear will both be among this first group of warriors. The four will take their horses and will ride with another warrior, a fifth, about halfway up the mountain. Here they will leave their horses, who will be tended to by the fifth warrior, for the entire time that they remain at the summit, the reason for this being that the warriors may at some point be needed down below. If such a situation arises, then they will not have to run down the entire mountain. They will be able to come to their horses, mount up, and ride down the mountain to assist their fellow warriors. Once the warriors reach the midpoint of the trail, the horse drop-off point, the sun will begin its climb. They will now continue on foot to join Eagle Fan at the top.

The warriors climb up the rocky trail to the point where the tall gray stones gleam with glints of sparkling gold flecks, like a glittering sheen on the high stone face. The tall gray granite billows up with outcroppings and rounded edges just near the summit. Saved By Bear reaches his hand out to touch the stone, to feel its warmth, its strength, and its honor. Inyan, the stone, is the oldest of the old people on Grandmother Earth. Inyan is everywhere near the top.

Saved By Bear feels the soothing fit of his moccasins upon his feet, stretching his toes upward. The soles of his feet grasp the rocks without pain. It is a gripping sensation, much like his brother the big horn sheep must feel when his hardened hoof grabs the crevice of the rock steadily and sure.

Moving forward, Saved By Bear feels the tendons in his shins burn as they expand to allow his feet to keep striving for the next available stone near the top of the rocky ledge. His elbow brushes the granite surface and scratches the outside of his buckskin sleeve. It breaks open, emitting a whiff of freshly exposed buckskin, which he recognizes, as his shirt used to smell that way when it was first made and worn. He misses the times of being new. Somehow, over time, things wear out, get old. This is true for all things. Even human beings.

The summit of the highest peak is the place to welcome the Thunder Beings, the Wakinyan, through an old doorway between the worlds.

The group of warriors ascend the last craggy ladder of rocks before reaching the top of the mountain. Just to the north-northwest, Saved By Bear sees Eagle Fan and the flat grassy circular area between the smaller ridges of stone walls facing north toward the Mato Paha. He knows that this grassy area is where the ceremony will be performed.

This is the mountain peak of Hinhan Kaga, the place of the Owl's Nest, the highest of the sacred sites. Mato Tipila, to the northwest, Mato Paha to the northeast, and Hinhan Kaga form a sacred triad representing the head of the buffalo bull. The Old Stone Warriors loomed to the southeast, standing at attention to guard the He Sapa and its inhabitants for millions of years past, and for all time. The great stone eagle is perched near to them on their southern shoulders. A flat stone mountain formation lies pure and clean to the east, the Six Grandfathers. The air smells clear and energetic, to blend with the high spirits in the hearts of the warriors.

Again, the ceremony to the spirits was intended to take place atop Owl's Nest. This place, this mountain amid the sacred He Sapa, is the closest to the clouds and the heavens. It is a place of vision, of prayer, of meeting, of hanbleceya. The trek to the high places had been made by the people for thousands of years. This was the mountaintop to which many of the elders and young alike had come on missions, on quests for vision, to pray, to seek answers, to seek help, to ask, and to seek and receive permission.

It can be a long, hard climb to the top if one is not motivated by prayer, by vision, or by the cannumpa. If the meaning and purpose behind the journey up to the stone heights of Owl's Nest is motivated by one's desire to speak with Creator or the spirits there, then the journey can be easy. It can be quick and less burdensome, because under such circumstances, one's legs and lungs are carried by the wings of Wakan Tanka, who assist in the journey. It is at times of burden and sorrow when the task may be slow and tedious. The spiritual weight upon one's shoulders sometimes makes a difference. Even if the burden is heavy on the heart and the spirit, the person carrying it can come to this place gifted by Creator and undergo a cleansing of spirit.

As the five warriors arrive at the summit, they are greeted by their brother and spiritual leader Eagle Fan. With a smile and confidence, he is willing to do for the warriors what he has been asked to do in his spiritual way.

Eagle Fan is a strong and a committed man. He is also a man who wants what these other warriors want. He knows that the role he is to play is crucial to their accomplishment and performance. So he will ask that the wisdom and the knowledge be opened to the warriors and self as they prepare to spend the entire day communing with everything that has ever been known on Turtle Island. The warriors will ask questions: "How are we going to perform? How are we going to feel? How are we going to react?" The strengths that each possesses will be stressed. Encouragement will be given by the spirits in attendance for this affair. These men will find self, and the reason why they have been chosen to be a part of the group. Each one will go through this in the coming days.

As the warriors ready for their first day atop Owl's Nest, Eagle Fan greets the sun in prayer and song. After this is finished, he begins smudging everybody to purify them. The warriors then take sage and bitterroot into their mouths to permit them to communicate honestly and with clarity, to speak openly and freely with one another from the human side and the spiritual side, as a connection must be established and trusted. These things are imperative given the deeds that each individual is being asked to do. During the day, the warriors will spend time in seclusion in order to receive. They will also spend individual time with Eagle Fan, asking questions and hearing any answers that have been given. He is there as the go-between and the provider of strength, courage, and commitment for the warriors. His prayers are very, very strong. The beings of the mountaintop pay attention, as they have not seen a human gathering in a while, and now they know why. The human being is suffering and hurting, and so are their own people. The other beings are watching and listening. These include the bighorn sheep, the white goats, the deer, the elk, the fox and the chipmunks, the badgers, the skunks, the rabbits, the cougars, the owls, and of course, the red tailed hawks and the wanbli. The warriors and Eagle Fan are also praying for the welfare of all kind on Grandmother Earth—Unci Maka and all her children.

The new people's society has had an effect, particularly with regard to the abuse of animals, plants, and such, which has heightened the conflict between cultures. Take wanbli, the eagle, for example. The eagle has always been a special sacred being to us. It delivers our prayers, watches over us, and shows courage and strength when a necessary conflict ensues. At the same time, eagles are caring, loving, compassionate beings that raise their families. Never to be hunted or killed. The symbol of these sacred spiritual beings, however, has been stolen and corrupted by the white Europeans. The eagle is on the white man's dollar bill and all of currency denominations. Whereas before, the wanbli was the being we called upon to hear and deliver our prayers and provide us with inner strength, now the image of the wanbli sits on the dollar bill, which is not often used properly. Given the circulation of currency, the image of the eagle is more visible to the white world and some other worlds than it is to the indigenous tribal people's world. This usurping of the image of the eagle is a breaking of the spirit and the culture of the Lakota. This breaking of the spirit is furthered by the white people's taking of our lands and resources, which allows them to amass more money, and by their imposing of taxes.

The warriors, on the other hand, seek to include significant beings in our life. We need to make sure that there is a parallel to our own lives so that we don't forget the service that we ask of them or the dependence that we have on them. Take the buffalo for example. To the Lakota, the buffalo is a major symbol of communal gatherings and of the management and maintenance of family units. Buffalo have the same feelings that humans have. They are beings that must be portrayed realistically. There would have been no battle and there would have been no people—there would have been nothing—had we not been able to access and utilize the tatanka people's wisdom and knowledge. The Lakota people respected the spiritual presence and the rituals, the individual parts of our sacred world.

The warriors are going to immerse themselves in the practice of asking, and are going to follow the directions that come from Creator as a result. Their time spent in He Sapa will be entirely of a spiritual nature. This is what the warriors and all the families agreed upon. It was agreed that we would fight this battle with the white man because of our belief in the sacredness of our life, our ceremonies, our He Sapa, Unci Maka, and our precious sites of sacredness. All of these matters have been a part of the preparation in this year before the ultimate battle. We want the world to understand that there is a preparation for the spirit, even in times of war, and that there is also a spiritual reward once you have performed according to your belief system and are satisfied with how you have gone about it.

Back up on the summit of Owl's Nest, the day moves forward. The warriors experience the most wonderful but also the most terrifying situations, visions, and dreams of their lifetimes. They believe that they will make a difference not only on the day of the coming battle but also in each day to come. Their optimism and tasks, and their tremendous support of life, will give them strength for the future.

As the day on top of Owl's Nest comes to a close, Eagle Fan addresses the warriors as men, first as sons and grandsons, then as husbands and spouses, and then as brothers and uncles. They play many roles for the people now. This is why it is vital that they develop the wisdom and knowledge to be successful in the upcoming battle. Not only will they be fighting for themselves and out of their own willingness to be warriors in defense of the people and their ways, but also they will be representing every man, woman, and child at this battle. They needed to understand what a child would feel, how a child would react to such torment and such denial. But they also need to remember that the mind is the primary reason they are on this mountaintop of wisdom and knowledge, this mountain named after the sacred owl and her nest. They need to control their emotions, their hurt, their pains, and their anger; otherwise, they will fail.

At the end of this day, the first wave of warriors come down from Owl's Nest Peak and go back to the temporary camp, feeling such pride in the position that they now have assumed. They now understood that they are the people. They are the word and the deed and the life of the people. They have committed themselves, from this day forward, to the wonder, peace, and joy of this world. To engage in this upcoming battle is not a good choice, but it is the only choice they feel they have left. Again, having finished on this first day, as the sun began to drop from sight, they give their thanks to Eagle Fan before turning and walking down toward their horses. Eagle Fan stands and watches them. Once the warriors disappear from his sight, he returns to the sacred altar he has prepared, sits down, and gives thanks for this day, knowing that he has three more days to do similar things for each group of warriors. He will not eat or drink during the days when he does these sacred things in preparation for the warriors and the people. He is a man who has been chosen to do this and to provide what is needed. He will be trusted and revered for everything that he has accomplished thus far for the warriors. The people know that he and his ways are as valuable as any weapon or soldier the warriors could strike down or take away. Together, the warriors will become a spiritual force, one that will have to be recognized and reckoned with in the very near future. The trust and the faith in one another within these warriors must be universal, even traveling across the tops of the greasy grass that grows on the battlefield they will go to. The lives of the people are in jeopardy. The lives of the people are being taken. These men have pushed this sadness aside so that their lives can be directed and full of purpose, rather than dwelling upon only the hurt and pain arising from the things happening to their people at the hands of the new people.

This spiritual process will be repeated for three days for the remainder of the warrior group. There are four the first day. On the second day there would be four more. There will be four on the third day, and three on the last day. And of course this preparation is done specifically at the top of this highest sacred mountain peak that the people called Owl's Nest, because it is the hill of wisdom and knowledge, going back to the sacred being, the owl, the symbol of wisdom and knowledge.

View the ceremonial party readying the altar, readying the ground, readying themselves. They are using sage, cedar, and sweetgrass to bring harmony and protection with their prayers and the *asking*. As if on the wings of wanbli, swooping overhead at ten thousand feet, the image zooms out of the present and into the area far above, to show the mountaintops, the forests, and the higher ridges. Then it zooms out higher still, showing the arc of the horizon and then looking down from space, just outside Grandmother Earth's atmosphere.

From high above, one sees the shape of the great sacred He Sapa, and as it looks to the beings who have passed this spot on Grandmother Earth many times before, during the billions of years gone past. It will look the same to those who will pass over her here in the future. Looking down, from above, one can see the clear shape of the human heart, the *canté* of the sacred He Sapa, Grandmother's heart. The heart is surrounded by the oval shape of the red-colored Great Racetrack around He Sapa.

He Sapa

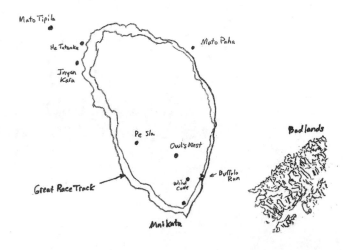

Then the view from the swooping and floating vision from far above begins to zoom down. The view from the Earth resumes slowly, like the swooping wanbli, once again settling and focusing on the group of Lakota who are readying themselves in the small grassy clearing on the top of Owl's Nest.

It is here where the young tall Dakota warrior known as Eagle Fan has prepared the sacred altar. Having readied the place, he is now cleansing the warriors with a healing spiritual bath of the smoke of burning sage, which bathes over the body of each man as he thrusts his open palms forward and pulls back, as if to cup the cleansing smoke to himself, leading it into his spirit. It is here, at the top of the world, at a high peak of connection, where another necessary part of the preparation is occurring. The stone tingles at the warriors' feet as their chests and hands buzz and vibrate with the energy of life and spirit.

They are going to reflect on themselves, and reinforce the strength and the confidence that they need to be the warriors they were called to be. Each warrior's strengths would be stressed during these times, and each would be recognized according to his positive attributes and abilities. The instructions stressed the individual's involvement in each part of the plan, none of which could be forgotten or be left undone if success was to be had. Without even one of the warriors, the battle would likely have a different outcome than the one planned.

During the seasons spent in the He Sapa, the warriors will reaffirm a belief and a practice not only with which they are familiar but also that they are now obligated to respectively seek and perform. There is a purpose for their visit to each sacred site, for example, strengthening and bringing the warrior into balance so that he can do what he is asked to do. From the waters that heal their bodies, to the sacred spiritual cave from which the people emerged at the origin, to the Old Stone Warriors and their advice and their experience, to the Owl's Nest, where everything that has ever been known and practiced can be shared. These are the areas, and these are the lessons and gifts that the warriors will keep and add to their pouch. A little bit today, a little bit tomorrow, and hopefully more in the future. Each warrior places his hands on the life that he is defending and which life is depending upon him to defend. The warriors must do this in a cleansed, purified fashion. They must be free of any torment. They must be free of self-wanting and guilt. There is no time and no space for them to be fallible in any way. They must believe in each step that they take, knowing that their fellow warriors also believe.

Everything that we have been told since the time of Bear Creek and throughout the seasons of their preparation period has been a spiritual education. We learned that the warrior is being provided for, that the warrior is needed, and that the warrior is the one to determine the outcome of something very crucial to our people's existence. We were taught these things so that when the time came for us to ride into battle, we would ride with our heads held high and with our spirits enriched and supported. Our fellow human beings will understand what we were going to do and how long it could take. The future was undetermined, but the future needed the Lakota in it. The warriors combined many gifts from Creator, including those from the human beings and the other beings. And we will walk this path. We will accomplish this for all of us.

———— ·((○))· ————

The time has come. It is now late May in the year 1876. The warriors have been in the sacred He Sapa for four entire seasons. Ever since the previous spring, they have lived and breathed, and prayed about and learned, all that there was to be learned. Their preparation is almost complete, at least the portion that was to be done in the He Sapa involving the sacred sites and the spirit of He Sapa. The warriors' hearts have blended with the heart of Unci Maka, her He Sapa. The warriors are now forever joined in purpose, intent, and life force. The *Protectors* have come to He Sapa and have listened. The *Protectors*, now filled with the sacred knowledge, must move forward, take the next step, the step that will take them west, and travel to the place upon which their preparation was focused, the place where their common destiny lies, not yet completed or fulfilled.

They will leave in the morning on the first day of travel, riding out from the western side of the He Sapa. They will take the less-known routes, the hidden trails and less-traveled ways. They will move mostly at night, many times using the light of the moon and the stars as a guiding beacon. This is the plan, part of the preparation. They must not be detected. Their journey must not be witnessed or known of. They will travel a deeply spiritual and historical route, yet there must be no traceable evidence of their journey. Their tracks must be covered and concealed where possible. Where they can ride through creek water, they will do that, as it is better than leaving hoofprints. When they can camp in a dense thicket, as is their preference, versus an open grassy riverbank, their night companions shall be the crickets and the owls.

The owl people know about them and their journey, for they are wise and filled with knowledge of many things. Their relatives from the He Sapa have spread the word, so the owls along the way shall assist the warriors and alert them to any danger or trespassers on their route. The coyotes, too, are well-informed. All of the four-legged and the winged ones—indeed, all of the nonhuman beings of the world—are hoping for the warriors' success. The wanbli will keep watch from above. The warriors' success will help all beings to live and survive as Creator intended.

It is the human beings the warriors are worried about. This is why all information about the mission, the journey, the preparation, and the spiritual plan must be kept from any humans who need not know. Many of the human beings cannot be trusted with such information, including some of the Lakota and their brother and sister tribes. Even some among the warriors' own people cannot be trusted, as many have been compromised by the government and the military. It is a dangerous thing to be too trusting.

The warriors intend to travel on the outskirts of areas where the people previously made camp or visited, staying away from the common routes that the people take on their usual and expected trips to the Greasy Grass valley. It is too risky for the warriors to travel where they may be seen and subsequently questioned about their purpose or their destination. If the warriors confront anyone, their group must be dismissed as a mere small hunting party. No one must know what they are doing apart from those who already know. The number of people who have been entrusted with the secret cannot be added to, as to do so is forbidden by the spiritual instructions and permission received from the Bear Creek ceremonies. No deviation from the plan can occur. The matter is too important.

On the morning of their departure from their sacred home territory in the He Sapa, the warriors gathered one last time at the base camp near Sage Creek. Eagle Fan led one last prayer of gratitude, thanking He Sapa and Unci Maka for keeping them all safe and committed. The prayer then turned its focus to the journey, the sacred tasks at hand, and those tasks to come. Eagle Fan sang his song of honor, his song of protection. The warriors prayed to the four directions, to Grandmother Earth, and to Grandfather Sky. Each drank of the clean water of the Grandmother. Each looked fondly at the only home he had had for the past four seasons. And then they all finished packing and loading the horses that would go with them to the Greasy Grass.

14

APPROACH

THE WARRIORS HAD BEGUN THEIR journey to Greasy Grass several weeks before the battle was to take place so that when they arrive, they would have plenty of time to adjust and assimilate to the surroundings. They will take the long route to the Greasy Grass area, riding north-northwest so they can use the bluffs, the different types of buttes, and the different types of cover. This is to ensure that the sixteen would not be encountered or even seen. To move in isolated areas and use camouflage was their plan. They would cross all the terrain cautiously and in a unified fashion. As they travel, there would also be the other groups of families traveling to the gathering area, going to the larger encampment. The goal of the greater group of Lakota was to arrive at the aboriginal campsite on the west side along the Greasy Grass River's lowlands, where the people had been setting up camp for the past hundreds of generations. This larger group would be taking the well-worn paths they usually took to reach the Greasy Grass river valley.

Again, the sixteen warriors will take the northern route so as to remain out of sight. The sixteen will cross the Rosebud Creek in a different place than would the moving encampment group. The warriors would cross the Wolf Mountains at a different time and by forging a new path. They will make the whole trip in seclusion, quitely, under cover, while at night, while camouflaged, and in silen ce. The availability of cover would be a primary focus every day as they ride.

The people often looked to the moon as a signal of the times. However, more so, the moon, and her phases helped to define moments. To be able to see what the territory looked like at night. To ride and hike during the night, instead of during the daylight, which happens when you choose to avoid detection of your movement. The moon was the light in the nighttime to serve as an illumination for those that seek the way while others sleep. The moon allows the sanctity of quiet and tranquility amongst most of the world. So that the concentrated and focused task at hand, in moving through the darkness, can be accomplished. Those beings that were nocturnal such as the owl, the coyote, the bats, the cougar, created the instruction for how the people can move themselves in the dark. But those same nocturnal beings afford the leeway and the clear passage for the warriors, as if knowingly wishing not to encumber them. So they do not intervene. But they do notice the movement, quietly... and they watch, and they know.

It was one of those bright summer nights under Creator's beautiful sky. The gift of the night sky must never be forgotten or forsaken. On this night, clumps of clouds moved overhead against the midnight-blue sky, the reliable nighttime canvas painted on Grandfather Sky for all to see.

The warriors were sitting around a campfire. Looking straight up, Saved By Bear watched the clouds form their shapes.

As he gazed up and caught the full moon rising in the southeast, sky, he noticed that the lighter-shaded clouds seemed to creep toward the bright edge of the circle of the moon. In the distance, he heard the midnight howl of the brother wolf. It soothed his senses and his mind.

While the longer wail was trailing off, with the next about to begin, Saved By Bear focused on the bank of clouds approaching the westernmost side of the bright moon. As the clouds drew closer, he noticed that the dark blue pillowy bank was splitting into five separate fingers, which seemed to slowly bunch up at the ends of each appendage. Each of these cloudy "fingertips" then formed into a snout. The five snouts thickened and lengthened. The five fingers of the cloud bank were now five heads of brother wolf, each with snout forward and mouth opening, baying at the full moon as if it were just beyond the tips of their noses. It was beautiful. It served as the perfect backdrop for what Saved By Bear heard in the moonlight chorus.

These were the things that he was used to witnessing in this beautiful land with the wide-open expansive night sky, ever since he was a young boy and began looking up toward the stars at night. He always thanked the spirits for granting him the gift of being able to look at things and being able to see that which may not be seeable by others. He had learned at a young age to see things with no restrictive lens of the obvious or normal expectation. He always thought that if he had not been taught by his grandmother to see, not just to look; then he might have missed these wondrous things that were put on display in Grandfather Sky and on other places on Earth for those who allow themselves to see with more than just their eyes. It was how he, Saved By Bear could look at a rock wall in the canyon and, without making much of an effort, at all, notice the face of an eagle with beak open, singing, at a nearby waterfall among the jagged and smooth surface of the wall of stone. It was as if the images would suddenly choose to expose themselves to him in all their natural glory, once he used his eyes and imagination with purpose, and when he saw with his heart and spirit.

The sudden howl from the distant rock once again brought his mind back from the cloud brothers, and back to the campfire in front of him, and to the task at hand awaiting him in the days to come. The wolf people were assuring the warriors of safe passage this night.

Once the sixteen warriors do arrive at Greasy Grass valley, they will be north of the *chosen hill* and the common encampment area along the west bank of the river. It is here, above the river and in the tree line, that they will stay for approximately a week and do their final preparation for the anticipated battle. They will stay completely out of sight, having absolutely no contact with anyone. Those in the Lakota encampment, when they arrive later, to the south, will have no idea who these warriors are. They will not know the sixteen are even there. The sixteen warriors, also, will have no idea who the other warriors in the Lakota encampment are. Those warriors are Spirit Horse's responsibility, as is which portions of the battle they will take care of. It is here, at this secluded camp, where the warriors will finalize their strategy of approach for once the day of confrontation arrives.

At night, the warriors will converse, making certain that all of them understand each man's individual position and responsibility, with a heavy emphasis on the role and duty of those who will lead the warriors onto the battlefield. These lead warriors, who are incredibly brave to lead and protect the rest of the warriors, are to be commended. They will make the decisions for those who follow behind them. The lead ones will be the ones to decide when to advance, pause, cease, or attack. The other warriors, including Swift Bear and Saved By Bear, will follow these lead warriors on foot, and eventually for the others, to follow on the horses.

The warriors will remain in hiding during the daylight hours, being basically invisible, but at nighttime, they will work, doing everything they can to prepare for the battle to come.

The Military Plan for Annihilation Moves Forward

The time period was May 17, 1876, through June 21, 1876. Gen. Philip Sheridan put together a grand plan based upon the failure of the Lakota hunting parties to "come in" and report to the agencies by January 31, 1876. When many of the Lakota, including the bands under Sitting Bull and Spirit Horse, the Hunkpapa and Mnincoju mostly, did not report to the agencies as ordered by President Grant's November 9, 1875, proclamation, they were officially declared to be hostiles. They were now considered *hostile* to the United States government. And therefore, these *hostiles* were now a matter to be dealt with by the Department of War.

General Sheridan had been selected by President Grant to prepare the war plan, the military campaign to deal with the *hostiles* as soon as practicable in the spring of 1876. There was little time to waste in light of the extreme public pressure to divest the Lakota of their gold-rich Black Hills. The treaty commissions to try to get the Lakota to agree to sell or cede the Black Hills to the United States had failed miserably, so war was imminent according to the U.S.. The country was nearly broke, and the gold was needed to bolster the nation's treasury, and to open up opportunities for those well-connected business interests to come in and scoop up the natural resources from the Lakota's sacred He Sapa.

Already, white miners such as John Pearson, Moses Manuel, Fred Manual, John Henry "Hank" Harney, and Alex Engh had obtained illegal mining claims in the northern areas in the heart of the Black Hills. Moses and Fred Manuel, Harney, and Engh obtained their mining claim in April 1876 despite the fact that the 1868 treaty prohibited this type of trespass. The white miners and other opportunists were bolstered by President Grant's initiative to pass the General Mining Act of 1872.

As set out previously, eventually, in June 1877, the Manuels, Harney, and Engh would sell their mining claim called Homestake Mine for $70,000 to mining executive/entrepreneur and financial opportunist George W. Hearst and his partners, San Francisco lawyers James Ben Ali Haggin and Lloyd Tevis (of Wells Fargo Company fame). Hearst and his corporate partners would take the originally illegally obtained Homestake Mine claim and turn it into a gold mine that would produce 10 percent of the world's gold, operate for 125 years, and pollute the environment. Homestake would end up extracting over forty million troy ounces of gold that rightfully belonged to the Lakota. In today's economy, that amount of gold would be worth over $51.42 billion. (not including the recent years from 2001 to the present, where private corporations continue to extract gold and silver out of the He Sapa).

In 1875 and 1876, the United States was determined to afford these entrepreneurs and financial barons the opportunity to seize the sacred land from the *stubborn Indians*. War was needed to do so, but there had to be a justification to start a war. There must be a provocation to provide a justification. The US government also needed a *legal* justification to take and occupy the Black Hills. The plan to do just that was now in place. The government's action of declaring Sitting Bull and the Lakota to be *hostiles* was the trigger. Sheridan was anxious to put his military plan into action. These things had already been discussed with Grant, and authorized.

That plan, once put into action, would come to be known as the Powder River Campaign of 1876. The simple purpose was to track, hunt down, and then annihilate all of the Lakota hostiles. Reports came in from the various Lakota agencies that Sitting Bull and Spirit Horse had called for a gathering of the hunting parties, planning for a move in the spring into the Powder River country in the Wyoming and Montana Territories.

Already, the military knew of the Lakota's propensity to travel to and spend months in the Powder River Territory, including in the Bighorn Mountains and the Little Bighorn Valley, known to the Lakota as the Greasy Grass valley. The Powder River country encompassed the area west and somewhat north of the Black Hills, which was part of the area of the 1851 *unceded hunting territories* and *unceded Indian territory* described within the eight-year-old 1868 Fort Laramie Treaty. (Art 5, 1851; Art. 16, 1868). This massive area, which included the mountains and river valley areas south of the Yellowstone ("Elk") River, west of the Powder River, and up to the eastern edge of the Bighorn Mountains and the Bighorn River, was one that the Lakota knew very well. They had been going to these places for thousands of years. The lands were part of their aboriginal territories, much like the He Sapa was. The Crow and Cheyenne frequented the valleys as well.

General Sheridan determined that this would be the most likely place to find the Lakota hostiles and any other unfortunate *Indian* bands that may be accompanying them. If the military could mount a movement of infantry, cavalry, and artillery, large enough to search for, track, hunt down, trap, and then attack and destroy them, then the campaign would be deemed a success. And the country needed a success. The United States, in the midst of a horrible financial quandary, was due to celebrate its centennial on July 4, 1876.

To accomplish this military strategy and achieve this outcome, Sheridan called in some of his best battle tacticians and some of his best *Indian-fighters*. Of course, Sheridan had to include his young protégé and admired understudy, Lt. Col. George Custer, and his Seventh Cavalry. Custer and the Seventh considered themselves to be the most elite of the *Indian-fighting* regiments.

Sheridan would also call upon his friend and colleague Gen. George Crook from the Wyoming Territory. Crook was a talented Civil War general and a veteran Indian-fighter. Sheridan needed to also call upon another Civil War hero veteran, Gen. John Gibbon from Montana Territory near Fort Ellis. Lastly, Sheridan needed to utilize the knowledge and sophistication of his good friend Gen. Alfred Terry, the man with a law degree. Terry would be the command head on the mission. Since Custer had recently gotten himself into trouble with the president and had caused turmoil, calling out the president's brother and the Secretary of Indian Affairs Belknap as corrupt idiots, he was not at all in the good graces of the president. Sheridan and Terry were able to convince Grant, just barely, to allow Custer to accompany the Seventh Cavalry. Sheridan and Terry had had to cash in some of their chips with Grant to get him to allow Custer to serve as troop leader of the Seventh, with General Terry to be the real command of the column, which would include the Seventh Cavalry.

Sheridan's plan was to use three main columns (prongs) of military for the approach into the Powder River country. General Crook and his cavalry, infantry, and cannons would approach from the south, after leaving from Fort Fetterman near the confluence of the Tongue River and Goose Creek in Wyoming. General Gibbon would bring 450 soldiers and scouts, mostly infantry, with Gatling gun groups, and approach from the northwest in Montana. The Third Column, coming from Fort Abraham Lincoln near Bismarck in Dakota Territory, would move west and then south. This Third Column would be headed by Terry, with Custer as the cavalry leader.

The strategy was to have Crook approach from the south at the same time as Terry and Custer moved toward the mouth of the Powder River.

Gibbon would travel down the Yellowstone River from Fort Ellis, and meet Terry and Custer at the mouth of the Powder. Meanwhile, Crook was intended to move into the Little Bighorn Valley from the south. Then all three columns would corner and then crush all of the Lakota before the *hostiles* could disperse and escape.

It seemed to be a sturdy plan. But the weather in the spring would not be cooperative.

Gibbon had already had his column of troops along the Yellowstone west of the Bighorn River since mid-April. They were temporarily stuck there on account of winter storms. Terry and Custer and their group of 925 troops, civilians, and scouts could not move out from Fort Lincoln until mid-May because of the cold, wet, snowy late spring weather.

Crook had already been in the Powder River area in March when he and Colonel Reynolds employed an attack, on March 17, against a camp of Cheyenne, believing it to be Spirit Horse's camp. This was a blunder. The Indians escaped, but the troops captured three hundred of their horses. However, within twenty-four hours, the Cheyenne took all the horses back from the troops in a nighttime raid. Crook was furious with Reynolds and threatened to bring him up on military charges.

Crook's column of approximately 1,100 infantry, with their big guns, moved out from Fort Fetterman on May 29, 1876. However, Crook would end up having an unforeseen confrontation with Lakota and Cheyenne warriors led by Spirit Horse in the early morning of June 17, 1876, near the headwaters of the Rosebud Creek on the eastern side of the Wolf Mountains. A six-hour battle ensued. Crook lost nine soldiers. He had no clear advantage. As will be discussed later, Crook decided to retreat.

As the Terry–Custer column, the Dakota Column, started out on May 17, 1876, from Fort Lincoln, the officers and the enlisted men would have no clue that the great military plan of Sheridan, implementing a three-prong attack, would end up with only two prongs when the situation came to a head near the Little Bighorn.

Fort Lincoln had been established in honor of President Lincoln following his death at the hands of an assassin. The site of the fort was along the big navigable Missouri River just miles south of the Dakota Territory city of Bismarck, which was a significant supply and trading center for the traders and military at the time. The site chosen for the fort was just above an aboriginal area of the Mandans, an indigenous band who called this area home. The site was also north of the other Missouri River military fort, called Fort Rice, which was a short distance away from the northern boundary of the Standing Rock Lakota Agency, which was located along the western bank of the Missouri. Standing Rock, formally known as the Grand River Agency, had been established in the 1868 Fort Laramie Treaty recognizing the aboriginal land holding and presence of the Lakota people called the Hunkpapa, (and some Yanktonai), the people of Sitting Bull. These were the people of the End of the Horn, one of the Lakota's seven main bands. This was the aboriginal home of the Sacred Stone along the river. The river and its fresh supply of water had been the lifeblood of the Hunkpapa people for many thousands of years. It is foretold that the *Water Spirit* will rise again from the river at a point in time when the Lakota need him the most. A time in need for protection; a time to defend based upon necessity.

Sitting Bull was one of the most recognizable and yet disliked Lakota leaders according to the US military and the white society as a whole. This was the case thanks to the heavily promoted misinformation about, fear of, and general prejudice against the Lakota and Indian people in general. The non-treaty-signing Lakota, of whom Sitting Bull was one, had been unfairly portrayed as *hostiles*. Also, the whites feared Sitting Bull because he was the manifestation of the *hostiles* as stereotyped in the US media, especially in the media of the midwestern section of the Great Plains at the time (such as the Bismarck Tribune).

The dislike of Sitting Bull and his Lakota followers, and of all bands of Lakota, was perpetuated by the US military's portrayal of the Hunkpapa Lakota leader as well. Sitting Bull, ever since the early 1850s, the beginning of the encroachment of the whites onto the Lakota's aboriginal homelands, was a vocal and easily recognized proponent of preserving the Lakota's traditional way of life, the free, sovereign, nomadic lifestyle that the Lakota were meant to live. The Hunkpapa leader was a gifted leader with a spiritual aura about him that allowed him to communicate with all beings through the natural energy of the spirit world. Sitting Bull was very outspoken, and was often quoted when speaking of how he viewed the natural world and the clash of cultures. Some of his famous quotations are as follows:

- "What white man can say I ever stole his land or a penny of his money? Yet they say I am a thief."
- "If we must die, we die defending our rights."
- "What treaty that the whites have kept has the red man broken? Not one."
- "Strangely enough, they have a mind to till the soil, and the love of possessions is a disease in them."
- "The earth has received the embrace of the sun, and we shall see the results of that love."
- "Each man is good in his sight. It is not necessary for eagles to be crows."
- "Let us put our minds together and see what life we can make for our children."
- "It is through this mysterious power that we too have our being, and we therefore yield to our neighbors, even to our animal neighbors, the same rights as we ourselves have to inhabit this vast land."

Because of his prominent position among his own people and among the Lakota in general, Sitting Bull was a force. When he chose to align with the young Mnincoju warrior by the name of Spirit Horse, the two men made a formidable pair, Sitting Bull with his spiritual and charismatic leadership abilities, and Spirit Horse with his finely honed experience in military tactics, protocol, planning, and strategy, a great source of battle knowledge and unlimited courage and fearlessness. Sitting Bull, however, would continue his efforts to seek peace and diplomacy with the United States and its military leaders, especially Custer, Grant, Sheridan, Terry, and Crook.

The US military, and especially the Dakota Territory military leadership, all at once feared, admired, and disdained the two Lakota leaders. The United States feared them for their notorious nature, their popularity among the Lakota people, and their innate ability to continue to frustrate the general policies of the US government. The United States and its officials were trying to tame and soothe the Indians so as to lure them into signing away all their land holdings and rights by agreeing to the so-called *treaties*. Many other Lakota headmen agreed to sign these treaties. Many Lakota believed that to be something that would lead to the future detriment of all the Lakota.

Terry, Sheridan, Grant, Sherman, and Custer all had personal feelings about the Lakota, and about men like Sitting Bull. In the 1860s through the time period of the lead-up to the Powder River Campaign of 1876, the US military became committed to removing, eliminating, annihilating, and destroying all of the Lakota, but especially Sitting Bull. Sheridan would be heard saying to Terry, "The only good Indians I ever saw were dead". Or stating that the US will "break" him [Sitting Bull and his people] (using the metaphor of a controlling owner breaking his horse, taming it so it can be ridden, or indicating how the controlling *master* breaks a *slave*, not to rebel or resist, leading the slave to merely submit and give in to the master's will).

A big part of the reason why the US military's hatred toward Sitting Bull and the Lakota intensified was the issue of the gold in the He Sapa. The desire to obtain the gold rose to prominence in the minds of the greedy government officials and private business vultures. The financial and mining interests were foaming at the mouth, wanting to get their hands on the Black Hills. No matter the desires, feelings, rights, or very lives of the Lakota, the United States was determined to possess the Black Hills at all costs, at any cost, whether in effort, in money, in lost lives, or in lost honor and humanity. It became an obsession for many in private business or in the US government and military. And the obsession spread like a dark poisonous snake had bitten them all, and had spread the vile poison of greed, vanity, covetousness, death and destruction. Having become overbearing, it soaked into the souls, minds, spirits, and what was left of the hearts, of the men calling the shots.

Ironically, even Custer acknowledged how the Indians likely felt about the encroachment of the whites, saying, "If I were an Indian, I would greatly prefer to cast my lot among those of my people who adhere to the free open plains, rather than submit to the confined limits of a reservation." However, in the same breath, unable to contain his arrogance and boundless self-aggrandizing, he said, "There are not enough Indians in the world to defeat the Seventh Calvary... ", or" I would be willing, yes glad, to see a battle every day during my life"..., :or," You ask me if I will not be glad when the last battle is fought, so far as the country is concerned I, of course, must wish for peace, and will be glad when the war is ended, but if I answer for myself alone, I must say that I shall regret to see the war end";or finally, "There are far more statues of soldiers out there than there are of civilians."

Spiritual Messages Are Sent

Throughout 1874, 1875 and 1876, what the military leaders, governmental officials, and their family members did not fully appreciate or understand were the ever-increasing messages that they were all receiving. Not so much by way of the written word in letters or notes. But the messages urging peace and diplomacy that the leaders and their families were receiving, were within their inner minds, their subconscious, and their spirits.

This was occurring because it was intended. It was actually a planned thing. Many Lakota medicine people and holy people, including Sitting Bull, were indeed sending spiritual messages to all of these leaders and their families. These messages advised them all, through the spirit, that war was not the answer. That peace and diplomacy was and would be still available as a workable means of resolving the intensity, and the violence and hatred toward the Lakota. That a peaceful, nonviolent coexistence was achievable, before it was too late. But the spiritual messages also, especially in the eighteen months from August 1874 to May 1876, included something else, namely that if these disputes between the whites and the Lakota were not resolved peacefully and without violence, if these men and their policies continued on the path of war with and destruction of the Lakota, then the Lakota would fully engage in that war and heap the consequences upon the whites. These messages came in the form of warnings. "We want peace and diplomacy. It can still happen. But if you choose to go to war against us, you will suffer the consequences. You will not prevail. You will be defeated. You will suffer great loss."

The messages and warnings were intended for the military leaders. However, those messages also affected those who were close to these men, including their families. There were signs that the messages were being received. They were being recognized but ignored, possibly out of spite, arrogance, disbelief, or indifference. But the messages could not be merely wiped away from the conscience, or from the spirit.

The Lakota made their first connections with the Custer family because of his position as a military leader. Sitting Bull had initiated that connection. The medicine, the energy, that was connected to Sitting Bull and which he sent out started the process of spiritually messaging Custer and other members of the military. This is how we make connections, by sending the *tun*, which is your medicine, your energy, that you give to the world. Those who come into contact with you when something is in the making or when something is occurring spiritually, then become a part of it also.

When the officers were at Fort Lincoln around Custer, and when Custer's cavalry were around him, they also felt this spiritual presence. They did not understand it, but they felt it. Their being able to feel this presence was why the soldiers and Custer all had an emotional sense of what was going to happen in this campaign. Because of Custer's commitment to chase, find and attack the Lakota, and what was going to occur, the other officers, and all their soldiers, also felt this presence. Maj. Marcus Reno and Capt. Frederick Benteen, knowing how headstrong Custer was in seeking glory of war for himself and in his own way, will let him fight as he chooses in the battle, because he had made his own decision as a commander. And this is where Reno and Benteen would follow protocol: they would allow Custer to do it on his own if he chose to. That is what the spirits on both sides want to happen on the day of the battle.

It is also clear that General Terry had some doubts in his own mind about this campaign. Even the renowned Indian-hater Sheridan showed signs of misgivings. It was clear that Crook felt it very strongly. Even Grant must have been haunted by these messages and warnings—after the fact. But it was absolutely clear that the intensity of the warnings was picked up on by Custer and his young wife, Libbie. Much of their conduct and behavior through May and June of 1876 resembled that of troubled people, troubled souls. They seemed edged with a certain feeling. Feelings like uncertainty, of fear, and with a sense of doom. As if they'd had a premonition of some sort that the Powder River Campaign of 1876 would turn out different from what they were expecting in so many ways.

Mrs. Elizabeth Custer was deeply affected by this particular military campaign that her husband was embarking upon. She surely was feeling the spiritual messages and warnings that had been sent by the Lakota, and also feeling a sense of despair and doom. She even insisted on riding with the troops and her husband on the first day's march. It is clear that Mrs. Custer was deeply affected by her feelings. She would write about her experiences, starting with those days, and continuing for the remainder of her life. She must have felt a certain amount of guilt of conscience. Some regret for not speaking up when she could have, to verbalize her fears, her emotions, her spiritual perceptions. To try to explain her misgivings to her husband before it was too late. But she did not do that. Fate and destiny would intervene. She would write about it for decades in an attempt to relieve her own guilt and regret, and in a bold attempt to resurrect and protect her husband's legacy in the passing years.

One important spiritual message that Libbie Custer later shared about the day the Seventh Cavalry departed Fort Lincoln, May 17, 1876, was both ominous and prophetic. She watched the two-mile-long train leave the fort under mostly cloudy skies, the sun breaking through as the cavalry train climbed the highlands to the west. This created an image, as if the men, their horses, and the wagons were climbing into the clouds, only to disappear as if they had never been there at all.

A fact that can perhaps serve as proof that Custer knew that this particular campaign would turn out to be different from all the others is that Custer had cut his hair. His long, flowing, somewhat curly reddish-blonde hair had been a symbol of his notoriety, stature, and character. Much like with Sampson, Custer's hair was a symbol of his strength. He knew and embraced the fact that he was known in Indian country as "Long Hair." He believed that his presence and his appearance would strike fear in the hearts of the Indians when they saw him approaching, and that the same would occur when they heard his favorite military charging theme, *Garryowen*. Custer's particular look was as important to him as his long list of deeds in war and killing. So it was a peculiar thing that he cut his long hair short, close to his scalp. Many of Custer's officers, including Tom Custer, Myles Keogh, Algeron Smith, and James Calhoun, wore buckskins like Custer did, and a large hat. It seems, quite frankly, that Custer felt the spiritual connection of the Lakota messages. By cutting his famous long hair, he was attempting to fool fate, to trick those who may have been looking for a long-haired cavalry leader wearing buckskin. By altering his appearance, he was trying to alter his fate.

Custer knew that this was a dangerous mission, the purpose of which was to try to find and destroy the warriors of the Lakota once and for all. After all the warnings, the direct communications from Sitting Bull, to leave the Lakota alone, Custer still politicked to pursue Sitting Bull and the Lakota, his desire to obtain the Black Hills and its gold being too great to ignore, the goal being too relevant to delay. To Custer, this was too valuable an opportunity for fame and glory for him to pass up.

Leaving Fort Lincoln

The enlisted men of the Seventh Cavalry at Fort Lincoln on May 17, 1876, were called to rise by revelry at dawn. The troops wore blue shirts, broad felt hats, cavalry boots, and blue or buckskin pantaloons. Each carried a rifle, usually a new springfield carbine, and a revolver. Around the waist of each man was an ammunition belt with sixty rounds for a Springfield carbine and a supply of revolver cartridges.

Most of the enlisted men were illiterate, unable to either read or write. So it was common for them to ask someone within their company who had the capability to write, to write letters to their family or loved ones for them. Many of the troops, being foreign born, could barely speak or understand English. As a result, communication among the troops and with their command, was an obvious problem. Many of the foreign-born enlisted men were either German, Polish, Russian, Scotch, Scandinavian, Irish, Italian, French, or some other nationality. There was a significant number of recruits from Switzerland. Two of those cavalry troopers were Charley Vincent from Lucerne and Alfred Hansen from Zurich. These two Swiss soldiers marched together most times and shared many stories of their homeland, of course in their native tongue. Both missed their families at home in Switzerland, and both agreed that they had enlisted because it was one of the few jobs that provided steady pay and was a dependable source of room, board and meals. There was little choice.

Charley Vincent was a spiritual man. He spoke often and quite fondly of his home. He remembered and spoke of the sacred mountain, Mt. Pilatus, and the home of the spiritual dragon that many believed lived in the mountain. Both men missed their homeland, and often spoke of regretting their decision to enlist. As they now found themselves in the vast Western Frontier, where they were expected to march and shoot or kill other human beings. They both realized that the US Army merely saw them as expendable tools of war, easily replaced by any of the new recruits that were constantly shipping in from overseas.

A majority of the enlisted men were new to the country and newly inducted into military service, meaning that these soldiers were not really familiar with where they were. They'd never seen the things that they were now seeing as they marched and followed Terry and Custer. These enlisted men may not have felt that killing other humans was the solution, but they had found no other alternative than to enlist in the military. Because of this, many of them exhibited certain emotions before and during battle. It was likely that their families back home missed them and prayed for them. These men likely had not expected to go to war when they enlisted. However, they now needed to accept the circumstance they were in. Many of the soldiers were recent immigrants who needed a way to earn money, a way to make a living. Many had enlisted out of necessity. And since many of them were novice soldiers, they were at a great disadvantage. They didn't know how to respond or react to much of what they encountered here, not the least because the terrain was completely different from what they were used to. Many of these soldiers were spiritual. Some were innocent, and some were in the army because no other choice was available. Many, including Charley Vincent, did not wish to be a part of the military at all.

During the 1860s and into the 1870s, European governments were shipping people, many times their undesirables, to the United States for the alleged purpose of helping the United States fight the Indians in the pursuit of manifest destiny. In the Powder River Campaign of 1876, approximately 150 of the cavalry soldiers were new recruits (greenhorns). Many could not even ride or shoot. They were therefore *expendable* in the eyes of the military. The US government policy was both arrogant and complacent. The military would be able to continue easily replenishing its troops, as there was a steady stream of newly arriving desperate people to serve as soldiers.

The Seventh Cavalry Regiment made up the majority of the combat strength of the Terry column that was to leave Fort Lincoln for the Powder River area in Montana. The regiment had 12 companies, including Custer's regimental band, whose leader was Felix Vinatieri. One company from the Sixth Infantry Regiment, Terry's headquarters detachment, was headed by Capt. Stephen Baker. There was one company from the Twentieth Infantry Regiment headed by Lt. William Low that had a battery of Gatling guns. Custer had hired 39 Crow and Arikira scouts in April and May who were commanded by Lt. Charles Varnum, who had been with Custer on many campaigns. Charley Reynolds, one of Custer's favorite scouts, was along as well. The total manpower count was 52 officers and 879 enlisted men, with 32 officers, and 718 enlisted men from the Seventh Cavalry alone.

Custer's brother Capt. Tom Custer, leader of the Seventh Cavalry's Company C, and Lt. James Calhoun, leader of the Seventh's Company L, were a part of the team. Calhoun was Custer's brother-in-law. Another of Custer's brothers, Boston Custer, and Custer's nephew Autie Reed, came along as civilian observers. Col. Samuel Sturgis's son Lt. James Sturgis was a new officer on his first officer's mission. Because Custer was a national celebrity in the eyes of the media, and because Custer enjoyed being close to the press, he brought along an embedded reporter from the *Bismarck Tribune*, Mark Kellogg, who also was a contributing writer for the *New York Herald*. Kellogg wanted to follow the exploits and planned to glorify the great victory for this potential rising media, social, and political star. Many believed Custer would use his final victory over the Lakota as a feather in his cap to make a run for the US presidency.

A supply steamboat, the *Far West*, would be commissioned and used to navigate the Yellowstone River, and any other river if needed, to further the campaign. In addition to hauling supplies, the boat would be used for transport and as a meeting place for the officers. The captain was Grant Marsh.

On the march out of Fort Lincoln, and for the remainder of the trip to the Powder River country, the Seventh Cavalry, in marching order, was divided into two columns: the Right Wing and the Left Wing. The Right Wing was commanded by Maj. Marcus Reno, and the Left Wing was commanded by Capt. Fredrick Benteen. Each wing was subdivided into two battalions of three troops each. Reno had marched with the Seventh on several previous campaigns, as had Benteen. Reno did not care much for Custer. Similarly, Benteen did not like his commanding officer that much either. Benteen had been with Custer during the 1868 Washita Massacre in Oklahoma, where a three-pronged method of attack had been used. Benteen was a strong-willed veteran officer. He and Custer had experienced differences in the past, including Custer's decision to leave Benteen's friend Maj. Joel Elliot and his men behind at the Washita.

On the day of departure from Fort Lincoln, Mark Kellogg wrote the following:

> Gen. George A. Custer, dressed in a dashing suit of buckskin, is prominent everywhere. Here, there, fitting to and fro, in his quick eager way, taking in everything connected with his command, as well as generally, with the keen incisive manner for which he is so well known. The General is full of perfect readiness for a fray with the hostile red devils, and woe to the body of scalp-lifters that comes within reach of himself and brave companions in arms.[18]

Lieutenant Colonel Custer was emulated by many, and despised by just as many others. When the Seventh Cavalry and the others departed on their thirty-five-day journey, neither the enlisted men nor

---

[18] Chorne, Laudi T., Following the Custer Trail of 1876, at 12.

the officers held back when expressing their bad feelings about Custer. For example, many of the enlisted men said that they resented Custer for granting most of the amenities, such as dining and sleeping under specially prepared canopies, and using the medical tent for officers' meals and taxidermy purposes, to his favored circle of people. Boston Custer was a civilian observer just along for the ride with his brothers George and Tom, yet he was being paid by the government at the rate of $100 per month, which was quite a bit more than the enlisted men's salary of $13 per month. Private Slaper of Company M expressed the common sentiment: "We are told that the men of the ranks did not appreciate Custer's bluntness toward them—which tended to be his usual manner."

Another private, Ewert, said, if only some of our leaders could see..."How officers lord it over the poor private or noncommissioned officer, how a man, constantly subjected to such treatment will at length lose his manhood and become little better than a cowardly slave! How unjustly, brutally and tyrannically the rank and file were treated."[19]

The accommodations for the enlisted men were meager in comparison to those for Custer and his circle of people.

> The pup tents, the enlisted men used for their shelter, were issued for three men to a tent, even though the tents were made for only two men. This presented crowded conditions in these little shelters, and robbed the troops of much needed rest …

> The officers however, had roomy wall-tents and folding cots, and suffer very little hardship. Most of the commissioned officers had their servants and orderlies to set up their camp and provide for their comforts. Custer had his black servant, Isaiah Dorman, who also acted as Custer's Interpreter, and his black cook, Mary Adams, who was along on the expedition. These were in addition to his striker and orderly.[20]

---

[19] Chorne, at 58.
[20] Chorne, at 59.

Dr. DeWolf advised that the commanding officers, primarily Custer, had little regard for ordinary troops, whether they were healthy or sick. Much like he did on the 1874 Black Hills expedition (the "Trail of Thieves" to the Lakota), Custer, when on the Powder River Campaign march, would commandeer the hospital tent for his hounds, or for taxidermy, leaving the sick troops to fend for themselves.[21]

Custer had no physical limitations and never succumbed to fatigue. It seemed that he hardly slept. He believed that every military man was capable of having the same level of stamina as he, and when a man did not measure up to Custer's expectations, which many could not, Custer was not forgiving. He believed that the men were shirking their duty. Because of this, many men under Custer's command commonly referred to him as "Hard Ass."

The trail followed by the Terry–Custer column led west, close along the Heart River. At one point on May 25, 1876, the column moved across and along the Green River several miles north and east of the present town of Dickinson. The infantry marching men, who usually fell behind, were happy to be able to stop and soak in the Green River's waters for a while. Custer was known as a hard driver, seemingly unconcerned with the well-being of the enlisted men's, needs or endurance levels. So even brief stops to rest and cool down were cherished by the hard-driven enlisted men.

The soldiers were already on edge as they neared the Little Missouri River. Before leaving Fort Lincoln, Terry had convinced the soldiers that the column would likely confront Lakota hostiles somewhere in the Badlands along the Little Missouri. Many of the soldiers therefore thought the campaign may end up being a short one. Given that they had encountered no enemy at all by this point, many of them had their hopes of a short mission dispelled, and now thought that the campaign would likely carry forth into the summer months. This had a diminishing effect on their morale. They were, of course, correct in their assessment, as things would turn out.

The relationship between Terry and Custer was becoming a contentious one. Custer wanted to move as far and as fast on their

---

[21] Chorne, at 59.

journey to Montana as he could, pushing the men and the livestock very hard. Terry did not agree with Custer's lack of concern for the soldiers. This was the type of sentiment held by some among Custer's ranks:

> It takes all kinds of o'men to make up an army … It takes a lot o'common fellows too … Jist privates, men that don't know nothing except what they're told to do, that kill and gits killed, and that the world never hars about. Jist privates we was, jist rough, strong young fellows ready to march all day, tired, hungry, thirsty, to go here, to thar, without understandin' why nothing except to shoot and shoot to kill.[22]

Sometime in the year 1875, Sitting Bull would receive spiritual messages from the Mnincoju ceremonies held near Bear Creek, and decided that a ceremony should be held near the sacred Deer Medicine Rock. As the hostilities toward the Lakota by the government and its military increased in 1876, Sitting Bull told the people that they needed to travel to the Powder River country.

The events leading up to the movement of the people were beginning to fall into place, set into motion in the time frame and sequence dictated by the instructions and spiritual messages, according to the signs. The connection with Creator, and the presence of Wakan Tanka in the everyday lives of the people, was strong. Maybe stronger than it had been in many years, at least ever since the whites had shown up and began encroaching upon the Lakota lands, specifically, the sacred He Sapa.

Word traveled fast among the people. The Lakota bands and the Cheyenne began to receive word that a calling was occurring. This was much more than what normally occurred season to season, when groups of people moved to follow the buffalo to the hunting grounds in the Powder River and Greasy Grass valleys north of the Shiny Mountains

---

[22] Chorne, at 94.

(the Bighorns). The Greasy Grass hunting areas were a common place to go every year because they were both beautiful and bountiful. Due to the intentional killing off of the tatanka, the herds were diminishing quite rapidly in the territories on or near the agencies. The herds would likely be more naturally abundant near the Powder River.

The areas around and near the Greassy Grass valley were known for its wonderful natural environment. It seemed as if the people and the land had been created for each other. Game was bountiful always, because of the clean, clear, fast-running rivers and creeks. There were vast meadows of tall grass for the herds of tatanka and the ponies. The natural flatlands, nestled against the rivers and surrounded by mountain ridges and bench cliff formations, served to protect the camps and herds from weather, the winds, and enemies. The areas of the Rosebud Creek and the Greasy Grass River were somewhat near the territories of the Crow, the longtime adversary of the Lakota and the Cheyenne.

The Crow lived much like the Lakota and the Cheyenne. In more modern times, and especially since the signing of the 1868 treaty involving the He Sapa and the surrounding hunting territories, the Lakota, the Cheyenne, and some of the other bands had viewed the Powder River, and the Rosebud and Greasy Grass River basins and valleys, as an important part of their *unceded hunting territories*, and *unceded Indian terriroty*. This was according to treaty stipulation.

The Crow seemed to be more agreeable than the Lakota or the Cheyenne to assimilating into white society and supporting the whites' efforts at ranching, farming, and industry in the 1860s and 1870s. In this manner, the Crow became more and more closely aligned with the government, the whites, and the armies of the whites. It seemed a natural alliance between the Crow and the oft-tempted encroaching armies of the whites. It was widely known throughout the 1800s that the Crow did not care for the Lakota. Particularly, the Crow were not happy about the fact that the Lakota and Cheyenne were specifically recognized as the true owners and possessors of the *unceded hunting territories* and *unceded Indian territory* to the east and north of the Bighorn Mountains. The Crow seemed hungry for what the Lakota had, in land and natural recognition as the Protectors of the He Sapa and Grandmother Earth. It was said by many, that the Crow feared the incredible strength and significance of the Lakota's spiritual awareness and connectivity to all things.

Over generations, a memorialized history of the Lakota and the Crow had developed, as clashes and conflicts between the two peoples occurred. Camps were raided, horses were taken, and horses were retaken. Hunting parties were intercepted, many coups were counted, and lives were taken, and lost. Many of the respected warriors of the Lakota were linked to stories of exhibiting bravery in their conflicts with members of the Crow.

Sitting Bull had come of age as a "feathered" warrior of the warrior societies. At age fifteen, he had a battlefield conflict with a Crow warrior. Sitting Bull won the conflict, having taken the Crow warrior's life.

So, the parameters of disagreement, conflict, and adversarial positioning had been set between the Lakota and the Crow long before the spring and summer of 1876.

Many males of the Crow tribe either had been taken into or voluntarily joined the US military. They had served mostly as Indian scouts for the armies of the Americans throughout the 1850s, 1860s, and 1870s. The Crow became a favorite of the white armies, frequently serving in the capacity of scouts, especially in the army campaigns against the Lakota and the Cheyenne, in part because the Crow's differences with the Lakota. Also, critically, the military preferred to use the ready-made adversaries of the Lakota, as they would likely be programmed to seek out and kill their adversaries, the Lakota. It seemed a natural choice of the government, which was determined to control or exterminate the Lakota and to steal their land and resources. Using the Crow was a handy means to help carry out that policy.

Deer Medicine Rock

Long ago, before the whites came to Turtle Island, before civilization, before time was kept, the place called Deer Medicine Rock was a place of sacred energy.

In June 1876, the people approached the site slowly from the east. They saw the rocky ridges of the hills surrounding the Rosebud valley and saw the long grass along the plain.

As the people got closer, they felt the energy and the power of the place, before it even came into view. It stood alone as a sandstone castle of rock overlooking the southern aspect of the Rosebud Creek and its valley below. Looking even further northwest, one could see the rocky column resembling an extraordinary seated horned owl facing south.

The magnetic pull on the people's hearts and spirits continued to attract the people to the rock. It had been told for many years that the south face of the Deer Medicine Rock had been struck by lightning. And that the lightning bolt had passed through the face of the rock so powerfully and so quickly that it left a crooked blue spiked trail that will remain there forever, encased within the rock itself. Left there to memorialize the significance of the holy and magical nature of the place, discernible by the people and all living beings. The lightning bolt struck the deer that had been etched there many, many years before, as a permanent etching for all time.

The stone columns of the rock symbolize the strong connection of Grandmother Earth to her beings. They are a remnant of a time that was at once more simple, and yet more advanced, when the Earth was recognized as a precious and giving Grandmother, not as a material thing to be used, taken from, raped, sold, or abused.

The rock speaks its own language. Not with words, but with feelings and emotions, and in the spirit. The ability to communicate with the energy of the rock is reserved for those open-minded, open-hearted believers who visit it. Those who fear neither the power nor the magic. To communicate with the rock and its power is to communicate directly with Wakan Tanka, as if the rock serves as a direct line for the connection, so that the unfiltered words, prayers, feelings, requests, and expressions of gratitude can pass from the being to the Creator without interruption. It was said also that at times during the dusk of night, the threshold of the spirit world could be seen in the medicine wheel boulder at the base of the rock.

For all these reasons, Sitting Bull, during the early summer season of 1876, chose to travel to the Deer Medicine Rock with the people. It was a time of uncertainty for the Lakota people. They suffered trials and tribulations on account of the encroaching white race whose armies were desperate to find, confine, and exterminate the people. The rock seemed the purely logical place to project the significance of the vision, the permission, and the messages received from Creator by the warriors.

The holy men and the warrior societies had held many secret ceremonies in the inipi and at the secret gatherings. The Mnincoju at Bear Creek had previously been provided the instructions and the spiritual permission for the battle with Custer, already. Much was learned of the old ways and how the old ways and beliefs needed to be followed at this time of pressure and anxiety for all the people. The pressing rush of the white humans was beginning to crush the people's minds, their hope, and their existence, but it had not yet crushed their spirit. The secret ceremonies at Bear Creek were intended to seek knowledge, understanding, and assistance. But also, to seek the spiritual technique and permission for the battle. That had all been done previously. But Sitting Bull needed to confirm this permission as an outward showing to the people.

When the people sought understanding and guidance from Wakan Tanka, it was done with respect, that the protection of the people was at stake. Something needed to be done to counterbalance the scales tipped in favor of the encroaching whites and their new ways and beliefs. The people did not understand how the whites could close their souls to all things good, and develop such narrow-minded focus as to seek out only that which would bring riches to themselves... such as the people's land, their hunting prey, their food, and their gold rocks. It was a mystery as to how these inhuman means of thinking and believing had such a stranglehold upon the will and the minds of so many of the oncoming whites. It was a mystery that needed to be understood, before it could be properly dealt with and resolved.

The mysterious driving force of the soul of many of the whites, was indeed foreign to the communal nature of the people, whose beliefs and values did not account for such things. The old ways of life were now clearly threatened, and the holy men and leaders feared that the whites' beliefs and devotions would infiltrate and dilute the people's minds, bodies, and spirits. The old ways were always utilized by the people to find their way back on to the proper path in life. The old ways were used to steady the direction of, and the means and methods of achieving the desired outcome. The old ways were a recognized tradition that followed strong principles and procedures in order stay true to the respect and honor of the Creator, and to know the right way of doing the right thing. The Creator intended that the people communicate in these old ways, as the Creator would respond with both seen and unseen guidance. The offerings were made to seek the Creator's gifts of knowledge, courage, intelligence, and understanding. And in this case, to present the vision of hope to the people which is to come from the permission of the Creator.

Sitting Bull, as the Hunkpapa spiritual leader, had received his own spiritual guidance and instruction concerning his role in what was to come. He had been instructed to make sure that the people who followed him, ended up at the Greasy Grass during the selected time. He had been chosen by the spirits to be present at the encampment at the time when his spiritual presence would serve the most good for what needed to be done. Sitting Bull knew that others had been chosen to carry out their own sacred spiritual instructions and duties. Sitting Bull had been entrusted with the duty and obligation to provide hope, will, and confidence to the people, so that their individual and collective spirits remained strong.

When the Lakota arrived in the Powder River country and made their way south and west along the Rosebud Creek, Sitting Bull, as he had been instructed, set up camp near the sacred Deer Medicine Rock. He was to perform a sun dance ceremony there to provide spiritual strength, energy, hope, and confidence to himself and the people during this time of uncertainty. Sitting Bull had been to the Deer Medicine Rock many times before and was quite familiar with the sacred site's power and connection. This is why it had been chosen as a point of ceremony along their path to the Greasy Grass valley. Spirit Horse knew this sacred site well too. He had a spiritual connection with the Owl Rock overlooking the Deer Medicine Rock. It was there, years ago, that he'd had a dream of his life and his death, a premonition that he'd etched into the Great Owl's rocky south wing.

On or about the eleventh day of June, well ahead of the arrival of any cavalry scouts or reconnaissance parties, Sitting Bull led the people to the Rosebud Creek valley and to the flatlands along its bending creek banks. It was here that the Lakota set up camp. They would be joined by more and more Lakota arriving from the east and north, many from the agencies in Dakota Territory. The Cheyenne also joined them, as their territories were nearby, also in the east.

On the first morning after his party's arrival, Sitting Bull began fasting and praying in preparation for the sun dance. He had his relative assist him in preparing his *scarlet blanket* as an offering to Wakan Tanka during the ceremony. One hundred pieces of Sitting Bull's flesh, fifty from each arm, were cut off by a bone knife and then offered to Wakan Tanka. The wounds were left open during his dance.

After two days of dancing and praying, Sitting Bull lay down on the ground. It was here that he indicated he received his vision confirming the spiritual permission previously granted. He saw soldiers falling into camp, with no ears. They resembled grasshoppers. When Sitting Bull awoke, he went to the southwest face of the Deer Medicine Rock and etched his vision. This he did to provide the hope and confidence to the people that Wakan Tanka and Creator were with them.

It would be several more days before the people began to move further south and west along the Rosebud, toward the passageway across the Wolf Mountains to the west. That passageway would lead into the lush fertile river valley of the Greasy Grass. According to his spiritual instructions, Sitting Bull needed to lead the people to this place to assemble their encampment. And then they were to wait.

On June 16, a group of a few hundred warriors led by Spirit Horse went ahead of the group of moving people to scout the passageway across the Wolf Mountain Pass. Late in the evening on June 16, Spirit Horse and several of the lead perimeter scouts saw an approaching column of cavalry and infantry coming from the southeast. They did not know it at the time, but this was General Crook's Wyoming Column seeking to find the *hostiles*. Spirit Horse advised the warriors that they would wait until early dawn of the next day, June 17, to meet the soldiers. It was a short, quiet night. Scouts were sent back to Sitting Bull to advise him to wait for word of the outcome.

The region known as the Powder River Territory consisted of the Yellowstone River flowing west to east along the northernmost edge. Flowing south to north into the Yellowstone River from the south were four rivers, with four large river valleys. From the west to the east, these rivers were the Bighorn River, the Rosebud Creek, the Tongue River, and the Powder River. Each of these four rivers had smaller tributaries that fed into them. The main tributary of the Bighorn River was the Little Bighorn River, known to the Lakota as the Greasy Grass River. The Lakota also knew the Yellowstone River as the Elk River.

On June 9, 1876, the Terry–Custer column had reached the point of rendezvous with Gen. John Gibbon. General Terry met with Gibbon aboard the steamer the *Far West* when it was docked along the Yellowstone at its confluence with the mouth of Rosebud Creek. In their discussion, Terry and Gibbon decided it was best to focus on the country between the Powder River to the east, and the Bighorn River to the west. But they needed further intelligence and reconnaissance to determine the likely whereabouts of the Lakota and Cheyenne encampment, which the army suspected was somewhere in this region. Terry studied the maps that had been created by the Raynolds expedition into the area in 1859 to survey the geography of the territory. It was left to General Terry to put together the plan of attack from this point forward. Of course, as of June 9, Terry and Gibbon did not know that their Third Column from the south, the Crook column, would run into a big problem at the headwaters of the Rosebud near the southern pass of the Wolf Mountains. Terry could not have anticipated that Crook's whole column from the south would be stopped. Terry certainly did not anticipate that the entire Crook column would retreat all the way to Goose Creek in Wyoming, or that Crook would not immediately send word to the other army commanders to indicate that the US Army's southern prong was no longer involved in the battle plan against the Lakota. The reasons why Crook chose not to warn the other combatants of his total withdrawal are uncertain, according to the official records. However, it does appear to the Lakota that the spiritual messages and warnings sent to the army leaders, was strong and real, in that consideration.

In any event, Terry decided that it was important to try to learn anything he could about the whereabouts of the *hostiles* and their encampments.

On June 10 in the morning, Terry ordered Major Reno to prepare six companies of cavalry, one Gatling gun, a group of scouts, and one hundred pack mules for a reconnaissance mission. Reno was to take rations enough for ten days. Reno and the soldiers were directed to ride to the west to the Tongue River and then go south to the mouth of the Tongue River. If Reno were to believe or know that the Indians were further west, then to separate his forces, sending one part of his command up the Tongue River to its headwaters, where they would cross to the headwaters of Rosebud Creek and then follow that stream back toward the Yellowstone. This mission was expected to take a good ten to twelve days.

Custer, of course, was upset with Terry, who would not allow Custer and his troops to go on this reconnaissance mission to try to locate the hostile encampment. Custer tried to change Terry's mind before Reno left. But Terry remained committed, assuring Custer that the entire Seventh Cavalry would march against the hostiles when the time came and saying that Custer would be the one to lead them. Terry knew that Custer was impatient and hard driving, and that he might try to seize the opportunity to run the men and the horses ragged on a mere reconnaissance mission, using them up before the necessary battle. This is why Terry thought Reno to be the better choice for this job.

Because the terrain involved was dry, hilly, and ravine filled, with many dips and rises, Reno chose to use the pack mules instead of the wagons. Mules are most certainly slower than horses, but they are extremely strong and sturdy, able to carry up to two hundred pounds of supplies each. Once they were guided or whipped into moving, the mules did quite well for this purpose. Also, mules can last a longer time and travel a greater distance without food and water than most horses can. However, it was still a harsh thing to watch as to how the packers and mule team handlers treated their beasts of burden. Most times, these men were mean and inhumane toward the mules. It struck a nerve with some, how the mules' burden would not suggest better treatment. They did not deserve such harsh treatment. The pack mule caretaker at

Fort Lincoln, Don Jorner, would be hopping mad once he learned how the Seventh was treating his mules.

As for Reno, the reconnaissance mission up the Tongue River was a welcome diversion from staying at camp with the other officers, namely, Custer. Reno was a civil war veteran but had mostly done administrative work since 1865. This would be his first work done in the field during the Indian-fighting operations. Terry had directed Reno to stay within the bounds of the territory between the Powder and the Tongue. However, as Reno and his search group went on, they saw signs of activity on the ground, in the form of tracks and abandoned campsites. So Reno decided to take his command group westward across the Tongue River valley, where they descended along Rosebud Creek and traveled toward the Yellowstone. Reno figured that by making the trek this way, he would cover more territory and be more sure of what was out there. However, the drawback and risk of this move was that it increased the possibility that the army's forces may be seen by the Lakota.

Having reached the confluence of the Yellowstone River and the Powder River by June 11, 1876, Terry was able to meet with the soldiers and officers to discuss his new plan of the approach. At this point in the Terry–Custer column's march, they had been gone 24 days and covered over 318 miles since leaving Ft. Lincoln. The enlisted men were happy to see that the steamboat *Far West*, with Captain Marsh, was there, because the boat carried a fresh supply of canned goods, new straw hats, ammo, forage provisions… and liquor. After clearing the area of rattlesnakes, the soldiers were allowed to partake of the liquor. They all were very thirsty. Indian scout leader Frank Gerard had forbidden the Arikira and Crow scouts from even going near the liquor tent. The trader who brought the liquor that day had set up in a large tent with partitions separating the enlisted men from the commissioned officers. The part set aside for the enlisted men was so filled with soldiers buying liquor, that it looked like a swarm of flies.

On June 14, Terry ordered Custer to take a column made up of companies from the Seventh Cavalry to rendezvous with Reno's reconnaissance group at the mouth of the Tongue. Captain Benteen would go along as well. It was here that the Seventh Calvary packed up, leaving behind their sabers, (their "long knives"),as they were considered useless in fighting the Lakota, and they made too much noise while the troops were moving. The mules were loaded down with supplies. The *Far West* was to follow the column, moving west along the Yellowstone. Custer and the remnants of the Seventh Calvary that were not with Reno, rode to the planned rendezvous point where they were to meet up with Reno's troops. On the way, on June 16, Custer came upon an abandoned Indian camp. There were several deceased bodies up on scaffolds, a practice to honor the dead. The troops decided to look at the bodies. In so doing, they ripped the blanket shrouds off the bodies and grabbed anything and everything that they thought was of value from the dead bodies. Custer, his brothers Tom and Boston, and even his nephew Autie Reed, participated in the desecration of the remains. Custer's interpreter Isaiah Dorman took items from one body and used the flesh from that body as bait for fishing. These acts, of course, were in violation of the moral and ethical standards of most every civilization. The Custer men took souvenirs to take home with them.

Custer's column arrived at the mouth of the Tongue River on June 17. Unbeknown to the army at the time, some ninety miles south along the Rosebud Creek, the southern prong of the three-pronged attack plan was being soundly whipped by a group of Lakota and Cheyenne warriors led by Spirit Horse. General Crook and his soldiers were involved in a six-hour battle, which resulted in a temporary standoff, until Crook decided to retreat and take his whole column back to Wyoming along the Goose Creek. He did not notify Terry, Gibbon, or Custer.

Prior to this time, June 17, all the military leaders, including General Crook, had been sent spiritual messages and warnings from the Lakota, urging them to use peace and diplomacy to resolve the dispute over the Black Hills. None of the US Army military brass were open enough about the situation to freely discuss the notion that they had all been warned ahead of time. But Crook, very likely, may have been a different story.

⸻ ◈ ⸻

George Crook graduated from West Point in 1852. He was viewed by his peers as a skilled military man. He had served in the Civil War, leading the Ohio Brigade at Antietam, and was a division commander at Chickamauga and in the Shenandoah Valley campaign. He attained the rank of brevet major general. Briefly before the Civil War, he did fight Indians on the California-Oregon border with the Fourth Infantry Regiment. After the Civil War, he was sent to the west to fight Indians.

As a military tactician, Crook prided himself on making himself more knowledgeable of his enemy before planning how to fight them. So in fighting out west, he would try to learn the techniques of the frontiersmen and the Indians by getting to know the plants, the terrain, the Indians' movements, and their habits of attack or retreat. He even tried to enlist as scouts, members of the same tribe of people he had planned to fight. Crook was a student and proponent of using a highly mobile, agile, tactical group of troops who were skilled in marksmanship. He preferred this type of fighting unit over a regiment that had large weapons and slow-moving teams or columns. Crook studied the indigenous peoples. He became aware of many of their personal tendencies and their social structures, having sought to teach himself as much as he could about how the Indian may think. When Crook was studying to learn more about his indigenous opponents, he ran straight into the fact that the Indians, in particular the Lakota, used prayers to the spirits. And to Wakan Tanka, asking for help, protection, and guidance in battle.

It was believed by many in and out of the military that Crook was different than most military commanders of the period in some respects. Notably in his having developed a degree of respect for his Indian opponents, believing that they were more than the savage animals or subhumans, that many or most in the military believed them to be.

Perhaps this is part of the reason why Crook encountered what he did when he accepted the appointment and commission to head up the Wyoming Column departing from Goose Creek and Fort Fetterman in the spring campaign of 1876.

It was believed by many of the Lakota, and especially many of their leaders and spiritual people, that when all of the spiritual messages were being sent out to the US Military and its officers in the year leading up to the Greasy Grass battle, that Gen. George Crook had a more specialized affinity than others, to be able to hear, feel, and know about the warnings while they were being sent out by way of the spiritual connection in the lead-up to the battle. And that it was Crook's willingness and intent to know more about the Lakota ways, that may have opened up his spirit, giving him the ability to receive the warnings and to know and accept them for what they were.

This would become more apparent than ever for Crook when he found himself matched up with the suddenly appearing Lakota and Cheyenne warriors led by Spirit Horse near the headwaters of Rosebud Creek on June 17, 1876. He seemed not to be totally surprised or caught off guard by the fierce opposition his forces encountered that day. He appeared calm and decisive. He seemed to react as if the outcome may have already been preordained. That the outcome was not his nor that of his troops to change that day…at that battle. He seemed to act in a way of a man, a soldier, who had calmly accepted his own fate and that of his regiment. It appeared that he was willing to fight, yet not attack; to react, yet not overreact; and to defend, then retreat. Not to press forward and not to potentially lose more, or most of his men's lives, or his own.

As it was, Spirit Horse and the Lakota and Cheyenne warriors presented an honorable and courageous stand against a heavily armed larger military force in Crook's column. The fight would last for hours and there were many acts of bravery and battle expertise exhibited by Spirit Horse and the warriors. It was during this conflict that a young Cheyenne woman named Buffalo Calf Road Woman would also show courage in rescuing her brother from the battlefield. The fighting eventually ceased.

In the end, Crook decided in his mind,…and likely in his heart,… and most uniquely, quite convincingly, in his spirit, that he must…

retreat. And take all of his men and his equipment, back to where they had come from: back to Goose Creek. This he did, eight days before the great campaign plan called for him to meet and converge with the Terry column from the northeast, and the Gibbon column from the northwest.

His decision was to go back to where he had started. And not to send a unit or scouts ahead to alert or warn the other columns. He did not hurry to the nearest telegraph station to wire the news or instructions to the other columns or the other commanders. No, Crook turned and went back to Goose Creek. In doing this, he saved the lives of most of his men, and likely his own.

Crook must have been at peace with his decision, because history notes that his men, upon returning to Goose Creek in Wyoming, calmly went fishing. As if it had all had been preordained. And according to the spiritual significance and overbearing presence of the message and permission received by Saved By Bear and the warriors at Bear Creek, directly from the Creator, it was something that Crook obviously was convinced, was preordained. That it was in fact, destiny. So he saved the lives of the men who he could. He listened. He heeded. He lived. And they all went fishing.

This may be the best explanation as to why Crook gave up so easily after being stopped cold and suddenly by Spirit Horse and his warriors at Rosebud Creek on the seventeenth. He did not feel like sacrificing himself and his men for Custer and his aspirations. Or, possibly, Crook realized that a military with mere guns and horses, could not match the spiritual strength of the Lakota that he was feeling, was waiting for the army at the Greasy Grass. Crook, by this point, had been a student of Lakota ways, so he may have had a more honest appreciation of what was to come.

Meanwhile, farther north, Custer, in a move of some significance, would decide to leave his regimental band behind at the mouth of the Powder River. Bandleader Felix Vinatieri had been with Custer on most of his recent campaigns, he and his band playing for the troops when there was downtime or the forces were being reviewed. But more importantly to Custer, Vinatieri and the band would come along on the raids or attacks so that the band could play Custer's favorite attack theme, *Garryowen*. Always for pomp and flair, it had to have been a tough decision for Custer to leave the band behind. The cavalry troops took the band's group of white horses for use in the upcoming pursuit and tracking of the hostiles. As for Vinatieri, he may have had a different perspective altogether as to when he and the band were left behind.

With an affinity for music, Custer was accustomed to having his own personal musicians and marching military band come along with him and his military unit on missions or outings, official or unofficial. He enjoyed the nuance of having a musical portrayal of his attachment's or company's approach to the enemy position. He felt as if the auditory presence of music, especially the right song, potentially added to the fear and anxiety of his enemy as he approached to fight. Custer envisioned that the added value of charging to a crescendo of horns and snare drums increased the pace and motivation of the soldiers and mounts under his command at the critical moment of truth—the point of initial engagement. Willing to use anything to gain an advantage over his enemy, Custer was always plotting and planning his next military move. Hoping to somehow make the present one more grand and dramatic than the previous one. To make the next one even better than the one before.

The added intrigue of the band's striking and its trumpeting beat made Custer feel as if he was more sophisticated than the other commanders. And certainly more sophisticated than his poor enemy, especially those *heathen redskins,* as he was known to say over the years of fighting Indians.

Custer had his favorite tunes, both for marching and for charging. He preferred a more melodious consistent tune such as *Boots and Saddles* for the march. However, when it came time to whip up the enthusiasm and of his charging troops and get them into killing mode, Custer greatly preferred the old Irish tune *Garryowen*. This song, he felt, fit his personality well, especially when he was leading his charge of cavalry along some western plain in an all-out sprint to the point of conflict and victory over his enemy, usually an unsuspecting camp of Indians.

The rhythm and melody of *Garryowen* made him feel so alive, even at a time when he was so close to such emotions and outcomes as death, mayhem, and suffering. It was as if he flew to the sound of the persistent fife and horn, and the determined rhythm of the melody as it cascaded in waves, much like his troops of cavalry would be doing over his soon to be vanquished enemies. Even Victory ("Vic") and Dandy, Custer's two personal mounts, seemed to enjoy and be energized by the sounds of the charge. As members of the horse nation, they too were motivated by the senses and energy, and were aware of their circumstances.

No one was better at leading his band in the *Garryowen* charge than Felix Vinatieri. The Italian immigrant was a tremendously talented bandleader and a prolific musician in his own right. He was a musician and songwriter-turned-bandleader, who happened to have been called to enlist in the US Department of the Army soon after the Civil War ended. As an immigrant, he saw serving in the army of his newly adopted country an act of respect and patriotism. When the army noticed his musical talents, they made him an army band member, and eventually a military bandleader.

It was during a concert at a fort in Yankton, Dakota Territory, that Lieutenant Colonel Custer first heard Vinatieri play and took notice of his God-given talents and his ear for the regimented synchronicity necessary for the military band style. Soon after that concert, Custer specifically requested that the young Italian be his bandleader to accompany him and the cavalry in the field. This is how it came to pass that Vinatieri was Custer's bandleader who went out on Custer's missions and expeditions in the mid-1870s, including the expedition into the Black Hills in 1874.

However, Vinatieri, at one point becoming upset with Custer's arrogant, flippant, and demanding style and personality, became reticent and reluctant to continue as Custer's personal bandleader. Vinatieri was to make one last march with Custer's Seventh Cavalry in the late spring of 1876, the last time he would willingly serve Custer. As fate would have it, Custer made the announcement of his decision to leave the band behind this time, after Vinatieri and the band had made the three-hundred-mile journey from Bismarck to the mouth of the Powder River in the unceded hunting territory of the Lakota. Despite his duty to his country and his military service, it is understandable that Felix Viniatari and his descendants to come, would be forever thankful for that decision.

⸻ ⦿ ⸻

Meanwhile, Custer's column moved up the Yellowstone and rendezvoused with Reno's men, who had returned from their ten-day scouting mission. On June 18, Reno reported to Terry that his troops had run across a big Indian trail up the Rosebud and had followed it until it crossed the mountains and appeared to go into the Little Bighorn Valley. Custer was upset with Reno because Reno did not provide specifics about the size of the trail and the direction it had traveled. Terry decided to move their camp up the Yellowstone to the mouth of the Rosebud Creek. Gibbon's column would be traveling down the Yellowstone to rendezvous there as well.

⸻ ⦿ ⸻

Custer, Reno, and Terry, and now Gibbon, all met up at the camp along the mouth of the Rosebud Creek on June 21. This was the moment when Terry finalized his plan to have Custer and the Seventh Calvary proceed south along the Rosebud and canvass for the hostiles in the valley, and then move south and west if necessary to drive the hostiles west and north into Gibbon's infantry and cannon group, which would arrive in the Little Bighorn Valley on June 26.

General Terry's Letter of Instructions

Headquarters Department of Dakota
(In the Field)
Camp at Mouth of Rosebud River
Montana Territory, June 22nd 1876.
Lieut. Col. G. A. Custer, 7th Cavalry.

Colonel:

The Brigadier-General Commanding directs that, as soon as your regiment can be made ready for the march, you will proceed up the Rosebud in pursuit of the Indians whose trail was discovered by Major Reno a few days since. It is, of course, impossible to give you any definite instructions in regard to this movement, and were it not impossible to do so, the Department Commander places too much confidence in your zeal, energy and ability to wish to impose upon you precise orders which might hamper your action when nearly in contact with the enemy. He will, however, indicate to you his own views of what your action should be, and he desires that you should conform to them unless you shall see sufficient reason for departing from them. He thinks that you should proceed up the Rosebud until you ascertain definitely the direction in which the trail above spoken of leads. Should it be found (as it appears almost certain that it will be found) to turn towards the Little Horn, he thinks that you should still proceed southward, perhaps as far as the headwaters of the Tongue, and then turn towards the Little Horn, feeling constantly, however, to your left, so as to preclude the possibility of the escape of the Indians to the south or southeast by passing around your left flank.

The column of Colonel Gibbon is now in motion for the mouth of the Big Horn. A soon as it reaches that point it will cross the Yellowstone and move up at least as far as the forks of the Big and Little Horns. Of course its further movements must be controlled by circumstances as they arise, but it is hoped that the Indians, if upon the Little Horn, may be so nearly inclosed by the two columns that their escape will be impossible. The Department Commander desires that on the way up the Rosebud you shall thoroughly examine the upper part of Tullock's Creek, and that you should endeavor to send a scout through to Colonel Gibbon's column, with information of the results of your examination. The lower part of the creek will be examined by a detachment from Colonel Gibbon's command.

The supply steamer will be pushed up the Big Horn as far as the forks if the river is found to be navigable for that distance, and the Department Commander, who will accompany the Column of Colonel Gibbon, desires you to report to him there not later than the expiration of the time for which your troops are rationed, unless in the meantime you receive further orders.

Very Respectfully,
Your obedient Servant,
Ed. W. Smith, Captain, 18th Infantry,
Acting Assistant Adjutant General.[23]

Terry's orders were detailed, but in the end these orders also allowed Custer leeway to use his discretion to quickly pursue the Indians should he see them. Custer was to set out on his march on the morning of June 22, with fifteen days' worth of rations to be loaded on the pack mules, consisting of hardtack, coffee, sugar, and twelve days' worth of bacon. Twelve mules were assigned for each troop. Each soldier was to carry one hundred rounds of carbine and twenty-four rounds of pistol ammunition. The horses and mules that had gone on the ten-day mission with Reno were still not refreshed, but it was Terry's decision not to delay further. He let Custer set out on the twenty-second anyway. On the night before Custer's departure, the Crow and Arikara scouts stepped up their death songs. It was quite obvious that the scouts were feeling the messages from the spirits at this time, being so close to the army leaders, especially Custer.

Custer had been given his orders by Terry to proceed from the mouth of the Powder River and up Rosebud Creek using the route taken by Maj. Marcus Reno a few days earlier. Custer was to scout for the camp of Lakota hostiles and engage them at his discretion. He and the Seventh Cavalry were to leave the camp at the Powder River early on the

---

[23] Dustin, The Custer Tragedy: Id.at 91.

morning of June 22. In order to travel light and as quietly as possible so as to not tip off the hostiles, which could cause them to disperse and escape, Custer decided that he would not take the Gatling guns, as they were too heavy and cumbersome. Custer decided he wanted to pack very light so that he and the Seventh could move as quickly and stealthily as possible. He instructed that rations be taken only for fifteen days, and that no sabers or other long knives be carried. He also would be without his military band, as they had already been left behind at the mouth of the Powder River.

On the morning of the twenty-second, as planned, Custer appeared dressed in his fringed yellow buckskin suit with a double-breasted shirt and his broad-brimmed grayish-white hat. He carried a Remington rifle with two white-handled pistols. All mounted up, Custer, Reno, Benteen, and the Seventh Cavalry, with 566 enlisted men, 35 Indian scouts, and 12 civilian scouts, plus 2 civilian relatives of Custer, the company went in front of Terry and Gibbon for review. Custer was on his horse Dandy, while Vic was in the horse column to follow. Dandy was the older of the two. Vic was the one Custer usually rode in battle. As the troops were leaving the camp, Gibbon yelled out to Custer, "Now, Custer, don't be greedy. Wait for us!" Custer waved his hand and said, "No, I will not." And then the Seventh trotted down the trail toward the winding southern stretch of the Rosebud. Custer and the Seventh Cavalry did not know that the sixteen warriors from the He Sapa were already waiting for them at the Greasy Grass.

After having arrived the previous night, many of the sixteen warriors rode down to the edge of the familiar rushing river, the Greasy Grass. Most were used to the river, having seen it many times, especially Saved By Bear, Swift Bear, and the Lakota warriors. The Dakota and Nakota were not as familiar with it, Buffalo Horn especially, as he had not been there since he was a child, which was not that long ago. He took in the beauty of the Greasy Grass valley and the river with wide eyes and a sense of awe and gratitude. "Beautiful," he said.

The warriors wanted to ride and walk through and over the land so as to get the layout, reconnecting and refamiliarizing themselves. They wanted to feel the ground beneath their moccasins. To reach down and grab a handful of the cool, clean water to splash on their faces and the backs of their necks. They desired to smell the sagebrush, which was heavenly thick. And to walk through, smell, and experience the movement of the tall greenish grass that is the namesake of the valley and the river. The grass leaves a sheen in its midst because of its unique nature.

As Saved by Bear gazed upon the flowing exposure of the grass up from a ford of a shallow crossing of the river, looking up toward the eastern ravine coulee on the opposite side, it seemed to him that the Greasy Grass was moving in waves up and down and side to side. Being pushed and stirred by the gentle breeze, the gentle breath, of Wakan Tanka. It was beautiful, as Buffalo Horn had said. It was also old. It was a hidden paradise among hidden paradises. A natural wonder among a land of natural wonders. He never tired of being here. Of seeing her in person, in the present. A slight buzzing sound near his ear brought him out of the near trance he had fallen into while appreciating where he was.

The quiet buzzing brought him back to the moment, back to the task at hand. He turned in the direction of the buzzing and caught a glimpse of his friend, his brother, Swift Bear kneeling down along the edge of the water with his left hand reaching for a stone that gave off a bluish hue. And as Saved By Bear focused on his friend, he saw him. The source of the buzzing: a big beautiful blue shaded dragonfly. He was hovering several feet in front of Swift Bear.

Saved By Bear stepped forward, toward the edge of the water to stand alongside his friend, who was still kneeling, still with his hand in the clear moving water. Saved By Bear thought to himself that he was thankful that it was he and Swift Bear who had been chosen by Creator to be here together. Two Lakota warriors. Two of the Dog Man warrior group. Two friends. Two brothers. Two spirits coordinated and granted the permission to act in a way to preserve all that is, and all that may ever be, of their way of life. They would do this for Unci Maka, and the Greasy Grass herself.

Swift Bear then stood. As he did so, the large blue dragonfly hovered and, with quick agility, moved between the two warriors. Then it quickly darted backward and down, swooping over the surface of the water and flying toward the chokecherry bush along the edge of the bank. The movement also caught Swift Bear's eye. The two Dog Man warriors watched the blue dragonfly as it again lifted, and darted in front of their faces. But now, the large dragonfly was joined by another large blue one, which flew by his side. They both came together to hover in front of the two Dog Man warriors. Here they were. The two Dog Man warriors standing on the banks of the Greasy Grass. About to embark upon the culminating journey of their sacred preparation over the past year. They were about to face a moment in their lives where they would be called upon to utilize everything they had learned and been taught. To achieve their goal. To fulfill the sacred permission.

And here were the two blue dragonflies. The symbol of the Dog Man. All four of them, now together. Saved By Bear stared at the beauty of design, color, and movement of the flying beings. And he understood. "Pilamaya ye," he said. As he did so, the two dragonfly brothers moved to the nearby chokecherry bush and hovered at the part hanging over the water's edge, the side facing the hilltop of the warriors'plans and preparation.

At the same time, Saved By Bear and Swift Bear saw them. The rest of them. There were sixteen of them. Clustered among the outer branches of the chokecherry bush. They were clinging to the bush, facing the same direction: west. They were all blue. All dressed the same. The dragonflies. The warriors saw this as another sign from the Creator. A sign of unity, and resolve. This is a vision that Saved By Bear would never forget. It signified the reason why they were here.

At once, all of the dragonflies lifted and hovered back, and then flew in unison to the east. Toward the slope. The slope leading up to the *hill*. And disappeared.

Saved By Bear put a hand on his brother's shoulder. No words were said. But as he turned to face the west, something in the distance caught his eye. It was a slight movement on the western horizon along the bench-style bluffs that bordered the western edge of the Greasy Grass River valley. Over there he looked. He brought his right hand up to shield his eyes from the rays of the overhead early summer sun, from his line of vision. And then he felt a warmth in his chest and a positive tingling running through there.

There it was. In the distance. Standing proudly, but watching them intently. Watching him. Watching over him. The white mane ruffled slightly in the breeze. And Saved By Bear felt comfort. Something he had been told, something he had been shown, long ago in the White Mountains was on the verge of becoming true. Saved By Bear closed his eyes momentarily to avoid the glare of the sun. When he opened them again, the figure was gone.

———————⊙———————

It was now seven days before the warriors would engage in their confrontation with the military. They had arrived at night, two nights prior. They had mostly stayed out of sight in the Wolf Mountains, except when they had come down to the river the day before. At dawn, they scouted west and south in the valley, looking for any type of activity. They wanted to be absolutely sure that no one was around. Not finding anyone, they believed they had a safe opportunity to scout the territory down by the river where the people's encampments were routinely set up. They also wanted to do some daytime reconnaissance to get the feel of the land and vegitation on the slopes leading up from the river. They were particularly interested in siting out the areas where they would need to conceal themselves the night before the battle, where they would lie in wait for their moment to arrive.

From their vantage point, they soaked in the surroundings. The warm summer breeze swooned up from the bench hills in the west and swooped down along the slope toward the Greasy Grass River. Bristles of sagebrush and sharp dry grass that had piled up along the river's edge flew by the group of warriors, blowing into the tough buffalo grass and chokecherry bushes on the west bank. Then, moving farther down the river's edge, the gentle breeze blew into the small thistles, causing them to bend and reach toward the water. Then flew over the surface of the water. The breeze picked up the loose dirt on the three-foot rise of the east bank and blew it up to the overhanging twenty-foot cliff looming on that side of the river. There, the chokecherry bushes shimmied. The breeze shot to the left and moved toward the open mouth of the coulee, running up the northeast side and over some small ash and pine trees. It blew through the needles and leaves, and then lit upon the built-up edge of the greasy grass. The greasy grass, very prevalent at this time of year, had grown quite thick here and there along the open areas rising up from the eastern riverbank. The light green and yellowish grass stands one and a half to two feet tall, amongst which periodic clumps of sagebrush, whitish and distinctive, pop up here and there.

The zephyr from the west stirs the greasy grass and caused it to sway, bend, and reflexively spring back, and then to do it all again. The blades bunch against each other and want to act independently but, for the most part, cannot. They are coaxed by the breeze to coordinate in their bending and swaying in random groupings, looking like a series of waves cascading in a flow of water. Resembling tumbling water moving up the hill, rather than down.

The grass moves in unpredictable patterns and stretches, bending and reaching, recoiling, springing left and springing right, and standing up tall. To only start the process again, moving in different cadences, to a different synchronicity, each time depending upon the volume and striking pressure of the warm summer breeze.

If one were to lay inside the moving waves, it is almost as if one could swim upstream or uphill as it was, easily with the massive upheaval and push of the waves of the greasy grass.

The tender touch and slap of green and yellow blades against each other can scarcely be heard by the human ear. But the blades know of their own individual and collective music. Their symphony being conducted and motivated by the conductor at their back and in their faces, all at once. The conductor is of course invisible to all. But the prominence and force are fully realized with each impending gust and burst. And the great rolling rapture of the grand wide sweep of the conductor's baton over the tips of his individual choir blades. They move as if a family of carpet strings reacting to being shaken out, like a giant rug in the huge grip and strength of the conductor. The Creator is the conductor.

If one were to dive into the flowing grass and attempt to float, one would be swept under by the undertow, and be hidden from view.

Hidden until the next gust were to slash the covers aside to expose the body within.

The movement of the greasy grass was magical. It was as if it were creating an illusion in and of itself to help conceal, and provide for the protection of those who did choose to swim within the embrace of its waves. The cloaking provided by the moving grass would serve as an additional shield of protection for the warriors.

As a means to practice their theory, several of the warriors crawled up and into the grass to create the image. One by one, they knew of the magic of the illusion, and of its powerful source. One by one they dove down to the greasy grass depths to allow themselves to be overtaken, then consumed, and to be hidden, and to be protected within. One by one, they could hide and move forward, without being seen as anything but the moving greasy grass itself. This was a benefit that came from the fact that the brothers—humans and plants—knew of and about each other. This was an old way of doing things. It was like riding a horse. A greasy-grass horse.

Saved By Bear and Swift Bear followed the vision and the plan set out before, according to the permission sought and granted. The assistance of the greasy grass was only one part of it. So they dived in and joined the others in the exercise of concealment, and moved forward uphill.

⊰⊱⊰⊱

While waiting for the day of destiny to arrive, the warriors observed the daily activities of the natural peoples that lived within or routinely visited the Greasy Grass valley. There were many. It was as it had always been. Among the natural peoples was the prairie chicken, a relative of the grouse people. A strong, proud being in its own right, who puts on a show for everyone to watch.

He knows that he is impressive. He knows that he is pretty and attractive. He needs to be. He often has to use his appearance during mating season in the spring. He is truly beautiful and proud, and confidently arrogant, when he wants to be. He knows the Lakota. His ancestors have shared the land and water with them for many, many years. They seem to always be fascinated by him and his kind, his ancestors and the little ones alike. He believes that it really is, and has been, all to do with the way he dances.

Creator was thoughtful and kind enough to cover him in thick, fluffy plumage. He shows this plumage proudly when he dances. And when he dances, he really dances. But he doesn't dance for just any old reason. It needs to be a special occasion, and that usually involves the females in the mating season, but sometimes just to show off his stuff.

He can stand, scratch, and preen with the best dancers in the territory. He considers the spring and summer to be the best time to dance, but he even does it in the fall to show that he can do it any time of the year. He really likes the prairie grass and the shorter nubs and stalks in the clearings. He has been living in the valley of the Greasy Grass for all his life, as have his ancestors. He knows that his own offspring and those of the Lakota will likely reside here as well, as long as Creator continues to provide his people with all the seeds and bugs that they need. And he is eternally grateful for that.

It seems that the hot late June sun is perfect for dancing, and he will be ready. He has seen the warriors in the area. Something is up, he knows. But he has his own plans, so he mustn't worry about what his two-legged Lakota brothers are doing along the Greasy Grass River.

But he is okay with whatever they're doing. He is okay with them. He actually likes it when they come to visit the Greasy Grass. They always bring the types of food that make for good scraps, which he eats from around the edges of the encampment—bits and pieces of bread and seeds and corn. The corn tends to make him puffier around the middle, more than he would like for his handsome appearance, but he can just dance it all off in the end.

He knows the Lakota like to watch him and the others when a dance of his kind occurs. He sees them. He watches them. They always seem to know and understand that they should not interrupt. He knows, as he has been assured by his parents, grandparents, and other ancestors, that that is their way. He remembers: *They respect us. They enjoy us. They accept us. They know us. They actually care about us. They will not attempt to destroy us or destroy our homes or food sources. They are our friends, of different mothers and fathers. And they have come to copy us.*

He has observed them at those moments as they were going about their ways, and has always been amused. He likes to watch them when they perform, just as they like to watch him when he performs. It is like a sharing of the shows with each of their people, the Lakota and the prairie chicken.

The Lakota speak of their dance as the fancy dance, the grass dance, but the prairie chicken knows that their dance is a copy of his people's dance, and even of his own personal dance moves. First, there is the way they adorn themselves, with all the feathers down their backs. Sure, other birds have feathers. He knows that some of those feathers have come from other birds. But then there are those leggings that the warriors and braves sometimes wear around their ankles and lower legs. He knows those leggings very well, as he sees them every fall season when he looks down (past his protruding breast and belly) to behold his own legs and feet. His leggings are the same as those the Lakota wear. Realizing this, makes him happy. This gives him another reason to puff out his chest and preen some more.

Days later, once the people of the encampment begin to arrive, he will wonder why there are all these people, tipis, and ponies in late June along the Greasy Grass—and all those red-tailed hawks.

———— ⊰⟨●⟩⊱ ————

Custer's movement south continued at a rapid pace, as Custer was accustomed to. He was used to pushing his troops in this manner. He was especially anxious to move forward in this campaign because of the circumstances resulting in his demotion from overall commander to company commander. However, it was clear that Terry trusted Custer by giving him the latitude and discretion to move against the hostiles should he get close enough to engage them.

On June 23, Custer and his soldiers moved into the Rosebud Creek valley heading south. It was during their stop along the creek that the troops observed evidence of a ceremony held by a group of Indians. The scouts who were with Custer determined that the camp showed evidence of a Lakota sun dance ceremony that had been held on this spot in the past week or so. Custer's scouts indicated to him that either the Lakota or Cheyenne, or both, had performed the sun dance here, within a quarter of a mile from the Deer Medicine Rock.

Whomever had performed the sun dance left the tree and the ties indicating the process. There was many hoofprints, lodge pole marks, and burned-out campfire rings indicating the presence of the people. Also, this gathering had been held near one of the Lakota and Cheyenne's sacred sites, the Deer Medicine Rock. The scouts with Custer viewed this as a bad sign.

Custer and his men camped for the night near the abandoned Lakota camp by the Deer Medicine Rock. The troopers reported seeing strange lights and hearing strange noises emanating from a spot near the rock. Custer was determined to push hard to pick up the trail before the Indians dispersed, like they always did. It should be noted at this time that Custer was used to carrying out sneak attacks on villages mostly made up of women, children, and old people. Custer rarely attacked a village or group of Lakota or Cheyenne when a large number of defending warriors were present. His expertise at fighting Indians is in the eye of the beholder.

———— ((◊)) ————

Meanwhile, also on June 23, the Sixth Calvary of infantry, with Gatling guns, was moving slowly toward the trail up the Bighorn River. Gibbon and Terry were in command, but a young seasoned officer by the name of Lt. James Bradley, the scout leader for the Gibbon column, was out in the lead of that strike prong. The Gibbon column was slower moving because their soldiers were on foot and hauling heavy cannons. Lieutenant Bradley, a veteran of the Civil War, had reenlisted in the army after the war and had been briefly assigned to a southern division to fight and control the hateful Ku Klux Klan. Now, the Sixth was still on schedule to rendezvous with the Seventh along the Little Bighorn on June 26.

———— ((◊)) ————

The last days and nights of preparation and waiting had come and gone. The rising of the sun tomorrow would bring the new day with the new history for Saved by Bear's people. Forever. But for now, there were some things to watch and some things to consider.

Mounted on his friend's strong back, standing in anticipation of what was to come, Saved By Bear was concealed atop the high ridge looking over the Greasy Grass River valley in the distance, and looking south across the buffalo-horn-shaped expansion of the camp. The two stood closely beside the other horse and rider. Saved By Bear's good friend and fellow Dog Man warrior Swift Bear leaned over the neck of his pony Spotted Smoke. They too realized the significance of the moments to come. Both riders looked south, scanning the valley and the large encampment stretching for a mile or so up and down the flatland along the western banks of the winding fast-moving river. Although they were too far away to hear or smell, Saved by Bear looked on and envisioned everything in the camp: the sweet smell of buffalo meat cooking over the campfire, the lifting sound of those washing and swimming in the water of the Greasy Grass, the familiar work song sung by the group of women tanning hides near the trees. These were the usual things in the early summer season, rich with smells and full of good hunting and festive camaraderie.

The warriors turned to each other, catching each other's eye. Then, as if in unison, they turned back to face the south, and then the east, gazing upon the Wolf Mountains about fifteen miles away. It was going to be hot today, the calm simmering beating rays of the early morning sun warming the tanned skin of their bare hands and faces, but not the rest of their buckskin-clothed bodies. The breeze lifted off the river and gusted in bursts before them, rustling the horses' manes and the two feathers on top of Saved By Bear's braided hair, the feathers standing straight up to symbolize the warrior's Dog Man status.

The two Dog Man warriors knew that they must remain concealed from all who would watch or scout for visitors, trespassers, or enemies, even from their own people in the encampment below. The group of sixteen warriors had been at the hidden base camp north of the Greasy Grass Valley for ten nights and nine days now. They had been doing most of their work at night, when they could move more freely and practice their foot speed and horse maneuvers. They had even gone down to the *pathway* area on the *hill* many days earlier to feel and know the bumps, ridges, and dips of the land, to determine the location of the trees and the sagebrush, and to discover what lines of vision were open. However, the spiritual instructions and their preparation had proven true as to all that was and to be. Now, on the morning before they were to move into position under the cover of night, the warriors had a chance to do some early daylight viewing, as long as they remained unseen and unnoticed. It was of vital importance that they not be seen. They could make out some things within the encampment since they were far away. Other things, they could only rely upon the memory of the traditions, and with their keen sense of imagination.

The encampment was a sight to behold in the early light of day. The people had now been at the Greasy Grass for three days and two nights, having moved the tipis slightly north each day to take advantage of the tall grazing grass for the two or three thousand ponies, which seemed to be constantly hungry and eating. Most of the large, moving, snorting, hoofing mass of the horse people were spread out in a long island of horse herd to the distant south and west of the two warriors and their mounts. The ponies were grazing in the grass along the bench-style ridge that rose about a half mile west of the westernmost edge of the people's encampment. In their elevated position to the northeast of the edge of the pony herd, Saved By Bear and Swift Bear had a wondrous view of some of the activity below, and beyond, to the rolling ridges and ravines beyond the quick river. They could see the large and long range of the Shiny Mountains on the southwest horizon in the distance. Their vantage point exposed to them a vivid scene of the large circles and layers of lodges of the families and people—Lakota, Hunkpapa, Sans Arcs, Oglala, Sicangu, Blackfeet, Cheyenne, and their own people, the Mnincoju.

The expanse of tipis were arranged in extended circles. The camp was laid out in the age-old fashion of the ancestors in honor of the Lakota's brothers the buffalo people. As always, the circles of tipi groups would follow the order of the peoples themselves, set up in the shape of the great buffalo horn. Since the Hunkpapa were the spirit people, they would occupy the southernmost point of the encampment, setting themselves up at the tip of the buffalo horn. They were the people of the end of the horn. Sitting Bull's lodge would be in that grouping, as foretold by the spirits.

Beyond the Hunkpapa tipi grouping at the southernmost tip of the great buffalo horn, to the north, would be the circle camp groupings of the Blackfeet. Directly to their north would be the Mnincoju grouping. The Mnincoju would be closest to the water, as they always were.

Beyond the Mnincoju grouping was the circle of lodges of the Sans Arcs just to the north along the river. To the north of the Sans Arcs, and nearly parallel to each other from the edge of the Greasy Grass, were the camp groupings of the Sicangu (Brule) and also the camp circles of the Oglala, being near the eastern edge of the Sicangu grouping and facing the river. Beyond the Oglala camp near the northernmost end of the long encampment of people, at the base of the great buffalo horn shape, would be the big circle of camp lodges of the Cheyenne.

The expansiveness of this camp was larger than anything Saved By Bear or Swift Bear had seen in the Greasy Grass valley in a while. They had seen some camps nearly as big before. This one was not an overly massive camp by any means, as there were people of many bands in the camp.

Saved By Bear knew that this was no ordinary time and this was no ordinary hunting expedition. This was one of those moments in the history of all the Lakota—and all the indigenous people of Turtle Island—that, the two warriors knew, would be talked about in stories told by future generations as they sat beside the campfire, as long as Creator's instructions were carried out as planned. Saved By Bear trusted in the spirit and knew no other way.

After Sitting Bull had led the groups of Lakota and Cheyenne to the encampment in the Greasy Grass River valley in the days leading up to the battle, they were joined by other, smaller groups of people. However, according to subsequent accounts, the numbers of those in the camp would be greatly overexaggerated.

The way the people would gather was predictable mostly in the times of peace. The numbers in the present encampment would be estimated and documented as being vast and overwhelming. However, these numbers would not be accurate. There were actually fewer people in the camp than history records. Since the number of the Lakota people had already been reduced drastically by war, starvation, disease, and genocide, the camp did not have the numbers that the government later claimed. It would be proven that the Lakota did not swarm or overwhelm the cavalry or Custer, by mere overwhelming numbers.

Seeking to gain a better vantage point by going slightly higher up the slope of the tree-lined northern ridge they were on, the riders carefully moved themselves back and faced the northeast. Then they started to carefully and quietly climb. Saved By Bear's heels nudged into Wildfire's ribs as they rose above the ridge. Wildfire knew not to go too fast. Saved By Bear had taught him this since he was a foal. The warrior's friend and companion for many years knew what was going on. The connection between the flesh of Saved By Bear and Wildfire's ribs and haunches, was solid. Coming to a slightly raised level beyond several groupings of pine trees, the mounted Lakota warriors slowed their ponies, turning once again toward the river to face the sun and the source of energetic activity in the encampment far below in the distance. Again, silently, they looked to the south. The west wind blew in Saved By Bear's face and ruffled Wildfire's mane. Both sets of eyes were focused in the early morning sun, knowing that their purpose was the same. Their hearts beat as one; their spirits, one of the two-legged and one of the four-legged, were together. Saved By Bear was Wildfire's friend, and Wildfire was his friend. Saved By Bear's hunka brother Swift Bear felt the same, as did Spotted Smoke. They knew no other language than what was in their blood at that moment, with thoughts of what was to happen here the next day.

Memories of the recent years filtered through Saved By Bear's mind. He thought to himself, as if speaking out loud to his own mind: *The Sacred Grandmother called for us to defend her. Nothing was more important. Wakan Tanka warned us of this coming time, and we gathered about it for many days, praying about what was to come. But time has now run out, as our invaders are close at hand. And the hand of Wakan Tanka is not idle, nor is Wakan Tanka's breath far from our senses. The very wind and energy that spawned us so many generations ago is breathing life into our lungs and our spirits, bringing us the courage and the motivation to stand before our invaders with the might, integrity, and commitment that so many before us have shown. We are not alone. We have never been alone. Even though our numbers, human and four-legged alike, have oftentimes been less than theirs, we knew in our hearts and in our spirits that we would be as one on the day of reckoning to come. Our will is strong, and our spirit is committed.*

In the stillness of these moments, before the preparation and permission of the two heyoka warriors would become reality, before the inevitable coming of the foretold events of the next day which were about to change everything, Saved By Bear looked inward. Reading his own thoughts, listening to his own spirit, and gauging his own reality, he allowed his mind to float to a previous time in his life. And his mind spoke to his spirit as one:

Our thoughts, my thoughts, stream back to the better days when we were free of the invaders and their greed and insistence. The good days of my youth, and Wildfire's early days, are long gone. We knew deep in our spirits that this day would come, and that they would come and keep coming. It was foretold and inevitable that this would happen. We never thought, however, that it would come to this.

The rainbows of life are frequent, yet they are far too elusive to truly grasp in your hands. My eyes when I was a young man caressed the beauty of Unci Maka, our Grandmother Earth, with frequency and regularity during my waking moments. Yet now, those rainbows seem more of a wishful illusion. I long to see the pristine beauty of the Wakinyan's summer rain and the rainbows, the cleansing of the sacred Grandmother Earth. I long for the moments of innocence and of connection to what is real and what is truly the purpose for breathing the air, smelling the fresh flowering sage and being a human being.

His eyes, although open and peering through the early morning haze into the valley, were momentarily blind, but in his longing search, his inner sight saw the majestic and proud beauty of the grassy hills and the rolling ridges of his homeland. Undeniably, his heart was screaming for a return to what had once been familiar, hoping to take him back to those moments when life was much more simple, direct, and truthful.

Saved By Bear's hands grasped his friend's mane. He felt Wildfire's anxiety and uncertainty through his shivers. Saved By Bear knew that Wildfire believed the same as he did: that things were different now, and that life would never be the same again. He clasped his legs around Wildfire's heaving chest in a way to show the horse that his rider knew the natural worry he felt, and also in a way to reassure his friend that the two of them were in it together, that Saved By Bear would not forsake him in this time of need and uncertainty.

His friend grunted in the manner that Saved By Bear had come to know as his signal to him that the horse was always ready to do his part for Saved By Bear when needed. Spoken words were not necessary between them, as the touch of their bodies communicated their spirit and their intent. Wildfire acknowledged Saved By Bear's signal with his familiar way, to let him know that they were in this together no matter what happened in the following days. Having ridden many trails and had traveled across many landscapes together through the years, they both cherished those moments, Wildfire being Saved By Bear's legs, and Saved By Bear being Wildfire's guide. The trust that Wildfire held for Saved By Bear in his heart and spirit mirrored that which Saved By Bear felt for Wildfire. Saved By Bear's trust in his horse was equal to Wildfire's trust in his rider. And both truly believed that they were destined to be here together at this precise moment in time, a time to be forever etched in our individual and collective memory, whether the outcome be good or bad. Wildfire would not charge into the battle tomorrow like some of his brothers would. He was too old for that. But he would ready himself to be there for the necessarily quick departure once the act is done and it is time to leave. Saved By Bear sits quietly on his friend's back and continues to ponder to himself as to what had been the reasons for the asking of the permission at Bear Creek. His thoughts go back momentarily to that time:

The natural and once dependable way of life had been altered by the encroachment of the whites.. To us, it was the height of the main gathering season. The tatanka usually ran thick in these days through the territory, and our time during this season was usually spent tracking and following them so as to take from the herds of tatanka while the chance was ripe, gathering what we would need—nothing more, nothing less. But now, we had been unnaturally separated from our routine on account of having to deal with the invaders. It was now imperative for us to protect our lands, our people, and our way of life. We had encountered the white people many times before, but we had rarely encountered them on our terms or in our strength. Before, we hadn't fully understood their motive, but now it appeared clear that their intent was to kill us all, to remove us from these lands, so they could build their roads, their forts, their railroads, their gold mines, and their safe passageways for their trespassing hordes, who usually followed their armies.

Humanity was at stake, and the humanity at stake was ours. The invaders had not shown humanity in their recent escapades across our territory. They desecrated the land and slaughtered the tatanka. It seemed as if their only purpose was to increase their own holdings for the purpose of increasing their own personal wealth. And we were, unavoidably, in the way of their plan.

But now things were different. Our elders and ancestors had not only envisioned this moment but also warned us of the same. Life was becoming too complicated now. When dealing with the occasional trespasser in the past, we commonly allowed the individuals to travel through our lands, believing that they were only transients whom we did not expect to stay for very long, let alone forever. We tolerated them because many, were lost souls and yet, were human beings. Our elders had advised us to be peaceful with them unless they took up arms against us, so we tolerated the occasional transgression into our territory, believing that the new treaty would at least protect our interests against any serious intrusion of the multitudes.

It seemed that even Wildfire knew that the transgressions of the white people, having become so frequent and so regular, were now an insurmountable problem for us all. The white people appeared to be staying longer, some even preparing to stay permanently, despite the obvious treaty violation and despite their Trail of Thieves into the He Sapa, which prompted an explosion in the number of trespassers.

Eight years prior, despite the reluctance by many of us not to make any treaties with the government, we had all been told by the Lakota who signed the treaty, that our lands would be safe and free forever. We were told that this sacred spiritual land was still ours to enjoy, celebrate, and savor, as always, despite the periodic transgressions of the foreigners. Some of the people believed, that the U.S. President, the "white father", would never lie to us, deceive us, or deprive us of our agreed upon freedom to travel over the land that was clearly set aside for our people's perpetual ownership, use and free and peaceful enjoyment. And that the white father would protect our rights with the force of his armies. Many of us objected to even the reference of a white father who may treat us as children within their control. But now, that white father was blatantly allowing his armies free trespass upon our territory, and allowing those same armies to corral and remove our people from the very lands that the treaty claimed to protect, at the expense of the ever increasing population of those who would come with their shovels, gold pans, wagons, and wares. We never expected those trespassers to actually believe that they could come in and stay without our knowledge and consent. The great heart and spirit of the He Sapa, as we know and believe, would never allow strange individuals to come in and claim any part of the herself to be taken, used or abused by any man who was not respectful of the true meaning of our Grandmother Earth and of her heart.

The reason for our present position on this hidden tree-lined ridgetop, now, had been foretold through ceremonies and visions, and was the result of our asking. It was the gift granted to us by Creator at the inipi ceremonies near Bear Creek in August of 1874, which was also when the spiritual permission had been given. We as a people hadn't truly anticipated the persistent resolve of the whites to be so blatant, so arrogant, so violating, in claiming parts of our territory as their own. And here was the United States government, as we have been told, dishonoring its commitments outlined in the new treaty, which was supposed to protect the boundaries of the Great Lakota Nation from encroachment by others. Many of us were not surprised that the government could not be trusted. We know that the government and its white father had made some concessions to the trespassers since they had found the gleaming rocks called "gold" last year, which they admired a great deal and were greedily hoping to obtain. We watched them looking for gold two summers ago in the He Sapa. This we knew when we sought and obtained the spiritual guidance from Creator, thereafter. This white father was no where near the type of father figure that could be trusted.

As he drifts back into the present, Saved By Bear sees that the sun is beginning to climb over the Wolf Mountains to the east, warming the easternmost knolls of grass in the valley. The greasiness shows clear on the grass and shimmers in the glancing rays of the bright sunshine. Wildfire shivered again from having to stand so long in a prone position, waiting. Saved By Bear listened to his spirit speak inwardly, once again:

We never wanted this. We never said to them that it was us versus them. We never said to them that we would try to harm them if they crossed the line. We never laid an ultimatum upon the invaders. But we did believe that they understood our discontent and our resolve once they did breach our sanctity. Ours is a culture of life and tolerance, not of violence and intolerance. To us, all of the beings of the Creator, even the whites, are worthy of dignity and respect from all the human beings. And yet they persisted. All the warnings sent out to the whites through the spirits and the ceremonies, all the warnings and the spiritual messages sent to Crook near the Shiny Mountains, all the warnings and spiritual messages sent out to the white father and his military officials, like Terry and Sheridan, all the warnings sent out to Custer and his young wife ... The warnings were sent out by Sitting Bull. The warnings were sent out by the Mnincoju holy men and the medicine people. Time and again, we said, "Leave us alone. We only want peace." We know not why they went back upon their word, or the word of the white father and his military puppet and exterminator, tempting us and pushing us to the point that we now find ourselves standing in this beautiful valley, waiting, and yet knowing.

Wildfire's nostrils flared as he inhaled. He knew the time was drawing near for them to let their instincts take over and act as Wakan Tanka intends and allows. Having prayed about this moment many times before, the warriors accepted and believed that Wakan Tanka had permitted them to place themselves in this position, preparing themselves for a battle with their white brothers' army. Saved By Bear listened to his spirit speaking to himself again:

We don't see or imagine the soldiers' faces or their individual lives. We have moved beyond that. Things have gone too far now. We must now see them for what they are. We have accepted the fact that they do not perceive our individual lives or spirits. They do not realize what they are in for if they persist in their mission, at this moment in time, in this event, for these reasons. The arrogant lieutenant colonel will be guided by his own prodding spirit to do what comes naturally to him, the great Indian-fighter. He will attack and pursue in the name of pride and glory—his own. Nothing on the physical earth will quench his desire to kill us all and eradicate our people from the face of Grandmother Earth. Custer is their golden symbol of bravery and conquest. He is the chosen one to do their bidding in their grand plan of our extinction. He is the face of their commitment, the face of their strength, the face of their future without us. And he is the face to us, of the evil force that we must remove ourselves if we are ever to survive as a people. He was the purpose of the plan. He was the object of the asking, of the instructions, of the preparation, of the permission. His presence was that which we prayed to Creator for, to be given the answers, the guidance, the help, the knowledge, and the permission, to remove forever. We were told he would come, and now he is on his way. We feel his spirit approaching. We can see his spirit and know he must come. It is time to act, time to save us all.

Now Saved By Bear and Swift Bear sat calmly behind the tree line on that high ridge, hidden from view of anyone in the valley, or behind them. They were overlooking the activity in the camp. A quiet resolve was preeminent in the air. They could hear each other breathing, and hear the slight shifting of the weight of their horses, from one leg to the other. No words are necessary. No encouragement is needed. No embellishment or exaggeration of the significance of what they were about to do is required. It is all understood. We know. We are ready. In the calmness of the moment, feeling the gentle breeze from the west again caress his cheek, Saved By Bear scanned the valley and the encampment. His eyes roamed over the points of contact and the points of conflict, reminding himself of the manner of entry, repulsion, defense, and pursuit, and the dim glowing presence of the *spiritual pathway*. And as he slowly closed his eyes, his thoughts take him forward in time to the moment of the gathering storm, the approach of the enemy. He hears the beginnings of the sounds of confrontation, hatred, violence, and war. And again, his spirit allows his mind to view what his closed eyes do not, can not. Within his spirit's vision, he sees them.

He sees them approaching the southern high pass through the Wolf Mountains, which they reach at daybreak. The Crow and Arikira scouts scurry up to the high ground to the overlook called the Crow's Nest. They look down toward the northeast across the valley of the Greasy Grass for the first time. Custer's scouts realize what it is that they have been feeling. What they have felt now touches their spirits in a way too powerful to ignore. There was reason why they are scared and feel doomed. They realize now that there is a very real reason why it was so easy and natural for them all to join in on the death songs the night before. Once the scouts see the Lakota encampment along the western bank of the Greasy Grass, and the vast number of ponies grazing, it becomes clear to them. The scouts are human beings, but they have also been exposed at points in their lives to the genuine strength of the spirit. And now the connection to the spirit is real, very real, and undeniably strong. The spiritual connection is direct and committed.

The Crow know better than the Arikira, because the Crow had experienced the Lakota spirit from the opposite perspective when the Lakota would choose to unite and bring strength and resolve in their spiritual way and commitment. The Crow had always felt vulnerable when the Lakota would call upon the old ways to bring forth the spiritual strength into the present. And the Crow scouts know that this is what they all are feeling at this moment, on this morning, in this valley, nearing the Lakota camp. The Crow and the Arikira know they will not be able survive this if they go along with their leader's plans.

Saved By Bear saw all this in his mind and felt it in his spirit before it actually happened. He knew that the spiritual connection is extremely strong right now and right here, in this place. It is as if the very Earth itself has absorbed the energy of the spirit. He is here for one purpose, as are the other fifteen warriors. Although he did not need to open his eyes, he opened them anyway when he felt his friend nudge him in the elbow. Swift Bear motioned down a ways toward the camp's perimeter, where a scouting team on horses was steadily moving, angling up toward the east, a fair distance beyond their general vicinity. So, despite their concealed presence and confident secrecy, Swift Bear and Saved By Bear nodded to one another and then squeezed their ponies in the ribs, indicating that they should back up and go down the other side of the ridge, and get on their way back to the hidden base camp. The horses calmly obliged, and all four were off, on a steady gait to meet with the others and make any final necessary preparations before their activities could start in earnest at nightfall.

———⫸•(◉)•⫷———

On the morning of June 24, Custer and his cavalry group followed their scouts, keeping a close eye on the Indian trail that was heading toward the headwaters of Rosebud Creek, where it met what was called Davis Creek. The trail then appeared to veer northeast across a ridge within the Wolf Mountains, later opening onto the valley of the Greasy Grass, the Little Bighorn, on the western slopes. By the night of June 24, Custer's column had ridden seventy-three miles in a little over two days. That was a lot of hot, hard, dusty riding. The men were exhausted, dirty, and anxious. The horses and the mules were also weary, having been driven hard by the demands placed upon them.

Just that afternoon, while the caravan of men, horses, and mules rode up and down the ravine-filled terrain along the Rosebud, the two Swiss soldiers who had become friends back at Fort Lincoln, were riding abreast of each other in the middle of the pack. The dust of the trail was caked on their clothes, and both men were sweating, periodically wiping the perspiration from their faces and eyes. Charley Vincent was twenty-seven years old, and his Swiss countryman friend Alfred Hansen was twenty-three. They felt most comfortable speaking in their native tongue as they rode. The Swiss language had varying dialects. (Actually, if one takes the time to listen to the Swiss language being spoken, then one realizes it has many similarities to the language spoken by Saved By Bear's people, the Mnincoju Lakota.) Vincent and Hansen again found themselves being swept up in memories of their homeland. Vincent said to Hansen that he wished to go back to Switzerland when his enlistment was done, to visit his family and to again look upon Mt. Pilatus, the sacred home of the spiritual dragon. He hoped that one day he could travel up and into the Bighorn Mountains to the west of this place to see how they compared to the Alps at home. Hansen just smiles and laughs, attempting to take his mind off this sticky, sweaty ride. But for the need of a job, neither man would be here on this journey.

Custer wants to keep riding through the night on the twenty-fourth, making no stops at all. However, his brother Tom and Dr. DeWolf both talked some sense into him, saying that his men, the scouts, and the livestock could not keep up with the torturous pace. It was as if Custer is determined to win some kind of a race in getting to the Indians' camp. He cannot contain his energetic anxiousness to meet his enemy, the *redskins,* as he often refers to them in his letters and other writings. When he used that term to describe the people, it is clear in his voice and demeanor that his intent is to delegitimize the Lakota as human beings. To point out that the Lakota *hostiles* are beneath him, certainly not as good as him or the people of his race.

The officers, including Reno and Benteen, notice a peculiar and distinct edginess about the colonel on this mission. It is as if he was facing something that he is unsure about, something that he does not know how to deal with. Something that he fears on a level heretofore unknown to him. An adversary that he has not yet faced. It is clear that his anxiety is not from the fear of battling Sitting Bull, since Sitting Bull no longer fights personally anymore. It is no longer his role. Custer suspects that Spirit Horse is with Sitting Bull, wherever the people are. Custer's anxiety appears to be about something altogether new. Among the other officers who can detect Custer's uneasiness are Capt. Myles Keogh and Col. William W. Cooke. Custer's personal assistant, Pvt. John Burkman, is also aware of Custer's anxiety. Custer has not even gone off on any impromptu hunting escapades while on this march, as he has a tendency to do on other missions. And many have been noticing the appearance of the owls. The owls have appeared even the day before the company left the Yellowstone, mostly in the darkness, but also in the dusk and early morning, for four nights in a row. The owls had been hanging around the marching cavalry train, hooting in a sporadic but consistent low tone.

Because of the fast pace set by Custer, the Seventh was appearing to be on schedule to cross the divide and get into the Little Bighorn Valley right on time to coordinate with Gibbon's arrival from the north on the twenty-sixth.

In the late afternoon of the twenty-fourth, Custer had called his scouts in, along with Lieutenant Varnum, and told them to scout across the ridge of the Wolf Mountains and see what was on the other side. The scouts had ridden on and done what was requested, returning before sundown. Again, two hoot owls would be heard not too far away from Custer's tent. Bloody Knife (one of the scouts) and Varnum came in to report. They said that the Lakota trail was fresh leading down toward the Little Bighorn River Valley and appeared to be intact, not split up. That meant it could be one big group. This caught Custer's attention immediately.

As the scouts left Custer's tent, they realized that he was obsessed with getting to that river valley as quickly as possible. They saw a look in his eyes, a trancelike expression with no emotion. But he did say that it was going to be easier to whip all of the Indians now that they were all in one place.

However, Custer had decided that instead of letting the troops sleep until first call (which came at 5:00 a.m.), they would start out at 9:30 p.m. on the twenty-fourth. This way, the caravan could get through the mountains at night without drawing attention to themselves. Custer called Reno and Benteen into his tent, and told them what was going to happen.

So at 9:15 on the evening of the twenty-fourth, the troops were wakened and told that the march would resume in fifteen minutes. There was much sighing and some slight groans, but most knew that it was not worth the punishment to complain. It was just another day, or night, under the command of George A. Custer, just another day of servitude under the hard-ass commander.

As everyone assembled at 9:30 p.m., including the noisy mules, Custer rode up and down the lines to make sure everyone was spry and motivated. Then he raised his hand, kicked Vic in the ribs, and rode forward. As the team started to move, a flash of horizontal lightning streaks ran across the western edge of the crest of the darkened Wolf Mountains. There was no rain. No hail. No wind. Just the stretching lightning reaching out across the night sky like a bright set of skeletal fingers seeking to grasp something, or someone, in the distance. The lightning would keep up this way for the next hour as the team moved into the mountains. No one else but a few of the scouts recognized them. The Wakinyan at work, showing the way. Showing the way for the man who must approach. For the man that must arrive.

Things had quieted down in the encampment along the Greasy Grass River as night fell on June 24, 1876. For the most part, the people in camp had settled in for the evening.

The sixteen warriors again move through the night to walk through some of what they have been practicing, but they have to be mindful not to be seen or heard, lest they lose the advantage and with it the chance to carry out the entire mission.

As the warriors anxiously await the time when their preparation can finally go into action, several of them, including Many Thunder and Touches Heart, are out away from the hidden base camp northeast of the northern edge of the encampment, riding very carefully and very quietly so as not to draw attention to their movement. As they draw nearer to the encampment, they mostly move very slightly close to the ground, and do not call out or signal to each other. They are there to protect their secrecy. Their plan must be kept secret until it actually occurs. To assure that there is no unplanned interruptions in the plan.

The night sky is clear. The full moon had already passed several days earlier, so the moon that remains in late June is less close, less bright. It makes for an easier time for one who moves in the darkness, hoping not to be seen or recognized.

Within the encampment, there is a din of voices and drums, including some singing, coming from the individual camp circles down on the flat river valley land above the western banks of the Greasy Grass River. There is no main event at this point, just a series of individual gatherings of Lakota within their own bands' tribal camp circles. The fire circles near the lodges are burning bright and giving off the scent of cooked meat and fresh sweet corn. The fires can be heard crackling with some periodic popping, because the people had to use the noisier-burning elm and birch trees from the tree lines near the river for firewood. These woods give off a denser smoke and do not burn as thoroughly as the preferred pine or ash. Some of the few children present still run from lodge to lodge, although it is quite close to their sleeptime. There are numerous groupings of tiospayes and others, forming circles around their individual group campfires.

It is with these sights, sounds and smells, that the visionary nightbird's view of the valley rises up from the ground level of the Lakota camp sites and lodges, and rises up, up and over and yet higher. So that what one sees as one continues to elevate up and over the entire encampment, is a singularly elongated encampment of the Lakota and Cheyenne, that is set up against the western banks of the fast moving, now moonlight gleaming, Greasy Grass River. The encampment is flanked to the west by the open flat land giving rise to a series of smaller bench style bluffs with gentle sloping grassy knolls climbing up to nearly flat summits. That is the area where the many ponies are kept and allowed to graze on the tall rich and thick grasses there.

The view goes further still up, and over and hovers straight up beyond the nighttime encampment of the people. In the darkness of the dusk and the fading natural light, the top view now looking straight down upon the tipis and the fires, reveals that for which the people have forever remained true to their earliest relatives and brothers, the tatanka, since time immemorial. That the Lakota still remember, still honor, still recognize and cherish, their permanent link to the buffalo nation.

For seen overhead in this manner, the one looking down upon the encampment can most certainly see the outline of it as efficiently delineated by the orange glow of the individual fires.

The encampment is set up and formed in the shape of a great buffalo horn. The tipis at the most southern end of the camp nearest the confluence of the Ash creek and the Greasy Grass River. The southern tip of the great buffalo horn is where the Hunkpapa Band of the Lakota is camped. This is where they must be because they are the spiritual people, the people of the "End of the Horn". In this group and in the 4th lodge in from the southern tip point, is the lodge of the holy man, the

Hunkpapa leader, Sitting Bull and his family of seven. It is preordained by the spiritual *Asking*, the spiritual messages and instructions given, and the spiritual permission received, that Sitting Bull must be present even though he is too old to fight in the battle. Still he must be present to assume the spiritual anchoring for the entirety of the larger group of the people, so that the spiritual energy remains present and constant. That is the holy man's role.

As the panning of the overhead view moves from the southern tip, toward the north and along the western most bank of the winding river, the view from above sees the encampment of the tipis and fires of the *"Protectors"*. The Mnincoju people. Saved By Bear's and Swift Bear's people. The Mnincoju are halfway down the great buffalo horn shape of the encampment, and closest to the river at its nearest point to the inner perimeter of the camp. The Mnincoju are the people of the water, it is known. They are the ones who are called for *protection*. They are the largest group of Warriors, young and old, but mostly young, on this trip.

As the view pans further in, and takes note of the camp circle groupings of the Oglala, the Sicangu (Brule), the Black Feet, even the Cheyenne nearest the northern most reaches of the buffalo horn, are seen. The overhead nighttime view moves beyond the edge of the camp, across the sparkling river flow, and onto and over the high cutting rugged bluffs which mostly line the eastern side banks of the river on the east. These bluffs rise and fall with the geographic topography of the landscape, but are clearly much more dramatic in visual and physical observation as a great contrast to the flat low land off of the western side of the river.

The overhead view then goes up and over, and beyond, to the north of the highest of the river bluffs and past the deepest coulee and ravines which cut into the high bluffs at points which allow narrower access to the river from the eastern approach. Then the view swoops more across the rolling hills between the bluffs and the higher ridges going north. It is here, that the overhead view slows and momentarily stops and hovers, to portray a slight and dim pulsing array of a yellowish gold light along the grassy gulleys leading through an open sloping area toward the ridge along the high point of the east part of the river valley. The pulsing golden light seems as if it is dimming and brightening to a rhythm all its own. Like it were breathing. But as the overhead view closes in on the highly vegetated areas of this sloped field before the eastern high ridge, the pulsing glow of the golden yellow seems to resemble the shape of the letter "L" with a large tip to the east. Like a glow which is pulsing. Beating. Something overhead that looks a lot like... a human arm bent at the elbow and facing up.

The overhead view, then settles back, rising yet again, and returns to swoop over the blazing fire induced outline of the great Horn. And this is how the night of the activity of the people in the encampment.... the night before, will end... the night before the morning of, the day of. The realization of the permission.

—————— ((●)) ——————

On June 24, 1876, the night before the battle, the warriors begin their final preparation. They will spend their time, painting their faces, making sure their weapons are ready, making sure there is enough of everything that was to be carried. After the preparation of each of the sixteen warriors is done, the thirteen warriors that will be on the battlefield will leave under the cover of darkness camouflaged by the natural surroundings and the darkness of nightfall. They will move silently like the owl, and with the precise ground navigation like the cougar. They will move into position and lie in wait for the battle to begin. And as the sun will begin to rise in the new morning, they all will already be in place.

Once these warriors have left, Eagle Fan, along with the two warriors who were to protect him and the horses, move to their spot of seclusion in preparation for the battle. The other thirteen would stay in their positions and wait for the coming confrontation with the Seventh Cavalry. Through the night, each warrior would go through things in his own mind and spirit, contemplating how, why, what and when, can we make this truly a difference in the lives of the people, and to honor the lives of those of their own people who have already suffered and died.

All sixteen wait for the sun to rise. And when the sun begins to come up, Eagle Fan will begin praying for the warriors, asking Creator and the spirits to help them accomplish their sacred deeds.

***

The night ride was treacherous for the cavalry, especially the mule teams, which were not exactly silent. They were also being whipped harshly. But the group did manage to navigate their way to a high western leading pass on the southern edge of the mountain range, with the help of the scouts.

Day began to break as they neared the highest pass. Having been marching for nearly seven hours, the men and their mounts were very tired, thirsty, and hungry, and uncertain as to what was going on. Finally Custer called for a halt. According to the plans made back at the *Far West*, Custer and his scouts had covered enough ground for today. They now would have time on the twenty-fifth to do some good reconnaissance of the territory, and locate the Indian camp if it was there. Then they would simply wait to rendezvous with Gibbon's column from the north, which was due to arrive in the morning on the twenty-sixth. It looked like Custer's luck was going to hold out, again. He silently praised himself for being such a masterful leader and having made it so far in so little time. However, he had not given any fair consideration to his troops and their horses, who were exhausted and badly in need of real rest.

Apparently Custer took pity on them. He called out for a rest, ordering his men to camp here at the mountain pass. This would allow the men to feed their horses and get a little sleep. But before Custer let himself go easy on everyone under his command, he summoned his brother Tom and advised him to get a group of scouts together and send them out to go up to a high point in the mountain pass to see what could be seen toward the river valley, and to make out a good route to get there from here.

The hoot owls had quit speaking a couple of hours ago. However, neither Custer nor any of the men noticed the two eagles quietly perched on a rocky enclave in the trees, overlooking the military team. But the two wanbli had noticed the humans for sure. They had actually begun flying over their heads for the last several miles, so high up in the sky that they were not noticeable.

Varnum took Reynolds, Gerard, Red Star, Bull and Mitch Bouyer with him. These men located the high point and then climbed up the stony surface, reaching the point where they could look north and west. Varnum had brought his standard-issue army field glasses with him. The two large eagles kept their keen eyes on the men, flying to the place that was known as the Crow's Nest and settling in among the nearby trees, from where they listened.

About the same time as the scouting party left, one of the officers and one of the privates rode back a ways on the trail, where some of the metal tack boxes had fallen off the mule pack. Their job was to pick them up and take them back to the camp area, as rations were valuable at this point. Plus, they did not want to leave clear evidence of the presence of the US Army in the area. When the soldiers arrived to the area of the lost tack boxes, they saw a Lakota and a Cheyenne, one of them crouched over the boxes, trying to open one. The soldiers panicked. Not wanting to create a disturbance, and yet not wanting to allow these Indians to get away and go alert any nearby camp of their presence, they did a stupid thing. The private took his gun out and shot toward the young one trying to open the box. The shots startled the men and they both ran into the trees, jumped on a horse, and galloped away at tremendous speed.

The sound of the gunshot alerted the soldiers in the camp at the pass. They had the same concern about having their presence detected. Custer had a very angry look on his face. It was about this time that Varnum came back from off the peak to gather Custer and take him to the Crow's Nest. So Custer quickly followed.

Custer and the Crow scouts, while looking through the field glasses and discussing the situation and the layout of the land in the valley below, did not see or notice the two eagles perched on the slope behind the enclave, toward the highest pinnacle of the rock outcropping. They had been quietly sitting there, listening and studying, undetected. The larger one, a great female golden, weighing thirty pounds and standing nearly three feet tall, had flown the Earth for twenty years now. The other, an elder bald with a pure white head and tail feathers, was smaller, but he claimed seniority over his friend. He had graced the skies over all of these territories for at least thirty-five years and had seen hundreds of movements of people and herds. He had seen a similar number of Lakota and Cheyenne camps erected and taken down in this very vicinity. Appreciative of the area for its magnificent beauty and hunting, he loved to visit these cliffs and fish the fast-moving river, after the snow melted especially. The beautiful valley was always rich with the songs, sounds, and prayers of the faithful; he and his family cherished that as well. This valley was a paradise for the wanbli and the Lakota.

Custer and his men paid no heed to the eagles, and carried on at the Crow's Nest in an animated discussion that led to one of the Crow scouts throwing up his hands and gesturing toward the valley, then quickly turning away in disgust. That would be Mitch Bouyer.

The scouts had been trying to convince Custer that a large village was out there, about fifteen miles to the northwest. Custer grabbed the field glasses from Varnum and peered that way. After several moments, he shook his head. "No, I don't see it."

One of the scouts gestured toward the Little Bighorn River in the distance and asked, "Don't you see the ponies?"

Custer, still peering through the glasses, but now squinting, said, "No. There is too much haze."

The scout interjected. "Look further west. Look for the worms moving in the grass." Custer still could not see.

Varnum said, "He means the ponies look like worms moving in the grass from here."

"I still don't see it," Custer replied, handing the glasses back. He turned to the scouts and said, "I believe you, I just can't see it. I will need to see for myself." And they started down from the rocky ledge.

Then suddenly, Custer's brother Capt. Tom Custer ran up to Custer and said, "General, we have been seen by a group of hostiles on the other side of the ridge. What do you wish that we do?"

The slim commander looked at his brother and then out over the vast valley below. He said, "We must attack now before they escape. Come on now, let's get snapping." With that, Custer and the group of soldiers and scouts jogged down the slope to their horses and comrades. It looked as if what the spirits had been telling the wanbli for some time now was about to occur. It came as no surprise to the wanbli.

15

ARRIVAL

CONCERNING THE SPIRIT, WHAT THE Lakota desire from our spirit is similar to what those on the opposite side also desire. We have hopes, we have dreams, and we have commitments. And to follow your spirit is to take a risk, as it could turn out to be either positive or negative.

After the warriors had prepared for the upcoming battle, all of them were connected spiritually and had realized the bond between spirit, knowledge, and a familiarity of what was to come. They recognized that their senses and feelings were aroused. The spirit affected everybody, so much so that it compelled them to react. Each person wanted to preserve what he or she believed in. The spiritual reaction was so strong that it affected the aspirations and desires of even the main military leaders. Things surfaced within their spirits and their minds. They would be willing to sacrifice any one of the other leaders just to preserve what they believed in and not to have to face death themselves.

There were parallels of this spiritual presence on the two opposing sides. If the white man had prepared spiritually like we had, then the outcome of the battle may have been completely different. It may have been like flipping from light to dark. The spirits of the cavalrymen may have received the exact same patterns of approach that the sixteen warriors received and thereby may have succeeded in exterminating their opponents, as they were used to doing. They may have followed the advice. The spirit would indeed have guided them to their own victory. The difference between the two sets of spirits was that one remained connected. The other had been forcibly removed from the place it had come from. This confrontation of spirit would be a critical factor in who would be victorious and who would be defeated.

The grass and the ground near the location of the plan, including the *hilltop* at the center of the preparation area, was alive with the natural signs of life. The beings that normally resided here were present and moving about. An hour before the battle was to begin, the warriors concealed in the grass, noticed a particular gathering that was occurring up on the *hilltop* that would serve as the focal point of the main encounter of their spiritual mission.

Saved By Bear could hear them before he could see them. The unmistakable melodious chirping and singing. The harmonious joining of voices and natural music. When he and Swift Bear peered through the sagebrush to get a closer look at the western edge of the sloping and cresting of the *hilltop*, they were able to see them. There was at least a hundred of them, some just sitting there, others jumping and hovering. All had gathered together in a show of unity, a show of meaning and message. The meadowlarks.

The meadowlarks (*tasiyagnupa*), a relation of and friend to the Lakota, always provided soothing feelings of calm and comfort, along with presence of mind and future. Through their song, they communicated a hope for all beings, including humans. They were a good representative of their winged brother. They had gathered here at this site, at this moment, to send a message to the warriors. They were an outward symbol from Creator indicating that all beings had joined with the warriors, standing with them as they honored their commitment and carried out their duty. They communicated the idea that all beings had chosen to be on the side of life and protection, not of war, depletion, destruction, and genocide. These winged ones also had a special bond with the Hunkpapa holy man, who is down in the encampment. He had spoken to them many times, in the past. And would again.

Saved By Bear and Swift Bear look at each other, and both close their eyes and just listen. It is a feeling of calm amid intensity, a feeling of hope where hopelessness hangs in the balance. A feeling of believing in a better world, and that a safer life, can be possible. The harmony of Unci Maka could survive and live on. As the sound of distant rumbling can be heard, the meadowlarks lift up in a blanket of winged motion and fly in unison over and above the two concealed Dog Man warriors hidden in the sagebrush. Then they turn and fly toward the mountains.

Mares' tails are in the sky. The shape of the long, wavy-shaped clouds linger overhead in the simmering heat of the midday sun, a reminder of the horse nation's ever-present kinship with the people. A remembrance of the events of the past, and a premonition of events of the present and the future. It was fitting that the light sparse clouds had assumed this form on this day, in light of all that the Lakota and the horse nation had been through together over the years and in recent times, and what they would go through today, at the time of fulfillment of the spiritual duty at hand.

The warriors had set up their secret camp inside the tree line. Eagle Fan had taken up his position after the other warriors, including Saved By Bear and Swift Bear, had left for the battlefield in the darkness prior to the day of the battle. Eagle Fan and the two warriors who were there to protect him and the horses, had moved out into an open area, away from the hidden camp. Eagle Fan did this so that he could be out in the open, in the sun, as he, being a sun dancer, faced the sun when he prayed. The sixteen warriors who had been chosen to fight this battle, the ones who had gone through all the preparation, the prayers, the ceremonies, and the training, everything involved in getting themselves ready, were all sun dancers. So they all knew the significance of what was being done for them by Eagle Fan as they were fulfilling their duties. At the time they were carrying out the things they had spent so much time, and so much effort, and so much spirit in preparing themselves.

———— ((◆)) ————

Custer could no longer rely on his plan to carry out a surprise attack on the Indian encampment. Once the Lakota and Cheyenne brought word back to the camp that they had seen some US military men, the people at the encampment would scatter in all directions, which would make them a hundred times more difficult to catch and kill. Custer's plan of attack would need to change. He would need to develop his strategy while on the run. There was no time for in-depth reconnaissance or coordination with any other unit. It was the Seventh's time. It was the Seventh's glory to be had. And if the Seventh were to bask in glory, then most of that glory will shine upon him.

So he gave the order: "Attack the village now. We will move down the Ash Creek toward the village area. Mount up. Let's go!"

The soldiers and scouts, although they were dead tired, reacted quickly to the order. All mounted up. Custer decided quickly to revert to an old reliable plan of attack he had used eight years earlier along the Washita River. It worked wonderfully there. He could see no reason why it would not do the same here. Custer quickly got on his Vic and rode to his officers. Dandy would remain behind with his striker John Burkman.

Custer quickly decided to divide up his command by companies. Reno would take command of Companies A, G, and M, about 140 soldiers, who would serve as the center column. Captain Benteen would lead the left column, consisting of Companies D, H, and K, with 115 officers and men. Captain McDougall would lead Company B as the escort for the pack train with all the ammo and supplies. Custer would take five companies with him: Companies C, I, and L, under Capt. George Yates, and Companies E and F, under Capt. Myles Keogh, who was riding his trusted horse Comanche.

Reno's column would ride along the eastern bank of Ash Creek, cross the Little Bighorn at the low point ahead, and attack the village from the south. Custer said his boys would provide support to Reno as needed. Benteen was ordered to divert south and then to the left to circle around to keep any of the *hostiles* from escaping in the direction of the Shiny Mountains to the southwest. McDougall would come up from behind Reno and Custer as quickly as possible with the mules and supplies. And Custer would do what he had done at the Washita: cover the northern perimeter, race to the northern edge of the camp, and strike back into the camp from there, where it would be a turkey shoot for Reno and Custer's men in the heart of the camp.

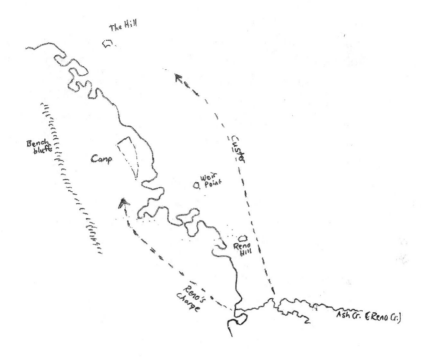

The Hill
Bench bluff
Camp
Weir Point
Custer
Reno
Reno Hill
Reno's Charge
Ash Cr. (Reno Cr.)

As he was giving these orders, Custer felt as if he had given the same orders before, in the same fashion—and not just at the Washita eight years earlier, but like it was...a dream. He scarcely had to think to say or mouth the words; that is how easily these orders came from him.

The men of the Seventh Calvary did not hesitate. They all followed orders and began to move in unison. Reno began his move along the opposite bank across from Custer's line. The two officers mimicked each other's movements for several miles.

———

The Army had been anxious to take up the positions according to the original multiprong column approach strategy, thinking and believing that they were going to surprise the *hostile Indians*. They made haste in traveling their respective routes, in anticipation of bloodshed, something in which Custer and his officers were well versed. Indeed, bloodshed was what they lived for at this point. Custer had been warned, having been contacted in the spiritual sense, and yet he is determined to follow his path, a path that we have given him. If he was true to self, then he will follow this path with every fiber of his being. It is that important for him to do so. He does not worry about defeat. He has really never suffered previously as a result of his arrogant battle approaches in the past.

In his haste to go to war to try to kill the people, Custer abandons his normal approach. He refused the offer of additional troops and weapons from General Gibbon. He decided not to have his soldiers bring their sabers. He also decided to leave behind his personal military band, which meant that there would be no music he so loved to hear as he charged into battle. He left behind the Gatling guns and the detail who manned them, believing he did not need them and that they would slow him down. He believes he is infallible, and that he is a god. So his approach is without care for the true well being of his soldiers. Custer is totally committed to war, and today this is his war entirely. He is at the center, the focal point of everyone's attention. And yet he is a man who is out of his mind.

These men who will fight for the United States government and its military were as committed as many of the Lakota, the warriors, are to their families. The white soldiers of Custer's Seventh Cavalry believe they are doing the right thing. They believe that they are there to support the United States in confiscating and controlling this new territory. However, by the sending of spiritual messages from the holy men and Sitting Bull suggesting a peaceful resolution to the differences between the two peoples, Lakota and white, the Lakota have shown a number of these soldiers what they are about to face. As a result, many of the soldiers fear the Lakota warriors.

The soldiers are human beings, common people themselves. They are fathers, sons, brothers, and uncles, individuals with emotions, and human frailties and faults. Any battle must be approached by the two sides. And during the time of the advance, which is usually brief, there is opportunity for reflection, thought, and memory, even hesitation and fear. Today, the soldiers have very little chance of feeling any emotions as they are rushed into a genocidal activity once again, something that many of them are all too familiar with. But there are human beings among these soldiers who do not feel the same as their leader. People such as these are the ones who give hope to humanity, nurturing the belief that one day there will be an end to war, especially wars fought to achieve a certain outcome, because of race, because of land, because of anything different from their own culture.

In the approach, Custer is in a self-centered state of mind. All that matters to him is his own existence. While he and the cavalry are riding and approaching the battlefield, he is drenched in sweat. His anxiety is running rampant inside him. His anticipation of carrying out his familiar routine of murder and genocide is almost like a shot of adrenalin. He needs this. He looks upon his soldiers and views them as inferior to himself. He yells at them, he hastens them, and he condemns them, because he is in an itching mood to go and they must accommodate his command and his attitude. By verbally and mentally oppressing and pushing his men, he is adding to their defeat. By making his gestures of disrespect, he is losing the battle as he approaches the battlefield. Possibly one of these reasons why his behavior is so intense is that years before, in his desire for war, he had been contacted by the spirit realm and had received the Lakota people's cautions and warnings about going to war, including the knowledge of what would happen if he did, which warnings he ignored. But now, those spiritual warnings and signs are spinning in his head like the wind blowing over the grass. The same thoughts, the same visions, occurring over and over in his head. He is in the state of mind where he will become defensive, where he will become the victim, and lose control.

<hr />

Custer's scouts stopped briefly at an abandoned tipi lodge just off the trail to investigate. Custer and his men stop too, as they reach this abandoned tipi site. Inside the lodge is a fully decorated burial area for a Lakota warrior who had obviously recently died. No one knew it at the time, but he had died from wounds suffered in the June 17 battle against Crook at the Rosebud.

Custer's men mounted up again, and they resumed their quick pace. Again, Custer felt as if he was riding along a path he had ridden before, although he had not been to the Greasy Grass before today. The feeling was not one of uncertainty. It seemed more like he was coming back…, coming home…. to a familiar place. There is a certain feeling of energy about him that he cannot explain, but that he cannot ignore either. It was as if he was being pulled or directed by some huge invisible hand that had taken he and Vic in its grasp and was cradling them in a way that was not overbearing but that seemed somewhat…. comforting.

The cavalry had now reached the point where the creek joined the Greasy Grass River. Custer did not even need to pull the reins to turn Vic to the right. He and his horse are now leading the men north along the high rise of the bluffs above the river basin. Vic can hear the rhythmic calling of the horse nation deep in his own spirit as he gallops toward his own destiny and the last moments of his life.

———————————

Reno and his men had reached the river crossing. They charged across the cold fast stream, making a tremendous splashing noise as 140 horses plowed through, and climbed up onto the western bank. And they moved into the flat river plain on the other side, and they turned north. Their pace picked up. The hooves on the dusty ground grew loud as a huge cloud of dust streamed up from behind the horses as they went.

Custer's right hand went up as a signal for all of his companies to follow. They rode at a brisk pace amid the rolling terrain and the tall grass. Custer's hearing diminished briefly. All became quiet to him for a moment, as he was now, for the first time, able to look off in the far distance to the north. Through the summer haze above the greasy grass, as he and Vic cut through it, he saw a rise in the far distance that attracted his attention. He no longer even guided his horse. As he stared at the highest ridge in the northern distance, he realized that that is where he must go. That is where he must lead his men. And then he noticed it. It was a dim pulsing, yellow-gold in color. He thought he even saw it move, as if it were breathing in and out. Now, for a moment, he could not even hear Vic's hoofbeats. He suddenly felt uncertain. Then, he felt the need to stop.

Custer pulled the reins tight. His hearing came back into focus, and he could hear the bugle of Reno's charge, and the beating of the horses' hooves in the valley. And he stopped his movement. All five companies stopped with him. He turned and looked at them. They all seemed to be waiting for him to say something. So he did. He said, "Hold!" He turned his gaze back toward Reno in the valley and watched his approach. Then he heard the first gunshots. Custer said, "There he goes! Let's get to work on our side."

From his vantage point on a high bluff looking to the northwest over the valley of the Little Bighorn, Custer could see portions of the encampment, and the place farther north where it seemed to end. The layout seemed familiar to him. The camp was here for the taking. Glory was at his fingertips. He decided that his Washita strategy was still workable. He turned to Cooke and asked for a messenger. Cooke yelled out for one, as Custer climbed off of Vic's back. A young private of Italian ancestry rode up quickly. His name was Giovanni Martini. He was the company trumpeter. He spoke very little English. Custer said to Cooke, "Take this message to Captain Benteen."

Cooke pulled out a pencil and hastily wrote out a message on a piece of paper as Custer dictated the words. Cooke then quickly handed the note to Martini, saying, "Go fast." The message read as follows:

Benteen. Come on. Big village. Be quick, bring packs.

W. W. Cooke.

P.S. Bring packs.

Custer paused briefly as if in thought, then took off his buckskin jacket and tied it under the back side of his saddle near the saddle bags. He was now wearing only his dark uniform shirt. He got back up on Vic. Raising his left arm again, he yelled, "We've got 'em, boys!" Then he spurred Vic hard in the shoulders. The horse jumped into a sprint and galloped toward the rise in the north, which was about two miles ahead. All five companies galloped briskly down and into the lower reach of the next dip in the grassy terrain. The tall grass appeared to part, as if making way for the riders.

⇒⇒ ·《◉》· ⇐⇐

Spirit Horse had told no one in the camp of what was to come. He'd only mentioned that everyone needed to have their weapons close and keep their lodges open. Most in camp did not know what was to occur or when. He had done his usual battle preparation that morning, in private this time, so no one would know that he was anticipating an attack or a battle. He smudged himself with sage. He put his spirit stone around his neck. He drew the red thunderbolt across his cheek. He asked for protection. Then he waited.

When he heard the thundering sound of the approaching hooves from the south, he knew the fight was under way. It was occurring exactly as he had been told in the instructions from the holy ones. He sprinted out of his lodge, jumped on his horse, and immediately called for all the warriors to come out and run to the south to meet the enemy. He rode hard toward the Hunkpapa camp at the end of the horn As he was riding by, he signaled and called out toward Sitting Bull's lodge. Sitting Bull came out of his lodge quickly and, seeing Spirit Horse, recognized that it was time. So he grabbed his cannumpa and jogged quickly with some of the women from the camp toward the western edge of the encampment, where he would pray and watch from the bench bluffs.

Spirit Horse yelled for the warriors to defend. At that moment, a wave of Hunkpapa, Mnincoju, Oglala, and Sicangu warriors emerged and started running or riding toward the south end of camp to meet the cavalry head-on. It seemed chaotic, but the warriors immediately went into protection mode and their spirits took over for their minds. They all trusted the warrior who stood up to lead them. They would follow his directions. The first battle of the conflict that day began with a flurry with Reno and his troops riding from the south toward the Hunkpapa lodges. Rifle shots rang out, arrows zipped and hoofbeats pounded the flatland on the eastern banks of the Greasy Grass. Dust and smoke rose and simmered in the air. The cries and shouting from the men in conflict signified the life and death nature of this meeting.

After confronting the attacking soldiers to the south of the Hunkpapa lodges, now it was time for Spirit Horse to sprint to the Cheyenne. He kicked his horse in the shoulders and warrior and horse quickly galloped toward the northernmost lodges of the Cheyenne relatives. He yelled for the warriors to quickly gather with him in the center lodge area. They obeyed. Spirit Horse spoke with conviction and urgency. The Cheyenne all listened intently.

Spirit Horse then urgently directed these warriors to get to the river's edge where the ravines dip in, and defend the camp when the soldiers would attempt to attack. The warriors quickly gathered and moved toward the banks of the Greasy Grass.

Reno's heart was pounding so fast that it felt like he was having an attack. His chest tightened and his throat constricted, his gut churning with anxiety and fear. Reno saw it within minutes of the horse charge. His companies were weary from the all-night march they'd made across the Wolf Mountains. The horses were tired and worn. The men of his command were also very tired, not in optimal condition to attack an Indian village, especially one where the Indians, it appeared, were prepared to actually fight back. This was not a village with just women, children, and old people. In this village were young capable fighters who were there as a difference, and who would fight against the cavalry. Reno was confronted by the wave of Lakota warriors who met him in the charge toward the southern tip of the horn of the camp. His men were forced to dismount and form a quick skirmish line. But they could not hold that line as the warriors seemed very strong and committed. So Reno yelled, telling his men to retreat. Then he got on his horse and quickly galloped into the trees to the east along the riverbank. Many of his soldiers followed him. Once there, Reno jumped off his horse, turned, and started firing at anything he could.

He looked nervously back and forth, from the edge of the camp to the edge of the tree line, so fast that his neck crooked to the left and jolted back to the right, the jerkiness blurring his vision momentarily and increasing the speed of the adrenaline running up and down his spine.

He had just ordered his men to dismount, not knowing if they heard him over the commotion of the gunfire and the beating hooves of all of the horses. But now, he could see a moving wall of approaching warriors bearing down on his position in the woods, coming fast from the southern edge of the camp. And the ponies, so many ponies, were running, with or without riders, all seeming to come at his face at once. His sweat poured out from under his white hat brim and down his brow, stinging his eyes. He noticed Bloody Knife to his right kneeling by his horse, aiming and shooting his rifle at the approaching wall of warriors and ponies.

Reno thought fleetingly of what Custer had said when he ordered the troops to divide: "Go and approach and attack the village from the south. I will support you."

A millisecond seemed like an hour as Reno's brain grasped upon the notion of support. Where? When? How? Then a bullet zoomed past his head. Zzzzzzzpp! His head jerked to the left and caught sight of one of the privates who was shot in the left side while trying to dismount, just fifteen feet in front and to the left of him. Bullets hit the log by his feet. Thump! Crack!

Bloody Knife fired again. The gunpowder rose to Reno's face, making his nose twitch. Reno raised his pistol in his right hand to aim at a young Lakota on a horse twenty feet in front of him, just below a small rise in the tree line.

Boom! A blast smashed into a horse next to Reno. The major fired frantically, missing the warrior by five feet. The pistol jerked back on his shoulder, the barrel nearly striking him in the eye on the recoil. He flexed his right elbow and aimed again.

Zzzzpdt! A shot whizzed by in front. Then he felt liquid and tissue strike him on the right side of his face, his neck, his chest, and his right shoulder. It was wet and sticky, and some quickly splashed into his right eye and onto his lower lip.

He turned slightly to his right, just catching sight of the body of the scout before it fell backward and to the left. It was then that Reno, seeing the hole in the center of Bloody Knife's forehead, knew that it was the scout's blood and brain matter on his own face and neck. The anxiety tripled in his chest. Reflexively, he yelled, "Mount up. Retreat!", not really even caring if he was heard or not.

⸻ ❊ ⸻

To the north, along the high ridge, Custer stopped his forward progression at a high bluff overlooking the river valley to gaze down upon the action involving Reno. Some of the soldiers had retreated into the trees. It appeared to be fierce fighting, almost hand to hand.

But Custer made no move to go there, or to send backup to help Reno's cause. He could not see the logic of doing so. He briefly thought of Major Elliot and the other seventeen soldiers at the Washita. And Benteen's reaction thereafter. But he quickly dispensed with the thought. It was not logical now to support Reno, not when Custer was overcome by the notion that he must try to strike the village by taking the next coulee downriver. Custer was determined to impose his will upon these people who dared warn him not to fight. But war and killing was his life. It was all he knew. He must prevail at all costs. He could think of nothing else. However, instead of taking the lead down the coulee, himself, he motioned for Captain Yates and Captain Keogh to take the lead, which they did, with Keogh and Comanche riding by down the slope. Both captains, with Smith and Calhoun, were wearing buckskin which Custer was known to wear on campaigns. Following the commanders, were Lt. James Sturgis and Lt. James Porter, with many of the companies' troops riding behind them. Custer let them pass him on their way down the coulee toward the river. He barely moved. He looked again at the distant *hill*. It appeared closer now, not so far. But still casting a slight dim glow. He blinked, believing it may be the dust or the dryness of his eyes.

As he tried to look away from the *hill* and toward the river, Custer caught a glimpse of the western sky above the river. It was as if the sky over there had been painted with clouds shaped like mares' tails, many, many mares' tails. Suddenly, a heavy volley of gunshots rang out from the coulee by the river. After several moments of heavy gunfire

exchange, soldiers on horseback were hurriedly riding up out of the
coulee in the opposite direction. Arrows were zipping behind them as
they rode, bullets taking down two or three at a time, along the way.

Many soldiers were falling, from the combat taking place. Smoke,
dust and gunfire filled the air. The cavalry that had retreated from the
coulee were being pursued by a large contingent of warriors from the
river. Those soldiers riding up toward Custer who was still near the
higher ridge, clustered together near the crest and turned to engage
their adversaries who were charging from the river and from the south.
They are seeing warriors springing up from their hiding places amid
the sagebrush and the shiny grass, as if they were, the grass. Custer and
his men fired many shots amidst the return of the warriors' gunfire and
arrows. Soldiers were dropping in significant numbers. Many fell from
their horses and either died or ended up on foot.

Seeing the imminent destruction of his companies, Custer realized
that the warriors' approach was forcing an opening to the north. Amidst
the loud and perilous conflict on this ridge, he once again viewed the
hill to the north. His men were taking heavy casualties in the lines in
front and all around him, and most were already dead or wounded. He
felt a strong presence within himself reminding him of the warnings he
had been receiving. Custer realized it was now or never to escape, and
he will choose to ride to a nonexistent northern defensive perimeter.

Quickly Custer turned Vic to the north and kicked him in the
flanks. Vic dashed in that direction, toward the high ridge. It could be a
good point of strategic defense, and to hide within the cloud of battle. A
group of riders sprinted from the ridge and followed their leader toward
the higher point to the north. Several stragglers that were not killed or
pinned down on the previous ridge, also frightfully ran through the
grass toward the north as well. It was the only escape route they could
see. Custer knew he had to get to that *hill*. That was where he must go.
That was where he must be. That was the place of his safe haven, his
salvation, his forgiveness, his deliverance.

Custer believed he could outrun the thrust of warriors that had come
up from the river, if he could just make it to that high *hill*. He spurred
Vic even harder. The horses and their riders galloped swiftly along the
high ridge leading to the *hill*. Custer looked over his shoulder to see the

large group of the soldiers with Calhoun cut off and surrounded at the rise on the ridge to the south he had just left. A roar of gunfire, cries and hoofbeats rose heavily from that crest. Very few of his companies now trailed him. He and his men fired their pistols at anything they could see. He turned his head back toward the *hill* in the north, and again felt the pulse in his chest, and energy, almost physical. He realized that the activities and the movements of the warriors were forcing him and his men further north, like a wave of water in a canal, toward the *hill*. The *hill* he felt. The *hill* that seemed to be calling to him. He quickly dispensed with the notion, convincing himself that he and his troops could fight their way out of anything. They were the Seventh. They were invincible. He was invincible.

But the energy that pulled him. It was a strong, strong feeling. So very strong.

———— «◉» ————

Spirit Horse did everything he could to do his part. To create a battle at the south end of the camp. His goal was to tie up two-thirds of the opposing forces there. To keep the majority of the battle with the soldiers to the south. And thereby force the action upon the lead remaining group of the cavalry. Spirit Horse was asked to prepare the strategy and organization for many battlefields. Miles of coordination moving as one believing force. This was his instructed role. And the plan was working as expected.

———— «◉» ————

The young Mnincoju warrior Sleeps Many had a long-standing relationship with his trusted friend the black and white mustang he rode toward the group of soldiers near the deep ravine. A crackling rifle shot zooms by Sleeps Many's right leg and hits with a smack into his friend's rib cage on the right side. He knows that Helps Out has been shot and wounded, because the young horse screams and veers to the left, tripping, stumbling, and then crashing to the dirt on the side of the ravine.

Sleeps Many's friend falls, with the warrior close behind. He rushes to his friend's side and puts his arm around his neck, his face next to the horse's neck and eye. Sleeps Many caresses his friend's face and mane as gunshots and chaotic action go on above and beside them. He will stay with his friend until the horse's spirit will rise and join those of his ancestors.

———— ((●)) ————

On the distant bluffs to the west, stood Sitting Bull. Praying. And watching. He looked on, realizing that what he had been told by his Mnincoju relatives from Bear Creek about the *asking* and the *permission* was now happening. He did not know the specifics about how, but it was becoming reality. He had been asked to be present when needed. He held tight to his cannumpa.

———— ((●)) ————

The power of the spirit and the power of prayer is being expressed in the oldest way possible by the holy man standing in the field north of the battlefield and the *hill*. He stands with both arms extended and palms turned up to Grandfather Sky. He is facing the battlefield. And the *hill*. Eagle Fan is praying to Wakan Tanka, the Creator. For the help. The courage. The guidance. The unity. The strength.... And the permission as foretold. The sound of the whistle of the wanbli is heard by Eagle Fan from above. He looks toward the sun. High above, three of the messengers are gliding in a circle with the gentle breeze and the breath of the Creator.

———— ((●)) ————

Along the high ridge running north, Custer and his troops, are dwindled in numbers. He and the few remaining with him, are panicked and shaken, and looking for somewhere to hide. Custer can now see over his shoulder that most of his companies have been cut off from him toward the south. They appear to be overrun by a large group of encircling and encroaching warriors. He and the few troops still with him, have been forced north, to the high *hill* he had seen in the distance. He swings his arm upward to urge those still with him to hurry forward to the higher ground. The strategic advantage. The place where they could regroup and hide from any charge from the river or the south.…. and to hunker down until the time when Benteen and Reno can come to help him. As he and Vic ride down into another dip before the next rise, an eagle's whistle is heard over the battlefield, off to the north..…. There appears to be a slight fog along the grass on the hilltop ridge now, which lies ahead. He bears down on Vic. The hoofbeats of all their horses rumble the ground across the large open area. As they run toward the *hill*.…. The *hill* that is calling.

⸺⸺◉⸺⸺

Saved By Bear smelled the yellow of the sun. His spirit was alive and energetic. He felt the energy in his chest and all along the blood running through his veins. He looked to his left and saw his great friend by his side. The strong scent of sage caressed his nostrils and reminded him of home. The movement over the high-running hilly ridge to the south caught his eye. He and Swift Bear sensed and felt the *pathway* opening up. So much had occurred so quickly. So suddenly. So dramatically. Their call to duty, his call to duty, filled his mind, his heart, and his spirit. Today was meant to happen. It was presented to the people from the Creator. The plan was made. The warriors summoned. The preparation was done. It all led to this place. This portal in time.

The sparse clouds to the west resembled mares' tails. For a brief moment, he remembered his white stone friend in the White Mountains. He remembered his spiritual commitment to protect his people, Grandmother Earth, and the sacred He Sapa. And time stood still for moment… a small moment in time, through all of the ancient and original history of all of the moments of time. And as the group of the horse-mounted soldiers rode briskly over the far ridge, the Creator shined that warm, nurturing light upon these warriors. Such as Creator had been doing since the beginning of time, since the beginning of the Grandmother Earth and the Grandfather Sky, and at the beginning of all things. All the moments of time forever, had arrived here, now. It had come to this.

Creator's strong will and great invisible hand had placed them here. It was the Creator all along. It always was. And always would be.

Now it was time to act.

16

OUR BATTLE

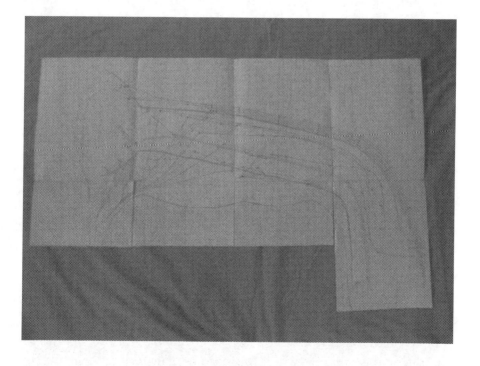

OUR BATTLE IS WELL UNDER way. The dust, the smoke, and the bodies combined create a spiritual presence with a life of its own. A haze of rolling clouds, ever moving and changing in size, are consuming the battlefield, advancing relentlessly, resembling a rushing tidal wave of element and warrior above the ground. This condition affects how far the eye can see, ranging from almost no visibility to limited clarity. Every second is a struggle to survive.

The air is filled with nonstop physical movement and mental anguish. The most prevalent factor is the energy or medicine being exchanged by warrior and soldier. This clouding causes periods of isolation and loss of control, making the combatants rely on instinct alone. Every member of the Seventh Calvary is experiencing true human emotion from deep within himself, knowing in his heart who he really is as a man, not as a soldier of war. Each will fight his personal battle guided by either mind or spirit. All have chosen to be here.

The sounds of the ground are dominated by the noise of the two-legged, noise coming from the rifle, the revolver, and mostly the mouths and lips of the soldiers. The cavalry is in utter chaos and confusion as they witness their companions brutally being taken down, listening to the horrific gasps and screams of those who fall into silence. The survivors scatter in desperation without leadership, or safety of retreat. Their bullets are discharged with no time to focus aim, randomly shot in every direction. Ammunition will run low for each soldier as the battle rages on. They each sense what it feels like to be pursued and murdered, just as the indigenous tribal nations felt at the hands of the US military. Their word *massacre*, once taken for granted, now has new meaning. The cavalry is overwhelmed and unorganized in field battle. Having expected such behavior, the warriors will exploit this advantage with the use of our traditional weapons. This is part of our commitment to be honorable red men.

The cloudy haze is moving up the hill and stretching across the entire field. On the north perimeter of the conflict, a portion of the haze leaves the main body and begins to roll over a meadow of prairie grass with scatterings of sagebrush. As the elements push forward, a number of bluffs on the right come into view which are in line going up the *hill*. The bluff at the bottom is where the meadow extends west, meeting the tree line by the river.

In the distance, near the northwest corner of this slope, is a large growth of sagebrush surrounded by meadow grass. It is visible briefly, and then it disappears, engulfed by the haze. The elements pass over the sagebrush, bringing it into the light. Visible now are two Lakota Dog Man warriors standing shoulder to shoulder directly behind it.

The warriors' appearance is intimidating in every respect. Dressed in leather head to toe, their leggings and shirts are embossed with the symbols of the Dog Man Society. Physically they are tall and well proportioned, much bigger than their enemies. Their weapons are the bow and arrow, a full quiver strapped to the back, and a waist belt with a stone club and a stone knife. Above each set of shoulders stand two eagle feathers pointed toward Grandfather Sky. The warriors' faces are uniquely painted in black and white symbolic designs chosen for this encounter. The most overpowering presence is their eyes, which show a commitment to life.

Mato Niyanpi and Mato Luzanhan are the indigenous names of these two Dog Man warriors. They have chosen to be here in defense of family, tradition, and culture for all Plains people. This is the consensus of our select group of warriors lying in wait.

The Dog Man has been mentored and trained in body, mind, and spirit to perform and know all phases in the circle of war. This method produces a superbly cross-trained athlete. His teachers were warrior society members with proven backgrounds and accomplishments worthy of respect. The mentoring duties have been passed from generation to generation, always to preserve and protect the people.

This battle of spirits was prepared for in parallel ways. Both sides have their own belief in practice and are guided by routine or ceremony considered necessary to ensure victory. We fight to save the spirit from being deadened or lost.

Battlefield warfare is a vital part of Lakota culture. Each of the various warrior societies had its own rituals, techniques, songs, and code of honor. When force was to be used, bloodshed and annihilation were not the intended outcomes of conflict. Diplomacy was the first step of approach used by our leaders. For years we had tried to honestly communicate to US officials that our rights were being stolen from us and denied by the treaties. Genocidal practice continued causing extreme pain and suffering. Our population was reduced, only a small percentage of our relatives surviving this extinction effort. Our concerns for life fell on the deaf ears of the United States government and military.

The reality of what is happening assaults every sense intensely. In the midst of this assault, one can either go mad or take control. The noise and commotion is endless, creating a feeling similar to when one hears a song being sung with a drumbeat. There is a total immersion of thought and perception. We remember occasions that were much more enjoyable, as we are absorbed in the pains of war.

Saved By Bear understands that the terrain of the field will require the warriors to run up and down over grass-covered knolls, into the rises and depressions, many of which will be encountered on the way to the top of the *hill*. Extreme physical conditioning and the use of instinct and finesse are survival necessities. The warriors' focus is on body, mind, and spirit as they prepare to take the first steps and enter the battle. With a quick glance, a meeting of their eyes, and a nod, Saved By Bear and Swift Bear acknowledge that their time has arrived.

Swift Bear turns to face west, as does Saved By Bear. Swift Bear reaches for the club on his waist belt, taking it into his right hand. Saved By Bear reaches to the left, grasping his knife with his right hand. As his arm comes back across his chest, it passes over a very special item: a beautifully adorned and quilled deer hide medicine pouch that is securely tied in front of the knife sheath on his waist belt. This was a gift for the Wakan (the sacred) from the women of life. Swift Bear raises his head to the sky in prayer, offering respect and honor to the Thunder Beings.

Swift Bear lowers his body to a semicrouching position and then takes off at a full sprint. Staying in stride just steps behind his left shoulder, Saved By Bear is close enough to be his brother's shadow as the two of them advance. They take about twenty of these long strides and then come to an abrupt halt, immediately turning to the left while rising to a standing position. Briefly, both understand where they are going, and feel what is to come for them as men and warriors. Saved By Bear senses he is on the way to the *hill*.

The two begin to walk forward in unison. Swift Bear extends his left hand in front of his body and connects with the ways of Grandmother Earth. Low clouding emerges from out of the dust and smoke, rapidly moving in their direction. The clouding turns to fog and mist as it passes over them. The spirits have arrived to present our senses with a guide. A spiritual path! Swift Bear's presence will keep the warriors' path open with his medicine and direction. He is the protector, our headman.

As they take their next step, a vision occurs. A mound-shaped aura becomes visible above the ground. Extending into the field ahead, it creates a bend to the left, heading toward the *hill*. Then it is blocked from view by the silhouette of the bluff. Perimeters form to the left and to the right. A red luminous line outlined by a yellow glow runs like a border through the grass and brush along each perimeter, emanating a haze of energy that fades in and out of view, with the deadly battle about to drift or fly through at any second.

The warriors feel the energy of the pathway provided to guide them. They will stay inside of and close to this clearly defined spiritual presence of support. To visualize this path, picture a man standing and facing you. He extends his left arm out at shoulder level, bends his elbow upward, and opens his hand, his palm exposed with his fingers pointed to the sky. This posture gives life to forces well beyond the comprehension of many human beings.

We wait no more! We are not here to fight with you; we are here to kill you. It is time to prove our traditional belief in the practice of who the true warrior is! Our surroundings are allies we depend upon. Unity provides strength and courage. This allows a connection and a spiritual awareness, as does knowing how to navigate the terrain as one constantly moving force advancing on Custer. From now on we communicate with our path, not with words. Toward the palm is where we journey.

Saved By Bear and Swift Bear bend their knees and continue to walk with the utmost caution. With rapid eye movements, they survey the areas to the left and right for threats. With weapons in hand, they know that only flesh and blood will get them to the *hill*. They see a figure. It is a warrior running, who then crosses in front of them, moving to the far right. Another trails and moves out front to cover the middle. A third stays on the left to cover the bluffs. The warriors are sprinting with the quickness of a lightning flash—here and then gone in an instant. Their moccasins look blurred as they glide through the grasses with bow and arrow in hand. Mastery of the bow is a very old tradition, although hand-to-hand combat is just as lethal for the victim. The warriors move with the ease and agility of the dragonfly. Our warriors are placed in protective positions because each possesses essential and specific strengths and abilities. Stamina for running is one of the most crucial abilities we must maintain.

The warriors slow down, assume a crouching position, and stop. Their backs and heads are visible to Saved By Bear. There is motion as each loads an arrow on the sinew for instant release. Saved By Bear and Swift Bear stop and crouch in the grass as well. All movement comes to a standstill. It is now that the senses are immersed in the intense ferocity of the battle, the sounds of life and death deafening the ears, the smells of the earth, the gun smoke, and the blood so overwhelming that they can be tasted. The warriors are ready for the soldier whom they will face in this tightly contained area. But there is an equally menacing foe, the stray bullet. This is a reality that must be accepted.

Saved By Bear looks across the field and sees the familiar sight of feathers. He gazes from side to side and then focuses on the center of the path. The warrior in the middle front position will initiate every advance. When he moves, we will move. He stands up, leans forward, and takes the first of about six quick sneaking steps. We are moving and keeping a proper distance while also maintaining visual contact, finishing with both feet planted squarely underneath us as we all come to a halt. After a quick check of our surroundings, we continue this cluster approach. This brings us closer to the bend. We are ready to depend heavily on our physical ability. There will be one more planned stop to gather spirit en route to the *hill*. The struggle is an endurance contest between warrior and soldier.

Observing the first phase of approach, our brothers are hidden from view. They wait for us to make the planned step that will be their signal to spring into action. We take that step, and they start to sprint toward the designated back and side lines to provide defense coverage. At the same time they are running through the field, our lead man slows and crouches, taking one long step at a time. This allows the others coming from behind to catch up to the rest. These warriors take position behind, to form the backside of the cluster formation, right, middle, and left. The first heads to the far right perimeter still behind

Saved By Bear. Another is coming toward the middle, behind and close to him. The third stays behind on left perimeter. As we continue at two different paces in preparation for the assault, the spirits unify our purpose in defending the human beings. We remember how you would ravage our people and pillage our lands, calling a massacre of innocents a fair and worthy political battle. You would celebrate and feast on yesterday's victory, but today your gut will be empty. We leave fear in the grass behind us.

In midstride, a soldier emerges from the clouding and appears on the path from the right, ahead of us. He is in a state of sheer panic and fear. Instantly, Blue Stone lunges forward into a sprint, drawing his bowstring to full tension. Closing the gap between him and the soldier is his responsibility. The soldier hurriedly steps backward and doesn't even see him. He is frantically trying to reload his rifle and concentrate at the same time. His head is rapidly moving from side to side. His mouth is open but there are no words, only deep breathing and exhaling is heard. This occurrence lasts mere seconds.

With the warrior in pursuit, Saved By Bear sees Comes From Star accelerate to fill the recently vacated right perimeter position. Then the soldier, seeing Blue Stone swiftly approaching, points the rifle in his direction and fires. The bullet misses its intended target. The soldier knows it is too late to try to reload. In stride, Blue Stone releases the arrow with confidence and accuracy. On instinct, we cautiously dash forward, maintaining the tight cluster so as to defend the perimeter.

The arrow passes by the barrel of the rifle. The young soldier's eyes fill with hurt and despair. The soldiers of his rank are the first expected casualties of a philosophical war. There is little value ascribed to their existence by the US military. They are seen as a body to be replaced by another in uniform. The sacrifice of life as a commodity.

When the arrow impales the soldier's chest, he falls to the ground, staring up into the uncluttered blue sky. Blue Stone rushes to take up position where the soldier has fallen, first to provide defense, and second to ensure the soldier has passed and is no longer a threat. Blue Stone will stay there as the rest move, and then he will take the back middle position after his kill.

Steadily pushing ahead, many gunshots are being heard. Swift Bear and Saved by Bear remain at the center of the cluster formation. Swift Bear then turns his head directly to the right, where there are no bodies to be seen. He knows a presence is on its way. Out of the haze comes the whizzing sound of a stray bullet. It seeks the direction of his and Saved By Bear's very next stride. Swift Bear extends his left arm and puts his left hand in front of his brother's chest as a caution, at the same time bending his upper torso backward. His reaction causes Saved By Bear to hesitate, and remain behind his left shoulder. Saved By Bear is kept out of the path of the bullet, which flies in front of Swift Bear's face, missing him by mere inches.

On the left perimeter facing the bluffs, Buffalo Horn has already come through, creating a focal point to lead us in the direction of the *hill*. The warrior covering the back of this perimeter is Elk Whistle, who stays behind Saved By Bear and keeps a steady pace. Warriors to the side and back securing the right perimeter are still sprinting as they enter the final expanse of the curve ahead. They must pick up speed as they pass through the lower portion of the bend, which will provide them with cover. Ahead on the right, Runs With Wind watches for movement as we move at full speed, preparing for the path to the *hill* to come into view, thus exposing the open field filled with rough terrain and the spoils of battle. The elements of heat and smoke combine to create another enemy of the physical, enveloping everyone like a second skin, bringing forth sweat and heightening the senses as each warrior draws another breath of foul air.

Running at different paces, we are almost ready to leave the bend. It is now that the path reveals the very top of the *hill* where we are to go. There is a section of ground covered in grass that is emanating the presence of life. All the warriors feel the energy within themselves. They are allowed only brief glimpses of this spot in the distance, due to the continual interruption of sight and the ability to focus. Saved By Bear sees the silhouettes of mounted soldiers coming from the right and beginning to assemble in this area. The horses are in distress because they are being held and beaten in an attempt to form a tight circle. The cries of the horses are sad to the ears. In rapid succession of gunfire, they are being murdered to provide protection for a pitiful self. As the bodies are falling to the ground in this act of desperation, Saved By Bear feels he has arrived. He too has a meeting of spirits to attend.

Penetrating the haze from our right, two soldiers come into view. The one closest to us scurries, and then looks back over his shoulder to where he has come from. A necklace dangles across his chest as he raises his revolver and fires into the unknown, knowing that his fate lies with the red man who reaches him first—a terrifying thought. Runs With Wind dashes through the grass in pursuit, arrow drawn. The soldier farther up the path is running away as fast as his legs are capable of carrying him. In pure survival mode, he is trying to escape with his life. His arms are flailing about as he heads toward the left perimeter and the bluffs beyond. He is not screaming, but is heard weeping as he fades from vision. Buffalo Horn bolts ahead and makes a quick, sharp left turn, disappearing into the haze, in anticipation of cutting the soldier off before he reaches the bluffs.

All warriors automatically start shifting to new positions of protection. Their moccasins lead them as they glide through the grass. They must maintain their presence on the north perimeter of the battle, pushing everyone back toward the main body. The warriors to the south are fighting bravely in honor of their commitment to life, just as we are. Comes From Star follows Runs With Wind, keeping his distance and securing the right perimeter with vision and speed. To the left, Elk Whistle picks up his pace, racing to fill the position out front so the warriors will have a visual point to gather their bearings and adjust their speed anywhere within the cluster.

Saved By Bear and Swift Bear continue their pace, with Red Whirlwind still on their right and behind them. Runs With Wind is nearing the soldier when the latter again looks over his shoulder, this time seeing his adversary. The soldier stops abruptly, turns, and stands up facing the warrior's approach. He begins to raise his revolver as if to shoot, but instead he opens his hand, letting the weapon fall to the ground. He reaches to his chest, where the necklace is weighed down by metal. It is a cross. He clasps it tightly and mumbles words not understood. It is his belief. Runs With Wind is very close and has already taken aim. He releases the arrow, watching the feathers spin and come to a halt in the soldier's chest. The soldier falls headfirst into the sea of grass. Runs With Wind goes to the body, pausing so that the others may move past him. Then he assumes a position at the back and toward the right of the perimeter.

Simultaneously, across the field, Buffalo Horn scampers through the dense clouding of smoke and dust, searching for the soldier. A figure comes into sight. He is walking, and then he stops and sits down in the grass. He crosses his arms and legs and stares in shock past Buffalo Horn. Upon witnessing this act of total submission, Buffalo Horn shifts his bow and arrow to his left hand while grabbing his stone club with the right. The man's stare expresses the innocence and curiosity of a child in dependent mode, asking for a new lesson to be taught. A compassionate death is given the soldier. A blow is delivered to the backside of his skull. He did not see.

Buffalo Horn twists his body while planting his feet and coming to a hasty stop. He is facing the opposite direction now. He lunges forward, running from the haze in order to catch sight of Saved By Bear. When he sees him, he puts the club away and readies his bow and arrow. As he secures the back left perimeter, he sees movement in the meadow's tree line far behind us.

This movement is the horse, stepping from silence, to a pounding gallop of breath and speed. He carries Spotted Horse on his back. They seek the right perimeter and take up the closest position to round the bend. A succession of entry occurs, each rider taking up position to the right of the horse ahead. Within seconds of each other come Flies Above, Strong Hand, Brave Dog, and Black Wolf, the remainder of our warrior band. The purpose of this tactical maneuver is to steadily sweep the ground ahead for stragglers or intrusions overflowing onto the path. The horse and man become one formidable entity. They comprise our most crucial element of offensive threat and aggression. Bound together in strength and trust, they are unparalleled in ability, and proven by accomplishment in the field.

Saved By Bear and the warriors now have a much broader view of the *hill* and the terrain in front of them. Still continuing at their individual paces of position, he sees Comes From Star's posture change to a leaning crouch as he begins to cautiously slow down. This is the signal for the rest of us to do the same. Our field of vision is clearer than before, with scatterings of clouding from dust and smoke. At times figures are seen scampering to and fro in a concentrated area below the top of the *hill*. They search for defensive positions in a frenzy, preparing for our encounter. Suddenly the ears are the first of the senses to heed the obvious change occurring as we advance. The gunfire is lessening, and sounds are sporadic.

Our moccasins seek sure footing in the grass as our pace is greatly reduced. The body is weary and tense, but unrelenting in desire. The legs are feeling the burn of overexertion and depletion of oxygen. The arms are heavy because of the incessant grasp on weapons and the use for balance on an unpredictable terrain. The heart is the muscle under the most strain, struggling with the emotions arising from good and bad thoughts.

All warriors come to a complete stop. They have been tightening the cluster by maintaining their watch toward the center of the cluster. They keep Saved By Bear and Swift Bear securely in the center. Each starts inhaling long and deep to control his breathing and catch a second wind. When their eyes meet to assess the formation, it is clear we have not suffered any casualties. Must refocus for what lies just ahead of us.

Comes From Star has decided that this interlude in time will be for recuperation of faculties. Our warriors cannot continue at such an exhausting pace. The risk must be taken. We focus on the need to absorb and replenish our energy from the strength of the path. The neck is the fastest-moving part of the body, constantly surveying the surroundings in every direction. The full use of peripheral vision is absolutely necessary at every position, enabling surveillance to become one eye of protection in full circle, prepared for combat with weapon or hand in an instant of need. Comes From Star waves his left hand in a sweeping motion over the grass tops. All warriors are anxious as they begin rising from their sneaking posture to take one step at a time. This crucial pause allows us time to regenerate our senses and an opportunity to time the arrival of our allies.

Saved By Bear looks into the gaps of coverage to the right. As his head pans to the left, his eyes lock on to our youngest, Buffalo Horn. He is the one who has seen much more than the rest of us have when it comes to witnessing the horrible evil deeds of contact with the white man. His early childhood was not as it should have been, as families were slaughtered and forced into the loss of tradition and culture. He grew up in a time of confusion, hurt, and pain that cannot be described, only experienced. With a commitment made, he is performing as he feels he must for Creator. The heart in his chest is very wise for such a young man. His ways are a part of us. He is our relative, a Nakota, chosen by his families and medicine people to represent everything in this world that they live for and believe in as human beings. He is their hope!

Saved By Bear need not turn and look far behind him to envision Eagle Fan standing alone in the grass facing our direction. Safely in seclusion and hidden from view, Eagle Fan has been in this position amid the heat since sunrise. His palms raised to the sun, he is in deep meditative prayer.

Protecting his presence at this place are Touches Heart and Many Thunder. Eagle Fan, a Dakota warrior, is the keeper of our sacred pipe, and the *bundle* prepared for this journey. His spiritual connection, wisdom, and belief are asked for by all extended families. Eagle Fan was chosen by a small number of our own trusted campfires. Then suddenly a transition from prayer to song occurs. A song that resonates mystery and beauty through the ground. He sings in honor and praise to the horse nation.

With a number of vigilant steps already taken, the body begins adjusting to conditions as we advance. The warriors' minds must also slow down thought and memory to bring awareness back to what is underfoot. All continue breathing deeply and steadily. We have been stepping at this pace for about ten seconds, remaining in a tight cluster. The haze comes and goes across our path, first moving very quickly and then slow enough to feel as though it is crawling over us. Custer and his remaining soldiers are now embedded in the grass, some below his position and some hiding behind the dead horses on the very top of the *hill*. Occasional gunfire comes from this position, as panic has taken over every one of the soldiers. They shoot in helpless abandon anywhere down the hill in front of them. Briefly, we are capable of seeing each other and the position each holds. The Seventh Cavalry look down from the top of the warriors' path, waiting in terror for our arrival. The human beings look up as we stride forward in confidence, to take down all soldiers protecting Custer, leaving him the focal point in the warriors' collective mind-set of elimination.

Saved By Bear scans what is visible ahead. He feels his duty will be upon him soon. His attention is centered on the soldiers out front in the grass. They provide him with a mental imprint of location to rely on. Among these soldiers he will look for the carbines closest to Custer. From their stationary crouched position, the soldiers fire and then reach down in the grass to retrieve cartridges that have been placed next to them. They are trying to reload faster. There are two on the right, one being just below the cover of dead horses and the other closer to us. Seeing these weapons is confirmation to Saved By Bear of his commitment to follow the rituals he had been instructed to perform. Saved By Bear prepares self and spirit for an encounter that will alter his existence and life force forever.

The warriors' physical state is improving with each step they take, preparing for the individual battles that each will call his own. Our cluster will soon be fragmented, leaving each warrior to fight one-on-one against the enemy, a do-or-die scenario for both sides. These spontaneous encounters will take place within seconds of one another across the field. We are about fifteen seconds at pace and still intact in formation. This strategic move has allowed us to gather our senses and personally strengthen the willingness to give every effort humanly possible for our cause.

A dense fog rushes over the path between the warriors and the cavalry. Obscuring everything, it blocks the view for both sides. The brothers are ready to put into practice the beliefs and power of the warrior. As we are in a state of temporary blindness, the ears lock onto a rumbling noise coming from behind us on our right side, the rhythmic sound of pounding hooves rapidly nearing our position. As the horses come closer and closer, they sound like thunder rising from the grass. This is a sign for the brothers to heed. Saved By Bear knows that seconds from now, it will be time for older brother to thrust his hooves into the ground along the path. We depend upon him. *Strike, leave your mark!* The fog clears just as Spotted Horse bursts onto the scene. Our field of vision is clearing as he crosses from right to left with great speed. He will be followed by other riders.

Elk Whistle sees this disruption of the soldier directly in front of him on left perimeter. He immediately takes off in his direction with bow drawn. While Elk Whistle is making his approach, the soldier rises from his crouched position with revolver in hand. He points his weapon toward the coming warrior. Just then Spotted Horse passes on his left side close enough to make a kill. The surprise of someone coming in another direction causes the soldier's finger to react too quickly. He pulls the trigger, sending the bullet over Elk Whistle's head. Elk Whistle decides this will be hand-to-hand combat. This soldier is confused, but upon readying himself, he knows this too. Both are eager to prove their manhood, as neither has ever backed down from a fight. The soldier draws his knife and faces Elk Whistle, waiting for him. He starts yelling and screaming in an unknown language as Elk Whistle nears. Their clash will be entirely physical, man conquering another man.

Elk Whistle places his bow and arrow in his left hand, and draws his knife. As he is about to make contact with the soldier, he tosses the bow and arrow forward into the grass, just feet in front of him. He leaps forward and leaves the ground, twists his body so it becomes parallel to the grass. When cross-body impact is made, the soldier's chest and stomach absorb the warrior's blow. He is forced backward to the ground, with Elk Whistle rolling on top and over his head as they both hit the earth hard. The soldier is on his back, stunned, the warrior is already on two feet. As the soldier tries to get up, Elk Whistle goes to a knee and grabs the soldier's head by the chin. Then he pulls upward and slits the soldier's throat. Hustling to grab his bow from the ground, leaving the arrow, he remains in position watching as Saved By Bear and Swift Bear advance.

Comes From Star is the closest to where the horses emerged between us and the cavalry. As Spotted Horse moves away left, he see a soldier crouched in the grass with his carbine. Then Flies Above comes and rides in front of Spotted Horse like a blur. He has seen the soldier. The horses rapidly move left. Flies Above is moving toward the soldier in quick strides, waiting for the remainder of our riders to open the field. He sees Strong Hand enter, also going left. To his right, Brave Dog and

Black Wolf are going up the right perimeter, alongside the soldiers below the hilltop. They rush by the first soldier Comes From Star is to face. The soldier is baffled by the presence of the horses coming and going with extreme speed and sound. They pass so close to him that he feels they could have easily trampled him to death. He must see the warrior approaching. He rises from the grass with carbine pointed forward, but only waist high. All warriors will choose a pace to keep moving forward and simultaneously remain aware of the enemy. Comes From Star sees a man staring at the surroundings as though he has connected spiritually with the path and his presence. He has heard of these Plains people and admires our ways of life. The soldier speaks in a tongue that has sounds somewhat familiar to our language. His words bring the dragonfly to mind, the symbol of our Dog Man Society. The soldier appears to be speaking to ancestors and beings in a faraway land. One of a sacred mountain, the home of the dragon. The spirit can be very powerful when shared with another being, as these two men have experienced.

Comes From Star is only yards away from the soldier. He feels on the inside for this man. He knows the soldier did not want to be here. He releases the arrow, and watches as it plunges into the center of the soldier's chest. His facial expression is not one of pain but one of relief to be able to return home. The soldier starts falling to his left, his head and eyes locked on that special feeling and sight coming from the sky. His body comes to rest, comforted by a blanket of grass. Comes From Star takes this position as he sees Red Whirlwind sprinting by on his right, heading to the second soldier on their perimeter. Saved By Bear remains cautious and patient.

The warriors and the soldiers are given a perfectly clear view of one another. The realization that they share a very small space. One approaching, the other one cowering in fear. There is no place to hide and not be seen, except to lay in the grass before your time. Saved By Bear checks left and right constantly, keeping a step behind Swift Bear. He sees our riders on the left forming a line and moving beneath the hilltop. From behind their dead horses, the soldiers fire two more shots. These will be the last shots fired. They are out of ammunition. The riders make a change in direction and gallop directly at instinctively chosen soldiers. The riders on the right are nearing the soldier with the carbine, who is in front of their fallen horses. The soldier rises to his feet, his head uncontrollably shaking and moving left and right.

Red Whirlwind sees this soldier and knows he has had a special journey to walk. This young man has carried a piece of the spiritual hope for humanity to this battlefield. There is hope in hopelessness. It is called commitment. He is not a warrior; he is a contributor to peace. This man deserves a warrior's death with honor. We would be brothers in a civilized world. Pilamaye. Red Whirlwind slows to take precise aim for the cleanest of kills. The soldier is standing with his carbine in his right hand. Red Whirlwind releases the arrow. The shot is accurate and fatal as it enters his chest. The soldier falls backward to the ground, his right arm outstretched and clutching the carbine. Soldier and carbine quickly disappear in the grass. Saved By Bear intently watches, knowing that this spot is exactly where he must go.

The rear protection group of warriors have witnessed the flurry of encounters thus far. They are beginning to move away from the path and toward the gathering point. Buffalo Horn runs from the behind left along the bottom slope of the *hill*. He will be followed by Blue Stone, Runs With Wind, Elk Whistle, and Comes From Star. They will exit the path behind Saved By Bear and Swift Bear, running toward the gathering point. Red Whirlwind will cross in front of Saved By Bear to trail the other warriors on foot.

The focus shifts to Strong Hand, who is now within feet of the soldier. He has his bow ready for release. The warrior's and soldier's eyes connect to reveal human nature's frailties. The soldier is trembling with his head buried in his chest. There will be no resistance. Does he remember the eyes of our women and children, when he had the upper hand? Their suffering is justified by the fear he will leave this world with. Strong Hand releases his arrow and watches as it enters the base of the soldier's neck, severing the artery. He falls to the side, clutching his neck with both hands upon impact with the ground. He will feel excruciating pain as he bleeds to death. This is the first kill by one of our mounted warriors. Each kill occurs within an instant of each other from left to right on the *hill*. Strong Hand exits, heading to the gathering point.

Flies Above is seen by the soldier through the point of his spear.

Flies Above has carried this weapon of choice for a reason. The spear is an extension of the hand. To touch and to feel the exchange of energy between enemies. This soldier does not believe, as he does. How could this *savage* navigate his way through battle and come for me? The military said this was not possible. But now this soldier was witnessing the truth of what these warriors and their families were capable of. Flies Above nudges his horse with a knee, and the horse leaps into the air, and twists sideways. What the soldier sees is a warrior dropping from the sky. His face is painted, weapon clutched and ready, from moccasin to shoulder in decorated flowing leather, atop a magnificent horse. The horse lands so close that his right front and back legs touch his dead relative's body. The horses would have preferred to deliver us into meetings of peace and diplomacy, rather than war and death. The soldier is so intimidated and scared by this presence that he attempts to stand up. His head and hands raise upward as his eyes make contact with Flies Above, watching as Flies Above leans forward and thrusts the spear through his heart. Then he pulls the spear out of his chest. The soldier collapses to his knees and then falls face first in the grass next to his dead horse. Flies Above follows Strong Hand and his horse, as they gallop by.

Stopping just feet in front of the soldier, the horse rears up on his hind legs and slams his front hooves on the ground. Spotted Horse has his bow drawn and arrow aimed at his enemy. The soldier is crouched over, his knees behind the belly of his dead horse. His body is convulsing; he is overcome with hysteria. His head is rolling from side to side, his hands appear to be grasping and pointing uncontrollably. His mouth stays open, but only his lower jaw moves up and down. He has nothing left, not even a scream. The United States military did not prepare him for this reality. Spotted Horse must shoot a clean and fatal arrow past the frantic motions of the soldier's arms. His fingers release the string, guided by instinct and expertise. In the blink of an eye, the arrowhead enters the soldier's chest. This has been a mental battle for each. The soldier falls forward over his knees and lands face first on the ground. He has passed. Spotted Horse follows Flies Above and quickly leaves the *hill*.

The horse carrying Brave Dog comes to a stomping and snorting halt as his bow is being drawn and aimed. He sees a soldier who is not a real man. He is a bad, undisciplined boy playing the game of genocide. Slaughtering the innocent, and obviously has no spirit to believe it is wrong. There are no more weapons, no more soldiers who can be ordered to die outfront by an officer's command. In truth, he is a weak, sorry example of mankind. The human beings disrespect him. This is evident in their behavior with the striking down of each soldier by a warrior. The soldier is kneeling on the ground. His head and shoulders are bent forward as he attempts to hide behind his dead horse. He raises his head to look at Brave Dog. He is terrified by his image. He covers his nose and mouth with his hands, and closes his tear-filled eyes. The warrior's fingers release the sinew; the arrow buries itself deep within the soldier's chest. The soldier falls forward with his face impacting the ground. Brave Dog will initiate the sweep behind the *hiltop* before exiting to the gathering point.

Four hooves dig into the ground only feet in front of a dead horse of another soldier. Black Wolf has timed his stop to position his left leg toward the soldier. He quickly draws his bow across the back of his horse and is ready to release his arrow. The soldier he sees is rising from a crouched position. His eyes are wide open as he stares at his foe. The eyes are expressive of the hatred and disdain he has for indigenous people. His is the dark disturbed mind of a murderer. He is angrily screaming and shouting nonstop. The facial expressions indicate that he is calling out obscenities. The spirit need not speak his language to understand the message implied by his fit of rage.

The soldier stands up to face Black Wolf. He raises his arm, his knife in hand, which he points and erratically thrusts into the air. His ranting is annoying like a crow squawking. Silence will be given. Black Wolf watches as his arrow passes by his fist, the arrowhead spinning and then piercing the soldier's chest. The force of the blow knocks him to his back on the ground. There is silence coming from the grass where he lays. Black Wolf will trail Brave Dog on the sweep behind and around the hilltop before exiting to the gathering point.

Red Whirlwind hurriedly exits in front of Saved By Bear and Swift Bear who are steadily running uphill. The remaining soldiers now realize that all but two of the warriors on foot have left the *hill*. There is no longer any back or side protection for Saved By Bear and Swift Bear.

The first set of horses is rapidly approaching the gathering point. Touches Heart and Many Thunder will bring horses to our warriors coming on foot. Looking to his right, over Swift Bear's shoulder, Saved By Bear sees Brave Dog riding beyond the fallen men and horses to finish the sweep around and behind the *hill*. He is followed by Black Wolf on his horse. They encircle the hilltop looking for the enemy, before they make their exit from the *hill* and head to the gathering point. The commitment of each of these warriors on foot and on horse is now fulfilled.

Mato Niyanpi and Mato Luzanhan know that they are entirely alone. They must believe in their *asking*. Looking into the open isolated area between the dead horses, they see no activity above the grass. The life is hiding from them. The two warriors will find and confront their enemy. They continue running, their instincts guiding them.

The two warriors see movement, a head rising above the belly of the first fallen horse to their left. After a brief look, a soldier drops from sight. Mato Luzanhan quickly steps in front of Mato Niyanpi with his club raised. Mato Niyanpi moves to the right without hesitation. They are headed in two different directions at this point. They will perform two sacred and separate acts of responsibility in the same seconds ahead.

Mato Luzanhan increases his speed to reach the soldier who has jumped to his feet with knife in hand. The soldier begins stomping with each stride he takes toward the oncoming warrior. He snarls at the top of his lungs and bares his teeth. His hair-covered face makes him look like an animal attacking its prey. The soldier's eyes are dark and ominous, the force of energy the Lakota oppose. His presence is that of many. This being is from evil seed of long ago. At the same time this is happening, Mato Niyanpi approaches the fallen soldier in search of the carbine that he carried to the battlefield. He puts his knife away, while his eyes search for the weapon by the body. He will arrive with just enough time to focus, grab with both hands, turn, and sprint to Mato Luzanhan.

Mato Luzanhan must stay on his feet. He cannot be in a physical brawl. He will use agility and finesse to avoid this attack. He backpedals to gain footing and almost comes to a complete stop. The soldier is taking his last step and begins to lunge forward with knife extended toward the warrior. Mato Luzanhan reacts by quickly sidestepping the blade, ensuring that this stabbing attempt fails. The soldier is pushed off balance by Mato Luzanhan's left arm extending and striking his shoulder with a downward motion. With club in hand, he raises his right arm and with excessive force, strikes downward. The club delivers a crushing blow to the soldier's skull, behind the ear. The soldier's momentum causes him to fall face first into the grass. His body slides to a standstill.

Mato Luzanhan begins a left pivot, and as he turns, a second soldier rises from the grass. This soldier comes to a hunched and standing position. Mato Luzanhan has not seen the soldier yet because his view is of Mato Niyanpi's movement.

Mato Niyanpi quickly comes to a stop beside the soldier. In front of him lays the carbine. He bends down and grabs the stock with his left hand. Next to the fallen man's hand is a cartridge, just inches away. Mato Niyanpi picks it up with his right hand. He rises and pivots with his right leg swinging away from this soldier. Both Mato Niyanpi and Mato Luzanhan see the man as they both turn to the center of the *hilltop*. They both know that this man is Custer. Each warrior has a different instruction, and his own manner of approach to get to Custer. Different angles and distances to cover. Mato Luzanhan is so close to him that he will not have to run. Mato Niyanpi is swiftly running and closing in on their position.

Custer is in shock upon seeing the two warriors rushing for him. His reaction is to start backing away in panic. Mato Luzanhan, stride for stride, closes in on him with sheer determination. Mato Niyanpi slows and readies the carbine, as his brother prepares for contact with Custer. Custer does not have a hat of any kind on his head. His hair has been cut short. He tries to hide its spirit. The name given to Custer by many tribal nations is Long Hair. This is applicable no longer! He will earn a given new name. He is clothed in the military uniform. He carries no weapon of any kind. Desperate and by himself, he is the last soldier.

Mato Luzanhan is directly in front of Custer. On his last stride, he is raising both arms with his palms facing him. He powerfully thrusts his hands forward into Custer's chest. The impact lifts him off the ground, shoving him backward, so he is now in midair above the grass. Mato Niyanpi will come to a stop when Custer lands on his back. With the honor of coup counting, Mato Luzanhan turns and runs from the top of the *hill*. Mato Luzanhan is forever a warrior. Kola is commitment.

As Custer lands on his back, hitting the ground very hard, he is dazed by the physical violence. He is gasping for air, trying to recover his senses. He tilts his head looking for the warrior, seeing only a horizon of grass and blue sky. Mato Niyanpi rises above him and comes to a complete stop. He looks down into the eyes of Custer. There is utter silence.

Custer sees through fear, like one experiencing an apparition or a ghost. Then, that of a warrior and a common man. The beauty and serenity of life surrounds Mato Niyanpi and Custer. Custer's facial expressions change from fear to a willful trusting release of self. A calm and accepting spirit for a newfound brother, Mato Niyanpi. There will be no more battlefield for these two human beings.

Mato Niyanpi points the gun at Custer's chest and pulls the trigger. The bullet draws blood as he begins to reload the chamber. The casing is discarded. The cartridge that the soldier has carried to this battle, is inserted into the chamber. The carbine is ready to take a second shot. This shot will be in the temple portion of Custer's skull, on the left side. His head absorbs the force of the bullet, leaving him facing the sky. Mato Niyanpi looks at him. He feels balance has come. He sees that peace has come, and it is shown on Custer's face. He lies in front of Mato Niyanpi as though he has fallen asleep. He can rest now, away from the turmoil and torture of a lost spirit; free from the evil ways of contact and behavior that dictated his life; ways that may have been against his heart in reality.

Mato Niyanpi crouches over Custer and removes his knife from the sheath. He reaches for Custer's left hand, grabbing and raising it above the grass. His knife slices across the flesh, taking a partial trigger finger at the joint. As he stands, he releases the hand, which drops back to the ground. He cups this piece of Custer in the palm of his left hand. He unties the sacred pouch and takes it off his waist belt. He opens the buckskin pouch, and places the finger inside. Then he pulls the pouch lace tight to close it, and ties it back on his waist belt. Mato Niyanpi stands alone, knowing he must offer prayer for the generations of suffering human beings. He asks for pity and understanding to rebuild our traditional and cultural lives. The time has come to speak to Wakan Tanka.

Far from sight at this time, Touches Heart is bringing Swift Bear his horse. Many Thunder waits with Mato Niyanpi's horse, for the time when he becomes visible in the distance. Custer lies in the grass. Mato Niyanpi is standing beside him. Even death is a healing for the mind and the physical presence. The spirit will live on. Custer is asked to go on a journey guided by Mato Niyanpi. He will be taught with patience to learn compassion and respect for another human being.

There is a feeling of harmony on the ground, in nature's surroundings, and in these men of the earth. It is as though the battle never existed at all. Mato Niyanpi raises his arms and turns west, away from the body of Custer. This is his last image of the Greasy Grass Battle. The victory is ours. He stands still as his eyes stare into the blue sky.

Mato Niyanpi was called upon by his relatives and Creator to perform this act of commitment and courage. Mato Niyanpi is the proud Lakota warrior who killed Lt. Col. George Armstrong Custer. In the taking of Custer's human presence from Unci Maka, Grandmother Earth, Mato Niyanpi will become, and continue to be, the spirit keeper of Custer.

Wakan Tanka, the Creator, called for this union for our future generations to learn from the past. Setting forth a pathway for unification and a workable peace between all cultures of the world. Mato Niyanpi must offer the prayers of families that have come with our bundle from the children, women, and men each with their own contributions of spirit. The prayers will be heard. The prayers will be sent in the directions of their *asking*. These prayers will bring mending to the broken hoop of the Lakota and to all people across the Earth.

Mato Niyanpi moves to the north, moves to the east, and then moves to the south. He lowers his head to Unci Maka, and then raises his head and arms directly to the sky of Tunkasila. He has completed the physical ritual of his vows. He turns and runs swiftly toward the bottom of the *hill.* Once there, he continues running toward the gathering point. As Mato Niyanpi leaves, he knows of one certainty: that through the eyes of any being, the only ones that could have witnessed this taking of life are not of the two-legged. We leave in peace, unity, tolerance and love, for the future of all the children and families of Grandmother Earth.

Running to the gathering point beyond the northern perimeter of the *hill,* Saved By Bear saw his friend and fellow heyoka Swift Bear waiting, already mounted on Spotted Smoke, and Many Thunder holding onto the reins of Wildfire. Saved By Bear sprinted forward to his companions. Upon reaching the spot, he quickly leapt up on Wildfire's back. Then all of the warriors quickly galloped off, leaving behind them the scene of the battle to which they had committed, and for which they had prepared for such a long time, and given so much of their lives and spirit.

The sixteen warriors and their horses rode off quickly to the northeast. Nearing the edge of the Wolf Mountains, they slowed to ensure that all were together and safe. As Saved By Bear turned Wildfire back to look upon those riders and horses behind him, he caught sight of something on the horizon. As his eyes focused through the haze of the dust and the golden aura still pulsing over the *hill* on the battlefield, he saw the image of his old friend against the horizon to the west.... The great white horse. The stone pony from the White Mountains. The great horse raised his head and tossed his mane, and nodded with a gentle yet strong affirmation of the horse nation, and the spirits of all of his people and their brothers and sisters. Then, the image slowly disappeared into the sun and brought a renewed jolt of spiritual energy bursting through Saved By Bear's chest. And he joined all of his warrior and horse brothers as they turned their hopes and determination toward getting back to their sacred haven. The He Sapa.

In the moments before the confrontation atop the chosen *hill*, Giovanni Martini had ridden hard to backtrack to the south to find Benteen. The young Italian immigrant soldier was carrying his urgent message. He really did not understand the words, as he did not speak English very well. He rode fast and hard, and finally saw the troops of Captain Benteen halted near Ash Creek, watering their horses.

After Custer had split his companies into four columns, Benteen had moved to the southwest as directed by Custer. He had been advised to watch out for Indians moving to escape to the south into the mountains or into the areas beyond the Little Bighorn Valley. Not finding any such Indians, Benteen turned back toward the trail along Ash Creek, the same trail that Custer and Reno had followed west and north toward the Little Bighorn River basin. The troops and their horses were hot, tired, and thirsty, so when they had come upon a low area stretching across the creek, Benteen had ordered a halt to water and rest the horses.

It was here that Martini approached from the north, galloping hard toward Benteen's location.

When the young trumpeter arrived with his handwritten note from Custer, he quickly rode up to Benteen and presented the message. Benteen took it from him, realizing the soldier was out of breath and did not fully know what to say. "It is General Custer." Benteen clasped the small paper in his gloved hand and unfolded it under the beating sun. The dust and nervousness of its message was apparent in the manner in which the note had been folded, crumpled, and squeezed. Benteen read it to himself, standing by his horse and not moving.

Captain Weir asked what the matter was. Benteen said nothing, except, "Mount up!" He then pointed out to Martini that his horse had been shot. And without further thought, Benteen ordered Martini to ride back to Captain McDougall and the pack mule train and advise them to come as quick as they could and follow his trail. Martini took off to the east on his wounded horse toward the direction of the movement of McDougall's mule train.

Instead of galloping at a fast pace, Benteen chose to move his troops forward along Custer's route at a medium pace. There was no apparent urgency to get to Custer. He did not even know for sure where Custer would be. So he angled toward the Little Bighorn seeking to run along the eastern ridge, the way that Custer had said he would go.

⎯⎯⎯⎯⎯⎯≈«(●)»≈⎯⎯⎯⎯

Reno's men were in utter chaos. When Reno had ordered the troopers to retreat across the Greasy Grass River on the eastern side, a mad scramble occurred among the soldiers on horseback and on foot. The warriors from the camp had pushed the troops back into the trees, and now, into the river, and across.

Reno was frantic to get away, to get across the river to higher ground. The soldiers who had not already been shot or struck down were all retreating across the fast-moving waterway. Reno himself managed to gain access to the east bank. Still on his horse, he spurred his mount to climb the steep loose ground leading up from the bank. He could hear the constant clap of gunshots and the whoosh of arrows slicing through the air.

The warriors were much more familiar with the ground and the water, than Reno and his men were. They knew this terrain well. They knew how to run and move within the contours. The warriors skillfully pressed hard and aggressively against the army men in all directions.

This was a day that these soldiers had not reckoned. To the warriors it was an opportunity to see and confront their white tormentors face-to-face for a change. As men. Men against men. It would not be soldiers raiding a vulnerable unsuspecting camp of women, children, and elders. Not this time. These were strong, athletic, able-bodied, battle-trained warriors. And the warriors were acting in the manner they had been always been trained to act, meeting their enemy in such a way as to exploit their weaknesses and vulnerabilities.

Now, on this day, these warriors in the southern part of the camp met the onslaught directly, right away, and stopped the cavalry cold. Once the warriors of the Sicangu and Mnincoju camps joined in, the numbers had grown to the point where the warriors could almost encircle the once attacking, now retreating, soldiers.

The warriors struck the soldiers down as they tried to cross the river or sought to escape by climbing up the slopes on the other side.

The soldiers' horses were set free from their masters as their masters fell away or slid off their backs.

Reno and many of his men needed support, but they had none. They could only run and seek cover. Shots rang out, bullets zoomed by, and men fell in random. Eventually, many of Reno's men were able to run or ride to a high point on a hill overlooking the river valley and the area where they had originally crossed the river to attack the village.

In a frenzy, Reno and some of the retreating troops gained the flat summit of this hill and sought to gain cover by shooting their horses. The cries and screams of horse nation again rose out and drifted across the threshold of the physical world, reaching out for the spirit world. The soldiers' makeshift breastworks were physically materializing, while the spirits of their dead mounts floated beyond the physical plane, seeking their merciful freedom.

This hill would be the place of temporary refuge for Reno and those of his troops who had survived the failed attack upon the encampment. This would be the site of their safe haven within the dust clouds, and the cocoon of their fear and anxiety, as they contemplated their own mortality.

———————◦◉◦———————

Captain Benteen and his companies heard the pressing conflict before they could see it. They picked up their pace and rode until they saw the conflict playing out before them on the distant hilltop, where cavalry soldiers were engaged in gun battle with approaching warriors. Upon seeing that action, Benteen called for a charge to the hilltop area. He recognized Reno's companies, or what was left of them, as the ones who were attempting to fend off the warriors along the lower slopes surrounding the hilltop to the west, south, and north.

Benteen and his mounted soldiers rode in from the east and immediately took up engagement, initially repelling the closest warrior contingents. They fought their way inside of Reno's perimeter, while holding the warriors at bay with periodic fire.

Benteen showed the note to Reno, and to Weir and Edgerly. No one said a word for several moments. Benteen cleared his throat and said, "I am not sure exactly what it means. Do we wait for the pack mule train? Do we search him out right away?" The mule train was a good mile and a half back down the trail with Captain McDougall.

It was at this point that Benteen and most of his men dismounted and began to build cover for themselves and for Reno's troops as well. They shot more of their own horses in the head, intending to use the bodies for the soldiers' breastworks—the likely fate that Vic had suffered earlier. Periodic gunfire and arrows struck within the perimeter. No one knew where Custer and his men were, although they were last seen heading to the north along the ridge leading off in that direction.

Benteen assumed control of the situation. Reno did not put up much objection. Reno was distraught and confused and seemed quite shaken. He still had the blood and tissue of Custer's favorite Indian scout on his neck and chest.

Captain Weir, a young aggressive officer in D Company, asked if anyone knew the whereabouts of Custer and his men. Reno and others pointed to the north, where gunfire and hostilities had been heard in the far distance.

As Reno and Benteen argued over what to do, Captain Weir decided in his own mind he would ride to the north toward the vicinity of the gunfire and obvious conflict, believing that Custer and his men were there in need of support. The young officer requested permission from Reno and Benteen to ride to the north to assist Custer, but they refused.

Weir disobeyed. He charged his horse off the hillside and rode hard past them, riding into the gradually sloping expanse of valley to the north in the direction of the earlier gunfire. Edgerly and several troops immediately charged after Weir, hoping to join him. Benteen then joined the group as well, riding fast to the north. They were speeding by a contingent of warriors hiding in the grass off to the left, avoiding the bullets and arrows best they could. Flanking away from that group of warriors, Weir and the riders behind him, whipped their horses hard. The urgent cadence of their hoofbeats revealed the haste and panic that the soldiers were feeling as they galloped across the open expanse toward the north.

Weir and the twenty or so mounted soldiers following him, rode about a mile to the north and up to the highest point Weir could see.

This was to have a better vantage point for looking to the north and trying to gain knowledge of Custer's whereabouts.

Once Weir gained the high hilltop, he pulled his field glasses out and looked toward the hilltops to the northeast, about four miles away. He saw movement, but mostly smoke and dust, and moving horses here and there, both with and without riders.

Suddenly, from the west and the coulee to their left, a large group of mounted warriors charged directly at them. Then more from the north, and from the east.

The soldiers who had gathered at this high point began to shoot back. After several minutes, they saw more warriors moving toward them on horseback, and some even coming on foot. Weir, Benteen, and the others were alone. Benteen gave the order to fall back to Reno's hill and rejoin the others. So the soldiers turned their mounts and sprinted back, using the route that they had just followed, leaning back now and then to fire over their shoulders. Two soldiers were hit and fell. One private was dragged along by his horse, his foot stuck in the stirrup. He did not survive.

As Weir, Benteen, and the riders who had gone with them, rejoined Reno on the hilltop, the army troopers settled in to a true defensive alignment to try to protect their high territory from the encroachment of the warriors from any direction. Reno was still missing many of his men. Unbeknown to him at the time, seventeen or so had concealed themselves in the timber by the river during the chaotic rush to retreat across the waters of the Greasy Grass.

Many who had made it to the hilltop from the river were wounded. Some were now dead or dying. There was quite a bit of crying and suffering. The US military men of the Seventh Cavalry were experiencing things that they were accustomed to inflicting upon their victims. Not vice versa. It was a change of fortune for the veterans, and a terrifying harsh new experience for the greenhorns. The cries and screams of mortality and imminent death sprang forth from their mouths in many different dialects.

This would be the area that these soldiers, the remnants of the Seventh Cavalry, would remain in to defend. This piece of highland was their salvation for the moment. There would be no charges made.

They would need to hang on, try to survive. And no one knew for sure, where he was. Custer.

Reno and Benteen, in the portions of the battles that they were involved in that day, had merely served in the capacity of carrying out events that had been spiritually foretold. Reno and Benteen were engaged by the warriors led by Spirit Horse, and never made any meaningful attempt to defend or fight alongside Custer. In a sense, it appears that they were somewhat satisfied that maybe Custer could or should be allowed to fend for himself because of his arrogance, and for the fact that neither of those two men really liked him. Essentially, history would show that neither Reno or Benteen exhibited much bravery. They retreated once they found themselves faced with a real warrior contingent. In the *conflicts* that they were accustomed to, the military usually attacked a camp of innocent women and children. In this case, the officers were relegated to serving in the capacity of blind bystanders to the main event. They could be described as being weak, having succumbed to the warriors and doing no more than holding their position, and that is as much as they did.

In the aftermath of the first day of clashing with the cavalry, deciding that it would be best for the warriors and the people to leave the battlefield so as not to have to encounter any more approaching troops, Sitting Bull made the decision to move the people to the Bighorns the next day. The people knew that the soldier groups that would be sure to come, would be able to take care of their own war dead that lay on the hills and near the river. His concern was for the well being and survival of his own people in the aftermath, and how to begin to heal from the events of the day and to comfort the families that needed it most right now.

On the night of June 25, 1876, the people held their mourning dance around a big fire. They mourned their losses, including the spirits of the people, the warriors, and the horses that had died. It was not a celebration of the victory as much as it was a recognition of those who had been lost. The purpose was to honor their memory and their bravery. To see it any other way would be to see a distortion of the people's commitment to the spirit world, and to the spirits of those who were lost in the battles.

17

SPIRIT KEEPER

WHEN THE BATTLE WAS FINISHED, Saved By Bear and the warriors begin their journey back to He Sapa. The reason they go back to He Sapa, is because there are things that they must finish spiritually in ceremony and as *wica*, as men, so that they can move forward with their lives. It takes three days of constant riding to pass nearby Mato Tipila and the buffalo shaped mountain. After one more day of riding, they enter into the sacred He Sapa.

When Saved By Bear and the other warriors arrive at the base camp, they realize all the things they have been allowed to come back home with: the emotions, memories, images, disappointments, and victories. Many things will be brought back with them from the Greasy Grass. These things need healing. These things need assistance from those who depended upon us. Now the warriors will depend upon them to help us cope, understand, and move forward in the new life that we have to live.

As an expected and natural consequence of fulfilling the permission granted from Creator to do what needed to be done at the Greasy Grass, it was necessary to take the lives of the soldiers encountered in the battle. Every warrior was touched by that consequence. With war and battle, injury and death are very real outcomes because both sides are armed and prepared to fight. The key for the warriors was to wait for the government and its military to act. Once the aggressive whites showed themselves and their bad motive and intent to kill all the Lakota people so as to remove them because they were an obstacle to those who wished to steal He Sapa and its resources, then it would be time for Saved By Bear and the other warriors to act.

The Creator granted the permission to the warriors and the people, to act when the government, and particularly Custer, came to the Greasy Grass to kill the people as one of the government's last critical steps in carrying out their grand plan of committing the genocide of the Lakota. Therefore, the warriors followed the instructions and acted upon the spiritual warnings and the fact that Custer and the government refused to respond in a manner of peace or diplomacy.

Now settled in at the base camp in He Sapa, each warrior begins taking care of himself, their horses, and everything that he owns at this time. Swift Bear has the right to take one of his eagle feathers that he wore while in battle, and to now clip a piece into it to represent counting coup on Custer, a feat he has earned. Saved By Bear puts a mark on his feather representing the taking of and caring for Custer and his spirit. The other warriors do similar things with their feathers according to what each encountered at the Greasy Grass.

According to the spiritual instructions, the warriors have honored their commitment and fulfilled their duty. They had entered the *spiritual pathway* and followed its energy and spirit to the *hill*. They had acted according to the spiritual plans laid out for Swift Bear by and through Creator. Just as they had done during their battle on the *hill*, they had climbed the *left arm* from the bicep, around to the elbow, through the forearm and wrist, and then on into the hand and its opened palm, where the deliverance of the goal of the spiritual instructions came to pass.

A sweat lodge ceremony will be performed, led by Eagle Fan, and all will attend. All warriors will be given the opportunity to understand how they must move forward, possibly coming to learn whom they will move forward with. The biggest benefit from this sweat lodge ceremony will be the wiping of the blood from their hands. They will be able to use their hands without guilt, remorse, or shame. They will be allowed to live as *wicasa*, as red men, as Lakota, as human beings, again. These are the duties required to finish the tasks that a warrior must do for his people, the Creator, themselves, and his family. This is the life that we have chosen to live and that we intend to live, forever.

The sacred prayer *bundle* was initially began and made a year or so before Saved By Bear's family was notified of, and the medicine people and leaders showed their support for, the move to go to this battle. The bundle was made from the ceremonies performed and all the necessary rituals. The bundle had been created to hold the items that were requested and needed for the Greasy Grass Battle. So this bundle was not a generational bundle, not one that had been passed down from family to family. This bundle was one that had been created specifically for the purpose of carrying forth the message and the *asking* of Creator, the spirits of the warriors and the families who participated, and the campfires of those who were willing to stand up for what they believed in. This is the ceremonial way of presenting the prayers, the hopes, the gratitude and honor, back to Creator for the culmination of the spiritual instructions and permission. This bundle was a very special bundle not only to the Lakota and other indigenous peoples, but to all peoples.

With Saved By Bear comes a piece of another human being: Custer. A portion of Custer's trigger finger is secured in the special pouch. Custer had had his finger on the trigger of the new country's military. He had his finger on the trigger of the genocide of the Lakota, the *Protectors*. His finger was on the trigger of the eventual destruction of Unci Maka. This object, this symbol of war, slaughter, greed, and domination, is to be taken into ceremony. When Custer was taken by Saved By Bear, Saved By Bear was instructed to place Custer's partial trigger finger in the pouch. The finger was then placed in the bundle, still in its pouch. And now that the warriors have returned to He Sapa, there is to be a ceremony for the warriors. In this ceremony, the pouch and the finger will be addressed. At that time, Eagle Fan will be the one running the ceremony. Eagle Fan will help the warriors become free from the things they had to do to another human being to let the people live. Another purpose of the ceremony will be to keep the bundle safe, and ready for the family of Saved By Bear, until one special day in the future where the family will walk forth with the sacred message of life which was borne out of the oral accounts and events culminating at the Greasy Grass battle. As a result, we will rely upon the spiritual side of life, through the generations, to continue now and into the future.

Creator will make the decision as to Saved By Bear's spiritkeeping of Custer. Saved By Bear will leave it to Unci Maka to decide where she will cradle him. The bundle will also be addressed and taken care of as well by Grandmother Earth. Then Saved By Bear will be finished. Saved By Bear has become Custer's spirit keeper. The spirit keeper of the one whom Creator granted the permission to remove from presence in the physical world on Unci Maka. As for Custer's spirit, Saved By Bear will take care of him and will nurture him. Saved By Bear will stand beside him, until one day in the future when the message and the *asking* is brought forth by family, again.

The Rhythm of Life Needs Cleansing and Healing

The Lakota had the original belief and the spiritual commitment, that "no warrior would be left behind" on the field of battle or in conflict. This was true whether the warrior was injured or killed.

Every warrior needed to be cared for when he came home from battle, no matter what. Part of the process of caring for each warrior in this way, was the warrior cleansing ceremony. The process that had been used for thousands and thousands of years. It was standard protocol for every warrior to heal from the violence of war. This specific ceremony is one that Creator gifted to the human being.

The tradition had been passed down through the generations of holy men and warriors throughout time. It was necessary for the survival of the people as a collective civilized society and community. It was also necessary for the sane, rational and complete survival of the individual warrior's mind, body, and spirit. It was done for the preservation of the spirit of the warrior, of the warrior society, of the warrior's family, and of the survival of the people themselves.

The cleansing needed to be done as soon as possible upon leaving the conflict or battle. It was not something to be put off or ignored. It will always follow the circumstances of battle when there has been killing. It must be performed when there has been the taking of a life. This ceremony was done once the warriors returned to the safety of the

He Sapa after the Greasy Grass Battle. Because of the relative nature of conflict and battle, many times lives were lost, enemies and friends killed, or violently and severely maimed or disabled. There were vicious, and many times unfamiliar or grotesque memories. The warriors often carried the psychological images of the war deep inside.

The warrior saw and experienced violent and disturbing things and events in the physical and mental sense. If he was not provided with a means of appropriately caring for the body and spirit after the fact, then he could fall into a long-lasting phase of unresolved and untreated wound to the body, the mind, the memory, the soul, and of his very life spirit.

To avoid potential long-lasting corruption of mind, body, and spirit, the cleansing ceremony was performed. This was viewed as a hopeful and satisfactory means of preserving the warrior as a human being and as a rational, reliable, functioning member of the society and community. The cleansing ceremony was done to protect him, his family, and his spirit, both now and in the future. The ceremony was done to preserve and restore the warrior's goodness of heart, belief, and presence, so that he could more easily return to carrying out his previous and existing role as warrior, leader, community member, friend, father, grandfather, uncle, spouse, and...Lakota.

This holistic cleansing was performed so that the people did not have to expend the extra time and effort to try to save the warrior from himself at some point in the future. For times when he might succumb to the torment or tragedy of allowing the vestiges of war, death, and inhumanity to fester or grow, and then erupt. If the potential psychological impact of having engaged in warfare was ignored, then there was the real danger that the warrior might threaten or harm other people within his community. Or he may even harm his own family and loved ones, physically, emotionally, and spiritually. This would defeat the whole purpose of the warrior having gone to battle to begin with: to protect the lives and way of life of his own nation, his own family.

The cleansing ceremony is performed in the inipi. It is a time when the warriors ask for healing from Creator. The warriors are prepared by smudging. They enter, carrying nothing made of altered metal into the lodge with them. This is because altered metal interferes with the spiritual connection and energy. Each warrior is prayed for by all the rest and by the ceremony leader. Each warrior has an opportunity to speak about how he feels about his experience in battle, in whatever language he speaks. The warriors are free to ask questions of Creator and the spirit world. The warriors are encouraged to leave the bad, violent things behind, and to pray and ask for rejuvenation of their former good, balanced life. Each individual warrior can now leave his pain and torment behind. He feels as if he is reborn as his former self. What he has seen and experienced in battle can now be accepted, and he can now move forward. Whatever feels appropriate and right to the warrior, and to the spirits, the warrior can do to free his own mind and spirit. He can then leave the ceremony with confidence and gratitude, and return home to the happinesss of family with the gifts of creation.

The Lakota believe that all peoples need help and guidance to heal their own warriors when the need arises. Providing such help and guidance allows the warrior to return home as the human being, rather than coming home with the ravages of war. This ceremony enables the warrior to live as a man.

━━━━◦《◉》◦━━━━

The cannumpa was the most vital part of the Greasy Grass Battle. The battle began through the cannumpa, and was advised and asked for through the cannumpa. The permission was relayed. It was received and acted upon. The cannumpa was the most viable weapon of the Lakota, as it allowed them to remain in existence. The cannumpa is full of prayer. It is all prayer, and hope, optimism, and the dreams of the people. It is used in a similar way as a weapon is used, to see if we can negotiate with the enemy and work on a lasting sensible peace. In this case, a peace between the new people and the old people of Turtle Island.

The use of the cannumpa was usually accompanied by prayer and requests for help from Creator. There were moments in history when prayer was necessary in order to battle evil. When the cannumpa was being used, it was essentially being used as a weapon of prayer.

━━━━◦《◉》◦━━━━

Throughout the meaningful sacred ceremonies that the warriors will undergo and perform in the He Sapa after their return, they will again use the drum, the sacred sound, the sacred rhythm. It is the old way.

Experience the heartbeat.

Each human being who is born knows and speaks of the sound of the heart from time to time. All of Grandmother Earth's peoples, including the winged and four-legged, undoubtedly know this too well, also. The sound, and more so, the feeling, is imprinted upon all our spirits very deeply. So that if one could view a picture of the soul or spirit, the picture and frames would come alive in a throbbing, moving tribute to the sound of life. The sound of our blood coursing through our veins.

The womb is sacred. It is the beginning of life and the comforting home of the helpless and vulnerable life it encases. All that is needed for sustenance, is conveyed, and received in this maternal home of homes. It is here where, throughout the millions and millions of years of life and birth, that the infant of the species first becomes physically, then mentally, and then ultimately spiritually, aware of the presence of Creator.

To be born of innocence into a not so innocent world, is to be the epitome of Wakan. The Creator designs things this way in order to grant a completely new and unblemished canvas, upon which the new life story begins to be painted. The colors and angles of life are new and inexperienced, and not yet provided with any opportunity to be dimmed, jaded, or torn. The Wakan nature, the wondrous spirit given herein, is the seed that is intended to sprout into the growing being that Creator has intended all along. If given the chance, the Wakan spirit will join the body to be born into a self-fulfilling prophecy of a good and honorable life and existence. One could only hope to experience, learn, and embrace one's free will, and to experience the magnificent and ultimate peak of one's existence: to love and to be loved.

The beat of the heart is the first and the most resounding call to life, that a being experiences. The beating heart is dependable, soothing, calming, assuring, and all-encompassing, like a warm blanket or robe. The heartbeat is absorbed by the new blood. The beat embraces the totality of the new spirit and soul, in love and protection. Never letting up, never letting go. If the young spirit could stay here forever, then it would be good enough. But the beating heart also serves as a call to courage and understanding. That there is more to do, more to experience, more to chance. The ability to love enhances the beat of the heart and its effect.

The heartbeat of the mother now matches the heartbeat of the new one. Soon they will separate, and then beat soundly, forever linked by the first sharing and nourishing. But thereafter, their heartbeats will echo individually and separately as an honor to Creator and free will.

All too soon the day comes when the sound of mother's heartbeat is overtaken by the newness of the other sounds. The sounds of the world screaming all around the new ears and within the new eyes' vision of the morning sun, and the original touch of new fingertips upon a very old, very trusted friend… Grandmother Earth. The new one has come home and is now a citizen of all that once was, and all that is to be, forevermore.

The birth of the new ones is many times accompanied by the beating of the drum. It was learned long ago by the wise ones, and first taught by Creator, that it is best to keep some things, the most important things, simple... and familiar.

The beating drum mimics the beating heart. The song remains the same. The mind and soul recognize the rhythm. This is the rhythm of life. The rhythm of the ancestors. The rhythm of Grandmother Earth. The drum beats. The heart beats. The rhythm flows. The blood flows. The beating drum carries forth as if blended with the bloodlines of the ancestors from all the generations before. This is the song of life. This is the sound of existence. This is the song and the story of life yet to be lived, to be told by the drum, and then by the heart.

Throughout the moments of life, the drum will sound. The beating of the drum will bring them back to the beginning, the beginning of their education, their structure, their beliefs, and the beginning of their lives themselves. Through the good times and the bad, through the laughter and the tears, and through the triumphs and the struggles, the truth of the drumbeats will bring them back. Back to the balance of life that was once there, and of which may have become unbalanced over time on account of trial and tribulation. An unbalancing of life may be tilted by unforeseen luck or tragedy, or some unexplained calamity, or by a regretful choice made by exercising free will.

It is as if the drumbeat is in fact the heartbeat. A strong, persistent, and constant, and reliable heartbeat, seeking to jump on the scales of imperfection, imbalance, injustice, inhumanity...And seeking to readjust the natural balance of a good and honorable life and existence by applying the counterweight of reason, compassion, and understanding. Seeking to right the natural balance to the appropriate recognition of the fundamental makeup of the scale of life itself. Seeking to bring home, the one, once new but now older and grown, to the ever-present home of the hope of the unbroken world; home to the balance provided by peace, tolerance, unity, and above all else, love.

Talented drumbeats can force one's foot to begin to move to the beat. But the most talented of drummers, cannot match the transference of energy in the natural sense, to force the heart and the spirit, to beat in time to the age-old rhythm of the balance of life.

Few humans to ever walk the Earth, have been gifted the talent to make music in such a way. Some have, and they have changed outcomes, changed minds, changed momentum, changed souls, and have changed the world.

Sometimes it takes only the simplest of drumbeats to move the people. Sometimes it takes the innocence of pure belief in a better life and a better world, to create the most magnificent of harmonies and rhythm. Sometimes, it only takes a small amount of people to create the drumbeat that causes an entire population to move as one. Sometimes it merely takes a single courageous, truthful, and honest drummer, to strike the stick against the hide, and to sound the original heartfelt beat, that stirs the consciousness and spirit, leading people to stand up, then to move, then to walk, then to run, and then to dance, as it was always meant to be.

If there has been a breaking of the world in any sense, it is never too late or too bleak for the time to pick up the stick and strike the hide, one more time for the hope and sake of all humanity and Grandmother Earth. For if there shall be the moment of the breaking of the world, much like the persistence of the beating drum of life and existence, so shall there be the moment, the right moment, for the healing of the world.

Creator has endowed each and every spirit and being of all the species on the Earth, with the power and the ability to be a drummer. To be the drummer. To be the mender. To be the healer. This is the way it has always been. We just need to listen for the beat of the heart.

Saved By Bear felt the beat of the heart. He heard the drum. He learned to follow the beat, to believe in it. This led him down the path of his life, where eventually, he was given the drumstick, and was granted permission to strike the hide, and to engage the rhythm of all of the beating hearts. For he was a healer. The heartbeat was needed at this time. At the time of the breaking of the world. It was time to act. The healing would come later, he was told.

18
VICTORY AND DEFEAT

THE CITIZENS OF THE NEW country were angry. They were provided a means and a method for feeling a collective loss of a rising hero, in Custer. The citizens were provided with a storyline which allowed them universally to feel, spread, and exert, a true rabid hatred for the *savages* who had done such things to Custer and the Seventh Calvary. A distorted and inaccurate storyline emerged from the valley of the Greasy Grass following the conflict. As has been the case throughout the history of man and the history of conflict, whoever it is that controls the story, controls the "truth" of the story, or at least what is perceived to be the truth of the story. Therefore, the history of the Greasy Grass Battle would be written by the people who chose to write it in a certain way. Take for example the headlines of the *Bismarck Tribune* on July 6, 1876, which read as follows:

TRIBUNE EXTRA.

BISMARCK, D.T., JULY 6, 1876.

MASSACRED

GEN. CUSTER AND 261 MEN THE VICTIMS.

NO OFFICER OR MAN OF 5 COMPANIES LEFT TO TELL THE TALE.

3 Days Desperate Fighting by Maj. Reno and the Remainder of the Seventh.

Full Details of the Battle.

LIST OF KILLED AND WOUNDED.

THE *BISMARCK TRIBUNE*'S SPECIAL CORRESPONDENT SLAIN.

Squaws Mutilate and Rob the Dead.

Victims Captured Alive Tortured in a most Fiendish Manner.

What Will Congress Do About It?

Shall This Be the Beginning of the End?

The *Bismarck Tribune*'s version of the story was the first version describing the battle as a "massacre" of Custer and his Seventh Calvary. That version started a long line of inaccurate and embellished propaganda news articles attempting to portray the Lakota as bloodthirsty evil savages who had massacred the innocent and vulnerable men of the Seventh Cavalry. The *Bismarck Tribune*'s reporting was heavily slanted against the Lakota, as it always had been. These inaccurate versions would be depicted as a massacre despite the fact, as clearly alluded to by Lt. James Bradley, that this was a bitterly contested fight to the death between the armed representatives of two civilizations.

⟫«◉»⟪

However, not found, written, or recorded in the *Bismarck Tribune*, or the *New York Times*, or any other newspaper, was something of this nature: "This was not a massacre... The Seventh Cavalry planned to come and kill all of us, and our families and children, in an effort to exterminate us. We only acted in accordance with the protection we had sought from Creator, and the permission that we were granted in return." That storyline, the truthful storyline, did not see the light of day for many years to come.

Lieutenant Bradley

In the aftermath of the Greasy Grass Battle, and especially within the first few days of the warriors' return to He Sapa, the warriors were occupied with cleansing themselves and their spirits and laying the bundle in the care of Unci Maka, who would determine its fate. Meanwhile, the story flashes back to the *hill* and the arrival of Lt. James Bradley from the Gibbon column. Bradley arrived a day and half after Custer's defeat. He was the first military man to enter the battlefield once the battle was over. He set foot upon it in the early morning of June 27, 1876. He was the first US military man of any rank, company, or unit to observe the bodies of the Seventh Cavalry, including Custer's. His initial observations and his account would be recorded in the *Helena Herald* (Montana) newspaper on July 25, 1876, thirty days after he gave his account to a news reporter. He would clearly indicate that he had observed these bodies, in particular that of Lieutenant Colonel Custer's, and saw what they looked like. He said Custer had a slight smile on his face and looked to be at peace. Bradley also said that the bodies of the cavalrymen had injuries that were usual and customary, similar to the injuries that always occurred in battle and war. He had not observed any mutilations of Custer or his men. That was what he reported. The Greasy Grass Battle was a very significant and great victory for the Lakota against the supreme power and strength of the United States military, and their top military unit and their top commander, which suffered the defeat, a defeat of total annihilation. The newspapers that ended up publishing stories of the Greasy Grass Battle, in particular the *Bismarck Tribune*, acknowledged this defeat. But of course, they later portrayed it as a "massacre" of Custer and his men of the Seventh Cavalry. The words of Lieutenant Bradley stated very clearly that this was not a "massacre." This was the end result of an armed conflict. The actual account of Lt. James Bradley describing the arrival at the Little Big Horn on June 26th and after, on June 27th begins as follows: The First News from Custer. "[On June 26,] we left the command on the ridge

overlooking the valley of the Little Big Horn, while Bradley, who was
on his scout, having struck the trail of the supposed four Indians, at
about the same time seeing a heavy smoke up the valley thought that
the Sioux village was ahead." What followed is so dramatic that it is
best told in Bradley's own words. The following is the actual account
of Lt. James Bradley, describing what he saw upon arriving at the Little
Bighorn on June 27:

> At the distance of less than two miles the trail struck
> the river and we [Bradley and several scouts] found
> that they had crossed there leaving behind a horse and
> several articles of personal equipment, indicating that they
> had fled in great haste. An examination of the articles
> disclosed to our great surprise that they belonged to some
> of the Crows whom I had furnished to Colonel Custer at
> the mouth of the Rosebud, which rendered it probable
> that the supposed Sioux were some of our own scouts
> who for some reason had left Custer's command and were
> returning to the Crow agency. While speculating on the
> circumstance, three men were discovered on the opposite
> side of the Big Horn about two miles away, apparently
> watching our movements. We at once signaled to them
> with blankets that we were friends, for a long time to no
> purpose, but when we were about to give up and seek
> some other method of communication with them, they
> responded by kindling a fire that sent up a small column
> of smoke indicating that they had seen the signals and
> trusted our assurances. We gathered wet sage brush and
> assured them with a similar smoke, and soon afterwards
> they came down to the river and talked across the stream
> with Little Face and one or two others who went down
> to meet them. While the interview went on I kept the
> remainder of the detachment on the bluffs. Presently our
> Indians turned back and, as they came, shouted out at the
> top of their voices a doleful series of cries and wails that
> the interpreter, Bravo, explained was a song of mourning
> for the dead. That it boded some misfortune there was

no doubt; and when they came up, shedding copious tears and appearing pictures of misery, it was evident that the occasion was of no common sort. Little Face in particularly wept with a bitterness of anguish such as I have rarely seen. For a while he could not speak, but at last composed himself and told his story in a choking voice, broken with frequent sobs. As he proceeded, the Crows one by one broke off from the group of listeners and going aside a little distance sat down alone, weeping and chanting that dreadful mourning song, and rocking their bodies to and fro. They were the first listeners to the horrid story of the Custer massacre, and, outside of the relatives and personal friends of the fallen, there were none in this whole horrified nation of forty millions of people to whom the tidings brought greater grief. The three men over the river were in truth a portion of the six scouts furnished to General Custer from my detachment; and this is the story they had told to Little Face; After Custer left the mouth of the Rosebud he had followed the Indian trail and yesterday struck the village on the Little Big Horn, the Sioux warriors letting him get close to the village and then Sallying forth in overwhelming numbers to meet him, defeating his command, and destroying all but a small portion who had been driven into the hills and surrounded by the Sioux, where the Crows left them fighting desperately. The corpses of Custer's men were strewn all over the country, and it was probable that before this that the last one was killed as it was impossible for the party who had taken refuge in the hills to hold out long, for the Sioux immensely outnumbered them and were attacking them in dense masses on all sides. Of the six Crows who had gone with Custer, three, Curly, White Swan and Half Yellow Face were missing and supposed to be killed. The fighting had occurred at the point where the smoke was then rising in our front. It was a terrible, terrible story, so different from the outcome we had hoped for this campaign, and I no longer wondered at the demonstrative sorrow of the Crows. My men listened to it with eager interest, betraying none of the emotion of the Crows, but looking at each other with white faces in pained silence too full of the dreadful recital to utter a word. Did we doubt the tale? I could not; there was an undefined vague something about it, unlooked for though it was, that commanded assent, and the most I could do was to hope that in the terror of the three fugitives from the fatal field their account of the disaster was somewhat overdrawn. But that there had been a disaster—a terrible disaster, I felt assured.

It was my duty to report it to General Terry, and being a matter of such importance I resolved to make the report in person, as I now saw the head of the column appearing over the ridge a couple of miles away. I therefore rode back until I met the command, which halted just before I came up, and narrated to the General the ghastly details as I received them from Little Face. He was surrounded by his staff and accompanied by Colonel Gibbon, who had that morning joined, and for a few moments there were blank faces and silent tongues and no doubt heavy hearts in that group, just as there had been among the auditors of Little Face at its rehearsal by him. But presently the voice of doubt and scorning was raised, the story was sneered at, such a catastrophy [sic] it was asserted was wholly improbable, nay, impossible; if a battle had been fought, which was condescendingly admitted might have happened, then Custer was victorious, and these three Crows were dastards who had fled without awaiting the results and told this story to excuse their cowardice.

General Terry took no part in these criticisms, but sat on his horse silent and thoughtful, biting his lower lip and looking to me as though he by no means shared in the wholesale skepticism of the flippant members of his staff. My imagination was busy supplying to my mind his train of thought, and it ran thus: "The story may not be true, when we have only to push on according to the original plan. It may be true, and then it becomes our duty to hasten to the rescue of the miserable remnant of Custer's command surrounded in the hills. If the savages have been able to destroy Custer's noble six hundred, what can we hope to accomplish with our paltry four? But we will do the best we can and rescue the wretched survivors or ourselves perish in the attempt." And as though it were the seal of authenticity to this bold attempt to divine the workings of this him, he cried "Forward!" and once more the column was in motion toward the foe.[24]

As mentioned earlier, Lt. Bradley, the commander of the Gibbon column's scouts, was the first white man to view the bodies of Custer and his men on the *hill*. Bradley was also the first US military man to lay eyes upon the bodies of the dead. His account indicated a lack of mutilations. He only viewed and recorded injuries consistent with the type that were usual in battle and war, wounds that were consistent with being struck by knives, spears, hatchets, or clubs. His story later appeared in the *Helena Herald* on July 25, 1876:

> Helena, M. T.
> July 25, 1876.

To the Editor of the *Herald*,

> In the presence of so great a disaster as that which overtook the regular troops on the Little Horn, and the consequent excited state of the public mind, and its eagerness to get hold of every detail, however minute, of that unfortunate affair, it is to be expected that many stories of a sensational character, having no foundation in truth, would obtain with the public. Of such character is that now going the rounds of the press to the effect that the Sioux had removed Custer's heart from his body and danced around it, a story related upon the authority of one Rain-in-the-Face, a Sioux Chief, who participated in the fight and

---

[24] Dustin, The Custer Tragedy: at p.171-72.

afterwards returned to his agency. Of the same character, also, is the sweeping statement as to the general shocking mutilation of the bodies of the soldiers who fell on that occasion. The bare truth is painful enough to the relatives and friends of these unfortunate men without the cruel and gratuitous exaggeration of their grief that must come from the belief that they had been horribly mutilated after death. It, therefore, seems to me worthwhile that these stories should receive emphatic contradiction, and being in a position to make such a denial, I address you this letter with that object.

In my capacity as commandant of the Scouts accompanying General Gibbon's column, I was usually in the advance in all his movements, and chanced to be upon the morning of the 27th of June, when the column was moving upon the supposed Indian village in the Little Horn Valley. I was scouting the hills some two or three miles to the left of the column upon the opposite bank of the river from that traversed by the column itself, when the body of a horse attracted our attention to the field of Custer's fight, and hastening in that direction the appalling sight was revealed to us of his entire command in the embrace of death.

This was the first discovery of the field, and the first hasty count made of the slain, resulting in the finding of 197 bodies reported to General Terry. Later in that day I was sent to guide Colonel Benteen of the 7th Cavalry to the field, and was a witness of his recognition of the remains of Custer. Two other officers of that regiment were also present and they could not be mistaken, and the body so identified was wholly unmutilated. Even the wounds that caused his death were scarcely discoverable (though the body was entirely naked), so much so that when I afterwards asked the gentlemen whom I accompanied whether they had observed his wounds, they were forced to say that they had not.

Probably never did hero who had fallen upon the field of battle appear so much to have died a natural death. His expression was rather that of a man who had fallen asleep and enjoyed peaceful dreams, than of one who had met his death amid such fearful scenes as that field had witnessed, the features being wholly without ghastliness or any impress of fear, horror or despair. He had died as he lived, a hero, and excited the remark from those who had known him and saw him there. "You could almost imagine him standing before you." Such was Custer at the time of his burial on the 28th of June, three days after the fight in which he had fallen, and I hope this assurance will dispose of the horrible tale of the mutilation and desecration of his remains.

Of the 206 bodies buried on the field, there were very few that I did not see, and beyond scalping, in possibly a majority of cases, there was little mutilation. Many of the bodies were not even scalped, and in the comparatively few cases of disfiguration, it appeared to me the result rather of the blow with a knife, hatchet, or war club to finish a wounded man, than deliberate mutilation. Many of Custer's men must have been disabled with wounds during the fight, and when the savages gained possession of the field, such would probably be mainly killed in the manner indicated. The bodies were nearly all stripped, but it is an error to say that Kellogg, the correspondent, was the only one that escaped this treatment. I saw several entirely clothed, half a dozen at least, who, with Kellogg, appeared to owe this immunity to the fact that they had fallen some distance from the field of battle, so that the Indians had not cared to go to them, or had overlooked them when the plundering took place.

The real mutilation occurred in the case of Reno's men, who had fallen near the village. These had been visited by the squaws and children and in some instances the bodies were frightfully butchered. Fortunately not many were exposed to such a fate. Custer's field was some distance from the village and appears not to have been visited by these hags, which probably explains the exemption from mutilation of those who had fallen there.

Yours truly,
James H. Bradley,
1st Lieut. 7th Inft.[25]

————— ⊰⟨◉⟩⊱ —————

If one were to believe the honest initial account of Bradley, himself a military officer, as to the absence of mutilations to or desecration of the bodies of the dead, then one must take into account the notion raised in the stories that came out later from the newspapers and military versions which described brutal mutilation and desecration of those bodies. And if one recognizes that if the bodies of Custer and his men were not mutilated or desecrated as of the early morning of June 27, then how is it that those bodies were mutilated or desecrated later, after Lieutenant Bradley's initial viewing and inspection of all of the bodies? One would need to ask: were the bodies actually mutilated or desecrated? And if so, who did it, after Bradley saw none on the morning of June 27? Why would anyone mutilate or desecrate the bodies of the dead, after Bradley had initially viewed and inspected them? What motive would be served by doing so? Why would anyone be allowed to mutilate or desecrate the bodies after Bradley initially viewed and inspected them? Who or what had the opportunity to mutilate or desecrate the bodies after Bradley's initial viewing? Were the bodies of the soldiers ever mutilated or desecrated, at any time? Or, were the stories of mutilation or desecration of the bodies just made up or fabricated by the military after the fact? Was that storyline made up so as to make the annihilation and defeat of the Seventh Cavalry seem more heinous or evil than it ever truthfully was? Or were those stories merely made up to serve as propaganda to generate hate, spite, and vengefulness in the hearts and minds of the public?

---

[25] Graham, The Story of the Little Big Horn: 1941, p.163-67

These are questions that logical and sensible human beings, including historians, must consider and decide for themselves.

Prayer at Mato Paha

After the warriors had finished their duties to fulfill the sacred instructions in the He Sapa to take care of the *bundle* and to cleanse themselves, their journey required one more stop: a visit to the most sacred of the sacred sites in He Sapa— Mato Paha. The sacred mountain of the Bear. This would be done to fulfill the spiritual instructions.

The warriors' trip to Mato Paha would be just a short visit to this very sacred site. They would not stay overnight. They would not plant anything of permanence. What they will do, is leave their prayers, experiences, hopes, and dreams with Mato Paha. Once the warriors properly cleansed and delivered the sacred bundle to Unci Maka's cradle, they convened one last time at the base camp, their last time to be together there. Then, they climbed up on their horses and set out to the north, riding through and near Pe Sla and past the clear high lakes in He Sapa.

It had been ten days since the Greasy Grass Battle. Since it was the middle of summer, near the beginning of the hotter summer season of the sun, the other beings are abundant in number along the way. The spirits had made them aware that the white armies would not disturb them here at this time. And Creator provided the opportunity for the beings of Unci Maka to express gratitude. The sight and smell of life is everywhere. The warriors will ride past the lakes, streams and foothills of the He Sapa, where the deer run and jump freely among the periodic antelope. At the higher elevations, the warriors see their sacred brothers of the Elkhead namesake, the elk, grazing in herds of hundreds, their large tall antlers breaching the lower branches of the tall pine trees on the slopes. Occasionally, the coyote will run by, looking to see the progress of the humans. Tatanka are prevalent everywhere along the grassy perimeter, grazing and lying about, fearful of neither man nor beast, just as tatanka always had been before the encroachment of the slaughterers on the plains.

The warriors were even blessed enough to see the medicine beings, the bears, near the stream running through the northern canyon. There are mothers with new cubs. Saved By Bear saw them, and for a brief moment remembered the story of his childhood. When the great mother grizzly had stepped forward to save him on that day long ago in He Sapa along that mountain creek. And how his mother, Iron Hat, spoke frequently about how he always needed to thank the mother bears when he saw them, because it was one of their kind long ago that had saved his life. So, true to his promise to his own mother, Saved By Bear waves his right hand in the direction of the mothers along the creek. Holding his arm extended, he threw his positive energy and good medicine toward them. All the bears, including the littlest of the little, stood on their hind paws as if to acknowledge their two-legged brothers on the horses. And to acknowledge the one who had sent the spiritual message to them, which struck directly to their hearts. As Saved By Bear lowered his arm back down to his side, he nodded their way. Nudging Wildfire in the sides with his moccasins, he couldn't help but share in the pride of the family of mato.

The birds, all kinds of the winged ones, were everywhere along the trek of the warriors to Mato Paha. It seemed as if they had all been instructed by Wakan Tanka to come out and greet these sixteen spirits that had been chosen to act in the defense of them all. The owls, the bluebirds, the sparrows, the wrens, the bright yellow finches, the full-breasted robins, the joyful warblers, the large and talkative meadowlarks, the doves, the blue herons, the killdeer, the turkey vultures, the osprey, the blackbirds, the cardinals, the blue jays, the orioles, the magpies, the pheasants, the grouse, the happy ducks, the blue hawks, the cranes, and the woodpeckers were all present in the air and along the way. However, the most noticeable of all the winged ones as the warriors neared the base of the sacred mountain to the north, were the red-tailed hawks and the large, beautiful wanbli. The hawks and the wanbli seemed to be congregating in great numbers along the low-lying areas near the mountain butte, or else swarming over and up upon, the summit and vicinity. It was as if they were having their own gathering of some sort. The warriors knew that word and spirit traveled fast among all the peoples of He Sapa. The sight of the red-tailed hawks was nothing new for Saved By Bear, as he had grown quite accustomed to, and quite fond of, their almost constant presence near him ever since he had befriended that mother hawk in the mountains. But the massive number of wanbli signified to all of the warriors that they were indeed embarking upon the final leg of their sacred spiritual journey and that Creator was going to ensure that there were more than enough of the messengers present to respond and to carry forth the great weight and significance of the spiritual messages that the warriors would ask to be carried forth and up.

One elder wanbli in particular took notice. He had followed the warriors ever since their arrival at the Greasy Grass valley before the battle. He was now following them on their return trip to He Sapa. He had seen many things over the past several weeks, as there had been so much to see, so much to hear, so much to know. He would forever remember the courageous spiritual deeds performed by the Protectors, these warriors, and in particular by the two Dog Man heyokas, Saved By Bear and Swift Bear.

When the warriors and their horses were crossing the small winding creek just south of the base of the sacred mountain, they saw a white thunderhead moving toward the summit of the sacred peak, from the west, the direction of the Wakinyan. Although the skies were mostly bright blue and uncluttered with clouds of any kind, the rolling, billowing blanket of the thunderhead moved as if it were a solitary warrior riding a white pony across the edge of the north side of He Sapa, heading directly for the sacred mountain, Mato Paha.

The warriors stopped. They saw what was coming, what was forming. They knew what was happening. So they got off their horses and allowed them to drink from the small creek briefly. Even the horses now, looked to the northwest and watched. All eyes, human and horse alike, were fixed upon the approach of the Wakinyan from the west.

As the large bank of clouds moved closer still to the summit, it seemed to roll into a shape, assuming the shape of a warrior mounted on his horse with a single feather hanging and the horse's mane streaming from behind, both of the warrior's hands securely holding the horse's mane, as if the cloud warrior and his loyal cloud horse were galloping toward the sacred mountain.

Each of the sixteen warriors saw this. No one took their eyes from it. They could not. It was too beautiful, too powerful, to look away from. The members of horse nation also recognized the joining of man and horse in the clouds, and also stood silent, watching. As the cloud bank hovered over the mountaintop, the cloud rolled again. Out of the center came horizontal medicine-colored (light blue) lightning bolts, streaking crosswise across the sky just over the summit. There was no rain, no wind, and no hail, just the presence, the spectacle… and the spirit of Wakinyan. Every warrior felt the pull in his chest, which moved through the arms, hands, and fingers, and into the soles of the feet. Swift Bear again felt it strongly in his left arm and hand. It was at this time that the Thunder Beings released a single massive bolt directly down and onto the top of Mato Paha. The loud clap and boom quickly followed. It was the voice of Wakinyan welcoming the warriors to the last phase of their destiny before the final journey home to the comfort of their own families. It was the spiritual signal that all was yet proceeding according to the spiritual plan and instruction of Creator. That all had proceeded as provided for by the spiritual permission granted to the warriors, and their people, from Creator. All permission granted and all instructions given, had been fulfilled. It was a good, welcoming sight, and feeling. And then the warriors all mounted up and headed forward, toward the mountain.

The group of sixteen rode their horses along the old trail that started at the southwest side of the mountain and bent around the edge near the creek bed. The lower area was where the large inipis had been built for use by the people when they came and visited the sacred mountain to pray, to hold ceremonies, and to perform the hanbleceya. There were no other humans near or on the mountain on this day, as the spirits had instructed. The bank of clouds remained, but all lightning activity ceased. The riders proceeded along the ages-old worn dirt trail that was wide enough for human and horse foot travel. The slight dust rose each time the horses' hooves struck into the soft, shiny granular dirt on the trail. The horses were also familiar with this trail. Again, the wanbli soared and swooped overhead from a distance, with their great expanse of full-spread wings allowing them to glide on the ever so slight early summer breeze. Among them was the Old One that had been following the warriors for so long.

When the riders and their horses reached the point where the midrange rises stretched out to the highest peak to the west, where the summit awaited, the warriors dismounted and tied their horses to the old pine tree that was used for these purposes. Then they set off on foot. Eagle Fan, as expected, led the way. The very narrow trail went around bends and curves, and clung to the steep side of the mountain. If one fell off the trail, it would be a long hard fall and tumble to the bottom. However, the warriors sensed on this day, according to the permission granted, that the great hand of the Creator would most likely catch them if they fell. Such was the spiritual importance of their sacred journey to the top today.

As a result of their extreme and determined training, preparation, and cleansing in the He Sapa over the past year, none of the sixteen warriors felt short of breath, weak in the legs, heavy of mind, or cluttered in purpose. They could have been climbing the mountain on trails where their moccasins barely touched the ground. In any event, they moved in a single sacred line along the edges of the mountainside in a circular, climbing, elevating sequence toward the summit.

As they reached the summit, Eagle Fan was the first to see the view to the west. He saw the great expanse of the beautiful, majestic dark colors of the He Sapa and the pristine lake below the sacred mountain. He momentarily felt his breath catch, taking in so much natural beauty and wonder all at once and quickly, like a thirsty man gulping down his first drink of cool, clear water after many days without. This view was always a sight to behold. And it was always the same. It was no wonder that this particular place, this peak, was commonly used as a place of hanbleceya for many thousands of years. It was fitting that Creator had instructed the warriors to come here for the last stage, on the last leg of their journey, before they would leave to be with their families.

As all sixteen came over the last rise to the summit, and beheld the full panoramic view of the scene, they reacted in the same way, in awe, gratitude, and comfort. Each took the time to breathe in deeply the fresh, clean, sweet-tasting air of Grandmother Earth. Eagle Fan motioned for them all to come forward and follow him to the southernmost edge of the summit, where a stone fire circle remained. Here and there in the several pine trees that grew on the summit, the warriors could see the tie bundles that had been left by their relations as offerings and prayer bundles for the spirits on previous treks to the sacred mountain. From this spot, and to the northwest, if one had the keen eye of a wanbli, one could just make out the Old Guardian, the old tree near the campsite just next to the Belle Fourche River up north. More than a year had passed since the warriors had last been there, since the last time Saved By Bear had communicated with the Old One and the two had shared their visions with each other when Saved By Bear placed his hands upon the old tree's trunk. Saved By Bear remembered his old friend as he gazed toward the north. The night owls will have some new and magnificent stories to share with the Old One the next time they land upon his sturdy and gentle limbs.

As all sixteen gathered around on the summit, Eagle Fan asked them to form a circle. Each did as instructed. Eagle Fan walked to the center of the group and then he turned toward the west. He raised both hands with palms extended and started to pray: "Creator, Wakan Tanka. We depend upon you. I depend upon you. We depend upon you. We pray for courage." The Wakinyan cloud bank was still there, floating high and off to the west of the summit. As Eagle Fan's hands were raised to the west, the cloud bank emitted a rumble of thunder. The warriors could feel it in their feet.

Eagle Fan then turned to his right, and in the same fashion raised his open hands to the north, and prayed. "Give us strength." A large wanbli with wings spread out wide swooped down within feet of Eagle Fan's raised hands, hovering just beyond his reach, and then flew to the east. Eagle Fan turned again to his right, facing the east now. "Creator, give us wisdom." The warm gentle breeze ruffled Eagle Fan's feather. A distant elk whistle could be heard from the tree-lined ridge. Eagle Fan turned to the right once more, and raised both hands to the south, saying, "Creator, we pray for unity." This time the howl of brother wolf could be heard from the south. At first sharp, the howl grew deep, drowning out the natural rhythm and symphony of the rest of the natural world. Eagle Fan turned again to the right, and again to the west. He looked down, and as he did so, he said, "Grandmother, Unci Maka. You are, and always have been, our grandmother. Tehicila. We love and cherish you, as you do us. We are here to give thanks to you for our lives, for our nourishment, for our everlasting bounty, and for our survival. We are here to join hands and spirits with you, to complete the sacred journey and to fulfill and preserve our sacred duty to protect you, as we have always been called upon to do. You know us. We know you. You trust us. We trust you. You honor us with your life, your grace, and your eternity. We honor you for all that we are, and all that we can ever be, here on the physical side of our existence. We will always be here to protect you, because without you, we cannot live." This time, he stood and turned his palms almost straight up. "Grandfather Sky, watch over us and provide the sun and night for energy and cover, and for our refreshment during the cleansing when it is needed."

Making a last singular gesture with his hands, Eagle Fan again looked to the west. It was then, with the gentle westerly wind blowing into his face and ruffling the stray dark hairs flowing across his forehead, he said, "Wakinyan. Wakan Tanka. We pray for protection for all of us and for our families, all of the families. And for Unci Maka and all of her children of all kinds. And we thank you for your blessing, your guidance, your protection, your promise. We pray for all beings, and for peace, unity, tolerance, and love."

Each warrior offered a small prayer at the same moment. "Mitakuye oyasin," each said. This is how it was done. This is how it was always done. This is what was done on this day, the last day, before the warriors departed for home after the fulfillment of their sacred journey. Each warrior had a chance to communicate individually with Creator, and with whatever spirit or ancestor he chose to communicate with, whether with verbal words or through silent thought or prayer. It was all offered. It was all received.

The messengers, swarming around the summit, now drifted and circled, flying ever higher into the bright blue sky, up and up, until each disappeared, on a journey to carry those prayers, those thoughts, to Creator. Among that group was the messenger from the Greasy Grass. And the soft thunder ceased, and the cloud dissipated.

As the summer breeze again drifted into the warriors' faces, blowing the sweet smell of sage and lilac into their noses, the warriors felt the connection. They saw the connection. They knew the connection. And they knew they had fulfilled their commitment to protect and preserve as a warrior is... intended to. At this point, all of the sixteen warriors issued one of the most heartfelt prayers of their lives. They bowed their heads in respect, honor, and celebration of their families, of their tradition and culture, and of Grandmother's children. They sent respect and honor to Creator for having been asked to represent the human beings in the battle: "Wakan Tanka, thank you for life." And just before they broke the circle, Eagle Fan gave each a small stone from the summit of this sacred mountain, so that each could carry a piece of the sacred mountain of Unci Maka with them for the rest of their lives, as a reminder of the strength and courage of the people of the sacred hoop on the journey home and, most importantly, as a reminder of the battle, and the spiritual pathway, as the permission of Creator had indicated and been fulfilled.

The sixteen gathered together one last time to view the beauty of the place... and the moment. Then much like a band of blood brothers, they come together. They shake hands. They hug each other. Then once again, they follow behind their spiritual leader, the noble, the strong, the holy, Eagle Fan. The Dakota warrior led them down the same narrow pathway to the place where their horses anxiously awaited them. The warriors mounted, and rode the rest of the way down. As they rode down the lower section, Eagle Fan began to sing the old songs of honor, gratitude, and hope—the old songs of integrity, life, and existence according to how a human being should exist.

Once the group of the sixteen warriors trailed off the sacred mountain, they turned to the east and the north, before embarking upon their long ride toward their individual homelands and their loving families. Toward their encounter with the eternal history and destiny of their people. And of humankind.

As the riders and their horses angle to the north and to the east to ride home, away from the sacred Mato Paha, a strong presence of something else is seeking attention. And like the ever-present wanbli, the view of the sixteen courageous warriors rises above them, reaching higher and higher. The rising view drifts back to the top of the sacred mountain briefly, floating over the summit, and then moving beyond to the greater expanse of the true and beating heart of Grandmother Earth, Unci Maka herself. And as the view from far above rises over the sacred He Sapa and lifts up and further beyond, into space, and looks down upon the shape of the heart, Her Heart. Then it becomes noticeable. We see the beings moving toward the heart of Grandmother in the He Sapa.... they are moving toward the Heart from all directions. The Buffalo from the north, the Turtle from the south, the Bear from the west, and the Magpie from the east. And as the view looks down upon Unci Maka and the He Sapa, a single cloud of dust rises from the edge of the Great Race Track surrounding the He Sapa. And soon another cloud of dust appears and joins the first. Then another. And another. ...and it is clear for all to see now... the importance of all life on Unci Maka, but especially to that of the human beings, the two-legged.... That the Race Track is active once more, after eons of time... and the Great Race around the He Sapa... is beginning again. The outcome is still uncertain. For the existence of all life on Unci Maka hangs in the balance.... once more.

THE END

EPILOGUE

MUCH OF THIS STORY DESCRIBES the history of Turtle Island and its people during the time of the middle to late 1800s. *Warrior Is* has taken you as far as the Greasy Grass Battle on June 25, 1876 and two weeks beyond those events.

All of the things Saved By Bear had done in his life, the hard things, the difficult things, the things he did for his family and his people out of love and necessity, the things he did in order to fulfill his destiny, were done for a reason. He never asked to be chosen to do these things. The duty and the obligation, and the honor, fell upon his shoulders, and fell heavily upon his spirit.

Despite the challenge, the preparation, and the extreme difficulty of carrying out what was asked of him, Saved By Bear knew that there would be no immediate recognition of his acts; no acknowledgment of the impact of his deeds; no public awareness, celebration, or honoring of what he had accomplished; and no chance for him to be condemned or ostracized by society. Since his deeds had to remain a secret, they had to remain unrecognized by the public.

If what he had done were to become known, before the appropriate time for honest revelation, then neither he nor his family would exist any longer. What Saved By Bear did, had to remain a solemn secret. Known only by those trusted in heart and spirit.. Those who silently thanked him and prayed that his spirit be protected all his life, and into the afterlife among the spirit of all of his people and ancestors who traveled the Milky Way. These people knew, and in time, some of Saved By Bear's close family came to know, from having been told of the story. Keeping this knowledge secret according to the sacred oath, until the moment in time when, through the appropriate prayer, preparation, and ceremony, the truth could and would finally be told.

The bigger picture of the outcome and the end result of the conflict that day at the Greasy Grass, was not that the Lakota and Cheyenne had prevailed. Or that they were successful in killing and removing the physical presence of Custer—the very symbol of white dominance and Lakota genocide. Or that the Lakota repelled, momentarily, the goals and advancement of white dominance over the indigenous peoples. It is now known and accepted as a part of history that the breaking of the world that occurred on June 25, 1876, was a history-changing event in so many ways. It was the single most devastating defeat of the US military in its efforts to control or eradicate the Lakota. But it was also a critical and legendary turning point in the then, present, lives of many. Custer, and the 260 or so soldiers of the US military, lost their lives. At least 65 Lakota and Cheyenne lost their lives. The US military suffered a humiliating and very public defeat, at the hands of a force that the mighty Seventh Calvary of the US Army was expected to easily handle and destroy.

But the greatest consequence of the events that occurred that day of June 25, 1876, and the events thereafter, had to deal with the will and the sanctity of survival. Had Custer, Reno, Terry, and Sheridan, accomplished their goal of exterminating all of the *hostile* Lakota at that time, then the world would have changed. The world would have been forever, and distinctly, different than it is now. The Lakota, to a man, to a woman, to a family, to a community... may not exist presently. The people, the families, and the individuals who were there at the Greasy Grass at that time in the history of the world, survived. They lived and persevered, because they sought, prayed for, and were blessed with, answers. They were gifted with the spirit as a guide and direction. They were given a vision of what was to come. How to deal with it. How to remove, or politically reverse, their own destruction and genocide. And they were given, above all else, the gift of having permission to change the course of the history.

Despite the fact that the Lakota way of life would be significantly restrained, controlled, and demoralized over the subsequent 141 years since the Battle of the Greasy Grass, it still remains a recognized truth, that but for the intervention of the Creator in the events at the breaking of the world, that the people who now breathe, and carry Lakota blood in their veins, still walk upon Grandmother Earth. We walk and breathe and act to serve her needs, to protect her against all evils and planned destruction, and to carry on with the duties of those honorable generations of ancestors who laid forward the way to walk and live as Creator intended:... in peace, unity, tolerance, and love.

The survivors of the people who sought and obtained the permission to stand up, and to act, back then, may be the gifts that sprang forward from the events and circumstances at the breaking of the world. The survivors are the ones who can come to the realization that they have a significant, a relevant, a predetermined, reason to exist, now, and forevermore. A reason to stand up themselves; to stand and to walk in the footsteps of those courageous and honorable ancestors who followed their spirits into immortality. And the day will come, and soon, when the ancestors of those brave and spiritual Lakota human beings, will feel the blood in their veins rush to their hearts. And the blood will join the energy of their spirits, in giving life to the moment of time when what was to be done, what needed to be done, what was asked to be done, what must be done, was,...done. And the descendants will feel their spirits rise up and unite with those of their relatives and ancestors. And especially with those that prayed, envisioned, prepared, then acted, under the guidance of the spirits to take action in the moment in time when they were asked to do so. So that those that follow, and will follow, can step within those deep, familiar footprints, and walk in the spiritual way. So they can take ahold of the hearts, the hands, and the spirits of all of their brothers and sisters of all races across Grandmother Earth, to step forward and together, in peace, unity, tolerance and love... for a better life, a better existence, a better world...To become a part themselves, all of them, in joining and Healing the Circle. This is what it meant then, what it meant later, what it means today, and what it will mean a thousand years from now..

If you have obtained a copy of *Warrior Is*, thank you. That means that you are at least curious enough to want to know more about Mato Niyanpi and his individual history. Please take a moment to recall that at the beginning of *Warrior Is*, you were asked to read his story, with an open mind, an open heart, and an open spirit. We hope you felt some things within your own heart and spirit while doing so.

Many things in his story describe the way things were during his life, from his viewpoint and from the viewpoint of his people. As a result, there is much within this story that shines a different light upon the events of history as they occurred, as they were perceived by Mato Niyanpi and the Lakota as they were happening, and upon the outcomes of these events. The story also mentions what the people experienced, what they learned from those events, and how those occurrences affected Mato Niyapi's life, the lives of the Lakota, their way of life, and all of history from that point forward.

Some readers may say that we are too harsh toward the United States and its government and military, and toward the white people and white society as a whole. That may be somewhat true. However, *Warrior Is* is Mato Niyanpi's story, our story, and our Lakota history. If the events and depictions thereof in this story reflect badly upon the historical conduct and beliefs of the United States, its officials, and white society as a whole during those times, then so be it. *Warrior Is* recounts how the Lakota saw and experienced what was happening during the time of westward expansion and manifest destiny. A very harsh time for the Lakota.

We have done our absolute best to honestly and accurately tell the story of Saved By Bear's life and the lives of his people, without trying to appease anyone in particular. This story is the truth as we know it to be, as told through the stories handed down within our family.

Like individuals, the United States, as a country, has every opportunity to change itself in the way it values the lives of individual human beings, of individual occupants of its borders, of human beings who are subject to its government's control and influence. The United States has always had this capability, as well as the opportunity to change itself. But the United States can only change according to the strength, courage, and will of those who have the power to change it. Those individuals who have the ability and opportunity to act, need to put words into action. But the country, its government, and its policies toward its peoples of all kinds, can only change if the American people and their government have the will, the courage, and the conscience, to do so.

A different world cannot be built by indifferent people.

If the United States is to survive as a nation with a benevolent society that has a benevolent purpose for its own people and the world, and as a member of the human family of Grandmother Earth, it must embrace its commitment and duty to be the beacon of hope, freedom, and liberty that it professes to be. The United States has done much good for the peoples of the world, at certain times, but it has also done horrible things to people of other countries and its own people, and has harmed Grandmother Earth. In order to truly embrace the duty and responsibility that the United States has, and takes upon itself as a leader of the free world, the United States, including its people, its government, and its society, must finally completely embrace the truth of its past. It must embrace all of the bad and destructive things that the U.S., its government, and its military, have done in the name of the United States and in the name of the American people. These destructive things, of course, include the enslavement of black people and the genocide of the indigenous peoples of Turtle Island. In the case of the Lakota, the purpose was to remove them from existence in order to steal their land and their natural resources.

Until the United States and its people truly embrace their real history, including the dark and sinister motives behind official government policies, for example, population displacement, assimilation, and genocide, this country may forever be seen as a country founded upon fraudulent principles and a hidden evil agenda. The United States may be viewed as being a nation that is interested in seeking only individual wealth, world domination, global annihilation and destruction. However, if the human beings who make up the population, including the government officials, those who serve in the military, and those who hold positions of power in private business in the fields of finance, communications, agriculture, energy, industry, and education, can see themselves as individual human beings and as citizens of Unci Maka, first, and as citizens of the United States second, then it is not too late for them to join the movement of humanity. It is not too late to join forces and to believe that we are all connected and really want the same things: life, liberty, and the pursuit of happiness. It is not too late to see, in a moment of spiritual clarity, that we are all related, *mitakuye oyasin*. If this movement of humanity, of the collective and individual soul and spirit, rises up to reach for and grasp the true collective destiny of survival and serving the common good, then all things, anything, can be achieved. Then can we truly see the vision, and the good and just path to healing the Circle, by embracing our own energy, destiny, and empathy according to the virtures of peace, unity, tolerance, and love. Just like the Creator of us all always intended for us to do.

If we unite and align our own interests with the good of Grandmother Earth and the rest of humanity, then we can defeat any opponent or meet any cause, no matter how powerful or intimidating it may be. If we take the lesson of the Greasy Grass Battle to heart, and if we look at and re-create the preparation of spirit undertaken by Saved By Bear, Swift Bear, and the fourteen other warriors, then we will see that it is the spirit that cannot be defeated. When we are in the midst of the preparation of the spirit, Creator is on our side and is the honorable, the good, the trusted, means of standing up, strong, proud, and together.

The world, as it existed then, needed to become broken. So that the pieces could be easily seen and understood. And so that one day, with the full commitment of the spirit, individually, and collectively, the moment of the breaking of the world, could lead to the healing of the world, for all, for all time.

Our hope is that as a result of this process that has taken place over the past 141 years, all beings will unify, especially all human beings and the children of the Creator, so that we can all one day soon turn to each other, look each other in the eye and the spirit, reach out our hands, our arms, and our hearts to each other. We can share and revive our individual traditions and our cultures in a hopeful and honest way. And embrace one another, and say with truth, honor, and hope in our voices and in our spirits, "Mitakuye oyasin, my friend, my brother, my sister." Then we can begin the wonderful process of healing the Circle of life.

At that time, each one of us, from all places, all origins, and all beginnings, and of all colors, all ethnicities, and all backgrounds, will happily prepare and then take part in our own grand wopila for us all. *Mitakuye oyasin!*

ACKNOWLEDGMENTS

Harley

I wish to honor the following people for their wonderful contributions of heart and spirit to my existence. I offer the utmost respect to each individual for his or her gift of wisdom and support. *Toksa ake* (until we meet again).

Mary Scar Leg Bagola is my grandmother. She was there for me before I was even born. Ready with a name and to present a spiritual path of coming teachings and growth, Grandmother Mary was the best example of a human being who believed in her ancestors' commitment to life. She brought two worlds together with her compassion and her understanding of body, mind, and spirit. Her wisdom in the ways of tradition and culture, combined with her acceptance of assimilating to a new people's way, made this possible. She loved family! When in her presence, one's spirit would experience feelings and truth. This is her bloodline connection as a Lakota woman who represents Wakan Tanka (Great Spirit) and the gift of all life. Unci (Grandmother), I love you! Thank you.

Unci Maka (Grandmother Earth), thank you for allowing me the opportunity to coexist with all nations of beings across the Plains and for giving me an appreciation for each separate family with a clearly defined life presence. Being one of the many species requires responsibility and leadership if one is to help maintain balance and harmony throughout the lands. You nurture us and provide for us the necessities for survival. The beauty and amazement of those you have given to us to be sisters and brothers of humanity are miracles of creation. I am proud to be called one of your human beings. Thank you.

Greg Dodd was a special childhood friend. He treated me like his own brother. His family was always kind and generous. Greg and I shared many experiences in a few short years. Our spirits were good together, and had a positive effect when interacting with others. Honesty and opinions were expressed on any topic that might come to mind. Smiles and happiness are associated with his memory. For a friendship that will last beyond this lifetime, I thank you, Greg.

Ben Tyon Sr., for his presence and encouragement during my first two years of high school. He gave positive insight and advice as I learned to cope with growing up as a teenager. I consider him an uncle for passing knowledge and tradition to the next generation as his grandfathers did. A very good man. Thank you.

Lyle Russman, for his mentorship and trustworthiness during my junior year in high school. Athletics would bring us together. Our friendship came first. It then evolved into a relationship resembling an adoption as I became a member of his family. We experienced through sports how each community treated its guests. After one of the first games, I was asked a question by Coach Russman: "Did you hear the racial slurs directed at you during the game?"

I answered, "Yes. I have heard those voices many times in my life." His face was full of hurt and pain for having witnessed such cruel, hateful behavior. He apologized for those people and regretted that I'd had the experience. We became close personal friends, and contributed positively to the spirit of the community as team members. Thank you.

The indigenous tribal people who started my teachings so I could learn about identity and self. To all people who care enough to share their tradition and culture with the world, as intended by Creator. This spiritual passage of medicine from generation to generation will eventually mend what has been broken in the sacred hoop of life. Human beings will find purpose and comfort as they pray and practice with one another in mind. When we believe in our hearts, there will always be enough for every family to prosper today and tomorrow. Thank you.

My heart speaks to my bloodline families since our first day on Unci Maka (Grandmother Earth). To my grandmothers and grandfathers who presented a path for me to walk. To my parents, Alverda Bagola Zephier and Harley D. Zephier, who cared for and raised me with love and compassion. To my sisters and brothers who shared their lives with me as we grew up together. To my sons for carrying good hearts and good deeds out to the people. To my granddaughters and grandsons, I give my love and appreciation for your presence in our families. I want your world to be safe and protected. I am always with you! You are my future. *Warrior Is* is for you and all the other children on earth. A one-world family makes us all related. Thank you.

Kathleen Good Iron, for her contributions in making *Warrior Is* become reality. Her time and effort, which she provided for months on end, is greatly appreciated and respected. She is a part of the writings from start to finish. A proud and accomplished woman, she is someone I am honored to know. Thank you.

Robin Zephier, my younger brother, for his belief in and commitment to the warrior way of life. His knowledge and his professional career in modern society meshes with his willingness to learn our ancestors' tradition and culture. He is an example to live by. His spirit comforts and assists me with unlimited compassion. His dedication to our family message comes from the heart of a red man. He carries the philosophy of his grandfathers, to protect and preserve family. I respect you immensely. Thank you.

Monika Andrist Zephier, for her presence and heart. She brought love and sharing of spirit to my life. She is my best friend and companion. Our good fortune is to be both teachers and students as we walk in this life together. You have given me much more than I ever imagined possible. You are the essence of a true human being. Love and gratitude always. Thank you.

Mitakuye oyasin.

Robin

It is an honor to be gifted with the knowledge and spirit of our ancestors and that of our great-grandfather Mato Niyanpi, and to take part in the telling of his story, which is really a story about all of us in one way or another. My love and respect goes out to all who have blessed us with their friendship, their guidance, their support, their prayers, and their love. The blood that runs through my veins has been a part of Grandmother Earth since the beginning of time. I feel it is a gift to be able to use what I have in this life, to create something that may at some point, some day, help another being to continue on to another sunrise and another sunset. I am thankful to be a child of Unci Maka and to feel her presence every day, everywhere. One truly embraces the beauty of life and creation when you view the mountain from afar, only to realize how truly significant and vast it is after you have put foot before foot, step by step, and found yourself at the summit to view the beauty of Unci Maka as one child amongst all of her children. This is part of what I take within my spirit, as my Great Grandfather, Mato Niyanpi, has shown to me. Thanks Grandpa. I love you.

I am eternally thankful to my teacher and mentor, my brother Harley L. Zephier, who has given much all of his life to help others. His kindness and wisdom permeate through me, through the pages and storylines of *Warrior Is*, and through the pages of those books to come. With love and the deepest gratitude and respect, thank you, Brother. Thank you for nurturing my spiritual thirst. Thanks to your loving wife, Monika, and all of the boys and girls (Pa Pa, Hoksila, Istà, Wica, Isota, Cahansa, Wasu, and Takosa), who treat me like one of their own every time we see each other. Sinte`, we will always remember you. I know you were there listening and watching as we worked.

To our grandmother Mary Scarleg Bagola, I wish to give thanks for being your grandson, and for the absolute and unconditional love and devotion to life and dignity you showed to me and continue to show me, as you continue to encourage and strengthen my spirit. I love you.

To our parents, Alverda Bagola Zephier and Harley D. Zephier. I can only say that I do not have the ability to truly express my love and gratefulness to the both of you for providing us, providing me, with an honorable and free pathway to discover my own path, and to see you constantly by the trail, holding my hand or guiding my steps when circumstances may seem tough or uncertain.

To my brothers and sisters. Darin Zephier and all of his loving family, including Buddie and the girls. You are a soulful rock of courage and integrity, Brother. To Loren W. Zephier and his family, thank you for your kindness, love, and dignity. To Lanni Zephier Smith, Lance,

Mercury, and their family (Deepak, Scrappy, and Sassy), you are a wonderful example for the Lakota families to emulate, and to embrace for your generosity, kindness, and talent. To Whitley Zephier, David, and family, including Eli, thank you very much for being my friends and supporters through many rough times and for celebrating the good. I always wish the best for you guys. For my sister Linda Montana and her family and Sage, bless you all. I appreciate your devotion to culture and to commitment of life and tradition, and thanks for always being so kind to me. The dance in the sky can still be heard and cherished. To Grandpa Whitley Bagola, thanks for your kindness, dignity, and infinite love. To Grandma Victoria Aungie Zephier and Grandpa Antoine "Tony" Zephier, I look forward to seeing you both again and giving you a hug while we sit around the campfire at the other side camp. To Snoopy, Jacquie, Buffy, Cindy, Teddy, Cante`, Miguel, Prints, Raleigh, Joshua and Beau, look for us in the big green meadow.

To Jared Zephier and his family (Steph, Sage, Reese, Taya, Madison, Mia and Bentley), and Derek Zephier and his family (Britnie, Chance, Brynn, Dawson and Myles), I love you all and wish for your strength, hope dignity and spirit in family, and your curiosity to see the beautiful things in life for what they are.

To my friends and colleagues who have touched and enriched my life through good times and not so good times. Jerry Jasinski and his family (Roy, Jade, Ben, Jacquee, Harry, and Sylvia)—thanks, Brother J, for your kind, thoughtful, humorous, eternal friendship and love. Marialee Neighbours and family, continue your work and dreams. Dr. Robert Schutz and family, thanks for all of your love, kindness, trust, friendship and generosity. David Blando and family—thank you, Dave, for being a good trusted friend and human being; you are not alone, and you are more than you ever imagined. Heidi, Kelsey, and Dylan Washenberger, remember always that you are a part of me and a part of your dad spiritually for all of the fantastic things that you will accomplish in life. Our paths will lead us to the journeys that John envisioned for us all. Percy and Joan Washenberger and family, your kindness and connectedness is a matter of grace and love, please embrace all that you have and cherish in the family. Tom Fritz and his family, Nanu Nanu, Jimmy. Dan Zerr and family, keep on singing and playing to the world, we are listening, and know your heart. Kevin Cleberg and family. Jon Berkley and family. Tim Pelkofer and family; David Red Cloud and family. Stay strong, Brother Mike; your people need you.

Our cousin Myron Bagola and family and siblings, you are the descendants of sacred, noble, caring human beings who are waiting for the fulfillment of your destinies. Your father's story awaits in the wings to be told. For Dave Johnson, Olga, and family, you will always have a special place in our hearts and spirits. I am eternally grateful for your friendship and trust, despite my phone bill. Thanks also to Bruce and Cherie Hintz; Marlin and Joni Kinzer; Rob and Diane Houdek and family; Tim and Marilyn Fisher and family; Jim and Leah Jeffries; Rich Kaudy and family; Al Shaefer and family; Greg and Darcy Mohr and family; Jim and Carrie DeForrest; Cindy Walsh and family, and Michael B.; Lowell Punt and family; Charlene and Don Wince and family; Perry Bushby; Greg Abdallah; Jack Fuhrman and family; Don Blyler; Coach Jim Stephenson and family; Sister Helen Freimuth, who encouraged the inner fire of storytelling in me when I needed it most; Shawn and Dan Pahlke and family; Mike Hoffman and family; Greg Eiesland and family;Vicki and Denny Bruski; Bruce Ellison; Don Bauermeister and family; Rob Dietz and family; Steve Strzelec; Frank Pommersheim for helping me see the light on the inequities and unfairness in the law toward the indigenous and the Lakota; Gerry Spence and family, thanks for your grandfatherly advice and those kind and comforting walks; Sonja Holy Eagle and family, and her Dakota Drum Company, thanks for all the kind and hopeful help; Maren Chaloupka and family (including the spirit of her loving father), and Riley Platt and family; Bob Hommel; Patrick McLain; Rafe Forman; Rolly Samp; Lily Mendoza and family and the Birdcage; Don Clarkson; Norm Pattis; Jim Nugent; Bart Costello; Anne Valentine; Toki Clark; Kenny Paige; John Sloan; Ken Turek, the Unknown Comic; John Taussig; Bob Rose; Dallas Laird; Macklin Johnson; Reggie Whitten; Uncle Richard Zephier, and Carol, Kira, Rick and Erin and family; John Nolte; Kaitlin Larimer; Milton Grimes; Bill Trine; Terry Pechota; Dr. Stuart Fromm; Mike Wilson; Jeff Viken and tiospaye; Barry Hogan; Aaron Eiesland; Seamus Culhane; Becky Purington; Jim Leach; Patrick Lee; Richard Gohn; Coach Tom Grassie; Stacey Levson; Ken James; Rick Johnson; Shawn DeGraff and family; Justin and Peg Crawford and family; Dave Balazs; Gary Montana; Rebecca Kidder; Jim Margadant; Karen Olson; Bob Ulrich; Michael Roche; Bill Dodge; Vonnie and Dick Lehrke and family; Ed and Sheila Albright; Veronica and Patrick Duffy and family; Duane and Carol Nelson; Pat and Homer; Alex and Michael next door; Greg Gruba; Delbert Schmidt and family; Kit McCahren; Dr. James Dye and staff; Dr. Warren Whalen and staff; Dr. Steve Roberts and staff; Steve Boone; Brian Manolis; Eric Rosenbaum; Doug Barthel; Dave Brenneman; Jim Cihak; Duane Tielke; Carl Richards; Randy Houska; Tim Haiar; Jeff Fransen; Brian Radke; Lawrence Larson; Steve Bormes; Dave Drapeaux; Thomas Boberg; Mike Miller and family, be proud to walk in your Dad's footsteps; Ken Kirk; Paul Haisch; Gerald Boyer; David Huss; Pat Donovan; David Bradsky; Bob Cihak; George Nelson; Jeffrey Maks and family; Arnie Laubach; Shiloh MacNally; Mike Stonefield; Tim Rensch; Matt Stephens; Matt Skinner; Brad Gordon; Dean Nasser; Jack Bailey; Michael Martin Murphey and family and Wildfire; Thom Hartmann and family and staff of the Thom Hartmann Program; Coach Gregg Popovich; David Bossart; Bob Van Norman; Dr. Malin Dollinger; Dave and Cathy Kaudy and family; Mark Weiler and family; Jean Scott and family; All of my friends and coworkers at the PCPDO; All the friends at Roncalli; Jody, Vanita, Colette, Mary, Nancy, Paula, Peggy, Jean, Gordie, Jason, Pat, Jeff, Pam, Cindy, Brigid, Tim, Andy, Don, Tony, Pete, Tim S., Donna, Jo, Terri, Pam, Paul, Betsy, Lisa, Carol, Jeff, Pam, Laura, Gary, Dave, Rita, Nadine, Todd, Diane, Steve, and Mike.

To my people at work, thanks for putting up with me. Jon LaFleur and family. Charlie Abourezk and family, thanks for all the years of partnership, love, support and endeavors, and your strong commitment to help people, including me. Mike Abourezk and family, with Ramey. Thanks for your help, Mike, and for allowing me to put up the Empathy—Heal the Circle billboard. Thanks also to Dan Holloway; Diana Kratovil; Lori Zens; Ilene Packard; Bre Jackson; Alex Pilcher; Kerri Desersa; Jennifer Snyder; Susie Blair; Chelsea Van Wyk and Ruger; Brenda and Rod Hubbard; Alicia Garcia; Mark Koehn and family.

Friends who have added much to my ability to survive in a sometimes hectic world: Gary Fye, Trudy and family, and Kim; Mike Strain and family, and Mick and the horse nation; Jim Abourezk and family—thanks for your vision, courage, and wisdom; Sam Eaglestaff and family, Sam thanks for lighting the path on the way to look at the old ways and old deals.

To John Doerner and Sharon Small, for your help and kindness in navigating the Little Bighorn waters, and for your insight. Tribute is owed to many of those that spent time and effort to study and learn more about the events and the prolonged mysteries inherent in what happened in the battles and in the times of suffering and turmoil, such as Fred Dustin, Col. W.A. Graham, Laudie Chorne, Alan Woolworth, Gary Anderson, William Millikan, Hugh Reilly, Patrick A. Lee, Sheldon Wolfchild, Sidney Keith, David Little Elk and Loren Bouten.

To friends such as Dorothy Thunder Bull, Ryan, and family; Bernadine Red Bear, "Bill," and family; the family of Cari Hill; Ferlin Dorian; Albert Six Feathers; Carilla Shot With Arrow; Leslie Demery; Teddy Poor Bear; Cheryl Buckman; Gus Scully and family and Judy; LaDonna Nieman, Ross, and family; Pam and Darryl Bayman; Tike Owens; Janine Polk and Mike; Roland Grosshans; Del and Vernice Blando; Don and Alberta Zephier and family (Mobridge 1963); Dr. Robert Bormes and his son Pete; Rich Hoffman; Oliver Jasinski; Jamie Zepp; Joel Van Dover; Lanny Krage; and Deryl Edwards Jr. and family.

To Ken Pavlish, by and with Betty, it is a blessing and a privilege to be a part of your family. To Kevin, Cheryl, Landon, Heather, Melanie, Mel, Garrett, Courtney, Noura, Paytynn, Jeremiah, Cindy, Tom, Sam, Melissa, Tim, and Jane, thank you for your love, friendship, and understanding.

To BJ Tillman and family, thanks for being there for me always and being a guiding spirit and foundation. To Kathy Good Iron and family. Kathy, this project would not have been possible without you and the strength, dignity, advice, Lakota awareness, cultural sensitivity, hard work, loyalty, and generosity that you have provided, which served as the backbone to our work in getting this done. You are a gift to the Lakota people, to your family, and to our ancestors.

To my beautiful, loving, and generous wife, Patti, and our little girls, JoJo and Marino. Patti, thanks for loving me, taking care of me, and supporting this dream. You are a gift from the heavens. I love you very much. JoJo, who keeps me busy, is a constant loving companion by my side, especially in the lonely and trying times, but mostly she makes us laugh and makes us appreciate family. Marino is our special spirit watching over us all from her place in the Milky Way. We miss you, baby girl. As I promised, I will find you.

Thanks to those who have helped us along the way. Thanks to Jeff Stevens, Sarah Disbrow, Kathi Wittkamper, Paolo Denton, Casey Martin, Heather Carter, Melanie Jacobs, Earl Thomas, and the staff at iUniverse for your kindness, open ears, and open hearts. And despite my misgivings, disappointment and my emphatic disagreement with how their corporation takes advantage of their employees by not paying them fairly and many times forcing them to use the public safety net at taxpayer expense, we must thank Wal-Mart. They were the only place that still sold the old-style cassette tape recorders and cassette tapes that Harley and I used in our hours and hours of discussion and recording of parts of this story. We just hope that their corporate behavior can become more empathetic and humane to all things that they influence, including Unci Maka. Since Wal-Mart is so big and influential, it is also an opportunity for the Walton family to step forward in the spirit of empathy for humanity and Grandmother Earth, to truly make a difference to help to turn the tide toward a better world for us all. Others will follow your lead if you strike the drum. That is a message for all of us to live by.

To all of our ancestors, thanks for making the loving and spiritual footprints for us to follow. To our descendants, please never forget who you are or where you come from. Keep the fire burning. Roots run deep. They are eternal and will connect with the brightness and nourishment of the new day. Try to be kind and benevolent when the opportunity comes, or even if your kindness is the hand on the door which opens up the universe of opportunity and hope for someone else..... take the chance, and open that door for them. We may see ourselves in the mirror on the other side of things one day. It is said that no one ever got lost just for following their dreams, or their heart. Dreams many times, offer the best trails for the journey ahead. My prayer for all of us, is that we keep walking that trail, together.

Mitakuye oyasin.

APPENDICES

APPENDIX A

CHRONOLOGY OF CRITICAL EVENTS

Billions of years ago, Creator creates the Universe and Wi, the sun, and Unci Maka, Grandmother Earth.

Life begins on Unci Maka.

Turtle Island forms.

Human beings emerge on Unci Maka.

Great Race occurs.

1 A.D.	Birth of Jesus Christ.
476 A.D.	Approximate fall of the Roman Empire.
1215	Magna Carta established in England, as a basis for English and American law.
1297	William Wallace of Scotland and his indigenious Scottish people rise up against the English ruling class.
1492	Columbus and European Spanish invade land in West Indies islands, part of North America and Turtle Island. Butchery, slavery, death and destruction begins.

1620	White immigrants (Pilgrims) seeking asylum in the New World, arrive on the eastern
	seaboard of North America and establish settlements upon indigenous lands.
	Massacre of the Lenape tribe near present day Bowling Green, NY on Manhatten Island.
	The Povonia Massacre along the Hudson River in N.Y.
	The Massacre at Corlears Hook on Manhatten Island, N.Y.
1763	October 7. Proclamation of 1763. The King of England issues this proclamation to the colonies in North America to prohibit white settlement west beyond the Appalachian Mountains.
1773	The Boston Tea Party. American colonists stage a revolt against the 1773 Tea Act, passed by the King of England. Revolutionaries dress up as "Indians" and break and spill containers holding thousands of pounds of tea into Boston Harbor as a revolt against corporate privilege and corporate tax breaks.
1776	July 4. United States of America makes its Declaration of Independence from Great Britain. The declaration refers to the indigenous people of Turtle Island as "merciless Indian savages." Many signing "founding fathers" owned slaves.
1778	First US "Indian" treaty was made with the Delaware Nation. It was eventually broken.
1787	Congress passes Northwest Ordinance declaring that the "land and property [of North American native peoples] shall never be taken from them without their consent."
1803	Louisiana Purchase is done between France and the United States, despite the fact that neither country owned any of the land west of the Mississippi River, and despite the fact that none of the Lakota, Nakota, or Dakota people were a part of any such "agreement."
1804	Meriwether Lewis and William Clark begin their expedition up the Mississippi and Missouri Rivers.

1825	Atkinson–O'Fallon mission signs peace treaties with Teton "Sioux" (Lakota) for the United States.
1830	The Indian Removal Act of 1830 becomes law. Andrew Jackson begins enforcement.
1830	*Cherokee v. Georgia* and *Worchester v. Georgia* cases go to US Supreme Court. The contention is that state law has no force over or effect on Indian reservations.
1831	Sitting Bull born along Yellowstone River (a.k.a. Elk River) in Montana Territory.
1837	September 29. First Treaty of Traverse des Sioux–Minnesota Territory (Dakota: Mdewakanton, Wahpeton, Wahpekute, Sisseton).
1837–1870	Smallpox epidemic spreads among and ravages whole indigenous populations in the Great Plains, killing millions of people. The virus was present on blankets given to the people, among other goods, by the white Europeans and the US government. It was a form of terrorism against the people.
1838	Trail of Tears of the Cherokee people; Hundreds die. One of many Trail of Tears events to come.
1840	Spirit Horse (II) born in the He Sapa near Rapid Creek.
1843	Oregon Trail opens, and the first wagon trains soon cross Lakota country on the Oregon Trail.
1849	Mato Niyanpi (Saved By Bear/Scar Leg) born in the He Sapa. Born as Brown Eagle.
	Mato Luzanhan (Swift Bear) born in the He Sapa.
	Gold rush in California.
	August 5. Second Treaty of Traverse des Sioux–Minnesota Territory (Dakota: Mdewakanton, Wahpeton, Sisseton, Wahpekute).

1851	September 17. First Fort Laramie Treaty between the United States and indigenous Plains tribes. Recognizes Lakota aboriginal ownership of sixty million acres of land, but allocates certain parts of the northern Powder River and Bighorn country to also include others bands, while legally recognizing hunting, fishing, and roaming rights of Lakota, forever, within the *unceded* Indian territory (including the Greasy Grass valley).
1852	Spirit Horse's hanbleceya atop Owl's Nest.
1854	August 17. Grattan Incident. US Cavalry Lieutenant Grattan confronts a Lakota band of Brule over the taking and killing of a white Mormon settler's lame cow by a visiting Mnincoju warrior. Conquering Bear offers restitution/compensation, but Grattan refuses and the military opens fire. All twenty-nine of the US soldiers are killed, fatally wounds Conquering Bear. A young warrior named Curly, a.k.a. Spirit Horse, is present. Many feel that this incident was the beginning of the long-standing period of conflict between the Lakota and the US government and its military—all over a single *cow*. The incident emphasizes that the government valued cattle more than Lakota human life.
1854	Half Breed land scrip authorized in Minnesota.
1855	September 3. General Harney and US troops slaughter eighty-six Lakota at Ash Hollow Massacre, a.k.a. Blue Water Creek Massacre (*outright butchery*), in direct retaliation for the Grattan Incident of 1854. Harney then purposefully marches near the He Sapa on his way to Fort Sully in Dakota. United States and Harney violate the terms of the 1851 Fort Laramie Treaty.
1856	Fights the Bear, Saved By Bear's father, performs a hanbleceya on Medicine Mountain in the Bighorn Mountains (the Shiny Mountains).
1857	Cheyenne warriors clash with US military along the Oregon Trail.

1858	Treaty with the Yankton (Dakota Territory). Yankton cede over six million acres of land in eastern Dakota Territory, except pipestone quarry.
1858	June 19. Third Treaty of Traverse des Sioux–Minnesota Territory (Dakota: Mdewakanton, Sisseton, Wahpeton, Wahpekute).
1859	July 20. Dakota scout Zephyr Rencountre guides an expedition team headed by Captain Raynolds to the Mato Tipila, Bear's Lodge. First known time that whites see sacred mountain of Bear's Lodge.
1860	April 13. Pony Express begins operation from Missouri to California.
1861–1865	Civil War of the United States. The Union of the North fights for the emancipation of the black Americans. The Confederacy of the South fights for secession from the Union in order to preserve its slavery-based economy.
1862	August 17, 1862. US war against Dakota begins with Dakota people's uprising in Minnesota, caused by United States breaching treaties of 1837, 1851 and 1858 with Dakota Indians (Sisseton, Wahpeton, Mdewakanton, Wahpekute).
	September. Battle of Wood Lake (Minnesota). Mdewakanton Leader Mankato, "Blue Earth," killed by cannonball.
	September. Battle of Birch Coulee (Minnesota).
	December 26. Thirty-eight Dakota warriors are hanged simultaneously in Mankato, Minnesota.
1862	Bounty of $25 for each Dakota scalp taken in Minnesota Territory offered by Gov. Alexander Ramsey.
1862–1865	Fort Snelling internment camp of the Dakota, including the "friendlies," loyal Mdewakantons. Prison camp is set at the base of Fort Snelling along the confluence of the Minnesota and Mississippi Rivers in present-day Minneapolis.

1863	February 3. Act abrogating all prior treaties with the Dakota bands, but granting eighty acres to each friendly Dakota and his or her heirs, forever. US government and US courts breach/violate the terms of said Act and do not provide the land.
1863	Discovery of gold around Bannock, Montana, encouraging white settlers, miners, and entrepreneurs to seek an economical route to the Montana goldfields, causing the United States to develop the Bozeman Trail.
1863	Mato Niyanpi performs a hanbleceya at Mato Paha in He Sapa.
1863	September 3. Whitestone Hill Massacre. US Cavalry led by Colonel Sully tracks Dakota to Hunkpapa territory (Dakota Territory [North Dakota]) north of Cannonball River and massacres three hundred Yanktonai, and also Hunkpapa and Blackfeet.
1864	Territory of Montana is established.
	July 28. Killdeer Mountain Battle. Over 150 Yanktonai, Blackfeet, and Hunkpapa killed by Sully's troops.
	November 29. Sand Creek Massacre (Colorado). Col. John Chivington and his gang of six hundred Colorado militia volunteers slaughter two hundred peaceful southern Cheyenne and Arapaho, two-thirds of whom are unarmed elders, women, and children. Chivington, when asked about why he had his men kill babies, replies, "Nits make lice." Entire camp wiped out, including peaceful leader Black Kettle, who had just returned from a peace meeting and flew a white flag over the camp. Victims scalped, pubic hair cut out, women split open, flesh souvenirs taken.
1864– 1866	Thirty-five hundred white miners, emigrant settlers, and others use the Bozeman Trail, traveling across territories belonging to Cheyenne, Arapaho, and Lakota.

1865	March 3. US Congress approves the act that authorizes the construction of four new wagon roads through Lakota territory. The Bozeman Trail is authorized west of Fort Laramie and entails the cutting up to Montana. This is a blatant violation of the Fort Laramie Treaty with the Lakota, in the name of the pursuit of gold.

March 3. US Congress approves the act that authorizes the construction of four new wagon roads through Lakota territory. The Bozeman Trail is authorized west of Fort Laramie and entails the cutting up to Montana. This is a blatant violation of the Fort Laramie Treaty with the Lakota, in the name of the pursuit of gold.

October 10. United States negotiates treaty with "friendly" Lakota bands, including Mnincoju.

Powder River expedition / Powder River invasion by US military, led by General Connor, who orders a punitive campaign against the Lakota, Cheyenne, and Arapaho for "harassing" miners and settlers along the Bozeman Trail.

August 13. Battle of "Crazy" Woman's Fork. First engagement between US military and Cheyenne in the Powder River invasion.

August 16. Battle of Powder River. On August 16, Pawnee scouts and Capt. Frank North attack a Cheyenne camp.

August 28. Battle of Tongue River. Connor attacks an Arapaho village of six hundred people on the Tongue River, mostly women, children, and old men.

September 1. Battle of Alkali Creek. Hunkpapa, Sans Arc, and Mnincoju fight Colonel Cole's column along Alkali Creek, Montana.

September 8. Battle of Dry Creek. Cheyenne, Lakota, and Arapaho fight Cole and Walker's group of two thousand solders along Dry Creek on Powder River, Montana Territory.

1866	United States enters into negotiations with *hostile* Lakota over travel routes to Montana. Red Cloud declares war when the United States moves to fortify the Bozeman Trail. Lakota confront military and annihilate Col. William Fetterman and his troops, in the Fetterman Fight on December 21, 1866, near Fort Kearney, Wyoming. Capt. William Fetterman and eighty-one US soldiers are killed in the battle.
1867	February 19. Treaty with the Sisseton and Wahpeton (Dakota Territory).
	August 1. Hayfield Fight. Lakota and Cheyenne confront military hay-cutting contingent from Fort C. F. Smith, Wyoming.
	August 2. Wagon Box Fight. Lakota and Cheyenne warriors confront soldiers from Fort Phil Kearney. The US troops turn back the Lakota and Cheyenne.
1868	April 29. Fort Laramie Treaty of 1868 confirms Great Sioux Reservation as permanent home of the Lakota Nation and preserves Powder River and Bighorn country as unceded hunting territory and unceded Indian territory.
	November 3. Ulysses S. Grant elected as president.
	November 27. Washita Massacre, Oklahoma Territory. Lt. Col. George A. Custer and the Seventh US Cavalry, including Capt. Frederick Benteen, attack a peaceful camp of Northern Cheyenne at dawn on a cold, snowy day. Custer uses the military tactic of splitting his regiments into three separate columns for the attack. Custer and his company ride around the perimeter of the camp to the north and circle back to cut off and cut into the heart of the encampment. Very few warriors are present, as most are out hunting. Two hundred men, women, children, and elders are slaughtered. All nine hundred of the Cheyenne's horses are rounded up and slaughtered as well.

1869	January. First Transcontinental Railroad is completed.
	New US president, Ulysses S. Grant, implements a Quaker Policy to deal with *Indian* issues (i.e., using Christianization to assimilate the Indians).
	Cheyenne River Agency established, encompassing four separate Lakota bands of Mnincoju, Blackfeet, Sans Arcs, and Two Kettle. Cattle industry eventually assumes primary power and influence over the agency lands and agency officials.
1872	Treaty with the Mississippi Sioux, Minnesota Territory (Mdewakanton, Wahpekute).
1872	May 10. General Mining Act instituted. Ulysses S. Grant instrumental in pushing this act into law because of his ties to the mining industry.
	August 16. Baker Fight. US General Stanley expedition to survey the Yellowstone Valley for the Northern Pacific Railroad. Lakota warriors led by Sitting Bull fight a battle with US forces led by Maj. Eugene Baker, near present-day Billings, Montana.
1870–1872	US government's policy of extermination of the buffalo begins and flourishes. Government seeks to eliminate the Lakota's main food source to further its genocidal policies.
1873	August 4. Segments of the Yellowstone Expedition commanded by Lt. Col. George Custer battle with Lakota on the north side of Yellowstone River (known as Elk River by the Lakota) near present-day Miles City, Montana.
	Barbed wire, Colt single-action army revolver, model 1873 Springfield carbine, and Winchester model 1873 are first introduced. US Army purchases these for western conflicts.

The dreaded Panic of 1873 hits the United States. The US economy experiences a severe financial recession, and nears bankruptcy and economic collapse. A quick significant influx of cash and financial opportunity is critically needed.

Black Elk has a vision on Owl's Nest Peak indicating his destiny to help his people.

1874   July–August. Custer expedition invades the He Sapa and discovers gold, in violation of the 1868 Fort Laramie Treaty. Lakota know it as the Trail of Thieves.

August–September. The Lakota engage in a spiritual *asking*, and receive permission received at Bear Creek to engage in battle with Custer and the US military.

1875   Trespassing immigrant miner John B. Pearson finds gold in Deadwood Gulch in the northern He Sapa. This happens at least one and a half years before the illegal taking of the Black Hills occurs in the "agreement" of February 28, 1877.

November. Indian Bureau issues official reports that the Lakota are upset about the government's breaching of the 1868 treaty by trespassing into the He Sapa, and about the failure of the government to deliver on any of its promises.

1875   November. Agency superintendents report that many Lakota have left the agencies to join Sitting Bull and Spirit Horse in the Powder River region area hunt.

Allison Commission attempts but fails to purchase or lease the He Sapa from the Lakota.

November 3. At a meeting in Washington, DC, President Grant makes the following statement to General Crook and General Sheridan: "No further resistance shall be made to miners going into the Black Hills." General Sherman writes to one of his subordinates, saying that if the miners wish to invade the Black Hills, then "I understand that the President and the Interior Department will wink at it."

November 9. Gen. Philip Sheridan writes a letter to Gen. Alfred Terry (the "Sheridan letter") stating the following:

> The President decided that while the orders heretofore issued forbidding the occupation of the Black Hills country, by miners, should not be rescinded, still no further resistance by the military should be made to the miners gong in: it being his belief that such resistance only increased their desire and complicated the troubles. Will you therefore quietly cause the troops in your Department to assume such attitudes as will meet the views of the President in this respect.
>
> P. H. Sheridan, Lieut. General.

1876 February 1. United States declares war on the Lakota and enters into the Powder River Campaign to hunt down and kill the *hostile* Lakota.

March 17. General Crook directs Col. Joseph Reynolds and US troops to attack a village of Northern Cheyenne, believing it to be Spirit Horse's camp. It is not.

April 9. Ten months before the formal *illegal taking* of the Black Hills by the United States occurred in the "agreement" of February 28, 1877, trespassing white miners Moses Manuel, Fred Manuel, John Henry "Hank" Harney, and Alex Engh find a "leed" of gold in the northern He Sapa and name it the Homestake Mine.

April. The Montana Column under the command of Col. John Gibbon departs Fort Ellis in Montana for the Powder River Territory with 450 infantry and cavalry, intending to join the two other US military columns hunting down the "hostile" Lakota.

1876

April. Crow, Arikira, and some Lakota are recruited to be Indian scouts for the US Army for its summer Powder River Campaign to track and eliminate the Lakota and Cheyenne led by Sitting Bull.

May 17. The Dakota Column under the command of Gen. Alfred Terry and Lt. Col. George A. Custer, with the US Seventh Cavalry, depart Fort Abraham Lincoln near Bismarck, North Dakota, for the Powder River Territory to hunt down the "hostile" Lakota.

May 29. The Crook column, under the command of Gen. George Crook, departs Fort Smith near Sheridan, Wyoming, for the Powder River Territory to join Gibbon's and Terry's columns, seeking to hunt down the *hostile* Lakota.

June 10. Maj. Marcus Reno is sent out on a ten-day reconnaissance mission in Powder River country.

June 12. Lakota and Cheyenne camp at Deer Medicine Rock, and Sitting Bull holds his *scarlet blanket* sun dance. Sitting Bull reveals his vision of soldiers falling into camp without ears. Sitting Bull already knows of the spiritual permission regarding the time of the upcoming battle. He etches his vision into the Deer Medicine Rock.

June 17. Battle of Rosebud. Brig. Gen. George Crook's Southern Column battles warriors of the Lakota and Cheyenne led by Spirit Horse along the Rosebud Creek in the Wolf Mountains. During the six-hour battle, nine soldiers and thirteen warriors are killed. Crook realizes that he must retreat and return to Wyoming at the fort along Goose Creek. This decision leaves only the Terry and Gibbon columns to confront the Lakota and Cheyenne.

June 22. Custer and the Seventh Cavalry leave the mouth of Rosebud Creek and seek to locate and engage the hostiles.

June 25. Lakota annihilate the Seventh US Cavalry and Lt. Col. George A. Custer in the Greasy Grass Battle at the Little Bighorn. Custer is killed on the *hill*.

June 26. Reno and Benteen pinned down on Reno Hill by Lakota and Cheyenne warriors.

June 26. Encampment of Lakota and Cheyenne depart the Greasy Grass valley to the southwest to the Shiny Mountains (Bighorn Mountains).

June 27 (morning). Gibbon column of US Army, including General Terry, arrives in the Greasy Grass valley. Lt. James Bradley, Gibbon's army scout leader, is the first white man and the first US military man to arrive at the scene on the hill where Custer and many of his Seventh Cavalry soldiers are found. Lieutenant Bradley reports the deaths of Custer and his 206 men, and specifically reports that the bodies of the deceased soldiers have not been mutilated or desecrated.

July 6. *Bismarck Tribune* publishes news of the defeat of Custer and the Seventh Cavalry at the Little Bighorn, the first official news announcement of the Greasy Grass Battle. Misrepresentation and propaganda ensue concerning the events at the Greasy Grass.

1877   June. California mining and business entrepreneur and financial opportunist George W. Hearst partners with San Francisco lawyers James Ben Ali Haggin and Lloyd Tevis (a founder of Wells Fargo Company) to purchase the unlawful mining interest and holding called Homestake Mine for $70,000. The mine will be operational for 125 years until 2001, and will produce 10 percent of the world's supply of gold at an estimated value in excess of $51.42 billion (40 million troy ounces @ $1,255.50/ounce).

APPENDIX B

A FULFILLMENT OF A LEGACY (HARLEY'S STORY)

THE STORY THAT I AM about to tell comes from the oral history given to me by Grandmother Mary, and given to her by her father, my great-grandfather Mato Niyanpi. It is the account of the holding of the Greasy Grass Battle.

My grandmother was always a very special and spiritual woman. She was revered by many of her relatives and peers throughout her life. She comes from a very, very good and committed bloodline. These people, traditionally, speak of feats and acts of courage, and improvement of the people's society. This story is of Great-Grandfather. My grandmother would approach my family soon after I was born to teach me. The reason that she began to instruct me, at such an early age, is that before I was even born, I was given a name. She was directed that this boy should be given this name because he would have a place in this story in the future. I recall being very, very young—one year of age—when my frequent contact with Grandmother began. My grandmother did not live that close to my family. The story begins on the occasions when she and I did come into contact with one another, on one of her visits, and continues during her visits throughout our lives. When I was about two, I noticed that my grandmother enjoyed drinking coffee. She would sit at the table and hold me. We would even drink coffee together. As we sat, we connected in a way many human beings refuse to understand or simply cannot understand. She would speak in her native tongue because she was raised speaking the Lakota language. Being such a young child, I found it easy to understand her, being that the first language I heard her speak was Lakota. Our connection was a spiritual connection. She began to tell me about a warrior, my great-grandfather, how his life was, what his life involved, and the significance of the events that he would participate in during a certain time frame, events that would change many, many people's lives. So throughout the years, I became informed by Grandmother's teachings and projections from the spiritual side. These projections, images, and goings-on from the spiritual side would not leave. Whether Grandma or other relatives were there, these things remained a piece of me. I was being told the story that one day, when I was ready and prepared to do so, would be released to the public and to the people of the world. My grandmother would tell me of things and occurrences, including the individuals who participated. She told me about acts and memories that would play roles in the future. As she explained through the early portion of my childhood, I began to understand who she was speaking of. I had never seen my great-grandfather in this world, but I felt his presence within my being. He and I were becoming one and the same, with a defined purpose to be achieved as I grew older. Grandma would tell me that Great-Grandfather was a man who performed an important act. He removed a human being of tremendous hatred and needless suffering in the Plains people's lives, a specific man who has risen through the ranks simply by destroying and taking advantage of the people as they were being forced to lose everything. His pursuit of fame would become strong enough to cause an entire tribal nation of people to become threatened and rely upon Creator for answers to their questions and the possible solution for their problem.

At the age of ten, I experienced something life-changing: I developed a physical ailment that almost took my life. During this time, the spirits of my great-grandfather and my ancestors helped me to survive so that I could continue to work toward carrying out the role that Great-Grandfather had asked me to fulfill. I was so sick at this time that I actually died on an operating table. But as we know and believe, we do not die simply because the physical body is exhausted and leaves. The spirit lives on. During this time of near death, I was allowed to see myself and the doctors and the nurses in the operating room from above, as though I was floating, in the most peaceful, serene setting of my life thus far. I felt as though I had never left this type of space before. I had not even wanted to leave it. As I was gazing down upon myself, in the midst of having an operation, I saw a light that was luminous but not bright. It was something that felt so comforting that I looked into it. Then I actually began to float in its direction. Whether I was ready to go to home or whether I was taking another step is not clear. But just as I began to move, I heard voices from behind me that said, "You cannot go. You must turn back. You have more to do." When the voices finished speaking, I was waking up in a recovery room in the hospital. And when I awoke from this experience, I knew that one day I would have to fulfill this asking and undergo personal preparation so as to leave this legacy of oral history.

This occurrence would take control of my existence, on an off, as I went about my daily routine at school, and my routines that were part of being a member of my family and society. It would be on my mind when I saw Indian people, how they were being treated, how we were being treated. I would say to myself, that one day I would be worthy to help. In the year following, I was immersed in this spiritual presence that had awakened another side of self. My visits with Grandmother continued. The major thing I focused on was to convince myself that I was truly needed on earth. It was a lot to try to comprehend for a child, thinking about the future, wondering how would I do what I had been asked to do and who would help me. Would there be any help at all? The way the people are today, they don't rely on tradition or the cultural way of enrichment.

In the fall and winter of the following year, I began to experience things that were not normal occurrences. I began to feel and see images of the people in situations where they depended upon Creator. Most of these visions were focused on ceremony and ritual, which I was totally unfamiliar with, other than having heard about them from my grandma. During this time frame, I engaged in self-analysis and self-evaluation, almost on a daily basis. A child's mind is curious, not so much analytical. With my near-death experience and the subsequent awakening of my spirit, I became able to understand much more than I ever could have simply by being told of the spirit world and the afterlife. I was able to understand these happenings that had not ever been explained to me. These happenings became clear because of something on the other side of this near-death experience, a piece that stuck with me once I returned to the physical realm. This strength that I was given would become a part of my existence. It would also be a big part of my life as I walked my path, moving toward the opportunity to express Great-Grandfather's asking from Creator. I would learn to perform and to help in the way that was given to me to do. I would have a much stronger way of connecting not only to the human being but also to every other being.

The ups and downs of this life teach you how to manage your mind and spirit. To appropriately pursue the asking and purpose, I moved to many geographical areas, as my spirit was always on a search for that place of comfort, that place of belonging, something that was easy for me to find almost anywhere I went. I had one of those gifts that Great-Grandfather possessed, the ability to communicate directly and personally with many beings. This was necessary when I wanted to convey a message. I had to have the presence to be able to speak, but more importantly the presence to practice so that others could observe how I did what I did, and why, and even ask the questions needed to give them a full understanding of something completely new.

My Grandmother finished telling me the specific details that I would need to do to bring the end of the story forth, I began to understand the role I was to play in our oral history. I must begin to find my identity as a Lakota. This identity would be the key to trying to rebuild what I had loss as a tribal person—the faith and the belief in myself and in others who are part of my life. The people who would help me along this route were many. They would come from so many facets of life that I could not describe them all. But most of the people who would come to me throughout my lifetime were concerned with and connected to Spirit, advisors to nurture me, provide me with teachings, and so forth. I did not encounter people such as this as regularly as I would have liked to. A majority of tribal people criticized and argued with one another over tradition and culture issues. Seeing them would become a personal choice for me, rather than a creational choice.

In my late thirties was when my personal calling truly began. One morning I traveled to He Sapa on personal business. I finished what I needed to do, and spent time enjoying the beauty of my surroundings. I drove home in the evening. As I was entering the Badlands, sweet grass entered my pickup. And along with this sweet grass came the word in Lakota: *hanbleceya*. Four times. The spirits were asking me to start my preparation as a warrior. I would go because of that asking.

My hanbleceya consisted of spending four days and four nights on this hill, fasting and praying. I ate no food and drank no water, contending only with self, Creator, and the ground. Green Grass was the location for this very sacred ceremony, the experience occurring under the full sun during the day and beneath the stars at nighttime. Many people shy away from the elements, heavily. But when you are up there, committed to stand, pray, and receive, your mind becomes focused to the point where you no longer belong on the outside. This is why Creator asks that the ceremony be of four days' duration, as this allows the body to become depleted and to suffer. The mind becomes exhausted, tired of the avenues it normally takes and tired of the analyzing of situations it normally does to ease or even remove the discomfort. The strongest part of your standing are the spirits, the support they provide and the connection they exhibit in aiding you toward your completion of this task. The hanbleceya is enduring, very confusing, and most of all very enlightening if you choose this way for self.

After the hanbleceya, I returned home. I had days to think over what I had experienced, seen, and heard. As my recuperation time was coming to an end, I heard a knock on my door. I walked to the door and opened it to find two of my uncles who are Dakota, standing there. They had driven all the way up from their tribal area, which is in southeastern South Dakota, to where I lived, on the western side of South Dakota. They explained their reason for coming after we greeted one another, shook hands, sat down, and began to have a cup of coffee together. The oldest uncle began by saying, "We are here on an asking. A sweat lodge was performed by our medicine people, and we were there included in this lodge. The sweat leader was told that the upcoming sun dance is going to go okay and well, but we need one man and his strength to help us complete this dance. There is turmoil, there is arrogance, there is selfishness, coming to this dance. The spirits have asked for you, Harley, to bring your strength to this dance. And far more important is the fact that you are being asked to become a sun dancer just like your great-grandfather."

My uncles and I sat and talked. I asked them, "Why did the spirits ask for me?" The uncle who had informed me of the asking replied, "Only the spirits know. We are just the messengers for that ceremony. We have come, if you decide to go, to bring you back. And we will dance at Pipestone, the home of the keepers of the stone, your relation. So we are here to ask and bring your presence and give you the opportunity to dance. And we will sit and wait for that decision."

My decision was to attend. It would be my honor to go. I know that this was one of the steps I must take.

My uncles gave instructions and encouragement in the variety of articles and tangible goods needed by a sun dancer. After lengthy discussions, I assembled belongings and acquired what I could to make this journey. I had only heard of the Sun Dance through my grandmother and a few other select people. Not all had described everything involved with this sacred ceremony for all people. I was to learn the experience of flesh and blood very soon. I was not afraid. I was willing to offer my human presence in strength and prayer.

We arrived at my uncle's home, which is located near Pipestone. The place where the dance will be conducted. The preparation to be a participant is followed in a step by step process. Swiftly the days pass and anxiety grows. The day has come to enter the sacred arbor as a man. What I need, they will provide. I'm here to dance. I must, it is on my path. I finished this sacred ceremony for the people to live. I received a greater understanding of people, prayer, and commitment. I will carry these teachings from Creator, as I walk in the direction of home.

I have spent many decades learning and understanding tradition and culture. The ceremonies, the daily practice and the interconnection of the spirit and the body have given me direction as I continued to ask for the assistance I needed to tell this story. My educated senses became very strong thanks to Grandmother's continuing efforts. Even though she is going to pass away and no longer be here in the physical realm, her spiritual guidance will remain. Her presence is very strong, having helped me and guided me through the process of helping the world come to understand the occurrence, and the people and the attitudes necessary to maintain a legacy. I eventually learned to trust the messages of Creator I received within. I followed like a child ready to learn, ready to do, and ready to be a part of a workable solution for our people.

When I began to write the story, I did so not only through memory, but also for the pain staking participation in the ceremony and Lakota culture. I will focus on the proper way of presenting this message. I was determined to follow and strengthen the story, as it was time for our family to acknowledge our responsibility and duty to carry this message. After many decades of keeping the secret of the Battle of Greasy Grass, Great-Grandfather asked his daughter that she and the family perform a ceremony for him and the warriors on Last Stand Hill. This was one of his last requests of the family on the physical plane. As a family unit, we arrived at the battlefield and performed a ceremony atop the hill. This was where the message was given that we should bring forth everything that we had to say. This ceremony was very special and enjoyable. Our job now is one for the present day. We are the representatives of that message. We are to convey in the best way possible the dream, and the realization, that all humanity will come to terms and will live civilly and mindfully. All my teachings throughout life are now put forth in words. And with our presence and our deeds, the rest of the message is left to the spirits who listen, who will act, and who believe that the message is worthy of their practice and commitment. Encouraging, learning and understanding tradition and culture of my tiospaye. I was determined to follow and strengthen the story, as it was time for our family to acknowledge our responsibility and duty to carry this message.

What this story offers to an individual is a spiritual presence, and even a beginning, which many have lived too long without. The Spirit is infectious. This is why many come from all over the world to the place at Greasy Grass. They are seeking the spirit of commitment, the spirit of hopes and dreams, and a way to appreciate life in peace and serenity, with proper protection. I think this is a longing of all human beings regardless of where they originate from.

The story of Greasy Grass serves as a stepping-stone for those people all across the world who are searching for something. These steps taken to make sure they feel the spirit of the story itself and find that it is actually pulling them, drawing them, leading them to want to know more, to feel more, to absorb the spirit. It's almost as if people find themselves thirsting in their spirit. In that sense, their searching leads them to want to know more.

APPENDIX C

REACHING OUT, I WILL SHOW YOU (ROBIN'S STORY)

THE STRONG, BEAUTIFUL LAKOTA WARRIOR stands facing the breeze on the mountaintop, the breeze blowing through his thick dark hair. He looks toward the setting sun, which slowly blankets the horizon above the distant mountains to the west.

The younger man is dressed in blue jeans and a faded flannel shirt. He is also looking to the west, his somewhat wavy hair, brown and graying slightly, blowing back behind his ears. Gently he turns his head to his right, and toward the Lakota warrior. He is sitting on the edge of the granite rocky peak, near the taller, older man's legs and feet. The younger man, in turning, catches the bright blue design of the dragonfly on the outside of the warrior's left buckskin pant leg. Then his dark brown eyes look up the warrior's body, taking it all in: his honor, his dignity, his peace, his presence…. his humanity. Until he reaches the man's face. His eyes see the dark weathered skin of his high resolute cheekbones, his strong angular jaw, his slightly full lips, his somewhat crooked and bumped nose. Then to his eyes. Those deep brown eyes, identical to his own, as those eyes stare outward to the west, toward the sunset, as the breeze ruffles a few strands of hair which have come loose from his tight braids.

The younger man's eyes search for, then catch onto the older brown eyes, and the older man meets his gaze. The eyes meet and connect. Much like their spirits have been connected, forever. The same blood of the strong Lakota warrior flows through and beats within the heart of the younger man. They are of the same people, of the same family, of the same lineage, of the same…. destiny.

His great-grandfather then smiles at the younger man and reaches out his rough-callused left hand. His fingers are unusually long and slender. Their fingers meet, and the warmth is shared. The great-grandson now knows why he is here…. now, at this moment. Why it has always been something that was meant to be. Something that was destined to happen. Something that must happen. Now. At this point in his life. At this point in their existence. At this point, again, at the time of the breaking of the world.

The strong hand and arm of his great-grandfather gently lifts the younger man to his feet, and the two stand side by side. His great-grandfather. The great respected and honorable Lakota Mnincoju warrior. The *heyoka*. One of the solemn Protectors. The warrior holds his great-grandson's gaze, and then turns again toward the west. They stand on the highest peak of the He Sapa, the sacred center of Grandmother Earth. Near the origin of their people. And they both look and see into the distance, into the wonderous scene of geography, of beauty, of time, and of life. Into the vast expanse of the spoken and unwritten stories of their ancestors and of Grandmother Earth herself. Into the beautiful and visible portrait of Creator's gift to all spirits. Silently, they both know, as they see with their eyes, but feel with their hearts. His great-grandfather's hand strongly grasps his own right hand. The warmth and the strength comforts the grandson.

Then, Great-Grandfather turns to him and speaks. He says, "Now is the time, Takoja. Now is the time to go forward and to begin the healing. Now is the moment to show those who have open hearts and open spirits and souls, what Creator has always intended for us all."

And the great warrior Mato Niyanpi turns to face the glowing sunset in the west once more.

"Come, Takoja." Grandfather takes his first step off the edge of the rocky peak…. and with his great-grandson's spirit in his hand…. he says, "Now, I will show you."

APPENDIX D

DOG MAN WARRIORS

THE DOG MAN WARRIORS WHO accompanied Mato Niyanpi in the Greasy Grass Battle, who committed to stand with him, are mentioned by name below. Following each warrior's name is his method of travel and the weapon he used during the battle; the emotion that he encountered in the soldiers on the *hill*, and/or during the conflict with the soldiers of the Seventh Cavalry; and/or the role he played. Note that the specific oyate name appears in parentheses after the warrior's name.

- Bluestone (Lakota)
  He travels on foot and uses the bow and arrow against the soldiers. The emotion he faces is the sacrifice of life.

- Runs With Wind (Lakota)
  He travels on foot and uses the bow and arrow against the soldiers. The emotion he faces is religious.

- Buffalo Horn (Nakota)
  He travels on foot, using the club as his weapon. Innocence is the emotion he encounters.

- Elk Whistle (Lakota)

He travels on foot. His weapon is the knife. The emotion he faces is arrogance.

- Comes From Star (Lakota)
  He travels on foot. His weapon is the bow and arrow. He is a very good man and a special warrior. The emotion of spirituality is present in his encounter. Spirituality is the very reason all human beings are on Earth.

- Red Whirlwind (Lakota)
  He travels on foot. His weapon is the bow and arrow. The emotion he faces is hopelessness.

- Strong Hand (Lakota)
  He is mounted on a horse. His weapon is the bow and arrow. The emotion he faces is fear.

- Flies Above (Lakota)
  He travels on a horse. His weapon is the spear. The emotion he faces is disbelief.

- Spotted Horse (Dakota)
  He is mounted on a horse. His weapon is the bow and arrow. The emotion he faces is insanity.

- Brave Dog (Lakota)
  He is mounted on a horse. His weapon is the bow arrow. The emotion he faces is cowardice.

- Black Wolf (Lakota)
  He is on a horse. His weapon is the bow and arrow. The emotion he faces is hatred.

- Swift Bear, a.k.a. Mato Luzanhan (Lakota)
  He travels on foot. His weapon is the club. The emotion he faces is evil.

- Saved By Bear, a.k.a. Mato Niyanpi (Lakota)

He travels on foot. The weapon he uses is one of the US Cavalry's own carbines. The state of being that he will bring to both sides, is peace.

- Touches Heart (Lakota)
  He is the protector of the bundlekeeper, one of two warriors called to do so. He travels on horse as a scout. His job is to protect the bundle keeper and the horses at the gathering point.

- Many Thunder (Lakota)
  Another of the scouts, he is on a horse. His job is to protect the bundlekeeper and the horses at the gathering point.

- Eagle Fan (Dakota)
  He travels by horse. He is the keeper of the bundle and the cannumpa.

These are the warriors who participate in the special *asking* of Creator. Each warrior is a very good man. All are members of the Dog Man Warrior Society.

APPENDIX E

IMAGE LIST OF PHOTOS, MAPS AND SKETCHES

Image

#1 Buffalo Parts (sketch by Robin L. Zephier), p.42

#2 White Mountains (photo by Robin L. Zephier), p.127

#3 White Stone Pony (sketch by Robin L. Zephier), p.132

#4 War Club (photo and art by Harley L. Zephier), p.138

#5 Warrior Shield (photo and art by Harley L. Zephier), p.140

#6 Red Tail Hawk (photo by Robin L. Zephier), p.148

#7 Black Tail Deer (sketch by Robin L. Zephier), p.169

#8 Map of Treaty land (1851 and 1868), (sketch by Robin L. Zephier), p.182

#9 Map of the Fort System (sketch by Robin L. Zephier), p.238

#10 Drum (photo and art by Harley L. Zephier), p.355

#11 Old Guardian along Belle Fourche River (sketch by Robin L. Zephier), p.378

#12 Split Drumstick Rock (sketch by Robin L. Zephier), p.382

#13 Stone Wanbli (photo by Patti J. Zephier), p.393

#14 Old Stone Warriors (photo by Patti J. Zephier), p.395

#15 Old Stone Warriors: Swift Bear's Arm (sketch by Robin L. Zephier), p.397

#16 On Top of Owl's Nest (sketch by Robin L. Zephier), p.410

#17 View from Above Heart Shaped He Sapa (sketch by Robin L. Zephier), p.415

#18 Sacred Sage Smudge on top of Owl's Nest (photo by Robin L. Zephier), p.416

#19 Prairie Chicken/Grouse (sketch by Robin L. Zephier), p.465

#20 Custer's Plan of Attack (sketch by Robin L. Zephier), p.493

#21 Greasy Grass Battle Diagram Map (photo and copyright by Harley L. Zephier), p.507

#22 Drum as heartbeat (photo and art by Harley L. Zephier), p.543

#23 Mato Paha/Bear Butte (photo by Patti J. Zephier), p.557

Appendix photos and images

a. Cahansa and Isota (photo by Harley L. Zephier), p.618

b. 7th Calvary troop movements map (sketch by Robin L. Zephier), p.618

c. Buffalo shaped mountain (photo by Robin L. Zephier), p.619

d. Thunder Butte (photo by Robin L. Zephier), p.619

e. Deer Medicine Rock (photo by Robin L. Zephier), p.620

f. Wanbli in flight by Wind Cave (photo by Patti J. Zephier), p.620

g. Mato Paha in morning mist (photo by Patti J. Zephier), p.621

h. Horses at Greasy Grass (photo by Robin L. Zephier), p.621

i. Horses watering at Greasy Grass River (photo by Robin L. Zephier), p.622

j. Tatanka on the run (photo by Robin L. Zephier), p.622

k. Tatanka at Wind Cave (photo by Patti J. Zephier), p.623

l. Wanbli straight on at Wind Cave (photo by Patti J. Zephier), p.623

m. Old Stone Warriors (photo by Patti J. Zephier), p.624

n. Old Stone Warriors (photo by Patti J. Zephier), p.624

o. Robin, JoJo & Kathy Good Iron, p.625
p. Lakota Travois setting (artwork and photo by Monika Andrist Zephier), p.625
q. List of Forts and Critical Events (See p.238, Image #9).

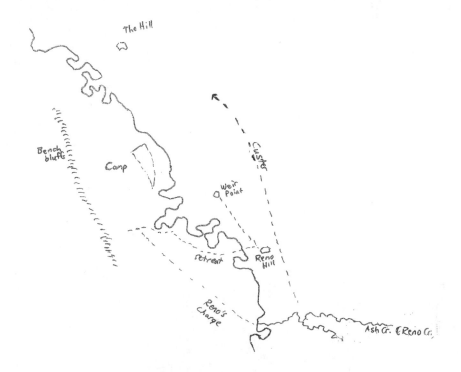

The Hill

Bench bluffs

Camp

Custer

Weir Point

retreat

Reno Hill

Reno's Charge

Ash Cr. & Reno Cr.

GLOSSARY

Akicita:	Warrior society for the Protectors; enforcers of the peace.
Ate`:	Father.
Cannumpa:	Sacred Pipe.
Cannumpa Wakan:	The Sacred Cannumpa; the Sacred Pipe.
Cante`:	Heart.
Cetan`:	Hawk.
Cikala:	Little; small.
Creator:	The First Spirit; Wakan Tanka.
Gi:	Brown.
Hanbleceya:	Man who stands on the hill and cries from self to the Creator.
Hau:	Hello; Greetings.
He:	Mountain.
Hehaka:	Elk.
He Sapa:	The Black Mountains; also referred to as Black Hills.
Heyoka:	Human being spiritually connected to the Wakinyan, the Thunder Beings; all spirit connection to creational beings.
Hinhan:	Owl.
Hinhan Kaga:	Owl's Nest; the home of the owl; sacred high mountain in He Sapa. (now known as "Black Elk Peak").

Hohwoju:	Subsistence for life through and by the water; original name for one of the oldest bands of Lakota people. The Mnincoju are extended family members.
Hoksila:	Boy.
Hoksila Wanbli:	Eagle Boy.
Ina:	Mother.
Indian:	An inaccurate description or label given to members of the peoples of the Lakota, Nakota and Dakota bands; a mistaken original reference given by early europeans to the aboriginal, indigenous and original inhabitants of Turtle Island.
Inipi:	Sweat lodge.
Inyan:	Stone, rock: the eldest of all Earth peoples.
Iyeska:	Interpreter between the human and the spirit worlds.
Keya:	Turtle.
Ke nunujela:	Turtle shell.
Kola:	Friend.
Lakota:	The Tetonwan people; the human being.
Mato:	Bear; medicine being.
Mato Luzanhan:	Bear swift; "Swift Bear".
Mato Niyanpi:	Bear, Saved By; "Saved By Bear" aka Scar Leg.
Mato Paha:	Bear Butte.
Mato Tipila:	Bear Lodge aka Devil's Tower.
Mitakuye Oyasin:	"All my relation"; akin to "we are all related".
Mni:	Water; the liquid of life.
Mni Kata:	Hot Springs, warm springs.
Mniluzanhan:	Fast water; fast creek, Rapid Creek.
Mnincoju:	Planters by the water/river.
Naca:	Leaders; leadership council.

Oceti:	Fire place; campfire.
Oceti Sakowin:	The Seven Council Fires of the Dakota, Lakota and Nakota..
Oki Inyanke Ocanku:	Racetrack; that which rings or surrounds He Sapa; the red-colored earth formation that runs around the perimeter of the He Sapa.
Osni:	Cold.
Paha:	Hill or butte.
Pejuta:	Medicine.
Pe Sla:	Sacred high meadow in He Sapa; center of Great Race Track.
Peji Sla:	Greasy Grass.
Pilamaye:	Thank you.
Pte Tali Yapa:	Buffalo Run.
Sa:	Red.
Sapa:	Black.
Sica:	Bad.
Sioux:	An inaccurate description or label given to members of the peoples of the Lakota, Dakota and Nakota; the word Sioux was a nickname derived from the Ojibwe word nadowessi (denoting a species of snake); the Ojibwe slang word was used and distorted by the Europeans.
Ska:	White.
Sota:	Many.
Sungila:	Fox.
Sungila Sapa:	Fox Black; "Black Fox".
Sunka:	Dog; sacred friend; "chien", in french.
Sunkawakan:	Horse.
Sunkmanitu Tanka:	Wolf.
Takoja:	Grandchild.
Tanka:	Large; great in any way.
Tasiyagnupa:	Meadowlark.

Tatanka:	Buffalo; buffalo people; bison; spirit of the buffalo.
Tehicila:	I cherish you; cherished.
Tesunka Witko:	"Crazy Horse"; known as "Spirit Horse" in this book.
Tiospaye:	Extended family.
Toksa Ake:	"Until next time"; akin to "until we meet again"; a Lakota phrase said to one another upon departing.
Tun:	The essence of a human being's life energy.
Tunkasila:	Grandfather; Grandfather to the grandchild; Grandfather Sky.
Turtle Island:	North America, Central America, and South American continents.
Unci:	Grandmother.
Unci Maka:	Grandmother Earth; Earth; our home planet.
Wakan:	Holy; spiritual; sacred; innocent; pure.
Wakan Gli:	Lightning; cleansing, rejuvenation of natural cycle; movement of Wakinyan (Thunder Beings).
Wakan Tanka:	Great Spirit; the Great Mystery; the Creator.
Wakinyan:	Thunder Beings; spirits who reside in the west direction.
Wakinyan Paha:	Thunder Butte.
Wakpa:	River.
Wakpa La:	Creek
Wanbli:	Eagle.
Wanbli Gi:	Eagle brown; "Brown Eagle".
Wanagi:	Spirit.
Wanagi Ta Canku:	Spirit Trail; Trail of Spirits; Spirit Road; Milky Way.

Wasi icu:	"Fat", "Takes" ("takes the fat, leaves nothing"; for their behavior against fellow beings; he won't just kill you, but will take everything from you, and leave nothing else); the behavior of the white peoples through history in the dealings with Lakota;
Wasna:	Sweet compounded cake made with ground buffalo or deer meat mixed with berry
Waste´:	Good; it is good.
Wasu:	Hailstone.
Wica:	Man.
Wicakiyuhapi:	The Big Dipper constellation; the Great Cup.
Wicasa:	Man; Red; Redman.
Wiconi:	Life.
Wolakota:	Peace.
Wojapi:	Sweet berry soup.
Wopila:	Ceremony for giving thanks.
Zuzeca:	Snake.

SOURCES

Chorne, Laudie J. *Following the Custer Trail of 1876.* Bismarck: Trails West Publishing, 2001.

Dustin, Fred. *The Custer Tragedy: Events Leading Up to and Following the Little Big Horn Campaign of 1876.* Ann Arbor: Edward Brothers, Inc., 1939 and 1965.

Reilly, Hugh J. *Bound to Have Blood: Frontier Newspapers and the Plains Indians.* Lincoln: Bison Books, 2011.

Anderson, Gary Clayton; Woolworth, Alan R. *Through Dakota Eyes: Accounts of the Minnesota Indian War of 1862.* St. Paul: Minnesota Historical Society Press, 1988.

Graham, Colonel W. A. *The Story of the Little Big Horn: Custer's Last Fight.* Harrisburg: Military Service Publishing Co., 1941.

Lee, Patrick A. *Tribal Laws, Treaties, and Government: A Lakota Perspective.* Bloomington: iUniverse, Inc., 2013.

Millikan, William. *The Great Treasure of the Fort Snelling Prison Camp.* Minnesota History Magazine, Spring 2010. St. Paul: Minnesota Historical Society 2010.

INDEX

A

Aborigines 22, 23, 191
Akicita 18, 92, 93, 94, 95, 110, 136,
    215, 340, 627
Ant People 226, 271
Arapaho 245, 256, 590, 591
Ash Hollow Massacre 84, 588
Australia 21, 22

B

Bad Face 239, 241, 245, 261, 262
Bagola, Mary Scar leg 19, 576
Bagola, Whitley 577
Base Camp 374, 382, 384, 385, 386,
    387, 388, 390, 392, 396, 400,
    402, 419, 469, 479, 482, 537,
    538, 557
Bear Creek 33, 36, 37, 103, 116, 260,
    263, 309, 325, 350, 353, 354,
    362, 363, 367, 369, 376, 378,
    385, 386, 390, 417, 419, 440,
    444, 453, 474, 475, 504, 594
Belle Fourche River 374, 378,
    562, 616
Benteen, Frederick 249, 432, 592
Bighorn Mountains/Shiny Mountains
    54, 115, 116, 117, 121, 122,
    160, 183, 246, 256, 425,
    440, 441, 470, 476, 480, 492,
    588, 597

Bighorn River 183, 425, 427, 447,
    468, 481, 488, 530
Bismarck 241, 324, 326, 327, 333,
    426, 427, 428, 436, 455, 547,
    548, 549, 596, 597, 633
Bismarck Tribune 241, 326, 327, 333,
    428, 436, 547, 548, 549, 597
Black Elk 84, 405, 406, 594, 627
Black Elk Peak 84, 627
Black Hills Expedition 322, 323, 439
Black Hills/He Sapa 5, 33, 84, 155,
    180, 183, 239, 246, 248,
    264, 266, 321, 322, 323, 324,
    326, 327, 328, 329, 331, 332,
    333, 334, 335, 336, 341, 342,
    343, 346, 361, 424, 425, 430,
    434, 439, 450, 455, 594, 595,
    596, 627
Black Tail Deer 615
Bloody Knife 481, 500, 501
Blue Earth/Mankato 205, 589
Blue Water Creek Massacre 84, 588
Bon Homme 257
Bouyer, Mitch 487, 488
Bow (Story of) x, 9, 24, 48, 61, 64,
    83, 106, 117, 126, 127, 139,
    140, 141, 142, 143, 144, 217,
    227, 228, 233, 306, 314, 509,
    511, 516, 520, 522, 523, 524,
    545, 551, 556, 558, 570, 606,
    611, 612, 633

Bradley, James 468, 548, 549, 550, 597

Brown Eagle 39, 57, 64, 65, 66, 68, 69, 70, 71, 72, 587, 630

Brule 80, 245, 261, 470, 484, 588

Buffalo 6, 7, 13, 22, 23, 30, 33, 34, 35, 36, 37, 38, 41, 42, 44, 45, 48, 53, 57, 58, 62, 66, 72, 73, 74, 75, 92, 117, 120, 126, 139, 141, 142, 144, 162, 168, 169, 172, 173, 183, 208, 223, 231, 234, 246, 252, 253, 254, 255, 256, 257, 258, 259, 260, 275, 280, 283, 287, 295, 315, 325, 346, 347, 348, 353, 356, 357, 358, 362, 371, 372, 374, 377, 381, 383, 384, 388, 396, 403, 410, 413, 440, 452, 459, 460, 462, 468, 470, 483, 484, 514, 515, 516, 517, 522, 537, 565, 593, 611, 615, 616, 629, 630, 631

Buffalo Run 7, 74, 172, 374, 381, 383, 629

Buffalo Shaped Mountain/Sheridan Mountain 255, 537, 616

Buffalo Slaughter 258

Bundle (Sacred) 557

C

Cahansa 250, 251, 252, 576, 616

Calhoun, James 434, 436

Campbell, Cecelia 208, 209

Cannumpa 33, 34, 35, 36, 37, 38, 46, 183, 184, 185, 223, 230, 260, 276, 278, 347, 348, 353, 354, 360, 362, 370, 371, 411, 498, 504, 542, 613, 627

Cattle industry 264, 265, 331, 593

Cherry Creek 103, 116, 162, 262, 263

Cheyenne People 251

Cheyenne River Agency 248, 259, 261, 262, 263, 264, 265, 321, 593

Chien River/Cheyenne River 162, 170, 248, 259, 261, 262, 263, 264, 265, 321, 593

Chosen Warriors (16) 247, 356, 357, 365, 370, 373, 381, 389, 399, 425, 446, 450, 507, 591, 593

Comanche (horse) 492, 501

Conquering Bear 80, 81, 82, 83, 104, 588

Creation ix, 3, 10, 12, 24, 124, 129, 150, 192, 229, 254, 269, 275, 301, 328, 333, 345, 406, 407, 542, 573, 576

Crook, George 426, 451, 452, 596, 597

Crow Creek 211, 214

Crow's Nest 478, 487, 488

Curly 81, 84, 104, 433, 551, 588

Custer, George Armstrong 248, 249, 528

Custer, Tom 434, 436, 488

D

Dakota People 34, 206, 210, 214, 357, 586, 589

Dakota Territory 84, 182, 211, 214, 240, 241, 257, 258, 259, 263, 333, 426, 427, 429, 446, 455, 589, 590, 592

Davenport 211, 213

Davis Creek 479

Deadwood Gulch 332, 333, 594

Deer Medicine Rock 404, 440, 442, 443, 445, 446, 467, 596, 616

Dickinson 439

Dog Man 110, 111, 113, 136, 137, 138, 262, 309, 325, 375, 381,

399, 460, 461, 468, 469, 491,
509, 521, 559, 611, 615
Dog Man Society 111, 375, 509, 521
Dog/Sunka 18, 31, 110, 111, 113,
136, 137, 138, 161, 230, 232,
233, 234, 235, 236, 262, 283,
284, 285, 286, 309, 314, 316,
325, 356, 375, 381, 399, 460,
461, 468, 469, 491, 509, 516,
520, 521, 523, 524, 525, 559,
611, 612, 615, 629
Dragonfly 111, 112, 113, 137, 460,
461, 512, 521, 607
Drumstick Rock 382, 616

E

Eagle Butte/Wanbli Paha 263, 270
Eagle Fan 152, 354, 356, 357, 360,
386, 387, 400, 401, 408, 409,
410, 411, 412, 413, 414, 416,
419, 485, 486, 491, 504, 518,
538, 539, 561, 562, 563, 564,
565, 613
Elk 18, 37, 38, 44, 45, 58, 65, 84,
117, 119, 126, 129, 137, 142,
144, 229, 231, 270, 275, 315,
320, 346, 356, 358, 381, 382,
405, 406, 412, 425, 447, 514,
515, 520, 522, 558, 563, 580,
587, 593, 594, 612, 627
Elk Head 37, 38
Elliot, Joel 249, 437
End of the Horn 261, 428, 470, 498
Engh, Alex 332, 424, 596

F

Family Stick 43
Far West 223, 437, 447, 449,
450, 486
Fetterman Fight 240, 592

Fights the Bear 64, 65, 97, 98, 116,
120, 121, 127, 158, 159, 162,
216, 293, 295, 296, 588
Fire Cloud 72, 77, 78, 79, 80,
215, 217
Fort Abraham Lincoln 426, 596
Fort Bennett 166, 263
Fort Ellis 426, 427, 596
Fort Fetterman 426, 427, 452
Fort Kearney 592
Fort Laramie 80, 81, 103, 182, 183,
239, 241, 242, 244, 245, 246,
247, 248, 256, 257, 259, 263,
266, 321, 324, 332, 338, 340,
341, 342, 425, 428, 588, 591,
592, 594
Fort Laramie Treaty of 1851 182
Fort Laramie Treaty of 1868 257, 592
Fort Rice 428
Fort Smith 596
Fort Snelling 206, 207, 210, 589
Fox/Sungila 110, 136, 396, 412, 629

G

Gibbon, John 426, 447, 596
Gold 21, 81, 153, 154, 155, 156, 157,
181, 182, 183, 190, 246, 248,
263, 265, 322, 323, 324, 327,
329, 330, 332, 333, 334, 341,
343, 344, 345, 346, 390, 391,
409, 424, 430, 434, 444, 474,
475, 476, 484, 496, 587, 590,
591, 594, 596, 598
Gold Rush 181, 182, 322, 327, 587
Goose Creek 426, 447, 450, 452,
453, 597
Grant, Ulysses S. 322, 328, 592, 593
Grattan Incident 80, 104, 588
Grattan, John 80
Greasy Grass ix, xi, 19, 96, 116, 122,
135, 183, 184, 246, 250, 332,

349, 356, 358, 361, 364, 365, 366, 368, 370, 372, 374, 375, 376, 386, 392, 399, 408, 414, 419, 420, 423, 425, 440, 441, 445, 446, 447, 452, 453, 459, 460, 461, 462, 463, 464, 465, 466, 467, 468, 469, 470, 471, 478, 479, 482, 483, 495, 496, 498, 499, 528, 531, 534, 537, 538, 539, 540, 541, 542, 547, 549, 558, 559, 564, 567, 568, 572, 588, 597, 599, 605, 606, 611, 616, 629

Greasy Grass River xi, 183, 250, 372, 376, 420, 441, 447, 461, 462, 466, 468, 471, 482, 483, 496, 531, 616

Greasy Grass Valley 122, 183, 246, 419, 423, 425, 440, 445, 459, 464, 469, 470, 559, 588, 597

Great Race 12, 13, 254, 279, 565, 585, 629

Great Sioux Reservation 182, 183, 263, 592

H

Hanbleceya 54, 115, 116, 118, 119, 120, 151, 222, 227, 260, 391, 408, 410, 561, 562, 588, 590, 603, 627

Harney, William 84

Hayfield Fight 240, 592

Heart River 439

He Sapa/Black Mountains/Black Hills xi, 5, 7, 12, 14, 16, 23, 33, 39, 41, 53, 64, 66, 74, 75, 84, 103, 107, 111, 116, 117, 120, 121, 123, 127, 145, 151, 152, 153, 156, 160, 161, 166, 167, 169, 170, 171, 172, 173, 176, 183, 222, 223, 228, 246, 248, 252,

254, 255, 256, 263, 264, 266, 275, 320, 321, 322, 323, 324, 325, 326, 327, 328, 331, 332, 333, 340, 341, 342, 343, 345, 346, 349, 351, 352, 359, 361, 362, 372, 373, 374, 375, 377, 378, 381, 382, 383, 384, 386, 387, 389, 390, 392, 393, 394, 401, 404, 406, 407, 408, 410, 413, 415, 417, 418, 419, 424, 425, 430, 440, 441, 459, 475, 476, 505, 529, 537, 538, 539, 541, 543, 549, 557, 558, 559, 560, 561, 562, 565, 587, 588, 590, 594, 596, 603, 608, 616, 627, 629

Heyoka 95, 104, 135, 145, 149, 150, 151, 165, 166, 278, 381, 390, 391, 472, 529, 559, 608, 627

Hinhan 14, 23, 84, 405, 410, 627

Hinhan Kaga 14, 23, 84, 405, 410

Homestake Mine 332, 424, 596, 598

Hopi 19

Horse Nation 62, 63, 134, 250, 252, 289, 290, 291, 292, 326, 386, 387, 388, 455, 491, 496, 518, 529, 532, 560, 579

Horse Training 135

Hot Springs/Mni Kata 23, 33, 374, 387, 388, 628

I

inipi/sweatlodge 25, 170, 222, 260, 277, 278, 363, 367, 374, 390, 396, 401, 444, 475, 541, 628

Inyan Kaga 14, 23, 33

Inyan/Stone 2, 5, 14, 23, 33, 34, 35, 121, 142, 152, 153, 164, 210, 271, 278, 283, 325, 383, 389, 396, 409, 628

Iron Hat 64, 65, 66, 69, 70, 71, 147, 152, 558
Iron White Man 103, 113, 118, 145, 149, 175, 215, 222
Isanti/Santee People 211
Isota 230, 231, 576, 616
Ista´ 314

J

Jackson, Andrew 202, 587
Johnson, Andrew 243

K

Killdeer Mountain 214, 590

L

Lenape tribe 193, 194, 586
Lincoln, Abraham 213, 426, 596
Little Missouri River 214, 439

M

Magpie 13, 559, 565
Mandan 214, 321, 428
Mankato /Blue Earth 181, 205, 213, 589
Mankato (City) 181, 205, 206, 213, 255, 427, 589, 593
Marsh, Grant 437
Martini, Giovanni 497, 530
Mato Cikala 72, 73, 75, 76, 78
Mato Luzanhan/Swift Bear 509, 525, 526, 527, 587, 612, 628
Mato Niyanpi/Saved by Bear ix, 19, 20, 26, 64, 72, 369, 509, 525, 526, 527, 528, 529, 569, 570, 575, 576, 587, 590, 599, 609, 611, 612, 628
Mato Paha/Bear Butte 14, 23, 33, 64, 121, 172, 222, 252, 374, 379,

381, 408, 410, 557, 558, 560, 565, 590, 616, 628
Mato Tipila/Bear Lodge 14, 23, 33, 253, 255, 256, 325, 410, 537, 589, 628
Medicine Mountain 54, 116, 117, 118, 119, 120, 121, 588
Medicine pouch 46, 283, 285, 510
Milky Way/Trail of Spirits/Wanagi Ta Canku 15, 80, 114, 119, 133, 161, 188, 223, 225, 235, 284, 285, 392, 567, 581, 630
Missouri River/Big Muddy River 211, 214, 262, 263, 427, 428, 439
Mitakuye Oyasin 10, 15, 27, 46, 297, 564, 571, 572, 575, 581, 628
Mni Kata/Hot Springs 14, 33, 374, 387, 388, 628
Mni/Water 1, 3, 4, 10, 14, 18, 21, 23, 27, 33, 53, 63, 99, 162, 172, 173, 183, 187, 205, 268, 275, 282, 374, 383, 384, 387, 388, 407, 417, 439, 534, 580, 628
Moon/Hanwi 15, 27, 53, 79, 118, 161, 173, 223, 282, 320, 393, 399, 418, 421, 422, 482
Mt. Pilatus 435, 479

N

Naca 74, 90, 91, 196, 215, 216, 340, 628
Nakota People 357
New People 5, 6, 36, 99, 100, 156, 177, 178, 179, 184, 186, 189, 190, 191, 192, 203, 204, 283, 303, 316, 321, 345, 358, 359, 371, 402, 412, 414, 542, 573
New Ulm 208, 209
New York Times 212, 213, 548
New Zealand 21, 191

O

Oglala 80, 172, 182, 237, 239, 241, 245, 261, 262, 470, 484, 498
Old Guardian 380, 381, 562, 615
Old Stone Warriors 171, 172, 374, 375, 392, 393, 394, 395, 396, 397, 400, 410, 417, 616, 617
Omaha Newspapers 248
Owl People 280, 418
Owl River/Moreau River 33, 116, 126, 162, 166, 167, 215, 230, 260, 262, 270, 325, 362, 367
Owl Rock 445
Owl's Nest/Hihan Kaga 14, 23, 33, 84, 116, 152, 171, 223, 225, 252, 327, 343, 375, 392, 403, 404, 405, 406, 407, 408, 410, 411, 413, 414, 415, 416, 417, 588, 594, 616, 627
Oyate 55, 56, 63, 85, 86, 90, 91, 110, 113, 136, 143, 196, 253, 383, 611

P

Pe Sla 14, 23, 33, 116, 120, 160, 557, 629
Pipe Keepers 34, 35, 36, 37, 38, 260, 353
Pipestone 34, 35, 215, 589, 604
Pleiades 1, 9, 10, 14, 15, 19, 22, 23, 32, 33, 261, 404, 406, 407
Powder River 126, 241, 243, 244, 255, 256, 343, 425, 426, 427, 430, 433, 436, 437, 439, 440, 441, 445, 447, 449, 453, 455, 458, 459, 588, 591, 592, 594, 595, 596
Powder River Campaign 343, 425, 430, 433, 436, 439, 595, 596

Powder River Country 243, 244, 255, 256, 425, 426, 437, 440, 445, 596

Q

Quaker Policy 593

R

Race Track/Oki Inyanke Ocanku 12, 565, 629
Rainbow 2, 22, 23, 473
Ramsey, Alexander 205, 211, 589
Raynolds, William F. 256
Red Cloud 182, 237, 239, 240, 241, 242, 243, 244, 245, 247, 333, 578, 592
Red Cloud Agency 239, 241, 245
Red Tail Hawk 615
Rencountre, Zephyr 256, 589
Reno, Marcus 366, 432, 437, 458, 596
Renville, Gabriel 210
Rosebud Creek 420, 427, 441, 443, 445, 447, 448, 449, 450, 452, 453, 456, 458, 467, 479, 597
Rosebud Creek Valley 445, 467

S

Sacred Cannumpa 34, 36, 37, 38, 183, 260, 276, 353, 354, 362, 371, 627
Sacred stone 34, 428
Sage xi, 46, 49, 51, 65, 72, 75, 116, 121, 170, 283, 374, 382, 383, 386, 388, 399, 411, 415, 416, 419, 473, 498, 505, 550, 564, 577, 616
Sami People 21
Sand Creek Massacre 241, 590
Santee/Isanti 211, 245

Saved By Bear/Mato Niyanpi ix, 20,
    26, 36, 38, 39, 48, 66, 72, 73,
    74, 75, 76, 77, 78, 79, 80, 85,
    88, 95, 102, 103, 104, 105,
    106, 107, 108, 113, 115, 116,
    118, 119, 120, 121, 122, 123,
    124, 125, 126, 127, 128, 129,
    130, 131, 132, 133, 135, 136,
    145, 146, 147, 148, 149, 152,
    158, 159, 160, 162, 163, 164,
    165, 167, 170, 171, 172, 173,
    174, 175, 176, 196, 215, 218,
    219, 220, 222, 223, 224, 225,
    226, 228, 229, 230, 231, 232,
    233, 236, 248, 260, 266, 270,
    271, 272, 273, 278, 283, 284,
    285, 292, 293, 296, 302, 307,
    309, 321, 325, 349, 350, 352,
    356, 357, 362, 363, 364, 366,
    367, 368, 369, 370, 372, 373,
    374, 375, 376, 377, 378, 379,
    380, 381, 382, 383, 384, 385,
    387, 390, 391, 394, 400, 402,
    409, 410, 421, 422, 423, 453,
    459, 460, 461, 462, 464, 468,
    469, 470, 471, 472, 473, 474,
    476, 477, 478, 479, 484, 490,
    491, 505, 510, 511, 512, 513,
    514, 515, 516, 517, 518, 519,
    520, 521, 522, 524, 525, 529,
    537, 538, 539, 540, 546, 558,
    559, 562, 567, 570, 572, 587,
    588, 612
Scar Leg ix, 573, 587
Seven Sacred Ceremonies 14, 35, 260
Seven Sacred Rites 33, 261
Seven Sacred Sites 23
Sheridan Letter 333, 595
Sibley, Henry H. 205, 214
Sioux 182, 183, 205, 206, 207, 209,
    210, 211, 212, 213, 245, 259,
    263, 331, 550, 551, 553, 587,
    589, 592, 593, 629
Sitting Bull 48, 57, 58, 321, 326,
    343, 349, 350, 364, 373, 423,
    425, 428, 429, 430, 431, 432,
    434, 440, 442, 443, 444, 445,
    446, 470, 471, 476, 480, 484,
    494, 498, 504, 535, 587, 593,
    594, 596
Spirit Horse 84, 103, 104, 105, 106,
    107, 173, 240, 364, 365, 366,
    367, 368, 404, 423, 425, 427,
    429, 445, 446, 450, 452, 453,
    480, 498, 499, 503, 535, 587,
    588, 594, 595, 597, 630
Spotted Smoke 167, 168, 169, 174,
    377, 386, 387, 468, 472, 529
Standing Rock Agency 259, 321
Steele, Franklin 205
Stone Wanbli 616
Sturgis, James 436, 501
Sully, Alfred 214
Sun Dance 21, 42, 151, 260, 374,
    385, 388, 389, 391, 445, 446,
    467, 596, 604
Sungila Sapa/Black Fox 396, 629
Sunkmanitu Tanka 286, 629
Sun Mountain 374, 382, 383, 384,
    385, 390
Sun/Wi xi, 10, 15, 21, 27, 33, 37, 41,
    42, 46, 53, 118, 121, 133, 145,
    148, 151, 158, 188, 223, 225,
    226, 233, 260, 282, 319, 320,
    351, 352, 359, 364, 374, 381,
    382, 383, 384, 385, 388, 389,
    390, 391, 397, 409, 411, 414,
    429, 433, 445, 446, 461, 462,
    465, 467, 468, 469, 471, 472,
    476, 485, 491, 504, 505, 518,
    529, 530, 544, 558, 563, 585,
    596, 603, 604, 607

Sweet Grass 354, 603
Swift Bear/Mato Luzanhan xi, 39, 95,
      103, 104, 106, 107, 108, 115,
      127, 131, 135, 151, 152, 160,
      162, 163, 164, 165, 166, 167,
      168, 169, 174, 175, 176, 283,
      309, 314, 315, 316, 325, 350,
      352, 356, 357, 362, 363, 364,
      366, 367, 370, 372, 375, 385,
      386, 387, 390, 391, 392, 394,
      396, 399, 400, 402, 408, 423,
      459, 460, 461, 464, 468, 470,
      472, 477, 478, 479, 484, 490,
      491, 505, 510, 511, 512, 513,
      514, 515, 517, 520, 521, 522,
      524, 525, 528, 529, 538, 559,
      560, 572, 587, 612, 616, 628
Switzerland 21, 434, 435, 479

T

Tehicila 347, 563, 630
Terry, Alfred 241, 323, 328, 426,
      595, 596
Thunder Butte 33, 230, 260, 263,
      616, 630
Tiospaye 38, 53, 55, 66, 85, 90, 91,
      118, 136, 143, 158, 166, 167,
      170, 172, 173, 218, 219, 260,
      274, 353, 354, 356, 483, 578,
      605, 630
Toksa Ake 86, 149, 169, 272, 373,
      400, 573, 630
Tongue River 121, 122, 426, 447,
      448, 449, 450, 591
Tun 50, 432, 630
Tunkasila 185, 528, 630
Turtle Island 4, 6, 7, 8, 11, 12, 14,
      20, 41, 53, 54, 62, 66, 85, 88,
      96, 99, 100, 101, 117, 118, 153,
      177, 180, 188, 189, 190, 191,
      192, 193, 194, 196, 197, 200,
      202, 203, 279, 290, 306, 309,
      310, 311, 312, 316, 322, 326,
      347, 371, 404, 406, 411, 442,
      471, 542, 567, 571, 585, 586,
      628, 630
Turtle Shell Circle 116

U

Unci Maka/Grandmother Earth xii, 1,
      2, 3, 4, 5, 6, 7, 9, 11, 12, 14, 23,
      24, 25, 33, 37, 48, 86, 98, 99,
      108, 118, 121, 122, 149, 157,
      188, 230, 260, 275, 279, 289,
      290, 320, 321, 326, 333, 343,
      351, 352, 353, 359, 369, 376,
      377, 379, 381, 384, 385, 389,
      391, 392, 405, 406, 407, 412,
      413, 418, 419, 460, 473, 491,
      528, 539, 540, 549, 557, 558,
      563, 564, 565, 571, 573, 574,
      576, 581, 585, 630

V

Varnum, Charles 436
Vincent, Charley 435, 479

W

Wagon Box Fight 240, 592
Wakan 6, 9, 14, 16, 23, 24, 28, 31,
      32, 33, 35, 47, 48, 60, 65,
      71, 86, 87, 88, 107, 108, 110,
      111, 115, 119, 124, 130, 160,
      176, 185, 205, 217, 219, 228,
      229, 230, 261, 267, 268, 269,
      279, 280, 281, 284, 285, 308,
      352, 374, 378, 381, 391, 411,
      440, 443, 444, 446, 451, 460,
      472, 476, 477, 504, 510, 528,
      544, 559, 562, 563, 564, 573,
      627, 630

Wakan Tanka/Great Spirit 9, 16, 24,
     28, 31, 32, 35, 47, 48, 60, 65,
     71, 86, 107, 110, 111, 115, 119,
     130, 160, 176, 185, 205, 217,
     219, 228, 229, 261, 267, 268,
     269, 279, 280, 281, 284, 285,
     374, 378, 381, 391, 411, 440,
     443, 444, 446, 451, 460, 472,
     476, 477, 504, 528, 559, 562,
     563, 564, 573, 627, 630
Wakinyan Paha 230, 630
Wakinyan/Thunder Beings 27, 33, 47,
     119, 150, 176, 185, 222, 230,
     233, 260, 276, 278, 379, 382,
     405, 409, 473, 482, 560, 562,
     563, 627, 630
Wanagi 14, 15, 223, 630
Wanagi Ta Canku 630
Wanbli/Eagle 6, 21, 39, 47, 57, 64,
     72, 117, 118, 130, 137, 152,
     172, 175, 223, 266, 267, 268,
     269, 270, 271, 272, 273, 380,
     393, 400, 412, 415, 416, 419,
     429, 486, 487, 488, 504,
     559, 561, 562, 563, 565, 616,
     628, 630
Warrior Cleansing Ceremony 540
Warrior Societies 110, 111, 136, 442,
     444, 509
Washita Massacre 250, 437, 592
Washita River 249, 250, 370, 492
Wasna 45, 121, 133, 165, 170,
     283, 631
Wasu/hail 315, 576, 631
Water Spirit 9, 428
White Buffalo Calf Woman 34, 35,
     36, 37, 38, 183, 260, 347,
     353, 362
White Mountains xi, 126, 127, 129,
     130, 132, 135, 292, 462, 505,
     529, 615

White River 74, 162
Whitestone Hill Massacre 590
White Stone Pony 129, 132, 133, 134,
     135, 615
Wiconi 1, 219, 631
Wildfire 127, 128, 129, 131, 132,
     133, 134, 174, 232, 233, 266,
     273, 292, 293, 296, 377, 386,
     387, 471, 472, 473, 474, 475,
     476, 529, 558
Willow 170, 278, 383, 385
Wind Cave 1, 6, 7, 14, 23, 33, 53,
     374, 381, 383, 384, 389,
     407, 616
Wolf Mountains 121, 122, 420, 427,
     446, 447, 462, 469, 476, 478,
     479, 481, 499, 529, 597
Wolf/Sunkmanitu Tanka 40, 57, 79,
     97, 98, 121, 122, 213, 234, 271,
     286, 287, 288, 289, 356, 420,
     421, 422, 427, 446, 447, 462,
     469, 476, 478, 479, 481, 499,
     516, 521, 524, 525, 529, 563,
     597, 612, 629
Wopila 52, 72, 105, 116, 121,
     572, 631

Y

Yankton 256, 258, 259, 261, 327,
     333, 455, 589
Yanktonai 172, 214, 256, 428, 590
Yates, George 492
Yellowstone (Elk) River 215, 425, 427,
     437, 447, 449, 587, 593

Z

Zephier, Alverda May Bagola 19,
     574, 576